Vivāha Saṁskāra
in Gṛhya-Sūtras of the Four Vedas

Vivāha Saṁskāra
in Gṛhya-Sūtras of the Four Vedas
— A Comparative Study of Marriage Ceremonies —

V.R. Anil Kumar

DK PRINTWORLD
Publishers of Indian Traditions

Cataloging in Publication Data — DK
[Courtesy: D.K. Agencies (P) Ltd. <docinfo@dkagencies.com>]

Anil Kumar, V.R., 1943-
Vivāha saṁskāra in Gr̥hya-sūtras of the four Vedas : a comparative study of marriage ceremonies / V.R. Anil Kumar.
p. cm.
Includes bibliographical references.
ISBN 9788124607497

1. Gr̥hyasūtras — Criticism, interpretation, etc. 2. Vedas — Rites and ceremonies. 3. Hindu marriage customs and rites. I. Gr̥hyasūtras. English & Sanskrit. II. Title.

DDC 294.538 23

First published in India, 2014
ISBN 13: 978-81-246-0749-7

Printed and published by:
D.K. Printworld (P) Ltd.
Regd. Office : *Vedaśrī*, F-395, Sudarshan Park
(Metro Station: Ramesh Nagar)
New Delhi – 110 015-11
Phones : (011) 2545 3975, 2546 6019; *Fax* : 2546 5926
e-mail : indology@dkprintworld.com
Web : www.dkprintworld.com

Dedicated to

the memory of
Dr S. Revathy,
Scholar, Guide and Friend

cruelly snatched away
in the prime of her life

Preface

THE Hindu marriage ceremony is a fascinating blend of elaborate rituals, joyous celebration, colourful dresses, sumptuous feasts, etc. with religious sanctity underlying the event. The way it is conducted follows traditions which are centuries old with *mantra*s and *śloka*s in Sanskrit being chanted at each step of the ceremony being carried out. While there are a few who understand the meaning and import of the rituals, the vast majority merely follow the instructions of the *purohita*s without understanding the significance of the rituals. This is mostly because of the fact that Sanskrit is not learnt by most people and also because it requires years of study to learn the meanings of *mantra*s and the relevance of rituals.

Having been fascinated by the marriage ceremony and having a desire to understand it fully, I decided to take up research on the topic. I got admitted as a full-time research scholar at the Department of Sanskrit, University of Madras.

I was fortunate that Prof. Dr S. Revathy guided me throughout the tenure of this research. Under her guidance and with the advice of other faculty members, I proceeded to collect material for my research. I thank her from the bottom of my heart. After preliminary studies, it was clear that the main sources of the rituals that a householder is expected to observe were the Gṛhya-Sūtras falling under Kalpaśāstra — one of the six limbs of Vedāṅga. I, therefore, decided to collect Gṛhya-Sūtra texts belonging to different branches of the four Vedas and conduct a comparative study of *vivāha saṁskāra*, the Hindu marriage ceremony as depicted in the Gṛhya-Sūtras.

Though there have been numerous branches of the four Vedas and texts written by *ṛṣis* and scholars pertaining to each branch, many of the texts have been lost. People followed different branches of the Vedas in different regions of India. Texts have been written for each of the branches. As time went by, some of the schools began to have fewer and fewer adherents and texts pertaining to them have become scarce.

I could collect texts of eighteen Gṛhya-Sūtras from various sources. Of these, one of them, *Kauthuma Gṛhya-Sūtra* of *Sāmaveda* does not contain much material on *vivāha*. The study is, therefore, confined to seventeen Gṛhya-Sūtras. Some of the texts were available in the bookshops but many were not. Apart from procuring the available texts from the bookshops, I was able to collect photocopies of texts from different sources. Among the many institutions which helped me were the Adyar Library, Kuppuswami Sastri Research Institute, Chennai; Oriental Research Institute, Mysore; Bhandarkar Oriental Research Institute, Pune; Vaidik Samshodhan Mandal, Pune; Deccan College, Pune; Manuscripts Library, University of Kerala, Tiruvananthapuram and Sri Sankara Samskrta Veda Pathasala of Mathur, Karnataka. I would like to place on record my immense gratitude to the authorities of these institutions for providing me photocopies of required texts. I was also able to refer many texts in the Hatcher Graduate Library of the University of Michigan, USA, thanks to Dr Madhav Deshpande who is a professor of Asian Studies at the University.

Books by foreign scholars such as W. Caland, Oldenberg, Maurice Winternitz and others with translations helped enormously in understanding the texts. The internet also proved to be a useful source. Especially, sites like those of Maharshi University of Management, sanskritdocuments.org, Ulrich Stiehl (sanskritweb.net) and others were very useful.

Many books on *vivāha* in languages such as Tamil, Kannada, Marathi and Hindi also proved useful.

The sources of the rituals are the Gṛhya-Sūtras. However, the contents are in the form of aphorisms (*sūtra*s) perhaps for ease of memorizing. Commentaries have been written for many of the texts explaining the content and context of the *sūtras*. From the commentaries evolved *prayoga*s and *paddhati*s, which laid down detailed instructions for conducting each *saṁskāra*. Over time, due to geographical and social factors, considerable changes took place in the way the rituals were performed. Further fragmentation in sects and castes also gave rise to more deviations. Though the underlying rituals are more or less similar in each of the Gṛhya-Sūtras, there have been many additions and changes in practice because of these developments. A comparative study of *vivāha saṁskāra* based on all the *prayoga*s and *paddhati*s would be too enormous a task. The very task of collecting all the material itself would take up a lot of time and expense. Even the collection of Gṛhya-Sūtras was not an easy task to accomplish.

It was therefore decided that a "Comparative Study of Vivāha Saṁskāras in the Gṛhya-Sūtras of the Four Vedas" with the extant material would be a worthwhile project. The bringing together of sections containing details of *vivāha saṁskāra* in all the extant Gṛhya-Sūtras at one place itself involved considerable effort. The sections have been presented with English translations, mainly with the help of existing English and Hindi translations. Where English translations were not available, as in the case of *Baudhāyana* and *Bhāradvāja Gṛhya-Sūtras*, help was rendered by Sri Venkatesa Avadhani of Mathur, Karnataka in translating the Sanskrit texts.

It was also difficult to get collections of *mantra*s used in the marriage ceremony. Most of the *mantra*s have their source in *Ṛgveda* and *Atharvaveda* but there are many which are not from these two. *Mantra Pāṭha of Āpastambins* by M. Winternitz was of great help. Also, the Hindi text, *Gṛhya-Mantra aur unkā Viniyoga* by Dr Krishnalal was extremely useful. *Chāndogya Mantra Brāhmaṇa* of *Sāmaveda* contains most of the *mantras*, though they may be of Ṛgvedic origin. Ekāgni Kāṇḍa contains *mantras* used in texts of *Kṛṣṇa Yajurveda*.

The thesis contains chapters on Introduction, An Overview of Scriptures, Vedāṅgas, Kalpaśāstra, Saṁskāras, Ṣoḍaśa Saṁskāras, Vivāha Saṁskāra, Sections of the Gṛhya-Sūtras dealing with Vivāha Saṁskāra with translations, comparison in the order and number of rituals, *mantras* used with their sources indicated wherever possible, differences in *mantras*, etc. The thesis contains Appendices giving collections of *vivāha mantras*.

I would like to express my gratitude to the authorities at the University of Madras for giving me permission to publish the thesis as a book.

I would like to thank Dr Siniruddha Das, Head of Department of Sanskrit, University of Madras for the encouragement and guidance provided. I would like to thank Dr G.U. Thite of the Bhandarkar Oriental Research Institute, Pune for the immense help and guidance given, Dr. Bhagyalata Pataskar of Vaidik Samshodhan Mandal, Pune for providing photocopies of texts and Dr S. Jagannatha of the Oriental Research Institute, Mysore. I would like to specially thank Sri Venkatesa Avadhani of Mathur, Karnataka for all the help in translating texts and clarifying doubts.

(***A Note on translations****: I have depended on existing translations,* bhāṣyas, *other writings and on the opinion of numerous scholars to get the translation right. However, since Mantras and Sūtras are extremely difficult to translate given the fact that one should be aware of the context and the* prayoga, *it is quite possible that there are errors and wrong interpretations in the printed translations. I appeal to scholars who are interested to kindly point out the discrepancies so that corrections can be incorporated in future editions.*)

Abbreviations

Āg.G.S.	*Āgnivesya Gṛhya-Sūtra*
Āp.Dh.S.	*Āpastamba Dharma-Sūtra*
Āp.G.S.	*Āpastamba Gṛhya-Sūtra*
Ās.G.S.	*Āśvalāyana Gṛhya-Sūtra*
ṚV	*Ṛgveda*
Ait.B.	*Aitareya Brāhmaṇa*
Apa.	*Aparārka*
AV	*Atharvaveda*
Bau.G.S.	*Baudhāyana Gṛhya-Sūtra*
Bhā.G.S.	*Bhāradvāja Gṛhya-Sūtra*
Ek.K.	Ekāgni Kāṇḍa
Gau.Dh.S.	*Gautama Dharma-Sūtra*
Go.G.S.	*Gobhila Gṛhya-Sūtra*
Hā.Dh.S.	*Hārīta Dharma-Sūtra*
Hi.G.S.	*Hiraṇyakeśin Gṛhya-Sūtra*
His.Dh.Ś.	*History of Dharmaśāstra*
Jai.G.S.	*Jaimini Gṛhya-Sūtra*
Kā.G.S.	*Kāṭhaka Gṛhya-Sūtra*
Kau.G.S.	*Kauśika Gṛhya-Sūtra*
Kauṣītaki.G.S	*Kauṣītaki Gṛhya-Sūtra*
Khā.G.S.	*Khādira Gṛhya-Sūtra*
Ma.Br.	*Mantra Brāhmaṇa*
Mā.G.S.	*Mānava Gṛhya-Sūtra*
Ma.Pā.	*Mantra Pāṭha*
Ma.Sm.	*Manu-Smṛti*

Mu.Up.	*Muṇḍaka Upaniṣad*
Śā.G.S.	*Śānkhāyana Gṛhya-Sūtra*
Śat.B.	*Śathapatha Brāhmaṇa*
Pā.G.S.	*Pāraskara Gṛhya-Sūtra*
SV	*Sāmaveda*
Tai.B.	*Taittirīya Brāhmaṇa*
Tai.Sa.	*Taittirīya Saṁhitā*
Tan.M.B.	*Tāṇḍya Mahābrāhamaṇa*
Vā.G.S.	*Vārāha Gṛhya-Sūtra*
Vai.S.S.	*Vaikhānasa Smārta-Sūtra*
VMS	*Vīra Mitrodaya Saṁskāra Prakāśa*
Vy.Sm.	*Vyāsa-Smṛti*
YV	*Yajurveda*

Contents

1

Introduction

Saṁskāras

SAṀSKĀRAS (sacraments) are rituals a Hindu is expected to perform at various events in his life. Beginning with conception and ending with funeral rites, *saṁskāra*s prescribe the way each activity is to be carried out. Offerings and oblations are required to be made in a prescribed manner at every event in order to propitiate gods to attain desired goals and to ward off evils and enemies. Even in the Vedic era, there was recognition of the existence of superhuman elements which affected a person's life. *Saṁskāra*s were developed to help one achieve one's goals in life by appeasing deities by offering sacrifices and performing rituals. Rituals represent an age when people followed religious injunctions assiduously. *Saṁskāra*s served as a link between spiritualism and the day-to-day life of the householder. While being an ascetic meant renunciation of all worldly things, *saṁskāra*s added spirituality to natural events of a householder and made the householder live a full materialistic life which was, however, infused with religious undertones. Because of the disciplinary and dhārmic nature underlying *saṁskāra*s one was guided towards living a life full of right values.

People in the Vedic period were expected to lead a disciplined life with various stages of life classified and *saṁskāra*s prescribed to be observed at every event in life. A highly-evolved ritualistic system guided people to carry out their lives in a systematic manner. The *āśrama* system described four stages in a person's life — (1) *brahmacarya,* (2) *gṛhastha,* (3) *vānaprastha,* and (4) *saṁnyāsa. Brahmacarya* was the stage of life from childhood to the end of studies. *Gṛhasthāśrama* was the stage of life when a person got married and led the life of a householder giving birth to and raising children. This was the period when he worked and earned money to satisfy his desires. *Vānaprasthāśrama* was the stage when at around the age of sixty years, one began philosophical contemplation. *Vānaprastha* means that one should go to the forest away from the worries of day-to-day life to seek spiritual knowledge. *Saṁnyāsa* is the stage when a person became totally detached from worldly goods and became immersed in his spiritual quest to attain *mokṣa.* The *āśrama* system reflected the transitional phases of a man from birth, studentship, being a householder, being philosophical and trying to achieve the ultimate, *mokṣa* (deliverance from re-birth). It acknowledged the transient nature of human life with its joys and sorrows, birth–growth–death cycle.

In *Manu-Smṛti* is the following *śloka:*[1]

चतुर्थमायुषो भागं वसित्वाद्यं गुरोः कुले ।
द्वितीयमायुषो भागं कृतदारो गृहे वसेत् ।
वनेषु च विहृत्यैवं तृतीयं भागमायुषः ।
चतुर्थमायुषो भागं त्यक्त्वा सङ्गान्परिव्रजेत् ॥

Having spent the first fourth part of his life in gurukula
The second fourth part in his own house with his wife
The third part in the forest
He should take saṁnyāsa *in the final part renouncing all wordly ties.*

During the four stages of life, one is required to follow the four principles of *puruṣārtha — dharma, artha, kāma* and *mokṣa.*

---

1 *Manu-Smṛti* IV.1.2.

While *dharma* (righteousness) is to be observed during all the four stages of life, *artha* and *kāma* are to be followed during *gṛhasthāśrama*. Efforts to attain *mokṣa* are to be made during *saṁnyāsa*. *Dharma* is a highly desired concept. Based on the concept of *ṛta* (natural justice), *dharma* became a guiding force in all activities of life. *Dharma* also meant carrying out one's duty judiciously in whatever situation or occupation one was placed in. The combination of righteousness and a sense of duty ensured that justice would be done.

The primary source of *dharma* is considered to be the Vedas.[2]

वेदो धर्म मूलम् । तद्विदां च स्मृतिशीले ॥

Veda is the source of *dharma*. And the practices and traditions of those who know and remember Vedas.

Saṁskāras were developed, inspired by the Vedas and the hymns in them. While Vedas did not contain rules and regulations for conducting rituals, they formed the basis for *saṁskāras* which came into being subsequently. *Saṁskāras* specified the way each step in a man's life was to be observed with specific procedures and *mantras*. The materials required for conducting the rituals, the way to establish the fire and the way to prepare the place where the rituals were to be conducted were clearly spelt out. A householder was expected to follow the rituals (*saṁskāras*) depicted in Gṛhya-Sūtras, which came to be written by *ṛṣis* belonging to different branches of the four Vedas.

As per Hārīta *saṁskāras* are classified into two types — *brāhma* and *daiva*.[3]

तथा च हारितः । द्विविधः संस्कारो भवति ब्राह्मो दैवश्च । गर्भाधानादिस्मार्तो ब्राह्मः । पाकयज्ञहविर्यज्ञसौम्याश्चेति दैवः । ब्रह्मासंस्कारसंस्कृत ऋषीणां

---

2 *Gau.Dh.S.* I.1.2.

3 *Ha.Dh.S.* XI.1.5.

समानतां सलोकतां सायुज्यं गच्छति । दैवेनोत्तरेण संस्कृतो देवानां समानतां सलोकतां सायुज्यं गच्छति । इति ।

> According to Hārīta, *saṁskāras* are of two kinds, *brāhma* and *daiva*. *Saṁskāras* beginning with *garbhādhāna* are called *brāhma*. *Pāka yajñas*, *havir yajñas* and *soma yajñas* are called *daiva*. A man who performs *brāhma saṁskāras* attains equality with *ṛṣis* and one who performs *daiva saṁskāras* attains equality with gods.

Every activity in life was marked by specific *saṁskāras* to be observed. The number and constituents of *saṁskāras* vary according to different *sūtrakāras*. In the beginning, the number of *saṁskāras* to be observed by the householder used to be around forty-eight.

According to Gautama, the forty-eight *saṁskāras* include the following:[4]

Garbhādhāna, puṁsavana, sīmantonnayana, jātakarma, nāmakaraṇa, annaprāṣana, caula, and *upanayana.* — Eight

Vedavratas — *mahānāmnī, mahāvrata, upaniṣadvrata,* and *godāna.* — Four

Samāvartana, Vivāha — Two

Pāka Yajñas — 1. *aṣṭaka*, 2. *pārvaṇa sthalipāka*, 3. *śrāddha* (*piṇḍapitṛ yajña*), 4. *śrāvaṇa karma*, 5. *āgrahāyana*, 6. *caitri*, and 7. *āśvayuji*. (This list varies from source to source. *Aupāsana* and *pratyāvarohaṇa* are included in some lists instead of *caitri* and *āśvayuji*.). — Seven

Mahā Yajñas — 1. *deva yajña*, 2. *pitṛ yajña*, 3. *bhūta yajña*, 4. *mānuṣya yajña*, and 5. *brāhma yajña*. — Five

Havir Yajñas — 1. *agnyādhāna*, 2. *agnihotra*, 3. *darśapurṇamāsa*, 4. *āgrayaṇa*, 5. *cāturmāsya*, 6. *niruḍhapaśu-bandha*, and 7. *sautrāmaṇi*. — Seven

[4] *Gau.Dh.S.* I.8.14-22.

Soma Yajñas — 1. *agniṣṭoma*, 2. *atyagniṣṭoma*, 3. *ukthya*, 4. *ṣoḍaśī*, 5. *vājapeya*, 6. *atirātra*, and 7. *āptoryāma*. — Seven

Ātmaguṇakas — 1. *dayā*: kindness, 2. *kṣamā*: tolerance, 3. *anasūya*: being without jealousy, 4. *śaucam*: cleanliness, 5. *anāyāsa*: doing things with a balanced mind without over exertion, 6. *māṅgalyam*: concentrating on the good and the auspicious, 7. *akārpaṇyam*: being generous and without greed, and 8. *aspruha*: having a mind devoid of desires. — Eight

*Ātmaguṇaka*s were included because it was felt that merely carrying out *saṁskāra*s without having dhārmic values would be futile. These eight qualities represent a high level of ethical values.

According to Aṅgiras, the following are the twenty-seven *saṁskāras*:[5]

गर्भाधानं पुंसवनं सीमन्तो बलिरेव च ।
जातकृत्यं नामकर्म निष्क्रमोऽन्नप्राशनं परम् ॥
चौलकर्मोपनयनं तद्व्रतानां चतुष्टयम् ।
स्नानोद्वाहौ चाग्रयणमष्टकाश्च यथायथम् ॥
श्रावण्यामाश्वयुज्यां च मार्गशीर्ष्यां च पार्वणम् ।
उत्सर्गश्चाप्युपाकर्म महायज्ञश्च नित्यशः ।
संस्कारा वियता ह्येते ब्राह्मणस्य विशेषतः ॥

Garbhādhāna, *puṁsavana*, *sīmantonnayana*, *viṣṇu bali*, *jātakarma*, *nāmakaraṇa*, *niṣkramaṇa*, *annaprāṣana*, *caula*, and *upanayana* (10); *vedavratas* 4; *samāvartana*, *vivāha*, *agrayaṇa* 3; and *aṣṭaka* 8.

According to Vyāsa, the following are the sixteen *saṁskāras*:[6]

गर्भाधानं पुंसवनं सीमन्तो जातकर्म च ।
नामक्रिया निष्क्रामोऽन्नप्राशनं वपनक्रिया ॥

---

[5] Quoted in *VMS*, vol. I.

[6] *Vy.Sm.* I.13.15.

कर्णवेधो व्रतादेशो वेदारम्भक्रियाविधिः ।
केशान्तः स्नानोद्वाहो विवाहोऽग्निपरिग्रहः ।
त्रैताग्निसङ्ग्रहश्चैव संस्काराः षोडश स्मृताः ॥

Garbhādhāna, puṁsavana, sīmantonnayana, jātakarma, nāmakaraṇa, niṣkramaṇa, annaprāṣana, caula, karṇa-vedha, upanayana, keśānta, samāvartana, vivāha, and *agni* sacrifices 3 are the sixteen *saṁskāras* of the ones who follow Smṛtis.

However, *yajñas, veda vratas* (except *godāna*) and *ātmaguṇakas* began to be excluded, as time went by, from the list of *saṁskāras* leaving sixteen *saṁskāras*. These are known as *ṣoḍaśa saṁskāras*. Even in the list of sixteen *saṁskāras*, there is difference of opinion among *sūtrakāras*. Some texts include *viṣṇu bali, śoṣyantī karma*, etc. *Karṇavedha, vidyārambha* and *vedārambha* appear to be the later additions.

THE CONSTITUENTS

The constituents of *saṁskāras* were Agni, water, prayers, sacrifices, magic and divination. Agni was the God through whom all gods were propitiated. The first two hymns of *Ṛgveda* are as follows:

अग्निमीले पुरोहितं देवमृत्विजम् ।
होतारं रत्नधातमम् ॥

Praise Agni, the priest, the God of *yajñas*, the holy one. The sacrificial priest, the giver of wealth.[7]

अग्निः पूर्वेभिर्ऋषिभि रीड्यो नूतनैरुत ।
स देवाँ इह वक्षति ॥

Agni is worthy of being praised by ancient as well as new *ṛṣis*, He will bring forth the gods here.[8]

---

7 *ṚV* I.1.1.1.

8 *ṚV* I.1.1.2.

Water was considered the utmost purifying agent. Importance was given to *ācamana* (ritual sipping of water) and bathing. At every important event, bathing was recommended as a purifier. Prayers were offered seeking numerous benefits. The Gāyatrī (Sāvitrī) *mantra* was recited on many occasions with *mahāvyāhṛtis*.

ॐ भूर्भुवस्स्वः ।
तत्सवितुर्वरेण्यम् ।
भर्गो देवस्य धीमहि ।
धीयो यो नः प्रचोदयात् ॥

Oṁ! *BHŪR* (*prāṇa*, earth, *sat*, existence), *BHUVAḤ* (*apāna*, sky, *cit*, consciousness), *SVAḤ* (*vyāna*, heaven, *ānanda*, bliss)

We pray to Him
That worthy God, Savitā,
Who can remove the ignorance from our minds
Who can stimulate of our intellect.

Sacrifices were offered to gods seeking blessings as well as material gains. It was believed that gods, like humans, were pleased with praises and offerings made to them and would grant the wishes of the one who performed the sacrifices. Sacrifices took many forms depending on the *saṁskāra* being conducted. Magic was prescribed in many cases to achieve desired results. *Atharvaveda* has many prescriptions using magic in *saṁskāras* like *śoṣyantī karma* and *jātakarma*, etc. respectively, for safe delivery of a child and a good future for the newborn.

Divination was used to try and understand the will of gods. Astrology was used as a tool for divination by the study of planets which represented different gods. Apart from choosing the most auspicious time and date for a particular *saṁskāra*, astrology began to be used for matching horoscopes for marriage, etc. in the post-Gṛhya-Sūtras period.

There have been many recensions or branches of the four Vedas and there have been Gṛhya-Sūtras for many of the branches. Though the underlying rituals remain unchanged, changes took place in the way *saṁskāra*s were conducted influenced by geographical and social aspects. Gṛhya-Sūtras texts that are still existing help us to study and understand the social customs of the times they were written in and to preserve heritage. There are eighteen Gṛhya-Sūtras texts available for study. While *Ṛgveda* has three Gṛhya-Sūtras, *Śukla Yajurveda* has one, *Kṛṣṇa Yajurveda* has nine, *Sāmaveda* has four and *Atharvaveda* one. Many other Gṛhya-Sūtras which are referred to in various texts and papers have been lost. *Paiṅgīya* and *Parāśara Gṛhya-Sūtras* of *Ṛgveda, Baijavāpa Gṛhya-Sūtra* of *Śukla Yajurveda* are some of the texts which are no longer available. Commentaries and translations are available for many of the Gṛhya-Sūtras. Some Gṛhya-Sūtras have more than one commentary. These help in understanding the rituals and their significance.

An Overview of Scriptures

In order to understand the background and evolution of Hindu marriage rituals, an overview of Hindu scriptures would be useful. Hindu literature can be broadly classified into two, namely, scriptures and secular writings. Scriptures include: Śrutis, Smṛtis, Itihāsas, Āgamas and Darśanas. Secular writings consist of Subhāṣitas, Kāvyas, Nāṭakas, Alaṁkāras, etc.

Śrutis

There has been a long tradition of teaching through the oral method. Śrutis literally means "that which is heard". Śrutis are considered to be revealed texts. Many Hindus believe that Śrutis are *anādi* and *apauruṣeya* — without beginning and divine (not man-made).

The four Vedas are considered to be Śrutis: *Ṛgveda, Yajurveda, Sāmaveda* and *Atharvaveda.*

Each Veda has four sections: Mantra Saṁhitas, Brāhmaṇas, Āraṇyakas and Upaniṣads.

There are four Upavedas:

— Āyurveda: The science of life and medicine.

— Dhanurveda: The science of archery and weaponry.

— Gāndharvaveda: The art of music and dance.

— Arthaśāstra: The science of statecraft and economics.

Smṛtis

Smṛti means that which is remembered. *Ṛṣis* who had mastered Vedas wrote Smṛtis in the form of manuals containing the essence of Vedas and laying down procedures to follow in day-to-day life. Among many, the following eighteen Smṛtis are considered the most important: Manu, Yājñavalkya, Parāśara, Viṣṇu, Dakṣa, Saṁvarta, Vyāsa, Śātātapa, Vasiṣṭha, Āpastamba, Śaṅkha-Likhita, Śaunaka, Hārīta, Yama, Gautama, Devala, Uśana and Atri.

Itihāsas or Epics

Rāmāyaṇa and *Mahābhārata* are the two great epics.

Supplementary Epics

Yoga-Vāsiṣṭha and Harivaṁśa are considered as supplementary epics.

Purāṇas

There are eighteen main Purāṇas and eighteen Upapurāṇas (among many) which are the most popular. They depict stories of the Trinity — Brahmā, Viṣṇu and Maheśvara. The stories project dhārmic values in the Vedas in a manner easily understood by the lay person through stories of gods and mortals.

Āgamas

There are three divisions of Āgamas — Śaiva, Vaiṣṇava and Śākta — and they contain procedures for temple building and details of temple rituals.

Darśanas or Philosophies

The six different philosophies are as follows: Nyāya, Vaiśeṣika, Sāṁkhya, Yoga, Pūrva-Mīmāṁsā, Uttara-Mīmāṁsā or Vedānta. The word Vedānta has become synonymous with philosophy.

Upaniṣads

Among many, thirteen Upaniṣads are considered the most important: *Īśāvāsya, Praśna, Muṇḍaka, Kena, Māṇḍūkya, Bṛhadāraṇyaka, Taittirīya, Aitareya, Chāndogya, Kaṭha, Maitrāyaṇī, Śvetāśvatara* and *Kauṣītaki.*

Vyāsa wrote *Brahma-Sūtra* distilling the essence of Vedas.

Brahma-Sūtra, Bhagavad-Gītā and Upaniṣads are called the *prasthāna traya* — the centrality of Hinduism.

Vedāṅgas

Six Vedāṅgas emerged out of Vedas dealing with different branches of knowledge.

1. Śikṣā (phonetics).
2. Vyākaraṇa (grammar).
3. Nirukta (etymology).
4. Jyotiṣa (astronomy).
5. Chandas (prosody metre).
6. Kalpa (rituals).

The first *khaṇḍa* of *Muṇḍakopaniṣad* contains the following verses mentioning the six parts of Vedāṅga:[9]

ब्रह्मा देवानां प्रथमः संबभूव विश्वस्य कर्ता भुवनस्य गोप्ता ।
स ब्रह्मविद्यां सर्वविद्याप्रतिष्ठामथर्वाय ज्येष्ठपुत्राय प्राह ॥१॥

The first among gods, Brahmā the maker of the universe
Protector of the earth came into being
He taught brahma-vidyā, *the basis of all knowledge*
To his eldest son, Atharva.

अथर्वणे यां प्रवदेत ब्रह्माथर्वा तां पुरोवाचङ्गिरे ब्रह्मविद्याम् ।
स भारद्वाजाय सत्यवहाय प्राह भारद्वाजोऽङ्गिरसे परावराम् ॥२॥

What was taught by Brahmā to Atharva
Atharva of old taught to Aṅgirā
He taught Bharadvāja Satyavāha
Bharadvāja taught Aṅgirasa the higher and lower knowledge.

शौनको ह वै महाशालोऽङ्गिरसं विधिवदुपसन्न पप्रच्छ ।
कस्मिन्नु भगवो विज्ञाते सर्वमिदं विज्ञातं भवतीति ॥३॥

Śaunaka, the great householder respectfully asked Aṅgirasa
What must one know to know brahma-vidyā?

तस्मै स होवाच ।
द्वे विद्ये वेदितव्ये इति ह स्म यद्ब्रह्मविदो वदन्ति परा चैवापरा च ॥४॥

He told him. The ones who know *brahma-vidyā* say, there are two types of knowledge, lower and higher.

तत्रापरा ऋग्वेदो यजुर्वेदः सामवेदोऽथर्ववेदः ।
शिक्षा कल्पो व्याकरणं निरुक्तं छन्दो ज्योतिषमिति ।
अथ परा यया तदक्षरमधिगम्यते ॥५॥

In it, the lower is the study of *Ṛgveda, Yajurveda, Sāmaveda* and *Atharvaveda*. Śikṣā, Kalpa, Vyākaraṇa, Nirukta, Chandas and Jyotiṣa. But the higher is that by which the imperishable (*akṣara*) is understood.

---

9 *Mun.Up.* I.1-5.

Kalpaśāstra

Kalpa is the branch of knowledge which deals with rituals in various forms. It is called *kara* (hand) of the Vedas. While other *aṅgas* represent knowledge, Kalpa represents activity to be carried out.

> छन्दः पादौ शब्दशास्त्रं च वक्त्रं कल्पं पाणी ज्योतिषं चक्षुषी च ।[10]
> शिक्षा घ्राणं श्रोत्रमुक्तं निरुक्तं वेदस्याङ्गान्याहुतानि षड् हि ॥

> Chandas is represented by feet, Śabdaśāstram (Vyākaraṇa) by the face. Kalpa by hand, Jyotiṣa by eyes, Śikṣā by the tongue and Nirukta by speech. These are the six parts (Vedaṅgas) of Vedas.

Kalpa-Sūtras are of four varieties: 1. Śrauta-Sūtras (sacrificial rituals as prescribed in the Vedas), 2. Gṛhya-Sūtras (domestic rituals), 3. Dharma-Sūtras (public laws), and 4. Śulba-Sūtras (geometrical specifications for *homa kuṇḍas*).

Many texts are understood to have been lost. *Baijavāpa Gṛhya-Sūtra* belonging to *Śukla Yajurveda* is not to be found though it finds mention in many of the books on Dharmaśāstra. There are references to *Parāśara Gṛhya-Sūtra* and *Paiṅgya Gṛhya-Sūtra* belonging to *Ṛgveda* but the texts are not available. Many of the texts have been critically edited by various scholars. Texts have been found in palm-leaf manuscripts in various scripts. Efforts have been made and are being made to preserve them in print and electronic forms. The following Kalpa-Sūtra texts are currently available

ŚRAUTA SŪTRAS

Ṛgveda	Aśvalayāna, Śāṅkhāyana
Kṛṣṇa Yajurveda	Āpastamba, Baudhāyana, Hiraṇyakeśi, Bhāradvāja, Vaikhānasa, Vādhūla, Mānava, Vārāha

---

10 *Śloka* 9 of *Ṛk Sarva* composed by six *guru-śiṣyas*.

Śukla Yajurveda	Kātyāyana (Pāraskara)
Sāmaveda	Khādira, Lāṭyāyana, Drāhyāyana, Jaiminīya
Atharvaveda	Kauśika

DHARMA-SŪTRAS

Ṛgveda	Vasiṣṭha
Kṛṣṇa Yajurveda	Āpastamba, Baudhāyana, Hiraṇyakeśi, Vaikhānasa
Śukla Yajurveda	—
Sāmaveda	Gautama
Atharvaveda	—

ŚULBA-SŪTRAS

All Śulba-Sūtras belong to *Yajurveda*.

Kṛṣṇa Yajurveda	Āpastamba, Baudhāyana, Hiraṇyakeśi, Mānava, Vārāha, Maitrāyaṇīya, Vādhūla
Śukla Yajurveda	Kātyāyana

GṚHYA-SŪTRAS

Ṛgveda	Āśvalāyana, Śaṅkhāyana, Kauṣītaki
Kṛṣṇa Yajurveda	Āpastamba, Baudhāyana, Hiraṇyakeśi, Bhāradvāja, Vaikhānasa, Mānava, Vārāha, Agniveśya, Kāṭhaka (Laugākṣi)
Śukla Yajurveda	Pāraskara
Sāmaveda	Khādira (Drāhyāyaṇa), Gobhila, Jaiminī, Kauthuma
Atharvaveda	Kauśika

Gṛhya-Sūtras

Gṛhya-Sūtras contain rituals to be followed by a householder which are generally called Smārta-Sūtras. While Śrauta-Sutras contain details of Vedic sacrifices and *yajñas* to be conducted, rituals to be performed by the householder are not included in them. Gṛhya-Sūtras are the texts which contain details of all *saṁskāras* to be followed by the householder. Gṛhya-Sūtras as well as other Sūtras are in the form of aphorisms for the sake of brevity. Since the oral teaching method was employed, the Sūtra form made it easier to memorize. Gṛhya-Sūtras contain details of how *saṁskāras* from *garbhādhāna* to *antyeṣṭi* are to be carried out. While some start with *vivāha saṁskāra*, being considered the most important *saṁskāra*, others start with *upanayana*. Smṛtis which appeared later further modified the *saṁskāras* influenced by sociological factors. Dharma-Sūtras are closely associated with Gṛhya-Sūtras sometimes overlapping each other.

A number of scholars have written commentaries on the original Sūtras to explain what is intended to be followed by the householder in observing the rituals. Devavrāṭa, Sudarśana, Gadādhara, Haradatta, Nārāyaṇa, Jayarāma, Rāmakṛṣṇa, Mātṛdatta, Kapardisvāmin, Bhavatrāta and Dārila are some of the commentators who have written on different Gṛhya-Sūtras. Though the Gṛhya-Sūtras prescribed the way each *saṁskāra* is to be observed, the Sūtra form made it difficult to understand all aspects of the procedures required. The commentaries on each Gṛhya-Sūtra elaborated on the Sūtras keeping in mind the context under which each *saṁskāra* was to be performed. From these emerged *pariśiṣṭas*, *prayogas*, *paddhatis* and *kārikās* which gave detailed explanations and also included ancillary activities like *saṁkalpa*, *Gaṇapatī Pūjā*, *nāndiśrādha* and *puṇyāha vācana*. Over time, though the basic rituals remained the same, additional features got included varying from area to area. Āpastamba in his Gṛhya-Sūtra mentions that the tradition prevailing in the area is to be followed. Cultural, sociological and geographical aspects affected the way *saṁskāras* evolved in different parts of the land with additions, deletions and modifications. The study of all the *pariśiṣṭas*, *prayogas*, *paddhatis* and *kārikās* will involve too large a canvas considering the differences which had cropped up in different regions. It is for this reason that this attempt confines itself to the comparative study of Gṛhya-Sūtras available. Out of these, *Kauthuma Gṛhya-Sūtra* belonging to *Sāmaveda* has not been considered as it does not contain much information on *vivāha saṁskāra*.

Regarding *mantras* used in various *saṁskāras*, some of the Gṛhya-Sūtras mention only the beginning line of the *mantra* (*pratīka*) while others quote the entire *mantra*. Most of the *mantras* can be traced to the 10th Maṇḍala of *Ṛgveda* and the 14th Kāṇḍa of *Atharvaveda*. There are variations in some of the *mantras* in different Gṛhya-Sūtras. Sources of some *mantras* are not clearly traceable. The *Mantra Pāṭha* of *Āpastambins*, *Mantra Brāhmaṇa* of *Sāmaveda*, *Āśvalāyana Mantra Vyākhyā* and *Ekāgni Kaṇḍa* are some of the texts with *mantra* collections. *Āgniveśya Gṛhya-Sūtra* contains a list of *mantras* in the main body of the text.

The period of Gṛhya-Sūtras is estimated to be during 800–300 BCE according to P.V. Kane.[11] In the recent past, a large number of Indian Indologists have studied the texts in detail and written books and presented papers in English and Indian languages. Many of the manuscripts were on palm leaves in scripts of many Indian languages such as Telugu and Grantha. These have been transliterated into the Devanāgarī script. Many of the Oriental research institutes around India and manuscript libraries are collecting and preserving the texts in different forms.

A number of Western scholars have studied Gṛhya-Sūtras and other texts and translated many of them into German, French and English. Among them are Willem Caland, Hermann Oldenberg, Maurice Winternitz, Friedirich Knauer, Maurice Bloomfield, Arthur Berriedale Keith, Adolf Freidrich Stenzler, George Bühler, Louis Renou, etc. Winternitz has published a collection of *mantras* referred in the *Āpastamba Gṛhya-Sūtra*

11 *His.Dh.Ś*, vol II, pt. I, p. ix.

called *The Mantra Pāṭha of Āpastambins*. It is the considered opinion of scholars that Gṛhya-Sūtras present a remarkable opportunity to understand the lives, attitudes and concerns of people and the society of the times they were written in. Gṛhya-Sūtras present a unique mirror to the society of ancient times and have indeed become recorded history. They help one understand the religious and spiritual nature of society of the times.

Ṣoḍaśa Saṁskāras

It is generally accepted that sixteen *saṁskāra*s are to be observed by a householder. Some of the texts do not include *antyeṣṭi* which is to be observed at funerals:

1. *Garbhādhāna* – Conception
2. *Puṁsavana* – Ritual for a male child to be born
3. *Sīmantonnayana* – Parting of hair of the pregnant wife
4. *Jātakarma* – Rituals at the time of the child's birth
5. *Nāmakaraṇa* – Naming ceremony
6. *Niṣkramaṇa* – Ritual when the child is taken out for the first time
7. *Annaprāśana* – Ritual when the child is given solid food for the first time
8. *Cūḍākarma* – The first hair cut of the child
9. *Karṇavedha* – Ear piercing
10. *Vidyārambha* – Teaching of alphabets for the first time
11. *Upanayana* – Ritual of wearing the sacred thread
12. *Vedārambha* – Beginning of the study of scriptures

13. *Keśānta (Godāna)* – Ritual for shaving the beard for the first time

14. *Samāvartana* – Ritual bath at the end of studentship

15. *Vivāha* – Marriage

16. *Antyeṣṭi* – Funeral rites

The first three, namely *garbhādhāna, puṁsavana* and *sīmantonnayana* are considered to be pre-natal *saṁskāras*. *Jātakarma, nāmakaraṇa, niṣkramaṇa, annaprāśana, cūḍākarma* and *karṇavedha* are considered to be *childhood saṁskāras*. *Vidyārāmbha, upanayana, vedārambha, keśānta* and *samāvartana* are considered to be educational *saṁskāras*. *Vivāha* and *antyeṣṭi* are *saṁskāras* of the householder.

The purpose of this research is to bring together all the extant Gṛhya-Sūtras and examine *vivāha saṁskāra* depicted in them comparatively. The sections dealing with *vivāha saṁskāra* have been reproduced in the original with translations in English. The texts have been collected from various sources, preference having been given to critical editions. Available translations in English and other languages have been adopted. A comparative study has been made with the number and order of rituals, the *mantras* recommended, etc. Collections of marriage *mantras* have also been provided in the Appendix section. Wherever possible, the sources of the *mantras* have also been indicated for reference.

2

Vivāha Saṁskāra

Vivāha saṁskāra (marriage) is considered the most important *saṁskāra*. Marriage as an institution was well established in ancient India and elaborate rituals were prescribed for conducting it. Promiscuous behaviour was not accepted socially and marriage was sacrosanct. Marriage was considered to be a religious obligation for a Hindu. Even in present times, *vivāha saṁskāra* is a highly important ritualistic event in the life of a Hindu. It is an exciting event for the couple getting married and their families. From ancient times, marriages have been arranged between families by the process of sending wooers to the house of the bride, going through the process of selecting her and in some cases with the exchange of gifts and money. Considerations such as caste, *gotra*, *sapiṇḍa* relationships and the qualities of the bride and the groom have played a part in choosing brides and grooms.

The word *vivāha* comes from the root *vaḥ* (to carry). Some other words meaning marriage are *pāṇigrahaṇa*, *pariṇaya*, *udvāha*, *upayāma*, etc. *Pāṇigrahaṇa* is the earliest ritual of marriage which is mentioned in *Ṛgveda*. Meaning holding of hand, *pāṇigrahaṇa* appears to have been common to many other cultures as a marriage ritual. *Pariṇaya* comes from *Agni Pariṇayana*, namely circumambulating the fire. *Udvāha* also comes from the root *vaḥ*. *Upayāma* means bringing closer referring to acquiring a bride to be part of the household. A lot of importance was given to the journey of the bride to her husband's home with elaborate rituals prescribed for it. It appears that for this reason, the word *vivāha* is the most commonly used one to represent marriage. All the Gṛhya-Sūtras use the word *vivāha* as the main heading when writing about the marriage ceremony. *Vivāha* represents the journey of the bride to her husband's house to become a partner in the stage of *gṛhasthāśrama* of her husband.

It is said in *Tāṇḍya Mahābrāhmaṇa* VIII.10.1:

> इमौ वै लोकौ सहास्तां तौ वियन्तावभूतां विवाहं विवाहवहै सह नावस्त्विति ।
>
> Heaven and earth were once together but they separated, then they said, "Let us have a marriage, let there be co-operation between us".

As Aparārka says:

> एवं उपयमनपाणिग्रहणशब्दवत् परिणयणशब्दोऽपि दण्डिन्यायेनैव कर्मसमुदाये शास्त्रेषु प्रयुज्यते ।
>
> With the words *upayāma* and *pāṇigrahaṇa*, *pariṇaya* also appears in the scriptures of rituals. — Aparārka, p. 91

Marriage rituals, which evolved in an era long gone past, are even today being practised with the basic elements unchanged. Marriage is an event involving not just the couple but families and friends as well. Marriage forms an important milestone as one steps into the life of a householder and prepares to start a family. It is also the vehicle to carry on the traditions of conducting religious obligations by performing *yajña*s, etc. for the well-being of the family as well as to please the souls of ancestors. Marriage is the first step in a man's life in *gṛhasthāśrama* which is considered by many to be the superior of the four *āśrama*s. *Gṛhasthāśrama* was an important stage in the development of man. A man was expected to fulfil his social responsibilities and desires by raising a family, earning money through his profession and ensure continuance of his lineage. Even though ultimately, the ideal goal would be to attain *mokṣa*, the seers of the Vedic age realized the practicality of life as a *gṛhastha*. *Gṛhasthāśrama* also fulfilled the innate desire to continue the human race by marriage and procreation.

What is marriage? According one ancient view, man and woman represent *Pradhāna Puruṣa* and *Prakṛti* and they come together in marriage to prolong creation. It was considered that a man has to get married and produce offspring to have lived a complete life.

> अर्धो ह वा आत्मनो यज्जाया तस्माद्यावज्जायां न विन्दते नैव तावत्प्रजायते असर्वो हि तावद्भवति । अथ यदैव जायां विन्दतेऽथा प्रजायते तर्हि हि सर्वो भवति ।
>
> The wife is indeed half of one's self; therefore, as long as man does not secure a wife and beget an issue, he remains incomplete. When a man gets a wife and begets progeny, only then he becomes complete.
>
> — *Śatapatha Brāhmaṇa* V.2.1.10
>
> तस्मात् पुरुषो जायां वित्त्वा कृत्स्नतरमिवात्मानं मन्यते ।
>
> Therefore a man, after securing a wife, regards himself as wholly complete. — *Aitareya Brāhmaṇa* I.2.5

A man needs to have a wife to complete religious duties as a householder. It is essential to have his wife with him to keep the household fire burning continuously. The household fire is called *gārhapatya* in *Ṛgveda* as mentioned in the *pāṇigrahaṇa* ritual. Marriage, therefore, becomes an important religious duty apart from being the vehicle to fulfil secular requirements of society. Importance was given to the wife in fulfilling the requirements of religious duties. It was a couple that performed religious duties. The wife was considered an essential part of such duties.

> अपत्यं धर्मकार्याणि शुश्रूष रतिरुत्तमा ।
> दाराधीनास्तथा स्वर्गःपितृणां आत्मनश्च ह ॥
>
> Offspring, religious rites, faithful service, highest conjugal happiness and heavenly bliss for one's ancestors and oneself depend on one's wife alone. — *Manu Smṛti* IX.28

Āpastamba in his Dharma-Sūtra states as follows emphatically:

जायापत्योर्न विभागो विद्यते । पाणिग्रहणाद्धि सहत्वं कर्मसु ।

A man and woman should perform religious acts together as a married couple and there is no question of separation between them. — *ĀP.Dh.S.* II.6.13.16,17

It is said that a man is born with three debts and these are repaid by: 1. studying Vedas (*brahmacarya*); 2. conducting *yajñas*; and 3. by begetting sons. Debts owed to *ṛṣis* are to be repaid by *brahmacarya*, to gods by conducting *yajña*s and to one's parents by begetting sons. A man needs to get married to beget sons and repay the debt owed to his father.

जायमानो वै ब्राह्मणस्त्रिभिर्ऋणवान् जायते ब्रह्मचर्येन ऋषिभ्यो यज्ञेन देवेभ्यः प्रजया पितृभ्यः ।

A man is born with three debts. Debts to *ṛṣis* are repaid by *brahmacarya*, to gods by *yajña*s and to one's father by producing sons. — *Tai.Sa.* VI.3.10.5

Ṛgveda is considered to be the oldest of scriptures known to mankind. According to Kane, the period of *Ṛgveda* is 4000 BCE. The earliest reference to marriage is in *Ṛgveda*. This is the marriage of Soma, the Moon with Sūryā, the daughter of Savitā, the Sun. The two Aśvins are sent to meet the Sun and negotiate the alliance. Savitā, the Sun knowing that Sūryā is happy with the alliance gives her to Soma.

सोमो वधूयुरभवदश्विनास्तामुभा वरा ।
सूर्यां यत्पत्ये शंसन्तीं मनसा सवितादादात् ॥

Soma, the Moon is desirous of a bride and the two Aśvins negotiated on his behalf with Savitā, the Sun for the hand of his daughter Sūryā. Savitā knowing that his daughter liked the alliance gave her to Soma. — *ṚV* X.85.9

Ṛgveda, in the 10th Maṇḍala, describes the steps in the marriage ritual and also contains many of the *mantra*s used in marriages. The early marriage rituals depicted in *Ṛgveda* are fairly simple and do not contain many of the features which were introduced later. Further steps were elaborated in *Atharvaveda*. Subsequently, all the *saṁskāras* including *vivāha* have been dealt with in detail in the Gṛhya-Sūtras. Gṛhya-Sūtras, belonging to different branches of all the four Vedas, specified the ways to conduct the *vivāha saṁskāras* in detail. Apart from the references in the Vedas, additions were subsequently made to the rituals making them more and more elaborate. Smṛtis which came later further modified the rituals. Sociological and geographical factors influenced the contents of the *saṁskāras*. Dharma-Sūtras, Purāṇas, Epics, *Kāma-Sūtra*, Kāvyas and Nāṭakas also depicted the marriage ceremony which influenced the way marriage was conducted in the later periods with additions and modifications.

Forms of Marriage

Gṛhya-Sūtras, Dharma-Sūtras and Smṛtis have described eight forms of marriage. They are Brāhma, Daiva, Prājāpatya, Ārṣa, Gāndharva, Āsura, Rākṣasa and Paiśāca. Some Gṛhya-Sūtras mention only six leaving out the last two. *Mānava Gṛhya-Sūtra* mentions only two types of marriages, namely — Brāhma and Śaulka (Āsura). Hiraṇyakeśī is silent on the types of marriages. The eight kinds of marriages were described for the first time in *Āśvalāyana Gṛhya-Sūtra*. Some scholars believe that this was a later interpolation. It is felt that the eight types were introduced only at the time of Dharma-Sūtras. It is the opinion of many scholars that the eight types of marriage do not refer to the marriage ceremony as such but to the way a bride is acquired by different sections of society. Marriage rituals had to be gone through as specified in Gṛhya-Sūtras after the acquisition of the bride in different ways. The types of marriages also indicated evolution of social norms over a period of time.

The eight types of marriages are described as follows:

Brāhma	:	The father gifts his daughter to a worthy bridegroom invited by him.
Daiva	:	The bride is given to a priest as part of sacrificial fee.
Prājāpatya	:	The bride is given in marriage to the worthy bridegroom who asks for her hand.
Ārṣa	:	The bridegroom gives a gift of a cow and a bull to the father of the bride in exchange for her hand.
Gāndharva	:	Marriage by mutual consent between the bride and the groom.
Āsura	:	The bride is purchased by the bridegroom from her father.
Rākṣasa	:	The bride is forcibly carried away by the bridegroom.
Paiśāca	:	Seduction of the bride while she is asleep or drugged.

Of these, the first four are considered superior to the rest. Brāhma type is considered most desirable. The types of marriages reflected the life styles of different sections in society and their occupations. Forcibly carrying away the bride, as in the Rākṣasa form of marriage, was prevalent among the warrior classes. Brāhma, Daiva and Prājāpatya forms were observed by the priestly classes. The order of the eight types varies in different Gṛhya-Sūtras. Some hold the view that there is hardly any difference between Brāhma and Prājāpatya forms of marriage. Gāndharva type of marriage has been exemplified in the marriage of Śakuntalā with Duṣyanta by Kālidāsa in his famous play, *Abhijñāna-Śākuntalam*. There are many instances of the Rākṣasa form of marriage in *Mahābhārata* and Purāṇas. It was believed that this form of marriage was accepted by kṣatriyas. However, this form of marriage was not approved by the Dharma-Śāstra writers but accepted as a social reality.

It was believed that children born after marriage of different forms brought different benefits to the family.

यथायुक्तो विवाहस्तथायुक्ता प्रजा भवति ।

The character of children will depend on the type of marriage gone through. — *Āp.Dh.S.* II.5.12.4

Āśvalayana (*Āś.G.S.* I.6.1) says that a son born of marriage of the Brāhma form will bring purification to twelve descendants and twelve ancestors on both sides, a son born of marriage of the Daiva form will bring purification to ten descendants and ten ancestors on both sides, a son born of marriage of the Prājāpatya form will bring purification to eight descendants and eight ancestors on both sides and a son born of marriage of the Ārṣa form will bring purification to seven descendants and seven ancestors on both sides. Others such as Manu and Gautama have similar views though they differ in the quantum of benefits arising out of different forms of marriage. Other forms of marriage were not expected to produce progeny of good character. On the contrary, they were said to produce sons who would bring disrepute to the families.

The word *svayaṁvara* appears in *Rāmāyaṇa, Mahābhārata* and other works such as *Raghuvaṁśa* and *Vikramāṅka Devacarita* of Bilhaṇa. The marriage of Sītā, Draupadī, Damayantī and others are examples of *svayaṁvara*. However, *svayaṁvara* was not included in the forms of marriage as it was felt that it was similar to *gāndharva vivāha*. Vīramitrodaya in his commentary on *Yājñavalkya Smṛti* says as follows:

त्वं मे पतिस्त्वं मे भार्येत्येवं कन्यावरयोः परस्परं नियमबन्धात् पित्रादिकर्तृकदाननिरपेक्षाद्यो विवाहः स गान्धर्व इत्यर्थः ।

Without expectations of action from parents, if the man and woman decide to accept each other as wife and husband, it is *gāndharva vivāha*.

Vivāha in the Vedas

Early marriage rituals as described in *Ṛgveda* were fairly simple. It appears that the main ritual was *pāṇigrahaṇa* which means holding of hands. The journey of the bride to her husband's house was given a lot of importance with rituals to be observed for getting the chariot ready, obstacles on the way, etc.

The rituals as described in *Ṛgveda* are the following:

- Negotiation and selection of the bride
- Selecting an auspicious day
- *Pāṇigrahaṇa*
- Carrying the bride to her new home in a chariot
- Consummation of the marriage

From the above, it is clear that child marriages were not prevalent in the early era. Consummation took place immediately after marriage and this meant that only girls who had reached puberty were ready for marriage. Child marriages came into vogue later in the Dharma-Sūtra and Smṛti periods.

Rituals mentioned in *Atharvaveda* are the following:

- Selecting an auspicious day
- Ritual bath of the bride
- *Pāṇigrahaṇa*
- *Aśmārohaṇa*
- *Lājā Homa*
- Journey to the groom's house
- Sitting on a bull's hide
- Consummation of marriage

Here one can notice that *aśmārohaṇa, lājā homa* and sitting on a bull's hide have been introduced. Other features like Saptapadī and Dhruva Arundhati Darśana were introduced subsequently. All rituals had specific goals as their purpose such as praying for longevity, faithfulness, good children, wealth, cattle, harmonious relationship, etc. Some rituals involved warding off of evil spirits, machinations of enemies and dangers while going on journeys, etc. Some Gṛhya-Sūtras mention the use of music, dance and musical instruments in the marriage ceremony. Expiation (*prāyaścitta*) is also part of *vivāha saṁskāra*. *Nāpita karma* has been mentioned in *Baudhāyana Gṛhya-Sūtra*.

Vivāha Saṁskāra does not figure prominently in *Yajurveda* and *Sāmaveda* even though Gṛhya-Sūtras, Dharma-Sūtras and Smṛtis belonging to these two Vedas describe *vivāha saṁskāras* in detail. *Yajurveda* deals mostly with Śrauta rituals while *Sāmaveda* is liturgical with emphasis on the musical aspect of *ślokas*. The marriage ceremony is also dealt with in Smṛtis, Purāṇas, Itihāsas, *Kāma-Sūtra*, Kāvyas and Nāṭakas, etc. However, the basis of all rituals is in Gṛhya-Sūtras. Smṛti texts which came after Gṛhya-Sūtras brought in many changes to the rituals. Different commentaries on Gṛhya-Sūtras have led to the establishment of *prayogas*, *paddhatis* and *kārikās* which explain the rituals and their contexts elaborately.

Gṛhya-Sūtras belonging to different Vedas generally are similar in content. The three Gṛhya-Sūtras of *Ṛgveda* — *Āśvalāyana*, *Śāṅkhāyana* and *Kauṣītaki* — do not have many differences except those influenced by geographical and local cultural factors. The ten available Gṛhya-Sūtras of *Yajurveda* show quite a bit of variations in content and complexity. *Baudhāyana Gṛhya-Sūtra* is the most elaborate of all the Gṛhya-Sūtras. The three Gṛhya-Sūtras of *Sāmaveda* follow a common trend. Only one Gṛhya-Sūtra belonging to *Atharvaveda* is available, namely *Kauśika Gṛhya-Sūtra*.

The sections dealing with marriage, *vivāha saṁskāra*, have been shown in the original in the following chapter of this book with translation in English. Attempts have been made to analyse the differences in the way marriage has been dealt with in each Gṛhya-Sūtra with comparisons of the constituents, order and *mantra*s used in the rituals. A separate chapter analyses the differences in the *mantra*s and the Appendix contains *mantra*s used by the different *sūtrakāra*s. It is hoped that the bringing together of all the available texts on *vivāha saṁskāra* in one place with the translations and the collections of *mantra*s would be useful for future researchers.

3

Gṛhya-Sūtras of Ṛgveda

THE sections of Gṛhya-Sūtras of *Ṛgveda* dealing with *vivāha saṁskāra* have been depicted with English translation in this chapter. The following Gṛhya-Sūtras belonging to *Ṛgveda* are extant: 1. *Āśvalāyana*, 2. *Śāṅkhāyana*, and 3. *Kauṣītaki*. Each has been dealt separately with text and translation. Translations of earlier scholars have been referred to.

Āśvalāyana Gṛhya-Sūtra

Āśvalāyana was a pupil of Śaunaka who is the author of *Daśa Granthas*. Āśvalāyana is said to have composed Śrauta-Sūtra in twelve *adhyāyas*, Gṛhya-Sūtra in four *adhyāyas* and the fourth Āraṇyaka. He is believed to have lived between 500 and 350 BCE. Devavrāṭa Devasvāmin wrote a commentary on *Āśvalāyana Gṛhya-Sūtra* followed by Naidhruva Nārāyaṇa. The following is the text of *Āśvalāyana Gṛhya-Sūtra* which deals with *vivāha saṁskāra*.

प्रथमोऽध्यायः (First Chapter)
चतुर्थं खण्डम्: (Fourth Section)

उदगयन आपूर्यमाणपक्षे कल्याणे नक्षत्रे चौलकर्मोपनयनगोदानविवाहाः ॥१॥
During the northern course of the sun, in the period of the waxing moon (*śukla pakṣa*), under an auspicious *nakṣatra*, the *saṁskāras* of *caulakarma*, *upanayana*, *godāna* (*keśanta*) and *vivāha* can be performed.

सार्वकालमेके विवाहम् ॥२॥
Some people opine that marriage can be conducted at all times.

तेषां पुरस्ताच्चतस्र आज्याहुतीर्जुहुयात् ॥३॥
Before the ceremonies, let him offer four *ājya* (ghee) oblations.

अग्न आयूंषि पवस इति तिसृभिः प्रजापते न त्वदेतान्यन्य इति च व्याहृतिभिर्वा ॥४॥
With three verses beginning with "Agni, you purify life" and one with "Prajāpati, none other than you" or with the *vyāhṛti*s (*bhūr bhuvaḥ svaḥ*).

समुच्चयमेके ॥५॥
Some say with the *mantra*s and *vyāhṛtis*.

नैके काञ्चन ॥६॥
Others say no oblations are required.

त्वमर्यमा भवसि यत्कनीनामिति विवाहे चतुर्थीम् ॥७॥
At the marriage, the fourth oblation should be offered with "Agni, you are Aryamā towards girls".

पञ्चमं खण्डम् (Fifth Section)

कुलमग्रे परीक्षेते ये मातृतः पितृतश्चेति यथोक्तं पुरस्तात् ॥१॥
Let him examine the family of the bride or groom, as it has been said before, "those who are from the father's side or from the mother's side".

बुद्धिमते कन्यां प्रयच्छेत् ॥२॥
The father should give the girl to an intelligent groom.

बुद्धिरूपशीललक्षणसम्पन्नामरोगामुपयच्छेतु ॥३॥
Let him marry a girl who is endowed with intelligence, beauty, moral conduct and one who is free from disease.

दुर्विज्ञेयानि लक्षणानीति ॥४॥
It is difficult to discern the qualities.

अष्टौ पिण्डान्कृत्वा ऋतमग्रे प्रथमं जज्ञ ऋते सत्यं प्रतिष्ठितम् । यदियं कुमार्यभिजाता तदियमिह प्रतिपद्यतां यत्सत्यं तद्दृश्यतामिति पिण्डानभिमन्त्र्य कुमारीं ब्रूयादेषामेकं गृहाण इति ॥५॥

Let him prepare eight lumps of earth and recite over the lumps the *mantra*: "In the beginning, right was established: On the right, truth is founded. For what purpose the girl is born, may she attain that here. What is true may be seen here." Then let him tell her to pick one of the lumps.

क्षेत्राच्चेदुभयतःसस्याद्गृह्णीयदन्नवत्यस्याः प्रजा भविष्यतीति विद्याद्गोष्ठात्पशुमती वेदपुरीषाद्ब्रह्मवर्चस्विन्यविदासिनो ह्रदात् सर्वसम्पन्ना देवनात्कितवी चतुष्पथाद्द्विप्रव्राजिनीरिणादधन्या श्मशानात्पतिघ्नी ॥६॥

If the girl chooses the lump from a field that produces two crops a year, he may know that her offspring will be rich in food. If from a cow stable, they will be rich in cattle. If from a Vedic altar, they will be rich in holy lustre. If from a pool which does not dry up, they will be rich in everything. If from a gambling place, they will be addicted to gambling. If from a place where four roads meet, they will be wandering in different directions. If from a barren ground, they will be poor. If she chooses the lump from a burial ground, she will cause the death of her husband.

षष्ठं खण्डम् (Sixth Section)

अलङ्कृत्य कन्यामुदकपूर्वां दद्यादेष ब्राह्मो विवाहः । तस्यां जातो द्वादशावरान्द्वादश परान्पुनात्युभयतः । ऋत्विजे वितते कर्मणि दद्यादलन्कृत्य स दैवो दशावरान्दश परान्पुनात्युभ्यतः । सह धर्मं चरत इति प्राजापत्योऽष्टावरानष्ट परान्पुनात्युभवतः । गोमिथुनं दत्त्वोपयच्छेत स आर्षः सप्तावरान्सप्त परान्पुनात्युभयतः । मिथः समयं कृत्वोपयच्छेत स गान्धर्वः । धननोपतोष्योपयच्छेत सः आसुरः । सुप्तानां प्रमत्तानां वाऽपहरेत्स पैशाचः । हत्वा भित्वा च शीर्षाणि रुदतीम् रुदद्भ्यो हरेत्स राक्षसः ॥१॥

The father may give away the daughter adorned with ornaments to the bridegroom with a libation of water. Such a marriage is called *brāhma vivāha*. A son born of this union will purify twelve descendants and twelve ancestors on both sides. He may give her away to an officiating priest having adorned her with jewels while a sacrifice with three Śrauta fires are going on. Such a marriage is called a *daiva vivāha*. A son from this marriage will bring purification to ten descendants and ten ancestors on both sides. If the bride and the groom observe the nuptial rites (dhārmic) together, the marriage is called *prājāpatya vivāha*. A son born of such a marriage will purify eight descendants and eight ancestors from both sides. If the father receives a bull and a cow from the groom for giving away the bride, such a marriage is called *ārṣa*. A son from this marriage purifies seven descendants and seven ancestors on both sides. If the bride and groom marry after mutual agreement, the marriage is called *gāndharva vivāha*. If the groom marries the girl after having satisfied her father with money, such a marriage is called *āsura*. If the groom carries off the bride while her people are asleep or inattentive, the marriage is called *paiśāca*. If he carries off the girl after killing her relatives and while she and relatives weep, the marriage is called *rākṣasa*.

सप्तमं खण्डम् (Seventh Section)

अथ खलूच्चावचा जनपदधर्मा ग्रामधर्माश्च तान्विवाहे प्रतीयात् ॥१॥
Now, various indeed are the customs of countries and villages. He should observe these at the wedding.

यत्तु समानं तद्वक्ष्यामः ॥२॥
What is commonly accepted is what we shall state.

पश्चादग्नेर्दृषदश्मानं प्रतिष्ठाप्योत्तरपुरस्तादुदकुम्भं समन्वारब्धायां हुत्वा तिष्ठन्प्रत्यङ्मुखः प्राङ्मुख्या आसीनाया गृभ्णामि ते सौभगत्वाय हस्तमित्यङ्गुष्ठमेव गृह्णीयद्यदि कामयित पुमांस एव मे जायेरन्नीति ॥३॥

Having placed to the west of the fire a stone and a water-pot to the north-east, he should sacrifice while she takes hold of him. Standing with his face to the west, while she is sitting with her face to the east, he should with the *mantra* "I seize your hand for the sake of happiness" seize her thumb if he desires that only male issues be born to him.

अङ्गुलीरेव स्त्रीकामः ॥४॥
Other fingers, if he is desirous of female children.

रोमान्ते हस्तं साङ्गुष्ठमुभयकामः ॥५॥

If he desires both male and female children, he should seize her hand on the hair-side together with the thumb.

प्रदक्षिणमग्निमुदकुम्भं च त्रिः परिणयञ्जपति । अमोहमस्मि सा त्वं सा त्वमस्यमोहं द्यौरहं पृथिवी त्वं सामाहमृक्त्वं तावेह विवहावहै । प्रजां प्रजनयावहै संप्रियौ रोचिष्णू सुमनस्यमानौ जीवेव शरदः शतमिति ॥६॥

He should lead her round the nuptial fire and the water-pot thrice. He should recite the *mantra*: "This am I (God), that are you. That are you (Goddess), this I am. I am the heaven, you are the earth. I am the song, you are the words. Come let us marry. Let us beget offspring. Loving, bright and with good minds may we live a hundred autumns."

परिणीय परिणीयाश्मानमारोहयतीममश्मानमारोहाश्मेव त्वं स्थिरा भव। सहस्व पृतनायतोऽभितिष्ठ पृतन्यत इति ॥७॥

Each time after he has taken her round the fire, he makes her tread on a stone reciting the *mantra* "ascend this stone; be firm like a stone, overcome enemies, tread the enemies down".

वध्वञ्जलावुपस्तीर्य भ्रात भ्रातृस्थानो वा द्विर्लाजानावपति ॥८॥

Having spread butter over the hands of the bride, her brother or a substitute should pour fried grain twice over her joined hands.

त्रर्जामिदग्न्यानाम् ॥९॥

Thrice for the descendants of Jamadagni.

प्रत्यभिघार्य हविः ॥१०॥

He should pour butter again over the sacrificial food.

अवत्तं च ॥११॥

And over what has been cut-off.

एषोऽवदानधर्मः ॥१२॥

This is the rule about the portions cut-off.

अर्यमणं नु देवं कन्या अग्निमयक्षत । स इमां देवोऽर्यमा प्रेतो मुञ्चातु नामृतः स्वाहाः । वरुणं नु देवं कन्या अग्निमयक्षत । स इमां देवो वरुणः प्रेतो मुञ्चातु नामृतः स्वाहा । पूषणं नु देवं कन्या अग्निमयक्षत । स इमां देवः पूषा प्रेतो मुञ्चातु नामृतः स्वाहेत्यविच्छिन्दत्यञ्जलीं स्रु चेव जुहुयात् ॥१३॥

For God Aryamā the girls have offered oblations to Agni. May he, God Aryamā release her from this and not that place. For God Varuṇa, the girls have offered oblations to Agni. May he, God Varuṇa release her from this and not that place. For God Pūṣaṇa, the girls have offered oblations to Agni. May he, God Pūṣaṇa release her from this and not that place. With these verses she should offer fried grain without opening her hand as if she did so with a spoon (*sṛk*).

अपरिणीय शूर्पपुटेनाभ्यां तूष्णीं चतुर्थम् ॥१४॥

Without being taken round the fire, she offers grain from the basket towards herself, silently a fourth time.

ओप्योप्य हैके लाजान्परिणयन्ति । तथोत्तमे आहुति न सन्निपततः ॥१५॥

Some lead the bride round each time after the fried grain has been poured out. Thus the last two oblations do not immediately succeed each other.

अथास्यै शिखे विमुञ्चति यदि कृते भवतः ॥१६॥

He then loosens her two locks of hair if they are tied.

ऊणरिस्तुके केशपक्षयोबद्धे भवतः "प्र त्वा मुञ्चामि वरुणस्य पाशात्" इति ॥१७॥

If two tufts of wool are tied around her hair on the two sides, he should release the right tuft first with the *mantra* "I release you from the noose of Varuṇa".

उत्तरामुत्तरया ॥१८॥

He releases the left tuft afterwards.

अथैनामपराजितायां दिशि सप्तपदान्यभ्युत्क्रामयति "इष एकपद्यूर्जे द्विपदो रायस्पोषाय त्रिपदी मायोभव्याय चतुष्पदी प्रजाभ्यः पञ्चपद्यृतुभ्यः षट्पदी

सखा सप्तपदी भव सा मामनुव्रता भव । पुत्रान्विन्दावहै बहूँस्ते सन्तु जरदष्टयः इति ॥"१९॥

He then makes her walk seven steps in the north-eastern direction with the following *mantra*: "One step for sap, two for energy, three for wealth, four for prosperity, five for offspring, six for seasons and be a friend with seven steps. So be devoted to me. Let us beget many sons who may reach old age."

उभयोः संनिधाय शिरसी उदकुम्भेनावसिच्य ॥२०॥

The priest then joins the heads of the bride and groom and sprinkles them with water.

ब्राह्मण्यश्च वृद्धाया जीवपत्न्या जीवप्रजाया अगार एतां रात्रीम् वसेत् ॥२१॥

She should dwell that night in the house of an aged brāhmaṇa woman whose husband and children are alive.

धृवमरुन्धतीं सप्तऋषीनिति दृष्ट्वा वाचं विसृजेत जीवपत्नीं प्रजां विन्देय इति ॥२२॥

When she sees the star Dhruva, the star Arundhati and the *sapta-ṛṣi maṇḍala*, let her break her silence and say, "may my husband live long and may I get children".

अष्टमं खण्डम् (Eighth Section)

प्रयाण उपपद्यमाने "पूषा त्वेतो नयतु हस्तगृह्य" इति यानमारोहयेत् ॥१॥

When the newly-wedded couple set out on the journey, let him make her mount the chariot with the *mantra* "May Pūṣaṇa lead you from here holding your hand".

"अश्मन्वतीरीयते संरभध्वम्" इत्यर्धर्चेन नावमारोहयेत् ॥२॥

With the *mantra*, "carrying stones, the river flows. Hold fast together" he should make her ascend a ship.

उत्तरणोत्क्रमयेत् ॥३॥

With the following *mantra*, let him make her descend.

"जीवं रुदन्ति" इति रुदत्याम् ॥४॥

He pronounces "the living one they bewail", if anyone weeps.

विवाहाग्निमग्रतोऽजस्रं नयन्ति ॥५॥
They carry the nuptial fire in front always.

कल्याणेषु देशवृक्षचतुष्पथेषु माविदन्परिपन्थिन इति जपेत् ॥६॥
At auspicious places, trees and crossroads he should murmur "let no robbers way lay us".

"वासे वासे सुमङ्गलीरियं वधूः" इतीक्षकानीक्षेत ॥७॥
At every house on the way, let him look at onlookers and pronounce "good fortune brings this bride".

"इह प्रियं प्रजया ते समृध्यताम" इत् गृहं प्रवेशयेत् ॥८॥
He should make her enter the house with the verse, "Here may your pleasure increase with offspring".

विवाहाग्निमुपसमाधाय पश्चादस्याऽऽनडुहं धर्माऽऽस्तीर्य प्राग्ग्रीवमुत्तरलोम तस्मिन्नुपविष्टायां समन्वारब्धायां । आ नः जनयतु प्रजापतिः इति चतसृभिः प्रत्युचं हुत्वा "समञ्जन्तु विश्वेदेवा" इति दध्नः प्राश्य प्रतिप्रयच्छेदाज्यशेषेण वाऽनक्ति हृदये ॥९॥
He should set up the nuptial fire in the house and then spread to the west of it a hide of a bull with its neck to the east and with the hair on top. He should offer oblations to the fire while she sits on the hide and takes hold of him with the four verses, "may Prajāpati create offsprings to us" and after each verse offer oblations. And with the verse, "may all gods unite", he partakes curds and offers a portion to her, or he besmears their two hearts with the rest of *ājya*.

अक्षारालवणाशिनौ ब्रह्मचारिणावलंकुर्वाणावधःशायिनौ स्याताम् ॥१०॥
From that time they should not eat spicy food, they should be celibate, wear no ornaments and sleep on the floor.

अत ऊर्ध्वं त्रिरात्रं द्वादशरात्रम् ॥११॥
This they should observe for three nights or twelve nights.

संवत्सरं वैक ऋषिर्जायत इति ॥१२॥
Or for one year according to some. A sage will be born to them.

चरितव्रतः सूर्याविदे वधूवस्त्रं दद्यात् ॥१३॥
When he has fulfilled his vow, he should give the bridal dress to one who knows the Sūrya hymn.

अन्नं ब्राह्मणेभ्यः ॥१४॥
He should give food to brāhmaṇas.

अथ स्वस्त्ययनं वाचयति ॥१५॥
Then he should cause them to pronounce *svastivacanas*.

नवमं खण्डम् (Ninth Section)

पाणिग्रहणादि गृह्यं परिचरेत्स्वयं पत्यापि वा पुत्रः कुमार्यन्तेवासी वा ॥१॥
Beginning with the wedding (*pāṇigrahaṇa*), he should worship the domestic fire himself, or his wife, son, daughter or a pupil.

नित्यानुगृहीतं स्यात् ॥२॥
The fire should be kept burning constantly.

यदि तूपशाम्येत्पत्नुपवसेदित्येके ॥३॥
If it goes out, the wife should fast. Thus say some.

तस्याग्निहोत्रेण ॥४॥
The rules in this regard are the same as in Agnihotra.

प्रादुष्करणहोमकालौ व्याख्यातौ ॥५॥
The time for setting the fire in a blaze and for sacrificing in it has already been explained.

हौम्यं च मांसवर्जम् ॥६॥
The sacrificial food should not contain meat.

कामं तु व्रीहियवतिलैः ॥७॥
If he likes he may perform the sacrifice with rice, barley or sesamum.

"अग्नये स्वाहा" इति सायं जुहुयात् "सूर्याय स्वाहा" इति प्रातस्तूष्णीं द्वितीये उभयत्र ॥८॥

He should sacrifice in the evening with the *mantra* "to Agni *svāhā*" in the morning with the *mantra* "to Sūrya *svāhā*" and silently for the second both times.

Śāṅkhāyana Gṛhya-Sūtra

Śāṅkhāyana is believed to be from the area of Gurjar (Gujarat). Nārāyaṇa wrote a commentary on *Śāṅkhāyana Gṛhya-Sūtra*. Ramachandra has written a *paddhati* on *Śāṅkhāyana Gṛhya-Sūtra*. Vāsudeva has written a commentary called *Śāṅkhāyana Gṛhya Saṅgraha*. The following is the text of the *Śāṅkhāyana Gṛhya-Sūtra* which deals with *vivāha saṁskāra*:

प्रथमोऽध्यायः (First Chapter)
पञ्चमः खण्डः (Fifth Section)

चत्वारः पाकयज्ञा हुतोऽहुतः प्रहुतः प्राशित इति ॥१॥
There are four kinds of *pāka yajñas — huta, ahuta, prahuta* and *prāśita*.

पञ्चसु बहिः शालायां विवाहे चूडाकरण उपनयने केशान्ते सीमन्तोन्नयन इति ॥२॥
On the five following occasions: *vivāha, cūḍākaraṇa, upanayana, keśānta* and *sīmantonnayana* in the outer hall.

उपलिप्त उद्धतावोक्षितेऽग्निं प्रणीय ॥३॥
To a place that has been smeared and elevated and sprinkled with water, he carries forward the fire.

निर्मन्थैके विवाहे ॥४॥
Which was started by attrition at the time of marriage, thus say some.

उदगयन आपूर्यमाणपक्षे पुण्याहे कुमार्यै पाणिं गृह्णीयात् ॥५॥
During the northern course of the sun, in *śukla pakṣa*, on an auspicious day he shall seize the hand of a girl (marry her).

या लक्षणसंपन्ना स्यात् ॥६॥
One who has good qualities.

यस्या अभ्यात्ममङ्गानि स्युः ॥७॥
Whose limbs are proportionate.

समाः केशान्ताः ॥८॥
Whose hair is smooth.

आवर्तावपि यस्यै स्यातां प्रदक्षिणै ग्रीवायाम् ॥९॥
Who should have at her neck two curls turned to the right.

षड् वीराञ्जनयिष्यतीति विद्यात् ॥१०॥
He shall know that such a girl will give birth to six manly children.

षष्टः खण्डः (Sixth Section)

जायामुपग्रहीष्यमाणोऽनृक्षरा इति वरकान् गच्छतोऽनुमन्त्रयते ॥१॥
He who is wishing to acquire a wife, sends the negotiators off to her father's house with the *mantra* "thornless may be the path".

अभिगमने पुष्पफलयवानादायोकुम्भञ्च ॥२॥
When they arrive they take flowers, fruits, barley and a pot of water.

"अयमहं भो इति" त्रिः प्रोच्य ॥३॥
They say, "here I am sir!" thrice.

उदिते प्राङ्मुखा गृह्याः प्रत्यङ्मुखा आवहमाना गोत्रनामान्यनुकीर्तयन्तः कन्यां वरयन्ति ॥४॥
After uttering these words, they ask for the girl in marriage and recite *gotra* names with the dwellers facing east and the visitors facing west.

उभयतो रुचिते पूर्णपात्रीमभिमृशन्ति पुष्पाक्षतयवहिरण्यमिश्राम् —
"अनाधृष्टमस्यानाधृष्टय़ देवानामोजाऽनभिशस्त्यभिशस्तिपा अनभिशस्तेयम्"
"अञ्जसा सत्यमुप गेषम" "सुविते मा धा" इति ॥५॥
When both sides have agreed, let them touch a vessel into which have been put flowers, *akṣata*, barley, fruits and gold and let them recite the *mantra*: "Undisturbed are you, the

undisturbable vigour of the gods, not cursed, protecting against a curse, unexposed to a curse. May I straightaway attain the truth. Put me into prosperity."

"आ नः प्रजामिति" त्वयि कन्याया आचार्य उत्थाय मूर्धनि करोति "प्रजां त्वयि दधामि, पशूँस्त्वयि दधामि, तेजो ब्रह्मवर्चसं त्वयि दधामिति" ॥६॥
With the verse, "let offspring be produced", the *ācārya* of the girl's family standing up places the vessel on the girl's head pronouncing, "offspring I give into you, cattle I give into you, splendour and holy lustre, I put into you".

सप्तमः खण्डः (Seventh Section)

प्रतिश्रुते जुहोति ॥१॥
When agreement has been announced, the bridegroom offers oblations.

चतुरस्रं गोमयेन स्थण्डिलमुपलिप्य ॥२॥
He besmears a quadrangular space with cowdung.

पूर्वयोर्व्दिशोर्दक्षिणां प्राचीं पित्र्ये ॥३॥
Let him consider the south-eastern direction if the rites belong to the manes (*pitṛ*).

उत्तरां दैवे ॥४॥
The northern direction if the rites belong to gods.

प्राचीमेवैके ॥५॥
The east according to some.

उदक्संस्थां मध्ये लेखां लिखित्वा ॥६॥
He draws in the middle of the sacrificial ground a line from south to north.

तस्यै दक्षिणत उपरिष्टादूर्ध्वामेकां मध्य एकामुत्तरत एकाम् ॥७॥
Upwards from this, to the south one line and in the middle to the north one line.

ता अभ्युक्ष्य ॥८॥
He sprinkles this with water.

"अग्निं प्रणयामि मनसा शिवनाऽयमस्तु सङ्गमनो वसूनाम् । मा नो हिंसीः स्थविरं मा कुमारं, शन्नो भव द्विपदे शं चतुस्पदे इत्यग्निं" प्रणीय॥९॥
Carries forward the fire with the *mantra*: "I carry forward Agni with genial mind; may he be the assembler of goods. Do no harm to us, to the old or to the young: Be a saviour to us, to men and animals."

तूष्णीं वा ॥१०॥
Or he carries it silently.

प्रदक्षिणमग्नेः समन्तात्पाणिना सोदकेन त्रिः प्रमार्ष्टि तत्समूहनमित्याचक्षते ॥११॥
Then he wipes with his wet hands three times round the fire, turning his right side to it. This they call sweeping together.

सकृदसव्यं पित्र्ये ॥१२॥
12. Once turning to his left if the rites belong to the manes.

अष्टमः खण्डः (Eighth Section)

अथ परिस्तरणम् ॥१॥
Now follows the strewing of the grass around the fire.

प्रागग्रैः कुशैः परिस्तृणाति त्रिवृत् पञ्चवृद्धा ॥२॥
He strews eastward pointing *kuśa* grass in three or five layers around the fire.

पुरस्तात् प्रथममथ पश्चाद् अथ पश्चात् ॥३॥
Beginning in the east, then to the west, then to the west.

मूलान्यग्रैः प्रच्छादयति ॥४॥
He covers the roots of the grass blades.

सर्वाश्चावृतो दक्षिणतःप्रवृत्तय उदक्संस्था भवन्ति ॥५॥
All rites are to be performed beginning in the south and ending in the north.

दक्षिणतो ब्रह्माणं प्रतिष्ठाप्य "भूर्भुवःस्वरिति" ॥६॥

He chants *bhūr bhuvaḥ svaḥ* after placing *Brahman* in the south.

सुमनोभिरलंकृत्य ॥७॥

Adorns him with flowers.

उत्तरतः प्रशीताः प्रणीय "को वः प्रणयति"ति ॥८॥

He carries forward the *praṇīta* waters on the north side chanting, "who carries you forward?".

सव्येन कुशानादाय दक्षिणेनापनौति ॥९॥

He takes *kuśa* grass with his left hand and arranges them with his right hand.

दक्षिणं जान्वाच्य ॥१०॥

Bending his right knee.

सव्यं पित्र्ये ॥११॥

The left when worshipping the manes.

नाज्याहुतिषु नित्यं परिस्तरणम् ॥१२॥

The strewing around of grass is not necessary in *ājya* offerings.

नित्याहुतिषु चेति माण्डूकेयः ॥१३॥

Or in regular offerings according to Māṇḍūkeya.

कुशतरुणे अविषमे अविच्छिन्नग्रे अनन्तगर्भे प्रादेशेन मापयित्वा कुशेन छिनात्ति "पवित्रे स्थ इति" ॥१४॥

He measures with the span of his hand two *kuśa* blades which are not unequal with unbroken points, bearing no young shoots and severs them from the roots with a *kuśa* blade, saying "purifiers are you".

द्वे त्रीणि वा भवन्ति ॥१५॥

There are two or three of these *kuśa* strainers.

प्रागग्रे धारयन् "वैष्णव्याविति" अभ्युक्ष्य ॥१६॥

He holds them pointing to the east and sprinkles them saying, "belonging to Viṣṇu".

कुशतरुणाभ्यां प्रदक्षिणमग्निं त्रिः पर्युक्ष्य ॥१७॥

With the two *kuśa* blades he sprinkles water around the fire thrice doing circumambulation.

"महीनां पयोऽसीति" आज्यस्थालीमादाय ॥१८॥

He brings the *ājya* pot with the words, "you are the milk of the cows".

"इषे त्वेति" अधिश्रित्य ॥१९॥

He puts *ājya* on the fire with the words, "for sap".

"ऊर्जे त्वेति" उदगुद्वास्य ॥२०॥

Takes it from the fire towards the north with, "for energy".

उदगग्रे पवित्रे धारयन्नङ्गुष्ठाभ्यां चोपकनिष्ठिकाभ्यां चोभयतः प्रतिगृह्योर्ध्वाग्रे प्रह्व कृत्वाज्ये प्रत्यस्यति । "सवितुष्ठ्वा प्रसव उत्पुनाम्यच्छिद्रेण पवित्रेण वसोः सूर्यस्य रश्मिभिरिति" ॥२१॥

And holding the two *kuśa* strainers pointing north, holding them on both sides with his thumbs and fourth fingers, he bends them down and dips them in *ājya* with the words, "By the will of Savitā, I purify you with this uninjured purifier and the rays of the good sun".

आज्यसंस्कारः सर्वत्र ॥२२॥

This preparation takes place each time.

नासंस्कृतेन जुहुयात् ॥२३॥

Let him not offer *ājya* which has not been so prepared.

स्रु वे चापः "सवितुर्व इति" ॥२४॥

He offers the water in the spoon with the words, "by the will of Savitā, I purify you".

ताः प्रणीताः प्रोक्षणीश्च ॥२५॥

This is called *praṇīta* and *prokṣaṇī* water.

नवमः खण्डः (Ninth Section)

स्रू वः पात्रम् ॥१॥
The *sruva* spoon serves as a vessel.

अर्थलक्षणग्रहणम् ॥२॥
Choose different things for different oblations as required.

सव्येन कुशानादाय दक्षिणेन मूलै स्रु वं "विष्णो र्हस्तोऽसीति" ॥३॥
Taking up the *kuśa* blades with the left hand and the *sruva* bottom with his right hand, he chants, "you are the hand of Viṣṇu".

स्रु वेणाज्याहुतीर्जुहोति ॥४॥
He offers *ājya* oblations with the *sruva* spoon.

उत्तरपश्चार्धादग्नेरारभ्याविच्छिन्न दक्षिणतो जुहोति "त्वमग्ने प्रमतिरिति" ॥५॥
From the north-west side of the fire, he continuously offers on the south side of the fire with the *mantra*, "you are the Agni full of foresight".

दक्षिणपश्चार्धादग्नेरारभ्याविच्छिन्नमुत्तरतो जुहोति "यस्येमे हिमवन्त इति" ॥६॥
From the south-west side of the fire, he continuously offers on the north side of the fire with the *mantra*, "To whom these snowy mountains".

आग्नेयमुत्तरमाज्यभागं सौम्यं दक्षिणम् ॥७॥
The northern *ājya* portion belongs to Agni and the southern to Soma.

मध्येऽन्या आहुतयः ॥८॥
In the middle are made oblations to others.

"अग्निर्जनिता स मेऽमू जायां ददातु स्वाहा" ॥ "सोमो जनिमान्त्स माऽमुया जनिमन्तं करोतु स्वाहा" "पूषा ज्ञातिमानन्त्स माऽमुष्यै पित्रा मात्रा भ्रातृभिर्ज्ञातिमन्तं करोतु स्वाहेति" ॥९॥
Agni is the begetter; may he give me her as my wife. Soma is rich in wives; may he make me rich with her as my wife.

Pūṣaṇa is rich in relations; may he make me well related to her father, mother, brothers, etc.

नाज्याहुतिषु नित्यावाज्यभागौ स्विष्टकृच्च ॥१०॥
At the *ājya* oblations, offering of two *ājya* portions and *sviṣṭakṛt* oblation is not constant.

नित्याहुतिषु चेति माण्डूकेयः ॥११॥
According to Māṇḍūkeya, not in constant oblations also.

महाव्याहृतिसर्वप्रायश्चित्त प्राजापत्यान्तरमेतदावापस्थानम् ॥१२॥
The place for insertion is the interval between the *mahāvyāhṛtis*, the general expiation and the oblation to Prajāpati.

आज्ये हविषि सव्ये पाणौ ये कुशस्तान् दक्षिणेनग्रे संगृह्य मूले सव्येन तेषामग्रं स्रू वे समनक्ति मध्यमाज्यस्थाल्यां मूलं च ॥१३॥
In *ājya* oblations, let him seize the *kuśa* blades in his left hand at the roots and his right hand at the points and let him wet the points in the *sruva* and the middle and the roots in the *ājya* pot.

अथ चेत् स्थालीपाकेषु स्रु व्यग्रं मध्यं स्रु वे मूलमाज्यस्थाल्याम् ॥१४॥
In *sthālipāka* oblations, the points are wetted in the *sruk*, the middle in the *sruva* and the roots in the *ājya* pot.

ताननुप्रहृत्य "अग्नेर्वासोऽसीति" ॥१५॥
He then throws them into the fire with the chant, "you are Agni's garment".

तिस्रः समिधोऽभ्याधाय ॥१६॥
He also puts in three pieces of wood.

यथोक्तं पर्युक्षणम् ॥१७॥
Water is sprinkled as stated.

अनाम्नामन्त्रास्वादिष्टदेवतासु "अमुष्यै स्वाहाऽमुष्यै स्वाहेति" जुहुयात् स्वाहारेण शुद्धेन ॥१८॥

In oblations where different deities are indicated with no specified texts, offerings are made with *svāhā,* "To (deity) Svāhā!"

व्याख्यातः पतिश्रुते होमकल्पः ॥१९॥
The ritual declared here is sacrifice to be made when the father's assent to give away the bride is declared.

दशमः खण्डः (Tenth Section)

प्रकृतिर्भूतिकर्मणम् ॥१॥
The standard for all sacrifices that procure happiness.

सर्वासां चाज्याहुतीनाम् ॥२॥
And for all *ājya* offerings.

शाखापशूनाम् ॥३॥
For the sacrifice of animals tied to a branch.

चरुपाकयज्ञानां च ॥४॥
And for offering of boiled cereals and cooked food.

त एते प्रयाजा अननुयाजा अनिला अनिगदा असामिधेनीकाश्च सर्वे पाकयज्ञा भवन्ति ॥५॥
These are performed, all offerings of cooked food, without *prayāja, anuyāja,* without invocation of Ilā, without *nigadā* recitation and without *sāmidhenī* verses.

तदपि श्लोकाः ॥६॥
There are also the following *śloka*s.

हुतोऽग्निहोत्रहोमेनाऽहुतो बलिकर्मणा ।
प्रहुतः पितृकर्मणा प्राशीतो ब्राह्मणे हुतः ॥७॥
An oblation is called *huta* if made by Agnihotra, *ahuta* if by *bali* offering, *prahuta* if by a sacrifice to the manes and *prāśīta* if deposited as an offering to a brāhmaṇa.

अनूर्ध्वज्ञु व्यूळजानुर्जुहुयात् सर्वदा हविः ।
न हि बाह्यहुतं देवाः प्रतिगृह्णन्ति कर्हिचित् ॥८॥

Without raising his knees, with spread knees let him always offer his oblation. For the gods never accept an offering that has been made holding the hand between the knees.

रौद्रं तु राक्षसं पित्र्यमासुरं चाऽऽभिचारिकम् ।
उक्त्वा मन्त्रं स्पृशेदप आलभ्यात्मानमेव च ॥९॥

But when he has repeated a text sacred to Rudra, to the *rākṣasa*s, to the manes, to the *asura*s or that which contains an imprecation, let him touch water and so also when he has touched his own body.

एकादशः खण्डः (Eleventh Section)

अथैतां रात्रीं श्वस्तृतीयां वा कन्यां वक्ष्यन्तीति ॥१॥

When the bride is to be carried away to the groom's house that night, or on the next, or on the third night.

तस्यां रात्र्यामतीते निशाकाले सर्वोषधिफलोत्तमैः सुरभिमिश्रैः सशिरस्कां कन्यामाप्लाव्य ॥२॥

On that night when the night is gone, they wash the girl up to her head with water made fragrant by herbs, fruits and scents.

तक्तमहतं वा वासः परिधाय ॥३॥

They make her wear a new garment which has not yet been washed.

पश्चादग्नेः कन्यामुपवेश्यान्वारब्धायां महाव्याहृतिभिर्हुत्वाऽऽज्याहुतीर्जुहोति॥ अग्नये सोमाय प्रजापतये मित्राय वरुणायेन्द्राण्यै गन्धर्वाय भगाय पूष्णे त्वष्ट्रे बृहस्पतये राज्ञे प्रत्यानीकायेति ॥४॥

Then the priest makes her sit down behind the fire; he sacrifices with the *mahāvyāhṛti*s and then he makes *ājya* oblations to Agni, to Soma, to Prajāpati, to Mitra, to Varuṇa, to Indra, to the Gandharva, to Bhaga, to Pūṣaṇa, to Tvaṣṭā, to Bṛhaspati and to the King Pratyānīka.

चतुस्रोऽष्टौ वाऽविधवाः शाकपिण्डीभिः सुरयाऽन्नेन च तर्पयित्वा चतुर् आनर्तनं कुर्युः ॥५॥

After they have fed four or eight *sumaṅgalīs* with lumps of vegetables, *surā* and food, let the *sumaṅgalīs* perform dances four times.

एता एव देवताः पुंसः ॥६॥
They worship the same deities on behalf of the man.

वैश्रवणमीशानं च ॥७॥
Also Vaiśravaṇa and Īśāna.

अतो ब्राह्मणभोजनम् ॥८॥
Then the feeding of brāhmaṇas.

द्वादशः खण्डः (Twelfth Section)

स्नातं कृतमङ्गलं वरमविधवाः सुभगा युवत्यः कुमार्यै वेश्म प्रपादयन्ति ॥१॥
The bridegroom who has bathed and for whom auspicious ceremonies have been performed is escorted by young and happy *sumaṅgalīs* to the house of the bride.

तासामप्रतिकूलः स्यादन्यत्राभक्ष्यपातकेभ्यः ॥२॥
To these he shall not behave disrespectfully except where forbidden food or a transgression is concerned.

ताभिरनुज्ञातोऽथास्यै वासः प्रयच्छति "रैभ्यासीदिति" ॥३॥
With their permission, he then gives her the garment with the *mantra*, "Raibhyasi".

"चित्तिरा उपबर्हणमिति" आञ्जनकोशमादत्ते ॥४॥
With the *mantra*, "mind is the cushion", he takes up the salve-box.

"समञ्जन्तु विश्वे देवा इति" समञ्जनीया ॥५॥
The *mantra* for anointing is: "May the Viśvedevās anoint."

"यथेय शचीं वावातां सुपुत्रां च यथाऽदितिं । अविधवां चापालामेवं त्वामिह रक्षातादिममिति" ॥ दक्षिणे पाणौ शललीं त्रिवृतं ददाति ॥६॥
With the *mantra*, "as this has protected Śaci, the beloved one and Aditi, the mother of noble sons and Apālā who was

freed from widowhood, may it protect you", he gives to her right hand the quill of a porcupine and a string of three twisted threads.

"रूपं-रूपमिति" आदर्श सव्ये ॥७॥
With the *mantra*, "shape by shape", a mirror in the left hand.

रक्तकृष्णमाविकं क्षौमं वा प्रतिसरं ज्ञातयोऽस्या बध्नन्ति "नीललोहितमिति" ॥८॥
Her relations tie a red and black woollen or linen cord with three gems with the verse, "*nīla lohitam*".

"मधुमतीरोषधीरिति" मधूकानि बध्नाति ॥९॥
With the verse, "Full of honey the herbs" the bridegroom ties to her body *madhūka* flowers.

विवाहे गामर्हयित्वा गृहेषु गां ते माधुपार्किक्यौ ॥१०॥
At the wedding after *arghya* ceremony, a cow is sacrificed. At the groom's residence after *arghya*, another cow is sacrificed. Both are *madhuparka* cows.

पश्चादग्नेः कन्यामुपवेश्यान्वाब्धायां महाव्याहृतिभिस्तिस्रो जुहोति ॥११॥
He makes her sit behind the fire and while she takes hold of him he makes three oblations with the *mahāvyāhṛtis*.

समस्ताभिश्चतुर्थी प्रतीयेतैतस्यां चोदनायाम् ॥१२॥
A fourth oblation with the three *mahāvyāhṛtis* is to be understood from this rule.

एवमनादेशे सर्वेषु भूतिकर्मसु पुरस्ताच्चोपरिष्टाच्चैताभिरेव जुहुयात् ॥१३॥
In this way, where no express rule is stated, in all sacrifices that procure happiness, one is to sacrifice before and afterwards with these same *mahāvyāhṛtis*.

त्रयोदशः खण्डः (Thirteenth Section)

"सम्राज्ञी श्वशुरे भवेति" पिता भ्राता वाऽस्यग्रेण मूर्धनि जुहति सृवेण वा तिष्ठन्नासीनायाः प्राङ्मुख्याः प्रत्यङ्मुखः ॥१॥
With the verse "be a queen over your father-in-law" her father or brother sacrifices with a sword's point over her

head or with the *sruva,* standing while she is sitting, with his face to the west while her face is to the east.

"गृभ्णामि ते सौभगत्वाय हस्तमिति" दक्षिणेन पाणिना दक्षिणं पाणिं गृह्णाति साङ्गुष्ठमुत्तानेनोत्तानं तिष्ठन्नासीनायाः प्राङ्मुख्याः प्रत्यङ्मुखः ॥२॥
"I seize your hand for the sake of happiness" with these words the bridegroom seizes with his right hand her right hand with the thumb, both hands being turned with the palms turned upwards, he standing while she is sitting, with his face to the west while her face is to the east.

पञ्च चोत्तरा जपित्वा ॥३॥
He murmurs the following five verses.

"अमोहमस्मि सा त्वं, सा त्वमस्यमोहं, द्यौरहं पृथिवी त्वं, ऋक्त्वमसि सामहं, सा मामनुव्रज्ञा भव, तावेह वि वहावहै, प्रजां प्र जनयावहै, पुत्रान्विन्दावहै बहून्, ते सन्तु जरदष्टय" इति ॥४॥
"This I am (God), that (Goddess) are you, that you are, this I am, heaven am I, earth are you, you are the verse, I am the song. Be attached to me. Let us marry. Let us beget offspring. Let us have many sons who may reach old age."

उदकुम्भं नवं भूर्भुवः स्वरिति पूरयित्वा ॥५॥
A new water-pot is filled with the words *bhūr bhuvaḥ svāḥ.*

पुन्नाम्नो वृक्षस्य सक्षीरान्त्सफलाशान्त्सकुशानोप्यः ॥६॥

In the water-pot the *ācārya* throws branches of *aśvattha, udumbara* with milky sap and fruits together with *kuśa* grass.

हिरण्यमिति चैके ॥७॥
And gold according to some.

तं ब्रह्मचारिणे वाग्यताय प्रदाय ॥८॥
And hands it over to a student who observes silence.

प्रागुदीच्यां दिशि ताः स्थेयाः प्रदक्षिणा भवन्ति ॥९॥
They should walk around this *stheyā* water placed to the north-east with their right sides towards it.

अश्मानं चोत्तरस्त उपस्थाप्य ॥१०॥
After a stone is placed towards the northern direction.

"एहि सूनरीति" उत्थाप्य ॥११॥
He makes rise with the verse, "come, joyful one".

"एह्यश्मानमा तिष्ठाश्मेव त्वं स्थिरा भव । अभि तिष्ठ पृतन्यतः सहस्व पृतनायत" इति ॥ दक्षिणेन प्रपदेनाश्मानमाक्रमय्य ॥१२॥
He makes her tread on the stone with her right foot with the verse, "come tread on the stone; be firm like a stone; tread the foes down; overcome your enemies".

प्रदक्षिणमग्निं पर्याणीय ॥१३॥
He then leads her round the fire.

तेनैव मन्त्रेण द्वितीयं वसनं प्रदाय ॥१४॥
With the same *mantra*, he gives her a second garment.

लाजाञ्छमीपलाशमिश्रान् पिता भ्राता वा स्यादञ्जलावावपति ॥१५॥
Her father or brother pours out fried grain mixed with *śamī* leaves into her joined hands.

उपस्तरणाभिधारण-प्रत्यभिधारणं चाज्येन ॥१६॥
Then spreading under and sprinkling over the grains and second sprinkling with *ājya*,

ताञ्जुहोति ॥१७॥
She sacrifices the grains.

चतुर्दशः खण्डः (Fourteenth Section)

"इयम्नार्य्युपब्रूते लाजानावपन्तिका । शिवा ज्ञातिभ्यो भूयासं चिरं जीवतु मे पतिः स्वाहेति" ॥ तिष्ठन्ती जुहोति पतिर्मन्त्रं जपति ॥१॥
"This woman, offering grains, prays thus, May I bring bliss to my relations; may my husband live long, *svāhā*" — while her husband recites this, she sacrifices standing.

अश्मक्रमणाद्येवं द्वितीयम् ॥२॥
Beginning with treading the stone, all the ceremonies are done second time.

एवं तृतीयम् ॥३॥
And in the same way, third time.

तूष्णींकामेन चतुर्थम् ॥४॥
Silently, if desired for the fourth time.

प्रागुदीच्यां दिशि सप्तपदानि प्रक्रमयति ॥५॥
They are made to take seven steps in the north-eastern direction.

इष एकपदी, ऊर्जे द्विपदी, रायस्पोषाय त्रिपदी, मायोभव्याय चतुष्पदी, पसुभ्यः पञ्चपदी, ऋतुभ्यः षट्पदी, सखा सप्तपदी भवेति ॥६॥
For sap with first step, for energy with second step, for prosperity with third step, for comfort with fourth step, for cattle with fifth step, for the seasons with sixth step. 'Be a friend' with the seventh steps.

तान्यद्भिः शमयति ॥७॥
Ācārya sprinkles water on those feet.

आपोहिष्ठीयाभिस्तिसृभिः स्थेयाभिरद्भिर्मार्जयित्वा ॥८॥
With the verse, *āpohiṣṭiya* he wipes them with the *stheyā* water.

मूर्धन्याभिषिच्य ॥९॥
And he sprinkles water on their heads.

गां ददामित्याह ॥१०॥
The bridegroom says, "I will give you a cow".

ब्राह्मणेभ्यः किञ्चिद्दद्यात् सर्वत्र स्थालीपाकादिषु कर्मसु ॥११॥
Let him give something to the brāhmaṇas each time at the *sthālīpāka*s and other rites.

सूर्यां विदुषे वाधूयम् ॥१२॥
He gives the bride's dress to one who knows the Sūrya hymn.

गौब्राह्मणस्य वरः ॥१३॥
A cow is the optional gift to be given by a brāhmaṇa.

ग्रामो राजन्यस्य ॥१४॥
A village by a kṣatriya.

अश्वो वैश्यस्य ॥१५॥
A horse by a vaiśya.

अधिरथं शतं दुहितृमते ॥१६॥
A hundred cows with a chariot he gives to a father who has only daughters.

याज्ञिकेभ्योऽश्वं ददाति ॥१७॥
To those versed in sacrificial rites, he gives a horse.

पञ्चदशः खण्डः (Fifteenth Section)

"प्र त्वा मुञ्चामीति" तृचं गृहात् प्रतिष्ठमानायाम् ॥१॥
The three verses, "I loosen you" when she departs from the house.

"जीवं रुदन्तेति" प्ररुदन्त्याम् ॥२॥
"They cry for the living" is chanted.

अथ रथाक्षस्योपाञ्जनं पत्नी कुरुते "अक्षन्नमीमदन्तेति" एतया सर्पिषा॥३॥
The wife then smears the axle of the chariot with butter with the *mantra*, "they ate and they drank".

"शुची ते चक्रे, द्वे ते चक्रे इति" चैताभ्यां चक्रयोः पूर्वया पूक्मुत्तरयोत्तरम्॥४॥
And with the two verses, "pure are your wheels", "your two wheels"; of the wheels the first with the first verse and the second with the second verse.

उस्रौ च ॥५॥
And the two bulls.

"खे रथस्येति" एतया फलवतो वृक्षस्य शम्यागर्तेष्वेकैकां वयान्निखाय॥६॥
After she has put, with the verse, "in the box of the wheel", a branch of a fruit-bearing tree into each of the holes meant for the pins.

नित्या वाऽभिमन्त्र्य ॥७॥
If the branches are already fixed, let her recite the *mantra*.

अथोस्रौ युञ्जन्ति "युक्तस्ते अस्तु दक्षिण" इति द्वाभ्याम्, "शुक्रावनड्वाहाविति" एतेनार्द्धर्चेन युक्तावभिमन्त्र्य ॥८॥

Then they harness the two bulls with the verses, "harnessed by the right one" with the bridegroom reciting the half verse, "the two white bulls" over them when they have been harnessed.

अथ यदि रथाङ्गं विशिर्येत छिद्येत वाऽऽहिताग्नेः गृहान् कन्यां प्रपाद्य ॥९॥
Should part of the chariot break or burst, let him take the girl to a house of one who keeps the sacred fire.

"अभि व्ययस्व खादिरस्येति" एतया प्रतिदद्यात् ॥१०॥
And repair the damage with the verse, "cover yourself with the *khādiras*".

"त्यं चिदश्वमिति" ग्रन्थिम् ॥११॥
A knot with the verse, "Him like a horse".

"स्वस्ति नो मिमीतामिति" पञ्चर्चं जपति ॥१२॥
He then recites the five verses, "May prosperity bring us".

"सुकिंशुकमिति" रथमारोहन्त्याम् ॥१३॥
"Adorned with the *kiṁśuka* flowers" when she mounts the chariot.

"मा विदन् परिपन्थिन इति" चतुष्पथे ॥१४॥
"May no waylayers meet us" at a crossroad.

"ये वध्व इति" श्मशाणे ॥१५॥
Near a cemetery, "That which is carried etc."

"वनस्पते शतवल्श" इति वनस्पतावर्द्धर्चं जपति ॥१६॥
Near a big tree, he recites: "O big tree with your hundred branches."

"सुत्रामाणमिति" नावमारोहन्त्याम् ॥१७॥
When she ascends a ship, "the good protectress".

अश्मन्वतीति नदीतरन्त्याम् ॥१८॥
When she crosses a river, "carrying stones".

अपि वा युक्तेनैव ॥१९॥
Optionally he also murmurs the same verse with the harnessed chariot.

"उद्व ऊर्मिरिति अगाधे" ॥२०॥
At deep places in the river, "up be your wave".

अप्रेक्षणं च ॥२१॥
At such places, let her not look out.

"इह प्रियमिति" सप्त गृहान् प्राप्तायाः कृताः परिहाप्य ॥२२॥
The seven verses, "here may delight" when she has reached the house omitting the verses already recited.

षोडशः खण्डः (Sixteenth Section)

आनाडुहमित्युक्तम् ॥१॥
A bull's hide — this has been declared.

तस्मिन्नुपवेश्यान्वारब्धायां पतिश्चतस्रो जुहोति ॥२॥
On that hide he makes her sit down and sacrifices while she takes hold of him with four oblations.

"अग्निना देवेन पृथिवीलोकेन लोकानामृग्वेदेन वेदानां तेने त्वा शमयाम्यसौ स्वाहा । वायुना देवेनान्तरिक्षलोकेन लोकानां यजुर्वेदेन वेदानां तेन त्वा शमयाम्यसौ स्वाहा । सूर्येण देवेन द्यौर्लोकेन लोकानां सामवेदेन वेदानां तेन त्वा शमयाम्यसौ स्वाहा । चन्द्रेण देवेन दिशां लोकेन लोकानां ब्रह्मवेदेन वेदानां तेन त्वा शमयाम्यसौ स्वाहा" ॥३॥

"With God Agni, with the earth world of worlds, with *Ṛgveda* of the Vedas: Therewith I appease you, *svāhā*!" "With God Vāyu, with the sky world of worlds, with *Yajurveda* of the Vedas: Therewith I appease you, *svāhā*!" "With God Sūrya, with the heaven of the worlds, With the *Sāmaveda* of the Vedas, therewith I appease you, *svāhā*!" "With God Candra, with the cardinal world of the worlds, with the *Atharvaveda* (*Brahmaveda* of the Vedas), therewith I appease you, *svāhā*!"

"भूर्या ते पतिघ्न्यलक्ष्मी देवरघ्नी जारघ्नी तां करोम्यसौ स्वाहेति" वा प्रथमया महाव्याहृत्या प्रथमोपहिता द्वितीयया द्वितीया तृतीयया तृतीया समस्ताभिश्चतुर्थी ॥४॥
"Bhūḥ, what harm dwells in you, bringing death to your husband, death to your husband's brother, that I make death-bringing to your paramour, *svāhā*!" Thus the first may be joined with the first, the second with the second and the third with the third, the fourth with all the three (*vyāhṛtis*) together.

"अघोरचक्षुरिति" आज्यलेपेन चक्षुषी विमृजीत ॥५॥
"With no evil eye", let him smear *ājya* on his eyes.

"कया नश्चित्र इति" तिसृभिः केशान्तानभिमृश्य ॥६॥
The bridegroom having touched the ends of her hair with the three verses, "how may us the resplendent one".

"उत त्या देव्या भिषजेति" चतुस्रोऽनुद्रुत्यान्ते स्वाहाकारेण मूर्धनि संस्रावम् ॥७॥
And having recited the four verses, "and those divine medicines" ending with *svāhā*, he pours out the remainder on her head.

अत्र हैके कुमारमुत्सङ्गमानयन्त्युभयतः सुजातम् "आ ते योनिमिति" एतया ॥८॥
Here some place a boy of good birth on both sides, on her lap, with the verse, "into your womb".

अपि वा तूष्णीम् ॥९॥
Or also silently.

तस्याऽञ्जलौ फलानि दत्त्वा पुण्याहं वाचयति ॥१०॥
Into the boy's joined hands, the bridegroom gives fruits and asks the brāhmaṇas to recite *puṇyāham*.

पुंसवतीह भवति ॥११॥
Thus she becomes the mother of male children.

"इहैव स्तमिति" सूक्तशेषेण गृहान् प्रपादयन्ति ॥१२॥
With the rest of the hymn, "Stay you both here" they make them enter the house.

सप्तदशः खण्डः (Seventeenth Section)

"दधिक्राव्णो अकारिषमिति" दधि संपिवेयाताम् ॥१॥
With the verse, "I praise Dadhikrāvṇa" let them drink curds together.

वाग्यतावासीयातामा ध्रुवदर्शनात् ॥२॥
Let them sit silent, when the sun has set, until the polar star (Dhruva) appears.

अस्तमिते ध्रुवं दर्शयति "ध्रुवैधि पोष्या मयीति" ॥३॥
After sunset, he shows her Dhruva with the verse, "be firm like Dhruva, prospering with me".

"ध्रुवं पश्यामि प्रजां विन्दयेति" ब्रूयात् ॥४॥
She will say, "I see Dhruva, may I get offspring".

त्रिरात्रं ब्रह्मचर्यं चरयाताम् ॥५॥
For three nights let them be celibate.

अधः शायीयाताम् ॥६॥
Let them sleep on the floor.

दध्योदनं संभुञ्जीयाताम् "पिबतञ्च तृप्णुतं चेति" तृचेन ॥७॥
Let them eat together cooked rice and curds with the three verses, "Drink and satiate yourselves".

सायंप्रातर्वैवाह्यग्निं परिचरेयाताम् "अग्नये स्वाहाऽग्नये स्विष्टकृते स्वाहेति" ॥८॥

Let them feed the nuptial fire, in the evening and morning with the words, "to Agni *svāhā*, to Agni Sviṣṭakṛt *svāhā*".

"पुमांसौ मित्रावरुणौ पुमांसावश्विनावुभौ ।
पुमानिन्द्रश्चाग्निश्च पुमांसं वर्धतां मयि स्वाहेति" ॥९॥
"Let the two men Mitra and Varuṇa, let the two Aśvins, let Indra and Agni make a male grow in me, *svāhā*."

दशरात्रमविप्रवासः ॥१०॥
Let them not travel out for ten days.

अष्टादशः खण्डः (Eighteenth Section)

अथ चतुर्थीकर्म ॥१॥
Now the rites of the fourth day.

त्रिरात्र निवृत्ते स्थालीपाकस्य जुहोति ॥२॥
When three nights have elapsed, he makes offerings of cooked food.

अग्ने प्रायश्चित्तिरसि त्वं देवानां प्रायश्चित्तिरसि ।
याऽस्याः पतिघ्नी तनूस्तामस्या अप जहि ॥
वायो प्रायश्चित्तिरसि त्वं देवानां प्रायश्चित्तिरसि ।
यास्याः अपुत्रिया तनुस्तामस्या अप जहि ॥
सूर्यं प्रायश्चित्तिरसि त्वं देवानां प्रायश्चित्तिरसि ।
यास्या अपशव्या तनुस्तामस्या अप जहि ॥
अर्यमणं नु देवं कन्या अग्निमयक्षत ।
सेमां देवो अर्य्यमा प्रेतो मुञ्चातु मामृतः ॥
वरुणं नु देवं कन्या अग्निमयक्षत ।
सेमां देवो वरुण पेतो मुञ्चातु मामृतः ॥
पूषणं देवो तु देवं कन्या अग्निमयक्षत ।
सेमां देवः पूषा प्रेतो मुञ्चातु मामृतः ॥३॥

"Agni, you are expiation: you are the expiation of the gods. The substance that exists that brings death to her husband, drive that away from her". "Vāyu, you are expiation: You are the expiation of the gods. The substance that exists that brings sonlessness, drive that away from her". "Sūrya, you are expiation: You are the expiation of the gods. The substance that exists that brings destruction of cattle, drive that away from her". "To God Aryamā, the girls have made sacrifice to Agni: May he, God Aryamā, loosen her from this and not from that place". "To God Varuṇa, the girls have made sacrifice to Agni: May he, God Varuṇa, loosen her from this and not from that place.""To god Pūṣaṇa, the girls have made sacrifice to Agni: May he, God Pūṣaṇa, loosen her from this and not from that place."

"प्रजापते" इति सप्तमी ॥४॥
The seventh oblation with the verse, "to Prajāpati".

सौविष्टकृत्यष्टमी ॥५॥
The eighth oblation with the verse, "to Sviṣṭakṛt".

Kauṣītaki Gṛhya-Sūtra

This is the third Gṛhya-Sūtra belonging to *Ṛgveda* presently available. It is very similar in content to *Śāṅkhāyana Gṛhya-Sūtra*. A commentary has been written on *Kauṣītaki Gṛhya-Sūtra* by Bhavatrāta. It has been found difficult to date this Sūtra. The following is the text of *Kauṣītaki Gṛhya-Sūtra* which deals with *vivāha saṁskāra*:

प्रथमोऽध्यायः (First Chapter)
प्रथमः खण्डः (First Section)

चत्वारः पाकयज्ञाः ॥२॥
There are four kinds of *pāka-yajñas*:

हुतोऽहुतः प्रहुतः प्राशित इति ॥३॥
huta, ahuta, prahuta and *prāśita*

पञ्चसु बहिः शालायाः ॥४॥
on the five following occasions: In the outer hall.

विवाहे चूडाकरण उपनयने केशान्ते सीमन्तोन्नयन इति ॥५॥
Vivāha, cūḍākaraṇa, upanayana, keśānta and *sīmantonnayana.*

उपलिप्योद्धत्य प्रोक्ष्य अग्निमुपसमाधाय ॥६॥
To a place that has been smeared and elevated and sprinkled with water, he carries forward the fire.

निर्मन्थ्यैके विवाहे ॥७॥
Which was started by attrition at the time of marriage, thus say some.

उदगयने आयूपूर्यमाणपक्षे पुण्याहे कुमार्यै पाणिं गृह्णीयात् ।
जाया लक्षण संपन्ना स्यात् ॥८॥
During the northern course of the sun, in *śukla pakṣa*, on an auspicious day he shall seize the hand of a girl (marry her), one who has good qualities.

यस्या अभ्यात्ममङ्गानि स्युः समाः केशान्ताः ॥९॥
Whose limbs are proportionate, whose hair is smooth.

आवर्तावपि यस्यै स्यातां प्रदक्षिणौ ग्रीवायां षड्वीरान् जनयिष्यतीति विद्यात् ॥१०॥
Who should have at her neck two curls turned to the right, he shall know that such a girl will give birth to six manly children.

द्वितीयः खण्डः (Second Section)

जायामुपग्रहीष्यमाणः अनृक्षराः इति वरकान् गच्छतोऽनुमन्त्रयते ॥१॥
He who is wishing to acquire a wife, sends the negotiators off to her father's house with the *mantra,* "thornless".

अभिगमने पुष्पफलयवानादाय उदकुम्भं च "अहमयं भो" इति त्रिः प्रोच्य वरिते प्राङ्मुखा गृह्याः प्रत्यङ्मुखा आवहमानाः कन्यां वरयन्ति इमाममुष्मा इत्थं गोत्राय इति ॥२॥
When they arrive they take flowers, fruits, barley and a pot of water. They say, "Here I am Sir!" thrice. After uttering these words, they ask for the girl in marriage, reciting *gotra* names with the dwellers facing east and the visitors facing west.

उभयतो रुचिते पूर्णपात्रीमभिमृशन्ति पुष्पाक्षतफलहिरण्यमिश्रान् । "अनाधृष्टमस्यानाधृष्यं देवानामोजो अभिशस्तिपा अनभिशस्त्यञ्जासा सत्यमुपगेषं सुविते मा धाः" इत्युत्थाय कन्याया आचार्यः "आ नः प्रजाम्" इति मूर्ध्नि निषिञ्चति "प्रजास्त्वयि दधामि। पशूंस्त्वायि दधामि। तेजो ब्रह्मवर्चस्यं त्वयि दधामि" इति च ॥३॥

When both sides have agreed, let them touch a vessel into which have been put flowers, *akṣata*, barley, fruits and gold and let them recite the *mantra*: "Undisturbed are you, the undisturbable vigour of the gods, not cursed, protecting against a curse, unexposed to a curse. May I straightaway attain the truth. Put me into prosperity." With the verse, "let offspring be produced", the *ācārya* of the girl's family standing up places the vessel on the girl's head pronouncing, "offspring I give into you, cattle I give into you, splendour and holy lustre, I put into you".

तृतीयः खण्डः (Third Section)

प्रतिश्रुते जुहोति ॥१॥

When agreement has been announced, the bridegroom offers oblations.

चतुरश्रं गोमयेन स्थण्डिलमुपलिप्य पूर्वयोर्विदिशयोः दक्षिणां प्राचीं पित्र्य उत्तरां दैवे प्राचीमेवैक उदक्संस्थां मध्ये रेखां लिखित्वा तस्या दक्षिणत उपरिष्टादूर्ध्वामेकां मध्य एकामुत्तरत एकां तामभ्युक्ष्य "अग्निं दधामि मनसा शिवेनायमस्तु सङ्गमनो वसूनाम्। मा नो हिंसीः स्थविरं मा कुमारं शं नो भव द्विपदे शं चतुष्पदे" ॥ इत्याग्निं प्रणीय तूष्णीं वा प्रदक्षिणम्। अग्नेः समन्तात् पाणिना सोदकेन त्रिः परिमार्ष्टि ॥२॥

He besmears a quadrangular space with cowdung. Let him consider the south-eastern direction if the rites belong to the manes (*pitṛ*). The northern direction if the rites belong to gods. The east according to some, he draws in the middle of the sacrificial ground a line from south to north. Upwards from this, he draws to the south one line and in the middle to the north one line. He sprinkles this with water. Carries forward the fire with the *mantra*: "I carry forward Agni with genial mind; may he be the assembler of goods. Do no harm to us, to the old or to the young: Be a saviour to us, to men and animals." Or he carries it silently. Then he wipes with his wet hands three times round the fire.

तत् समूहनमित्याचक्षते ॥३॥
This they call sweeping together.

सकृदपसव्यं पित्र्ये ॥४॥
Once turning to his left if the rites belong to the manes.

अथ परिस्तरणम् ॥५॥
Now the strewing of grass around the fire.

दक्षिणेन कुशानादाय सव्येनापनोति ॥६॥
Takes the *kuśa* blades with his right hand and arranges them with his left.

दक्षिणं जान्वाच्य प्रागग्रैः कुशैः परिस्तृणाति ॥७॥
Bending on his right knee, he strews the grass pointing to the east.

त्रिवृत् पञ्चवृद्वा ॥८॥
In three layers or five layers.

पुरस्तात् प्रथमम् ॥९॥
Beginning with the east.

अथ पश्चान्मूलान्यग्रैः प्रच्छादयति सर्वाश्चावृतो दक्षिणतः प्रवृत्तय उदकसंस्था भवन्ति ॥१०॥
Then to the west and he covers the roots of the grass blades with the points. All rites are performed beginning in the south and ending in the north.

सकृदपसव्यं पित्र्ये ॥११॥
Turning his left side to the fire, in offering to the manes.

नाज्याहुतिषु नित्यं परिस्तरणम् ॥१२॥
Strewing of grass is not necessary for regular *ājya* offerings.

नित्याहुतिषु वा ॥१३॥
Not for regularly done oblations also.

चतुर्थः खण्डः (Fourth Section)

दक्षिणतो ब्रह्माणं प्रतिष्ठाप्य उदपात्रं वा "भूर्भुवः सुवः" इत्युत्तरतः प्रणीताः कुशनरुणे अविषमे अविच्छिनाग्रे अनन्तगर्भे प्रादेशेन कुशेन चिनत्ति "पवित्रे स्थः" इति ॥१॥
He places the *Brahman* or the water-pot on the south side chanting, *bhūr bhuvaḥ svaḥ*. Carries forward the *praṇīta* waters on the northern side. He measures two *kuśa* blades with unbroken points, bearing no young shoots in them and severs them with a *kuśa* blade saying, "purifiers are you".

द्वे त्रीणि वा भवन्ति ॥२॥
There are two or three of the *kuśa* strainers.

"वैष्णव्यौ" इत्यभ्युक्ष्य "त्वं विदश्वम्" इति प्रदक्षिणग्रन्थिम् ॥३॥
Saying, "belonging to Viṣṇu" he sprinkles water and "you are the horse of knowledge" he goes round the fire.

प्रागग्रे धारयन् आज्यस्थाल्या उपरि "महीनां पयोऽसि" इत्याज्यं निर्वपति॥४॥
He holds them with their points to the east over the *ājya* vessel and saying , "you are the milk of the cows" he sprinkles *ājya*.

उदीचोऽङ्गारान्निरूह्य "इषे त्वा" इत्याधिश्रित्य त्रिरवद्योत्य कुशतरुणे प्रत्यस्य "ऊर्जे त्वा" इति त्रिरुदगुद्वास्याङ्गरान् प्रत्यूह्य अङ्गुष्ठोप-कनिष्ठिकाभ्यामूर्ध्वाग्रे प्रह्वीकृत्य आज्ये प्रत्यस्य त्रिरुत्पुनाति "सवितुष्ट्वा प्रसव उत्पुनाम्यच्छिद्रेण पवित्रेण वसोः सूर्यस्य रश्मिभिः" इति ॥५॥
Keeping the charcoal on the north saying, "You are the sap", he makes three portions and saying, "You are the energy", he takes *kuśa* shoots and mixes with the three parts of charcoal. Seizing them with his two thumbs and little fingers, he bends them down with the points upwards and dips them into the *ājya* saying, "By the impulse of the Savitā, I purify you with this uninjured purifier with the rays of the good sun".

आज्यसंस्कारः सर्वत्र ॥६॥
This preparation of *ājya* takes place each time.

नासंस्कृतेन जुहुयात् ॥७॥
Let him not offer *ājya* which has not been prepared thus.

स्रुवे चापः "सवितुर्वेः" इति ॥८॥
Also the waters in the *sruva* spoon, he purifies saying, "by the impulse of Savitā, I purify you".

ताः प्रोक्षणीः स्रुवं प्रतितप्य कुशैः संमृज्य पुनः प्रतितप्य निधाय एवं स्रुचं च सस्थालीपाके आपः प्रणीताः प्रोक्षणीश्च ॥९॥
The waters and spoon are heated and grass gathered, again heated. Similarly, *sruk* and water for *sthālipāka*. The water is called *praṇīta* and *prokṣaṇī*.

स्रुचः पात्रमर्थलक्षणग्रहणम् ॥१०॥
Sruva and the vessel should be chosen according to each oblation.

पञ्चमः खण्डः (Fifth Section)

दक्षिणेन कुशानादाय सव्येनापनोति ॥१॥
Taking up *kuśa* blades with his right hand, he spreads them with his left.

दक्षिणं जान्वाच्य परिधिभिस्त्रिभिरच्छिन्नाग्रैरग्निं परिदधाति ॥२॥
Bending on his right knee, he spreads three layers of grass as limits around the fire.

पश्चाद् दक्षिणत उत्तरतश्च ॥३॥
On the west, south and the east.

अलंकृत्य कुशतरुणाभ्यां प्रदक्षिणमग्निं त्रिः पर्युक्षति "महान्त कोशम्" इति॥४॥
With the bride decorated and flowers around Agni, he makes three circumambulations and sprinkles water with shoots of the *kuśa* grass chanting 'The treasure of God'.

हुत्वा च ॥५॥
Offering oblations also.

ते अनुप्रहरति ॥६॥
He sprinkles water and offers oblations following the right sequence.

तूष्णीं सकृदपसव्यं पित्र्यै ॥७॥
Once silently on the left to the manes.

अभिघारितमिध्ममग्नौ जुहोति "स्विध्मा यदूनधितिः" इति ॥८॥
He offers ghee as fuel on it saying, "accept this fuel".

"विष्णोर्हस्तोऽसि" इति दक्षिणेन मूले स्रुवम् ॥९॥
Chanting "you are the hands of Viṣṇu", he offers oblations holding the end of the *sruva* spoon in his right hand.

स्रुवेणाज्याहुतीर्जुहोति ॥१०॥
He offers ghee with the *sruva* spoon.

स्रुचा स्थालीपाकं द्विरवद्यति ॥११॥
With *sruva*, he offers cooked rice twice.

त्रिर्जामदग्न्यानाम् ॥१२॥
For descendants of Jamadagni, the offerings are to be made thrice.

उपस्तरणाभिघारणप्रत्यभिघारणं च स्थालीपाके आ स्विष्टकृतः ॥१३॥
Sprinkling ghee, re-sprinkling and offering of cooked food are for *sviṣṭakṛt* Agni.

उत्तरार्धात् स्विष्टकृतः ॥१४॥
The latter half is for *sviṣṭakṛt*.

द्विरभिघारयति ॥१५॥
Offerings are made twice.

न प्रत्यनक्ति ॥१६॥
No ghee is offered after *sthālipāka* offering.

उत्तरपश्चार्धादग्नेरभ्याविच्छिन्नं दक्षिणपूर्वार्धे जुहोति "त्वमग्ने प्रमतिः" इति॥१७॥
Beginning from the north-west side of the fire, he offers *ājya* continuously on the south side saying, "You, Agni are full of foresight".

दक्षिणपश्चार्धादग्नेरारभ्याविच्छिन्नमुत्तरपूर्वार्धे जुहोति "यस्येमे हिमवन्तः इति"॥१८॥
Beginning from the south-west side of the fire, he offers *ājya* continuously on the north side saying, "To whom these snowy mountains".

आघारौ ॥१९॥
Sprinkling of *ājya*.

आग्नेयमुत्तरमाज्यभागं सौम्यम् दक्षिणम् ॥२०॥
To Agni belongs the northern *ājya* portion and to Soma belongs the southern portion.

"अग्ने यं यज्ञम्" "इमं यज्ञम्" इति ॥२१॥
"To Agni that sacrifice", "this sacrifice".

"अग्नये स्वाहा" "सोमाय स्वाहा" इति वा ॥२२॥
"To Agni *svāhā*", "to Soma *svāhā*", etc.

मध्ये अन्या आहुतयः ॥२३॥
In between to other deities.

नाज्याहुतिषु नित्यावाज्यभागौ स्विष्टकृच्च ॥२४॥
At the *ājya* oblations, the offering of the two *ājya* portions and of the *sviṣṭakṛt* oblation is not standing (*nitya*).

नित्याहुतिषु चेति च माण्डूकेयः॥२५॥
Nor in the standing oblations, according to Māṇḍūkeya.

"अग्निर्जनिना स मेऽमूं जायां ददातु स्वाहा । सोमो जनिमान् स मामुया जनिमन्तं करोतु स्वाहा । पूषा ज्ञातिमान् स मामुष्यै पित्रा मात्रा भ्रातृभिर्ज्ञातिमन्तं करोतु स्वाहा" इत्याज्येन ॥२६॥
"Agni is the begetter; may he give me her as my wife. Soma is rich in wives; may he make me rich with her as my wife.

Pūṣaṇa is rich in relations; may he make me well related to her father, mother, brothers, etc. with ghee."

महाव्याहृतिसर्वप्रायश्चित्तान्तरमेतदावापस्थानमाज्यहविषि ॥२७॥
The place for insertion is the interval between the *mahāvyāhṛtis*, the general expiation and the oblation to Prajāpati.

व्याहृतिं स्विष्टकृतोः स्थालीपाके ॥२८॥
At the offering of *sthālīpāka* to *sviṣṭakṛt*, chant the *vyāhṛtis*.

"ततं म आपः" "उद्वयं तमसस्परि" "उदुत्यम्" "चित्रम" "इमं मे वरुण" "तत्त्वा यामि" "त्वं नो अग्ने" "स त्वं नो अग्ने" "त्दस्तु मित्रावरुणा" "वषट्ते विष्णो" "इष्टेभ्यो वषळनिष्टेभ्यः" "यत दुरिष्ट्यै निष्कृत्यै" "दौराध्यै ऋद्ध्यै" "देवीभ्यस्तनूभ्यः" "यत इन्द्र भयामहे" "त्वं नः पश्चात्" "अद्याद्याश्वश्वः" "सूर्यो नो देवस्पान्तु" "भूर्भुवःस्वः" "अयाश्चाग्ने" इति सर्वप्रायश्चित्ताहुतीर्हुत्वा मनसा प्राजापत्यं महाव्याहृतयश्चतस्र इत्येता आहुतीर्हुत्वा सव्ये पाणौ ये कुशास्तान् दक्षिणाग्रे संगृह्य सव्येन तेषामग्रं स्रुवे समनक्ति मध्यमाज्यस्थाल्यां मूलं च । अथ चेत् स्थालीपकेषु स्रुच्यग्रं मध्यमं स्रुवे मूलमाज्यस्थाल्यांताननुप्रहृत्य "अग्नेर्वासोऽसि" इति समिधोऽभ्याधाय यथोक्तं पर्युक्षणनमनुप्रहृत्य परिधीन्नवा नित्ये प्रणीताः परिगृह्य दिशो व्युदुक्षति त्रिस्त्रिः प्राच्यां प्रथममेवं प्रदक्षिणं प्रतिदिशमूर्ध्वं च प्राची निनीय उदीचीर्वा ताः स्पृष्ट्वा प्राणान्मुखं च संमृशति । उत्सर्जनं ब्रह्मणः ॥२९॥
Chanting names of various deities, expiation is offered, keep Prajāpati in the mind, chant *mahāvyāhṛtis* four times. Seize the *kuśa* blades in the left hand at the roots with the right hands at their points, wet the points in *ājya* in *sruva*, points in the *sruk* and the roots in the *ājya* pot, chanting "Agni's garment you are". As mentioned, sprinkle water on the limits with the *praṇīta* waters thrice beginning with the east and go round the fire and sprinkle in each direction and touches the *prāṇa*. The ritual of releasing water using palm is the duty of brāhmaṇas.

षष्ठः खण्डः (Sixth Section)

व्याख्यातः प्रतिश्रुते प्रकृतिर्भूतिकर्मणम् ॥१॥
It has been stated that standards are formed for all sacrifices that procure happiness.

सर्वासां चाज्याहुतीनाम् शाखापशूनाम् चरुपाकयज्ञानां च ॥२॥
And for all *ājya* offerings, for the sacrifice of animals tied to a branch and for offering of boiled rice and cooked food.

अनाम्नातमन्त्रास्वादिष्टदेवतासु "अमुष्यै स्वाहा" इति शुद्धेन ॥३॥
Oblations for which only the deities are indicated, but no texts prescribed, are to be made with the word *svāhā*, "To such and such a deity *svāhā*!, etc."

यदि पाकयज्ञाः समानकालाः स्युरावापस्थाने प्रधानान्येवावर्तयेदानुपूर्व्येण ॥४॥
If *pākayajña* offerings are to be made at the same time, they have to be inserted between *pradhāna homas* (*avāpa*).

त एते अप्रयाजा अननुयाजा अनिळा अनिगदा असामिधेनीकाश्च सर्वे पाकयज्ञा भवन्ति ॥५॥
These are performed, all the offerings of cooked food, without *prayāja* and *anayāja* oblations, without invocation of Ilā, without *nigada* recitation and without *sāmidhenī* verses.

तदपि श्लोकाः ॥६॥
Here also the verses:

हुतोऽग्निहोत्रहोमेनाऽहुतो बलिकर्मणा ।
प्रहुतः पितृकर्मणा प्राशीतो ब्राह्मणे हुतः ॥
अनूर्ध्वज्ञु व्यूळजानुर्जुहुयात् सर्वदा हविः ।
न हि बाह्यहुतं देवाः प्रतिगृह्णन्ति कर्हिचित् ॥
रौद्रं तु राक्षसं पित्र्यमासुरं चाऽऽभिचारिकम् ।
उक्त्वा मन्त्रं स्पृशेदप आलभ्यात्मानमेव च ॥७॥

An oblation is called *huta* if made by Agnihotra, *ahuta* if by *bali* offering, *prahuta* if by a sacrifice to the manes and *prāśīta* if deposited as an offering to a brāhmaṇa. Without raising his knees, with spread knees let him always offer his oblation. For the gods never accept an offering that has been made holding the hand between the knees. But when he has repeated a text sacred to Rudra, to *rākṣasas*, to manes, to *asuras* or that which contains an imprecation, let him touch water and so also when he has touched his own body.

सप्तमः खण्डः (Seventh Section)

अथैतां रात्रीं श्वस्तृतीयां वा कन्यां वहिष्यपन्तीति तस्यां रात्र्यामतिते निशाकाले सर्वसुरभिमिश्रैः फलोत्तमैः सशिरस्कां कन्यामाप्लाव्य रक्तमहतं वासं परिधाप्य प्रदक्षिणमग्निं पर्याणीर्य पश्चादग्नेः कन्यामुपवेश्य आघारावाज्यभागौ हुत्वा अग्नये सोमाय प्रजापतये मित्राय वरुणाय इन्द्राय इन्द्राण्यै गन्धर्वाय भगाय पूष्णे त्वष्ट्रे बृहस्पतये राज्ञे प्रत्यानीयेति ॥१॥

When the bride is to be carried away to the groom's house that night, or on the next or on the third night, on that night when the night is gone, they wash the girl up to her head with water, made fragrant by herbs, fruits and with scents. They make her wear a new garment which has not yet been washed. Then the priest makes her sit down behind the fire, he sacrifices with the *mahāvyāhṛtis* and then he makes *ājya* oblations to Agni, Soma, Prajāpati, Mitra, Varuṇa, Indra, Gandharva, Bhaga, Pūṣaṇa, Tvaṣṭā, Bṛhaspati and the King Pratyānīka.

चतस्रोऽष्टौ वा अविधवाः शाकपिण्डिभिः सुरयान्नेन च तर्पयित्वा चतुरा नर्तनं कुर्युः ॥२॥

After they have fed four or eight *sumaṅgalīs* with lumps of vegetables, *surā* and food, let the *sumaṅgalīs* perform dances four times.

एता एव देवताः पुंभ्यो वैश्रवणमीशनं च ॥३॥

They worship the same deities on behalf of the man. Also, Vaiśravaṇa and Īśāna.

ततो ब्राह्मणभोजनम् ॥४॥

Then the feeding of brāhmaṇas.

अष्टमः खण्डः (Eighth Section)

स्नातं कृतमङ्गलं वरमविधवाः सुभगा युवत्यः कुमार्यै वेश्म प्रपादयन्ति । तासामप्रतिकूलः स्यादन्यत्राभक्ष्यपातकेभ्यः ॥१॥

The bridegroom, who has bathed and for whom auspicious ceremonies have been performed, is escorted by young and happy *sumaṅgalīs* to the house of the bride. To these he shall not behave disrespectfully except where forbidden food or a transgression is concerned.

ताभिरनुज्ञातोऽथास्यै वासः प्रयच्छति "रैभ्यासीत" इति ॥२॥

With their permission, he then gives her the garment with the *mantra, "raibyasi"*.

"युवं वस्त्राणि" इत्यस्मै ॥३॥

And the *mantra,* "these dresses".

"चित्तिरा उपबर्हणम्" इत्यञ्जनकोशमादत्ते ॥४॥

With the *mantra,* "Mind is the cushion" he takes up the salve-box.

"समञ्जन्तु विश्वे देवाः" इति समञ्जनीया ॥५॥

The *mantra* for anointing is, "May the Viśvedevās anoint".

"यथेयं शचीं वावातां सुपुत्रां च यथादितिम् । अविधवां चापालामेवं त्वमिह रक्षतु" ॥ इति दक्षिणे पाणौ शललीं त्रिवृतां ददाति ॥६॥

With the *mantra,* "as this has protected Śaci, the beloved one and Aditi, the mother of noble sons and Apālā who was free from widowhood, may it protect you" he gives to her right hand the quill of a porcupine and a string of three twisted threads.

"रूपं रूपं" इत्यादर्शं सव्ये ॥७॥

With the *mantra,* "shape by shape", a mirror in the left hand.

रक्तकृष्णमाविकं क्षौमं वा त्रिमणिं प्रतिसरं ज्ञातयोऽस्या बध्नन्ति "नीललोहितम्" इति ॥८॥

Her relations tie a red and black woollen or linen cord with three gems with the verse, *"nīla lohitam"*.

"मधुमतीरोषधीः" इति मधूकानि बध्नाति ॥९॥

With the verse, "full of honey the herbs" the bridegroom ties to her body *madhuka flowers.*

विवाहे गामर्हयित्वा गृहेषु गतेषु कान्ताणां माधुपर्किक्यः ॥१०॥

At the wedding one cow, when the *arghya* ceremony has been performed; in the house one cow; these are the *madhuparka* cows.

न त्वेवामांसोऽर्घ्यस्स्यादधियज्ञमधिविवाहम् ॥११॥

In principal *yajñas* and *vivāhas*, meat offering is not made.

कुरुत इत्येव ब्रूयात् ॥१२॥

It is said that he will make offerings himself (of other than meat).

"ब्रहस्पतये त्वा मह्यं वरुणो ददातु । सोऽमृतत्वमशीय । त्वद्राष्ट्रयोरधिमयो मह्यं प्रतिगृह्णते" इति वाससी प्रतिगृह्य परिधायोपस्पृश्य "कोऽदात् । कस्मा अदात्" इति कन्याम् ॥१३॥

With the *mantra "bṛhaspataye tvā"* he hands over the garment to the girl. He touches the garment with the *mantra, "ko adāt, kasmāt adāt"*.

"सम्राज्ञी श्वशुरे" इति पिता भ्राता वास्यग्रेण मूर्धनि जुहोति । स्रुवेणावतिष्ठन्नासीनायाः प्राङ्मुख्याः प्रत्यङ्मुखः ॥१४॥

With the verse "be a queen with your father-in-law" her father or brother sacrifices with a sword's point over her head or with the *sruva*, standing while she is sitting, with his face to the west while her face is to the east.

हुत्वान्वारब्धायां महाव्याहृतिभिर्हुत्वा समस्ताभिः चतुर्थी प्रतीयेतैतस्यां चोदनायामेवमनादेशे ॥१५॥

He sacrifices with the *mahāvyāhṛtis* four times with cooked oblation offered for her.

सर्वेष्वेव तु भूतिकर्मसु पुरस्ताच्चोपरिष्टाच्चैताभिरेव जुहुयात् ॥१६॥

After sacrificing with the *vivāha homas*, let him sacrifice with the *mahāvyāhṛtis*.

"एहि सूनरी" इत्युत्थाप्य "गृभ्णामि ते सौभगत्वाय हस्तम्" इत्युतानेन दक्षिणेन पाणिनोत्तानं दक्षिणं पाणिं गृह्णाति साङ्गुष्ठं प्राङ्मुख्याः प्रत्यङ्मुखस्तिष्ठन् ॥१७॥

After reciting "come, joyful one" and "I seize your hand for the sake of happiness" with these words the bridegroom seizes with his right hand her right hand with the thumb, both hands being turned with the palms upwards, he standing while she is sitting, with his face to the west while her face is to the east.

पञ्च चोत्तरा जपति "अमोहमस्मि सा त्वं सा त्वमस्यमोहम् द्योरहम् पृथिवी त्वम् सामाहम् ऋक्त्वम् तावेव विवाहवै प्रजां प्रजनयावहै पुत्रान् विन्दावहै बहूंस्ते सन्तु जरदष्टयः" इति ॥१८॥

He murmurs the following five verses. "This I am (God), that are you (Goddess), that you are, this I am, heaven am I, earth are you, you are the verse, I am the song. Be attached to me. Let us marry. Let us beget offspring. Let us have many sons who may reach old age."

उदकुम्भं नवम् "भूर्भुवः स्वः" इति पूरयित्वा पुनामस्य वृक्षस्य सक्षीरान् पलाशान् सकुशानोप्य हिरण्यं चेत्येके । तं ब्रह्मचारिणे वाग्यताय प्रदाय प्रागुदीच्यां दिशि ताः स्थेयाः प्रदक्षिणा भवन्ति । दक्षिणत एकेषाम् ॥१९॥

A new water pot is filled with the words *bhūr bhuvaḥ svaḥ*. In the water pot the *ācārya* throws branches of *aśvattha*, *uḍuṁbara* with milky sap and leaves together with *kuśa* grass. Gold according to some. And hands it over to a student who observes silence. They should walk around this *stheya* water placed to the north-east with their right sides towards it. Some say towards the right.

अश्मानं चोत्तरत उपस्थाप्य "एहि सूनरी" इत्युक्त्वा "एह्यश्मानमातिष्ठ। अश्मेव त्वं स्थिरा भव । अभितिष्ठ पृतन्यतः । सहस्व पृतनायतः" इति दक्षिणेनास्याः प्रपदेनाश्मानक्रमय्य "विश्वा उत त्वया वयम्" इति प्रदक्षिणमग्निं पर्याणिय तेनैव मन्त्रेण द्वितीयं वसनं प्रदाय ॥२०॥

After a stone is placed towards the northern direction, he makes her rise with the verse "come, joyful one". He makes her tread on the stone with her right foot with the verse, "come tread on the stone; be firm like a stone; tread the foes down;

overcome the enemies". He then leads her round the fire. With the same *mantra*, gives her a second garment.

लाजान् शमीपालमिश्रान् पिता भ्राता वा अस्या अञ्जलावापयति ॥२१॥
Her father or brother pours out fried grain mixed with *śamī* leaves into her joined hands.

उपस्तरणाभिघारणे प्रत्यभिघारणं लाजेषु ॥२२॥
Then spreading under and sprinkling over the grains and second sprinkling with *ājya*.

तान् जुहोति "इयं नार्यपब्रूते लाजानावपन्तिका । शिवा ज्ञातिभ्यो भूयासं चिरं जीवतु मे पतिः । स्वाहा" इति तिष्ठन्ती जुहोति ॥२३॥
She sacrifices the grains. "This woman, offering grains, prays thus, May I bring bliss to may relations; may my husband live long, *svāhā*!" This she sacrifices standing.

पतिर्मन्त्रं जपति ॥२४॥
While her husband recites.

अश्माक्रमणादेवं द्वितीयमेवं तृतीयं तूष्णीं कामेन चतुर्थम् ॥२५॥
Beginning with treading the stone, all the ceremonies are repeated twice. And in the same way, thrice. Silently, if desired for the fourth time.

"प्रजापते न त्वदेतानि" इति प्राजापत्यं हुत्वा "यत्पाकत्रा" इति स्विष्टकृतं च सर्वत्र ॥२६॥
With the *mantra*, "*prajāpate na tvat*" he sacrifices and with "*yatpakatrā*" he sacrifices to *sviṣṭakṛt* and all with *vyāhṛtis* four times.

"अग्नये स्विष्टकृते स्वाहा" इति वा ॥२७
With "*agnaye sviṣṭakṛte*" he sacrifices to all.

उदङ् सप्तपदानि प्रक्रमयेत् । "इष एकपदी । ऊर्जे द्विपदी । रायस्पोषाय त्रिपदी । मायो भव्याय चतुष्पदी । प्रजाभ्यः पञ्चपदी । ऋतुभ्यः षट्पदी । सखा सप्तपदी भव" इति । "विष्णुस्त्वा नयतु" इति सर्वत्रानुषजति ॥२८॥

He makes them take seven steps. For sap with first step, for energy with second step, for prosperity with third step, for comfort with fourth step, for cattle with fifth step, for the seasons with sixth step. Be a friend with seventh step. With each they follow with "let Viṣṇu carry you forward".

आपोहिष्ठीयाभिस्तिसृभिः स्थेयाभिरद्भिर्मार्जयित्वा मूर्ध्न्यवसिच्य ब्राह्मणेभ्यः किंचिद् दद्यात् ॥२९॥

With the verse, "*āpohiṣṭa*" he wipes them with the *stheya* water. And he sprinkles the water on their heads. He should give something to the brāhmaṇas.

सर्वत्र स्थालीपाकादिषु कर्मसु ॥३०॥

After carrying out *sthālīpāka* rites,

आचार्याय वरं ददातीत्याह ॥३१॥

give *dakṣiṇā* to the *ācārya*, it is said.

सूर्यां विदुषे वा धूयम् ॥३२॥

He gives the bride's dress to one who knows the Sūrya hymn.

गोर्ब्राह्मणस्य वरः ॥३३॥

A cow is the optional gift to be given by a brahmaṇa.

ग्रामो राजन्यस्य ॥३४॥

A village by a kṣatriya.

अश्वो वैश्यस्य ॥३५॥

A horse by a vaiśya.

अधिरथं शतं दुहितृमते ॥३६॥

A hundred cows with a chariot to a father who has only daughters.

ज्ञेभ्योऽश्वं ददाति ॥३७॥

To those versed in sacrificial rites, he gives a horse.

नवमः खण्डः (Ninth Section)

"प्र त्वा मुञ्चामि" इति तिसृभिः गृहान् प्रतिष्ठमानायाम् ॥१॥
The three verses, "I loosen you" when she departs from the house.

"जीवां रुदन्ति" इति रुदत्याम् ॥२॥
If she begins to cry, "they cry for the living" is uttered.

अथ रथाक्षस्योपाञ्जनं पत्नी कुरुते "अभिव्ययस्व खदिरस्य सारम्" इत्येतया सर्पिषा ॥३॥
The wife then smears the axle of the chariot with butter with the verse, "Cover yourselves with *khadiras*".

"शुची ते चक्रे" "द्वे ते चक्रे" इति चक्रयोः ॥४॥
And with the two verses, "pure are your wheels", "your two wheels", of the wheels.

पूर्वया पूर्वमुत्तरयोत्तरम् ॥५॥
The first with the first verse and the second with the second verse.

उस्रौ च ॥६॥
And the two bulls.

"खे रथस्य" इत्येतया फलवतो वृक्षस्य शम्याकत्रेष्वेकैकां वैयां निधाय नित्यावभिमन्त्र्य अथोस्रौ युञ्जन्ति "युक्तस्ते अस्तु दक्षिणः" इति द्वाभ्याम् ॥७॥
After she has put, with the verse, "in the box of the wheel", a branch of a fruit-bearing tree into each of the holes meant for the pins. If the branches are already fixed, let her recite the *mantra*. Then they harness the two bulls with the verses, "harnessed by the right one" with the bridegroom reciting the half verse.

"शुक्रावनड्वाहौ" इत्येतेनार्धर्चेन युक्तावभिमन्त्र्य "सुकिं शुकम्" इति रथमारोहन्त्याम् ॥८॥
"The two white bulls" over them when they have been harnessed. "Adorned with the *kiṁśuka* flowers" when she mounts the chariot.

अग्निष्ठस्त्वग्रतो गच्छेत् ॥९॥
Let him go to first one who keeps the sacred fire.

"मा विदन् परिपन्थिनः" इति चतुष्पथे ॥१०॥
"May no way layers meet us" at a crossroad.

"ये वध्वः" इति श्मशाने ॥११॥
Near a cemetery, "That which is carried etc."

"वनस्पते शतवल्शः" इति वनस्य तावर्धर्चं जपति ॥१२॥
Near a big tree, he recites, "O big tree with your hundred branches".

अथ यदि रथाङ्गं विशीर्येत छिद्येत वा आहितग्नेर्गृहं कन्यां प्रवेश्य "यं ऋते" इत्येतया संदध्यात् । "त्यं चिदश्वम्" इति ग्रन्थिम् "स्वस्ति नो मिमीताम्" इति पञ्चर्चं जपति ॥१३॥
Should part of the chariot break or burst, let him take the girl to a house of one who keeps the sacred fire with the *mantra*, "that season which". A knot with the verse, "him like a horse". He then recites the five verses, "may prosperity bring us".

"सुत्रामाणम्" इति नावमारोहन्त्याम् ॥१४॥
When she ascends a ship, "the good protectress".

"अश्मन्वतीः" इति नदीं तरन्त्याम् ॥१५॥
When she crosses a river, "carrying stones".

यदि वा युक्तेनैव "उद्व ऊर्मिः" इत्यगाधे प्रेक्षणं च ॥१६॥
Optionally he also murmurs the same verse with the harnessed chariot. At deep places in the river, "up be your wave". At such places, let her not look out.

"इह प्रियं प्रजया ते समृद्ध्याताम्" इति सप्त गृहान् प्राप्तायाम् ॥१७॥
The seven verses, "here may delight" when she has reached the house.

कृताः परिहाप्य ॥१८॥
Omitting the verses already recited.

दशमः खण्डः (Tenth Section)

गृहान् प्रपद्य पश्चादग्नेरानडुहे चर्मण्युपविश्य दर्भेष्वन्वारब्धायां पतिश्रतस्रो जुहोति "अग्निना देवेन पृथिवीलोकेन लोकानामृग्वेदेन वेदानां तेन त्वा शमयाम्यसौ स्वाहा", "वायुना देवेनान्तरिक्षेण लोकेन लोकानां यजुर्वेदेन वेदानां तेन त्वा शमयाम्यसौ स्वाहा", "सूर्येण देवेन दिवो लोकेन लोकानां सामवेदेन वेदानां तेन त्वा शमयाम्यसौ स्वाहा", "चन्द्रेण देवेन दिशां लोकेन लोकानां ब्रह्मवेदेन वेदानां तेन त्वा शमयाम्यसौ स्वाहा" इति ॥१॥
After reaching the house, he makes her sit on a bull's hide and after strewing *kuśa* grass he sacrifices. "With God Agni, with the earth world of worlds, with *Ṛgveda* of the Vedas; therewith I appease you, *svāhā*!" "With God Vāyu, with the sky world of worlds, with *Yajurveda* of the Vedas; therewith I appease you, *svāhā*!" "With God Sūrya, with the heaven of the worlds, with the *Sāmaveda* of the Vedas, therewith I appease you, *svāhā*!" "With God Candra, with the cardinal world of the worlds, with the *Atharvaveda* (*Brahmaveda* of the Vedas), therewith I appease you, *svāhā*!".

"भुर्या ते पतिघ्न्यलक्ष्मी देवरघ्नी जारघ्नी तां करोमि तेऽसौ" इति वा ॥२॥
"*Bhūḥ*, what harm dwells in you, bringing death to your husband, death to your husband's brother, that I make death-bringing to your paramour, *svāhā*!."

द्वितीयया महाव्याहृत्या द्वितीया उपहिता ॥३॥
Thus the second *vyāhṛti* may be joined with the second.

तृतीयया तृतीया ॥४॥
And the third with the third.

समस्ताभिः चतुर्थी ॥५॥
The fourth with all the three (*vyāhṛtis*) together.

"अघोरचक्षुः" इत्याज्यलेपेन चक्षुषी विमृज्य "कया नश्चित्र आभुवत्" इति तिसृभिः केशान्तानभिमृश्य "उत त्या दैव्या भिषजा" इति चतस्रो जपित्वा मूर्धनि संस्रावम् ॥६॥
"With no evil eye", let him smear *ājya* on his eyes. The bridegroom having touched the ends of her hair with the

three verses, "how may us the resplendent one". And having recited the four verses, "and those divine medicines" ending with *svāhā,* he pours out the remainder on her head.

अत्र हैके कुमारमुत्सङ्गमानयन्त्युभयतः सुजातम् "आते योनिम्" इत्येतयर्चा ॥७॥
Here some place a boy of good birth on both sides, on her lap, with the verse, "into your womb".

अपिवा तूष्णीमेव ॥८॥
Or also silently.

तस्याञ्जलौ फलानि दत्वा पुण्याहं वाचयति ॥९॥
Into the boy's joined hands, the bridegroom gives fruits and asks the brāhmaṇas to recite *puṇyāham.*

"पुंसुवती ह भव" इति ॥१०॥
"Become the mother of male children."

वाचंयमावास्तामा ध्रुवस्य दर्शनात् ॥११॥
Let them sit silent, when the sun has set, until the polar star (Dhruva) appears.

नक्षत्रेषु दृश्यमानेषुं ध्रुवं दर्शयति ॥१२॥
When the stars appear, he shows her Dhruva.

"ध्रुवैधि पोष्या मयि" इति "ध्रुवं पश्यामि" इति "ध्रुवां विन्देय" इति ब्रूयात् ॥१३॥
With the verse, "Be firm like Dhruva, prospering with me". She will say, "I see Dhruva, may I get offspring like Dhruva".

"दधिक्राव्णो अकारिषम्" इति देध्योदनं सह भुञ्जीयाताम् "पिबतं च तृष्णुतं च" इति तृचेन च ॥१४॥
With the verse, "I praise Dadhikrāvṇa" let them drink curds together.

त्रिरात्रमधःशायिनावक्षारालवणाशिनौ स्याताम् ॥१५॥
For three days they should sleep on the floor and eat food without spices and salt.

एवमेवाध्वनि ॥१६॥
Similarly during travel.

न सह भुञ्जीत ॥१७॥
Not eat together.

संवत्सरं न मिथुनमुपेयातां द्वादशरात्रं षड्रात्रम् ॥१८॥
Let there be no intercourse for one year, twelve nights or six nights.

त्रिरात्रमन्ततः ॥१९॥
After the end of three nights.

सायंप्रातर्वैवाहिकमग्निं परिचरेयातां यवैर्व्रीहिभिर्वा ॥२०॥
Let them feed the nuptial fire with barley and grains.

"अग्नये स्वाहा" इति सायम् ॥२१॥
In the evening with the words "to Agni *svāhā*".

"सूर्याय स्वाहा" इति प्रातः ॥२२॥
And in the morning with the words, "to Sūrya *svāhā*".

"अग्नये स्विष्टकृते स्वाहा" इत्युभयोः ॥२३॥
In the evening and morning with the words, "to Agni *svāhā*, to Agni Sviṣṭakṛt *svāhā*".

"पुमांसौ मित्रावरुणौ पुमांसावश्विनावुभौ । पुमानिन्द्रश्चाग्निश्च पुमांसं वर्धतां मयि । स्वाहा ॥ इति पूर्वो गर्भकामः" ॥२४॥
"Let the two men Mitra and Varuṇa, let the two Aśvins, let Indra and Agni make a male child grow in me, *svāhā*." So says one who has wishes to have children.

दशरात्रमविप्रवासः ॥२५॥
Let them not travel out for ten days.

एकादशः खण्डः (Eleventh Section)

अथ चतुर्थ्यां त्रिरात्रे निवृत्ते स्थालीपाकस्य जुहोति ॥१॥
In *caturthī karma*, when three nights have elapsed, he makes offerings of cooked food.

पयसि स्थालीपाकः पाकयज्ञेषु ॥२॥
Milk and cooked food to be used in the *pākayajña*.

वचनादन्यत् ॥३॥
Others are by reciting (necessary *mantra*).

"अग्ने प्रायश्चित्तरसि त्वं देवानां प्रायश्चित्तिरसि यास्याः पतिघ्नी तनूस्तामस्या अपजहि स्वाहा" ॥ "वायो प्रायश्चित्तिरसि त्वं देवानां प्रायश्चित्तिरसि यास्या अपुत्र्या तनूस्तामस्या अपजहि स्वाहा" ॥ "सूर्यं प्रायश्चित्तिरसि त्वं देवानां प्रायश्चित्तिरसि यास्या अपशव्या तनूस्तामस्या अपजहि स्वाहा" ॥ "अर्यमणं नु देवं कन्या अग्निमयक्षत" । "स इमां देवो अर्यमा प्रेतो मुञ्चातु नामुतस्स्वाहा" ॥ "वरुणं नु देवं कन्या अग्निमयक्षत" । "स इमां देवो वरुणः प्रेतो मुञ्चातु नामुतस्स्वाहा" ॥ "पूषणं नु देवं कन्या अग्निमयक्षत" । "स इमां देवः पूषा प्रेतो मुञ्चातु नामुतस्स्वाहा" ॥ "प्रजापते न त्वत्" इति सप्तमी ॥४॥
"Agni, you are expiation: you are the expiation of the gods. The substance that exists that brings death to her husband, drive that away from her." "Vāyu, you are expiation: you are the expiation of the gods. The substance that exists that brings sonlessness, drive that away from her." "Sūrya, you are expiation: you are the expiation of the gods. The substance that exists that brings destruction of cattle, drive that away from her". "To God Aryamā, the girls have made sacrifice to Agni: may he, God Aryamā, loosen her from this and not from that place". "To God Varuṇa, the girls have made sacrifice to Agni: may he, God Varuṇa, loosen her from this and not from that place". "To God Pūṣaṇa, the girls have made sacrifice to Agni: may he, God Pūṣaṇa, loosen her from this and not from that place." The seventh oblation with the verse, "to Prajāpati".

सौविष्टकृत्यष्टमी ॥५॥
The eighth oblation with the verse, "to *sviṣṭakṛt*".

4

Gṛhya-Sūtras of Yajurveda

YAJURVEDA is divided into *Śukla Yajurveda* and *Kṛṣṇa Yajurveda*. While *Kṛṣṇa Yajurveda* has a number of Gṛhya-Sūtras available, *Śukla Yajurveda* originally had two Gṛhya-Sūtras, namely, Pāraskara and Baijavāpa. There have been references to *Baijavāpa Gṛhya-Sūtra* in many texts but it has not been possible to obtain the text. Only *Pāraskara Gṛhya-Sūtra* is available presently belonging to *Śukla Yajurveda*.

Pāraskara Gṛhya-Sūtra

Pāraskara Gṛhya-Sūtra follows both the Kāṇva and Mādhyandina branches of *Yajurveda*. Commentaries on *Pāraskara Gṛhya-Sūtra* have been written by Harihara, Gadādhara, Jayarāma and Rāmakṛṣṇa among others. Pāraskara is also known as Kātyāyana. The following is the text of *Pāraskara Gṛhya-Sūtra* pertaining to *vivāha saṁskāra*.

प्रथमं काण्डम् (First Chapter)
चतुर्थी कण्डिका (Fourth Section)

चत्वारः पाकयज्ञा हुतोऽहुतः प्रहुतः प्राशित इति ॥१॥
There are four kinds of *pākayajñas*: *huta*, *ahuta*, *prahuta* and *prāśita*.

पञ्चसु बहिःशालायां विवाहे चूडाकरण उपनयने केशान्ते सीमन्तोन्नयन इति ॥२॥
In the outer hall on five occasions: *vivāha*, *cūḍākaraṇa*, *upanayana*, *keśānta* and *sīmantonnayana*.

उपलिप्त उद्धतावोक्षितेऽग्निमुपसमाधाय ॥३॥
On an elevated place which has been smeared and sprinkled with water, the fire is established.

निर्मन्थ्यमेके विवाहे ॥४॥
According to some, the fire is started by attrition at marriages.

उदगयन आपूर्यमाणपक्षे पुण्याहे ॥५॥
Marriages are to be conducted during the northern course of the sun, in *śukla pakṣa*, on an auspicious day.

कुमार्याः पाणि गृह्णीयात् ॥६॥
Let him marry a girl.

त्रिषु त्रिषूत्तरादिषु ॥७॥
Under the three stars which begin with the three *uttaras* — 1. Uttarāphālgunī (Hastā, Citrā), 2. Uttarāṣāḍhā (Śravaṇā, Dhaniṣṭhā), 3. Uttarābhadrā (Revatī, Aśvinī).

स्वातौ मृगशिरसि रोहिण्यां वा ॥८॥
Or under Svāti, Mṛgaśirā, Rohiṇī.

तिस्रो ब्राह्मणस्य वर्णानुपूर्व्येण ॥९॥
As per *varṇāśrama*, three wives (brāhmaṇa, kṣatriya or vaiśya) are allowed for a brāhmaṇa.

द्वे राजन्यस्य ॥१०॥
Two for a kṣatriya (kṣatriya or vaiśya).

एका वैश्यस्य ॥११॥
One for vaiśya (vaiśya).

सर्वेषां शूद्रमप्येके मन्त्रवर्जम् ॥१२॥
A śūdra girl for all, according to some, but married without uttering Vedic *mantras*.

अथैनां वासः परिधापयति — "जरां गच्छ परिधत्स्व वासो भवाकृष्टीनामभिशस्तिपावा । शतं च जीव शरदः सुवर्च्चा रयिं च पुत्राननुसंव्ययस्वायुष्मतीदं परिधत्स्व वास इति" ॥१३॥

He makes her put on the garment with the verse: "Live to old age, be a saviour of the family against curses. Live 100 years virtuously, clothe yourself in wealth and children, put on this garment being blessed."

अथोत्तरीयं "या अकृन्तन्नवयँय्या अतन्वत याश्च देवीस्तन्तूनभितो ततन्थ। तास्त्वा देवीर्जरसे संव्ययस्वायुष्मतीदं परिधत्स्व वास" इति ॥१४॥

Then the upper garment: "The goddesses who spun, wove and spread the garment and who drew out the threads on both sides, may the goddesses clothe you for a long life. Blessed with life, put on this garment."

अथैनौ समज्जयति — "समञ्जतु विश्वेदेवाः समापो हृदयानि नौ । सम्मातरिश्वा सन्धाता समु देष्ट्री दधातु नौ" इति ॥१५॥

Then the bride and groom are made to face each other with the verse: "Let Viśvedevās and let waters unite these hearts. May Mātariśvan and Deṣṭrī bring us together."

पित्रा प्रत्तामादाय गृहित्वा निष्क्रमति — "यदैषि मनसा दूरं दिशोऽनु पवमानो वा हिरण्यवर्णो वैकर्णः स त्वा मन्मनसां करोत्वित्यसौ इति" ॥१६॥

The bridegroom holds the hand of the bride who has been given away by her father and leaves with the verse: "When you wander far away in your mind like the wind, let the golden-winged Vaikarṇa make your heart live in mine."

अथैनौ समीक्षयति — अघोरचक्षुरपतिघ्न्येधि शिवा पशुभ्यः सुमनाः सुवर्च्चाः वीरसूर्देवकामा स्योना शन्नो भव द्विपदे शं चतुष्पदे सोमः प्रथमो विविदे गन्धर्वो विविद उत्तरः । तृतीयोग्निष्टे प्रतिस्तुरीयस्ते मनुष्यजाः । सोमोऽददद् गन्धर्वाय, गन्धर्वोददद‌ग्नये । रयिं च पुत्रांश्चादादग्निर्मह्यमथो इमाम् । सा नः पूषा शिवतमामैरय सा न ऊरू उशती विहर । यस्यामुशन्त प्रहराम शेपं यस्यामु कामा बहवोनिविष्ट्या इति ॥१७॥

He then makes them look at each other while the groom recites: "With no evil eye, not bringing death to your husband, bring luck to the cattle, be full of joy and vigour. Give birth to heroes, be godly and friendly. Bring luck to men and animals." "Soma has acquired you first, after him the *gandharva*, Agni is third and fourth is man." "Soma gave you to *gandharva*, *gandharva* to Agni. With you Agni has given me wealth and children." "That woman who has been purified by Agnihotra and Upasana, I enter her with many desires."

पञ्चमी कण्डिका (Fifth Section)

प्रदक्षिणमग्निं पर्याणीयैके ॥१॥
According to some, after leading the bride around the fire (giving the garment, etc.).

पश्चादग्नेस्तेजनीं कटं वा दक्षिणपादेन प्रवृत्योपविशति ॥२॥
Having pushed with his right foot a bundle of grass or a mat to the west of the fire, he sits down.

अन्वारब्ध अघारावाज्यभागौ महाव्याहृतयः सर्वप्रायश्चित्तं प्राजापत्यं स्विष्टकृच्च ॥३॥
While she touches him, the following oblations are made: the two *aghāra* oblations, the two *ājya* portions, the *mahāvyāhṛtis*, the general expiation, the *prājāpatya* and the *sviṣṭakṛt* oblations.

एतान्नित्यं सर्वत्र ॥४॥
These are regular at every sacrifice.

प्राङ् महाव्याहृतिभ्यः स्विष्टकृद् अन्यच्चेदाज्याद्धविः ॥५॥
If the sacrificial offering is other than *ājya*, the *sviṣṭakṛt* comes before the *mahāvyāhṛtis*.

सर्वप्रायश्चित्त प्राजापत्यान्तरमेतदावापस्थानं विवाहे ॥६॥
The place for insertion of peculiar oblations is the interval between the general expiation and the oblation to Prajāpati during marriage.

राष्ट्रभृत इच्छञ्जयाभ्यातानाँश्च जानन् ॥७॥
He may make oblations with *rāṣṭrabhṛt* formula if he likes and with the *jayā* and *abhyatana* formulae, if he knows them.

येन कर्मणेर्त्सदिति वचनात् ॥८॥
Because it has been said, "by what sacrifice he wishes to attain success".

चित्तं च चित्तिश्चाकूतं चाकूतिश्च विज्ञातं च विज्ञातिश्च मनश्च शक्वरीश्च दर्शश्च पौर्णमासं च बृहच्च रथन्तरं च । प्रजापतिर्जयानिन्द्राय वृष्णे प्रायच्छदुग्रः पृतनाजयेषु । तस्मै विशः समनमन्त सर्वाः स उग्रः स इहव्यो बभूव स्वाहा इति ॥९॥

Sentience and the sentient, the substance of intent and intent, the basis of learning and learning, the mind, the sensory organs, the rituals of Darśa and Pūrṇamāsa, the *sāmas* of *bṛhat* and *rathantara*, were all given to Indra the one who causes rain by Prajāpati. People who were engaged in battling enemies received these as worthy of offering as *havya*. *Devas* and *asuras* were fighting each other. Indra and Prajāpati went there speedily and gave these Jayā *mantras* to *devas*. *Devas* having carried out these Jayā *homas* were able to defeat the *asuras*. Those engaged in contests will emerge victorious if Jayā *homas* are carried out and opponents will be defeated.

अग्निर्भूतानामधिपतिः स माऽवत्विन्द्रो ज्येष्ठानां, यमः पृथिव्या, वायुरन्तरिक्षस्य, सूर्यो दिवश्चन्द्रमा नक्षत्राणां, बृहस्पतिब्रह्मणे, मित्रः सत्यानां, वरुणोऽपाम्, समुद्रः स्रोत्यानामन्नटम् साम्राज्यानामधिपति तन्मावतु, सोम ओषधीनां, सविता प्रसवानाम्, रुद्रः पशूनां, त्वष्टा रूपाणां, विष्णुः पर्वतानां, मरुतो गणानामधिपतयस्ते मावन्तु पितरः पितामहाः परेवरे ततास्ततामहाः। इह मावन्त्वस्मिन्ब्रह्मण्यस्मिन् क्षत्रेऽस्यामाशिष्यस्यां पुरोधायामास्मिन्कर्मण्यस्यां दवेहूत्याम् स्वाहेति सर्वत्रानुषजति ॥१०॥

The *abhyātāna* formula runs thus: "May Agni, the first among lords, protect me. May Indra, the lord of the elders, Yama of the earth, Vāyu of the air, Sun of the heaven, Moon of the *nakṣatras*, Bṛhaspati of the *Brahman*, Mitra of the truth, Varuṇa of the waters, the sea, of the rivers, food, the lord of royalty, protect me. May Soma of the herbs, Sāvitrī of impulses, Rudra of cattle, Tvaṣṭā of forms, Viṣṇu of mountains, Marut the lord of the hosts protect me. May the fathers, the grandfathers, the former, the later, the fathers, the grandfathers protect me in the power of holiness, in this wordly power, in this prayer, in this purohitship, in this invocation of the gods, *svāhā*."

"अग्निरैतु प्रथमो देवतानाम् सोऽस्यै प्रजां मुञ्चतु मृत्युपाशात् । तदयं

राजा वरुणोऽनुमन्यतां यथेयां स्त्री पौत्रमघं न रोदात्स्वाहा । इमामग्निस्त्रायतां गार्हपत्यः प्रजामस्यै नयतु दीर्घमायुः । अशून्योपस्था जीवतामस्तु माता पौत्रमानन्दमभिविबुध्यामियाम् स्वाहा । स्वस्ति नो अग्ने दिव आपृथिव्या विश्वानि धेह्ययथा यजत्र । यदस्यां महि दिवि जातं प्रशस्तं तदस्मासु द्रविणं धेहि चित्रम् स्वाहा । सुगन्न पन्थां प्रदिशन्न एहि ज्योतिष्मद्धेह्यजरन्न आयुः । अपैतु मृत्युरमृतश्च आगाद्वैवस्वतो नो अभयं कृणोतु स्वाहा" इति ॥११॥

He then makes other oblations with these texts: "May Agni come here, the first of gods. May he release the offspring of this wife from the fetters of death. May this king Varuṇa grant that this wife may not weep over distress caused through her sons, *svāhā*." "May Agni *gārhapatya* protect this woman. May he lead her offspring to old age. With fertile womb, may she be the mother of living children. May she experience delight in her sons, *svāhā*." "Make, Agni, all ways of heaven and earth blissful to us, O you who are worthy of sacrifices. What is great born on this earth and praised in heaven that bestow on us, rich treasures, *svāhā*."

परं मृत्युविति चैके प्राशनान्ते ॥१२॥

With the verse, "Another way, O death" after eating the remnants of the sacrificial food, according to some.

षष्ठी कण्डिका (Sixth Section)

कुमार्या भ्राता शमीपलाशमिश्राँल्लाजानञ्जलिनाञ्जलावावपति ॥१॥

The girl's brother pours out of his joined hands into her joined hands fried grains (*lājā*) mixed with *śamī* leaves.

ताञ्जुहोति संहतेन तिष्ठती अर्यमणं देवं कन्याऽग्निमवक्षत । स नो अर्यमा देवः प्रेतो मुञ्चतु मा पतेः स्वाहा । इयं नार्युपब्रूते लाजानावपन्तिका । आयुष्मानस्तु मे पतिरेधन्तां ज्ञातयो मम स्वाहा । इमाँल्लाजानावपाम्यग्नौ समृद्धिकरणं तव । मम तुभ्य च संवननं तदग्निरनुमन्यतामियम् स्वाहा इति ॥२॥

This she sacrifices with firmly joined hands, standing while the verses are being recited: "To the God Aryamā the girls have made sacrifice to Agni. May he, God Aryamā, loosen us from here and not from the husband, *svāhā*." This woman strewing grains, prays thus, "May my husband live long:

May my relations be prosperous, *svāhā*". "These grains I throw into the fire: May this bring prosperity to you and may it unite me with you. May Agni grant us that, *svāhā*."

अथास्यै दक्षिणं हस्तं गृह्णाति साङ्गुष्ठं, गृभ्णामि ते सौभगत्वाय हस्तं मया पत्या जरदष्टिर्यथाऽऽसः । भगोऽर्यमा सविता पुरन्धिर्मह्यं त्वाऽदुर्गार्हपत्याय देवाः । अमोऽहमस्मि सा त्वं सा त्वमस्यमोऽहम् । सामाहमस्मि ऋक्त्वं द्यौरहं पृथिवी त्वं तावेहि [व] विवहावहै सह रेतो दधावहै प्रजां प्रजनयावहै पुत्रान् विन्द्यावहै बहून् ते सन्तु जरदष्टयः संप्रियौ रोचिष्णु सुमनस्यमनु पश्येम शरदः शतं जीवेम शरदः शतं श्रृणुयाम शरदः शतमिति ॥३॥

He then seizes her right hand together with the thumb with the verse, "I seize your hand for the sake of happiness, so that you may live to an old age with me, your husband. Bhaga, Aryamā, Savitā, Puraṁdhi have given you to me so that we may rule our house". "This am I (God), that are you (Goddess), That are you, this am I, The song am I, the words you are. Heaven am I, Earth are you". "Come, let us marry. Let us beget offspring. Let us acquire many sons and may they reach old age. Loving, bright with genial minds may we see 100 autumns, may we live 100 autumns and may we hear 100 autumns."

सप्तमी कण्डिका (Seventh Section)

अथैनामश्मानमारोहयत्युत्तरतोऽग्नेर्दक्षिणपादेन — आरोहममश्मानमश्मेव त्वं स्थिरा भव । अभितिष्ठ पृतन्यतोऽवबाधस्व प्रुतनायत इति ॥१॥

He then makes her thread on a stone, to the north of the fire, with her right foot while reciting the verse: "Tread on this stone; be firm like a stone; tread the foes down; turn away enemies."

अथ गाथां गायति — "सरस्वति प्रेदमव सुभगो वाजिनीवती । या त्वा विश्वस्य भूतस्य प्रजायामस्याग्रतः । यस्यां भूतं समभवद्यस्यां विश्वमिदं जगत् । तामध्य गाथां गास्यामि या स्त्रीणामुत्तमं यश" इति ॥२॥

He then sings a song. "Sarasvatī! Promote this marriage, O gracious one, bountiful one, beautiful one, you whom we sing first of all that is, in whom what is, has been born, in whom the whole world dwells — that song I will sing today which will be the highest glory of women."

अथ परिक्रामतः — "तुभ्यमग्रे पर्यवहन्त्सूर्यां वहतु ना सह । पुनः पतिभ्यो जायां दाग्ने प्रजया सहेति" ॥३॥
Then they go round the fire with the verse sung by the bridegroom: "To you who they have in the beginning carried round Sūryā (Savitā's daughter) with the bridal procession, May you give back, Agni, to the husbands the wife together with offspring."

एवं द्विरपरं लाजादि ॥४॥
The rites are repeated twice again, beginning with *lājā homa*.

चतुर्थं शूर्पकुष्टया सर्वाल्लाँजानावपति–भगाय स्वाहेति ॥५॥
The fourth time she pours the whole fried grain by the edge of the basket into the fire with the words, "to Bhaga *svāhā*".

त्रिः परिणीता प्राजापत्यं हुत्वा ॥६॥
He leads her around the fire three times and sacrifices to Prajāpati.

अष्टमी कण्डिका (Eighth Section)

अथैनामुदीचीम् सप्त पदानि प्रक्रामयति "एकमिषे द्वे ऊर्जे त्रीणि रायस्पोषाय चत्वारि मायोभवाय पञ्च पशुभ्यः षड् ऋतुभ्यः सखे सप्तपदा भव सा मामनुव्रता भव" ॥१॥
Then he makes her step forward in the northern direction seven steps with the words, "One for sap, two for energy, three for prosperity, four for comfort, five for cattle, six for seasons. Be a friend with me with the seventh step, be one with me."

विष्णुस्त्वा नयत्विति सर्वत्रानुषजयति ॥२॥
The words, "may Viṣṇu lead you" are added after each step.

निष्क्रमणप्रभृत्युदकुम्भं स्कन्धे कृत्वा दक्षिणतोऽग्नेर्वाग्यतः । स्थितो भवति ॥३॥

When they are exiting, a man who holds a water pot on his shoulder stands silent on the south of the fire.

उत्तरत एकेषाम् ॥४॥
North according to some.

तत एनां मूर्द्धन्याभिषिञ्चति "आपः शिवाः शिवतमाः शान्ताः शान्ततमास्तास्ते कृण्वन्तु भेषजमिति" ॥५॥
From the pot he sprinkles her with water on her head with the *mantra*: "The blessed, the most blessed waters, the peaceful ones, may they give you health."

आपोहिष्ठेति च तिसृभिः ॥६॥
And with the three verses, "you waters are".

अथैनाम् सूर्यमुदीक्षयति तच्चक्षुरिति ॥७॥
He then makes her look at the sun with the verse, "that eye".

अथास्यै दक्षिणाम् समधि हृदयमालभते — "मम व्रते ते हृदयम् दधामि मम चित्तमनुचित्तं ते अस्तु मम वाचमेकमना जुषस्व प्रजापतिष्ट्वा नियुनक्तु मह्यम्" इति ॥८॥
He then touches her heart, reaching over her right shoulder with the verse: "Into my will I take your heart; your mind shall follow my mind; in my word you shall rejoice with all your heart; may Prajāpati unite us."

अथैनामभिमन्त्रयते — "सुमङ्गलीरियं वधूरिमाम् समेत पश्यत सौभाग्यमस्यै दत्त्वा यथाऽस्तं विपरेतनेति" ॥९॥
He then recites over her: "Come look at this auspicious bride, give her good fortune and go to your houses."

तां दृढपुरुष उन्मथ्य प्राग्वोदग्वाऽनुगुप्त आगार आनडुहे रोहिते चर्मण्युपवेशयति "इह गावो निषिदन्त्विहाश्वा इह पूरुषाः। इहो सहस्रदक्षिणो यज्ञ इह पूषा निषीदतु" इति ॥१०॥
A strong man lifts her up from the ground and sets her down on a red bull's hide in an eastern or northern direction with the words: "Here may the cows sit down, here the

horses, here the men. Here may sacrifice with 1000 gifts, here may Pūṣaṇa sit down."

ग्रामवचनं च कुर्युः ॥११॥
Do what the village people tell them what should be done.

विवाहश्मशानयोर्ग्रामं प्राविशतादिवचनात् ॥१२॥
It is said that at weddings and funerals, listen to what the village people say.

तस्मात्तयोर्ग्रामः प्रमाणमिति श्रुतेः ॥१३॥
For Śruti says, "on those two occasions, what the villagers say is the authority".

आचार्याय वर ददाति ॥१४॥
He gives a gift to the teacher.

गौर्ब्राह्मणस्य वरः ॥१५॥
A cow is the gift for a brāhmaṇa.

ग्रामो राजन्यस्य ॥१६॥
A village is the gift for a kṣatriya.

अश्वो वैश्यस्य ॥१७॥
A horse is the gift for a vaiśya.

अधिरथं शतं दुहितृमते ॥१८॥
Hundred cows with a chariot is the gift to a father who has only daughters.

अस्तमिते ध्रुवं दर्शयति — "ध्रुवमसि ध्रुवं त्वा पश्यामि ध्रुवैधि पोष्ये मयि ।
मह्यं त्वाऽदाद् बृहस्पतिर्मया पत्या प्रजावती संजीव शरदः शतम्" इति ॥१९॥
After sunset, he shows her the Dhruva star with the verse: "Firm are you; I see you the firm one. Be firm with me, O thriving one." "Bṛhaspati has given you to me; obtaining offspring through me, live 100 autumns."

सा यदि न पश्येत्पश्यामीत्येव ब्रूयात् ॥२०॥
If she is not able to see (Dhruva), let her say, "I see, I see".

त्रिरात्रमक्षारालवणाशिनौ स्यातामधः शयीयाताम् संवत्सरं न मिथुनपेयातां द्वादशरात्रां षड्रात्रं त्रिरात्रमन्ततः ॥२१॥
Through a period of three nights they shall eat no saline food; they shall sleep on the floor; through one year they shall refrain from intercourse, or for twelve nights, or six nights, or at least three nights.

नवमी कण्डिका (Ninth Section)

उपयमनप्रभृत्यौपासनस्य परिचरणम् ॥१॥
Beginning with the wedding, worshipping of *aupasana* fire is prescribed.

अस्तमितानुदितयोः ॥२॥
After sunset and before sunrise.

दध्ना तण्डुलैरक्षतैर्वा ॥३॥
With curds, rice and barley.

अग्नये स्वाहा प्रजापतये स्वाहेति सायम् ॥४॥
In the evening with, "to Agni *svāhā*, to Prajāpati *svāhā*".

सूर्याय स्वाहा, प्रजापतये स्वाहेति प्रातः ॥५॥
In the morning with, "to Sūrya *svāhā*, to Prajāpati *svāhā*".

पुमाँसौ मित्रवरुणौ पुमाँसाविश्विनावुभौ पुमानिन्द्रश्च सूर्यश्च पुमाँसं वर्ततां मयि पुनः स्वाहेति पूर्वां गर्भकामा ॥६॥
"Men are Mitra and Varuṇa; Men are the two Asvins; Men are Indra and Sūrya; may a man be born in me, *svāhā*." With these words, the wife who is desirous of having male children offers oblations.

दशमी कण्डिका (Tenth Section)

राज्ञोऽक्षभेदे नद्धविमोक्षे यानविपर्यासेऽन्यस्यां वा व्यापत्तौ स्त्रियाश्चोद्वहने तमेवाग्निमुपसमाधायाज्यँ संस्कृत्येहरतिरिति जुहोति नानामन्त्राभ्याम् ॥१॥
If the axle of a king's chariot breaks, or something that is bound loosens itself, or if another accident happens when a bride is carried home, he establishes the same fire, prepares

ājya and sacrifices two *ājya* oblations separately with the two *mantras*, "Here is joy".

अन्यद्यानमुपकल्प्य तत्रोपवेशयेद्राजानां स्त्रियं वा प्रतिक्षत्र इति यज्ञान्तेनात्वाहार्षमिति चैतया ॥२॥

Having got ready another chariot, he should make the king or the woman sit down thereon with the *mantra*, "in royal power" down to the word, "in sacrifice" and with, "I have seized you".

धुर्यौ दक्षिणा प्रायश्चित्तिः ॥३॥

The two animals that draw the chariot constitute the sacrificial fee.

ततो ब्राह्मणभोजनम् ॥४॥

Thereafter the feeding of brāhmaṇas.

एकादशी कण्डिका (Eleventh Section)

चतुर्थ्यामपररात्रेऽभ्यन्तरतोऽग्निमुपसमाधाय दक्षिणतो ब्राह्मणमुपवेश्योत्तरत उदपात्रं प्रतिष्ठाप्य स्थालीपाकं श्रपयित्वाऽऽज्यभागाविष्ट्वाऽऽज्याहुतीर्जुहोति ॥१॥

On the fourth night after the wedding, towards morning, he establishes the fire, assigns seat to the south of it to the brāhmaṇa, places a pot of water to the north, cooks a mess of sacrificial food, sacrifices the two *ājya* portions and makes other oblations with the following *mantras*.

अग्ने प्रायश्चित्ते त्वं देवानां प्रायश्चित्तिरसि ब्राह्मणस्त्वा नाथकाम उपधावामि याऽस्यै पतिघ्नी तनूस्तामस्यै नाशय स्वाहा । वायो प्रायश्चित्ते त्वं देवानां प्रायश्चित्तिरसि ब्राह्मणस्त्वा नाथकाम उपधावामि याऽस्यै प्रजाघ्नी तनूस्तामस्यै नाशय स्वाहा । सूर्य प्रायश्चित्ते त्वं देवानां प्रायश्चित्तिरसि ब्राह्मणस्त्वा नाथकाम उपधावामि याऽस्यै पशुघ्नी तनूस्तामस्यै नाशय स्वाहा । चन्द्र प्रायश्चित्ते त्वं देवानां प्रायश्चित्तिरसि ब्राह्मणस्त्वा नाथकाम उपधावामि याऽस्यै गृहघ्नी तनूस्तामस्यै नाशय स्वाहा । गन्धर्व प्रायश्चित्ते त्वं देवानां प्रायश्चित्तिरसि ब्राह्मणस्त्वा नाथकाम उपधावामि प्रायश्चित्ते त्वं देवानां प्रायश्चित्तिरसि ब्राह्मणस्त्वा नाथकाम उपधावामि याऽस्यै यशोघ्नी तनूस्तामस्यै नाशय स्वाहेति ॥२॥

"Agni, expiation. You are the expiation of the gods. I, the brāhmaṇa, entreat you desirous of protection. Remove that which dwells in her which brings death to her husband, *svāhā*." "Vāyu, expiation. You are the expiation of the gods. I, the brāhmaṇa, entreat you desirous of protection. Remove that which dwells in her which brings death to her children, *svāhā*." "Sūrya, expiation. You are the expiation of the gods. I, the brāhmaṇa, entreat you desirous of protection. Remove that which dwells in her which brings death to cattle, *svāhā*." "Candra, expiation. You are the expiation of the gods. I, the brāhmaṇa, entreat you desirous of protection. Remove that which dwells in her which brings destruction to the house, *svāhā*." "Gandharva, expiation. You are the expiation of the gods. I, the brāhmaṇa, entreat you desirous of protection. Remove that which dwells in her which brings destruction to fame, *svāhā*."

स्थालीपाकस्य जुहोति प्रजापतये स्वाहेति ॥३॥
He sacrifices with cooked portion with, "To Prajāpati *svāhā*".

हुत्वा हुत्वैतासामाहुतीनामुदपात्रे सं स्रवान्त्समवनीय तत एनां मूर्द्धन्यभिषिञ्चति — "या ते पतिघ्नी प्रजाघ्नी पशुघ्नी गृहघ्नी यशोघ्नी निन्दिता तनूर्जारघ्नीं तत एनां करोमि सा जीर्य त्वं मया सहासाविति" ॥४॥
After sacrificing, he pours the remainder into a water pot and from that he sprinkles on her head with the verse, "The evil substance which dwells in you that brings death to your husband, death to your children, death to cattle, destruction of the house, destruction to fame, that I change into one that brings death to your paramour. Thus you live with me for hundred years."

अथैनां स्थालीपाकं प्राशयति "प्राणैस्ते प्राणान्त्संदधाम्यस्थिभिरस्थीनि माँसैर्माँसानि त्वचा त्वचमिति" ॥५॥
He then makes her eat the cooked food with the verse, "I add breath to your breath, bones to your bones, flesh to your flesh and skin to your skin".

Gṛhya-Sūtras of Kṛṣṇa Yajurveda

Kṛṣṇa Yajurveda has the maximum number of Gṛhya-Sūtra texts presently available among the four Vedas. These are the following: Āpastamba, Hiraṇyakeśin (Satyāṣāḍha), Baudhāyana, Vārāha, Mānava, Agniveśya, Bhāradvāja, Kaṭhaka (Laugākṣī) and Vaikhānasa. This section presents texts pertaining to *vivāha saṁskāra* in these Gṛhya-Sūtras.

Āpastamba Gṛhya-Sūtra

Āpastamba Gṛhya-Sūtra belongs to Taittirīya branch of *Kṛṣṇa Yajurveda*. It is understood that Āpastamba hailed from the Āndhra region of south India. Commentaries have been written on the Gṛhya-Sūtra by Haradatta and Sudarśanācārya. The following is the text of the *Āpastamba Gṛhya-Sūtra* which deals with *vivāha saṁskāra*.

प्रथमः पटलः (First Chapter)
द्वितीयः खण्डः (Second Section)

शम्याः परिध्यर्थे विवाहोपनयनसमावर्तनसीमन्तचौलगोदानप्रायश्चित्तेषु ॥ २॥
As *paridhis* (boundaries), yoke pins are used at the *vivāha, upanayana, samāvartana, sīmantonnayana, caula, godāna* (*keśānta*) and expiatory ceremonies.

सर्व ऋतवो विवाहस्य शैशिरौ मासौ परिहाप्योत्तमं च नैदाघम् ॥१२॥
All seasons are fiṭ for marriage except for two months of winter and the last month of summer.

सर्वाणि पुण्योक्तानि नक्षत्राणि ॥१३॥
All *nakṣatras* which are said to be pure are fit for marriage.

तथा मङ्गळानि ॥१४॥
And for all auspicious ceremonies.

आवृतश्चास्त्रीभ्यः प्रतीयेरन् ॥१५॥
One should learn from women the ceremonies and the customs prevailing.

इन्वकाभिः प्रसृज्यन्ते ते वराः प्रतिनन्दिताः ॥१६॥
Under the Invakās (Mṛgaśirā *nakṣatra*), the wooers, who go to the girl's father, are sent out. Such wooers are welcome.

तृतीयः खण्डः (Third Section)

मघाभिर्गावो गृह्यन्ते ॥१॥

Cows are provided in Māgha.

फल्गुणीभ्वां व्यूह्यते ॥२॥

Marriage is celebrated under the Phālguṇī month.

यां कामयेत दुहितरं प्रिया स्यादिति तां निष्टयायां दद्यात्प्रियैव भवति नेवतु पुनरागच्छतीति ब्राह्मणावेक्षो विधिः ॥३॥

A father who wishes his daughter to be dear to her husband should give her in marriage under the Niṣṭya (Svāti) *nakṣatra;* Then she becomes dear to her husband; she does not return to her father's house as has been said in Brāhmaṇas.

इन्वकाशब्दो मृगशिरसि ॥४॥

Invakā means Mṛgaśirā.

निष्टयाशब्दस्स्वातौ ॥५॥

Niṣṭya means Svāti.

विवाहे गौः ॥६॥

At the wedding one cow.

गृहेषु गौः ॥७॥

In the house one cow.

तया वरमतिथिवदर्हयेत् ॥८॥

With the first cow he should prepare an *arghya* reception for the groom as for a guest.

योस्यपचितस्तमितरया ॥९॥

With the other for a person whom he reveres.

एतावद्गोरालम्भस्थानमतिथिः पितरो विवाहश्च ॥१०॥

The arrival of a guest, Aṣṭaka sacrifice, ceremonies for fathers and marriage are occasions for killing a cow.

सुप्तां रुदन्तीं निष्क्रान्तां वरणे परिवर्जयेत् ॥११॥

Let the wooer avoid a girl who sleeps, or cries or has left home.

दत्तां गुप्तां द्योतामृषभां शरभां विनतां विकटां मुण्डां मण्डूषिकां साङ्कारिकां रातां पालीं मित्रां स्वनुजां वर्षकारीं च वर्जयेत् ॥१२॥

And let him avoid one who has been given to another, and who is guarded by her relations, one who has a wicked look, one who is built like a bull, a bald-headed girl, one whose skin is like a frog, a girl who has gone over to another family, a girl given to many sensual pleasures, one who has too many friends, one who has a fine younger sister, or whose age is too near that of the bridegroom.

नक्षत्रनामः नदीनामा वृक्षनामाश्च गर्हिता ॥१३॥

Girls who are named after *nakṣatras*, rivers or trees are to be avoided.

सर्वाश्च रेफलकारोपान्ता वरणे परिवर्जयेत् ॥१४॥

All girls whose names have *r* or *l* as the last but one letter are to be avoided.

शक्तिविषये द्रव्याणि प्रतिच्छन्नान्युपनिधाय ब्रूयादुपब्रुस्पृशेति ॥१५॥

If possible, he should place the following objects hidden before the girl and say to her, "touch".

नानाबीजानि सँसृष्टानि वेद्याः पाँसून् क्षेत्राल्लोष्टँ शकृच्छ्मशानलोष्टमिति॥१६॥

Different kinds of seeds mixed together, loose earth from an altar, a field, cow dung and an earth clod from a cemetery.

पूर्वेषामुपस्पर्शने यथालिङ्गामृद्धिः ॥१७॥

If she touches one of the former objects, it portends prosperity accordingly.

उत्तमं परिचक्षते ॥१८॥

The last is regarded as objectionable.

बन्धुशीललक्षणसम्पन्नामरोगामुपयच्छेत ॥१९॥

Let him marry a girl of good family and character with auspicious characteristics and of good health.

बन्धुशीललक्षणसम्पन्नश्श्रुतवानरोग इति वरसम्पत् ॥२०॥
Good family, a good character, auspicious characteristics, learning and good health are the accomplishments of a bridegroom.

यस्यां मनश्चक्षुषोर्निबन्धस्तस्यामृद्धिर्नेतरदाद्रियेतेत्येके ॥२१॥
A girl who is pleasing to his mind and his eyes, will bring happiness to him. Let him disregard other things, according to some.

द्वितीयः पटलः (Second Chapter)
चतुर्थः खण्डः (Fourth Section)

सुहृदस्समवेतान्मन्त्रवतो वरान् प्रहिणुयात् ॥१॥
Let him send out his wooers, friends who have assembled and versed in the *mantras*.

तानादितो द्वाभ्यामभिमन्त्रयेत ॥२॥ (प्र सु ग्मन्ता . . . ,अनृक्षरा ऋजवः . . .)
He should recite over them the first two verses.

स्वय दृष्ट्वा तृतीयां जपेत् ॥३॥ (अभ्रातृघ्नीं वरुणापतिघ्नीं . . .)
When he himself has seen the girl, let him recite the third verse.

चतुर्थ्या समीक्षेत ॥४॥ (अघोरचक्षु . . .)
With the fourth, let him behold her.

अङ्गुष्ठेनोपमध्यमया चाङ्गुल्यादर्भं संगृह्योत्तरेण यजुषा तस्या भ्रुवोरन्तरं संमृज्य प्रतीचीनं निरस्येत् ॥५॥ (इदमहं या त्वयिं पतिघ्न्यलक्ष्मिस्तां निर्दिशामि ॥)
Let him hold with his thumb and fourth finger a *darbha* grass and let him wipe the space between her eyebrows with the next verse and let him throw it away towards the west.

प्राप्ते निमित्त उत्तरां जपेत् ॥६॥ (जीवां रुदन्ती विमयन्तो . . .)
If an omen such as the weeping of the bride or her relations, let him murmur the next verse.

युग्मान्समवेतान्मन्त्रवत उत्तरयाद्भ्यः प्रहिणुयात् ॥७॥ (व्युक्षक्रूरमुदन्ताप आस्यै . . .)
With the next verse, let him send an even number of persons who are there and who are versed in the *mantra*s to fetch water.

उत्तरेण यजुषा तस्याशिशरसि दर्भेण्वं निधाय तस्मिन्नुत्तरया दक्षिणं युगच्छिद्र प्रतिष्ठाप्य छिद्रे सुवर्णमुत्तर्यान्तर्धायोत्तराभिः पञ्चभिस्स्नापयित्वोत्तरयाऽहतेन वाससऽऽच्छाद्योत्तरया योक्त्रेण सन्नहयति ॥८॥ (अर्यम्णो अग्निं परिं यन्तु . . . , खेऽनसः खे रथः . . . , शं ते हिरण्यँ . . . , हिरण्यवर्णाः शुचयः . . . , हिरण्यवर्णाः शुचयः . . . , यासाँ राजा . . . , यासाँ देवा . . . , शिवेन त्वा . . . , परि त्वा गिर्वणो . . . ,अ॒शासाना सौमनसं . . .)
With the next *mantra*, he places a round piece of *darbha* network on her head. On that, with the next verse he places a right yoke hole. On this hole he lays with the next verse a piece of gold, and washes her with the next five verses, so that the water runs over that gold and through the yoke hole. With the next verse, he causes her to dress in a fresh garment and with the next, he girds her with a rope.

अथैनामुत्तरया दक्षिणे हस्ते गृहित्वाऽग्निमभ्यानीयापरेणाग्निमुदगग्रं कटमास्तीर्य तस्मिन्नुपविशत उत्तरो वरः ॥९॥ (पूषा त्वेतो नयतु . . .)
Then he takes hold of her with the next verse by her right hand, leads her to the fire, spreads a mat, west of the fire, so that the points of the blade in it are directed towards the north, and on this mat they both sit down, the bridegroom to the north.

अग्नेरुपसमाधानाद्याज्यभागान्तेऽथैनामादितो द्वाभ्यामभिमन्त्रयेत ॥१०॥ (सोमः प्रथमो . . . , सोमो ददद्गन्धर्वाय . . .)
After the ceremonies have been performed from the putting of wood on the fire to the *ājyabhāga* oblations, he recites over her the first two verses of the third *anuvāka*.

अथास्यै दक्षिणेन नीचा हस्तेन दक्षिणमुत्तानं हस्तं गृह्णियात् ॥११॥
Then he should take with his right hand palm down, her right hand which she holds palm up.

यदि कामयेत स्त्रीरेव जनयेयमित्यङ्गुलिरेव गृह्णीयात् ॥१२॥
If he wishes that only daughters may be born to him, he should seize only the fingers without the thumb.

यदि कामयेत पुंस एव जनयेयमित्यङ्गुष्ठमेव सोभीवाङ्गुष्ठमभिव लोमानि गृह्णाति ॥१३॥
If he wishes that only sons may be born to him, he seizes the thumb. He takes her hand so as just to touch her thumb and the hairs on her hand.

गृभ्णाति त इत्येताभिश्चतसृभिः ॥१४॥ (गृभ्णामि ते सुप्रजस्त्वाय . . . ते ह पूर्वे . . . , सरस्वति प्रेदमव . . . , य एति प्रदिशस्सर्वा . . .)
With the four verses, "I seize your hand".

अथैनामुत्तरेणाग्निं दक्षिणेन पदा प्राचीमुदीचीं वा दिशमभि प्रक्रमयत्येकमिष इति ॥१५॥ (एकमिषे . . .)
He then makes her step forward with her right foot, to the north of the fire, in an easterly or northerly direction, with the *mantra*, "one step for sap".

सखेति सप्तमे पदे जपति ॥१६॥ (सखा सप्तपदा भव सखायौ सप्तपदा बभूव . . .)
At her seventh step, he murmurs, "be a friend".

पञ्चमः खण्डः (Fifth Section)

प्राग्घोमात्प्रदक्षिणमग्निं कृत्वा यथास्थानमुपविश्यान्वःरब्धायामुत्तरा आहुतीर्जुहोति सोमाय जनिविदे स्वाहेत्येतैः प्रतिमन्त्रम् (गन्धर्वाय . . . , अग्नये . . . , कन्यला पितृभ्यो . . . , प्रेतो मुञ्चाति . . . , इमां त्वमिन्द्र . . . , अग्निरेतु प्रथमो . . . , इमामग्निस्त्रायतां . . . , मा ते गृहे . . . , द्यौस्ते पृष्ठँ . . . , अप्रजस्तां पौत्रमृत्युं . . . , इमं मे वरुण . . . , तत्त्वा यामि ब्रह्मणा . . . , त्वं नो अग्ने वरुणस्य . . . , स त्वं नो अग्नेऽवमो . . . , त्वमग्ने अयास्यया . . .) ॥१॥
Having gone round the fire so that their right sides are towards it, they sit down in their former position and while she takes hold of him, he offers the oblations with the *mantra*, "To Soma who has given me my wife *svāhā*!" one oblation with each *mantra*.

अथैनामुत्तरेणाग्निं दक्षिणेन पदाऽश्मानमास्थापयत्यातिष्ठेति (आतिष्ठेममश्मानमश्मेव . . .) ॥२॥
He then makes her, to the north of the fire, to tread with her right foot on a stone with the *mantra*, "tread . . .".

अथास्या अञ्जलावुपस्तीर्य द्विर्लाजानोप्याभिघारयति ॥३॥
Having "spread under" *ajya* into her joined hands, he pours roasted grains twice into her hands and sprinkles *ājya* over it.

तस्यास्सोदर्यो लाजानावपतीत्येके ॥४॥
Some say her brother pours the grains into her hands.

जुहोतीयं नारीति (इयं नार्युपब्रूते . . .) ॥५॥
Sacrifices with the verse, "This woman".

उत्तराभिस्तिसृभिः प्रदक्षिणमग्निं कृत्वाऽश्मानमास्थापयति यथा पुरस्तात् ॥ ६॥
Having gone round the fire, with three verses he makes her tread on the stone as before.

होमश्चोत्तरया (तुभ्यमग्रे पर्यवहन् . . . , पुनः पत्नीमग्नि . . . , विश्वा उत त्वया वयं . . . , आतिष्ठेममश्मानमश्मेव . . .) ॥७॥
And the oblation with the next verse.

पुनः परिक्रमणम् (अर्यमणं नु देवं . . .) ॥८॥
Again going round the fire.

आस्थापनम् (तुभ्यमग्रे पर्यवहन् . . . , पुनः पत्नीमग्नि . . . , विश्वा उत त्वया वयं . . . , आतिष्ठेममश्मानमश्मेव . . . , त्वमर्यमा भवसि . . .) ॥९॥
To tread on the stone.

होमश्चोत्तरया (तुभ्यमग्रे पर्यवहन् . . . , पुनः पत्नीमग्नि . . . , विश्वा उत त्वया वयं . . .) ॥१०॥
The process is repeated with oblations.

पुनः परिक्रमणम् ॥११॥
The process is repeated with oblations once again.

जयादि प्रतिपद्यते ॥१२॥
He starts the oblations beginning with *jayā homa*.

परिषेचनान्तं कृत्वोत्तराभ्यां योक्त्रं विमुख्य तां ततः प्र वा वाहयेत्प्र वा हारयेत् (प्र त्वा मुञ्चामि . . . , इमं विश्यामि . . .) ॥१३॥

After performing the rites down to the sprinkling of water round the fire and having untied the rope with the next two verses, he should make her depart from her father's house in a vehicle or should have her taken away.

समोप्यैतमग्न्मनुहरन्ति ॥१४॥

Having put the marriage fire in a vessel, they carry it behind the couple.

नित्यः ॥१५॥

The fire should be kept constantly.

धार्यः ॥१६॥

The fire should be kept constantly.

अनुगतो मन्थ्यः ॥१७॥

If it goes out, it should be lit by attrition.

श्रोत्रियागाराद्वाहार्यः ॥१८॥

Or should be fetched from the house of a holy man.

उपवासश्चान्यतरस्य भार्यायाः पत्युर्वा ॥१९॥

If the fire goes out, either the husband or the wife should fast.

अनुगतेऽपि वोत्तरया जुहुयान्नोपवसेत्(अयाश्चाग्नेऽस्यनभिशस्तीश्च . . .) ॥ २०॥

Or he may sacrifice with the next verse and not fast.

उत्तरा रथस्योत्तम्भनी (सत्येनोत्तभिता . . .) ॥२१॥

The next verse is for putting the chariot in position.

वाहावुत्तराभ्यां युनाक्ति दक्षिणमग्रे (युञ्जति ब्रध्नां . . . , योगे योगे . . .) ॥२२॥

With the next two verses, he puts the two animals to the chariot, first the right one.

आरोहतीमुत्तराभिराभिमन्त्रयते (सुकिँशुकँ . . . , उदुत्तरमारोहन्ती . . . , सम्राज्ञी श्वशुरे भव . . . , स्नुषाणाँ श्वशुराणां . . .) ॥२३॥

When she mounts the chariot, he recites over her the next verses.

सूत्रे वर्त्मनोर्व्यवस्तृणात्युत्तरया नीलं दक्षिणस्यां लोहितमुत्तरस्यां (नीललोहिते भवतः) ॥२४॥

With the next verse, he spreads out two threads in the wheel tracks, a dark blue one in the right and a red one in the left track.

ते उत्तराभिरभियाति (ये वध्वश्चन्द्रं . . . , मा विदन्परिपन्थिनो . . . , सुगं पन्थानं . . . ,) ॥२५॥

With the next verses, he walks on these tracks.

तीर्थस्थाणुचतुष्पथव्यतिक्रमे चोत्तरं जपेत् (ता मन्दसाना मनुषो . . .) ॥२६॥

And when they pass by bathing places, posts, crossroads, let him murmur the verse.

षष्टः खण्डः (Sixth Section)

नावमुत्तरयामुमन्त्रय ते (अयं नो मह्याः . . .) ॥१॥

When they are going in a boat, he recites the verse.

न च नाव्यांस्तरती वधुः पश्येत् ॥२॥

And let the wife not see the crew when they are crossing.

तीर्वोत्तरां जपेत् (अस्य पारे निर्ऋथस्य . . .) ॥३॥

After they have crossed, let him murmur the next verse.

श्मशानाधिव्यतिक्रमे भाण्डे रथे वा रिष्टेऽग्रेरुपसमाधानाद्याज्यभागान्ते–ऽन्वारब्धायामुत्तरा आहुतीर्हुत्वा जयादि प्रतिपद्यते परिषेचनान्तं करोति (यदृते चिदभिश्रिषः . . . , इडामग्ने पुरुदँसँ . . . , इमं मे वरुणा, तत्त्वा यामि, त्वं नो अग्ने, स त्वं नो अग्ने, त्वमग्ने अयासि)॥४॥

If they have to pass over a cemetery, or if any article or chariot is damaged, the ceremonies from the putting of wood on the fire down to the *ājyabhāga* oblations are performed and while she takes hold of him, he offers the oblations with the *mantras*, then starts the *jayā* and other oblations and performs the rites down to the sprinkling of water round the fire.

क्षीरिणामन्येषां वा लक्ष्मण्यानां वृक्षाणां नदीनां धन्वनां च व्यतिक्रम उत्तरे यथालिङ्गं जपेत् (ये गन्धर्वा . . . ,या ओषधयो . . .) ॥५॥

If they pass by trees with milky sap or by other trees that serve as marks, by rivers or by deserts, he should murmur the next two verses accordingly.

गृहानुत्तरया संकाशयति (सं काशयामि . . .)॥६॥

With the next verse, he shows her the house.

वाहावुत्तराभ्यां विमुञ्चति दक्षिणमग्रे (आ वामगन्त्सुमति . . . , अयं नो देवस्सविता . . .) ॥७॥

With the next two verses, he unyokes the two animals, the right one first.

लोहितं चर्मानडुहं प्राचीनग्रीवमुत्तरलोम मध्येऽगारस्योत्तरयाऽऽस्तीर्य गृहान्प्रपादयन्नुत्तरां वाचयति दक्षिणेन पदा (शर्म वर्मेदमा . . . , गृहान्भद्रान्त्सुमनसः . . .)॥८॥

Having, with the next verse, spread out in the centre of the house a red bull's skin with the neck to the east and hair on top, he makes her recite the verse, while he makes her enter the house with her right foot.

न च देहलीमभितिष्ठति ॥९॥

And she does not stand on the threshold.

उत्तरपूर्वदेशेऽगारस्याग्नेरुपसमाधानाद्याज्यभागान्तेऽन्वारब्धायामुत्तरा आहुतीर्हुत्वा जयादि प्रतिपद्यते परिषेचनान्तं कृत्वोत्तरया चर्मण्युपविशत उत्तरो वरः (आगन्गोष्ठं . . . , अयमग्निगृहपति . . . , प्रजाया आभ्यां . . . , तेन भूतेन . . . , अभि वर्धतां . . . , इहैव स्तं मा . . . , ध्रुवैधि पोष्या . . . , त्वष्टा जायां . . . , इमं मे वरुणा,तत्त्वा यामि, त्वं नो अग्ने, स त्वं नो अग्ने, त्वमग्ने अयासि)(इह गावः प्र . . .) ॥१०॥

In the north-east part of the house the ceremonies from the putting of wood on the fire to the *ājyabhāga* oblations are performed and while she takes hold of him, he offers oblations with the *mantras*; then, he starts the *jayādi* oblations and performs rites down to sprinkling of water round the fire. Then they sit down on the skin with the verse, the bridegroom to the north.

अथास्याः पुँस्वोजीवपुत्रायाः पुत्रमङ्क उत्तरयोपवेश्य तस्मै फलान्युत्तरेण यजुषा प्रदायोत्तरे जपित्वा वाचं यच्छत्या नक्षत्रेभ्यः (सोमेनादित्या . . .) (प्रस्व स्थः प्रेयं . . .) (सुमङ्गलीरियं . . .)॥११॥

He then places with the verse, the son of a wife who has only sons and whose children are alive in her lap, gives fruit to the child with the next *mantra*. Then he and his wife observe silence till the stars appear.

उदितेषु नक्षत्रेषु प्राचीमुदीचीं वा दिशमुपनिष्क्रम्य उत्तराभ्यां यथालिङ्गं धूवमरुन्धतीं च दर्शयति (ध्रुवक्षितिर् . . . , सप्तर्षयः प्रथमां . . .) ॥१२॥

When the stars have appeared, he goes out of the house with her in an easterly or northerly direction and shows her the Polar star and Arundhatī with the verses.

तृतीयः पटलः (Third Chapter)
सप्तमः खण्डः (Seventh Section)

अथैनामाग्नेयेन स्थालीपाकेन याजयति ॥१॥

He then makes her offer the sacrifice of *sthālīpāka* sacred to Agni.

पत्न्यवहन्ति ॥२॥

The wife removes husk from the rice grains out of which this *sthālīpāka* is prepared.

श्रपयित्वाऽभिघार्य प्राचीनमुदीचीनं वोद्वास्य प्रतिष्ठितमभिघार्यग्नेरुप-समाधानाद्याज्यभागान्तेऽन्वःरब्धायां स्थालीपाकाज्युहोति ॥३॥

After he has cooked the *sthālīpāka*, and has sprinkled *ājya* over it and has taken it from the fire towards the east or the north and has sprinkled *ājya* over it while it stands, the ceremonies from putting the wood on the fire to the *ājyabhāga* oblations are performed while she takes hold of him, he sacrifices that of the *sthālīpāka*.

सकृदुपस्तरणाभिघारणे द्विरवदानम् ॥४॥

The spreading under and sprinkling of *ājya* over are done once. Two *avadāna*s (portions) are taken.

अग्निर्देवता स्वाहाकारप्रदानः ॥५॥

Agni is the first deity of the oblation made with *svāhā*!

अपि वा सकृदुपहत्य जुहुयात् ॥६॥

Or he may sacrifice after having taken out a portion with the *darvi* spoon.

अग्निस्स्विष्टकृद्द्वितीयः ॥७॥

Agni *sviṣṭakṛt* is the second deity.

सकृदुपस्तरणावदाने द्विरभिघारणम् ॥८॥

At the *sviṣṭakṛt* oblation, the spreading under and taking an *avadāna* are done once and sprinkling of *ājya* twice.

मध्यात्पूर्वस्यावदानम् ॥९॥

The *avadāna* of the first deity is taken from the middle of the *sthālīpāka*.

मध्ये होमः ॥१०॥

It is offered over the centre of the fire.

उत्तरार्धादुत्तरस्य ॥११॥

The second *avadāna* is taken from the northern part.

उत्तरार्धपूर्वार्धे होमः ॥१२॥

It is offered over the eastern part of the fire.

लेपयोः प्रस्तरवत् तूष्णीं बर्हिरङ्क्त्वाग्नौ प्रहरति ॥१३॥

Having silently anointed a part of the *barhis* by dipping it into the remains of the *sthālīpāka* and *ājya* as in the Śrauta ritual for the part of the *barhis* called *prastara*, he throws that part of the *barhis* into the fire.

सिद्धमुत्तरं परिषेचनम् ॥१४॥

The rule regarding the second sprinkling of water around the fire is valid here.

तेन सर्पिष्मता ब्राह्मणं भोजयेत् ॥१५॥

He gives the remains of that sacrificial food with ghee to a brāhmaṇa to eat.

योस्यापचितस्तस्मा ऋषभं ददाति ॥१६॥

Whom he reveres. To him he makes the present of a bull.

एवमत ऊर्ध्वं दक्षिणावर्जमुपोषिताभ्यां पर्वसु कार्यः ॥१७॥

In the same way, they should sacrifice a *sthālīpāka* from then onwards on the days of new and full moon after having fasted with the exception of the gift.

पूर्णपात्रस्तु दक्षिणेत्येके ॥१८॥

Some say that a vessel full of grains is the gift.

सायं प्रातरत ऊर्ध्वं हस्तेनैते आहुती तण्डुलैर्यवैर्वा जुहुयात् ॥१९॥

From then onwards, he should offer in the morning and evening with his hand these two oblations of rice, grains or barley.

स्थालीपाकवद्दैवतम् ॥२०॥

The deities are the same as described in the *sthālīpāka*.

सौरी पूर्वाहुतिः प्रातरित्येके ॥२१॥

Some say that the first oblation in the morning is sacred to Sūrya.

उभयतः परिषेचनं यथा पुरस्तात् ॥२२॥

Before and after the oblations, the sprinkling of water around the fire as stated above.

पार्वणेनातोऽन्यानि कर्माणि व्याख्यातान्याचाराद्यानि गृह्यन्ते ॥२३॥

Apart from the rituals of *pārva* (new and full moon) which are *sthālipāka* for a married man, other ceremonies such as Sarpabali etc. are derived from practice, it is understood.

यथोपदेशं देवताः ॥२४॥

The deities are as stated above.

अग्निं स्विष्टकृतं चान्तरेण ॥२५॥

Having their places between Agni *sviṣṭakṛt*.

अविकृतमातिथ्यम् ॥२६॥

The sacrifice of a cow on the arrival of a guest without alterations.

वैश्वदेवे विस्वे देवाः ॥२७॥

The deities of Vaiśvadeva or Viśvedevās.

पौर्णमास्यां पौर्णमासी यस्याम् क्रियते ॥२८॥

Of the ceremonies performed on full moon days, the full moon day on which they are performed.

अष्टमः खण्डः (Eighth Section)

उपाकरणे समापने च ऋषिर्यः प्रज्ञायते ॥१॥

At the opening and concluding ceremonies of Vedic study, the *ṛṣi* who is indicated of the chapter which they study is the deity to whom the ceremony belongs.

सदसस्पातिर्द्वितीयः (सदसस्पतिमद्भुतं . . .) ॥२॥

The *sadasaspati* is second.

स्त्रियानुपेतेन क्षारलवणावरान्नसंसृष्टस्य च होमं परिचक्षते ॥३॥

They reject a sacrifice performed by a wife or by one who has not had the *upanayana* and a sacrifice of spicy food or a mixture of despised food.

यथोपदेशं काम्यानि बलयश्च ॥४॥

Sacrifices connected with special wishes and *bali* sacrifices should be performed as advised.

सर्वत्र स्वय प्रज्वलितेऽग्नावुत्तराभ्यां समिधावादध्यात् (उद्दीप्यस्व . . . , मा नो हिंसी . . .) ॥५॥

Whenever the fire flames itself, he should put two pieces of wood in it with the verses.

आगन्मा श्रीः श्रीगार्गाविति वा ॥६॥

Or with the *mantra*: "Let fortune reach me! May fortune come to me."

एतदहर्विजानीयद्यर्भार्यामावहते ॥७॥
Let him notice the day on which he brings his wife home.

त्रिरात्रमुभयोरधश्शय्या ब्रह्मचर्यं क्षारलवणवर्जनं च ॥८॥
From that day through three nights they should sleep on the floor, be chaste and avoid food with salt and spices.

तयोश्शय्यामन्तरेण दण्डो गन्धलिप्तो वाससा सूत्रेण वा परिवीतस्तिष्ठति ॥ ९॥
Between their sleeping places a staff is kept which is anointed with perfumes and wrapped round with a garment or thread.

तं चतुर्थ्यापररात्र उत्तराभ्यामुत्थाप्य प्रक्षाळ्य निधायाग्नेरुपसमाधाना-द्याज्यभागान्तेऽन्वारब्धायामुत्तरा आहुतीर्हुत्वा जयादि प्रतिपद्यते परिषेचनान्तं कृत्वापरेणाग्निं प्राचीमुपवेश्य तस्याशिशरस्याज्यशेषाद्व्याहृति-भिरोङ्कारचतुर्थाभिरानीयोत्तराभ्यां यथालिङ्गं मिथस्समीक्ष्योत्तरयाऽऽज्यशेषेण हृदयदेशौ संसृज्योत्तरास्तिस्रो जपित्वा शेषँ समावेशने जपेत् (उदीर्ष्वातो विश्वावसो . . . , उदीर्ष्वातः पतिवति . . .) (अग्ने प्रायश्चित्ते . . . , वायो प्रायश्चित्ते . . . , आदित्य प्रायश्चित्ते . . . , प्रजापते प्रायश्चित्ते . . . , प्रसवोश्चोपयामश्च . . . , मधुश्च माधवश्च . . . , चित्तं च चित्तिश्चाकुतं च . . .) (भू स्वाहा भुव स्वाहा सुव स्वाहोँ स्वाहा) (अपश्यं त्वा मनसा चेकितानं . . . , अपश्यं त्वा मनसा दीध्यानाँ . . .) (समञ्जन्तु विश्वे देवा . . .) (प्रजापते तन्वं . . . , आ नः प्रजां . . . , तां पूषञ्छिवतम . . .) आ रोहोरुमुप . . . , आर्द्रयारण्या . . . , अहं गर्भमदधां . . . , पुत्रिणेमा कुमारिणा . . . , वीतिहोत्रा कृतद्वसू . . .) ॥१०॥
In the last part of the fourth night he takes the staff with the verses, washes it and puts it away; then the ceremonies from putting of wood on the fire down to *ājyabhāga* oblations are performed and while she takes hold of him, he sacrifices the oblations with the *mantras*; then he starts the oblations beginning with *jayā homa* and performs the rites down to the sprinkling of water round the fire. Then he makes her sit down to the west of the fire, facing the east and pours some *ājya* of the remains on her head with the three *vyāhṛtis* and the word *oṁ* as the fourth. Then they look at each other with

the next two verses, according to the characteristics; with the next verse he applies the regions of their hearts with the remains of the *ājya;* then he murmurs the next verses and should murmur the rest of the *anuvāka* when cohabiting with her.

अन्यो वैनामभिमन्त्रयेत ॥११॥
Or another person should recite the *anuvāka* over her.

यदा मलवद्वासाः स्यादथैनां ब्राह्मणप्रतिपिद्वानि कर्मणि सँशास्ति यां मलवद्वाससमित्येतानि ॥१२॥
During her monthly periods he instructs her about things forbidden to her contained in the Brāhmaṇa in the section, "a menstruous woman".

रजसः प्रादुर्भावात् स्नातामृतुसमावेशन उत्तराभिरभिमन्त्रयये (विष्णुर्योनि कल्पयितु . . . , गर्भं देहि . . . , हिरण्ययी . . . , यथेयं पृथिवी . . . , यथा पृथिव्य . . . , विष्णो श्रेष्ठेन . . . , नेजमेष परा मत . . . , व्यस्य योनिं . . . , आ ते गर्भो . . . , करोमि ते प्रजापत्यमा . . . , पुमाँस्ते पुत्रो . . . , यानि भद्राणि . . . , कामप्रमृध्यतां . . .) ॥१३॥
After her periods, he should, when going to cohabit with her, recite over her after she has bathed, the next verses.

Hiraṇyakeśī Gṛhya-Sūtra

Hiraṇyakeśī was an adherent of *Kṛṣṇa Yajurveda* and is also known by the name Satyāṣāḍa. He belonged to the Taittirīya branch of *Kṛṣṇa Yajurveda*. According to Kane, his period is during 800–400 BCE. *Hiraṇyakeśī Gṛhya-Sūtra* has two *praśna*s under which there are *paṭala*s and sections. Mātṛdatta has written a commentary on this Gṛhya-Sūtra. The following is the text of *Hiraṇyakeśī Gṛhya-Sūtra* referring to *vivāha saṁskāra.*

प्रथमः प्रश्नः (First Praśna)
षष्ठः पटलः (Sixth Chapter)

ऊनविंशः खण्डः (Nineteenth Section)

समावृत्त आचार्यकुलान्मातापितरौ बिभृयत् ॥१॥

After he has returned from the teacher's house, he should support his father and mother.

ताभ्यामनुज्ञातो भार्यामुपयच्छेत्सजातां नग्निकां ब्रह्मचारिणीमसगोत्राम् ॥ २॥
With their permission, he should take a wife belonging to the same caste, a maiden who is a virgin belonging to a different *gotra*.

अह्नः पञ्चसु कालेषु प्रातः संगवे मध्यंदिनेपराह्णे सायं वैतेषु यत्कारी स्यात्पुण्याह एव कुरुते ॥३॥
Whatever he intends to do, he should do on an auspicious day only, during the five times of the day, namely, morning, forenoon, midday, afternoon or in the evening.

अग्निमुपसमाधाय परिधानन्तं कृत्वा वधूमानीयमानां समीक्षते । सुमङ्गलीरियं वधूरिमां समेत पश्यत । सौभाग्यमस्यै दत्त्वायाथास्तं विपरेतन ॥ इति ॥४॥
Having put wood on the fire, set the limits and performed the preparatory rites, he looks at the bride who is led to him with the verse: "Auspicious ornaments does this woman wear. Look at her and having brought luck to her, go back to your houses."

दक्षिणतः पतिं भार्योपविशति ॥५॥
The bride sits to the right side of the bridegroom.

आचान्तसमन्वारब्धायां परिसिञ्चति यथा पुरस्तात् ॥६॥
After she has sipped water, she touches him and he sprinkles water round the fire as before.

व्याहृतिपर्यन्तं कृत्वा जुहोति । अग्निरैतु प्रथमो देवतानां सोस्यै प्रजां मुञ्चतु मृत्युपाशात् । तदयं राजा वरुणोनुमन्यतां यथेयं स्त्री पौत्रमघं न रोदात् । स्वाहा ॥ इमामग्निस्त्रायतां गार्हपत्यः प्रजामस्यै नयतु दीर्घमायुः। अशून्योपस्था जीवतामस्तु माता पौत्रमानन्दमभिप्रबुध्यतामियम् स्वाहा ॥ मा ते गृहे निशि घोष उत्थादन्यत्र त्वद्रुदत्यः संविशन्तु । मा त्वं विकेश्युर आवधिष्ठा जीवपत्नी पतिलोके विराज प्रजां पश्यन्ती सुमनस्यमानाम् । स्वाहा ॥ द्योस्ते पृष्ठं रक्षतु वायुरूरू अश्विनौ च स्तनं धयतस्ते पुत्रान्सविताभिरक्षतु । आ वाससः परिधानाद्बृहस्पतिर्विश्वे देवा अभिरक्षन्तु पश्चात् । स्वाहा ॥ अप्रजस्तां पौत्रमृत्युं पाप्मानमुत वाधम् । शीर्ष्णाः

स्रजमिवोन्मुच्य द्विषद्भ्यः प्रतिमुञ्चामि पापम् । स्वाहा ॥ देवकृतं ब्राह्मणं कल्पमानं तेन हन्मि योनिषदः पिशाचान् । क्रव्यादो मृत्यूनधरान्पादयामि दीर्घमायुस्तव जीवन्तु पुत्राः । स्वाहा ॥ इति ॥७॥

After he has performed the rites down to the oblations made with *vyāhṛtis*, he sacrifices with the *mantras*: "May Agni the first of gods come here. May he release the offspring from the fetter of death. May the great king Varuṇa grant that this wife may not weep over distress through her sons, *svāhā*!" "May no noise coming from you arise in the house at night. May the she-goblins, the weeping ones take their abode in another woman. May you not be beaten at the chest at your behest by Vikeśī. May your husband live and may you shine in your husband's world, beholding your genial offspring, *svāhā*!" "May heaven protect your back, Vāyu, your thighs and the Aśvins your breast. May Sāvitrī protect your suckling sons." "Until the garment is put on them, may Bṛhaspati guard them and Viśvedevās afterwards."

इमं मे वरुणा ॥ तत्त्वा यामि ॥ त्वं नो अग्ने ॥ स त्वं नो अग्ने ॥ त्वमग्ने अयासि ॥ प्रजापते ॥ इति हुत्वाश्मानमास्थापयति । आतिष्ठेममश्मानमश्मेव त्वं स्थिरा भव । प्रमृणीहि दुरस्यून्सहस्व पृतनायतः ॥ इति ॥८॥

After he has sacrificed with the verses, "This O Varuṇa", "For this I entreat you", "You Agni", "Thus you Agni", "You Agni are quick", "Prajapati"— he makes her tread on a stone with the verse, "Tread on this stone; like a stone be firm. Destroy those who seek to do you harm; overcome your enemies."

अपरेणाग्निं द्वयान्दर्भान्पूर्वापरानुदगग्रान्संस्तीर्य तेष पूर्वापराववतिष्ठेते ॥९॥

To the west of the fire he strews two layers of *darbha* grass pointed northwards, one more to the west, the other to the east. On these both they station themselves, one to the west and the other more to the east.

विंशः खण्डः (Twentieth Section)

प्राङ्मुखः प्रत्यङ्मुख्या हस्तं गृह्णीयात्प्रत्यङ्मुखः प्राङ्मुख्या वा । यदि कामयेत पुंसो जनयेयमित्यङ्गुष्ठं गृह्णीयात् । यदि कामयेत स्त्रीरित्यङ्गुलीः ।

यदि कामयेतोभयं जनयेयमित्यमीव लोमान्यङ्गुष्ठं सहाङ्गुलिभिर्गृह्णीयात् । सरस्वति प्रेदमव सुभगे वाजिनीवति । यां त्वा विश्वस्य भूतस्य प्रजायामस्यग्रतः ॥ गृह्णामि ते सुप्रजास्त्वाय हस्तं मया पत्या जरदष्टिर्यथासत् । भगो अर्यमा सविता पुरन्धिर्मह्यं त्वादुर्गार्हपत्याय देवाः ॥ इति ॥१॥

Facing the east, while she faces the west or facing the west while she faces the east, he should seize her hand. If he desires to have male children, he should seize her thumb; if he desires female children, her other fingers; if he desires both male and female, let him seize the thumb together with the other fingers with the hairs on the hand on the top. He should recite the two *mantras*: "Sarasvatī! Promote this undertaking, O, gracious one, rich in studs, you whom we sing first of all that is". "I seize your hand that we may be blessed with offspring, that you may live to old age with me, your husband. Bhaga, Aryamā, Savitā, Puraṁdhi have given you to me that I may become a householder with you."

तामग्रेण दक्षिणमंसं प्रतीचीमभ्यावृत्याभिमन्त्रयते । अघोरचक्षुरपतिघ्न्येधि शिवा पशुभ्यः सुवर्चाः । जीवसूर्वीरसूः स्योना शं न एधि द्विपदे शं चतुष्पदे ॥ तां नः पूषञ्छिवतमामेरयस्व यस्यां बीजं मुनुष्या वपन्ति । या न ऊरू उशती विस्रयातै यस्यामुशन्तः प्रहरेम शेपम् ॥ सोमः प्रथमो विविदे गन्धर्वो विविद उत्तरः । तृतीयो अग्निष्टे पतिस्तुरीयोहं मनुष्यजाः ॥ सोमोददाद्गन्धर्वाय गन्धर्वोग्नयेददात् । पशूंश्च मह्यं पुत्रांश्चाग्निर्ददात्यथो त्वाम् ॥ अमूहमस्मि सा त्वं द्यौरहं पृथिवी त्वं सामाहमृक्त्वं तावेहि संभवाव सह रेतो दधावहै पुंसे पुत्राय वेत्तवै रायस्पोषाय सुप्रजास्त्वाय सुवीर्याय ॥ इमां त्वमिन्द्र मीढ्वः सुपुत्रां सुभगां कुरु । दशास्यां पुत्रानादेहि पतिमेकादशं कुरु ॥ इति ॥२॥

He makes her turn around, from left to right so that she faces the west and recites over her the *mantra*, "With no evil eye, not bringing death to your husband, bring luck to the cattle, be full of joy and vigour. Give birth to living children, give birth to heroes, be friendly. Bring us luck, to men and animals. Thus, Pūṣaṇa, lead her to us, the highly blessed one, into whom men pour forth their sperm, into whose thighs men would cause bleeding and desire to beat their organs." "Soma has acquired you first: After him the *gandharva*: Third is Agni. Fourth am I, your human husband." "Soma has given her to the *gandharva*, *gandharva* to Agni. Agni gives me cattle and children besides you. I am this (God), that (Goddess) you are; I am the heaven; you are the earth; I am the song, you are the words. Come let us unite so that we may beget male children for the sake of increased wealth, of blessed children and strength. Bountiful Indra, bless this woman with sons and fortune. Give her ten sons and make her husband the eleventh."

तां यथायतनमुपवेश्याथास्या अञ्जलावाज्येनोपस्तीर्य लाजान्द्विरावपति । इमाँल्लाजानावपामि समृद्धिकरणान्मम । तुभ्यं च संवननं तदग्निरनुमन्यतामयम् ॥ इति ॥३॥

After he has made her sit down in her proper place, and sprinkled *ājya* into her joined hands, he twice pours fried grains into them with the verse: "This grain I pour into your hands; may it bring prosperity to me and may it unite us. May Agni grant us that."

अभिघार्य । इयं नार्युपब्रूतेग्नौ लाजानावपन्ती । दीर्घायुरस्तु मे पतिरेधन्तां ज्ञातयो मम । स्वाहा ॥ इति तस्या अञ्जलिना जुहोति ॥४॥

After he has sprinkled *ājya* over the grains in her hands, he sacrifices holding her hands with the verse, "This woman strewing the grains into the fire". She prays thus: "May my husband live long; may my relations be prosperous, *svāhā*!"

उदायुषा ॥ इत्युत्थाप्य । विश्वा उत त्वया वयं धारा उदन्या इव । अतिगाहेमहि द्विषः ॥ इति प्रदक्षिणमग्निं परिक्रम्य तथैव लाजानावपति ॥ ५॥

Having made her rise with the verse, "up with life" and having circumambulated the fire with the verse, "may we find our way with you through all hostile powers as through streams of water" — he pours fried grain into her hands and sacrifices as before.

द्वितीयं परिक्रम्य तथैव लाजानावपति ॥६॥

Having circumambulated a second time, he pours fried grain into her hands and she sacrifices, as before.

तृतीयं परिक्रम्य सौविष्टकृतीं जुहोति ॥७॥

After the third circumambulation, he sacrifices to *sviṣṭakṛt*.

अत्रैके जयाभ्यातानान्राष्ट्रभृत इत्युपजुह्वति यथा पुरस्तात् ॥८॥
Here some add oblations such as *jayā, ābhyātāna* and *rāṣṭrabhṛta* as before.

तामपरेणाग्निं प्राचीमुदीचीं वा विष्णुक्रमान्क्रामयति ॥९॥
To the west of the fire, he makes her step forward in an easterly or northerly direction the steps of Viṣṇu.

अथैनां संशास्ति । दक्षिणेन प्रक्रम्य सव्येनानुपक्राम मा सव्येन दक्षिणमातिक्रमीः ॥ इति ॥१०॥
He says to her: "Step forward with the right foot and follow with the left. Do not put the left before the right."

एकविंशः खण्डः (Twenty-first Section)

एकमिषे विष्णुस्त्वान्वेतु । द्वे ऊर्जे विष्णुस्त्वान्वेतु । त्रीणि व्रताय विष्णुस्तान्वेतु । चत्वारि मायोभवाय विष्णुस्तान्वेतु । पञ्च पशुभ्यो विष्णुस्तान्वेतु । षड्रायस्पोषाय विष्णुस्तान्वेतु । सप्त सप्तभ्यो होत्राभ्यो विष्णुस्तान्वेतु । इति ॥१॥
"One step for sap, may Viṣṇu lead you, second step for energy, may Viṣṇu lead you, third step for vows, may Viṣṇu lead you, fourth step for comfort, may Viṣṇu lead you, fifth step for cattle, may Viṣṇu lead you, sixth step for prosperity, may Viṣṇu lead you, seventh step for rituals, may Viṣṇu lead you."

सप्तमं पदमवस्थाप्य जपति । सखायौ सप्तपदाबभूव सख्यं ते गमेयं सख्यात्ते मा योषं सख्यान्मे मा योष्ठाः ॥ इति ॥२॥
After the seventh step, he murmurs: "With seven steps, we have become friends. May we attain mutual friendship. May I not be separated from your friendship. May you not be separated from my friendship."

अथास्या दक्षिणेन पादेन दक्षिणं पादमवक्रम्य दक्षिणेन हस्तेन दक्षिणमंसमुपर्युपर्यन्ववमृश्य हृदयदेशमभिमृशति यथा पुरस्तात् ॥३॥
He then puts his right foot on her right foot, moves his right

hand down over her right shoulder and touches the place of heart as before.

प्राणानां ग्रन्थिरसि स मा विस्रसः ॥ इति नाभिदेशम् ॥४॥
And the place of her navel with the *mantra*: "You are the knot of all breath; do not loosen yourself."

तामपरेणाग्निं प्राचीमुपवेश्य पुरस्तात्प्रत्यङ् तिष्ठन्नद्भिः प्रोक्षति । आपो हि ष्ठा मयोभुवः ॥ इति तिसृभिः । हिरण्यवर्णाः शुचयः पावकाः ॥ इति चतुसृभिः । पवमानः सुवर्जनः ॥ इति चैतेनानुवाकेन ॥५॥
After he has made her sit down to the west of the fire, so that she faces the east, he stands to the east facing west and sprinkles her with water with the three verses, "O waters, you are wholesome", with the four verses, "the gold coloured, clean, purifying waters" and with the *anuvāka*, "the purifier, the heavenly one".

अत्र बीजान्यधिश्रयन्ति ॥६॥
Now they pour seeds of rice, etc. on the heads of the groom and the bride.

सप्तः पटलः (Seventh Chapter)
द्वाविंशः खण्डः (Twenty-second Section)

तां ततः प्रवाहयन्ति प्र वा हारयन्ति ॥१॥
Then they let her depart in a vehicle from her father's house, or let her be carried away.

समोप्यैतमग्निमनुहरन्ति ॥२॥
They carry the nuptial fire behind the newly-married couple.

नित्यो धार्यः ॥३॥
It should be kept constantly.

अनुगतो मन्थ्यः श्रोत्रियागाराद्वाहार्यः ॥४॥
If it goes out, a new fire should be lit by attrition or be brought from the house of a *śrotriya*

उपवासश्चानुगते भार्यायाः पत्युर्वा ॥५॥

If the fire goes out, the husband or the wife should fast.

आगारं प्राप्यथैनां संशास्ति । दक्षिणं पादमग्रेहितर देहलिं माधिष्ठाः ॥ इति ॥६॥
When they reach his house, he says to her, "Cross the threshold with your right foot first; do not stand on the threshold".

पूर्वार्धे शालायां न्युप्योपसमादधाति ॥७॥
In the eastern part of the hall, he keeps the fire and puts wood on it.

अपरेणाग्निं लोहितमानडुहं चर्म प्राचीनग्रीवमुत्तरलोमास्तृणाति ॥८॥
To the west of the fire, he spreads a red bull's skin with the neck to the east and with the hair on top.

तस्मिन्प्राङ्मुखावुदङ्मुखौ वोपविशतः । पश्चात्पतिं भार्योपविशति । इह गावो निषीदन्त्विहाश्वा इह पुरुषाः । इहो सहस्रदक्षिणोपि पूषा निषीदतु ॥ इति ॥९॥
On that skin they both sit down facing east or north. The wife sits behind her husband with the verse, "Here may the cows sit down, here the horses, here the men. Here may Pūṣaṇa also with a thousand gifts."

वाचंनियसावासाते आ नक्षत्राणामुदयात् ॥१०॥
They sit silently until the stars appear.

उदितेषु नक्षत्रेषु प्राचीमुदीचीं वा दिशमुपनिष्क्रम्य । देवीः षडुर्वीः ॥ इति दिश उपतिष्ठते ॥११॥
When the stars have appeared, he goes out of the house in an easterly or northerly direction and worships the four directions with the *mantra*, "You goddesses, you six wide ones".

मा हास्महि प्रजया ॥ इति नक्षत्राणि ॥१२॥
He worships the stars with the verse, "May we not be deprived of our offspring".

मा रधाम द्विषते सोम राजन् ॥ इति चन्द्रमसम् ॥१३॥

The moon with the verse, "May we not get into the power of one who hates us, O King Soma".

सप्तर्षयः प्रथमां कृत्तिकानामरुन्धती ये ध्रुवतां ह निन्युः । षट्कृत्तिकामुख्ययोगं वहन्तीयमस्माकं भ्रजत्वष्टमी ॥ इति सप्तर्षीनुपस्थाप्य ध्रुवमुपतिष्ठते । ध्रुवक्षितिर्ध्रुवयोनिर्ध्रुवमसि ध्रुवत स्थितम् । त्वं नक्षत्राणां मेथ्यसि स मा पाहि पृतन्यतः ॥ नमो ब्रह्मन्णे ध्रुवायाच्युतायास्तु नमो ब्रह्मणः पुत्राय प्रजापतये नमो ब्रह्मणः पुत्रेभ्यो देवेभ्यस्त्रयस्त्रिंशेभ्यो नमो ब्रह्मणः पुत्रपौत्रेभोङ्गिरोभ्यः ॥ यस्त्वा ध्रुवमच्युतं सपुत्रं सपौत्रं ब्रह्म वेद ध्रुवा अस्मिन्पुत्राः पौत्रा भवन्ति । प्रेष्यान्तेवासिनो वसनं कम्बलानि कंसं हिरण्यं स्त्रियो राजानोन्नमभयमायुः कीर्तिर्वर्चो यशो बलं ब्रह्मवर्चसमन्नाद्यमित्येयातानि मयि सर्वाणि ध्रुवाण्यच्युतानि सन्तु ॥१४॥

He worships the *sapta ṛṣi maṇḍala* with, "The seven *ṛṣi*s who have led to firmness she, Arundhatī, who stands first among the six Kṛttikās — may she the eighth one, who leads the conjunction of the moon with the six Kṛttikās, the first among conjunctions shine upon us!" Then he worships Dhruva star with the *mantra*, "Firm dwelling, firm origin. The firm one are you, standing on the side of firmness. You are the pillar of the stars; protect me against my enemies." "Adoration to the *Brahman*, immovable one! Adoration be to *Brahman*'s son, Prajāpati! Adoration to the *Brahman*'s children to the thirty-three gods! Adoration to the *Brahman*'s children and grandchildren and to the Aṅgiras!" "He who knows you as the firm, immovable *Brahman* with his children and grandchildren, with such a man children and grandchildren will firmly dwell, servants and pupils, garments and blankets, bronze and gold, wives and kings, food, safety, long life, glory, renown, splendour, holy luster and the enjoyment of food. May all these things firmly and immovably dwell with me!"

त्रयोविंशः खण्डः (Twenty-third Section)

ध्रुवं त्वा ब्रह्म वेद ध्रुवोहमस्मिँल्लोकेस्मिंश्च जनपदे भूयासम् ॥ अच्युतं त्वा ब्रह्म वेद माहमस्माल्लोकादस्माच्च जनपदाच्च्योषि द्विषन्मे भ्रातृव्योस्माल्लोकादस्माच्च जनपदाच्च्यवतताम् । अक्षोषं त्वा ब्रह्म वेद माहमस्माल्लोकादस्माच्च जनपदाच्चेष्टिषि द्विषन्मे भ्रातृव्योस्माल्लोकादस्माच्च

जनपदाछेष्टिताम् । अव्यथमानं त्वा ब्रह्म वेद माहमस्माल्लोकादस्माच्च जनपदाद्व्यथिषि द्विषन्मे भ्रातृव्योस्माल्लोकादस्माच्च जनपदाद्व्यथताम् ॥ नभ्यं त्वा सर्वस्य नभ्यमहमस्य जनपदस्य भूयासम् । मध्यं त्वा सर्वस्य वेद मध्यमहमस्य जनपदस्य भूयासम् । तन्तिं त्वा सर्वस्य वेद तन्तिरहमस्य जनपदस्य भूयासम् । मेथीं त्वा सर्वस्य वेद मेथ्यहमस्य जनपदस्य भूयासम् । नाभिं त्वा सर्वस्य वेद नाभिरहमस्य जनपदस्य भूयासम् । यथा नाभिः प्राणानां विषूवानेवहमहं विषूवान् । एकशतं तं पाप्मानमृच्छतु योस्मान्द्वेष्टि यं च वयं द्विष्मो भूयांसि मामेकशतात्पुण्यान्यागच्छन्तु ॥ इति ॥१॥

"I know you as the firm *Brahman*. May I become firm in this world and in this country. I know you as the immovable *Brahman*. May I not be moved away from this world and from this country. May he who hates me, my rival, be moved away from this world and country. I know you as the unshaken *Brahman*. May I not be shaken from this world and country. May he who hates me, my rival, be shaken off this world and country. I know you as the unfalling *Brahman*. May I not fall from this world and country. May he one who hates me, my rival, fall from this world and country. I know you as the nave of the universe. May I become the nave of this country. I know you as the centre of the universe. May I become the centre of this country. I know you as the string that holds the universe. May I become the string that holds this country. I know you as the pillar of the universe. May I become the pillar of this country. I know you as the navel of the universe. May I become the navel of this country. As the navel is the centre of the *prāṇa*s, thus I am the navel. May hundred and onefold evil befall him who hates us and whom we hate. May more than hundred-and-onefold merit fall to my lot."

अत्र मनोज्ञेन संभाष्यागारं प्राप्याथैनामाग्नेयेन स्थालीपाकेन याजयति ॥ २॥

Having spoken there with a person that he likes, he causes her to sacrifice a mess of cooked food.

पत्न्यवहन्ति ॥३॥

The wife husks the rice grains for *sthālīpāka*.

श्रपयित्वाभिघार्योद्वास्याग्नये हुत्वाग्नये स्विष्टकृते जुहोति ॥४॥
She cooks the *sthālīpāka*, sprinkles *ājya* on it, takes it to the fire and sacrifices to Agni and then to Agni Sviṣṭakṛt.

तेन ब्राह्मणं विद्यावन्तं परिवेवेष्टि ॥५॥
With that he entertains a learned brāhmaṇa whom he reveres.

योस्यापचितो भवति तस्मा ऋषभं ददाति ॥६॥
To that brāhmaṇa he makes a present of a bull.

नित्यमत ऊर्ध्वं पर्वस्वाग्नेयेन स्थालीपाकेन यजते ॥७॥
From that time he constantly sacrifices on the days of full moon and new moon a mess of cooked food sacred to Agni.

नित्यं सायं प्रातर्व्रीहिभिर्यवैर्वा हस्तेनैते आहुती जुहोति । अग्नये स्वाहा ॥ प्रजापतये स्वाहा ॥ इति ॥८॥
Everyday in the morning and evening he sacrifices with his hand the following two oblations of rice or barley: "To Agni *svāhā*! To Prajāpati *svāhā*!"

सौरीं पूर्वां प्रातरेके समामनन्ति ॥९॥
Some say that the morning oblations should be to Sūrya.

त्रिरात्रमक्षारलवणाशिनावधःशायिनावलंकुर्वाणौ ब्रह्मचारिणौ वसतः ॥ १०॥
For a period of three nights they should eat no saline food, sleep on the floor, wear no ornaments and be chaste.

चतुर्थामपररात्रेग्निमुपसमाधाय प्रायश्चित्तिपर्यन्तं कृत्वा नव प्रायश्चित्तीर्जुहोति ॥११॥
In the fourth night, towards morning, he puts wood on the fire, performs regular ceremonies down to expiatory oblations and sacrifices nine expiatory oblations with the following *mantras*.

चतुर्विंशः खण्डः (Twenty-fourth Section)

अग्ने प्रायश्चित्ते त्वं प्रायश्चित्तिरसि ब्राह्मणस्त्वा नाथकाम उपधावामि यास्यै घोरा तनूस्तामितो नाशय स्वाहा ॥ वायो प्रायश्चित्ते त्वं प्रायश्चित्तिरसि

ब्राह्मणस्त्वा नाथकाम उपधावामि यास्यै निन्दिता तनूस्तामितो नाशय स्वाहा ॥ आदित्य प्रायश्चित्ते त्वं प्रायश्चित्तिरसि ब्राह्मणस्त्वा नाथकाम उपधावामि यास्यै पतिघ्नी तनूस्तामितो नाशय स्वाहा ॥ आदित्य प्रायश्चित्ते वायो प्रायश्चित्तेऽग्ने प्रायश्चित्तेऽग्ने प्रायश्चित्ते वायो प्रायश्चित्त आदित्य प्रायश्चित्ते ॥ इति ॥१॥

"Agni! Expiation! You are expiation. I, the brāhmaṇa, entreat you desirous of protection. What is terrible in her drive that away from her, *svāhā*!" "Vayu! Expiation! You are expiation. I, the brāhmaṇa, entreat you desirous of protection. What is blameful in her drive that away from her, *svāhā*!" "Āditya! Expiation! You are expiation. I, the brāhmaṇa, entreat you desirous of protection. What dwells in her that is death-bringing to her, drive that away from her, *svāhā*!" "Āditya! Expiation! Vāyu Expiation! Agni Expiation! Agni Expiation! Vāyu Expiation! Āditya Expiation!"

हुत्वाथास्यै मूर्ध्नि संस्रावं जुहोति । भूर्भगं त्वयि जुहोमि स्वाहा ॥ भुवो यशस्त्वयि जुहोमि स्वाहा ॥ सुवः श्रियं त्वयि जुहोमि स्वाहा ॥ भूर्भुवः सुवस्त्विषिं त्वयि जुहोमि स्वाहा ॥ इति ॥२॥

Having sacrificed these oblations, he then pours the remainder as an oblation on her head with the *mantra*, "*Bhuḥ*! I sacrifice fortune over you, *svāhā*! *Bhuvaḥ*! I sacrifice glory over you, *svāhā*! Suvaḥ! I sacrifice beauty over you, *svāhā*! *Bhūr bhuvaḥ suvaḥ*! I sacrifice brightness over you, *svāhā*!"

अत्रैवोदपात्रं निधाय प्रदक्षिणमग्निं परिक्रम्यापरेणाग्निं प्राचीमुदीचीं वा संवेश्यास्यै योनिमभिमृशति । अभि त्वा पञ्चशाखेन शिवेनाविद्विषावता । साहस्रेण यशस्विना हस्तेनाभिमृशामसि सुप्रजास्त्वाया ॥ इति ॥३॥

There near the fire he places a water pot, walks a round the fire and the water pot, makes her lie down to the west of the fire facing east or north and touches her *yoni* with the *mantra*, "We touch you with five forked, auspicious, unhostile, thousandholdedly blessed, glorious hand that you may be rich in offspring!"

अथैनामुपयच्छते । सं त्वा सं हृदयानि सं नाभिः सं त्वचः । सं त्वा कामस्य योक्त्रेण युञ्जान्यविमोचनाय ॥ इति ॥४॥

He then cohabits with her with the *mantra*, "United is our soul, united our hearts, united our navel, united our skin. I will bind you with the bond of love; that shall be unbreachable."

मामनुव्रता भव सहचर्या मया भव । या ते पतिघ्नी तनूर्जारघ्नीं त्वेतां करोमि । शिवा त्वं मह्यमेधि क्षुरपविर्जारिभ्यः ॥ इति ॥५॥
He then embraces her with the *mantra*, "Be devoted to me; be my companion. What dwells in you that is death-bringing to your husband, that I make death-bringing to your paramours. Bring luck to me; be a sharp-cutting destroyer to your paramours."

अथास्यै मुखेन मुखमीप्सते । मधु हे मध्विदं मधु जिह्वा मे मधुवादिनी । मुखे मे सारघं मधु दत्सु संवननं कृतम् ॥ चाक्रवाकं संवननं यन्नदीभ्य उदाहृतम् । यद्युक्तो देवगम्धर्वस्तेन संवनिनौ स्वके ॥ इति ॥६॥
He then seeks her mouth with his mouth, with the verses, "Honey! Lo! Honey! This is honey! My tongue's speech is honey; in my mouth dwells the honey of the bee; on my teeth dwells concord." "The magic charm of concord that belongs to *cakravāka* birds, that is brought out of the rivers, of which the divine *gandharva* is possessed, thereby we are concordant."

त्रिरात्रं मलवद्वससा ब्राह्मणव्यातानि व्रतानि चरति ॥७॥
A woman who has her menstrual period, keeps through a duration of three nights the observances prescribed in the Brāhmaṇa.

चतुर्थ्यां स्नातां प्रयतवस्त्रामलंकृतां ब्राह्मणसंभाषामाचम्योपव्हयते ॥ ८॥
In the fourth night, the husband having sipped water, calls the wife who has taken a bath, who wears a clean dress and ornaments and spoken with a brāhmaṇa to himself with the following verses.

पञ्चविंशः खण्डः (Twenty-fifth Section)

विष्णुर्योनिं कल्पयतु त्वष्टा रूपाणि पिंशतु ॥ आसिञ्चतु प्रजापतिर्धाता

गर्भं दधातु ते ॥ गर्भं देहि सिनीवालि गर्भं देहि सरस्वति । गर्भं ते अश्विनावुभावाधत्तां पुष्करस्रजौ । हिरण्ययी अरणीं यं निर्मन्थतो अश्विना । तं ते गर्भं हवामहे दशमास्याय सूतवे ॥ यथाग्निगर्भा पृथिवी द्यौर्यथेन्द्रेण गर्भिणी । वायुर्यथा दिशां गर्भ एवं दधामि ते ॥ यस्य योनिं प्रति रेतो गृहाण पुमान्पुत्रो जायतां गर्भो अन्तः । तं माता दश मासो बिभर्तु स जायतां वीरतमः स्वानाम् ॥ आ ते गर्भो योनिमेतु पुमान्बाण इवेषुधिम् । आ वीरो अत्र जायतां पुत्रस्ते दशमास्यः ॥ करोमि ते प्रजापत्यमा गर्भो योनिमेतु ते । अनूनः पूर्णो जायतामनन्धोऽश्लोणोऽपिशाचधीरः ॥ यानि प्रभूणि वीर्याण्वृषभा जनयन्तु नः । तैस्त्वं गर्भिणी भव स जायतां वीरतमः स्वानाम् ॥ यो वशायां गर्भो यश्च वेहतीन्द्रस्तं निदधे वनस्पतौ । तेन त्वं गर्भिणी भव सा प्रसूर्धेनुगा भव ॥ सं नाम्नः ॥ चाक्रवाकम् ॥ इति च ॥१॥

"May Viṣṇu make your womb ready; may Tvaṣṭā frame the shape of the child; may Prajāpati pour forth the sperm; may Dhātrī give you conception!" "Give conception, Sinīvāli; give conception, Sarasvatī! May the two Aśvins, wreathed in flowers give conception to you". "The embryo which the two Aśvins produce with their golden kindling-sticks, that embryo we call into your womb, that you may give birth to it in ten months." "As the earth is pregnant with Agni, as the heaven is pregnant with Indra, as Vāyu dwells in the womb of the regions, thus I place an embryo into your womb." "Open your womb; take in the sperm; may a male child, an embryo, be begotten in the womb. The mother bears him ten months; may he be born, the most valiant of the kin." "May a male embryo enter your womb as an arrow enters the quiver; may a man be born here, your son after ten months". "I do with you that which is sacred to Prajāpati; may an embryo enter your womb; may a child be born without deficiency, with all its limbs, not blind, not lame, not sucked out by *piśāca*s." "By the superior powers which the bulls shall produce for us, thereby you become pregnant; may he be born, the most valiant of his kin." "Indra has laid down in the tree the embryo of the sterile cow and of the cow that prematurely produces; thereby you become pregnant; be a well breeding cow". Our names are united. We are concordant like the *cakravāka* birds.

भूः प्रजापतिनात्वृषभेण स्कन्दयामि वीरं धत्स्वासौ । भुवः प्रजापतिनात्वृषभेण स्कन्दयामि वीरं धत्स्वासौ । सुवः प्रजापतिनात्वृषभेण स्कन्दयामि वीरं धत्स्वासौ ॥ इति वीरं हैव जनयति ॥२॥

He should cohabit with her with the *mantras*, "Bhūḥ, through Prajapāti, the highest bull, I pour forth the sperm; conceive a valiant son. Bhuvaḥ! Through Prajāpati, the highest bull, I pour forth the sperm; conceive a valiant son. Suvaḥ! Through Prajāpati, the highest bull, I pour forth the sperm; conceive a valiant son." Thus he will gain a valiant son.

सर्वाण्युपगमनानि मन्त्रवन्ति भवन्तीत्यात्रेयः ॥३॥

The *mantras* should be repeated whenever they cohabit, according to Ātreya.

यच्चदौ यच्चर्ताविति बादरायणः ॥४॥

Only the first time and after her monthly periods, says Bādarāyaṇa.

Baudhāyana Gṛhya-Sūtra

Baudhāyana Gṛhya-Sūtra belongs to the Kaṭha branch of *Kṛṣṇa Yajurveda* under a further division of Vājasaneya. The Gṛhya-Sūtra is divided into four *praśnas* with each *praśna* having chapters. Bhāvasvāmi and Govindasvāmi have written commentaries on *Baudhāyana Dharmaśāstra* of which *Baudhāyana Gṛhya-Sūtra* forms a part. The following is the text of chapters of *Baudhāyana Gṛhya-Sūtra* dealing with *vivāha saṁskāra* with English translation.

प्रथम प्रश्नः (First Praśna)
प्रथम अध्यायः (First Chapter)

विवाहं व्याख्यास्यामः ॥१३॥

Let us study the rites of marriage.

उदगयन आपूर्यमाणपक्षे पुण्ये नक्षत्रे युग्मान् ब्राह्मणान् वरान् प्रहिणोति

"प्रसुग्मन्ता धियसानस्य सक्षणि वरेभिर्वरॉं अभि षु प्रसीदतः । अस्माकमिन्द्र उभयं जुजोषति यत्सौम्यस्यान्धसो बुबोधति" इति ॥१४॥
During the northern course of the sun, during the period of the rising moon under an auspicious *nakṣatra*, two brāhmaṇas are sent to look for a bride with the verse, "Indra sends his fast horses to the service of the expectant worshipper, propitiating by suitable means. Indra is gratified by both our oblations and praises when he savours the food presented by the offerer of Soma".

यतोऽनुमन्त्रयते "अनृक्षरा ऋजवस्सन्तु पन्था येभिस्सखायो यन्ति नो वरेयम् । समर्यमा सम्भगो नो निनीयात्सञ्जास्पत्यँ सुयममस्तु देवाः" इति ॥१५॥
They chant the *mantra*: "Let the paths that our friends travel for the wooing be thornless and smooth. Let Aryamā and Bhaga lead us: O gods! Let the union of husband and wife be successful."

अथ यदि दक्षिणाभिस्सह दत्ता स्यान्नात्र वरान् प्रहिणुयात् ॥१६॥
Where the bride is given away with offerings, there is no need for further offerings for the groom.

तां प्रतिगृह्णीयात् प्रजापतिस्स्त्रियां यशः इत्येताभिष्षड्भिरनुच्छन्दसम् ॥१७॥
Let the bridegroom accept these with six *mantras* beginning with, "Prajāpati is women's fame".

सर्वे मासा विवाहस्य ॥१८॥
All months are suitable for marriages.

शुचितपस्तपस्यवर्जमित्येके ॥१९॥
Some say the months of Śuci (Āṣāḍha), Tapas (Māgha) and Tapasyā (Phālguna) are to be avoided.

रोहिणी मृगशीर्षमुत्तरे फल्गुनी स्वातीति विवाहस्य नक्षत्राणि ॥२०॥
Rohiṇī, Mṛgaśirā, Uttarā, Phālgunī and Svāti are auspicious stars for marriages.

पुनर्वसू तिष्यो हस्तश्श्रोणा रेवतीत्यन्येषां भूतिकर्मणाम् ॥२१॥

Punarvasu, Tiṣyā, Hastā, Śravaṇā and Revatī are suitable for other auspicious ceremonies.

यानि चान्यानि पुण्योक्तानि नक्षत्राणि तेषु पूर्वेद्युवर्द्धिपूर्तेषु युग्मान् ब्राह्मणान् भोजयेत् ॥२२॥
If other stars have been declared auspicious, then before the *puṇyāha vācana,* let two Brāhmaṇas be fed.

प्रदक्षिणमुपचारः ॥२३॥
Going around the Agni is the practice.

पुष्पफलाक्षतमिश्रैर्यवैस्तिलार्थमुपलिप्य दध्योदनं सम्प्रकीर्य दक्षिणं जानुं भूमौ निधाय सव्यमुद्धृत्य "इडा देवहूः" इति जपित्वा "नान्दीमुखाः पितरः प्रियन्ताम्" इति वाचयित्वा "अद्य विवाहः" इति ब्राह्मणानन्नेन परिविष्य "पुण्याहं स्वस्ति ऋद्धिम्" इत्योङ्करपूर्वं त्रिस्त्रिरेकैकामाशिषो वाचयित्वा स्नातोऽहतवासो गन्धानुलिप्तस्स्रग्वी भुक्तवान् प्रतोदपाणिपदातिर्गत्वा वधूज्ञातिभिरतिथिवदर्चितस्स्नातामहतवाससां गन्धानुलिप्तां स्रग्विणीं भुक्तवतीमिषुहस्तां दत्तां वधूं समीक्षते "अभ्रातृघ्नीं वरुणापतिघ्नीं बृहस्पते। इन्द्रापुत्रघ्नीं लक्ष्म्यं तामस्यै सवितस्सुव" इति ॥२४॥
Having smeared sesame seeds with a mix of flowers, fruits, *akṣata,* offering a mix of curds and rice, having knelt with the right knee on the ground, worn the sacred thread (on the left), having chanted the verse, "for Goddess Iḍā" he makes the brāhmaṇas say, "let *nāndimukha* ancestors be pleased" and "today is the marriage" and having fed the brāhmaṇas with cooked rice, he makes them to recite thrice, "puṇyāham, svasti and ṛddhi", he takes bath and wears new (unwashed) clothes, wears garland with sandal paste on it, he goes to the bride's place as a guest and worshipper he looks at the bride who has bathed and worn new clothes and garland with the *mantra,* "her, not brother-slaying, O Varuṇa, not husband-slaying, O Bṛhaspati; O Indra, not children-slaying, she who is Lakṣmī, bring her to us O Savitā".

तयेक्ष्यमाणो जपति "अघोरचक्षुरपतिघ्न्येधि शिवा पतिभ्यऽस्सुमनास्सुवर्चाः। जीवसूर्देवकामा शं नो भव द्विपदे शं चतुष्पदे" इति ॥२५॥
He chants: "With no evil eye, not bringing death to your husband, bring luck to the cattle, be full of joy and vigour.

Give birth to heroes; be godly and friendly. Bring luck to men and animals."

अथैनामन्तरेण भ्रुमुखेण दर्भेण सम्मार्ष्टि "इदमहं या त्वयि पतिघ्न्यलक्ष्मिस्तां निर्दिशामि" इति ॥२६॥
Then he touches the space between her brows with the *darbha* grass with the *mantra*, "here I indicate as a mark of good fortune for your husband".

दर्भं निरस्याप उपस्पृश्याथैनां दक्षिणे हस्ते गृह्णाति "मित्रोऽसि" इति ॥२७॥
Keeping away the *darbha*, he sprinkles water and with his right hand he holds her with the *mantra*, "you are my friend".

अथैनां देवयजनमुदानयति "एकमिषे विष्णुस्त्वाऽन्वेतु। द्वे ऊर्जे विष्णुस्त्वाऽन्वेतु। त्रीणि व्रताय विष्णुस्त्वाऽन्वेतु। चत्वारि मायोभवाय विष्णुस्त्वाऽन्वेतु। पञ्च पशुभ्यो विष्णुस्त्वाऽन्वेतु। षड्रायस्पोषाय विष्णुस्त्वाऽन्वेतु। सप्त सप्तभ्यो होत्राभ्यो विष्णुस्त्वाऽन्वेतु" इति ॥२८॥
Then he makes her step forward with the *mantra*: "First step for sap, let Viṣṇu take you along. Second step for energy, let Viṣṇu take you along. Third step for *vratas*, let Viṣṇu take you along. Fourth step for happiness, let Viṣṇu take you along. Fifth step for cattle, let Viṣṇu take you along. Sixth step for wealth, let Viṣṇu take you along. Seventh step for friendship and for sacrifices, let Viṣṇu take you along."

सप्तमं पदमुपसङ्गृह्य जपति "सखायस्सप्तपदा अभुम सव्यं ते गमेयं सख्याते मा योषं मा योष्ठाः" इति ॥२९॥
With the seventh step taken he says: "We will become friends, you are the woman by my side, my companion."

द्वितीयः अध्यायः (Second chapter)

आवेद्यार्घ्यं कुर्यात् ॥१॥
Arghya is prepared for those who have come.

मध्येऽगारस्योदीचीनप्रतिपेवणा एरका उपस्तृणाति ॥२॥
In the middle of the hall towards the north, he spreads the mat of *erakā* grass.

तास्वहतानि बहुगुणान्युत्तरदशानि वासांस्यास्तीर्य तेष्वृत्विजः प्राङ्मुखा उपविशन्ति ॥३॥

Spreading a new cloth of good quality with its border on top on the northern side, he makes the holy men sit facing east.

उत्तरपूर्वे देशेऽगारस्य प्राक्कूलान् दर्भान् संस्तीर्य तेष्वर्घ्यद्रव्याणि संसादयति ॥४॥

On the north-east of the hall, after spreading *darbha* grass, the materials for *arghya* are kept.

यावन्त ऋत्विजस्तावन्ति कांस्यानि पात्राणि सापिधानानि तावतः कूर्चान् ॥ ५॥

As per the number of *ṛtvijas*, as many brass vessels with lids are kept with *kūrca* grass.

द्वायन्यौ परिग्रहणीयौ कूर्चौ ॥६॥

Two other bundles of *kūrca* grass are kept.

दधि मधु घृतमापः पयो वस्त्रयुगानि कुण्डलयुगानि ॥७॥

Curds, honey, ghee, water, milk, clothes and vessels are kept.

यस्यै गोः पयश्चमसः स्रगलङ्करणीयं चेति ॥८॥

The cow whose milk is used is kept with decoration of garlands.

पवित्रे कृत्वा तूष्णीं संस्कृताभिरद्भिरुत्तानानि पात्राणि कृत्वा प्रोक्ष्य कूर्चं कांस्यं निधाय तिरःपवित्रण् मध्वानयति ॥९॥

Silently having made *pavitra* (ring of *kuśa* grass worn on the finger for sprinkling), he keeps the vessels upright and sprinkles them with pure water and keeps the brass vessels on *kūrca* grass and fills them with honey over the *kūrca* grass kept across.

दधि पयो वा द्वितीयं स द्विवृत् ॥१०॥

Curds and milk have to be poured twice.

घृतं तृतीयं स त्रिवृत् ॥११॥

Third, ghee must be poured thrice.

यद्वितीयं तच्चतुर्थं स चतुर्वृत् ॥१२॥
What was poured the second time should be poured on the fourth time, four times.

आपः पञ्चमीस्स पाङ्कः ॥१३॥
On the fifth, water should be poured.

वर्षीयसा तेजोमयेनापिधाय नानापुरुषा अर्घ्यद्रव्याण्याददते अन्वगनुसंव्रजता ॥१४॥
From the elders, many people receive the *arghya* materials kept in lustrous lids.

"कूर्चः" इति कूर्चं प्राह ॥१५॥
He recites, "*kūrca*" looking at the *kūrca*.

तत "सुकूर्च्:" इतीतरः प्रतिगृह्णाति ॥१६॥
The other receives saying, "*sukūrca*".

तं प्रदक्षिणं पर्यस्योदगावृत्त उपविशति ॥१७॥
He goes round with his right towards it and sits down.

पुरस्ताद्वैनं प्रत्यञ्चमुपोहते "राष्ट्रभृदस्याचार्यासन्दी मा त्वद्योषम्" इति ॥१८॥
He gathers it from behind, turning it around with the *mantra*, "*rāṣṭrabhṛta*, etc."

अथास्मा उदपात्रमादाय कूर्चाभ्यां परिगृह्य पाद्या आप इति प्राह ॥१९॥
He then holds the water vessels with *kūrca* and says water for the feet.

ता अभिमन्त्रयते "आपः पादावनेजनीर्द्विषन्तं नाशयन्तु मे ॥ अस्मिन् कुले ब्रह्मवर्चस्यानि" इति ॥२०॥
He recites the *mantra*: "Let the water wash the feet and destroy the poison. Let our lineage shine with *brahma-varcas*."

दक्षिणं पादं पूर्वं ब्राह्मणाय प्रसारयति । सव्यं शूद्राय ॥२१॥
He puts out the right foot to the brāhmaṇa first and left foot to the śūdra.

स्त्री प्रक्षाळयति पुमानभिषिञ्चति । निवपरीतमित्येके ॥२२॥

The man pours the water and woman washes the feet. Some say, it is the other way.

नियमात् पत्नीयजमानौ जङ्घे धावयतः ॥२३॥
As a rule, the couple washes the legs from ankle to knee.

अवनेक्तुः पाणी सम्मृशति "मयि महो मयि भगो मयि भर्गो मयि यशः" इति ॥२४॥
The bridegroom touches the hand that washes with the *mantra,*"O Bhaga make me great, make me fortunate, make me radiant, make me famous".

अथाप उपस्पृश्य "मयीन्द्रियं वीर्यम्" इत्युरःप्रत्यात्मा नं प्रत्यभिमृशते ॥२५॥
Then after touching the water, he touches his chest with the *mantra,* "give me Indra's virility, etc".

अपो व्रीहिभिर्यवैर्वा समुदायुत्य तथैव कूर्चाभ्यां परिगृह्यार्हणीया आप इति प्राह ॥२६॥
He then adds to the barley, grains, etc. with *kūrca* and holds it saying, "water".

ता अभिमन्त्रयते "आम आगाद्वर्चसा यशसा संसृज पयसा तेजसा च । तं मा प्रियं प्रजानां कुर्वधिपतिं पशूनाम्" इति ॥२७॥
He worships that water with the *mantra*: "O Lord of the waters! Established in the manner described above you render me glorious and endow me with divine radiance. Let the best among your subjects give me love and happiness. Let me be the master of such animals as cows and horses and let my body be free of illness and acts of violence."

एकदेशमञ्जलावानीयमनुमन्त्रयते "विराजोऽसि विराजो दोहमशीय। मम पद्याय विराज" इति ॥२८॥
He takes some water in his joined hands and chants, "O vital resplendent water! make my path resplendent".

अतिशिष्टाः प्राचीर्निनीयमाना अनुमन्त्रयते "समुद्रं वः प्रहिणोम्यक्षिताः

स्वां योनिमपि गच्छत । अच्छिद्रः प्रजया भूयासं मा परासोचि मत्पयः" इति ॥२९॥
He carries the remaining water to the north-east and chants: "I send you forth to the ocean; go to your own lair. Unbroken let nothing harm my brothers and children."

अथ तथैव कूर्चाभ्यां परिगृह्योपस्तरणिया आप इति प्राह ॥३०॥
Then holding the *kūrca* grass spread there, he says "water".

ताः पिबति "अमृतोपस्तरणमसि" इति ॥३१॥
He takes a sip with the chant, "you are the nectar".

त्रिराचामेत् त्रिः परिम्रुजेत् । द्विरित्येके ॥३२॥
He takes *ācamana* (sip) thrice and leaves water. Some say twice.

आचान्तायापावृत्तय तथैव कूर्चाभ्यां परिगृह्यार्घ्य इति प्राह मधुपर्क इति वा ॥३३॥
Having been purified by the water, he takes hold of the *kūrca* grass as before and says, *arghya* and *madhuparka*.

मधुपर्कं प्रोक्तमनुमन्त्रयते "त्रय्यै विद्यायै यशोऽसि यशसो यशोऽसि ब्रह्मणो दीप्तिरसि । तं मा प्रियं प्रजानां कुर्वधिपतिं पशूनाम्" इति ॥३४॥
After saying *madhuparka*, he chants: "You are famed for the three types of knowledge, famous are you, you are the light towards the *Brahman*. Make my dear children the lords of the cattle."

तामुभाभ्यां हस्ताभ्यां प्रतिगृह्णाति "देवस्य त्वा सवितुः प्रसवेऽश्विनोर्बाहुभ्यां पूष्णो हस्ताभ्यां प्रतिगृह्णामि" इति ॥३५॥
He takes them (*kūrca* grasses) with both hands and says: "O *madhuparka*! By the grace of the sun and the power from the shoulders of Aśvins and derived from the hands of Pūṣaṇa, I accept you with my hands thus invigorated and energized."

तस्मिंश्चित् किञ्चिदापतितं स्यात्तदङ्गुष्ठेन च महानाम्न्या चोपसङ्गृह्येमां दिशं निरस्यंति "नेष्टावृद्धिं कृन्तामि या ते घोरा तनूः । तया तमाविश योस्मान् द्वेष्टि यं च वयं द्विष्मः" इति ॥३६॥

If a little bit of the *madhuparka* spills, he takes it with his thumb and middle finger and says, "I will not destroy my desires nor will I do anything cruel. With you I will face my enemies and our ill-wishers".

अथाप उपस्पृश्य सर्वाभिरङ्गुलीभिस्समुदायुत्य प्राश्नाति "यन्मधुनो मधव्यं परममनाद्यं वीर्यम् । तेनाहं मधुनो मधव्येन परमेणान्नाद्येन वीर्येण परमोऽन्नादो मधुव्योऽसानि" इति ॥३७॥
Then he touches water and bringing all his fingers together he sips *madhuparka* with the chant: "O celestial beings! The luscious sweetness which lights up the body despite all passage of time and circumstance; which is the quintessence of all primary juices and which will be the cause of my sweetness."

त्रिः प्राश्य त्रिरनुपिवेच्छेषं च कुर्यात् ॥३८॥
He sacrifices thrice and drinks thrice and keeps some remainder.

य आत्मनः श्रेयांसमिच्छेत्तस्मै शेषं दद्यादिति ॥३९॥
He gives the remainder to those who are his well-wishers.

आचान्तायापावृत्ताय तथैव कूर्चाभ्यां परिगृह्यापिधानीया आप इति प्राह ॥४०॥
After sipping water and sprinkling it around, he takes the same *kūrca* blades and says, "the water that is covered".

ताः पिबति "अमृतापिधानमसि" इति ॥४१॥
He drinks that water saying, "you are the hidden nectar".

त्रिराचामेत् त्रिः परिमृजेत् । द्विरित्येके ॥४२॥
He takes *ācamana* (sip) thrice and leaves water. Some say twice.

आचान्तायापावृत्ताय गौरिति गां प्राह ॥४३॥
After sipping water and sprinkling it around, he says, "cow" pointing to the cow.

तामनुमन्त्रयते "गौरस्यपहतपाप्माऽप पाप्मानं नुद मम चामुष्य च"इत्युपवेत्तुर्नाम गृह्णाति ॥४४॥
He chants: "With this sacrifice of the cow, let our sins be driven away, mine and of belonging to my family."

नाना महर्त्विग्भ्यो गाः प्राह ॥४५॥
He declares that the cows are for many holy men.

एकां होतृकेभ्यः ॥४६॥
Also for people belonging to the same *gotra*.

सर्वेभ्यो वैकामविभवत्वात् ॥४७॥
Or he offers one cow to all together.

यः प्राह तस्मा उपाकरोत्येकदेशं वपायै जुहोति "अग्निः प्रथमः प्राश्नातु स हि वेद यथा हविः । शिवा अस्मभ्यमोपधीः कृणोतु विश्वचर्षणिः" इति ॥४८॥
He takes a part of the omentum and sacrifices with the *mantra*: "Let Agni eat it first for he is the Veda and he is the *havis*: let the auspicious hide our universal thirst."

एकदेशमुपहरति तत् प्राश्नाति "अग्निः प्रथमः प्राश्नातु स हि वेद यथा हविः । अरिष्टमस्माकं कृणोत्वसौ ब्राह्मणो ब्राह्मणेषु" इति ॥४९॥

He takes another part of the omentum and sacrifices with the *mantra*: "Let Agni consume it first for he is the Veda and he is the *havis*: Let our dwellings be made perfect with brāhmaṇas."

अथ यदुत्स्रक्ष्यन् भवति तामनुमन्त्रयते "गौर्धेनुभव्या माता रुद्राणां दुहिता वसूनां स्वसाऽऽदित्यानाममृतस्य नाभिः । प्रणुवोचं चिकितृषे जनाय मा गामनागामदितिं वधिष्ट । पिबतूदकं तृणान्यत्तु । ओमुत्सृजत" इति ॥५०॥
In case the cow is to be freed, he worships it with the *mantra*: "This beautiful animal is the mother of Rudras, daughter of Vasus. She is the sister of the Ādityas and she is the source of nectar. I tell the host he must not kill this innocent cow for my sport and pleasure. Let it drink water and eat grass. *Oṁ*! Release the cow."

तस्यामुत्सृष्टायां मेषमजं वाऽऽलभते ॥५१॥
In the place of the cow, a goat may be used.

आरण्येन वा मांसेन ॥५२॥
Or any meat from the forest.

न त्वेवामांसोऽर्घ्यस्स्यात् ॥५३॥
That which is without meat will not become *arghya*.

अशक्तो पिष्टान्नं संसिद्ध्येत् ॥५४॥
One who is not capable of providing meat may prepare flour-mixed cooked rice.

सिद्धे "भूतम्" इति प्राह ॥५५॥
Once ready, he says, "elements".

तत् "सुभूतम्" इति इतरः प्रत्याह ॥५६॥
Others will respond and say, "good elements".

तदभिमन्त्रयते "भूतं सुभूतं सा विराट् तन्मा क्षायि तन्मेऽशीय तन्म ऊर्जं धा ओं कल्पयत" इति ॥५७॥
Then he chants: "She is the queen of all elements, let her bring fame, energy and wealth to me."

चतुरो नानागोत्रान् ब्राह्मणान् भोजयतेत्येव ब्रूयात् ॥५८॥
After feeding four brāhmaṇas of different *gotras*, he says.

तेषु भुक्तवत्स्वन्नमस्मा उपहरति ॥५९॥
What is left after they have eaten will be eaten by me.

तत्प्राश्नाति "विराडसि विराडन्नं विराड्विराजो मयि धेहि" इति ॥६०॥
He eats it and chants: "You are the ruler, the rice is the ruler, make me a royal too."

भुक्तवद्भ्यो वस्त्रयुगानि कुण्डल्युगानि यस्यै गोः पयश्रमसः स्रगलङ्करणीयमिति च दद्यात् । एकधनं पष्ठौहां दम्यावित्येके ॥६१॥
After eating he gives the one, who decorates the cow with garland, etc., two sets of clothes and two vessels. Some people say give a bagful of money.

प्राङ्मधुपर्कादलङ्करणमेके समामनन्ति ॥६२॥
Some people say that giving *madhuparka* is equivalent.

महयेदृत्विजमाचार्यं चात्मानं वा महयति यस्संमृत्विजमाचार्यं च महयत्येवमेवंव्रता वा आत्यन्तिकास्स्युः पतितोऽननूचान इति निमित्तानि ॥६३॥
Worship the learned scholars and dear ones, worship the good holy men, worship those observe religious practices continually. It is said that those who do not study Vedas fall down.

वरणेऽग्न्याधेयप्रभृतिषु चैषामृत्विजं स्मरेत् ॥६४॥
Let the groom remember the holy men who begin Agnyādheya sacrifice.

तथैते अर्घ्या ऋत्विक् श्वशुरः पितृभ्यो मातुल आचार्यो राजा वा स्नातकः प्रियो वरोऽतिथिरिति ॥६५॥
There those, who are worthy of *arghya* are holy men, father-in-law, mother, teacher, king and one who has finished Vedic studies, are treated as guests dear to the groom.

संवत्सरपर्यागतेभ्य एवं कुर्यात् विवाहे वराय ॥६६॥
Within a year of studies let the marriage of the groom take place.

अथर्त्विग्भ्यः कर्मणिकर्मणि ददाति ॥६७॥
The holy men are given *madhuparka* at every Śrauta ritual.

चतुर्थः अध्यायः (Fourth Chapter)

अथास्या उपोत्थाय दक्षिणेन दक्षिणमंसं प्रविताहुमन्ववहृत्य हृदयदेशमभिमृशति — "मम हृदये हृदयं ते अस्तु मम चित्ते चित्तमस्तु ते। मम वाचकमेकमनाः शृणु मामेवानुव्रता सहचर्या मया भव" इति ॥१॥
Then he makes her rise and with his right hand over her right shoulder, he touches her heart and says: "Let your heart be one with mine, your mind be one with my mind. Listen to my sayings with concentration, become my devoted friend."

अथास्यै दक्षिणे कर्णे जपति ॥२॥
Then he whispers in her right ear.

"मां ते मनः प्रविशतु मां चक्षुर्मामु ते भगः मयि सर्वाणि भूतानि मयि प्रज्ञानमस्तु ते" ॥३॥
"Let your mind enter into me, let your brilliance enter my eyes, let all the elements be in my awareness."

"मधुगो मध्वगाहे जिह्वा मे मधुवादिनी। मुखे मे सारघं मधु दत्सु संवननं कृतम्" ॥४॥
"Let my tongue be honeyed. Let the honey make my face a pleasant one."

"चाक्रवाकं संवननं यन्नदीभ्य उदाहृतम्। यद्वित्तौ देवगान्धर्वौ तेन संविननौ स्वः ॥५॥
"The *cakravāka* bird taking pleasure from the rivers is an example." "Money and *devagandharvas* cause pleasure."

"स्पृशामि तेऽहमङ्गानि वायुरापश्च मा परः । मां चैव पश्य सूर्यं च मा चान्येषु मनः कृथाः" ॥६॥
"I touch your limbs apart from air and water. Look only at the sun apart from me and do not think of anyone else."

"सोमः प्रथमो विविदे गन्धर्वो विविद उत्तरः। तृतीयो अग्निष्टे पतिस्तुरीयस्ते मनुष्यजाः" ॥७॥
"Soma is the first and then the *gandharvas*. The third one is Agni and fourth is man."

"सोमोऽददद्गन्धर्वाय गन्धर्वोऽददददग्नये । रयिं च पुत्रांश्चा दादग्निर्मह्यमथो इमाम्" ॥८॥
"Soma gave her to *gandharva* (Sūrya), *gandharva* to Agni. For the sake of wealth and children, Agni has given her to me."

"सरस्वति प्रेदमव सुभगे वाजिनीविति । तां त्वा विश्वस्य भूतस्य प्रगायामस्यग्रतः" इति ॥९॥
"Sarasvatī! Promote this marriage, O gracious one, bountiful one, beautiful one, you whom we sing first of all."

अथास्यै दक्षिणेन नीचा हस्तेन दक्षिणमुत्तानं हस्तं साङ्गुष्ठमभीव लोमानि गृह्णाति — "गृभ्णामि ते सुप्रजस्त्वाय हस्तं मया पत्या जरदिष्टिर्यथाऽसः। भगो अर्यमा सविता पुरन्धिर्मह्यं त्वाऽदुर्गार्हपत्याय देवाः" इति ॥१०॥
Now he takes her right hand with his right hand with the thumb and the hairy outer portion with the *mantra*, "I take your hand mine so that we may live up to old age. The gods Bhaga, Aryamā, Savitā and Puraṁdhi have given you to me so that I may become a householder."

अथैनां प्रदक्षिणमग्निं पर्याणयति — "परित्वाऽग्ने पुरं वयं विप्रं सहस्य धीमहि। धृषद्वर्णं दिवोदिवे भेत्तारं भङ्गुरावतः" इति ॥११॥
Then he makes her circumambulate the fire with the *mantra*: "We worship you O Agni, the accomplisher of rites, the sage of fearful colours, day-by-day destroyer of the treacherous."

अथ तथोपविश्यान्वारब्धायामुपयमनीर्जुहोति ॥१२॥
Then he sits down close to her and sacrifices.

"अग्ने शर्ध महते सौभागाय तव द्युम्नान्युत्तमानि सन्तु। सञ्जास्पत्यं सुयममाकृणष्व शत्रूयताभितिष्ठा महांसि स्वाहा" ॥१३॥
"O Agni for our well-being let your blessings be good. Let our household be smooth and enemies be defeated," *svāhā*!

"सोमाय जनिविदे स्वाहा" ॥१४॥
To Soma who has given me my wife, *svāhā*!

"गन्धर्वाय जनिविदे स्वाहा" ॥१५॥
"To *gandharva* who has give me my wife, *svāhā*!

"अग्नये जनिविदे स्वाहा" ॥१६॥
"To Agni who has given me my wife, *svāhā*!

"कन्यला पितृभ्यो यती पतिलोकमव दक्षिणमदास्थ स्वाहा" ॥१७॥
"Young girls of their fathers who are being sent with *dakṣiṇā* to go to their husbands' world, *svāhā*!"

"प्रेतो मुञ्चाति नामुतस्सुबद्धाममुतस्करत्। यथेयमिन्द्रमीढ्वस्सुपुत्रा सुभगा सती स्वाहा" ॥१८॥

"I release her from here (father's house), not from there (husband's house). I make her well bound there, that she, O gracious Indra, may we be rich in sons and be fortunate, *svāhā*!"

"इमां त्वमिन्द्र मीढ्वस्सुपुत्रां सुभगां कुरु। दशाभ्यां पुत्रानाधेहि पतिमेकादशं कृधि स्वाहा" ॥१९॥
"O Indra, make this woman fortunate and have good sons. Give her ten sons and make her husband the eleventh, *svāhā*!"

"अग्निरैतु प्रथमो देवतानां सोऽस्यै प्रजां मुञ्चतु मृत्युपाशात् । तदयं राजा वरुणोऽनुमन्यतां यथेयं स्त्री पौत्रमघं न रोदात् स्वाहा" ॥२०॥
"O Agni, the first among gods, release this woman's children from the death trap. Let King Varuṇa agree so that she does not weep due to distress caused to her sons, *svāhā*!"

"इमामग्निस्त्रायतां गार्हपत्यः प्रजामस्यै नयतु दीर्घामायुः । अशून्योपस्था जीवतामस्तु माता पौत्रमानन्दमयि प्रबुध्यतामियं स्वाहा" ॥२१॥
"Let the *gārhapatya* (household) Agni protect her and carry her children to long life. Let this mother with the full body have children living and have pleasure through her children, *svāhā*!"

"मा ते गृहे निशि घोष उत्थादन्यत्र त्वद्रुदत्यस्संविशन्तु। मा त्वं विकेश्युर अवधिष्टा जीवपत्नी पतिलोके विराज पश्यन्ती प्रजां सुमनस्यमानां स्वाहा" ॥२२॥
"Let there be no noise in your house in the night, let women who cry and demonize go to some other place. Do not be a woman without hair (widow), shine in your husband's house with a living husband with a pleasant mind and seeing children, *svāhā*!"

"अप्रजस्तां पौत्रमृत्यं पाप्मानमुत वाऽघम्। शीर्ष्णस्स्रजमिवोन्मुच्य द्विषद्भ्यः प्रतिमुञ्चामि पाशं स्वाहा" इति ॥२३॥
"Being childless, losing children to death, sadness and sin, I release them like removing a garland from the head and put them on my enemies, *svāhā*!"

अथैनामुत्थाप्योत्तरेणाग्निं दक्षिणेन पदाऽश्मानमास्थापयति "आतिष्ठेममश्मानमश्मेव त्वं स्थिरा भव । अभितिष्ठ पृतन्यतस्सहस्व पृतनायतः" इति ॥२४॥

Then he makes her stand up to the north of the fire and puts her right leg on the stone and makes her stand with the *mantra*: "Stand on this stone and be firm like it. Stand up to your enemies and destroy your ill-wishers."

अथास्या अञ्जलावुपस्तीर्य तस्यास्सोदर्यो द्विर्लाजानावपति ॥२५॥

Then joining her hands together, her brother pours fried grains into them.

तानाभिघार्य जुहोति — "इयं नार्युपब्रूतेऽग्नौ लाजानावपन्ती । दीर्घायुरस्तु मे पतिर्जीवातु शरदश्शतं स्वाहा" ॥२६॥

She offers the fried grains to the fire with the *mantra*, "This woman is offering fried grains to Agni. Let my husband have a long life and live to see hundred autumns, *svāhā*!"

अथैनां प्रदक्षिणमग्निं पर्याणयति "तुभ्यमग्रे पर्यवहन् सूर्याम् वहतुना सह । पुनः पतिभ्यो जायां दा अग्ने प्रजया सह" इति ॥२७॥

Then he makes her go around the fire with the verse: "The gods have brought Sūrya's chariot to take you round the fire. Agni, again give the husband a wife with children."

तथाऽऽस्थापयति तथा जुहोति ॥२८॥

As he pours the fried grains, she offers oblations.

अथैनां पुनः प्रदक्षिणमग्निं पर्याणयति "पुनः पत्नीमग्निरदादायुषा सह वर्चसा । दीर्घायुरस्या यः पतिस्स एतु शरदशतम्" इति ॥२९॥

Again he makes her go round the fire with the verse: "Agni, give again the wife with long life with lustre. Let her live long with her husband and see hundred autumns."

तथैवास्थापयति तथैव जुहोति ॥३०॥

As he pours the fried grains, she offers oblations.

अथैनां पुनरेव पर्याणयति "विश्वा उत त्वया वयं धारा उदन्या इव । अतिगाहेमहि द्विषः" इति ॥३१॥

Then he makes her go round the fire again with the verse, "just as the flow of waters submerges everything, we will with you get rid of enemies".

अथ तथोपविश्यान्वारब्धायां जयानभ्यातानान्राष्ट्रभृत इति हुत्वा अथामात्यहोमान् जुहोति ॥३२॥

Then sit together touching each other and carries out Jayā, Abhyātāna, Rāṣṭrabhṛta sacrifices and then Ātya *homa*.

अथ प्राजापत्यान् जुहोति "प्रजापते न त्वदेतान्यन्यः" इति ॥३३॥

Then he worships Prajāpati with, "to Prajāpati who is not different from these".

अथ सौविष्टकृतं जुहोति "यदस्य कर्मणोऽत्यरीरिचं यद्वा न्यूनमिहाकरम्। अग्निस्तत्स्विष्टकृद्विद्वान् सर्वं स्विष्टं सुहृतं करोतु मे। अग्नये स्विष्टकृते सुहुतहुत आहुतीनां कामानां समर्धयित्रे स्वाहा" इति ॥३४॥

Then the Sviṣṭakṛt *homa* is conducted: "When his *karmas* are released or when the word nothing is said, let the learned of the Sviṣṭakṛt make me clean and good hearted. To Agni, to Sviṣṭakṛt, I offer to fulfil desires with this good offerings, *svāhā*!"

अथ स्रुवेण परिधीननक्ति ॥३५॥

With the spoons he sets the *paridhīs* (limits).

अथ परिस्तरात्समुल्लिप्याज्यस्थाल्यां प्रस्तरवत् बर्हिरक्त्वा तृणं प्रच्छाद्याग्नावनुप्रहरति ॥३६॥

Then smearing the area and establishing the *ājya* plates, he spreads grass around the fire.

अथ शम्या अपोह्य तथैव परिषिञ्चति। "अन्वमंस्थाः, प्रासावीः" इति मन्त्रान्तान् सन्नमयति ॥३७॥

Then he sprinkles water and with *śamī* branches sweeps. "At once, in the forefront."

अथ प्रणीताद्भ्यो दिशो व्युन्नीय ब्रह्मणे वरं ददामिति गां ब्राह्मणेभ्यः ॥३८॥

Then after wetting with water in both directions, he says:

"give a gift to brāhmaṇas" and gives cows to brāhmaṇas.

एष आघारवान् दर्वीहोमः ॥३९॥
This is *darvīhoma* with clarified butter.

अथापरः — परिसमूह्य पर्युक्ष्य परिस्तीर्याज्यं विलाप्योत्पूय स्रुक्स्रुवं निष्टप्य सम्मृज्य स्रुचि चतुर्गृहीतं गृहीत्वा सर्वान् मन्त्रान् समनुद्रुत्य सकृदेवाहुतिं जुहोति ॥४०॥
After this, gathering and sprinkling with butter, cleansing the vessels and ladles holding the *sruci*, he sacrifices with all the *mantras* being recited.

अग्निस्स्विष्टकृद्द्वितीयः ॥४१॥
Sacrifice Agni Sviṣṭakṛt, second.

द्विर्जुहोति द्विर्निमार्ष्टि द्विः प्राश्नात्युत्सृप्याचामति निर्लेढी त्येष आग्निहोत्रिकः ॥४२॥
He worships twice, applies butter twice, eats twice, sips water, not licking says *agnihotrikas*.

अथापरः — परिसमूह्य पर्युक्ष्य परिस्तीर्य प्राकृतेन हविषा यावदाम्नातमाहुतीर्जुहोत्येष ह्यपूर्वः ॥४३॥
After this, he collects materials, sprinkles and sacrifices with *havis* as per traditions established earlier.

तत्रोदाहरन्ति — आघारं प्रकृतिं प्राह दर्वीहोमस्य बादरिः । अग्निहोत्रिकं अथाऽऽत्रेयः काशकृत्स्नस्त्वपूर्वताम् ॥ इति ॥४४॥
There the example is given, "Bādari has said that ghee is the nature of *darvīhoma*". Agnihotrikas are "Ātreya, Kāśa, Kṛtsna for completion of *satva*".

पञ्चमोऽध्यायः (Fifth Chapter)

तां न मिथस्सांदयेदनादेशात् ॥१॥
Do not consider it a myth because it is not declared.

अनुनयन्त्येतमग्निम् ॥२॥
Carry the fire behind.

अथैनां पितुरङ्कादुद्वहति, गुरुर्वा — "ये वध्वश्चन्द्र वहतुं यक्ष्मा यन्ति जनाँ अनु । पुनस्तान्यज्ञिया देवा नयन्तु यत आगताः" इति ॥३॥

Then she is carried either by her father or *guru* — May the adorable Gods drive back the diseases which come from the people who follow the bride's golden car to the places where they come from.

अथैनां दक्षिणे हस्ते गृहीत्वा स्वरथमारोप्य स्वान् गृहानानयति "पूषा त्वेतो नयतु हस्तगृह्याश्विनौ त्वा प्रवहतां रथेन । गृहान् गच्छ गृहपत्नी यथाऽसो वशिनी त्वं विदथमावदासि" इति ॥४॥

Then he takes her right hand and having mounted the chariot he takes her to the house — "O bride, let Pūṣaṇa holding your hand take you out, let the two Aśvins bring you to my home. Go to your home in the chariot, as is done, become a housewife, let your relations have love towards you and carry out the rituals."

पन्थानुमन्त्रयते "सु गं पन्थानमारुक्षमरिष्टं स्वस्तिवाहनम् । यस्मिन् वीरो न रिष्यत्यन्येषां विन्दते वसु" इति ॥५॥

The roads are worshipped. "Let the travel be smooth, protect the chariot against danger. Where the heroes do not get hurt, Vasu will get hold of others."

ओषधिवनस्पतयो नद्यो वनान्यनुमन्त्रयते — "या ओषधयो या वनस्पतयो या नद्यो यानि धन्वानि ये वना । ते त्वा वधु प्रजावतीं प्रत्वे मुञ्चन्त्वंहसः" इति ॥६॥

He chants when comes across herbal trees, rivers, forests — "Those herbs, rivers, fields, trees, bows; let these defend you, possessing progeny for your husband, against demons."

अथ जायमानीय स्वान् गृहान् प्रपादयति — "भद्रान् गृहान् सुमनमः प्रपद्येऽवीरघ्नी वीरवतस्सुवीरान् । इरां वहतो घृतमुक्षमाणास्तेष्वहं सुमनास्संविशानि" इति ॥७॥

Now having brought his wife, he enters his house — "Bring into the house your good mind and enter for the sake of brave children."

अथैनामानडुहे चर्मण्युपवेशयति — "इह गावः प्रजायध्वमिहाश्वा इह पुरुषाः । इहो सहस्रदक्षिणो रायस्पोषो निषीदतु" इति ॥८॥
Then he makes her sit on a bull's hide — "May the men, children and horses born here in abundance and the cows may grow their clan. Let the one who provides the thousand contributions and wealth be enshrined here."

अत्राभ्याममात्यास्स्तोक्माण्यारोपयन्ते ॥९॥
Here his confidants throw water and *akṣata*.

अथ वाचं यच्छतः आ नक्षत्राणामुदयात् ॥१०॥
Then they remain silent till stars are seen.

अथाहोरात्रयोस्सन्धिमनुमन्त्रयते — "नीललोहिते भवतः कृत्या सक्तिर्व्यज्यते । एधन्तेऽस्या ज्ञातयः पतिर्बन्धेषु वध्यताम्" इति ॥११॥
In the evening they chant, "Krutyā (goddess of destruction, etc.) becomes blue-red. Her relations will thrive and her husband will be bound as a householder."

अथोदितेषु नक्षत्रेषूपनिष्क्रम्य ध्रुवमरुन्धतीं च दर्शयति ॥१२॥
Then when they appear, they go out and she is shown the pole star and the Arundhatī star.

"ध्रुवोऽसि ध्रुवक्षितिर्ध्रुवमसि ध्रुवतस्स्थितम् । त्वं नक्षत्राणां मेथ्यसि स मा पाहि पृतन्यतः" इति ध्रुवम् ॥१३॥
"You are Dhruva, Dhruva's horizon, Dhruva's fixedness. You are the pole of the stars, protect me from enemies."

"सप्त ऋषयः प्रथमां कृत्तिकानामरुन्धतीं यद्ध्रुवतां ह नित्युः । षट्कृत्तिका मुख्ययोगं वहन्तीयमस्माकमेधत्वष्टम्यरुन्धती" इत्यरुन्धतीम् ॥ १४॥
"The first among Kṛttikās established by the seven *ṛṣi*s: that eighth one, Arundhatī, six Kṛttikās and Candra, be our guide."

अथ विवाहस्यारुन्धत्युपस्थानात् कृत्वा व्रतमुपौति — "अग्ने व्रतपते उपयमनं व्रतं चरिष्यामि तच्छकेयम् तन्मे राध्यताम् । वायो व्रतपत आदित्य व्रतपते व्रतानां व्रतपते उपयमनं व्रतं चरिष्यामि तन्मे राध्यानाम्" इति ॥१५॥
Then having brought Arundhatī closer to her, he observes

vrata. "To Agni, the lord of *vratas*, I will observe the marriage *vrata*, I will offer it to you. To Vāyu, the lord of *vratas*, Āditya, the lord of *vratas*, I offer the marriage *vrata* to you."

उभौ जायापती व्रचारिणौ ब्रह्मचारिणौ भवतोऽधश्शयाते ॥१६॥
Both husband and wife observe celibacy and sleep on the floor.

तयोश्शय्यामन्तरेणोदुम्बरदण्डो गन्धानुलिप्तो वाससा सूत्रेण वा परिवीतस्तिष्ठत्यापक्कहोमात् ॥१७॥
In between them, a staff, smeared with sandal paste and tied with a cloth string around it, is made to stand with *pakka homa*.

चतुर्थ्यां निशायां हुते पक्कहोमे व्रतं विसृज्य दण्डमुत्थाप्यति — "ऊर्जः पृथिव्या अध्युत्थितोऽसि वनस्पते शतवल्शो विरोह । त्वया वयमिषमूर्जं वदन्तो रायस्पोषेण समिषा मदेम" इति ॥१८॥
On the fourth night after performing *pakka homa*, giving up the *vrata*, the staff is removed — "You have sprung up from the energy of the earth, *vanaspati* spread hundred branches. From you we will draw sap, energy and health. Pray let us be happy."

अथैनं वध्वै प्रयच्छति — "प्रजया त्वा संसृजामि मासरेण सुरामिव" इति ॥१९॥
Then he gives the staff to the wife — "I will join you for the sake of children just like rice gruel is mixed with *surā*."

तं वधूः प्रतिगृह्णाति — "प्रजावती भूयासम्" इति ॥२०॥
The wife holds the staff and says — "I will become child bearing."

अथैनं वराय प्रयच्छति — "प्रजया त्वा पशुभिस्संसृजामि मासरेण सुरामिव" इति ॥२१॥
Then she hands it over to her husband — "I will join you for the sake of children and cattle just like rice gruel is mixed with *surā*."

तं वरः प्रतिगृह्णाति — "प्रजावान् पशुमान् भूयासम्" इति ॥२२॥
He takes it from her — "I will be with children and cattle."

अथैनं स्थूणादेशे निधायान्तिकेन प्रतिपद्यते ॥२३॥
Then they keep the staff with pillars and return inside.

प्रसिद्धमुपसंवेशनम् ॥२४॥
Then intercourse takes place.

श्वोभूते दण्डमादाय पुण्याहं वाचयित्वाऽप्सु विसर्जयति ॥२५॥
In the morning, they bring the staff and after reciting *puṇyāhaṁ* leave it in water.

अथ देवयजनोल्लेखनप्रभृत्याग्निखात् कृत्वा पक्काज्जुहोति — "अग्निमूर्धा, भुवः" इति द्वाभ्याम् ॥२६॥
Then with the beginning with *deva yajña*, settling the fire *pakka homa* is carried out — "The top of Agni, heaven, etc."

स्विष्टकृतत्प्रभृति सिद्धमाधेनुवरप्रदानात् ॥२७॥
With Sviṣṭakṛt *homa* they keep a cow ready for *dakṣiṇā*.

स एष पार्वणो भवति ॥२८॥
Similarly, every full moon and dark moon.

अथास्तमित आदित्येऽन्योमलङ्कृत्योपरिशय्याम् शयते ॥२९॥
Then at sunset, after worshipping Āditya and others, they sleep on cots.

अथ वधूमभिमन्त्रयते — "सुमङ्गलीरियं वधूरिमां समेत पश्यत । सौभाग्यामस्यै दत्वायाथास्तं विपरेतन" इति ॥३०॥
Then they chant at the bride — "She is decorated with ornaments. Look at her the fortunate one and go on your way."

अथैनां सर्वसुरभिगन्धया मालया युनक्ति — "सं ना मनस्सं हृदयानि सं नाऽभि सं तनुत्यजः । सं त्वा कामस्य याक्त्रेणे युञ्जत्यविमोचनाय" इति ॥३१॥
Then he garlands her with many scented garland — "Let

this bring our minds, hearts, navels and bodies together. Let this release you from the chains of your desire."

षष्ठः अध्यायः (Sixth Chapter)

आनयन्त्येतमग्निं ॥१॥
Let the Agni be brought.

अथ देवयजनोल्लेखनप्रभृत्याप्रणीताभ्यः कृत्वा पक्वमोदनं पायसं वा याचति ॥२॥
Then with the beginning of *deva yajña*, performing up to *praṇīta* rituals, he asks for cooked rice (*khīra*).

तमभ्युक्ष्याग्नावधिश्रयतिं ॥३॥
He offers the cooked food as sacrifice into the fire.

आज्यं निर्वपति ॥४॥
He keeps the *ājya* prepared.

अथाज्यमधिश्रयति ॥५॥
Then he warms the ghee.

उभयं पर्यग्नि कृत्वा मेक्षणं स्रुवं च संमार्ष्टि ॥६॥
Making two fires, he cleans the sacrificial ladle and vessel.

अथैतं चरुं श्रपयित्वाऽभिधार्योदञ्चमुद्वास्य प्रतिष्ठतभिघारयति ॥७॥
Then he cooks in the vessel and sprinkles ghee over it after keeping it out and covers with a cloth with its border on top.

परिधानप्रभृत्याग्निमुखात् कृत्वा पक्वाज्जुहोति ॥८॥
After establishing the borders around the fire, he carries out *pakka homa*.

स एवमेव सर्वेषां स्थालीपाकानां चरुकल्पः ॥९॥
He similarly prepares all the *sthālīpāka* preparations.

"यस्त्वा हृदा कीरिणा मन्यमानः" इति पुरोनुवाक्यामनूच्य "यस्मै त्वं सुकृते जातवेदः" इति याज्यया जुहोति ॥१०॥
He recites the *anuvākas*: "From that man who worships with

sincerity and respect, calls you again and again, for good deeds O Jātaveda" he sacrifices with *ājya*.

अथाज्याहुतिरुपजुहोति ॥११॥
He offers oblations with ghee (*upahoma*).

"अग्ने प्रायश्चित्ते त्वं देवानां प्रायश्चित्तरसि ब्राह्मणस्त्वा नाथकामः प्रपद्ये याऽस्यां पतिघ्नी तनूः प्रजाघ्नी पशुघ्नी लक्ष्मिघ्नी जारघ्नीमस्यै कृणोमि स्वाहा" ॥१२॥
"Agni! Expiation! You are the expiation of gods. I, the brāhmaṇa, entreat you desirous of protection. What is terrible in her that will destroy her husband, children and wealth, I will make it die young, *svāhā*!"

"वायो प्रायश्चित्ते . . . कृणोमि स्वाहा" ॥१३॥
"Vāyu! Expiation! You are the expiation of gods. I, the brāhmaṇa, entreat you desirous of protection. What is terrible in her that will destroy her husband, children and wealth, I will make it die young, *svāhā*!"

"आदित्य प्रायश्चित्ते . . . कृणोमि स्वाहा" ॥१४॥
"Āditya! Expiation! You are the expiation of gods. I, the brāhmaṇa, entreat you desirous of protection. What is terrible in her that will destroy her husband, children and wealth, I will make it die young, *svāhā*!"

"प्रजापते प्रायश्चित्ते . . . कृणोमि स्वाहा" इति ॥१५॥
"Prajāpati! Expiation! You are the expiation of gods. I, the brāhmaṇa, entreat you desirous of protection. What is terrible in her that will destroy her husband, children and wealth, I will make it die young, *svāhā*!"

पक्वादेव स्विष्टवतीभ्यां सौविष्टकृतम् ॥१६॥
With well-made cooked food, he performs Sviṣṭakṛt *homa*.

लाजैरितरत्र ॥१७॥
Lājā and other *homas* here.

"हव्यवाहमभिमातिषाहं रक्षोहणं पृतनासु जिष्णुम् । ज्योतिष्मन्तं दद्यितं पुरन्धिमग्निं स्विष्टकृतमाहुवेमोम् । स्विष्टमग्ने अभि तत् पृणाहि विश्वदेव पृतना अभिष्य । उरुं नः पन्थां प्रदिशन् विभाहि ज्योतिष्मद्धेह्यजरं न आयुस्स्वाहा" इति ॥१८॥

"I offer this *havis* for the protection of my loved ones and destruction of enemies. I offer to Puraṁdhi, Agni who carry the two lights (sun and moon) with this Sviṣṭakṛt *homa*."

जयपभृति सिद्धमाधेनुवरप्रदानात् ॥१९॥

He carries out the *homas* beginning with Jayā with the gift of a cow.

अथाज्यशंषेण हिरण्यमन्तर्धाय मूर्ध्नि संस्रावं जुहोति — "भूस्स्वाहा भुवस्स्वाहा सुवस्स्वाहा भूर्भुवस्सुवस्स्वाहा" इति ॥२०॥

With the remnants of the *ājya*, keeping gold piece in it, smearing it on her head, he worships with, "Bhū *svāhā*! Bhuvaḥ *svāhā*! Suvaḥ *svāhā*! Bhūrbhuvasuvaḥ *svāhā*!"

अथैनां प्रदक्षिणमग्निं पर्याणयति — "अर्यम्णो अग्निं परियन्तु क्षिप्रं प्रतिक्षन्तां श्वश्रुवो देवराश्च" इति ॥२१॥

Then he makes her go around the fire — "Let her go around Aryamā and Agni to reach her husband's house quickly awaited by her in-laws."

अथ श्रीमन्तमागारं सम्मृष्टोपलिप्तं गन्धवन्तं पुष्पवन्तं धूपवन्तं दीपवन्तं तल्पवन्तं दिक्षु सर्पिस्सूत्रेन्धनप्रद्योति तमुदकुम्भादर्शोच्छिरसं प्रपाद्य तस्मिन्नेनां सवेश्य तस्या अन्तिके जपति ॥२२॥

Then in the well-decorated hall with smearing of sandal paste, flowers, incense, lights, mirror, seats and sprinkled with ghee and filling water vessels, provided with pillows, he makes her lie down and offers oblations.

"उदीर्ष्वातो विश्ववसो नमसेडामहे त्वा । अन्यामिच्छ प्रफर्व्यं सं जायां पत्या सृज । उदीर्ष्वातः पतिवती ह्येषा विश्वावसु नमसा गीर्भिरी । अन्यामिच्छ पितृपदं व्यक्तां स ते भागो जनुषा तस्य विद्धि" इति ॥२३॥

"I salute you, Viśvāvasu in the forefront with Iḍā Agni. Make this lascivious girl desired by others my wife. I salute you,

Viśvāvasu of this married woman, I salute Sarasvatī. I take this beautiful woman from her father by breaking her relation with her father."

अथैनामुपसंवेशयति — "प्रजापतिस्स्त्रियां यशः" इत्येतया ॥२४॥
Then he has intercourse with her — "Prajāpati will bring fame to women."

अथास्यास्स्तोकोर्तिं विवृणोति — "प्रजायै त्वा" इति ॥२५॥
Then he ejaculates inside her — "For the sake of your children."

सा यद्यश्रु कुर्यात्तामनुमन्त्रयते — "जीवां रुदन्ती विमयन्तो अध्वरे दीर्घामनुप्रसितिं दीधियुर्नरः । वामं पितृभ्यो य इदं समेरिरे मयः पतिभ्यो जनयः परिष्वजे" इति ॥२६॥
If she cries, he chants — "They cry for the living: They lead away the sacrifice; the men send their thoughts after a long reach; what is lovely for the fathers who came together: joy for the husbands for embracing the wife."

सप्तमः खण्डः (Seventh Chapter)

ब्राह्मणेन ब्राह्मण्यामुत्पन्नः प्रागुपनयनाज्जात इत्यभिधीयते ॥१॥
It is said that a brāhmaṇa is born from a brāhmaṇa after *upanayana*.

उपनीतमात्रो व्रतानुचारी वेदानां किञ्चिदधीत्य ब्राह्मणः ॥२॥
One who has the thread ceremony done and does *sandhyā-vandanā*, etc. and knows a little bit of Veda is called brāhmaṇa.

एकां शाखामधीत्य श्रोत्रियः ॥३॥
One who has studied one branch of Vedas is called a *śrotriya*.

अङ्गाध्याय्यनूचानः ॥४॥
One who has studied Vedāṅgas is called *anūcāna*.

कल्पाध्यायी ऋषिकल्पः ॥५॥
One who has studied *kalpa* is called Ṛṣikalpa.

सूत्रप्रवचनाध्यायी भ्रूणः ॥६॥
One who has studied *sūtras* is called *bhrūṇa*.

चतुर्वेदादृषिः ॥७॥
One has studied the four Vedas is called a *ṛṣi*.

अत ऊर्ध्वं देवः ॥८॥
Higher than the above is called a *deva*.

अथ यदि कामयेत श्रोत्रियं जनयेयमित्याऽरुन्धत्युषस्थानाकृत्वा त्रिरात्रमक्षारलवणाशिनावधश्शयिनौ ब्रह्मचारिणावासते ॥९॥
If he desires to have a *śrotriya* as a son, he should after Arundhatī *darśana*, observe *vrata* for three nights eating bland food, sleeping on the floor, being a celibate.

अहतानां च वाससां परिधानं सायं प्रातश्चालङ्करणमिषु प्रतोदयोश्च धारणमग्निपरिचर्या च ॥१०॥
With new dresses and garments, carrying a whip and an arrow, he should go round the fire in the hall in the morning and evening.

चतुर्थ्यां पक्वहोम उपसंवेशनं च ॥११॥
On the fourth day he should perform *pakka homa* and have intercourse.

अथ यदि कामयेतानूचानं जनयेयमिति द्वादशरात्रमेतद्व्रतं चरेत् ॥१२॥
If he desires to have an *anūcāna* as a son, he should observe *vrata* for twelve nights.

व्रतान्ते पक्वहोम उपसंवेशनं च ॥१३॥
At the end of the *vrata*, he should perform *pakka homa* and have intercourse.

अथ यदि कामयेत ऋषिकल्पं जनयेयमिति मासमेतद्व्रतं चरेत् ॥१४॥
If he desires to have a Ṛṣikalpa as a son, he sholud observe *vrata* for one month.

व्रतान्ते पक्वहोम उपसंवेशनं च ॥१५॥

At the end of the *vrata*, he should perform *pakka homa* and have intercourse.

अथ यदि कामयेत भ्रूणं जनयेयमिति चतुरो मासानेतद्व्रतं चरेत् ॥ १६॥
If he desires to have a *bhrūṇa* as a son, he should observe *vrata* for four months.

व्रतान्ते पक्वहोम उपसंवेशनं च ॥१७॥
At the end of the *vrata*, he should perform *pakka homa* and have intercourse.

अथ यदि कामयेत ऋषिं जनयेयमिति षण्मासानेतद्व्रतं चरेत् ॥१८॥
If he desires to have a *ṛṣi* as a son, he should observe *vrata* for six months.

व्रतान्ते पक्वहोम उपसंवेशनं च ॥१९॥
At the end of the *vrata*, he should perform *pakka homa* and have intercourse.

अथ यदि कामयेत देवं जनयेयमिति संवत्सरमेतद्व्रतं चरेत् ॥२०॥
If he desires to have a *deva* as a son, he should observe *vrata* for one year.

व्रतान्ते पक्वहोम उपसंवेशनं च ॥२१॥
At the end of the *vrata*, he should perform *pakka homa* and have intercourse.

अथ यदैषा मलवद्वासास्स्यात् — "नैनया सह संवेदत न सहासीत नास्या अन्नमद्याद्ब्रह्महत्यायै ह्येषा वर्णं प्रतिमुच्यास्तेऽथो खल्वाहुरभ्यञ्जनमेव न प्रतिगृह्यं काममन्यत्" इति ॥२२॥
If she is having her monthly periods — "Do not have intercourse, do not sit with her, do not eat food cooked by her; she will sit having applied *brahmahatyā* colour: Do not take offerings, or carry out rubbing with oil, other desires are not prohibited."

नैनामुपेयात् ॥२३॥
Do not have intercourse with her.

नारण्ये ॥२४॥
Let her not go to the forest .

न पराचीम् ॥२५॥
Let her not turn her face away in disgust.

न स्नाति ॥२६॥
Or have a bath.

नाभ्यङ्क्ते ॥२७॥
Or have rubbing of the body.

न प्रलिखते ॥२८॥

Or scratch herself.

नाङ्क्ते ॥२९॥
Or apply collyrium to her eyes.

न दत्तो धावते ॥३०॥
Or brush her teeth.

न नखानि निकृन्तते ॥३१॥
Or cut her nails.

न कृणात्ति ॥३२॥
Or cut cloth.

न रज्जुं सृजति ॥३३॥
Or make ropes.

न पर्णेन पिबति ॥३४॥
Or drink from leaves.

न खर्वेण पिबति ॥३५॥
Or drink from a brass vessel.

"तस्यै खर्ववस्तिस्रो रात्रिर्व्रतं चरेदञ्जलिना वा पिवेदखर्वेण वा पात्रेण प्रजायै गोपिथाय" इति ब्राह्मणम् ॥३६॥

She will get a dwarf as a child, if she goes against the above. On the third night, perform *vrata*: Let her drink from her joined hands, or a non-brass vessel for the protection of children.

चतुर्थ्यां स्नातायां निशायामलङ्कृत्य शयनेऽभिमन्त्रयते — "विष्णुर्योनिं कल्पयतु त्वष्टा रूपाणि पिंशतु । आसिञ्चतु प्रजापतिर्धाता गर्भं दधातु ते" ॥३७॥
On the fourth day after bathing in the night after decorating her he chants on the bed: "Let Viṣṇu create your *yoni*, let Tvaṣṭā give you beauty: Let Prajāpati sprinkle you, let the god give you the embryo."

"यथाऽग्निगर्भा पृथिवी द्योर्यथेन्द्रेण गर्भिणी । वायुर्यथा दिशां गर्भ एवं गर्भं दधातु ते" ॥३८॥
"Similar to Agni has given to Pṛthivī, the sky has become pregnant because of Indra, like Diśā has because of Vāyu, God give her embryo."

गर्भं धेहि सिनीवालि गर्भं धेहि सरस्वति । गर्भं ते अश्विनौ देवावाधत्तां पुष्करस्रजा" ॥३९॥
"Give her embryo, Sinīvālī, give her embryo, Sarasvatī: Let the Aśvins decorate with a garland of lotuses."

"हिरण्ययी अरुणी यं निर्मन्थतो अश्विना । तंते गर्भं दधाम्यहं दशमे मासि सूतवे" ॥४०॥
"That churned from gold and reddish brown by Aśvins, give me that embryo for delivery after ten months."

"नेजमेष परापत सपुत्रः पुनरापत । अस्यै मे पुत्रकामायै गर्भमाधेहि यः पुमान्" इति ॥४१॥
"O Nejameṣa Deva! If through my future son, you become a bad son, stay away from me. If you desire to become a good son, give her a good embryo."

अथैनां परिष्वजति — "अमूहमस्मि सा त्वं द्योरहं पृथिवी त्वं रेतोऽहं रेतोभृत्त्वं मनोऽहमस्मि वाक्त्वं सामाहमस्मि ऋक्त्वं तावेहि सम्भवाव सह रेतो दधावहै पुंसे पुत्राय वेत्तवै रायस्पोषाय सुप्रजास्त्वाय सुवीर्याय" इति ॥४२॥
Then he addresses her — "I am this (God), you are that

(Goddess); I am the heaven, you are the earth; I am the sperm, you are the sperm receptacle; I am the mind, you are the speech; I am the song, you are the lyric; let us get together, I will give my sperm; let us have male children who are wealthy, good and heroic."

आत्मानं प्रत्यभिमृषते — "अहं गर्भमदधामोषधीष्वहं विश्वेषु भुवनेष्वन्तः । अहं प्रजा अजनयन्पितृणामहं जनिभ्यो अपरिषु पुत्रान्" इति ॥४३॥
He touches himself — "I have impregnated herbal trees, I have impregnated all the animals, I have created my lineage on earth, I have given birth to sons through women."

अथैनामुपैति — "तां पूषच्छिवतमोमरयस्व यस्यां बीजं मनुष्या वपन्ती । या न ऊरू उशती विस्रयातै यस्यामुशन्तः प्रहरेम शेफम्" इति ॥४४॥
Then he has intercourse — "That seed which has been given to man by Pūṣaṇa and Śiva for immortality, that I will plant by beating with my organ in her spread thighs."

स एवमेव चतुर्थीप्रभृत्याषोडशीमुत्तरामुत्तरां युग्मामुपैति ॥४५॥
Like this, beginning from the fourth day, he has intercourse on even days and beyond.

प्रजानिश्श्रेयसमृतुगमनमित्याचार्याः ॥४६॥
Gurus say till she has her periods.

सर्वाण्युपगमनानि मन्त्रवन्ति भवतन्ति बोधायनः ॥४७॥
During all the time let *mantras* be chanted says, Baudhāyana.

यच्चदौ यच्चर्ताविति शालिकिः ॥४८॥
Mantras to be chanted during intercourse for the first time and after every monthly period, says, Śāliki.

अष्टमः अध्यायः (Eighth Chapter)

अथाभ्यां पञ्चमेऽहनि नापितकर्म कुर्वन्ति ॥१॥
On the fifth day, *nāpita karma* is carried out.

नापितेन पयोदनं दत्वा ग्रामात्प्राचीं वोदीचीं वा दिशमुपनिष्क्रम्य यत्रैकमुदुम्बरमूलं पश्यन्ति तं प्रदक्षीणं परिसमूह्य प्रदक्षिणं गन्धैरनुलिम्पन्

जपति — "यथा त्वं वनस्पत ऊर्जा अभ्युत्थितो वनस्पते । शतवलूशो विरोहस्येवमहं पुत्रैश्च पशुभिश्च सहस्रवलूशा वि वयं रुहेम" इति ॥२॥
After giving the barber milk and cooked rice, they go in the easterly or northerly direction till they find the root of a *udumbara* tree, they go round it, smear it with sandal paste and chant — "O Vanaspate! like you give energy to the plants; like hundred shoots coming out, give us children and cattle through a thousand shoots."

सुमनोभिः प्रच्छादयति — "यथा त्वं वनस्पते फलवानस्येवमहं पुत्रैश्च पशुभिश्च फलवान् भवानि" इति ॥३॥
With the offer of flowers, he requests — "Like you give fruits to the trees, give us fruits like children and cattle."

अत्रैव त्रिवृताऽन्नेन बलिमुपहरति ॥४॥
Here, he offers cooked rice, milk and honey and sacrifices.

मन्त्रं चोदाहरन्ति — "ऊर्जस्वान् पयस्वान् पयसा पिन्वमानोऽस्मान् वनस्पते पयसाऽभ्याववृत्स्व" इति ॥५॥
He chants the *mantra* — "Drinking the milk with energy and sweetness, Vanaspate make our life sweet."

अन्नं संस्कृत्य ब्राह्मणान् सम्पूज्याशिषो वाचयित्वा जानुदध्नमुदकमवतीर्य प्राचीनदशेनाहतेन वाससौ मत्स्यान् गृह्णतो ब्रह्मचारिणं पृच्छतो "ब्रह्मचारिन् किं पश्यसि" इति ॥६॥
Feeding brāhmaṇas with the cooked rice and getting the good wishes recited, they stand in the water up to the knees and sprinkle curds and water in the eastern direction and, with new clothes, hold a fish and ask the *brahmacārī* — "*Brahmacārī* what do you see?"

स पृष्टः प्रतिब्रूयात् "पुत्रांश्च पशूंश्च" इति ॥७॥
He answers from behind: "I see children and cattle too."

अथैनाम् मत्स्यानुदुम्बरमूले बकानां बलिमुपहरति — "धीर्घायुत्वाय वर्चसे" इति ॥८॥
Then at the root of the *udumbara* tree he offers the fish to the cranes — "For the sake of long life and lustre."

अत्रैव निर्माल्यानि परिभुक्तानि वासांसि प्रतिसरांश्च प्रतिमुच्योदुम्बरशाखायां संसृज्य ॥९॥

Here he removes the *kaṅkana*, dresses, etc. and ties them round the branches of the *udumbara* tree.

अथावगाह्यान्योन्यस्य पृष्ठे धावयित्वोदकान्तं प्रति यौति — "प्रतियुतो वरुणस्य पाशः प्रत्यस्तो वरुणस्य पाशः" इति ॥१०॥

Then taking a dip in the water and they rub and sprinkle water on each other and chant — "Get released from the fetters of Varuṇa, get released from the fetters of Varuṇa."

अन्योन्यमलङ्कृत्य वासांसि परिधायाहतेन वाससा वेति ॥११॥

He decorates the loved one with new red clothes and garments.

यानेन पद्भ्यां वा गृहं गत्वा प्रक्षाळितपाणिपादावप आचम्य वाग्यतौ शयनमारभेते ॥१२॥

Going home in a vehicle or by foot, after washing feet with water, sipping water, they sleep together quietly.

श्वोभूते वैश्वदेवेन प्रतिपद्यते ॥१३॥

In the morning they invoke Vaiśvadevas.

मासिश्रद्धेन चापरपक्षे ॥१४॥

Similarly during monthly *śrāddha* and during full moon and new moon.

Vārāha Gṛhya-Sūtra

Vārāha Gṛhya-Sūtra belongs to the Maitrāyanīya branch of *Kṛṣṇa Yajurveda*. It appears to be closely associated with *Mānava Gṛhya-Sūtra* and *Kāṭhaka Gṛhya-Sūtra*. Gaṅgādhara and Vasiṣṭha have written *paddhati*s on *Vārāha Gṛhya-Sūtra*. According to some scholars, it can be dated to first and second century CE. *Vārāha Gṛhya-Sūtra* unlike others starts the *saṁskāra* section with *jātakarma* and ends with *sīmantonnayana*. The following is the section of *Vārāha Gṛhya-Sūtra* dealing with *vivāha saṁskāra*:

दशमः खण्डः (Tenth Section)

विनीतक्रोधस्सहर्षः महिषीं भार्यां विन्देता नन्यपूर्वां यवीयसीम् ॥१॥
Let the groom, who has controlled anger and is happy, choose a queenly bride who is not in any other's possession and one who is young.

असमानप्रवरैर्विवाह ॥ ऊर्ध्वं सप्तमात्पितृबन्धुभ्यः पञ्चमान्मातृबन्धुभ्यो बीजिनश्च ॥२॥
Let her be from a different *gotra* from his. Let her be a seven times removed from his father and five times from his mother as a relative.

कृत्तिकास्वातिपूर्वैरिति वरयेत् ॥३॥
Let him marry under the stars Kṛttikā, Svāti and Pūrvā (Āṣāḍha, Bhādrapada and Phālgunī).

मृगशिरश्श्रविष्ठोत्तरफाल्गुणित्युयमेत् ॥४॥
Mṛgaśirā, Rohiṇī, Śravaṇā, Dhaniṣṭhā and the stars beginning with Uttarā (Āṣāḍha, Bhādrapada and Phālgunī) are auspicious for marriage.

पञ्च विवाहकारकाणि भवन्ति — वित्तं रूपं विद्या प्रज्ञा बान्धमिति ॥५॥
The bride's father will look at the following aspects of the groom: money, looks, education, intelligence and family.

एकालाभे वित्तं विसृजेत् । द्वितीयालाभे रूपं तृतीयालाभे विद्यां प्रज्ञायां तु बान्धवा विवन्दते ॥६॥
If all five qualities are not present, he can overlook money. Second, he can overlook looks, third, education if he is intelligent and from a good family.

अनृक्षरा ऋजवः सन्तु पन्था येभिस्सखायो यन्ति नो वरेयम् । समर्यमा सं भगो नो निनीयात् सञ्जास्पत्यं सुयममस्तु देवाः ॥ इति वरकान्व्रजतोऽनुमन्त्रयते ॥७॥
They chant the *mantra*: "Let the paths that our friends travel for the wooing be thornless and smooth. Let Aryamā and Bhaga lead us: O gods! Let the union of husband and wife be successful."

बन्धुमतीं कन्यामस्पृष्टमैथुनामुपयच्छेतानग्निकाम् श्रेष्ठाम् ॥८॥

Let her be one who does not have relation with another, be of another *gotra*, be a virgin.

विज्ञानमस्यै कुर्यात् । चतुरो लोष्टानाहरेत् — सीतालोष्टं वेदिलोष्टं गोमयलोष्टं स्मशानलोष्टं च ॥९॥

To find out her goodness do the following. Get four mud lumps. From a ploughed field, altar, cowshed and cemetery.

एतेषामेकं गृह्णिष्वेति ब्रूयात् । स्मशानलोष्टं चेद्गृहणीयान्नोपयच्छेतम् ॥१०॥

From these, ask her to take one. If she takes the lump from the cemetery, do not choose her.

असंसृष्टामधर्मेणोपयच्छेत् । ब्राह्मेण श्लोकेन वा ॥११॥

Choose one who is not associated with unethical values. Marry as per Brāhma or Ārṣa form of wedding.

शतमिति रथं दद्याद्गोमिथुनं वा ॥१२॥

Give a chariot with 100 gold pieces or a bull and a cow or both.

उभयाँस्तेजनीष्वासजेज्जन्यान्कौमारिकाश्च । पूर्वे जन्याः स्युरपरे कौमरिकाः ॥१३॥

Give clothes which bring pleasure to her and to her parents. First, to her parents and then to her.

चतुरो गोमयपिण्डान्कृत्वा द्वावन्येभ्यस्तथान्येभ्य इति प्रयच्छेत् ॥१४॥

Lumps of cow dung are prepared with two being held by the bride's parents and two by the bride.

धनं न इति ब्रूयुः । पुत्रपशवो न इति जन्याः ॥१५॥

Let the parents of the bride declare, "no money". The groom's parents say, "no cattle".

"ददानि" । प्रतिगृह्णनीति त्रिर्ब्रह्मदेयाम् ॥१६॥

"Will I give." Thrice holding the lumps.

कृतेनाँसेना विसङ्केसेयुः ॥१७॥

The lumps are then broken up.

त्रिरानन्दं मागधो ह्वयेत् ॥१८॥
This kind of practice is called *trirānanda* by the people of Magadha.

एकादशः खण्डः (Eleventh Section)

षडर्घ्यार्हा भवन्ति — ऋत्विगाचार्यो विवाह्यो राजा स्नातकः प्रियश्चेति ॥ १॥
Six people are worthy of *arghya* offerings — *purohita*, teacher, groom, *rājā*, one who has completed studies and a dear one.

अप्राकरणिकानापरिसंवत्सरादर्हयन्ति । अन्यत्र याज्यात्कर्मणे विवाहच्च ॥ २॥
Those who are not directly involved in the rituals are worthy of offerings once a year. Those *purohitas* who take part in *yajñas* are also worthy of offerings. At weddings, they are offered *madhuparka* first.

न जीवपितृकोऽर्घ्यं प्रतिगृह्णीयात् ॥३॥
Those whose fathers are alive may not be offered *arghya* at weddings.

अथैनमर्हयन्ति ॥५॥
Now they are worthy of these.

काँस्ये चमसे वा दधनि मध्वासिच्य वर्षीयसाऽपिधाय, "विराजो दोहोऽसि विराजो दोहमशीय मयि दोहः पद्यायै विराज" इति मधुपर्कमाहियमाणं प्रतीक्षते ॥५॥
With brass spoons, these people (those who are worthy once a year), do *ācamana* with curds and honey first having approached the *pūjā* area. With the *mantra*, "O water! you are the essential sweetness of the elemental liquid born of Cosmic Infinitude. Pray grant me the same delicious beauty and embellish my feet with loveliness by washing them clean."

सावित्रेण विष्टरौ परिगृह्य, "राष्ट्रभृदसीत्यासन्द्यामुदगग्रमास्तृणाति" ॥६॥
Having received the spread grass, he recites, *raṣṭrabhṛt*.

"अहं वर्ष्म सदृशानामुद्यतामिव सूर्यःइदमहं तमधरं करोमि यो मा कश्चाभिदासति" त्येकस्मिन्नुपविशति ॥८॥
"I am the body similar to the rising sun." With the *mantra*, "I

am bringing down whoever harasses me". And he sits on the seat provided.

"मा त्वद्योषमित्यन्यतरमधस्तात्पादयोरुपकर्षति" ॥८॥
With the *mantra*, "may I not withdraw from you", he pushes the spread grass over his feet.

विष्टरमासीनायैकं त्रिः प्राह ॥९॥
Having been seated, the *mantra* is repeated thrice.

नैव भोःइत्याह ॥ न मा रिषामेति ॥१०॥
The *mantra*, "*naiva bho*!" is muttered. We are not holy men.

आचमनीयाः प्रथमाः प्रतिपद्यन्ते ॥११॥
Those have sipped water will start first.

"अमृतोपस्तरणमसीत्याचामति" ॥१२॥
With the *mantra*, "spread out nectar you are" he sips water.

पद्येन पादौ प्रक्षालयति ॥१३॥
He washes his feet with water.

स्पृशत्यर्घ्यम् ॥१४॥
He touches the *arghya* water.

ततः प्रणयति ॥१५॥
He brings it there.

सावित्रेणोभयतोविष्टरं मधुपर्कं प्रतिगृह्य "आदित्यास्त्वा पृष्ठे सादयामि"ति भूमौ प्रतिष्ठाप्यावसाद्य "सुपर्णस्य त्वा गरुत्मतश्चक्षुषाऽवेक्षे" इत्यवेक्ष्य नमो रुद्राय पात्रसदे" — इति प्रादेशेन प्रतिदिशं व्युद्दिश्याङ्गुष्ठेनोपमध्यमया च "मधु वाता ऋतायत" इति तिसृभिस्संसृजति ॥१६॥
Touching the *arghya* water, and washing the feet, holding the *madhuparka* vessel, chanting the *mantra*, "I will hold you behind Āditya", and keeping it on the ground he chants "see with your eyes the golden bird with the golden feathers" and saying, "hail Rudra! who lives in the cup" the *madhuparka* is sprinkled in all the directions with the right thumb dipped thrice.

"सत्यं यशः श्रीर्मयि श्रीरश्रयतामिति त्रिः प्राश्नाति भूयिष्ठम्" ॥१७॥
With the *mantra*, "truth, fame and wealth I seek" he sprinkles *madhuparka* on the floor.

सुहृदयेऽवशिष्टं प्रयच्छति ॥१८॥
He hands over the vessel with the remnants of the *madhuparka* to a friend.

"अमृतापिधानमसीत्या"चामति ॥१९॥
He sips water with the *mantra*, "the nectar is covered".

असिविष्टरपाणिर्गां प्राह ॥२०॥
Holding in his hands a sword he offers a cow to his guest.

"हतो मे पाप्मा पाप्मानं मे हत । यां त्वा देवा वसवोऽन्वजीविषुरादित्यानां स्वसारं रुद्रमातरम् । दैवीं गामादितिं जनानामारभन्तामर्हतामर्हणाय" । ओ३म् कुरुतेति संप्रेष्यति ॥२१॥
"Destroyed is my sin: Destroy my sin. In whom the gods reside, the mother of Rudra, the sister of Ādityas, seize her who is Aditi, to feed the deserving." Saying *oṁ*! He summons the butcher.

चतुरवरान्ब्राह्मणान् नानागोत्रानित्येकैकं पश्वङ्गं पायसं वा भोजयेत् ॥ २२॥
Feed four brāhmaṇas belonging to different *gotra*s with parts of cow's meat (*khīra*).

यद्युत्सृजेत् — "माता रुद्राणां दुहिता वसूनां स्वसादित्यानामृतस्य नाभिः । प्र नु वोचं चिकितुषे जनाय मा गामनागामदितिं वधिष्ठ" । ओ३म् उत्सृजत तृणान्यत्तूदकं पिबतु इत्युक्ते पशुमालभते ॥२३॥
If he wishes to release the cow, he does so with the *mantra*, "Mother of Rudra, daughter of Vasus, sister of Ādityas and the navel of immortality, in the midst of learned people, I shall say: Do not kill the guiltless cow, which is Aditi. *Oṁ*! Let it loose, let it eat grass and drink water". Saying this, he releases the cow.

शं नो मित्र इति पाणी प्रक्षाल्य यथार्थम् ॥२४॥
Saying "let my friends be happy" he washes his hands and does whatever he wants.

द्वादशं खण्डम् (Twelfth Section)

अथालङ्करणम् । "अलङ्करणमसि सर्वस्मा अलं भूयासम्" ॥१॥

Now dressing up is done. "You are the decoration. May I be adequate for everyone."

"प्राणापानौ मे तर्पयामि समानव्यानौ मे तर्पयामि उदानरूपे मे तर्पयामि चक्षुःश्रोत्रे मे तर्पयामि सुवर्चा अहमक्षिभ्यां भूयासं सुवर्चा मुखेन सुश्रुत्कर्णाभ्यामिति" गन्धाछादने ॥२॥

With the *mantra*, "satiate my *prāṇa* and *apāna*, satiate my *samāna* and *vyāna*, satiate my *udāna* and beauty, may I become splendid of face, may I come to hear well with my ears", she touches herself and takes new dresses smeared with sandal paste.

"परिधास्ये यशो धास्ये दीर्घायुत्वाय जरदिष्टरस्मि । शतं च जीव शरदः पुरूचीर्वसूनि चाय्यो विभजाय जीयाम्" ॥ इत्यहत वास आछाद्याग्निं प्रज्वाल्य व्याहृतिभिर्वीहियवान्हुत्वा मङ्गलान्याशासेत् ॥३॥

With the verses, "I shall put on glory, I shall wear this garment for the sake of long life. May we live to old age and see hundred autumns", she wears the garment after sacrificing chanting *vyāhṛtis*, with barley, rice husk, etc.

त्रयोदशं खण्डम् (Thirteenth Section)

अथ प्रवदने कन्यामुपवसितां स्नातां सुशिरस्कामहताऽनाच्छिन्नदशेन वाससा संवितां संस्तीर्णस्य पुरस्ताद्विहितानि वादित्राणि विधिवदुपकल्प्य पुरस्तात्स्विष्टकृतः वाचे पथ्यायै पूष्णे पृथिव्या अग्नये सेनायै धेनायै गायत्र्यै त्रिष्टुभे जगत्या अनुष्टुभे पङ्क्त्यै विराजे राकायै सिनीवाल्यै कुहै, त्वष्ट्र आशायै सम्पत्त्यै भूत्यै निर्ऋत्या अनुमत्यै पर्जन्याय अग्नये स्विष्टकृते च जुहुयात् ॥१॥

Now they say that the bride having fasted, bathed including her head, clothed in new clothes will be asked to sit on the spread grass near the fire, arrange the selected musical instruments and Sviṣṭakṛt sacrifice will be carried out. Sacrifices will be made to Pathyā, Pūṣaṇa, Pṛthvī, Agni, Senā, Dhenā, Gāyatrī, Jagatī, Anuṣṭup, Paṅkta,Virāja, Rākā, Sinīvālī, Kuhvā, Tvaṣṭā, Āśā, Saṁpatti, Bhūtā, Niruktā, Anumatī, Parjanyā, Agni and Sviṣṭakṛt.

आज्यशेषेण पाणी प्रलिप्य कन्याया मुखं संमार्ष्टि–प्रियां करोमि पतये देवराणां श्वशुराय च ॥ रुच्यै त्वाग्निस्संसृजतु रुचिष्या पतये भव ॥ सौभाग्येन त्वा संसृजत्विळा देवी घृतपदीन्द्राण्यग्नाय्यश्विनी राट् । वागिला द्योररुन्धती ॥ इति च॥२॥

With the remnants of the *ājya* smeared on the hands, besmear the bride's face with the *mantra*, "I will please", referring to the husband, his brothers and sisters and in-laws. Bring brightness, Agni! Let the husband become lustrous. With prosperity, bring together Vilā Devī, Indra, Agni, Aśvinīs, Raṅgvāgilā, Heaven, Arundhatī.

सर्वाणि वादित्राण्यभिमन्त्रयते ॥ या चतुर्धा प्रवदत्यग्नौ या वाते या बृहत्युत । पशूनां या ब्राह्मणे न्यदधुः शिवा सा प्रवदत्विह ॥ इति॥३॥

Now all the musical instruments are worshipped. She recites, "with four ways" addressing Agnis, wind and the giants. All the instruments are decorated and she recites, "cattle, brāhmaṇa become auspicious".

सर्वाणि वादित्राण्यलङ्कृत्य कन्या प्रवादयते — "शुभं वद दुन्दुभे सुप्रजास्त्वाय गोमुख । प्रक्रीडन्तु कन्यास्सुमनस्यमानास्सहेन्द्राण्या सवयसः सनीडाः । प्रजापतिर्यो वसति प्रजासु प्रजास्वन्वते सुमनस्यमानाः । स इमाः प्रजां रमयतु प्रजात्यै स्वयं च नोरमतां शं दधानः ॥" इति॥४॥

With the *mantra*, "Speak the good" she plays the instruments wishing for good children and cattle. Let the bride play with flowers, control of senses, etc. Let the children living with Prajāpati, bless us with good children. Let she entertain the people with her playing.

प्रवदन्ति कारालिकानि ॥५॥

So says, Kārālika.

कन्यामुदकेनाभिषिञ्चेत् ॥६॥

Let her be sprinkled with water.

चतुर्दशं खण्डम् (Fourteenth Section)

खे रथस्य खेऽनसः खे युगस्य शतक्रतोः । अपालामिन्द्रस्त्रिः पूर्त्यवकृणोत्सूर्यत्वचसः ॥ इत्यथास्या अहतः वासः प्रयच्छति ॥१॥

"In the hole of the yoke of the chariot, in the hole of the cart, O! you, who has hundred powers, you cleansed Apālā with water thrice and made her skin as bright as the sun", her new (unwashed) clothes he brings.

अथैनां दर्भशुल्वेन संनह्यति —"सं त्वा नह्यामि पयसा पृथिव्याः सं त्वा नह्याम्याद्भिरोषधीभिः । सं त्वा नह्यामि प्रजया धनेन सह संनद्धा सुनुहि भागधेयम् ॥" इति॥२॥

Now he ties the *mekhalā* of grass around her with the verse: "I tie with the milk of the earth, I tie you with water and herbal plants, I tie you with children and money, you take all this together and be fortunate."

अथैनाँ वाससोऽन्तं ग्राहयित्वाऽभ्युदानयति — "अघोरचक्षुरपतिध्न्येधि। एहि शिवा पशुभ्यः सुमना सुवर्चाः। दीर्घायुपत्नी प्रजया स्वर्विदिन्द्रप्रणयीरुप नो वस्तुमेहि ॥३॥"

Now, he holds her dress and says: "Do not look at your husband with evil eyes that may kill. Look with a clean and virtuous mind so that our cattle are blessed. Be a long living wife with loving looks for children and belongings."

समूहनोल्लेपनोद्धननावेक्षणमित्याग्नकाले भूमिसँस्कारात्सर्वत्र यथानिमित्तम् ॥४॥

Collect all that is required for sacrifice such as paste, planks as per practice.

पश्चादग्नेः कटे तेजन्याः वा दर्भेष्वासनम् ॥५॥

To the west of the fire, place a bamboo cot or a seat of *darbha* grass.

शुचौ भूमिप्रदेशे शमीशमकश्यामाकानां प्रियङ्गुदूर्वागौरसर्षपाणाँ यथालाभगन्धसक्षीरफलवद्भ्यो वनस्पतिभ्यो हरित्पर्णकुशयवादिभिश्चान्नै-र्या ओषधयः। समन्या यन्तीत्यनुवाकेन शं नो देवीरिति च सहिरण्यापोऽभिमन्त्र्य प्रणीतोदकुंभं प्रणयेत् ॥६॥

On cleaned floor keeping *śamī* and other woods, good and soft *dūrvā* grass, mustard, water, as available sanḍal, *khīra*, fruits, herbs, green leaves mixed rice, plants, etc. With *anuvākas* blessed be us by gods, he worships the gold filled pot of *praṇīta* water.

तं लाजाहुतीषु हूयमानासु भ्राता ब्रह्मचारी वोद्गृह्य धारयेद् दक्षिणतश्च ॥७॥
The material for *lājā homa* may be carried by her brother or a *brahmacārī* to the south of the fire.

लाजान्सँस्कृतान्शमीपर्णमिश्रान्शूर्पेण दक्षिणतो माताऽन्या वाऽविधवा ॥ ८॥
The fried grains mixed with *śamī* leaves are carried in a basket to the south (of the fire) by the mother or any *sumaṅgalī*.

आज्यँ सँस्कृत्य ब्रह्माणमामन्त्र्य समिधमाधायाधारावधार्याज्यभागौ हुत्वा ॥९॥
With the "Brahmaṇa" *mantra*, the *ājya* is cleaned and kindling the fire with wood, holding part of the *ājya*, it is sacrificed.

अथ जुहोति — "अग्नये जनविदे स्वाहा । सोमाय जनविदे स्वाहा । गन्धर्वाय जनविदे स्वाहा । सोमः प्रथमो विविदे गन्धर्वो विविद उत्तरः । तृतीयोऽग्निष्टे पतिस्तुर्योऽहं मनुष्यजाः॥ स्वाहा ॥ सोमाऽददद्गन्धर्वाय गन्धर्वोऽददग्नये । रयिं च पुत्राँश्चादादग्निर्मह्यमथो इमाम् ॥" इति॥१०॥
He sacrifices — "To Agni who gave me my wife, *svāhā*! To Soma who gave me my wife, *svāhā*! To *gandharva* who gave me my wife, *svāhā*! Soma knew her first, *gandharva* knew her next, the third is Agni, I, a man, am the next in the form of husband as the fourth. Soma gifted her to *gandharva*, *gandharva* to Agni, I was gifted by Agni for the sake of wealth and children."

हिरण्यगर्भ इत्यष्टाभिः प्रत्यृचमाज्याहुतीर्जुहुयात् ॥११॥
With the *mantra*, "Hiraṇyagarbha" he sacrifices eight times the *ājya* portions.

येन कर्मणेर्त्सेत्तत्र जयाञ्जुहुयादिति जयानाँ श्रुतिः । त्वा यथोक्तम् । आकूत्यै त्वा स्वाहा । भूत्यै त्वा स्वाहा । कामायै त्वा स्वाहा । रक्षायै त्वा स्वाहा । समृधे त्वा स्वाहा । समृद्ध्यै त्वा स्वाहा । ऋचा स्तोमम् । प्रजापतये । भूः स्वाहा । अयाश्चाग्नेऽसीति च ॥१२॥
Śrutis say that sacrifices for success are followed by the Jayādi sacrifices. It is done as said. "Ākūti *svāhā*! Bhūta *svāhā*! Kāma *svāhā*! Rakṣā *svāhā*! Samṛdha *svāhā*! Ṛcā *svāhā*!

Prajāpataye *svāhā*! Bhūḥ *svāhā*!" He sacrifices sitting in front of the fire.

उत्तरतोऽग्नेर्दर्भेषु प्राचीं कन्यामचस्थाप्य पुरस्तात्प्रत्यङ्मुख उपयन्ता "देवस्य ते सवितुः प्रसवेऽश्विनोर्बाहुभ्यां पूष्णो हस्ताभ्याँ हस्तं गृह्णाम्यहमसा"वित्यथास्या उपनयनवद्ध्स्तं नीचारिक्तमरिक्तेन — गृह्णामि ते सौभगत्वाय हस्तं मया पत्या जरदष्टिर्यथासत् । भगो अर्यमा सविता पुरन्धिर्मह्यम् त्वादुर्गार्हपत्याय देवाः ॥ ऊर्ध्वा वाक्समभवत्पुरा देवासुरेभ्यः । यां त्वा विश्वस्य भूतस्य प्रागायाम्यस्या अग्रतः ॥ सरस्वति प्रेदमव सुभगे वाजीनावति । येन भूतँ समभवद्येन विश्वामिदं जगत् । तामद्य गाथां गास्यामो या स्त्रीणामुत्तमं मनः ॥ सा त्वमस्यमोऽहमोऽहमसि सा त्वम् । द्योरहं पृथिवी त्वं बृहदहं रथन्तरं त्वम् । रेतोऽहमस्मि रेतोधृक्त्वम् ॥ सामाहमस्मि ऋक्त्वं मनोऽहमस्मि वाक्त्वम् । सा मामनुव्रता भव सा मामनुप्रजायस्व ॥ प्रजाँ सृजावहा उभौ पुँसे पुत्राय कर्तवे । श्रियै पुत्राय वेथवेह सूनृते" ॥ इति ॥१३॥

To the north of the fire, he makes the bride sit on the *darbha* grass, sitting facing west, he chants the *mantra*: "With the blessing of the God Savitā, I take her from the shoulders of the Aśvins and the hands of Pūṣaṇa" and does her *upanayana* (*pāṇigrahaṇa*) with the following *mantras*: I hold your blessed hand so that you will be my wife till old age. The gods, Bhaga, Aryamā, Savitā and Puraṁdhi have gifted you to me so that I may become a householder. From above the gods are uttering their blessings. Sarasvatī! One having plants which will do good everyone, one who is in the forefront to look after all beings in this world, I worship you to take care of this event also. One who is the bright reflection of all women's good minds, one from the beginning of creation is representing all forms, one in whom all beings are dependent, I sing praises of that Sarasvatī". "You are her (Goddess), this I am (God), heaven I am, earth you are, Bṛhad I am, Rathantara you are, sperm I am, sperm receiver you are, song I am, lyric you are, mind I am, word you are. Let her be my follower. Let her bear my children. Let us together have male children, children who are fortunate."

प्रदक्षिणमग्निं परिणयेत् ॥१४॥

They go around the fire.

पश्चादग्नेर्दर्भेष्वश्मानमवस्थापयति — आतिष्ठेममश्मानमश्मेव त्वँ स्थिरा भव । कृण्वन्तु विश्वे देवा आयुष्टे शरदः शतम् ॥ इति ॥१५॥

To the west of the fire on *darbha* grass, he places a stone. He says: "Stand on the stone so that you become as firm as the stone. Let the gods make you live to see hundred autumns."

अत्रैवास्या द्वितीयाँ वासः प्रयच्छति ॥१६॥

Now he brings her second set of clothes.

उपर्यग्नावञ्जलौ लाजान्भ्राता ब्रह्मचारी वोपस्तीर्ण आवपेत् ॥१७॥

Then let her brother or a *brahmacārī* take fried grains in both hands and sacrifice in the fire.

तानभिघारितानविच्छिन्दनी जुहुयात् । कर्तानुमन्त्रयते — "इयं नार्युपब्रूते लाजानावपन्तिका । दीर्घायुरस्तु मे पतिरेधान्तां ज्ञातयो मम ॥ अर्यमणं नु देवं कन्याग्निमयक्षत । सोऽस्मान्देवोऽर्यमा प्रेतो मुञ्चातु मामुत ॥ स्वाहा ॥ इति ॥१८॥

Let her sprinkle the fried grains on the fire without break. She chants: "Let me, this woman who is offering fried grains, pray for my husband's long life and good relation with me. O Aryamā, the god to whom this woman prays with devotion, release her from the bonds of her parents but not from her husband's."

वीरसूर्जीवपत्नीर्भूयासमिति सर्वत्र वाचयेत् ॥१९॥

Let him become a hero with a living wife.

तुभ्यमग्रे पर्यण्यँ सूर्याँ वहुतना सह । पुनः पतिभ्यो जायां दा अग्ने प्रजया सह ॥ इति द्वितीयं परिणयेत् ॥२०॥

"I have brought Sūrya's chariot to go around you. Again I pray to you, Agni to give this husband a wife with children." Then they go around the fire for the second time.

एवमेव तृतीयम् । अवस्थापनप्रभृति समानम् । "पूषणं नु देवम् । वरुणं देवम्" इति होमौ । "कन्याग्निमयक्षते" ति समानम् ॥२१॥

Similarly a third time. The procedure is same as before. "I sacrifice to God Pūṣaṇa, I sacrifice to Varuṇa."

कामेन चतुर्थीं पूरयित्वा द्विरभिघार्योत्तरार्धपूर्वार्धे जुहुयात् ॥२२॥

If they wish, they can repeat a fourth time, let her sprinkle fried grains in the first and second half.

अथैनां प्राचीँ सप्त पदानि प्रक्रमयति — एकमिषे विष्णुस्त्वां नयतु । द्वे ऊर्जे । त्रीणि रायस्पोषाय । चत्वारि मायोभवाय । पञ्च प्रजाभ्यः । षड् तुभ्यः । सप्त सप्तभ्यो होत्राभ्यः ॥ विष्णुस्त्वा नयत्वीति द्वितीयप्रभृत्यनुषजेत्। सखी सप्तपदी भव सख्यं ते गमेयँ सख्यात्ते मा रिषिमिति सप्तम एनां प्रेक्षमाणा समीक्षते ॥२३॥

Then he makes her take seven steps to the east — first step for sap — let Viṣṇu lead you; second step for energy, let Viṣṇu lead you; third step for wealth, let Viṣṇu lead you; fourth step for health, let Viṣṇu lead you; fifth step for children, let Viṣṇu lead you; sixth step for seasons, let Viṣṇu lead you; seventh step for riuals, let Viṣṇu lead you. Let them repeat following the first one. He says be my friend with the seventh step; let me go as your friend, do not harm me. The seventh step will look after her.

"प्र त्वा मुञ्चातु वरुणस्य पाशाद्येन त्वाबध्नात्सविता सुशेवः । धातुश्च योनौ सुकृतस्य लोके हृष्टा सँ सह पात्या भूयासम् ॥" इति शुल्वँ विस्रँस्योदकुम्भेन मार्जयन्ते — पुनन्तु मा पितरं इत्यनुवाकेन । आपोहिष्ठीयेनेत्येके ॥२४॥

"I release you from the bondage of Varuṇa through which the almighty Savitā had bound you. In the good world made from the creator's womb, let me with my wife be happy". Then releasing the thread, she is made to bathe. Again, with the verse, *mā pitaram*. Some say with the verse, "O water God".

सुमङ्गलीरियँ वधुरिमाँ समेत पश्यत । सौभाग्यमस्यै दत्वा यथार्थँ विपरेतन ॥ इति ॥२५॥

This bride is a *sumaṅgalī*, all of you look at her together. Give her your blessings and return to your places with auspicious minds.

स्थालीपाकेन शेषो व्याख्यातः ॥२६॥

It is said that the rest with cooked food (*sthālīpāka*).

"पृथक्त्वेत् । येन द्यौरुग्रे"त्येवंप्रभृतय उद्वाहे होमाः स्युः । नापाणिग्रहणे लाजाः । समानं प्रक्रमणं मार्जनं च ॥२७॥

Beginning with "Separately. In the skies." Carry out the *vivāha homa*. No *pāṇigrahaṇa* and *lājā homa*. Similarly, going around the fire also.

पञ्चदशं खण्डम् (Fifteenth Section)

"अङ्कौ न्यङ्कावभितो रथँ ये ध्वान्ता वाता अग्रमभि ये संपतन्ति । दूरेहेतिः पतत्री वाजीविनाँस्ते नोऽग्नयः पप्रयः पारयन्तु" ॥ इति चक्रमभिमन्त्रयते ॥१॥

They chant the *mantra* addressing the wheels of the chariot: "You who are from the wood of fuels, one who moves around in sacred fires, one who is in the speed of the far travelling winds, one who is static in the grains, please protect all the parts of the chariot."

"सुकिँशुकँ शल्मलिं विश्वरूपँ हिरण्यवर्णँ सुधुरँ सुचक्रम् । आरोह सूर्ये अमृतस्य पन्थाँस्तेन याहि गृहान्स्वस्ति ॥ इत्यारोपयेत् ॥२॥

They make her mount the chariot with the *mantra*, "Bride! mount the chariot which is decorated with *kiṁśuka* and made of *śalmali* and other wood, of beautiful shape, golden coloured, go to your husband's place to make it an immortal and happy household".

"उप मायन्तु देवता उप ब्रह्म सुवीर्यम् । उप क्षत्रं च यद्बलमुप मामैतु यद्बलम्" ॥ इति प्रयास्यन्जपति ॥३॥

"O goddesses, bring me the good potency of the brāhmaṇa, bring me the strength of the kṣatriya." So she chants during the travel.

"अनु मायन्तु देवता अनु ब्रह्म सुवीर्यम् । अनु क्षत्रं च यद्यशमनु मामैतु यद्यशं" ॥ इति प्राञ्चं प्रयाप्य प्रदक्षिणमावृत्य यथार्थलक्षण्यँ वृक्षं चैत्यँ वोपतिष्ठेत ॥४॥

"O goddesses, bring me the good potency of the brāhmaṇa. Bring me the fame of the kṣatriya." She moves towards the east and goes round as per practice and sits.

"नमो रुद्रायैकवृक्षसद" इत्येकवृक्षे जपति । "ये वृक्षेषु शष्पिञ्जरा" इति च ॥५॥

When she sees big trees, she chants, "I worship you Rudra in the trees". "The red like grass of the trees."

"नमो रुद्राय चतुष्पथसद" इति चतुष्पथे । "ये पथां पथिरक्षय" इति च ॥६॥
At crossroads, "I worship you Rudra in the crossroads".

"नमो रुद्राय श्मशानसद" इति श्मशाने । "ये भूतानामधिपतय" इति च ॥७॥
At cemeteries, "I worship you Rudra in the cemeteries".

"नमो रुद्राय पात्रसद" इति पिबन् । "ये अन्नेषु विविध्यन्तीति" च ॥८॥
Taking a sip, she chants "I worship you Rudra in the vessel". "The variety in the cooked rice."

"ये तीर्थानी"ति तीर्थे ॥९॥
"The waters", near water bodies.

यत्रापस्तरितव्या आसीदति — "समुद्राय वयुनाय सिन्धूनां पतये नमः । नदीनाँ सर्वासां पित्वे जुहुता विश्वकर्मणे । विश्वहादाभ्यँ हविः" ॥ इत्यप्सूदकाञ्जलीर्जुहुयात् ॥१०॥
Where they cross rivers — "I worship you the husband of the seas and the moving rivers, I worship Viśvakarmaṇa to whom sacrifices are made, to whom *havis* is offered all over."

यावताँ सखायानँ स्वस्तिमिच्छेत्तावत् उदकाञ्जलीर्जुहुयात् — "अमृतमास्ये जुहोम्यायुः प्राणे परिदधामि । अमृतं ब्रह्मणा सह मृत्युं तरेम । प्रासहादितीष्टरस्यादितिरेव मृत्युन्धय"मिति त्रिराचमेत् ॥११॥
From whom she wishes to have a smooth and good journey, she worships with both hands filled with water. "I worship you with nectar, I worship you with my breath, with *brahma-vidyā* I will cross death. Please take away my fear with Śakti, and grant me release from death." They sip thrice.

द्विः परिमृजेत् ॥१२॥
They should worship twice.

यद्यक्षा शम्याणिर्वा रिष्येत तत्रैवाग्निमुपसमाधायाग्नेयेन स्थालीपाकेनेष्ट्वा जयप्रभृतिभिश्चाज्यस्य पुरस्तात्स्विष्कृतः ॥१३॥
If the wooden pins of the axle get released, they should

make a fire and worship with cooked food, Jayādi *homa*s and later Sviṣṭakṛt *homa*.

अपरस्याह्नः संधिकाले गृहान्प्रपादयेत् ॥१४॥

Let her enter the house of her husband at the beginning of the evening.

रथाध्यौपासनात्संततामुलपराजीँ स्तृणाति ॥१५॥

From the chariot, *ulapa* grass is spread.

तयाभ्युपैति ॥१६॥

He leads her to the house.

"गृहानहँ सुमनसः प्रपद्येऽवीरघ्नी वीरवतः सुशेवा । इराँ वहन्ती घृतमुक्षमाणाँस्तेष्वहँ सुमनाः सँविशामि ॥ इत्यभ्याहिताग्निंसोदकं सौषधमावसथं प्रपध्ये(त) । रेवत्या रोहिण्या यद्वा पुण्योक्तम्" ॥१७॥

I enter the house with a good mind, which is the house of heroes who are well endowed. I bring cooked rice, ghee with which we will reside with a good mind.

आनडुहे चर्मण्युपविश्य ॥१८॥

Let her sit on the bull's hide.

अथास्या ब्रह्मचारिणं जीवपितृकं जीवमातृकमुत्सङ्गमुपवेशयत् ॥१९॥

On her lap place a boy whose parents are alive.

फलानामञ्जलिं पूरयेत्तिलतण्डुलानाँ वा ॥२०॥

Give rice and fruits in his hands.

"अच्युता ध्रुवा ध्रुवपत्नी ध्रुवं पश्येम विश्वत" इति ध्रुवं जीवन्तीँ जयप्रभृतिभिश्चाज्यस्य पुरस्तात्स्विष्टकृत आज्यशेषे दध्यासिच्य "दधिक्राव्णो अकारिषम्" इति दध्नः पुमाँस्त्रिः प्राश्नाति ॥२१॥

You are the steady Dhruvapatnī. Let us all see the Dhruva star. They see Dhruva after Jayādi and Ājya *homa*s and then Sviṣṭakṛt *homa*. Pouring curds in the remnants of *ājya*, a woman with a son says, "I worship Jaṭharāgni who is the Vaiśvānara who churns the curds, who decorates our mouths with Vidyā and long life".

"चक्रमिवानडुहः पदं मामेवान्वेतु ते मनः । मां च पश्यसि सूर्यं च मा चान्येषु मनस्कृथाः ॥ चाक्रावाकं सँवसनं तन्नौ सँवननं कृतम्" ॥ इत्यवशिष्टं जायायै प्रयच्छति ॥२२॥

"Like the wheels of the chariot which follow the footsteps of the bulls, let your mind follow mine. You are looking at me and Sūrya. Do not look at anyone else. Like the *cakravāka* birds become one, let our minds become one." With this he gives the remnants to his wife.

तूष्णीँ सा प्राश्नाति ॥२३॥

She takes it silently.

सँवत्सरं मुदा तौ ब्रह्मचर्यं चरतः । द्वादशरात्रम् त्रिरात्रमेकरात्रँ वा ॥ २४॥

Practise celibacy for one year. Or twelve nights or three nights or one night.

एवमेव चतुर्थ्यां कृत्वा "हिरण्यगर्भ" इत्याष्टाभिः स्थालीपाकस्य हुत्वा जयप्रभृतिभिश्चाज्यस्य पुरस्तात्स्विष्टकृतः ॥२५॥

Observe similarly the *caturthī* with the *mantra*, "Hiraṇyagarbha". And worship with Jayādi and Ājya *homas* followed by Sviṣṭakṛt *homa*.

अथास्याः सव्येऽँसे "पूषा ते ग्रन्थिं ग्रथ्नात्विति वाससो ग्रन्थिं क्रियमानमनुमन्त्रयते ॥२६॥

Now to her left he worships the knot tying her dress with the *mantra*, "Pūṣaṇa your knot, I loosen".

चतस्रोऽविधवाः कुर्वन्ति । ताभ्यो हिरण्यं ददाति ॥२७॥

Four *sumaṅgalīs* will undress her. Gold is given to them.

सँवत्सरं न प्रवसेत् । द्वादशरात्रं त्रिरात्रमेकरात्रँ वा ॥२८॥

Do not travel for one year. Or twelve nights, or three nights, or one night.

Mānava Gṛhya-Sūtra

Mānava Gṛhya-Sūtra belongs to the Maitrāyaṇīya branch of *Kṛṣṇa Yajurveda*. It appears to be closely associated with *Vārāha Gṛhya-Sūtra* and *Kāṭhaka Gṛhya-Sūtra*. Aṣṭāvakra (perhaps a pseudonym) has written a *Bhāṣya* on *Mānava Gṛhya-Sūtra*. It is considered to be a contemporary of *Kāṭhaka Gṛhya-Sūtra*. The following is the text of *Mānava Gṛhya-Sūtra* which deals with *vivāha saṁskara*.

सप्तमः खण्डः (Seventh Chapter)

भार्यां विन्दते ॥३॥
He takes a wife.

कृत्तिका स्वाति पूर्वैरिति वरयेत् ॥४॥
Let him seek a bride under the *nakṣatra*s Kṛttikā, Svāti, Pūrvāphālgunī, Pūrvāṣāḍhā and Pūrvabhādrapada.

रोहिणीमृगशिरः श्रवणश्रविष्ठोत्तराणीत्युमयमे तथोद्वाहे यद्वा पुण्योक्तम् ॥५॥
Under Rohiṇī, Mṛgaśirā, Śravaṇā, Śraviṣṭhā (Dhaniṣṭhā) or the three Uttarā *nakṣatra*s (Phālgunī, Āṣaḍha, Bhādrapada) which are considered auspicious for marriage.

पञ्च विवाहकारकाणि भवन्ति वित्तँ रूपँ विद्या प्रज्ञा बान्धव इति ॥६॥
There are five characterisitics for marriage: wealth, beauty, knowledge, intellect and relationship.

एकालाभे वित्तँ विसृजेद् द्वितीयालाभे रूपं तृतीयालाभे विद्यां प्रज्ञायां बान्धव इति च विवहन्ते ॥७॥
If one has to be given up, let him leave wealth, if two let him leave beauty, if three let him leave out knowledge. There is a dispute about intellect and relationship.

बन्धुमतीं कन्यामस्पृष्टमैथुना मुपयच्छेत समानवर्णामसमानप्रवराँ यवीयसीं नाग्निकाँ श्रेष्ठाम् ॥८॥
He should marry a girl of a good family, who is a virgin, who belongs to the same caste, who is not of the same *gotra*, who is yet to reach puberty.

विज्ञानमस्याः कुर्यादष्टौ लोष्ठानाहरेत्सीता — लोष्ठ वेदिलोष्ठं दूर्वालोष्ठं गोमयलोष्ठं फलवतो वृक्षस्याधस्ताल्लोष्ठं श्मशानलोष्ठ मध्वलोष्ठमिरीणलोष्ठमिति ॥९॥

To know (test) her: He should take eight clods of earth, from a ploughed field, from an altar, from a *darbha* grass field, from cow dung, from below a fruit-bearing tree, from a cemetery, from a road and from saline soil.

देवागारे स्थापयित्वाथ कन्यां ग्राहयेत् यदि श्मशानलोष्टं गृह्णीयादध्वलोष्ठमिरीणलोष्टँ वा नो पयमेत् ॥१०॥
Having put them in a temple, he makes her pick one of them. If the clod taken is from the cemetery, road or the saline soil, he should not marry her.

संजुष्टां धर्मेणपयच्छेत ब्राह्मेण श्लोकेन वा ॥११॥
If approved, he should marry her as per *brāhma vivāha* with *śloka*s.

शतमिति रथं दद्याद् गोमिथुनँ वा ॥१२॥
He should give her 100 cows or a couple of bulls and cow.

अष्टमः खण्डः (Eighth Section)

पश्चादग्नेश्चत्वार्यासनान्युपकल्पयीत ॥१॥
To the west of the fire arrange four seats.

तेषूपविशन्ति पुरस्तात्प्रत्यङ्मुखो दाता पश्चात्प्राङ्मुखः प्रतिग्रहीता दातुरुत्तरतः प्रत्यङ्मुखी कन्या दक्षिणत उदङ्मुखो मन्त्रकारः ॥२॥
On these they sit down: On the eastern side with his face to the west, the giver (father of the bride); on the western side with his face to the east, the receiver (bridegroom); to the north of the giver with her face to the west, the bride; to the south with his face to the north, the *purohita*.

तेषां मध्ये प्राक्तूलान्दर्भानास्तीर्य काँस्यमक्षतोदकेन पूरयित्वा अविधवास्मै प्रयच्छति ॥३॥
Having strewn *darbha* grass with their ends pointing east in the middle, having filled a brass vessel filled with *akṣata* water, a *sumaṅgalī* gives the vessel to the groom.

तत्र हिरण्यम् ॥४॥
In that gold pieces are kept.

अष्टौ मङ्गल्यान्यावेदयति ॥५॥
He announces eight auspicious things.

मङ्गल्यान्युक्त्वा ददामि प्रतीगृह्णामिति त्रिब्रह्मदेया पिता भ्राता वा दद्यात् ॥६॥
When the auspicious things have been announced, the father or the brother of the bride should give her away, if she marries according to the Brāhma form of marriage, saying the words "I give" thrice and the receiver accepts with the words "I accept" thrice.

सहिरण्यानञ्जलीनावपति धनाय त्वेतिदाता पुत्रेभ्यस्त्वेति प्रतिग्रहीता तस्मै प्रत्यावपति ॥७॥
The giver gives handful of gold pieces with the words "for the sake of wealth" and the receiver gives them back with the words "for the sake of children".

चतुर्व्यतिहृत्य ददाति ॥८॥
Having repeated four times, he gives her away.

सावित्रेण कन्यां प्रतिगृह्य प्रजापतय इति च "क इदं कस्म अदादिति सर्वत्रानुषजति कामैतत्त" इत्यन्तम् ॥९॥
After having accepted the girl with the Sāvitra verse, he says: To Prajāpati, etc. "Who has given this to whom? Love has given it to love. Love is the giver and love is the receiver." For love, I accept you.

समाना वा आकूतानीति राह जपन्त्यान्तदनुवाकस्य ॥१०॥
"Let our designs be the same, hearts be the same, minds be the same" so he worships ending with an *anuvāka*.

खे रथस्य खे नसः खे युगस्य शतक्रतो अपालामिन्द्रस्त्रिः पूर्त्यवकृणोत्सूर्यत्वच मिति तेनोदकाँस्येन कन्यामभिषिञ्चेत् ॥११॥
"In the hole of the chariot, in the hole of the cart, in the hole of the yoke, O you with hundred powers, you who made after having cleansed her thrice, Apālā's skin as bright as the sun", he sprinkles water from the vessel on her.

नवमः खण्डः (Ninth Section)

षडर्घ्यार्हा भवन्त्यृत्विगाचार्यो विवाह्यो राजा स्नातकः प्रियश्चेति ॥१॥

There are six persons worthy of *arghya* reception: a priest officiating, a teacher, a person related by marriage, a king, a *snātaka* and a friend.

अप्राकरणिकान्वा परिसंवत्सरादर्हयन्ति ॥२॥

They do not honour those who are not connected with the subject, before a year has elapsed.

प्राकरणिकाः कर्त्तारः सदस्याश्च वृताः ॥३॥

Persons, connected with the subject, who are honoured more than once a year, are the priests and *sadasya*s who are invited.

न जीवत्पितृकोऽर्घ्यं प्रतिगृह्णीयादितिश्रुतिरथवा प्रतिगृह्णियात् ॥४॥

According to Śruti, those whose fathers are living should not receive an *arghya* reception. Or should receive, according to my opinion.

अथैनमर्हयन्ति ॥५॥

Then they give them (those worthy), the reception.

काँस्ये चमसे वा दधि मधु चानीय वर्षीयसा पिधायाचमनीयप्रथमै प्रतिपद्यन्ते ॥६॥

In a brass cup a mixture of curds and honey is made, covered with a lid and after sipping water, they come near.

"विराजो दोहोसि विराजो दोहमशीय मयि दोहः पद्यायै विराजः कल्पतामित्येकैक" माह्नियमाणं पर्तीक्षते ॥७॥

"O water! You are the essential sweetness of the elemental liquid born of Cosmic Infinitude. Pray grant me the same delicious beauty and embellish my feet with loveliness by washing them clean."

सावित्रेन विष्टरं प्रतिगृह्य "अहं वर्ष्म सदृशानामुद्यतामिव सूर्यः । इदं तमभितिष्ठामि यो मा कश्चाभिदासतिति" जपति ॥८॥

Having received the spread grass with the Sāvitra-verse, he murmurs the *mantra*: "I am the highest among my peers as the sun is among the stars. Here I step upon him, whosoever harasses me."

राष्ट्रभृदसीत्याचार्य आसन्दीमनुमन्त्रयते ॥९॥
A giver of royal power are you, the seat of an *ācārya*.

मा त्वा दोष इत्यधस्तास्पादयोर्विष्टरमुपकर्षति ॥१०॥
May I not withdraw from you, he puts under his feet another layer of grass.

विष्टर आसीनायै कैकं त्रिः प्राह ॥११॥
While he is sitting on the grass, the host announces to him every requisite thrice.

नैव भो इत्याह नम आर्षेयायेति श्रुतिः स्पृशत्यर्घ्यम् ॥१२॥
He does not greet the guest with Bho but says, "Hail to the venerable One" according to Śruti and then he touches the *arghya* water.

पाद्येन पादौ प्रक्षाल्य सावित्रेण मधुपर्कं प्रतिगृह्य प्रतिष्ठाप्यावसाय्य "नमो रुद्राय पात्रसदे नमो रुद्राय पात्रसद" इति प्रादेशेनाध्यधि प्रतिदिशं प्रदक्षिणं सर्वतोऽभ्युद्दिशति ॥१३॥
Having washed his feet with *pādya* water, having accepted *madhuparka* with the Sāvitra-verse, having put it down and having uncovered it, he points upwards, at each quarter, in every direction, from east to west, with the words: "Hail to Rudra who resides in the vessel! Hail to Rudra who resides in the vessel!"

"मधुवाता ऋतायत" इति तिसृभिरङ्गुल्या प्रदक्षिणं प्रत्यृचं त्रिरायौति ॥१४॥
With his fingers he stirs the *madhuparka* thrice with each verse, "for the righteous, the winds blow sweetness".

अमृतोपस्तरणामसीत्युपस्तरति ॥१५॥
"You are the layer of nectar" and he spreads it (*madhuparka*).

"सत्यं यशः श्रीर्मयि श्रीः श्रयतामिति" मधुपर्कं त्रिः प्राश्नाति ॥१६॥
With the verse, "truth, glory and wealth may rest on me", he eats thrice from *madhuparka*.

अमृतापिधानमसीत्याचामति ॥१७॥
With "you are the covering for nectar", he sips water.

सुहृदेऽवशिष्टं प्रयच्छति ॥१८॥
He gives the remainder to a friend.

असि पाणिर्गां प्राह ॥१९॥
Keeping a hand on the sword, he announces a cow to the guest.

"हतो मे पाप्मा पाप्मानं मे हत ॐ कुरुत" इति प्रेष्यति ॥२०॥
"Destroyed is my sin; destroy my sin; *Oṁ*! Slaughter it" he summons the butcher.

चतुरो ब्राह्मणान्नानागोत्रान् भोजयते ॥२१॥
Feed four brāhmaṇas of different *gotras*.

पश्वङ्गं पायसं वा कारयेन्नामांसो मधुपर्क इति श्रुतिः ॥२२॥
Part of the cow's flesh (*khīra*): Śruti says: Let the *madhuparka* not be without meat.

यद्युत्सृजेन्माता रुद्राणां दुहिता वसूनां स्वसादित्यानाममृतस्य नाभिः । प्रनुवोचं चिकितुषे जनाय मागा मनगा मदितिं वधिष्ट । भूर्भुवः स्वरोमुत्सृजतु तृणान्यत्तु ॥२३॥
When he lets the cow loose, he should do so with the verse, "The mother of Rudras, the daughter of Vasus, the sister of Ādityas, the navel of immortality, in the midst of people who understand me, I shall say, Do not kill the innocent cow, which is Aditi. *Bhūr, bhuvḥ, svah*! *Oṁ*! Let it loose, let it eat grass".

अथालंकरणमलंकरणमसि सर्वस्मा अलं मे भूयासम् ॥२४॥
Now she puts on a garment with the words, "You are an ornament: May I be adequate for everyone".

प्राणापानौ मे तर्पय समान व्यानौ मे तर्पय उदानरूपे मे तर्पय सुचक्षा अह मक्षिभ्यां भूयासं सुवर्चा मुखेन सुश्रुत्कर्णाभ्यां भूयासमिति यथालिङ्गमङ्गानि सँस्पृशति ॥२५॥

With the verses, "satiate my *prāṇa* and *apāna*, satiate my *samāna* and *vyāna*, satiate my *udāna* and beauty; may I come to see well with my eyes; may I become splendid of face; may I hear well with my ears", she touches respective parts of her body.

अथ गन्धोत्सदने वाससी ॥२६॥
Now the scented dresses are readied.

परिधास्ये यशो धास्ये दीर्घायुत्वाय जरदष्टिरस्तु शतं जीवमेशरदः पुरूची रायस्पोषमभिसँव्ययिष्ये यशसा माऽद्यावा पृथिवी यशसेन्द्रा बृहस्पती यशो भगश्च मारिषद्यशो मा प्रति मुच्यताम् इत्यहतँ वासः परिधत्ते ॥२७॥
With the verses, "I shall put on glory, I shall wear this for long life; may I attain old age, may we live to see hundred autumns; I shall wrap myself up in increasing wealth; with glory to me, heaven and earth, Indra and Bṛhaspati; may glory and good fortune not be lost to me, may glory not be lost", she puts on the garment.

कुमार्याः प्रमदने भगमर्यमणं पूषणं त्वष्टारमिति यजति ॥२८॥
With the regard to the pleasure spots of the bride, he offers oblations to Bhaga, Aryamā, Pūṣaṇa and Tvaṣṭā.

प्राक्स्विष्टकृतश्चतस्रो अविधवा नन्दीरुपवादयन्ति ॥२९॥
Before the Sviṣṭakṛt *homa*, four *sumaṅgalī*s sing Nandī songs.

अभ्यन्तरे कौतुके देवपत्नीर्जयति ॥३०॥
In the interior of *kautuka* (dressing room), he offers oblations to the wives of gods.

दशमः खण्डः (Tenth Section)

प्रागुदञ्चं लक्षणमुद्धृत्यावोक्ष्य स्थण्डिलं गोमयेनोपलिप्य मण्डलम चतुरस्त्रं वा अग्निं निर्मथ्याभिमुखं प्रणयेत् तत्र ब्रह्मोपवेशनम् ॥१॥
Having made a mark by drawing lines in the north-eastern direction and having sprinkled water and smeared the square or round *sthaṇḍila* with cow dung and having kindled the fire by attrition, he carries the fire towards it.

दर्भाणां पवित्रे मन्त्रवदुत्पाद्येमँस्तोम मर्हत इत्याग्निं परिसमुह्य पर्युक्ष्य परिस्तीर्य पश्चादग्नेरेकवद्बार्हिःस्तृणाति ॥२॥

Having prepared two blades of *darbha* grass as per the verse, having swept the fire together with the verse, "*Oṁ*! Jātaveda deserving this praise", having sprinkled with water and having strewn *darbha* grass around it, he spreads a single layer of *darbha* grass to the west of the fire.

उदक् प्राक् तूलान्दर्भान्प्रकृष्य दक्षिणांस्तथोत्तरानग्रेणाग्निं दक्षिणैरुत्तरानवस्तृणाति ॥३॥

Having pulled some grass from the southern and northern ends of which the ends are turned partly to the north and partly to the east, he strews them to the east of the fire, the southern ones upon the northern ones.

दक्षिणतोऽग्नेर्ब्रह्मणे सँस्तृणात्यपरँ यजमानाय पश्चार्द्धे पत्न्यै अपरमपरँशाखोदकधारयोर्लाजा धार्याश्च पश्चाद्युगधारस्य च ॥४॥

To the south he strews a layer of grass for the brāhmaṇa, and another one for *yajamāna*, to the west for the wife, separate ones for the branch bearer, water carrier and the woman carrying the fried grains and to the west he strews one for the yoke bearer.

स्योना पृथिवी भवेत्येतवस्थाप्य शमीमयीः शम्याः कृत्वान्त-र्गोष्ठेऽग्निमुपसमाधाय भर्त्ता भार्यामभ्युदानयति ॥५॥

Having installed them with the verse: "Be kind, O earth, etc." having prepared *paridhis* of *śamī* wood, having kindled a fire in the cowshed, the groom leads the bride to the fire.

वाससोन्ते गृहीत्वा — "अघोर चक्षुरपतिघ्न्येधि शिवा पशुभ्यः सुमनाः सुवर्चाः वीरसूर्देवकामा स्योना शं नो भव द्विपदे शं चतुस्पदे" इत्यभिपरिगृह्याभ्युदानयति ॥६॥

Having seized the rim of garment while embracing her, he pronounces, "Be not of evil eye, nor bringing death to your husband, but bring luck to the cattle, be kindly disposed and full of splendour: give birth to heroes, love to the gods, be friendly, bring luck to our two-footed ones and four-footed ones". He leads her to the fire.

उत्तरेण रथँ वाऽनो वानुपरिक्रम्यान्तरेण ज्वलनवहनावतिक्रम्य दक्षिणस्यां धुर्युत्तरस्य युगतन्मनोऽधस्तात्कन्यामवस्थाप्य शम्यामुत्कृष्य हिरण्यमन्तर्धाय हिरण्यवर्णाः शुचय इति तिसृभिरद्भिरभिषिच्य अत्रैव बाणशब्दं कुरुतेति प्रेष्यति ॥७॥

Having gone round a chariot or a cart placed to the north of the fire, they go between the fire and the chariot/cart; having placed the bride under the left yoke-hole in the right pole, he pulls out the pin, puts a piece of gold therein and sprinkles water on her through the hole with the verse, "Gold-coloured, pure, etc. and the two following". Then he summons the players, makes the sound of lutes resound.

अथास्यै वासः प्रयच्छति — "या अकृन्तन्या अतन्वन्या अवाहरन् याश्चाग्नादेव्योऽन्तानभितोऽततनन्त । तास्त्वादेव्यो जरसे सँव्ययन्त्वायुष्मतीदं परिधत्स्व वासः" — इत्युहतँ वासः परिधाप्यान्वारभ्याघारावाज्यभागौ हुत्वा "अग्नये जनविदे स्वाहेत्युत्तरार्धे जुहोति सोमाय जनविदे स्वाहेति दक्षिणार्द्धे गन्धर्वाय जनविदे स्वाहेति" मध्ये ॥८॥

Then he gives her a garment. Having made her put this new garment with the verse: "The divine women, who spun, who spread, who wove, who drew out on both sides the ends of the garment, may these goddesses wrap you up into old age; blessed with life put on this garment, having grasped her from behind, having offered the two *āghāra*s and the two *ājyabhāga*s, he offers an oblation with the words: "To the knower of Agni, *svāhā*!, In the southern part with the words: to the knower of Soma, *svāhā*! And in the middle of the fire with the words: to the knower of *gandharva*, *svāhā*!"

युक्तो वह यदाकूतमिति द्वाभ्यामग्निँयोजयित्वा नक्षत्रमिष्ट्वा नक्षत्रदेवताँयजेत्तिथिं तिथिदेवतामृतुमृतुदेवतां च ॥९॥

Having stirred up the fire with the verse, "to whom we have set to work, Jātavedas, take away our oblations; know this as it is being done here; your are a healer, a protector of medicines; may we obtain by you, cows, horses and men, *svāhā*!" and the verse, "what purpose, etc.", he offers oblations to the *nakṣatra* and the deity of *nakṣatra*, to the *tithi* and the deity of *tithi*, to the season and the deity of the season.

सोमोददद्गन्धर्वाय गन्धर्वो दददग्नये । रयिं च पुत्रांश्चादादग्निर्मह्यमथो इमाम् अग्निरस्याः प्रथमो जातवेदाः सोऽस्याः प्रजा मुञ्चतु मृत्युपाशात् । तदिदं राजा वरुणोऽनुमन्यताम् । यथेदँस्त्रीपौत्रमगन्म रुद्रियाय स्वाहा — इति हिरण्यगर्भ इत्यष्टाभिः प्रत्यृचमाज्याहुतीर्जुहुयात् ॥१०॥

"Soma has given you to *gandharva* and *gandharva* to Agni. Agni has given to me wealth and sons and this woman. May Agni, the first of gods, Jātavedas, release this woman's children from the fetters of death. May King Varuṇa grant that now this woman shall not face distress through her sons, *svāhā*!" — and with eight verses "The golden womb etc.".

येन च कर्मणेच्छेत्तत्र च जयान् जुहुयात् जयानां च श्रुतिस्ताँयथोक्ताम् । आकूत्यै त्वा स्वाहा, भूत्यै त्वा स्वाहा, प्रयुजे त्वा स्वाहा, नभसे त्वा स्वाहा, अर्यम्णे त्वा स्वाहा, समृध्यै त्वा स्वाहा, जयायै त्वा स्वाहा, कामाय त्वा स्वाहेत्यृचा स्तोमं प्रजापतय इति च ॥११॥

At each sacrifice whereat he wishes to obtain success, he should make oblations with the Jayā — formulae. So it is said of Jayā *homa* in Śruti. For intentions, *svāhā*! For the sake of prosperity, *svāhā*! For the sake of acquisition, *svāhā*! For the sake of sky, *svāhā*! For Aryamā, *svāhā*! For the sake of welfare, *svāhā*! For victory, *svāhā*! For desire, *svāhā*! By the Ṛk, by praise for Prajāpati!

शुचिः प्रत्युङ्ङुपयन्ता ताँसमीक्षस्वेत्याह ॥१२॥

With a pure mind, he turns towards her and says to her: "behold me".

तस्याँ व्रते ते हृदयं दधातु मम चित्तमनुचितं तेऽस्तु मम वाचमेकमना जुषस्व प्रजापतिष्ट्वा नियुनक्तुमह्याम् — इति ॥१३॥

While looking at her, he chants: "May he place your heart in mine, may your will follow my will, may you rejoice in my words, with your whole world, may Prajāpati join you to me."

का नामासीत्याह ॥१४॥

He asks her: "What is your name?"

नामधेये प्रोक्ते देवस्य त्वा सवितुः प्रसवेऽश्विनोर्बाहुभ्यां पूष्णो हस्ताभ्याँहस्तं गृह्णाम्यसाविति हस्तं गृह्णन्नाम गृह्णाति । प्राङ्मुख्याः प्रात्यङ्मुख ऊर्ध्वस्तिष्ठन्नासीनाय दक्षिण मुत्तानं दक्षिणेन नीचारिक्त मरिक्तेन — यथोन्द्रोहस्तमग्रहित् सविता वरुणो भगः । गृभ्णामि ते सौभगत्वाय हस्तं मया पत्या जरदृष्टिर्यथा सत् । भगो अर्यमा सविता पुरन्धि र्मह्यं त्वादुर्गार्हपत्याय देवाः । याग्रे वाक् समवदत पुरा देवासुरेभ्यः । तामद्य गाथां गास्यामो या स्त्रीणामुत्तमं मनः । सरस्वति प्रेदमव सुभगे वाजिनीवति यां त्वा विश्वस्य भुतस्य भव्यस्य प्रगायाम्यस्याग्रतः । अमोह मस्मि सा त्वं सा त्वमस्यप्यमोहम् ॥ द्योरहं पृथिवी त्वमृक् त्वमसि सामाऽहम् रेतोह मस्मि रेतो धत्तम् ॥ ता एव विवाहवहै पुँसे पुत्राय कर्त्तवै । श्रीये पुत्राय वेधवै ॥ रायस्पोषाय सुप्रजस्त्वाय सुवीर्याय ॥ इति॥१५॥

After she has said her name, he pronounces her name, while seizing her hand with the verse: "By the impulse of God Savitṛ, with the arms of the two Aśvins, with Pūṣaṇa's hands, I seize your hand" (her name) while her face is turned eastward and his westward, while he is standing upright and she is sitting, her right hand upwards and his downwards, her hand which is not empty, with his hand which is not empty. After seizing her hand he chants: "In the same manner in which Indra, Savitṛ, Varuṇa and Bhaga have seized her hand, I seize your hand for the sake of happiness, in order that you may live to old age with me your husband; Bhaga, Aryamā, Savitṛ and Puraṁdhi, the gods have given you to me for making me a householder." "The words which were sung in olden times for gods and *asura*s, that song we shall sing today, sung about the highest glory of women — Sarasvatī, promote this (our undertaking), O gracious one, you who are rich in horses, you whose praise we sing first of all, that is and will be — This I am (God), that (Goddess) are you: that are you, this I am, heaven am I, earth are you, Ṛk are you, the song am I, sperm am I, sperm bearer you are; come, let us marry for begetting sons, for the sake of wealth, beauty, many children who will be heroic."

अभिदक्षिणमानीयाग्नेः पश्चात् — एतमश्मानमातिष्ठतमश्वेव युवां स्थिरौ भवतम् कृण्वन्तु विश्वे देवा आयुर्वां शरदः शतम् । इति दक्षीणाभ्याम् पभ्द्यामश्मानमास्थापयति ॥१६॥

After going round the fire, he makes them both step onto a stone with their right feet with the verse: "Come step you both on this stone; be firm like a stone; may Viśvadevas make you both live to see hundred autumns."

यथेन्द्रः सहेन्द्राण्या अवारुहद् गन्धमादनात् । एवं त्वमस्मादश्मनो अवरोह सह पत्न्या ॥१७॥
With the verse: "In the same way that Indra together with Indrāṇī descended from the Gandhamādana, likewise you must descend from this stone together with your wife."

आरोहस्व समे पादौ प्र पूर्व्यायुष्मती कन्ये पुत्रवती भव । इत्येवं द्विरास्थापयति ॥१८॥
"Mount together so that she will have long life with children." They are made to mount the stone twice.

चतुः परिणयति ॥१९॥
He leads them round the fire four times.

समितं संकल्पेथामिति पर्याये ब्रह्मा ब्रह्मजपं जपेत् ॥२०॥
At each *pradakṣiṇā*, the brāhmaṇa murmurs the *brahmajapam*: "Be united, be one, be friendly to each other, radiant, with kindly thoughts, clothing yourselves in food and strength."

एकादशः खण्डः (Eleventh Section)

ततो यथार्थं कर्मसन्निपातो विज्ञेयः ॥१॥
Now the purpose of combination of actions is explained.

अर्यम्णेऽग्नये पूष्णेऽग्नये वरुणाय च व्रीहीन् यवान्वाऽभिनिरूप्य प्रोक्ष्य लाजा भृज्जति ॥२॥
Having offered rice or barley corn to Aryamā, Agni, Pūṣaṇa and Varuṇa, he prepares fried grains.

मात्रे प्रयच्छति स जाताया अविधवायै ॥३॥
He gives them to the mother of the bride or a woman relative who is a *sumaṅgalī*.

अथास्यै द्वितीयं वासः प्रयच्छति तेनैव मन्त्रेण ॥४॥

He gives her another garment with the same *mantra*.

दर्भरज्वा इन्द्राण्याः संनहनमित्यन्तौ समायम्य पुमाँसं ग्रन्थिं बध्नाति ॥५॥
Having drawn together the ends with a rope of *darbha* grass with the words, "the cord of Indrāṇī", he ties a male knot.

"सं त्वा नह्यामि पयसा पृथिव्याः संत्वा नह्याम्यद्भिरोषधीभिः । सं त्वा नह्यामि प्रजया धनेन सा सन्नद्धा सुनुहि भगधेयम् ॥" इत्यन्तरतो वस्त्रस्य योक्त्रेण कन्यां संनह्यते ॥६॥
With the verse, "I gird you with the milk of the earth, I gird you with water and herbs, I gird you with offspring and wealth; may you, being girded acquire prosperity and wealth", he girds her with a yoke-rope under the upper garment.

अथैनान्युपकल्पयते शूर्पं लाजा इषीका अश्मान माञ्जनम् ॥७॥
He then prepares the following: Winnowing basket, fried grains, blades of grass, a stone and an eye-shadow.

चतसृभिर्दर्भेषीकाभिः शरेषीकाभिर्वा समुञ्जाभिः सतूलाभिरित्येकैकया त्रैककुभस्याञ्जनस्य संनिकृष्य वृत्रस्यासि कनीनिकेति भर्त्तुर्दक्षिणमक्षि त्रिः प्रथम माङ्क्ते तथा परं तथा पत्न्याः शेषेण तूष्णीम् ॥८॥
Having taken portions of the eye-shadow, which comes from the mountain of Trikakubha and four blades of *darbha* grass or four reed stalks which are provided with *muñja* grass and with their panicles, once with each of them with the words, "*vrata*'s eye pupil you are" the *purohit* first anoints the right eye of the bridegroom thrice and then the other eye; then with the remainder the eyes of the bride in silence.

दिशि शलाकाः प्रविध्यति "यानिरक्षाँस्यभितो व्रजन्त्यस्या वध्वा अग्निसकाश मागच्छन्त्याः तेषामहं प्रतिविध्यामि चक्षुः स्वस्ति वध्वै भूतपतिर्दधातु" ॥ इति ॥९॥

He thrusts pieces of wood in all directions with the verse: "The demons who wander on all sides towards this woman who is approaching the fire, of them I pierce their eyes; may the lord of the earth grant prosperity to this woman."

लाजाः पश्चादग्नेरुपसाद्यशमीपर्णैः सँयुज्य शूर्पे समं चतुर्धा विभज्याग्रेणाग्निं पर्याहृत्य लाजाधार्यै प्रयच्छति ॥१०॥

Having placed the grain to the west of the fire, having mixed it with *śamī* leaves, having divided it in the winnowing basket into four equal parts, and having to the east of the fire handed over the winnowing basket, he gives it back to the *lājādhārī*.

लाजा भ्राता ब्रह्मचारी वाञ्जलिनाञ्जल्योरावपति ॥११॥

The bride's brother or a *brahmacārī* scatters the grain with his two hands joined together into their hands.

उपस्तरणाभिघारणैः संपातं ता अविच्छिन्नैर्जुहुतः । अर्यमणं नु देवं कन्या अग्निमयक्षत सोस्मान्देवोऽर्यमा प्रेतो मुञ्चातु मामुतः स्वाहा ॥ तुभ्यमग्रे पर्यवहन्त्सूर्यां वहतुना सह । पुनः पतिभ्यो जायां दा अग्नेः प्रजया सह ॥ पुनः पत्नी मग्निरदादायुषा सह वर्चसा । दीर्घायुरस्या यः पतिर्जीवाति शरदः शतम् ॥ इयं नार्युपब्रूतेऽनौलाजावपन्तिका । दीर्घायुरस्तु मे पतिरेधन्तां ज्ञातयो ममेति ॥१२॥

They offer the residue of the spreadings and the pouring together without opening their hands with the verses — To God Aryamā the girls have sacrificed and to Agni; may he God Aryamā set us free from here (father's house) but not from there (husband's house), *svāhā*! For you in the beginning they have carried round Sūrya in the bridal procession: may you give back, Agni, to the husbands their wives together with offspring — Agni has given back the wife with long life and splendour; he who is her husband, may he live a long lifetime, a hundred autumns; this woman who is strewing fried grains into the fire prays thus; may my husband live a long time; may my relationship be prosperous.

एवं पूषाणं नु देवं वरुणं नु देवम् ॥१३॥

Similarly, she offers to God Pūṣaṇa and God Varuṇa.

येन द्यौ रुग्रेत्यादय उद्वाहे होमा जयाभ्यातानाः संततिहोमा राष्ट्रभृतश्च ॥१४॥

At the Udvāha *homa*, oblations should be made with the

verses, "by whom the dreaded earth". And with the Jayā, Abhyātāna, Santati and Rāṣṭrabhṛt *mantras*.

आकूताय स्वाहेति जयाः प्राची दिग्वसन्त ऋतुरित्यभ्यातानाः । प्राणादपानँ संतन्विति संततहोमा ऋता षाड्ऋतधामेति द्वादशराष्ट्रभृतश्च ॥ १५॥
Jayā *homa* begins with, "to intuition, *svāhā*!"; Abhyātāna begins with, "the eastern quarter! spring! season!; Santati *homa* with, "may you out of *prāṇa* with *apāna*"; Rāṣṭrabhṛt with, "Supporting Ṛta, he whose law is truth!"

त्रातारमिन्द्रँ विश्वादित्या इति माङ्गल्ये ॥१६॥
With *māṅgalya* verses, offers are made to Indra, the protector, and all the Ādityas.

लाजाः कामे न चतुर्थँ स्विष्टकृतमिति ॥१७॥
She offers a fourth oblation to Sviṣṭakṛt with Kāma.

अथैनां प्राचीँ सप्तपदानि प्रक्रमयत्येकमिषे द्वे ऊर्जे त्रीणि प्रजाभ्यश्चत्वारि रायस्पोषाय पञ्च भवाय षड्तुभ्यः — सखा सप्तदीभव सुमृडीका सरस्वती । सा ते व्योम संदृशी । विष्णुस्त्वा मुन्नयत्विति सर्वत्रानुषजति ॥१८॥
Then he makes her take seven steps in the eastern direction, "First step for sap, second for energy, third for offspring, fourth for prosperity, fifth for welfare, sixth for the seasons, the seventh step to be a friend. Be very gracious Sarasvatī! May we not be removed from your sight." With each step, he subjoins the words, "let Viṣṇu lead you".

पश्चादग्ने रोहिते चर्मण्यानडुहे प्रागग्रीवे लोमतो दर्भानास्तीर्य तेषु वधूमुपवेशयत्यपि वा दर्भेष्वेव ॥१९॥
He makes the bride sit to the west of the fire on a red bull skin with its neck eastward, with the hairs on top after spreading *darbha* grass on it.

इमँ विष्यामि वरुणस्य पाशँ यज्जग्रन्थ सविता सत्यधर्मा । धातुश्च योनौ सुकृतस्य लोके रिष्टां मा सह पत्या दधातु" ॥ इति योक्त्रपाशँ विषाय वाससोऽन्ते बध्नाति ॥२०॥
With the verse: "I loosen this knot of Varuṇa, which Savitṛ whose ordinances are true, has fastened. In the lap of Dhātṛ,

in the world of good deeds, unhurt with my husband may he place me", she loosens the yoke rope and binds it again on the inside of her upper garment.

अ नुमतिभ्याँ व्याहृतिभिश्च त्वन्नो अग्ने, स त्वन्नो अग्ने, अयाश्चाग्नेसीति च ॥२१॥

He offers oblations with the Anumatī verses and *vyāhṛtis*, "Let Anumatī today approve our offering among the gods and also Agni, the oblation bearer".

शमीमयीस्तिस्त्रोऽक्ताः समिधः समुद्रादूर्मिरित्येताभिस्तिसृभिः स्वाहाकारान्ताभिरादधाति ॥२२॥

He puts three sticks of *śamī* wood on the fire smeared with ghee with the three verses, "From the ocean the sweet wave has arisen" ending with *svāhā*!

अक्षत सक्तूनां दध्नश्च समवदयेदँ हविः प्रजननं म इति च हुत्वा वि ते मुञ्चामि रशनाँ वे रश्मीनिति च हुत्वा पवित्रे नु प्रहृत्याज्येनाभिजुहोति ॥२३॥

After having taken portions of *akṣata* and curds and offered them with the verses, "this oblation may it be bringing forth for me", he says, "I loosen your strap, your ropes and your harness".

एधोऽस्येधिषीमहीति समिधमादधाति । समिदसि समेधिषीमहीति द्वितीभ्याम् ॥२४॥

He puts one fuel stick on the fire with the words, "you are prosperity, may we prosper" and a second one with the words, "you are a fuel-stick, may we prosper with you".

कुम्भादुदकेनापोहिष्ठीयाभिर्मार्जयन्ते ॥२५॥

With water from the vessel, they cleanse themselves with the verses, "you are waters".

वरो दक्षिणा ॥२६॥

The priest is given suitable fee.

द्वादशः खण्डः (Twelfth Section)

सुमङ्गलीरियँ वधूरिमां समेत पश्यतः । सौभाग्यमस्यै दत्वायाथास्त्वं विपरेतन ॥ इति प्रेक्षकान्व्रजातोऽनुमन्त्रयते ॥१॥

He addresses the on-lookers before they go home, with the verse: "This woman wears auspicious ornaments; come up to her and look at her; having brought luck to her, go back to your houses."

अत्रैव सीमन्तं करोति त्रीश्येतया शलल्या समूलेन वा दर्भेण सेनाहनामेत्येतया ॥२॥

Then he performs the *sīmanta* ceremony of parting of the hair with a white porcupine quill having three white spots or with a *darbha* stalk together with the root with the verse, "Sena is your name".

अथाभ्यञ्जन्ति — अभ्यज्य केशान् सुमनस्यमानाः प्रजावरीर्यशसे बहुपुत्रा अघोराः । शिवा भर्त्तुः श्वशुरस्यावदायायुष्मतीः श्वश्रूमतीश्चिरायुः ॥ इति ॥३॥

Then they anoint her hair with the verse, "having anointed their hair, being kind, having children, for the sake of splendour, having many sons, not having evil eye, being kind to their husbands, their in-laws, living a long life".

जीवोर्णयोपसमस्यति — समस्य केशानवृजिनानघोरान् शिखा सखिभ्यो भव सर्वाभ्यः । शिवा भव सुकुलोह्यमाना शिवा जनेषु सहवाहनेषु ॥ इति ॥४॥

He ties her hair with wool from a living animal with the verse: "Having tied your hair which is not deceitful or of evil eye, be kind to all your *sakhīs*; be kind, you who are of good family, now that you are married, be kind among living beings and when you are in the vehicles."

अथैनौ दधिमधु समश्नुतो यद्वा हविष्यँ स्यात् ॥५॥

Then they take curds and honey or food which is fit for sacrifice.

तस्य स्वस्ति वाचयित्वा समाना वा आकूतानीति सह जपन्ति ॥६॥

Having got Svasti recited, they murmur, "united are your wills".

उभौ सह प्राश्नीतः ॥७॥
The two of them eat together.

त्रयोदशः खण्डः (Thirteenth Section)

पुण्याहे युङ्क्ते ॥१॥
On an auspicious day, he harnesses the horses.

युञ्जन्ति ब्रध्नमिति द्वाभ्याँ युज्जमानमनुमन्त्रयते दक्षिणमथोत्तरम् ॥२॥
With the two verses, "they harness the horses with the *mantras* first to the right horse and second to the left one".

अहतेन वाससा दर्भैर्वा रथँ संमार्ष्टि ॥३॥
With a new cloth or *darbha* grass, he cleans the chariot.

अङ्कून्यङ्कवभितो रथँ ये ध्वान्ता वाता अग्निमभिये संचरन्ति दूरे हेतिः पतत्री वाविनी वाँस्ते नोऽग्नयः पप्रयः पालयन्तु इति चक्रे अभिमन्त्रयते ॥ ४॥
With the verse, "the two curves, the two bows on both sides of the chariot, which move forward along the rushing wind, the far darting one, the winged one, which drives swift mares, may these fires, the protectors protect us", he addresses the wheels of the chariot.

वनस्पते विड्वङ्ग इत्याधिष्ठानम् ॥५॥
With the verse "O tree, be strong of limb, etc.", he addresses the seat of the chariot.

सुकिँशुकँ शल्मलिँ विश्वरूपँ हिरण्यवर्णँ सुवृतँ सुचक्रम् आरोह सूर्ये अमृतस्य लोकँ स्योनं पत्ये वहतं कृणुष्व ॥ इत्यारोहयति ॥६॥
With the verse, "well adorned with *kiṁśuka* flowers, of *śālmali* wood, of various forms, gold coloured, running well, having good wheels, O Sūrya, mount this car, the world of *amṛta*; make the bridal procession agreeable for the husband", he makes her mount the chariot.

अनुमायन्तु देवता अनुब्रह्म सुवीर्यम् । अनुक्षत्रं तु यद्बल मनुमामैतु मद्यशः ॥ इति प्राङ्भिप्रयाय प्रदक्षिणमावर्त्तयति ॥७॥

With the verse, "may the deities follow me, may *Brahman* with manly vigour follow me, may power, strength and glory follow me", he makes the chariot turn round from left to right after having gone forward in the eastern direction.

प्रतिमायन्तु देवताः प्रतिब्रह्म सुवीर्यम् । प्रतिक्षत्रं तु यद्बलं प्रति मामैतु यद्यशः ॥ इति यथास्तँ यन्तमनुमन्त्रयते ॥८॥

With the verse, "May the deities come to me, may *Brahman* with manly vigour come to me, may power, strength and glory come to me".

अमङ्गल्यं चेदतिक्रामति अनुमायन्त्विति जपति ॥९॥

When he passes an inauspicious place, he murmurs, "may the deities follow me".

"नमो रुद्राय ग्रामसद" इति ग्रामे इमा रुद्रायेति च ॥१०॥

Near a village he murmurs, "glory to Rudra who resides in the villages".

"नमो रुद्रायैक वृक्षसद" इत्येकवृक्षे । "ये वृक्षेषु शष्पिञ्जरा" इति च ॥११॥

Near a single tree, he murmurs, "glory to Rudra who resides in the trees". "He who is inside the green cage."

"नमो रुद्राय श्मशानसद" इति श्मशाने । "ये भूताना मधिपतय" इति च ॥१२॥

Near a cemetery, he murmurs, "glory to Rudra who resides in cemeteries". "Rudras who are the lords of all beings."

"नमो रुद्राय चतुष्पथसद" इति चतुष्पथे । "ये पथां पथि रक्षय" इति च ॥१३॥

At a crossing, he murmurs, "glory to Rudra who resides in crossroads". "Rudras who protect the roads."

"नमो रुद्राय तीर्थसद" इति तीर्थे । "ये तीर्थानि प्रचरन्तीति" च ॥१४॥

At a water way, he murmurs, "glory to Rudra who resides in water". "Rudras who make the waters move."

यत्रापस्तरितव्या आसीदति समुद्राय वैणवे सिन्धूनां पतये नमः । नमो नदीनाँ सर्वासां पत्ये । विश्वाहा जुषताँ विश्वकर्मणामिदँ हविः स्वः स्वाहेत्यप्सूदकाञ्जलीन्निनयति । अमृतं वा आस्ये जुहोम्यायुः प्राणेऽप्यमृतं ब्रह्मणा सह मृत्युन्तरति । प्रासहादिति रिष्टिरिति मुक्तिरिति मुक्षीयमाणः सर्वं भयं नुदस्व स्वाहेति त्रिः परिमृज्याचामति ॥१५॥

When he reaches a river crossing, he pours out into the water handfuls of water with the words, "to the ocean, to the child of Veṇu, the waters of the world, glory; glory to the lord of all waters, may this oblation always be pleasant, to Viśvakarman, *svaḥ, svāhā*!" With the words, "I sacrifice *amṛta* in my mouth and *amṛta* and long life in my *prāṇa*; may they both cross death together with *Brahman*; with Aditi, Iṣṭi and Mukti who give deliverance, drive away all fear", he sips water thrice.

यदि नावा तरेत् सुत्रामाणमिति जपेत् ॥१६॥

When he crosses the river in a boat, he murmurs, "may we be protected".

यदि रथाक्षः शम्याणीवा रिष्येतान्यद्वा रथाङ्गं तत्रैवाग्निभुपसमाधाय जयप्रभृतिभिर्हुत्वा सुमङ्गलीरियँ वधूरिति जपेत् वध्वा सह वधूँ समेत पश्यत ॥१७॥

If the axle, yoke pins or any other part of the chariot are damaged, then after having made the fire, he sacrifices with Jayā and other *homa*s and says. "This woman wears auspicious ornaments: together with the bride, he says, come up to her and behold her."

व्युत्क्रामतः पन्थां जरितां जवेन शिवेन वैश्वानर इडयास्याग्रतः । आचार्यो येन येन पथा प्रयाति तेन तेन सह ॥ इत्युभावेवोक्रामतः ॥१८॥

At the parting of roads, the two of them take different roads, with the verse: "With kind speed Vaiśvānara with the ground in front. Along which road, the teacher always goes, go in that road with him."

गोभिः सहास्तमिते ग्रामं प्रविशन्ति ब्राह्मणवचनाद्वा ॥१९॥
They enter the village after sunset along with the cows or as the brāhmaṇa says.

चतुर्दशः खण्डः (Fourteenth Section)

अपरस्मिन्नन्ह संधौ गृहान्प्रतिपादयति ॥१॥
At twilight the next day, he takes her inside the house.

प्रतिब्रह्मन्निति प्रत्यवरोहति ॥२॥
With the words, "I rest on *Brahman*", he descends from the chariot.

मङ्गलानि प्रादुर्भवन्ति ॥३॥
Auspicious objects are shown.

गोष्ठात्सन्ततामुलपराजिँ स्तृणाति ॥४॥
He strews *ulapa* grass from the cowshed continuously from the chariot to the house.

रथादध्योपासनात् येष्वध्येति प्रवसन्येषु सौमनसं महत् । तेनोपव्हयामहे ते नो जानन्त्वागतम् ॥ इति तथाभ्युपैति ॥५॥
With the verse, "To whichever house the traveller returns from a journey, where there is comfort, that house we invoke; may it know us as we approach", he walks over the grass layer towards the house with his bride following.

"गृहानहँ सुमनसः प्रपद्ये वीरँहि वीरवतः सुशेवा इराँवहन्ती घृतमुक्षमाणास्तेष्वहँ सुमनाः सँवसाम्" ॥ इत्यभ्याहिताग्निँ सोदकँ सौषधमावसथं प्रतिपद्यते रोहिण्या मूलेन वा यद्वा पुण्योक्तम् ॥६॥
"I enter the house which is pleasant, which is full of heroes, with my husband, I bring food to the house which drips with ghee, kindly disposed." She enters the house which has the fire kindled, water and plants are ready under the stars, Rohiṇī or Mūlā or whichever is said to be auspicious.

पश्चादग्ने रोहिते चर्मण्याडुहे प्राग्ग्रीवे लोमतो दर्भानास्तीर्य तेषु वधूमुपवेशयत्यति वा दर्भेष्वेव ॥७॥

To the west of the fire, he makes the bride to sit down upon a red bull skin of which the neck is turned eastward, on the hairy side after having strewn it with *darbha* grass or he makes her sit on *darbha* grass only.

अथास्यै ब्रह्मचारिणामुपस्थ आवेशयति — सोमेनदित्या बलिनः सोमेन पृथिवी मही असौ नक्षत्राणामेषामुपस्थे सोम आहितः ॥ इति ॥८॥

Then he makes a *brahmacārī* to sit in her lap with the verse, "Through Soma are the Ādityas strong, through Soma the earth is great; he, Soma is put in the lap of these *nakṣatras*".

अथास्य तिलतण्डुलानां फलमिश्राणामञ्जलिं पूरयित्वोत्थाप्याथास्यै ध्रुवमरुन्धतीं जीवन्तीँ सप्तऋषीनिति दर्शयेत् ॥९॥

Then after having filled the boy's hands with a mixture of sesamum seeds, rice and fruits, he makes him stand up and he makes her look at the pole star, Dhruva and Arundhatī and the *saptaṛṣi maṇḍala*.

अच्युता ध्रुवा ध्रुवपत्नी ध्रुवं पश्येम सर्वतः ध्रुवासः पर्वता इमे ध्रुवा स्त्री पतिकुलेयम् ॥ इति तस्यां समीक्षमाणायां जपति ॥१०॥

He chants: "Unshakeable, steadfast, a steadfast wife may she be, may we look steadfast all around; steadfast are the mountains, steadfast may this woman in the family of her husband."

श्वोभूते प्राजापत्यं पयसि स्थालीपकँ श्रपयित्वा तस्य जुहोति । आज्यशेषे दधिसमानीय तेन हुतशेषेण ॥११॥

On the next day, he offers milk and cooked food to Prajāpati. Also, with the remnants of *ājya* mixed with curds.

"चक्रीवानडुहौ वा मे वाङ्मैतु ते मनः चाक्रवाकँ सँ वननं तन्नौ सं वननं कृतम्" — इति यजमानस्त्रिः प्राश्नात्यवशिष्टं तूष्णीं पत्नी ॥१२॥

"As the wheels of the chariot follow the footsteps of the bulls, may your mind follow me. Like the concord of *cakravāka* birds let our minds become one." So saying he partakes while his wife does so silently.

अपरान्हे पिण्डपितृयज्ञः स व्याख्यातः ॥१३॥
In the afternoon, *piṇḍapitṛ yajña* is carried out as explained.

सँवत्सरं ब्रह्मचर्यं चरतो द्वादशरात्रं त्रिरात्रमेकरात्रं वा ॥१४॥
Let them practice celibacy for one year, twelve nights, three nights or one night.

अथास्यै गृहान् विसृजेत् ॥१५॥
Then he should give her the authority over the house.

योक्त्रपाशं विषाय तौ संनिपातयेत् — "अपश्यं त्वा मनसा चेकितानां तपसो जातं तपसो विभूतम् — इह प्रजामिह रयिँरराणः प्रजायस्व प्रजया पुत्रकाम ॥ अपश्यं त्वा मनसा दीध्यानां स्वायां तनूँ ऋत्विये बाधमानम् । उप मामूच्चा युवतिर्बभुयाः प्रजायस्व प्रजया पुत्रकामे ॥ प्रजापतिस्तन्वं मे जुषस्व त्वष्टा देवैः सहमान इन्द्रः । विश्वेदेवैर्ऋतुभिः सँ विदानः पुँसां बहूनां मातरौ स्याव ॥ अहं गर्भ मदधामोषधीष्वहँ विश्वेषु भुवनेष्वन्तः । अहं प्रजा अजनयं पृथिव्या अहं जनिभ्यो अपरिषु पुत्रान् ॥" इति स्त्र्यादिव्यत्यासं जपति ॥१६॥
Having untied the yoke rope, they lie down together and in turn murmur the verses, "I saw you observing in your mind what is born of *tapas*, what has come into existence from *tapas;* granting here offspring and wealth, propagate yourself through offspring, O you, who are desirous of sons, I saw you while you were desiring in your mind, and praying for our own body, in the time proper for procreation; approach me powerfully, young woman, propagate yourself through offspring, O you, who are desirous of sons; Prajapati, may you be delighted in my body, and Tvaṣṭā and powerful Indra and other gods, accompanied by all gods and seasons; may we be the parents of many sons; I impregnated the plants, I impregnated all creatures; I begot offspring in the earth, I shall beget sons for women in future nights."

करदिति भसदमभिमृशति ॥१७॥
Pronouncing the words, "May it bring forth", he touches her private parts.

जननीत्युपजननम् ॥१८॥

Pronouncing the words, "May it beget" she touches his organ.

बृहदिति जातं प्रतिष्ठितम् ॥१९॥

At the word, "Great" sperm is ejaculated.

एतेन धर्मेण ऋतावृतौ संनिपतयेत् ॥२०॥

In this manner, he has intercourse with her after each menstrual period.

Agniveśya Gṛhya-Sūtra

Agniveśya Gṛhya-Sūtra belongs to the Taittirīya branch of *Kṛṣṇa Yajurveda*. It is supposed to be one of the four divisions of the Vādhūla School. It is said that this Sūtra is posterior to *Baudhāyana* and *Bhāradvāja Gṛhya-Sūtra*. Agniveśya is considered to be a disciple of Śāṇḍilya, Ānabhimlāya and Gārgya.The following is the text of the *Āgniveśya Gṛhya-Sūtra* which deals with *vivāha saṁskāra*.

प्रथमः प्रश्नः (First Praśna)
पञ्चमोऽध्यायः (Fifth Chapter)

The fifth chapter lists the *mantras* used in *vivāha saṁskāra* without the details of *prayogas* they refer to.

"अनृक्षरा ऋजवः सन्तु पन्था येभिः सखायो यन्ति नो वरेण्यम् । समर्यमा संभगो नो निनीयात् सञ्जास्पत्यं सुयममस्तु देवाः" । अयं कूर्चः । "मयि गृह्णाम्यग्रे अग्निं रायस्पोषाय सुप्रजस्त्वाय सुवीर्याय । मयि प्रजां मयि वर्चो दधाम्यरिष्टाः स्याम तनुवा सुवीराः । यो नो अग्निः पितरो हृत्स्वन्तरमर्त्यो मर्त्यों आविवेश । तमात्मन् परिगृह्णीमहे वयं मा सो अस्मां अवहाय परागात्"। "भूर्भुवःस्वः । प्रजापतिः स्त्रियां यशो मुष्कयोरदधात् सपम् । कामस्य तृप्तिमानन्दं तस्याग्ने भाजयेह मा । मोदः प्रमोद आनन्दो मुष्कयोर्निहितः सपः । सृत्वेव कामस्य तृप्याणि दक्षिणानां प्रतिग्रहे । मनसश्चित्तमाकूतिं वाचः सत्यमशीमहि । पशूनां रूपमन्नस्य यशः श्रीः श्रयतां मयि । यथाहमस्या अतृपं स्त्रियै पुमान् यथा स्त्री तृप्यति पुंसि प्रिये प्रिया । एवं भगस्य तृप्याणि यज्ञस्य काम्यः प्रियाम् । आदित्यः सत्यभोमिति । आपस्तत् सत्यमाभरन् । यशो यज्ञस्य दक्षिणाम् ।

असौ मे कामः समृध्यताम्"। "आपो हि ष्ठा मयोभुव" इति तिसृभिः, "हिरण्यवर्णाः शुचयः पावका" इति चतसृभिः, "पवमानः सुवर्जनः" इत्येतेनानुवाकेन । "या अकृन्तन्नवयन् या अतन्वत याश्च देवीरन्तानभितोऽददन्त। तास्त्वा देवीर्जरसा संव्ययन्त्वायुष्मतीदं परिधत्स्व वासः । परिधत्त धत्त वाससैनां शतायुषीं कृणुत दीर्घमायुः । बृहस्पतिः प्रायच्छद्वास एतत् सोमाय राज्ञे परिधातवा उ। जरां गच्छासि परिधत्स्व वासो भवा कृष्टीनामभिशस्तिपावती । शतं च जीव शरदः सुवर्चा रायश्च पोषमुपसंव्ययस्व। "परीदं वासो अधिपाः स्वस्तयेऽभूरापीनामभिशस्तिपावति। शतं च जीव शरदः पुरूचीर्वसूनि चार्यो विभजासु जीवति।" अनया सह मया कर्माणि कर्तव्यानि। प्रजाश्चोत्पदयितव्याः। तदर्थमेनां परिणेष्ये। "इन्द्राय नमः । अग्नये नमः । यमाय नमः । निर्ऋतये नमः । वरुणाय नमः । सोमाय नमः । ईशानाय नमः । ब्रह्मणे नमः । अद्भ्यो नमः । अग्नये नमः। आत्मने नमः" । "अदितेऽनुमन्यस्व । अनुमतेऽनुमन्यस्व । सरस्वतेऽनुमन्यस्व । देवसवितः प्रसुव" । "अयं त इध्म आत्मा जातवेदस्तेनेध्यस्व वर्धस चेद्ध वर्धय चास्मान् प्रजया पशुभिर्ब्रह्मवर्चसेनानाध्येन समेधय स्वाहा । प्रजापतये स्वाहा । इन्दाय स्वाहा । अग्नये स्वाहा । सोमाय स्वाहा । भूः स्वाहा । भुवः स्वाहा । स्वः स्वाहा । भूर्भुवःस्वः स्वाहा" । "या तिरश्री निपद्यसेऽहं विधरणी इति । तां त्वा घृतस्य धारया जुहोति वैश्वकर्मणि" स्वाहा । यानूची निपद्यसेऽहं विधरणी इति । तां त्वा घृतस्य धारया अग्नौ संराधन्यै देव्यै स्वाहा। प्रसाधन्यौ देव्यै स्वाहा" ॥१॥

"युक्तो वह जातवेदः पुरस्तादग्ने विद्धि कर्म क्रियमाणं ययेदम्। त्वं भिषग् भेषजस्यासि कर्ता त्वया गा अश्वान् पुरुषान् सनेमि स्वाहा । विरुपाक्षाय स्वाहा। दन्तान् जये स्वाहा। विरूपाक्षमहं यजे निजङ्गं शबळोदरम्। यो मायं परिबाधते श्रियै पुष्ट्यै च तस्मै स्वाहा। परिबाध मा विबाधिष्ठा मा विबाध विबाधिथाः । निर्ऋत्यै त्वा पुत्रमाहुः स नः कर्माणि साध्य स्वाहा । सदस्पतिमद्भुतं प्रियमिन्द्रस्य काम्यम् । सनिं मेधामयासिषं स्वाहा । यावन्तो देवास्त्वयि जातवेदः स्रियं चोद्घ्नन्ति पुरुषस्य कर्म। तेभ्य एतद्धूयते भागधेयं ते मा तृप्तास्तर्पयन्तु कामैः स्वाहा । आकूत्यै त्वा कामाय त्वा समृधे त्वा । पुरो दधे अमृतत्वाय जीवसे स्वाहा । आकूतिमस्यावसे। काममस्य समृद्ध्यै । इन्द्रस्य युञ्जते धियः स्वाहा । आकूतिं देवीं मनसः पुरो दधे । यज्ञस्य माता सुहवा मे अस्तु । यदिच्छामि मनसा स कामः । विदेयमेनद्धृदये निविष्टं स्वाहा"। "इष्टेभ्यः स्वाह। वषडनिष्टेभ्यः स्वाहा। भेषजं दुरिष्ट्यै स्वाहा। निष्कृत्यै स्वाहा। दौराध्यै स्वाहा। देवीभ्यस्तनूभ्यः स्वाहा। ऋद्ध्यै स्वाहा। समृद्ध्यै स्वाहा"। "चित्ताय स्वाहा । चित्तये स्वाहा । आकूताय स्वाहा । आकूत्यै स्वाहा । विज्ञाताय स्वाहा । विज्ञानाय स्वाहा । मनसे स्वाहा । शकरीभ्यः स्वाहा । दर्शाय

स्वाहा । पूर्णमासाय स्वाहा । बृहते स्वाहा । रथन्तराय स्वाहा । प्रजापतिर्जयानिन्द्राय वृष्णे प्रायच्छदुग्रः पृतनाज्येषु । तस्मै विशः समनमन्त सर्वाः स उग्रः स हि हव्यो बभूव स्वाहा" । "अग्निर्भुतानामधिपतिः स मावतु स्वाहा । पितरः इन्द्रो ज्येष्ठानामधिपतिः स मावतु स्वाहा । यमः पृथिव्या अधिपतिः स मावतु स्वाहा । वायुरन्तरिक्षस्याधिपतिः स मावतु स्वाहा । सूर्यो दिवोऽधिपतिः स मावतु स्वाहा । चन्द्रो नक्षत्राणामधिपतिः स मावतु स्वाहा । बृहस्पतिर्ब्रह्मणोऽधिपतिः स मावतु स्वाहा । मित्रः सत्यानामाधिपतिः स मावतु स्वाहा । वरुणोऽपामधिपतिः स मावतु स्वाहा । समुद्रः स्त्रोत्यानामधिपतिः स मावतु स्वाहा । अन्नँ साम्राज्यानामधिपति तन्मावतु स्वाहा । सोम ओषधीनामधिपतिः स मावतु स्वाहा । सविता प्रसवानामधिपतिः स मावतु स्वाहा । रुद्रः पशूनामधिपतिः स मावतु स्वाहा । त्वष्टा रुपाणामधिपतिः स मावतु स्वाहा । विष्णुः पर्वतानामधिपतिः स मावतु स्वाहा । मरुतो गणानामधिपतयस्ते मावन्तु स्वाहा । पितरः पितामाहाः परेऽवरे ततास्ततामहा इह मावत । अस्मिन् ब्रह्मचारिन् क्षत्रेऽस्यामाशिष्यस्यां पुरोधायामस्मिन् कर्मस्यां देवहूत्यां स्वाहा" । "ऋताषाड़्तधामाग्नि-गन्धर्वस्तस्यौषधयोऽप्सरस ऊर्जो नाम स इदं ब्रह्म क्षत्रं पातु ता इदं ब्रह्म क्षत्रं पान्तु तस्मै स्वाहा । ताभ्यः स्वाहा । सँहितो विश्वसामा सूर्यो गन्धर्वस्तस्य मरीचयोऽप्सरस आयुवो नाम स इदं ब्रह्म क्षत्रं पातु ता इदं ब्रह्म क्षत्रं पान्तु तस्मै स्वाहा । ताभ्यः स्वाहा । सुषुम्नः सूर्यरश्मिश्चन्द्रमा गन्धर्वस्तस्य नक्षत्राण्यप्सरसो बेकुरयो नाम स इदं ब्रह्म क्षत्रं पातु ता इदं ब्रह्म क्षत्रं पान्तु तस्मै स्वाहा । ताभ्यः स्वाहा । भुज्युः सुपर्णो यज्ञो गन्धर्वस्तस्य दक्षिणा अप्सरसः स्तवा नाम स इदं ब्रह्म क्षत्रं पातु ता इदं ब्रह्म क्षत्रं पान्तु तस्मै स्वाहा । ताभ्यः स्वाहा । प्रजापतिर्विश्वकर्मा मनो गन्धर्वस्तस्यर्कूसामान्यप्सरसो वह्नयो नाम स इदं ब्रह्म क्षेत्रं पातु ता इदं ब्रह्म क्षत्रं पान्तु तस्मै स्वाहा । ताभ्यः स्वाहा । इषिरो विश्वव्यचा वातो गन्धर्वस्तस्यापोऽप्सरसो मुदा नाम स इदं ब्रह्म क्षत्रं पातु ता इदं ब्रह्म क्षत्रं पान्तु तस्मै स्वाहा । ताभ्यः स्वाहा" । "अग्निरेतु प्रथमो देवतानां सोऽस्यै प्रजां मुञ्चतु मृत्युपाशात् । तदयँ राजा वरुणोऽनुमन्यतां यथेयं स्त्री पौत्रमघं न रोदात् स्वाहा । इमामग्निस्त्रायतां गार्हपत्यः प्रजामस्यै नयतु दीर्घमायुः । अशून्योपस्था जीवतामस्तु माता पौत्रमानन्दमभिप्रबुद्ध्यतामियं स्वाहा । मा ते गृहे निशि घोष उत्थादन्यत्र त्वद्रुदत्यः संविशन्तु । मा त्वं विकेश्युर आवधिष्ठा जीवपत्नी पतिलोके विराज पश्यन्ती प्रजां सुमनस्यमानां स्वाहा" ॥ "स्तनन्धयतस्ते पुत्रान् सविताभिरक्षतु । आ वाससः परिधानाद् बृहस्पतिर्विश्वदेवा अभिरक्षन्तु पश्चात् स्वाहा । अप्रजस्तां पौत्रमृत्युं पाप्मानमुत वाघम् । शीर्ष्णः स्रजमिवोन्मुच्य द्विषद्भ्यः प्रतिमुञ्चामि पाशं स्वाहा । ब्राह्मणं देवकृतं कल्पमानं तेन हन्ये निषदः पिशाचात् । क्रव्यादो मृत्युरधरान् पातयामि दीर्घमायुस्तव जीवन्तु पुत्रान् स्वाहा ।" "शन्नो देविरभिष्टय

आपो पीतये शंयोरभिस्रवन्तु नः ।" "देवस्य त्वा सवितुः प्रसवेऽश्विनोर्बाहुभ्यां पूष्णो हस्ताभ्याम् । हस्तेन हस्तं गृभ्णामि सौभगत्वाय मया पत्या जरदिष्टिर्यथासत्" । "भगो अर्यमा सविता पुरन्धिस्ते त्वा देवा अदुर्मह्यं पत्नीम् । अघोरचक्षुरपतिघ्न्येधि शिवा पशुभ्यः सुमनाः सुवर्चाः । यां पूषन् शिवतमामेरयस्व यस्यां बीजं मनुष्या वपन्ति । या न ऊरू उशति विस्रयातै यस्यामुशन्तः प्रहरेम शेफम् । सोमोऽददात् गन्धर्वाय गन्धर्वोऽग्नयेऽददात् । पशूंश्च मह्यं पुत्रांश्च ददावग्निरथो त्वा असावहम् । सोमः पथमो विविदे गन्धर्वो विविद उत्तरः । तृतीयो अग्निष्टे पतिस्तुर्योऽहं मनुष्यजाः । सरस्वति प्रेदमव सुभगे वाजीनीवति । तां त्वा विश्वस्य भूतस्य प्रगायामस्यग्रतः" । "आतिष्ठेममश्मानमश्मेव त्वं स्थिरा भव । प्रमृणीहि दुरस्यून् सहस्व पृतनायतः । विश्वा उत त्वया वयं धारा उदन्या इव । अतिगाहेमहि द्विषः" ॥२॥

"इमान् लाजानावपामि समृद्धिकरणान्मम । मम तुभ्यं च संवननं तदग्निरनुमन्यताम् । भगेन त्वा संसृजामि मासरेण सुरामिव । इयं नार्यपब्रूते अग्नौ लाजानावपन्ती । दीर्घायुरस्तु मे पतिरेधन्तां ज्ञातयो मम स्वाहा । इमं मे वरुण श्रुधी हवमद्या च मृडय । त्वामवस्युराचके स्वाहा । तत्वा यामि ब्रह्मणा वन्दमानस्तदाशास्ते यजमानो हविर्भिः । अहेडमानो वरुणेह बोध्युरुशंस मा न आयुः प्रमोषीः स्वाहा" । "त्वन्नो अग्ने वरुणस्य विद्वान् देवस्य हेडोऽवयासिसीष्ठाः । यजिष्ठो वह्नितम शोशुचानो विश्वा द्वेषाँसि प्रमुमुग्ध्यस्मत् स्वाहा । स त्वं नो अग्नेऽवमो भवेती नेदिष्ठो अस्या उषसो व्युष्टौ । अवयक्ष्व नो वरुणं रराणो वीहि मृडिकं सुहवो न एधि स्वाहा । त्वमग्ने अयास्ययासन्मनसा हितः । अयासन् हव्यमूहिषेऽयानो धेहि भेषजं स्वाहा। प्रजापते न त्वदेतान्यन्यो विश्वा जातानि परिता बभूव । यत्कामास्ते जुहुमस्तन्नो अस्तु वयँ स्याम पतयो रयीणां स्वाहा । यन्म आत्मनो मिन्दाभूदग्निस्तत्पुन-राहार्जातवेदा विचर्षणिः स्वाहा । पुनरग्निश्चक्षुरदात् पुनरिन्द्रो बृहस्पतिः । पुनर्मे अश्विना युवं चक्षुराधत्तमक्ष्योः स्वाहा । अनाज्ञातं यदाज्ञातं यज्ञस्य क्रियते मधु । अग्ने तदस्य कल्पय त्वं हि वेत्थ यथातथं स्वाहा । पुरुषसम्मितो यज्ञो यज्ञः पुरुषसम्मितः । अग्ने तदस्य कल्पय त्वं हि वेत्थ यथातथं स्वाहा । यत्पाकत्रा मनसा दीनदक्षान यज्ञस्य मन्वते मर्त्तासः । अग्निष्टद्धोता क्रतुविद्विजानन् यजिष्ठो देवां ऋतुशो यजाति स्वाहा ।" "पाहि नो अग्न एनसे स्वाहा । पाहि नो विश्वेदसे स्वाहा । यज्ञं पाहि विभावसो स्वाहा । सर्वं पाहि शतक्रतो स्वाहा । भुरग्नये च पृथिव्यै च महते च स्वाहा । भुवो वायवे चान्तरिक्षाय च महते च स्वाहा । सुवरादित्याय च दिवे च महते च स्वाहा । भूर्भुवः स्वश्चन्द्रमसे च नक्षत्रेभ्यश्च दिग्भ्यश्च महते च स्वाहा । नमो देवेभ्यः स्वधा पितृभ्यो भूर्भुवस्वर्महरों स्वाहा । ॐ स्वाहा । भूः स्वाहा । भुवः स्वाहा । स्वः स्वाहा । भुर्भुवःस्वः स्वाहा ।

यदस्य कर्मणोऽत्यरीरिचं यद्वा न्यूनमिहाकरम्। अग्निष्टत् स्विष्टकृद्विद्वान् सर्वं स्विष्टं सुहुतं करोतु मे । अग्नये स्विष्टकृते सुहुतहुते सर्वहुते सर्वप्रायश्चित्ताहुतीनां कामानां समर्धयित्रे स्वाहा" । "अदितेऽन्वमंस्थाः । अनुमतेऽन्वमंस्थाः । सरस्वतेऽन्वमंस्था । देव सवितः प्रासावीः" । "अग्ने व्रतपते व्रतं चरिष्यामि तच्छकेयं तन्मे राध्यताम् । वायो व्रतपते व्रतं चरिष्यामि तच्छकेयं तन्मे राध्यताम् । आदित्य व्रतपते व्रतं चरिष्यामि तच्छकेयं तन्मे राध्यताम् । व्रतानाम् व्रतपते व्रतं चरिष्यामि तच्छकेयं तन्मे राध्यताम्" । "अमूहमस्मि सा त्वं सा त्वमस्यमूहं ऋगहमस्मि साम त्वं द्योरहं पृथिवी त्वम् । मम हृदये हृदयं ते अस्तु । मम चित्ते चित्तमस्तु ते। मम वाचमेकमनाः श्रुणु । मामेवानुव्रता सहचर्या मया भव । चाक्रवाकं संवननं यन्नदीभ्य उदाहृतम् । यद्देवगन्धर्वो वित्तः संवननं तेन संवनिनौ स्वः।" एकमिषे विष्णुस्त्वान्वेतु द्वे ऊर्जे विष्णुस्त्वान्वेतु त्रीणि व्रताय विष्णुस्त्वान्वेतु चत्वारि मायोभवाय विष्णुस्त्वान्वेतु पञ्च पशुभ्यो विष्णुस्त्वान्वेतु षड् रायस्पोषाय विष्णुस्त्वान्वेतु सप्त सप्तभ्यो होत्राभ्यो विष्णुस्त्वान्वेतु । सखायौ सप्तपदाबभूव सख्यं ते गमेयं सख्यात्ते मा योषं सख्यान्मे मा योष्ठाः । "सप्तऋषयः प्रथमां कृत्तिकानामरुन्धतीम् । ध्रुवतां ये ह निन्युः । षट् कृत्तिका मुख्ययोगं वहन्तीयमस्माकं भ्राजत्वष्टमी । ध्रुवं नमस्यामि मनसा ध्रुवेण ध्रुवं नो सख्यं दीर्घमायुश्च भुयात् । अद्रुग्धावस्मिंश्च परे च लोके ध्रुवं प्रविष्टौ स्याम शरणं सुखार्तौ । शन्न एधि द्विपदे शं चतुष्पदे। इह गावो निषीदन्त्विहाश्वा इह पुरुषाः । इहो सहस्रदक्षिणो अधिपूषा निषीदतु" ॥४॥

"अग्ने प्रायश्चित्ते त्वं देवानां प्रायश्चित्तिरसि ब्राह्मणस्त्वा नाथकाम उपधावामि यास्यै पतिघ्नी तनूस्तामितो नाशयामसि स्वाहा । वायो प्रायश्चित्ते त्वं देवानां प्रायश्चित्तिरसि (ब्राह्मणस्त्वा नाथकाम उपधावामि) यास्यै पुत्रघ्नी तनूस्तामिते नाशयामसि स्वाहा । आदित्य प्रायश्चित्ते त्वं देवानां प्रायश्चित्तिरसि ब्राह्मणस्त्वा नाथकाम उपधावामि यास्यै पशुघ्नी तनूस्तामितो नाशयामसि स्वाहा । सर्व प्रायश्चित्ते त्वं प्रायश्चित्तिरसि ब्राह्मनस्त्वा नाथकाम उपधावामि योस्यै पतिघ्नी पुत्रघ्नी पशुघ्नी निन्दिता तनूस्तामितो नाशयामसि स्वाहा" । "अग्ने व्रतपते व्रतमचारिषम्" इत्यादि "व्रतानां व्रतपते व्रतमचारिषम्" इत्यन्तम् । आवाभ्यां दम्पतिभ्यां स्वस्ति भवन्तो ब्रुवन्तु । युवाभ्यां दम्पतिभ्यां स्वस्ति। "तशिने शिवेन त्वाभिमृशति हस्तेनाविद्विषाणिना । यथा न विद्विषेमहि" न हि ये च कदाचन । ऋषभेण स्कन्दामि व्यस्य योनिं पतिरेतो गृहाण । पुमांस्त्री जायतां गर्भो अन्तः । आ ते योनिं गर्भ एतु पुमांसं गर्भमाधत्स्व । यन्तुभ्यं शिमिवाससि पुमांस्ते पुत्रो नारितं पुमाननुजायताम् । स संवर्धतां गर्भो दशमे मासि सूतवे" ॥ अनृक्षराऋजवःसन्तुपन्था युक्तोवहजातवेद स्तनन्धयतस्तस्तेपुत्रान् इमाल्लाँजानावपामि अग्नेप्रायश्चित्ते पञ्च ॥५॥

षष्ठोध्यायः (Sixth Chapter)

अथ समावृत्ते भार्यामुपयच्छेत । प्रजातन्तुं मा व्यवच्छेत्सीः इति गुरुशासनात् सर्वाङ्गिनीं मनोज्ञां यवीयसीं ब्रह्मचारिणीं कन्याम् असगोत्राम् मातुरसपिण्डां अनुक्तामगर्हिताम् नक्षत्रनदीवृक्षाभिधानासंयुक्ताम् । अथ दूतान् प्रहिणोति अनृक्षरा ऋजव इति । वधूमन्तं याचयति अमुष्मै अमुकगोत्राय अमूममुकगोत्रीं धर्मप्रजार्थं वधूं ददातु इति । तथेत्युक्ते वधूम् । आपूर्यमाणपक्षे पुण्ये नक्षत्रे शोभनान्यगाराणि कल्पयित्वा बद्धकौतुकः कृतमङ्गलस्वस्त्ययनः पदातिवधूगृहं गत्वा गृहीतमधुपर्कः उद्धननाध्यसम्भारसम्भरणान् कृत्वा लाजानश्मानमहतं वासश्च संभृत्य ब्रह्मप्रवेशनाद्यापरिधानन्तं करोति । एतस्मिन् काले वधूं बद्धकौतुकां कृतपुण्यानिनीं यज्ञोपवीतिनीमाचान्तामग्नेमुत्तरेण परेण च गत्वा दक्षिणतः प्राचीं तिष्टन्तीं वरोऽग्नेरुत्तरेण पूर्वेण च गत्वा पुरस्तात् प्रत्यक् तिष्ठन् सपवित्रेन पाणिना व्याहृतिभिः प्रजापतिः स्त्रियाम् इति षड्भिरेनां दक्षिणत उदङ्मुखस्तिष्ठन् अमूम् अमुकगोत्रीम् अमुष्मै अमुकगोत्राय तुभ्यं प्रजासहत्वकर्मभ्यः प्रतिपादयामि इति वधूमताद्भिर्दत्तां प्रतिगृह्णाति स्त्रीधनं च ।

"आपो हि ष्ठा मयोभुव" इति तिसृभिः, "हिरण्यवर्णाः शुचयः पावका" इति चतुसृभिः, "पवमानः सुवर्जन" इत्येतेनानुवाकेन मार्जयित्वा यथाप्रपन्नम-परेणाग्निमुपवेश्याथैनामहतं वासः परिधापयति पूर्वं निधाय "या अकृन्तन्नवयन्" इति तिसृभिः । "परिदं वास" इत्येतया अभिमन्त्रयते। अथैनामाचान्तां दक्षिणतः प्राचीमुपवेश्य तस्यामन्वारब्धायां गन्धादिनाग्निमलङ्कृत्य परिशिञ्चति "अदितेऽनुमन्यस्व" इति दक्षिणतः प्राचीनम्, "अनुमतेऽनुमन्यस्व" इति पश्चादुदीचीनं, "सरस्वतेऽनुमन्यस्व" इति उत्तरतः प्राचीनं, "देव सवितः प्रसुव" इति सर्वतःप्रदक्षिणं परिषिच्य ऊर्ध्वं "समिधावनूयाजार्थं चादधाति" । इध्मदेवोद्धृत्य दक्षिणं परिधिमग्निं चान्तरेण उत्तरं परिधिं चाग्निं चान्तरेण प्रणीताप्रणयनेऽनूयाजार्थं चादधाति । "अयं त" इध्मम् अक्त्वाभ्यदधाति । अप उपस्पृश्य, इध्मस्य मूलमुपसंस्पृश्य दर्व्यां जुहोति "प्रजापतये स्वाहा" इत्युदञ्चम्, "इन्द्राय स्वाहा" इति प्राञ्चम् आघारावाघार्य । आज्यभागौ जुहोति "अग्नये स्वाहा" इति उत्तरतः, "सोमाय स्वाहा" इति दक्षिणतः । मध्ये व्याहृतिभिर्हुत्वा "या तिरश्ची निपद्यसेऽहम्" इति त्रयोदशाहुतीर्जुहोति ॥१॥

Let him seek a bride after *samāvartana*. With the advice of the *guru*, "do not break your lineage", he chooses a bride who has all limbs in order, pleasing to look at, younger, unmarried who is not of the same *gotra*, not *sapiṇḍa* from mother's side, not committed to a household, he walks to the house of the bride and having partaken *madhuparka*, one who is not named after a *nakṣatra*, river or tree. Then he sends his messengers with the *mantra*, "let the paths that our friends travel for the wooing be thornless and smooth". The messengers ask the bride's father, "please give this bride of . . . (name) of . . . (*gotra*) of. . . . (*gotrī*) for the sake of good children". Then the girl is spoken for.

During *śukla pakṣa*, under an auspicious star, having made a decorated *paṇḍāl*, having conducted the premarital ceremony (tying a marriage thread on the hand, etc.) with auspiciousness and happiness, he walks to the bride's house, and holding the *madhuparka* vessel, gathering good quality material required such as fried grains, the stone, new clothes, he prepares the dresses for *brahmapraveśa*, etc. During this time, the bride after tying a marriage thread on her hand is led after the wearing of the sacred thread and sipping water from the north-west of the fire and made to stand at the south-east of the fire; the bridegroom goes from the north-east of the fire and stands in the west opposite the bride and with the *pavitra* water recites the *vyāhṛtis* and murmurs, "Prajāpati of the women", six times; to the south of these, facing north, the bride's parents and say we give this . . . (name) of . . . (*gotra*) to you for the sake of progeny and receive the *strīdhana*.

With the *anuvākas*, "O water you bring happiness", three times, "gold coloured, clean and holy", four times, "sacred fire, etc.", water is rubbed on the bride and as said before, she is made to sit to the west of the fire and given new clothes with the *mantra*, "those goddesses who have prepared this cloth, etc.", thrice. They worship with the *mantra*, "having worn this dress, etc.". After sipping water, she is made to sit down on the south-east side, and sprinkled with the scent laden, pure water with the *mantra*, "Aditi permits this woman" from the south-east, "Anumatī permits this woman" from the north-west, "Sarasvatī permits this woman" from the north-east, with "From God Savitā release" all round: sprinkling on top, they give fuel, etc. for the sacrifice. Gathering the fuel to the south and making circles, and with gaps on the south, he gives *praṇīta* waters for the sake of the sacrifice. With the *mantra*, "this you are", he worships the fuel. Having touched the water and the ends of the fuel, he sacrifices with the spoon, "to Prajāpati *svāhā*!" from the north, "to Indra *svāhā*!" from the east towards the hall. He sacrifices the parts of the *ājya* with "to Agni *svāhā*!" from the north and "to Soma *svāhā*!" from the south. In the middle, after sacrificing with the *vyāhṛtis*, recites the *mantra*, "that lady who says, I am the one bearing, etc.", he sacrifices thirteen times.

अथाष्टौ समृद्धिहोमान् जुहोति "इष्टेभ्यः स्वाहा" इति । अथ जयाञ्जुहोति "चित्तं च चित्तिश्च" इत्येवं वा जुहोति । नानास्रुवाहुतीः "चिताय स्वाहा चितये स्वाहा" इत्येवम् । अथाभ्यातानाञ्जुहोति "अग्निर्भूतानामधिपतिः स मावतु स्वाहा" इति । अथ प्राचीनावीतं कृत्वाधिवदते "पितरः पितामहा" इति । उपवीती भूयो भवति । स एवमेतान् सप्तदशाभ्यातानान् साधिवादान् जुहोति । अथ स्वाहाकृताः षड् राष्ट्रभृतो जुहोति । "ऋताषाडृतधामा" इति । "अग्निरेतु प्रथम" इति षड् प्रधानाहुतीर्जुहोति । "शन्नो देवीरभिष्टय" इत्युभौ मार्जयते । अथास्य दक्षिणेन हस्तेन दक्षिणं हस्तं साङ्गुष्ठं गृह्णात्यभीवलोमानि "देवस्य त्वा" इति । अथोपोत्थापयति "भगो अर्यमा" इत्येताभिः पञ्चभिः । अत्रासौशब्दप्रथमया नाम गृह्णीयात् । उत्तरेणोत्तरार्धपरिधिसन्धिमश्मानं निधाय दक्षिणेन पादेन वधूमास्थापयति "आतिष्ठेममश्मानम्" इति । "विश्वा उत त्वया वयम्" इति प्रदक्षिणमग्निं परिक्रामतः । अथास्या अञ्जलावुपस्तीर्य द्विर्लाजानावपति । त्रिः पञ्चावत्तिनाम् । "इमान् लाजानावपामि" इति । अभिधार्य दर्व्या संसृजति "भगेन त्वा संसृजामि" इति । अथ जुहोति "इयं नारी" इति ॥२॥

Then he performs *samṛddhi* oblations with the verse, "to the chosen gods, *svāhā*!"; then he performs the Jayā *homa* with, "mind and thinking, *svāhā*!"; with many spoons, he offers, "for the mind and to the mind, *svāhā*!"; then he performs the *abhyātāna* oblations with the verse, "to Agni who is the lord of all beings, protect me, *svāhā*!"; then changes his *yajñopavītam* to *prācīnāvidhi*, he offers oblations, "to my fathers and grandfathers, *svāhā*!"; he wears the *yajñopavītam* in the normal fashion and sits down. He similarly performs seventeen Abhyātāna *homas* successfully. Then he performs six Rāṣṭrabhṛt *homas* with *svāhās*, with "Agni is the friend of the seasons, seasons are his place, etc.". With the *mantra*, "Agni is the first", he performs six *pradāna* sacrifices. With the verse, "Let the blessings of the goddesses be there", both purify themselves with water. Then he holds her right hand with his right hand including the thumb and with the hairs on the hand, with the verse, "you belong to gods". Then he makes her rise with the verse, "Bhaga, Aryamā, etc." five times. Then he takes her name for the first time. Keeping a stone on the northern half of the *paridhi*, he makes her stand on it with her right foot with the verse, "Stand on this stone, etc." With the verse, "The gods have brought Sūrya's chariot for us to go together", they go around the fire. Then he makes her join her hands together and pours fried grains in them twice with the verse, "I pour fried grains in these". Gathering the *darvi* spoons, he chants, "I am gathering because of Bhaga". Then he sacrifices with the verse, "this woman".

एवं द्वितीयमास्थाप्य परीत्य जुहोति । तथा तृतीयम् । यथायतनमुपवेश्य अनूयाजसमिधमदाय दर्व्या वारुण्यौ चाग्निवारुण्यौ भेषजवनस्पतिं प्राजापत्यं सौविष्टकृतं च हुत्वा पुरस्तात् स्विष्टकृतं प्रायश्चित्तं जुहोति "यन्म आत्मन" इति पञ्च । "पाहि नो अग्न एनस" इति चैषोऽनुवाकः । अत्र महाव्याहृतिभिर्हुत्वा "भुरग्नये च पृथिव्यै च महते च स्वाहा" इति अत्रैव प्रणवं जुहुयाद् व्याहृतिभिः समस्ताभिश्च ॥३॥

Similarly he sacrifices the second time after making her stand up and circumambulate the fire. Similarly a third time. Making her sit down and collecting the wood for the sacrifice, he offers oblations with the *darvi* spoon to Varuṇa, Agni-Varuṇa, medicinal herbs, Prajāpati, Sviṣṭakṛt and later performs the expiatory oblations to Sviṣṭakṛt with the *mantra*, "that mind which of the soul", five times. Also with the *anuvāk*, "Agni! protect us from making mistakes". Here offering the *mahāvyāhṛtis*, he sacrifices with the *mantra*, "To Bhūr, Agni and Mahat, *svāhā*!" He offers oblations to *praṇava* and *vyāhṛtis* and all the others.

अथ मध्यमं परिधिमक्त्वा दक्षिणार्धं च, अप उपस्पृश्य उत्तरार्धं च परिस्तरणेभ्योऽर्धमर्धमादाय दर्व्यामग्रमनक्ति मध्यं च, आज्यस्थाल्यां

मूलमनक्ति। पुनरपि दर्व्यामग्रं मध्यं च, आज्यस्थाल्यां मूलमनक्ति । पुनरपि आज्यस्थाल्यां मूलं, मध्यं चाग्रं च दर्व्याम् । तृणं निधायाप उपस्पृश्य शिष्टमग्नौ प्रहरेत् । "नात्यग्रं प्रहरेत् यदत्यग्रं प्रहरेद्" इति ब्राह्मणम् । त्रिरुद्यत्य तृणमप्यनुप्रहरेत् । अङ्गुलिं त्रिरुद्यम्य प्राणस्थानं चक्ष्वादि संमिश्य परिधिनादाय मध्यं प्रथमं प्रहरेत् । युगपद् दक्षिणमुत्तरं च । ऊर्ध्वे समिधौ प्रहरति । उत्तरार्धमङ्गारेषूपोहति । संस्रावेणाभिजुहुयात् । अथ परिषिञ्चति । यथा पुरस्ताद् "अन्वमंस्थाः प्रासावीः" इति मन्त्रान्तान् सन्नमति ।४॥

Then establishing the southern half of the area from the fire with wooden *paridhis* in the middle, touching water, he establishes the upper half also with the *ājya* plate in the beginning and *darvi* spoons in the middle. He repeats this thrice. Having strewn grass and touching water he offers the remnants to Agni. "*Nātyagraṁ praharet yadatyagraṁ praharet*" says the brāhmaṇa.

प्रणिताप्रणयनमादायाग्रेणाग्निं परिहृत्य दक्षिणेनाग्निं चाश्मानो देशे निधाय यथाशक्ति दक्षिणां ब्रह्मणे दत्त्वा प्रागादि प्रतिदिशं तूष्णीं मार्जयते । किञ्चिदवसिच्य हस्तेन मार्जयेत् । "आपो हि ष्ठा मयोभुव" इति तिसृभिः, "हिरण्यवर्णाः शुचयः पावका" इति चतसृभिः, "पवमानः सुवर्जन" इत्येतानुवाकेन "कयानश्चित्र आभुवद्" इति तिसृभिः, "प्राजपत्यं पवित्रम्" इति द्वाभ्याम् । एतस्मिन् काले ब्रह्मा यथाप्रपन्नमुपनिष्क्रामणमिति । प्रायश्चित्तादि आ ब्रह्मण उपनिष्क्रामणात् "सर्वदर्वीहोमानामेष समानम्" । अत्र गुरुवे वरं ददाति ।५॥

Bringing the marriage water to the front of the fire and sprinkling it, to the south of the fire keeping the stone, to the extent possible, giving *dakṣiṇā* to brāhmaṇas, from the east he washes in all directions, silently. Sprinkling a little, he washes with his hands. With the *mantras*, "O water you are happiness", thrice; "golden coloured and pure", four times. With the *anuvāk*, "wind for good growth", "for whom this picture is drawn", thrice; "Prajapati is pure", twice. During this time, Brahmā as mentioned goes away. Beginning with expiation, the going of brāhmaṇas is equal to *homas* with all the spoons. Then he gives *dakṣiṇā* to the *guru*.

अथ देवतानामुपतिष्ठते "अग्ने व्रतपते व्रतं चरिष्यामि" इत्येतैः । "अमूहमस्मि"

इत्यथास्या दक्षिणे कर्णे जपति । अथास्या दक्षिणेन हस्तेन दक्षिणमंसमुपर्युपरि अवमृश्य हृदयदेशमभिमृशति — "मम हृदये हृदयं ते अस्तु" इति द्वाभ्याम् । अथापरेणाग्निमिदंविष्णुक्रमात् प्रक्रयामि "एकमिषे विष्णुस्त्वान्वेतु" इति । मनाग् दक्षिणं पूर्वं पादं प्रहरति । सव्येनानुनिष्क्रामति । अत्रैव सप्तमं पदं विक्रमते । नाग्निमति प्रच्यवते । "सखायौ सप्तपदाबभूव" इति सप्तमे पदे जपति ।६॥

Then he establishes the gods with the *mantra*, "O Agni! God of *vratas*, I will carry out the *vrata*". He whispers into her right ear, "I am this". Then with his right hand going round her shoulder he touches her chest (heart) with the *mantra*, "Let your heart be in mine", twice. Then to west of the fire, he makes her take steps with the *mantra*, "First step for sap, let Viṣṇu carry you", he makes her step with her right foot first and finish with the left foot. Similarly, they take seven steps. They will cross the boundaries of Agni. With the seventh step, he chants, "with the seventh step become friends".

अथापरेणाग्निमुदङ्मुखस्तिष्ठन् सप्तऋषीनुपतिष्ठते "सप्त ऋषयः प्रथमां कृत्तिकानाम्" इति । अथ "ध्रुवं नमस्यामि" इति । मुहूर्तमुपविश्य औपासनाग्निमाहवनीयाकारे कुण्डे निधायात्र सदस्या आशिर्वादं कुर्वन्ति । अथ व्रजं प्रपद्यते । अथास्या दक्षिणेन हस्तेन दक्षिणं पाणिं परिगृह्य दक्षिणं द्वारेयीमभिमृशति "शन्न एधि द्विपदे शं चतुस्पद" इति । एवमुत्तराम् । अगारं प्रविश्यानडुहे चर्मण्युत्तरे लोम्न्युपविशति "इह गावो निषीदन्तु" इति । ज्ञातिसम्भाषावासाते ।७॥

Then to the west of the fire with face turned to the north, they see the *saptarṣi maṇḍala* with the *mantra*, "Seven *ṛṣis* with Kṛttikā being first". At the right time, having brought the *aupāsana* fire in a vessel, the people present bless the couple. They then walk to the cowshed. Then he takes her right hand in his right hand, he touches the southern door with the *mantra*, "Let the two-footed and four-footed prosper". Similarly, with the northern door. Entering the house, they make her sit on a bull's hide with the hair on the upper side, "Here cows are not allowed". The couple enter into conversation with the relations.

ब्रह्मचारिणावलंकुर्वणौ त्र्यहं व्रातं चरे यातामक्षारलवणमशमीधान्यं भुञ्जानावधःशायिनावसंवर्तमनौ सहचर्याताम् । सायंप्रातरौपासने जुहोति व्रीहिभिर्यवैर्वा । सायं प्रथममग्निमुपसमाधाय परिस्तीर्य प्रक्षाळ्य स्थालीं निष्टप्य सम्मृज्य एकमुष्टिं व्रीहीनोप्य पर्यग्नि कृत्वा गन्धपुष्पैरग्निमलंकृत्य इन्द्रयाग्नये यमाय निर्ऋत्यै वरुणाय वायवे सोमायेशानयेति प्रागादि प्रतिदिशं पश्चादात्मानमलंकृत्य अप उपस्पृश्य सपवित्रपाणिः "अदितेऽनुम्न्यस्व" इति परिषिच्य समिधमभ्याधाय प्रज्वलयित्वा हस्तेन व्रीहीन् जुहुयाद् "अग्नये स्वाहा, प्रजापतये स्वाहा" इति सायं, "सूर्याय स्वाहा, प्रजापतये स्वाहा" इति प्रातः । "अदितेऽन्वमंस्था" इति परिषिच्य "कनीयस्तस्य पूर्वं हुत्वोत्तरं भूयो जुहुयाद्" इति ब्राह्मणम् । एवमौपासने जुहोति । अथापरं पत्नीं भोजयेत् । तस्मान्नित्यो धार्योऽनुगतो मन्थ्यः श्रोत्रियागाराद्वाहार्यः । प्रायश्चित्तम् जुहोति "अथाश्चाग्नेरनभिशस्तीश्च सत्यमित्वमया असि । अयसा मनसा धृतोऽयसा हव्यमूहिषेऽयानो धेहि भेषजं स्वाहा" इति ।८॥

The *trirātra vrata* is observed with celibacy, avoiding food with spices and salt and sleeping on the ground. Aupāsana *homa* is observed in the evening and morning with rice, barley, etc. In the evening establishing the fire, having washed the *sthālī*s, taking rice grains in one fist and pouring into the fire, then decorating her up with sandal paste, flowers, he worships, "To Indra, Agni, Yama, Nirṛtya, Varuṇa, Vāyu, Soma, Īśāna on all sides beginning with the east, later decorating himself, touching water, he sprinkles with the *mantra*, "Aditi! do not go away" and "his younger first and then he worships" according to brāhmaṇas. Similarly, he conducts the Aupāsana *homa*. Then he makes his wife eat. From that takes cooked rice, etc. followed by churning and feeds *śrotri*s in the hall. Then he observes expiation, "To Agni who is blameless and with truth and illusion. With an iron mind and determined mind take this *havis* and give us health, *svāhā*!"

त्र्यहे पर्यपेते निश्यग्निप्रतिष्ठापनादि प्रसिद्धं दार्विहोमिकमा राष्ट्रभृद्भ्यो विवाहग्रकृतिं नयेल्लाजादिसम्भारवर्जं प्रतिग्रहमार्जनवासःपरिधानवर्जम् एवमेष सर्वेषां विवाहप्रकृतिम्। आकालं प्रायश्चित्तम् जुहोति "अग्नये प्रायश्चित्त" इति चतुसृभिः । वारुण्यादि समानम् । व्रतविसर्गः ।९॥

It is known that the night fire is established and will be gone round thrice. Darvi *homas*, Rāṣṭrabhṛt, etc. are done in the beginning of the wedding and Lājā *homa*, *pāṇigrahaṇa*, bathing, wearing of clothes, etc. are during the wedding. Later, he performs expiation with, "To Agni you are expiation", four times. Similarly to Varuṇa. Then *vrata* is over.

अथ व्रतं विसृजते "अग्ने व्रतपते व्रतमचारिषम्" इत्ये(तैः) । अथ पुन्याहं वाचयित्वा "आवाभ्यां दम्पतिभ्यां स्वस्ति भवन्तो ब्रुवन्तु" इति । "युवाभ्यां दम्पतिभ्यां स्वस्ति" इति प्रतिवचनम् । अथास्या उपस्थमभिमृशति "शिवेन त्वाभिमृशामि" इति । प्रतिसंविशाति "ऋषभेण स्कन्दामि" इति । रत्यन्तं कृत्वा जपेत् "आ नो योनिं गर्भ एतु" इति तिसृभिः । एवमेव मासि मास्यृतुवेलायां संतिष्ठते भार्योपयमनम् ॥१०॥

After finishing the *vrata* with "Agni! God of *vratas*, I have done the *vratas*" *puṇyāham* will be read out, "Let this couple be fortunate and happy. This couple will be, is said in return. He then touches her private parts, "With auspiciousness I touch you. He makes intercourse with the *mantra*, "With the shoulders of a bull". After the intercourse he chants, "Let this *yoni* create the embryo". Similarly at end of her monthly periods, he makes intercourse.

अथसमावृत्तेभार्यामुपयच्चेत अथाष्टौसमृद्धिमाञ्जुहोति एवंद्वितीयमास्थाप्य त्रीणि ॥११॥

Then after a bath he takes his bride and carries out eight *samṛddhi homas*. Similarly, thrice in the second month.

Bhāradvāja Gṛhya-Sūtra

Bhāradvāja Gṛhya-Sūtra belongs to the Taittirīya branch of *Kṛṣṇa Yajurveda*. Though a commentary is available, name of the commentator is not known. The following is the text of the *Bhāradvāja Gṛhya-Sūtra* which deals with *vivāha saṁskāra*:

प्रथमः प्रश्नः (First Praśna)
एकादशः खण्डः (Eleventh Chapter)

चत्वारि विवाहकरणानि वित्तं रूपं प्रज्ञा बान्धवमिति ॥१॥
There are four aspects in choosing a bride: wealth, beauty, intelligence and relations.

तानिन्चेत्सर्वाणि न शक्नुयाद्वित्तमुदस्येत् ॥२॥
If you cannot find all the aspects, you can leave out wealth.

ततो रूपं ॥३॥
Similarly beauty.

प्रज्ञायां च बान्धवे च विवदन्ते ॥४॥
Intelligence and relations are accepted.

बान्धवमुदस्येदित्येक आहुः ॥५॥
Some say that relations also can be ignored.

अप्रज्ञेन हि कः संवासः ॥६॥
Who can live with someone who is not intelligent?

अथैतदपरं न खल्वियमर्थेभ्य ऊह्यते प्रजननार्थोऽस्यां प्रधानः स योऽलं संलक्षणाय स्यात्स तामावहेत यस्यां प्रशस्ता जायेरन् ॥७॥
It is said that one does choose a girl for money alone. The main purpose is to beget children. It is enough if the girl is with features which will help beget good children.

न स्वपन्तीमुपगृह्णीत न चरन्ती ॥८॥
Do not marry a girl who is sleeping when you visit or one who goes out.

प्रथममभ्यागच्छन्नामङ्गल्यानि मङ्गल्यानि परिपृच्छेत् ॥९॥
When you visit the bride's house do not ask inauspicious questions.

चतुरो लोष्टानाहरेद्वेदिलोष्टं गोमयलोष्टं सीतालोष्टं श्मशानलोष्टमिति तामाहैषामेकमादत्स्वेति ॥१०॥
Get four lumps of mud prepared, one from an altar, one

from a cowshed, one from a ploughed field and one from a cemetery and ask her to choose one.

सा चेद्वेदिलोष्टमाददीताध्यापकं यायजूकं जनयिष्यतीति विद्यात् ॥११॥
If she chooses the lump from the altar, she will give birth to a son who will be a teacher, one who carries out frequent *homas*, etc.

यदि गोमयलोष्टं बहुपशुं जनयिष्यतीति विद्यात् ॥१२॥
If she chooses the one from the cowshed, they will be rich in cattle.

यदि सीतालोष्टं कृष्टराधिकं जनयिष्यतीति विद्यात् ॥१३॥
If she chooses from the lump from a ploughed field, they will have a lot of fields.

यदि श्मशानलोष्टमादहनशीक्षाणि परिख्योतेति विद्यात् ॥१४॥
If she chooses the one from a cemetery, there will be misery due to burning, etc.

नैनामुपगृह्णीत ॥१५॥
Do not marry if she chooses the one from the cemetery.

अथ खलु बहूनि लक्षणानि भवन्ति ॥१६॥
Then there are many features of a bride.

श्लोकं तु लाक्षणा उदाहरन्ति "यस्यां मनोऽनुरमते चक्षुश्च प्रतिबद्यते । तां विद्यात्पुण्यलक्ष्मीकां किं ज्ञानेन करिष्यति ॥" इति॥१७॥
The *śloka* on features says, "The one whom the mind likes which fixes ones eyes on her, marry her as a Lakṣmī, what other knowledge is required?"

उदगयन उदगृह्णीत विज्ञायत उदगयनं देवानामिति दैवं पुनरिदं कर्म ॥ १८॥
Get married in the northern movement of the sun. The period belongs to gods and is fit for good rituals.

द्वादशः खण्डः (Twelfth Chapter)

दक्षिणायन इत्यपरं विज्ञायते दक्षिणायनं पितृणामिति पितृसंयुक्तं पुनरिदं कर्म ॥१॥

Dakṣiṇāyana is said to belong to the manes and therefore is suitable for rituals involving manes.

पूर्वपक्ष उपगृह्णीत विज्ञायते पूर्वपक्षो देवानामिति दैवं पुनरिदं कर्म ॥ २॥
Śukla pakṣa belongs to *deva*s and is suitable for rituals involving *deva*s including marriage.

अपरपक्ष इत्यपरं विज्ञायतेऽपरपक्षः पितृणामिति पितृसंयुक्तं पुनरिदं कर्म ॥३॥
Kṛṣṇa pakṣa belongs to the manes and therefore is suitable for rituals involving manes including marriage.

पूर्वाह्ण उपगृह्णीत विज्ञायते पूर्वाह्णो देवानामिति दैवं पुनरिदं कर्म ॥४॥
Forenoon belongs to the gods and therefore is suitable for rituals involving gods including marriage.

मध्यंदिनमुपगृह्णीत विज्ञायते मध्यंदिनमृषीणामित्यृषिसंयुक्तं पुनरिदं कर्माथापि विज्ञायते तस्मान्मध्यंदिने सर्वाणि पुण्यानि संनिपतितानि भवन्तीति ॥५॥
The midday is said to belong to *ṛṣi*s and is therefore suitable for all auspicious ceremonies including marriage.

अपराह्ण उपगृह्णीत विज्ञायतेऽपराह्णः पितृणामिति पितृस्संयुक्तं पुनरिदं कर्माथापि विज्ञायते भगस्यापराह्ण इति भगसंयुक्तं पुनरिदं कर्मथापि विज्ञायते तस्मादपराह्णे कुमार्यो भगमिच्छमानाश्चरन्तीति ॥६॥
The afternoon is said to belong to the manes and therefore is suitable for rituals involving manes including marriage. Afternoon is said to belong to Bhaga and is suitable for marriage.

पुण्याह उपगृह्णीतापि वै खलु लोके पुण्याह एव कर्माणि चिकीर्षन्ते तस्मादश्लीलनामंश्चित्रे नावस्येन्न यजेत यथा पापाहे कुरुते तादृगेव तदिति परिचष्ट एव पापाहं विज्ञायते खलु ॥७॥
Under an auspicious star it is good to conduct the marriage. Those desirous of doing auspicious rituals should not perform rituals under undesirable stars. They have to reject undesirable stars for rituals.

एकेषामिन्वकाभिः प्रसृज्यन्ते ते वराः प्रतिनन्दिताः ॥८॥

Some *ācāryas* say that a bride who has been chosen under Invakā (Mṛgaśirā) star will bring happiness to the bridegroom with her family.

मघाभिर्गावो गृह्यन्ते॥९॥

During Māgha month, the bride's people will give cows to the groom.

फल्गणीभ्यां व्यूह्यते ॥१०॥

In Phālguna month, they are taken away. Marriage is performed in Māgha and the bride is taken to her husband's house in Phālguna.

यां कामयेत दुहितरं प्रिया स्यादिति तां निष्ट्यायां दद्यात्प्रियैव भवति नैव तु पुनरागच्छतीति विज्ञायते ॥११॥

One who treats the daughter as a favourite should give her away under Svāti *nakṣatra*. She will become dear to her husband and will not return to her father's house, it is said.

त्रयोदशः खण्डः (Thirteenth Chapter)

तत आह स्नापयतैनामिति ॥१॥

After the *madhuparka*, she is brought by her relatives for ritual bathing.

स्नातायै वाससी प्रयच्छति या अकृन्तन्नवयन्या अतन्वत याश्च देविरन्तानभितोऽददन्त । तास्त्वा देवीर्जरसे संव्ययन्त्वायुष्मतीदं परिधत्स्व वासः इति ॥२॥

After she has bathed, she is given new clothes with the marks, 'those who weave . . .'. Thus she will have the blessing of the goddess for long life.

आथैनां परिधापयति परिधत्त धत्त वाससैनां शतायुर्षीं कृणुत दीर्घमायुः । बृहस्पतिः प्रयच्छद्वास एतत्सोमाय राज्ञे परिधातवा उ ॥ जरां गच्छासि परिधत्स्व वासो भवा कृष्टीनामभिशस्तिपावती । शतं च जीव शरदः सुवर्चा रायश्च पोषमुपसंव्ययस्व ॥३॥

She is made to wear the new clothes by her relations saying that she will live 100 years. They bless her saying, "You will live to see hundred autumns with lustre, wealth and well-being".

परिहितानामभिमन्त्रयते परीदं वासो अधिधाः स्वस्तयेऽभूरापीनामभिशस्तिपावती ।
शतं च जीव शरदः परूचीर्वसूनि चार्या विभजासि जीवती इति ॥४॥
After she is dressed, Svasti is recited and she is blessed. "Live to see hundred autumns."

अथास्या अग्रेणा ज्ञातिकुलमग्निमुपसमाधायाघारावाघार्याज्यभागौ जुहोत्यग्नये जनिविदे स्वाहेत्युत्तरार्धपूर्वार्ध सोमाय जनिविदे स्वाहेति दक्षिणार्धपूर्वार्ध ॥५॥
Then her relatives will prepare the fire and sacrifices with ghee with, "to Agni who gave me my wife, *svāhā*!" in the north-east and "To Soma who gave me my wife, *svāhā*!" in the south-east.

तत एता आहुतीर्जुहोति भूः स्वाहा भुवः स्वाहा सुवः स्वाहा भूर्भुवः सुवः स्वाहा या तिरश्ची यानूची संराधन्ये प्रसाधन्ये सदसस्पतीं युक्तौ वह जातवेद इति ॥६॥
Then sacrifices are made with *vyāhṛtis*, "Bhūḥ *svāhā*! Bhuvaḥ *svāhā*! Suvaḥ *svāhā*! and Bhurbhuvaḥsuvaḥ *svāhā*!" Seeking the blessings of Jātavedas.

जयाभ्यातानान्राष्ट्रभृत इति ॥७॥
Jayā, Abhyātāna and Rāṣṭrabhṛt *homa*s are conducted.

एता आहुतीर्जुहोति ॥८॥
Sacrifices are made as per normal practice.

चतुर्दशः खण्डः (Fourteenth Chapter)

अग्निरैतु प्रथमो देवतानां सोऽस्यै प्रजां मुञ्चतु मृत्युपाशात् । तदयं राजा वरुणोऽनुमन्यतां यथेयं स्त्री पौत्रमघं न रोदात्स्वाहा ॥ इमामग्निस्त्रायतां गार्हपत्यः प्रजागरयै नयतु दीर्घमायुः । अशून्योपस्था जीवतामस्तु माता पौत्रमानन्दमभिप्रबुध्यतामियं स्वाहा ॥ मा ते गृहे निशि घोष उत्थादन्यत्र त्वद्रुदत्यः संविशन्तु । मा त्वं विकेश्युर आवधिष्ठा जीवपत्नी पतिलोके विराज पश्यन्ती प्रजां सुमनस्यमानां स्वाहा ॥ द्योस्ते पृष्ठं रक्षतु वायुरूरू अश्विनौ च स्तनं धयन्तं सविताभिरक्षतु । आ वाससः परिधानाद्बृहस्पतिर्विश्वे देवा अभिरक्षन्तु पश्चात्स्वाहा ॥ अप्रजस्तां पौत्रमृत्युं पाप्मानमुत वाघम् ।

शीर्ष्णः स्रजमिवोन्मुच्य द्विषद्भ्यः प्रतिमुञ्चामि पाशं स्वाहेति पूर्णा पश्चादिमं मे वरुणा तत्त्वा यामि त्वं नो अग्ने स त्वं नो अग्ने त्वमग्ने अयास्ययाश्चाग्नेऽस्यनभिशस्तीश्च यदस्य कर्मणोऽत्यरीरिचं ॥१॥

"Agni! You are the first among gods, release her children from the fetters of death. King Varuṇa bless her so that she does not cry due to losing her children. Take this housewife who maintains the *gārhapatyāgni* and her children to long life. Let there be no noises in her house in the night to make her cry. Let her not be without hair (widow), let her be a living wife in her husband's world and see children with a good mind, *svāhā*! Let heavens protect her behind, Vāyu her thighs, Aśvins her breasts, Savitā her nipples. By wearing these clothes, let Bṛhaspati, Viśvedeva protect her, *svāhā*! Let her not suffer not having children, loss of children, and other sinful dangers. By removing the garland from her head, I release her from her enemies, passions *svāhā*! This woman is your sister, Varuṇa, to Agni I hand over for protection."

प्रजापत इत्युत्तमां हुत्वा ॥२॥

Offer sacrifices to Prajāpati and other gods.

गुरवे वरं ददाति ॥३॥

He gives a gift to the *guru*.

पञ्चदशः खण्डः (Fifteenth Chapter)

अपरेणाग्निं द्वयान्दर्भन्पूर्वापरानुदगग्रान्स्तृणाति तेषु पूर्वापरावुपतिष्ठेते ॥ १॥

To the west of the two sets of *darbha* grass are spread and on that facing west stands the bride and facing east stands the groom.

प्राङ्मुखः प्रत्यङ्मुख्या हस्तं गृह्णीयादित्येकं प्रत्यङ्मुखः प्राङ्मुख्या इत्यपरम् ॥२॥

The groom facing east takes the hand of the bride who is facing west.

अथैनयोः प्रैषकृदञ्जली उदकेन पूरयति ॥ ३॥

Then he fills water in her joined hands.

अथास्याञ्जलिनाञ्जलावुदकमानयति शं नो देवीरभिष्ट्य आपो भवन्तु पीतये । शं योरभिस्रवन्तु न इति ॥४॥

He pours water into her hands with, "Let the goddesses good wishes become water; let the water flow with auspiciousness".

अथास्या दक्षिणेन हस्तेन दक्षिणं हस्तमभिवाङ्गुष्ठमभीव लोमानि गृह्णाति देवस्य त्वा सवितुः प्रसवेऽश्विनोर्बाहुभ्यां पूष्णो हस्ताभ्यां ॥ हस्तेन ते हस्तं गृह्णामि सौभगत्वाय मया पत्या जरदिष्टिर्यथासः । भगो अर्यमा सविता पुरन्धिस्ते त्वा देवा अदुर्मह्यं पत्नीम् ॥ अघोरचक्षुरपतिध्न्येधि शिवा पशुभ्यः शन्तमा प्रजायै । क्षुरपविर्जारिभ्यो जीवसूर्वीरसूः स्योना मह्यं त्वादुर्गार्हपयाय देवाः ॥ तां नः पूषञ्छिवतममेरयस्व यस्यां बीजं मनुष्या वपन्ति । या न ऊरू उशती विस्रयातै यस्यामुशन्तः प्रहरेम शेफम् ॥ सोमः प्रथमो विविदे गन्धर्वस्ततोऽपरः । तृतीयो अग्निष्टे पतिस्तुरीयस्ते मनुष्यजाः ॥ सोमो ददद्गन्धर्वाय गन्धर्वोऽग्नये ददत् । रयिं च पुत्रांश्चादादग्निर्मह्यमथो इमाम् । सरस्वति प्रेदमव सुभगो वाजिनीवति । तां त्वा विश्वस्य भूतस्य प्रगायामस्यग्रत इति ॥५॥

Then he holds her right hand with his right hand including the thumb and the back of the hand with hairs saying, "You belong to the god, Savitā's womb, the two Aśvins shoulders and Pūṣaṇa's hands". "I hold your hand in mine for good fortune and grow old as your husband. Bhaga, Aryamā, Savitā and Puraṁdhi have given you to be my wife." Do not cast evil eyes to cause the death of your husband, let there be good in the cows and peace in the children. With Kṣurapavi sacrifice I ask you gods to make me a householder. That seed which belongs to Pūṣaṇa and is auspicious, this man is using. I beat with my organ quickly her genital organ when her thighs are spread. Soma is the first, then *gandharva*. Third is Agni and the fourth is man as husband. Soma gave her to *gandharva*, *gandharva* to Agni. For the sake of wealth and children, Agni gave her to me. Sarasvatī make her suitable to be a strong person with energy.

अथैनौ ब्रह्माभिमन्त्रयते समितं संकल्पेथां सं वां सृजामि हृदये । संसृष्टं मनो अस्तु वां संसृष्टः प्राणो अस्तु वां इति ॥६॥

Then they chant the *brahma mantra* and resolve that they will take each other in their hearts. Let their minds and breaths mingle.

अथैनामश्मानमास्थापयत्यतिष्ठेममश्मानमश्मेव त्वं स्थिरा भव । प्रमृणीहि दुरस्यून्सहस्व पृतनायत इति ॥७॥

Then he makes her stand on a stone saying: "Be unmoving like the stone. Cause death to the evil minded and face enemies with strength."

प्रदक्षिणमग्निं परिणयति विश्वा उत त्वया वयं धारा उदन्या इव । अतिगाहेमहि द्विषः इति ॥८॥

He takes her around the fire saying: "We will be like the flow which submerges everything, we will suppress our enemies".

अथास्या भ्राताञ्जलिनाञ्जलावुपस्तीर्णाभिघारितान्लाजानावपतीयं नार्युप्रब्रूतेऽग्नौ लाजानावपन्ती । दीर्घायुरस्तु मे पतिरेधन्तां ज्ञातयो मम ॥ भगेन त्वा संसृजामि मासरेण सुरामिव इति ॥९॥

Then her brother pours fried grains into her holded hands and mixed with ghee, she offers the grains to Agni. "Let my husband live long, let my relations flourish. I join you with happiness like rice gruel is mixed with *surā*."

आथैनां वाचयतीमान्लाजानावपामि समृद्धिकरणान्मम । तुभ्यं च संवननांस्तदग्निरनुमन्यतामियं स्वाहेति ॥१०॥

Then he recites: "I offer fried grains for the sake of prosperity. Let me be one with you with the blessings of Agni."

एवमेव त्रिरास्थापयति त्रिः परिणयति त्रिरावति ॥११॥

Similarly, Aśmārohaṇa, Agni *pariṇayana* and Lājā offerings are made thrice.

अथैनां प्राचीं वोदीचीं वा ॥१२॥

Then he takes her away in the eastern or northern direction.

षोडशः खण्डः (Sixteenth Chapter)

सप्त पदानि प्रक्रमयत्येकमिषे विष्णुस्त्वान्वेतु द्वे ऊर्जे विष्णुस्त्वान्वेतु त्रीणि

व्रताय विष्णुस्त्वान्वेतु चत्वारि मायोभवाय विष्णुस्त्वान्वेतु पञ्च पशुभ्यो विष्णुस्त्वान्वेतु षड्रायस्पोषाय विष्णुस्त्वान्वेतु सप्त सप्तभ्यो होत्राभ्यो विष्णुस्त्वान्वेतु इति ॥१॥

He makes her take seven steps with, "First step for sap, second for energy, third for *vratas*, fourth for happiness, fifth for cattle, sixth for wealth, seventh for rituals". At each step, "Let Viṣṇu lead you" is recited.

सप्तमे पदे समीक्षमाणो जपति सखा सप्तपदा भव सखायौ सप्तपदाबभूव। सख्यं ते गमेयं सख्यात्ते मा योषं सख्यान्मे मायोष्ठा इति ॥२॥

At the end of the seventh step he says, be my friend, let us be friends for life.

आथास्या दक्षिणमंसं प्रति बाहुमन्ववहृत्य हृदयदेशमभिमृशति "मम हृदये हृदयं ते अस्तु मम चित्ते चित्तमस्तु ते। मम वाचमेकमना शृणु मामेवानुव्रता भव सहचर्या मया भवेति" ॥३॥

Then he takes his hand round her right shoulder and touches her heart saying, "Let your heart be in mine, your mind in my mind. Listen with concentration to what I say, be my follower, my companion."

अथास्यै दक्षिणं कर्णमाजपति मां ते चित्तं प्रविशतु मां चक्षुर्मामु ते मनः। मयि सर्वाणि भूतानि मयि प्रज्ञानमस्तु ते। मधु हे मध्वागाहे जिह्वा मे मधुवादिनी। मुखे मे सारघं मधु दत्सु संवननं कृतम्॥ चाक्रवाकं संवननं यन्नदीभ्य उदाहृतम्। यद्देवगन्धर्वो वितस्तेन संवनिनौ स्वः। मां चैव पश्य सूर्यं च मान्येषु मनः कृथा इति ॥४॥

Then he whispers in her right ear, "Let me enter your mind, let my eyes enter your mind. All my body and mind be in your senses. Let your speech like honey on my tongue. With the honey from the bees, let my face be pleasing. Let there be concord like with the *cakravāka* birds. Like the *devas* and *gandharvas*. Look at me as you regard the sun and think of me similarly."

सप्तदशः खण्डः (Seventeenth Chapter)

अथास्याः स्वधितिं मूर्ध्नि धारयन्हिरण्यं वोदकुम्भेनावसिञ्चत्यापो हि ष्ठा

मयोभुव इति तिसृभिर्हिरण्यवर्णाः शुचयः पावका इति चतुसृभिः पवमानः सुवर्जन इत्येतानुवाकेन ॥१॥

Then on her head gold coins are kept and from a vessel water is sprinkled with the *mantra*, "O water make her happy", thrice. "Golden coloured, clean and holy", four times and with the *anuvāka*, "O wind blow favourably".

अवसिच्य यथार्थं वहन्ति ॥२॥

After the sprinkling, the bride is carried away as usual in a chariot, etc.

ऊह्यमानामनुमन्त्रयते — "ये वध्वश्चन्द्रं वहतुं यक्ष्मा यन्ति जनामनु । पुनस्तान्यज्ञिया देवा नयन्तु यत आगता" इति ॥३॥

After changing (her dress) they chant: "The bride is carried by Candra, let her diseases be carried by others. Let the gods who have been worshipped take her where she is welcome."

अथैनां गृहानुह्यानुडुहे रोहिते चर्मण्युपवेशयतीह गावो निषीदन्त्विहाश्वा इह पुरुषाः । इहा सहस्रदक्षिणोऽभि पूषा निषीदत्विति ॥४॥

Then after she enters the house, she is made to sit on a red skin of a bull. Here men gift her cows. Here Pūṣaṇa will grant her 1,000 gifts.

अथैनामग्नेयेन स्थालीपाकेन याजयति ॥५॥

Then he makes her offer sacrifice to Agni with *sthālīpāka*.

अथैतस्य स्थालीपाकस्योपहत्याभिघार्य जुहोत्यग्नये स्वाहाग्नयेऽग्निवते स्वाहयग्नेऽन्नादाय स्वाहाग्नये स्विष्टकृते स्वाहेति ॥६॥

Then from the *sthālīpāka* taking the remainder of cooked food, he worships: "To Agni, *svāhā*! To Agni and to the one with Agni *svāhā*! To Agni and the one who gave the cooked rice, *svāhā*! To Sviṣṭakṛt, *svāhā*!"

यावज्जीवमेतमग्निं व्रीहिभिर्यवैर्वा सायं प्रातः परिचरत्यग्नये स्वाहेति सायं पूर्वानाहुतिं जुहोति प्रजापतये स्वाहेत्युत्तराम् ॥७॥

To the eternal fire, he offers rice grains, or barley, saying "to Agni *svāha*!" in the morning and evening, first to Agni and then to Prajāpati.

सौरी पूर्वां प्रातरेके समामनन्ति ॥८॥
Some say offer oblations in the morning to Sūrya.

अत्यौपासनः ॥९॥
Then the Aupāsana *homa* is carried out.

नित्यः ॥१०॥
Constantly.

धार्यः ॥११॥
By the living.

अनुगतो मन्थ्यः ॥१२॥
The fire for the *homa* should be prepared by attrition.

श्रोत्रियागाराद्वाहार्यः ॥१३॥
Where it was a hall belonging to a *śrotrī*, there also.

अन्यतरस्य चैतदहरुपवासः ॥ १४॥
If unable, she should fast.

अष्टादशः खण्डः (Eighteenth Chapter)

अष्टाम्यां पर्वाणि चोपवसति ॥१॥
On *aṣṭamī*s and new and full moon days, they fast.

आग्नेयेन स्थालीपाकेन पर्वसु यजते ॥२॥
During *parvaṇa*, they worship with cooked food in the south-east.

वाग्यत आस्त आ नक्षत्राणामुदयात् ॥३॥
They remain silent till the appearance of the stars.

उदितेषु नक्षत्रेषु वत्समन्वारभ्योत्थापयत्युदायुषा स्वायुषेति ॥४॥
When the stars appear, he makes her rise touching her and they go out.

अथैनां ध्रुवमरुन्धतीमन्यानि च नक्षत्राण्यभिवीक्षयति नमो ब्रह्मणे ध्रुवायाच्युतायास्त्वित्येतेनानुवाकेन ध्रुवमुपतिष्ठते ध्रुवक्षितिर्ध्रुवयोनिर्ध्रुवमसि

ध्रुवत स्थितम् । त्वं नक्षत्राणां मेथ्यसि स मा पाहि पुतन्यत इति सप्तर्षयः प्रथमां कृत्तिकानामरुन्धतीं ध्रुवतां ये ह नित्युः । षट्कृत्तिका मुख्ययोगं वहन्तीयमस्माकं भ्राजत्वष्टमीत्यरुन्धतीम् ॥५॥

Then he shows her Dhruva, Arundhatī and other stars with the *anuvāka*: "I salute you Brahmā, Dhruva who is unmoving and firm: Dhruva you are the source of constancy. You are the pole of stars, protect us from enemies. The first star among Kṛttikās is Arundhatī whose steadfastness is eternal. Please make our relationship similar."

त्रिरात्रमक्षारलवणाशिनावधःशायिनो ब्रह्मचारिणौ भवतः ॥६॥

For three nights they observe *vrata*, eating bland food, sleeping on the floor and practising celibacy.

अथ चतुर्थ्यामपररात्रेऽत्तरागारेऽग्निमुपसमाधाय जयाभ्यातानात्राष्ट्रभृत इति हुत्वता आहुतीर्जुहोत्यग्ने प्रायश्चित्ते त्वं देवानां प्रायश्चित्तिरसि ब्राह्मणस्त्वा नाथकामः प्रपद्ये । यास्यां पतिघ्नो तनूः प्रजाघ्नी पशुघ्नी लक्ष्मिघ्नो जारघ्नीमस्यै तां कृणोति स्वाहा ॥ वायो प्रायश्चित्त आदित्य प्रायश्चित्ते प्रजापते प्रायश्चित्ते त्वं देवानां प्रायश्चित्तिरसि ब्राह्मनस्त्वा नाथकामः प्रपद्ये । यास्यै निन्दिता तनूस्तामितो नाशयामसि स्वाहेति ॥७॥

Then on the fourth night, he establishes the fire on the northern side of the hall and carries out Jayā, Abhyātāna and Rāṣṭrabhṛt *homa*s. He carries out expiation of gods: "Agni you are the expiation of the gods, our desires are met by you. What is in her that may kill her husband, cattle and wealth, destroy it. Vāyu, you are expiation, Āditya, you are expiation, Prajāpati, you are expiation. Destroy the evil in her body."

एकोनविंशः खण्डः (Nineteenth Chapter)

अथैनां तूष्णीं हिंकृत्य वाग्यत उपेत्यामूहमस्मि सा त्वं द्योरहं पृथिवी त्वं सामाहमृक्त्वं तावेहि संभवाव सह रेतो दधावहै पुंसे पुत्राय वेत्तवै रायस्पोषाय सुप्रजस्त्वाय सुवीर्यायति ॥१॥

Then silently he holds her and says, "I am this (God), you are that (Goddess), heaven I am, earth you are, I am the song, you are the lyric, let us get together, I give my sperm for begetting children. For the sake of good children, heroes, wealth and happiness."

अथास्या अपवृत्तर्थोऽपवृत्तर्थायै मुखेन मुखं संनिधाय प्राणित्येतं पाणामपानिहीति ॥२॥

Then he embraces, brings his face to her face, and breathes together with her.

तं सा प्रत्यपानि ॥३॥

She reciprocates.

अथास्या आचान्तोदकायै पाणी प्रक्षाल्यभिमृशति करद्दधच्छिवेन त्वा पञ्चशाखेन हस्तेनाविद्विषवता साहस्रेण यशस्विनाभिमृशति सुप्रजस्त्वायेति भसद्देशं ॥४॥

Then sipping water, washing his hand touches her, I touch you with auspicious hand, without enemity, happily for the sake of good children.

यदा मलवद्वासाः स्यादथैनां ब्राह्मणप्रतिषिद्धानि व्रतानि सँशास्ति या मलवद्वासमिति ॥५॥

If her dress is dirtied, he makes her do the *brāhmaṇa pratiṣiddha vrata*s.

अथ चतुर्थ्यां स्नातां प्रयतवस्त्रां ब्राह्मणसंभाषां सं ते मनसा मन इत्येतेनानुवाकेनोपसंविशति ॥६॥

Then on the fourth day, they bathe and wear different clothes and with the *anuvāka*, "My mind in yours", he has intercourse with her.

सर्वाण्युपायनानि मन्त्रवन्ति भवन्तीत्याश्मरथ्यः ॥७॥

During all the acts, *mantra*s are recited.

यच्चदौ यच्चर्तावित्यालेखनः ॥८॥

What is carried out in the first intercourse is repeated after every monthly menstruation.

Kāṭhaka Gṛhya-Sūtra

Kāṭhaka Gṛhya-Sūtra belongs to the Kaṭha (Kāṭhaka) branch of *Kṛṣṇa Yajurveda*. It is also known under the name *Laugākṣi Gṛhya-Sūtra*. Devapāla and others have written commentaries on the Gṛhya-Sūtra. The following is the text of *Kāṭhaka Gṛhya-Sūtra* which deals with *vivāha saṁskāra*.

द्वितीयोऽध्यायः (Second Chapter)
चतुर्दशी काण्डिका (Fourteenth Section)

उदगयने भार्यां विन्देत ॥१॥
Get a bride during the northern course of the sun.

कृत्तिकास्वातिपूर्वैवरयेत् ॥२॥
Marry under Kṛttikā, Svāti and stars beginning with Pūrva (Pūrvā Phālgunī, Pūrvāṣāḍhā, Pūrvabhadrā).

लक्षणिना लक्षणानि परिक्षयेत् ॥३॥
Examine the features of the bride (before selection).

भागधेयमपि वा पिण्डैः परिक्षयेत् ॥४॥
Select from her background or using lumps of mud.

वेद्याः सीताया ह्रदयद्गोष्ठादादेवनादादहनाच्चतुष्पथादिरिणात्संभार्यं नवमम्। ऋतमेव परमेष्ठ्तं नात्येति किञ्चन। ऋत इयं पृथिवी श्रिता सर्वामिदमियमसौ भूयादिति ॥५॥
Make nine lumps of mud: eight from an altar, a ploughed field, a reservoir, a cowshed, a gambling den, a cemetery, crossroads, an arid place and the ninth one made from the mixture of all the above. Chanting the *mantra*, keep the lumps on the floor and make them all similar.

कन्याया नाम गृहीत्वा सर्वतः कृतलक्षणान्पिण्डान्पाणावादाय कुमार्या उपनामधेयेतेषामेकं गृहाणेति ब्रूयात् पूर्वेषां चतुर्णामेकं गृह्णतीमुपयच्छेत् ॥६॥
Taking her name, arranging the prepared lumps, ask her to give a name and pick one of the lumps. Earlier all the lumps would be kept in a square.

संभार्यमपीत्येके ॥७॥
Some say mix them all together.

रोहिणी मृगशिरः श्राविष्ठोत्तरा इत्युपयमे ॥८॥
Marry under Rohiṇī, Mṛgaśirā, Śraviṣṭhā (Dhaniṣṭhā), Uttarā stars.

यद्वा पुण्योक्तं ॥९॥
Or whenever it is said to be auspicious.

पञ्चदशी काण्डिका (Fifteenth Chapter)

अथ ब्राह्मदेयायाः प्रदानविधिं वक्ष्यामः ॥१॥
We will study the procedures as per Brāhma and other types of marriages.

शुद्धपक्षस्य पुण्याहे पर्वणि वेदगग्रान्दर्भानास्तीर्य तेषूपविशतः प्राङ्मुखः प्रतिगृहीता सामात्यः प्रत्यङ्मुखः प्रदाता ॥२॥
During the *śukla pakṣa* on an auspicious day, on a spread of *darbha* grass, the parents of the bride sit facing west and the groom facing east.

मध्ये प्रागग्रोदग्रान्दर्भानास्तीर्य तेषूदकं सन्निधाय ब्रीहियवानुप्य दक्षिणत उदङ्मासीन ऋत्विगुपयमनं कारयेत् ॥३॥
In the centre to the east, *darbha* grass is spread and water and rice grains are kept and *purohitas* sitting to the south will conduct the marriage.

समेतेष्वाह ददानीति प्रतिगृह्णामीति त्रिरावेदयते ॥४॥
The *purohitas* ask the father of the bride to say, "I offer my daughter" thrice, and groom says "I will accept" thrice.

एतद्वः सत्यमितुक्त्वा "समाना वः" "सं वोमनांसि" इति ऋत्विगुभ्यौ समीक्षमाणो जपति ॥५॥
"This giving is true and equal" say the *purohitas*. They ask the parents of the groom to observe.

षोडशी काण्डिका (Sixteenth Chapter)

अथ शुल्क देयायाः ॥१॥

Now the giving of bride price in the case of Asura type of marriage.

हिरण्यं व्यतिहरतः ॥२॥

Gold is given by the groom's father.

प्रजाभ्यस्त्वेति प्रददाति ॥३॥

Groom's father gives the gold saying, "for the sake of children".

रायस्पोषादय त्वेति प्रतिगृह्णाति ॥४॥

The bride's father receives saying, "for the sake of wealth".

कंसे हिरण्यं समुप्य "हिरण्यवर्णाः" इति चतसृभिः समवमृशन्ते ॥ ५॥

Keeping the gold in a brass vessel, it is touched four times chanting, "golden coloured".

सप्तदशी काण्डिका (Seventeenth Chapter)

गौदानिकैमन्त्रैः कन्यामलंकृत्य चतुष्पादे भद्रपीठे प्रागासीनायाश्चतस्रोऽविधवा माता पिता च गुरुः सप्तमस्तां सहस्रच्छिद्रेण पवित्रेण स्नापयित्वाहतेन वाससा प्रच्छाद्य स्थालीपाकस्य जुहोतीन्द्राण्यै कामाय भगाय ह्रियै श्रियै लक्ष्म्यै पुष्ट्यै विश्वावसवे गन्धर्वराजाय स्वाहेति ॥१॥

With the *mantra*, "*godānika*" the bride is decorated and made to sit on a seat with four legs. On the opposite side will be four *sumaṅgalīs*. On the left her mother and on the right her father. In the front, her *guru* who will conduct the marriage as the seventh. The bride is bathed and made to wear new clothes and oblations are offered with cooked food to Indra, Kāma, Bhaga, Hriya, Śriya, Puṣṭi, Viśvāvasavas, king of *gandharvas*, *svāhā*!

नाडीं तूणवं मृदङ्गं पणवं सर्वाणि च वादित्राणि गन्धोदकेन समुपलिप्य कन्या प्रवादयते "स्वनं वद दुन्दुभे सुप्रजस्त्वाय गोमुख । प्रक्रीड्न्तु कन्याः सुमनस्यमानाः सहेन्द्राण्या कृतमंगलाः" ॥ इति ॥२॥

With all the musical instruments such as *nāḍī*, *tūṇa*, *paṇa* and *mṛdaṅga* sprinkled with sandal paste, they play to the bride with the *mantra*: "Sing pleasantly like a bee for the sake of good children. Let the bride sing and dance with a good mind with happiness created by Indrāṇī."

प्रतिसखि प्रक्रीडयत्येकमहर्द्वे वाहोरात्रे ॥३॥
Let her female companions sing and dance through the night.

अष्टादशी काण्डिका (Eighteenth Chapter)

यज्ञियस्य वृक्षस्य प्रागायतां शाखां सकृदाच्छिन्नां सूत्रतन्तुना प्रच्छाद्य सावित्रेण कन्यायै प्रयच्छति "या तेऽलक्ष्मीर्मातृमयी पितृमयी संक्रामणी सहजा वापि काचित्तां तिष्येण सह देवतया निर्भजामि निर्दुणामि सा द्विषन्तं गच्छतु तिष्यबृहस्पतिभ्यां नमो नमः" इति ॥१॥
From the trees which are fit for worship, branches are cut into pieces and tied with thread and with *vyāhṛtis* given to the bride with the *mantra*: "That which represents Lakṣmī, mother, father togetherness, natural, I worship those goddesses with Tiṣya. Let her enemies be finished. I salute Tiṣya, Bṛhaspati."

तस्या उत्सर्गः स्थावरोदके शुचौ वा देवतायतने ॥२॥
With water sprinkled, the branches are released. The place where gods are kept is cleaned.

एकोनविंशति काण्डिका (Nineteenth Chapter)

अथातो हविष्यकल्पं व्याख्यास्यामः ॥१॥
Let us now study Haviṣya *kalpa*.

दशवार्षिकं ब्रह्मचर्यं कुमारिणां द्वादशवार्षिकं वा ॥२॥
For girls, *brahmacarya* is observed up to ten years or twelve years.

ब्रह्मचर्यान्ते गन्धर्वे देवकुले वा द्वावग्नी प्रज्वाल्य द्वौ पशू उपाकरोत्यर्यम्णे दक्षिणं प्राजापत्यमुत्तरम् ॥३॥

At the end of the *brahmacarya*, establish two fires in the place where gods are kept and offer two cows — in the south to Aryamā and in the north to Prajāpati.

असंभवे त्वेकपशुः ॥४॥
If it is not possible, one cow is enough.

तण्डुलैर्वा कुर्यात् ॥५॥
Or with rice flour.

यथास्थानं पशुर्यथास्थानमवदानानि तथा हविः ॥६॥
Where *ājya* offerings are usually kept, there the cows are kept as *havis*.

अग्निं सोमं वरुणं मित्रमिन्द्रं बृहस्पतिं स्कन्दं रुद्रं वात्सीपुत्रं भगं भगनक्षत्राणि कालीं षष्ठीं भद्रकालीं पूषणं त्वष्टारं महिषिकां च गन्धाहुतिभिर्यजेत ॥७॥
Worship with sandal, etc. Agni, Soma, Varuṇa, Mitra, Indra, Bṛhaspati, Skanda, Vatsīputra, Bhaga, Bhaga *nakṣatras*, Kālī, Ṣaṣṭhī, Bhadrakālī, Pūṣaṇa, Tvaṣṭā, Mahiṣikā.

विंशी काण्डिका (Twentieth Chapter)

अथातो हविष्य पुण्याहः ॥१॥
Now the Haviṣya Puṇyāha ritual.

उदकान्तं गत्वा यथोपपत्ति वा पयसि स्थालीपाकं श्रपयित्वा सर्वगन्धैः फलोत्तरैः सशिरस्कां स्नापयित्वाहतेन वाससा प्रच्छाद्य स्थालीपाकस्य जुहोतिन्द्राणी वरुणानि गन्धर्वाण्युदकान्यग्निर्जीवपुत्रः प्रजापतिर्महाराजः स्कन्दोऽर्यमा भगः प्रजानक इति ॥२॥
Going as near the water as possible, with *khīra* prepares *sthālīpāka* and with sandal paste and scents take a bath over the head, wears new clothes and carries out Sthālīpāka *homa* to Varuṇa, *gandharvas*, Agni, Prajāpati, Skanda, Aryamā, Bhaga and Prajānaka, etc.

एकविंशी काण्डिका (Twenty-first Chapter)

यामेव द्वितीयां रात्रिं कन्यां विवाहयिष्यन्स्यात्तस्यां रात्र्यामतीते निशाकाले

नवां स्थालीमाहृत्य पयसि स्थालीपाकं श्रपयित्वा सर्वगन्धैः फलोत्तरैः सशिरस्कां स्नापयित्वहतेन वाससा प्रच्छाद्य स्थालीपाकस्य जुहोत्यग्नये सोमाय मित्राय वरुणायेन्द्रायोदकाय भगायार्यम्णे पूष्णे त्वष्ट्रे राज्ञे प्रजापतये इति ॥१॥
The father of the bride who wishes to give her away in the second night, he should perform Sthālīpāka *homa* after bathing her with sandal paste and scents over the head with oblations to Agni, Soma, Mitra, Varuṇa, Indra, Bhaga, Aryamā, Pūṣaṇa, Tvaṣṭā, King Prajāpati, etc.

एता एव देवताः पुंसः कुम्भं वैश्रवणमीशानं च यजेत् ॥२॥
Similarly to gods Puṁsa, Kumbha, Vaiśravaṇa, Īśāna.

द्वाविंशी काण्डिका (Twenty-second Chapter)

चतस्त्रोऽष्टौ वाविधवाः शाकपिण्डीभिः स्त्रियोऽन्नेन च ब्राह्मणान्भोजयित्वा वीणागायिभिः सह संगायेयुरपिवा चतुरो नर्तनं कुर्यात् "क्रीडं वः शर्धो मारुतमनर्वाणं रथेशुभम् । कण्वा अभिप्रगायत" ॥ इति ॥१॥
Four or eight *sumaṅgalīs* belonging to a group after feeding brāhmaṇas with cooked rice, sing with *vīṇā* players, four of them dance, "let us dance boldly like the wind around a chariot".

अक्षतसक्तूनामग्निं पुष्टिपतिं प्रजापतिं च यजेत "अग्निना रयिमश्नवत्पोषमेव दिवेदिवे। यशसं वीरवत्तमम्" ॥ "प्रजापते नहि त्वत्" इति च ॥२॥
With rice grains and barley they worship Agni, Puṣṭipati and Prajāpati chanting:, "Give us wealth and happiness everyday. Fame and bravery."

सर्वत्रोद्वाहकर्मस्वनादिष्टदैवतेष्वग्निं पुष्टिपतिं प्रजापतिं च यजेत ॥३॥
They worship all the gods of marriages along with Agni, Puṣṭipati and Prajāpati.

त्रयोविंशी काण्डिका (Twenty-third Chapter)

अथ प्रास्थानिक कर्म ॥१॥
Now the *prāsthāna* (when the bridegroom enters his father-in-law's house for marriage).

तस्मिन्यथोक्तमुपसमाधाय जयप्रभृतिभिर्हुत्वा पश्चाद्भगिनी सिचं गृह्णाति शस्त्रं गृहीत्वा ॥२॥

In that as said, fire is established and *homa*s are performed beginning with Jayā and then he holds the border of the dress and the implement.

पूषा मेति यान्ति यत्रोदकम् ॥३॥

They seek Pūṣaṇa's help as they go towards the groom's house.

शन्नो देवीरित्युपस्पृश्य प्राची दिगिति यान्ति यथादिशम् ॥४॥

Let the goddesses bless us they say, touch the water and proceed in the eastern direction.

चतुर्विंशी काण्डिका (Twenty-fourth Chapter)

षडर्घ्या भवन्त्याचार्य ऋत्विग्राजा विवाह्यः प्रियः स्नातक इति ॥१॥

There are six person worthy of receiving *arghya* — *guru*, *purohita*, king, bride, groom, friend and *snātaka* (*brahmacārī* who has finished studies).

अथैनमर्हयन्ति ॥२॥

These are offered *arghya* during the ceremony.

आदौ च कर्मणः ॥३॥

Those are conducting the ceremonies are offered first.

अर्घ्यमुदकं सौषधं दर्भा इति ॥४॥

Arghya will be water, grains like rice and barley, and *darbha* grass.

कंसे चमसे वा दध्यासिच्य मधु च वर्षीयसा पिधाय विष्टराभ्यां परिगृह्य पाद्यप्रथमैः प्रतिपद्यन्ते ॥५॥

With a brass spoon, *madhuparka* is sprinkled from a closed big vessel, keeping hold of the grass seat, the feet are washed first.

मयि दोहोऽसि विराजो दोहः पाद्यायै विराजो दोहमशीयेत्याह्रियमाणमनु-मन्त्रयते ॥६॥

O water, you are great, you are splendorous milk, please be present when the feet are being washed.

विष्टरोऽसि मातरि सीदेति विष्टरमास्तीर्य तस्मिन्नुपविशति ॥७॥

Saying "you are the seat of the earth" and spreading the grass seat, they are made to sit on the seat.

विष्टर आसीनायैकैकं त्रिः प्राह ॥८॥

Those sitting should say thrice: *pādyam, pādyam, pādyam, viṣṭaram, viṣṭaram, viṣṭaram, madhuparkam, madhuparkam, madhuparkam.*

नैव भोरित्याह न मार्षेति ॥९॥

During the ceremony personal address such as Bho and Mārṣa are not used.

शन्नो देवीरित्यपोऽभिमन्त्र्य पाद्याभिः प्रक्षालयते दक्षिणं पादमवनेनिज इदमहमस्मिन् कुले ब्रह्मवर्चसं ददाम्युत्तरं पादमवनेनिज इदमहं मां मयि तेजो वीर्यमन्नाद्यं प्रजां पशून् ब्रह्मवर्चसं ददामि ॥१०॥

With the *mantra*, "by the desire of *devīs*, let this water be fit", he washes the feet. Washing the right foot, he says, "give lustre to our lineage" and then the left foot saying, "give us lustre, strength, food, children, cattle and *brahmavarcas*".

आपोहिष्ठीयाभिरर्घ्यं परिगृह्य सावित्रेण मधुपर्कं विष्टरोऽस्यन्तरिक्षमधिविश्रयस्वेति विष्टरमवकृष्योरु त्वेत्यपसार्य तच्चक्षुरिति वीक्ष्य पृथिव्यास्त्वेति विष्टरे निधाय मधु वाता ऋतायते इति तिसृभिः प्रदेशिन्या प्रदक्षिणमालोडयति ॥११॥

With the *mantra*, "O great water who will give us happiness" holding the *arghya* vessel, with *vyāhṛtis*, he keeps it on the grass seat, with a knife he cuts the *madhuparka* and with his thumb mixes it up, chanting thrice.

वसवस्त्वाग्निराजानो भक्षयन्तु पितरस्त्वा यमराजनो भक्षयन्तु रुद्रस्त्वा सोमराजानो भक्षयन्त्वादित्यास्त्वा वरुनराजानो भक्षयन्तु विश्वे त्वा देवा बृहस्पतिराजानो भक्षयन्त्विति प्रदक्षिणं प्रतिमन्त्रं पात्रस्यान्तेषु लेपान्निर्मार्ष्टि ॥१२॥

He keeps churning the *madhuparka* with *mantra* at every rotation, "let Vasus and Agni eat, let the manes and Yama eat, let Rudra and Soma eat, let Āditya and Varuṇa eat, let

Viśvedevās and Bṛhaspati eat" and smears the lip of the vessels with the fingers.

यन्मधुनो मधव्यस्य परमस्यान्नाद्यस्य परममन्नाद्यं रूपं तेनाहं मधुनो मधव्यस्य परमस्यान्नाद्यस्य परमोऽन्नादो मधव्यो भूयासं त्रय्यै विद्यायै यशोऽसि श्रियै यशोऽसि यशसे ब्रह्मणे दीप्तिरसि सत्यश्रीर्यशः श्रीर्मयि श्रीः श्रीः श्रयतामिति मधुपर्कस्य चतुष्प्राश्नात्यङ्गुष्ठद्वितीयाभिः कनिष्ठया प्रथममेवमनुपूर्वं सर्वाभिस्तदवशिष्टं सुहृदे प्रयच्छति ॥१३॥

That *madhuparka* which is the best, sweet fit for *anna-prāśana*, which has the shape suitable for *anna-prāśana*, I want to become that. With his thumb and each finger, he makes four parts. Then with the thumb and little finger first and then with his thumb and ring finger he makes separate portions in the middle. That he gives to his close friend, younger brother first.

आचामत्यमृतोपस्तरणमसीति ॥१४॥

He sips water saying, "you are the spread of nectar".

तस्मा असिपाणिर्गां प्राह ॥१५॥

Then he brings the cow to kill for the *madhuparka*.

तां शास्ति ॥१६॥

He kills the cow.

मम चामुष्य च पाप्मानं जहि हतो मे पाप्मा पाप्मानं मे हत ॥१७॥

I destroy the sins of this house, the sins of the sinners.

ॐ कुरुतेति ॥१८॥

He chants *oṁ*.

चतुरो नानागोत्रान् ब्राह्मणान्भोजयेदेष आद्योपायः ॥१९॥

Feed four brāhmaṇas of different *gotras* with the *madhuparka*.

यद्युत्सृजेन्माता रुद्राणामिति जपेत् माता रुद्राणां दुहिता वसूनां स्वसादित्यानाममृतस्य नाभिः । प्र नु वोचं चिकितुषे जनाय मा गामनागामदितिं वधिष्ट ॥ सूयवसाद्भगवती हि भूया अथो वयं भगवन्तः स्याम । अद्धि तृणमघ्न्ये विश्वदानी पिब शुद्धमुदकमाचरन्ती ॥२०॥

If he desires to release the cow, he chants, "Mother of Rudras, daughter of Vasus, sister of Āditya and the source of nectar". I will say to the learned do not kill this cow who is innocent. Hey cow, eating good grass become fortunate and let us be fortunate. Move around eating good grass and drinking clean water.

ओमुत्सृजत तृणान्यत्त्वित्युक्त्वा तामुत्सृष्टां पशुमंगं वा ॥२१॥
With *oṁ* he releases the cow saying "eat grass".

नामांसो मधुपर्कः स्यादिति ह विज्ञायते ॥२२॥
There cannot be *madhuparka* without meat.

अपिवा घृतौदन एव स्यात् ॥२३॥
Or you can use cooked rice with ghee.

पञ्चविंशी काण्डिका (Twenty-fifth Chapter)

अनृक्षरा ऋजवः सन्तु पन्था येभिः सखायो यन्ति नो वरेयम् । समर्यमा सं भगो नो निनीयात् सं जास्पत्यं सुयमस्तु देवा इत्युदाहारं प्रहिणोति ॥ १॥
They chant the *mantra*, "Let the paths that our friends travel for the wooing be thornless and smooth". "Let Aryamā and Bhaga lead us: O gods! Let the union of husband and wife be successful."

शमीशाखया सपलाशया पिधायाहरेत् ॥२॥
With the branches of *śamī* wood, bearing fruits, he brings a water vessel with lid.

एतासामेवापामुदकार्थान् कुर्वीत ॥३॥
Only this water is used for bathing the bride.

शन्न आपो धन्वन्या शन्नं सन्त्वनूप्याः । शन्नः समुद्रिया आपः शमु नः सन्तु कूप्या या इमा इत्यकेवलाभिरद्भिः स्नातां या अकृन्तन्या अवयन्या अतन्वत याश्च देवीरन्तां अभितोऽततन्थ । तास्त्वा देवीर्जरसा संव्ययन्त्वायुष्मतीदं परिधत्स्व वास इत्यहतं वासः परिधाप्याशासानेत्यन्तरतो मौञ्जेन दार्भेण वा योक्त्रेण सन्नह्यति ॥४॥

With the *mantra*: "Blessed is this water, flowing and from a holy source." They bathe the bride with the water and clothe her with new clothes with the chanting of the *mantra*s and a girdle of *mauñjī* grass is tied around her.

प्रेतो मुञ्चामि नामृतः सुबद्धाममृतस्करम् । यथेयमिंद्र मीढ्वः सुपुत्रा सुभगासति ॥ पूषा त्वेतो नयतु हस्तगृह्याश्विनौ त्वा प्रवहतां रथेन । गृहान्गच्छ गृहपत्नी यथासो वशिनी त्वं विदये मा वदासि ॥ मा विदन्परिपंथिनो य आसीदन्ति दम्पती । सुगोभिर्दुर्गमतीतामपद्रान्त्वरातय इत्युदानीयोक्तं वाससः कर्म ॥५॥

"I release you from the fetters of your parents' house and not from your husband's. O Indra make this woman have good children and fortune. Let Pūṣaṇa carry you holding your hand and let the Aśvins carry you in a chariot. Go to his house to become a housewife and rule, and do not become a slave. People in the street do not obstruct the groom and the bride who are on their way."

आचारिकाणि ॥६॥

Whatever is the practice of the area is carried out.

तूष्णीं निर्मन्थ्यं भ्राष्ट्रत्सान्तपनं यत्र दीप्यमानं वा बहिरग्निमुपसमाधाय परिसमूह्य पर्युक्ष्य परिषिच्य परिस्तीर्याज्यं विलीनोत्पूतं कृत्वाघारादाज्यभागान्तं हुत्वापरेणाग्निमनो रथं वावस्थाप्य योगे योग इति युनक्ति दक्षिणमितर-मुत्तरमितराम् ॥७॥

Silently prepare a fire with attrition where there is light or outside and gather grass and spread around the fire and sacrifice in the fire with clean, thin butter. To the west of the fire, bring the chariot and chanting, "Let union take place" the groom comes to the right and the bride to the left.

तूष्णीं विमुच्य खे रथस्य खेऽनसः खे युगस्य शतक्रतो । अपालामिन्द्रस्त्रिष्पूत्वा करोतु सूर्यवर्चसमिति हिरण्यं निष्टर्क्यं बद्ध्वध्याधि मूर्धनि दक्षिणस्मिन्युगतर्मण्यद्भिरवक्षारयते शं ते हिरण्यं शमु सन्त्वापः शं ते मेथी भवतु शं युगस्य तर्म । शं त आपः शतपवित्रा भवन्त्वेना पत्या तन्वा संसृजस्वेति ॥८॥

Silently releasing, he chants: "In the hole of the chariot, in the hole of the cart, in the hole of the yoke, you have done 100 things. Indra, you cleansed Apālā to make her skin brilliant like the sun. Though the hole in the yoke where gold is kept, water is poured on her head so that she shines like gold, like clear water. Let this pure water make her 100 times pure."

दक्षिणतः पुमान् भवति ॥९॥
To her right stands the groom.

अथ जुहुयात्यग्नये जनिविदे स्वाहा सोमाय जनिविदे स्वाहा गन्धर्वाय जनिविदे स्वाहेति ॥१०॥
Then he offers oblations to "To Agni who gave me my wife, *svāhā*! To Soma who gave me my wife, *svāhā*! To Gandharva who gave me my wife, *svāhā*!"

आयुषः प्राणं संतन्विति संतनीर्जुहोति ॥११॥
With the *mantra*, "let longevity, breath be mine" he worships eleven times.

जयाभ्यातानान् राष्ट्रभृतश्च ॥१२॥
He performs Jayā, Abhyātāna and Rāṣṭrabhṛt *homa*s.

तानि यथोक्तम् ॥१३॥
And others as instructed.

आधिपत्यानि जुहोति ॥१४॥
He worships the lords.

आकूत्या इति त्रिभिस्त्वेत्यन्तैर्हिरण्यगर्भ इत्यष्टाभिः पत्यृचं भूः स्वाहेति महाव्याहृतिभिश्चतसृभिरग्न आयूंषीत्याग्निपावमानीभिस्तिसृभिर्हुत्वा हुत्वा मूर्ध्नि संपातानवनयेत् ॥१५॥
With the *mantra*, "Intentions", thrice and at the end of that eight times with, "Hiraṇyagarbha" then with the *mahāvyāhṛtis* four times and with "*āyūṁṣī*" thrice, he offers oblations and smears the remnants of the *ājya* on her head.

या ते पतिघ्नी तनूरपतिघ्नीं ते तां करोमि स्वाहा या तेऽपुत्रिया तनूः पुत्रियां

ते तां करोमि स्वाहा या तेऽपशव्या तनूः पशव्यां ते तां करोमि स्वाहेति त्रिभिः ॥१६॥

"One who has the powers to kill her husband, I will make her powerless to kill, one who cannot bear children, I will make her bear children, one who is cattleless, I will make her have cattle."

उदगग्नेर्दर्भेषु प्राचीमवस्थाप्य शुचिः पुरस्तात्प्रत्यङ्ङुपयन्ता देवस्य सवितुः प्रसवेऽश्विनोर्बाहुभ्यां पूष्णो हस्ताभ्यां हस्तं गृह्णामीति हस्तं गृह्णाति दक्षिणमुत्तानं साङ्गुष्ठं नीचारिक्तमरिक्तेनैवं सव्यं सव्येन ॥१७॥

In the south-east direction *darbha* grass is spread and the bride is made to stand facing east and the bridegroom standing facing west holds her hand saying, "With the impulse of Savitā, you are brought here in the shoulders of Aśvins, hands of Pūṣaṇa". He holds her right hand with the thumb upwards, not left with left hand.

गृह्णामीति चतस्रो वरं वाचयति गृभ्णामि ते सुप्रजस्त्वाय हस्तौ मया पत्या जरदष्टिर्यथासः । भगो अर्यमा सविता पुरन्धिर्मह्यं त्वादुर्गार्हपत्याय देवाः ॥ तां पूषञ्छिवतमामेरयस्व यस्यां बीजं मनुष्या वपन्ति । या न ऊरू उशति विश्रयाते यस्यामुशन्तः प्रहराम शेपम् ॥ सोमो ददद्गन्धर्वाय गन्धर्वो दददग्नये । रयिं च पुत्रांश्चादादग्निर्मह्यमथो इमाम् ॥ सोमः प्रथमो विविदे गन्धर्वो विविद उत्तरः । तृतीयो अग्निष्टे पतिस्तुरियोऽहं मनुष्यज इति ॥१८॥

He chants four times, "I hold your hands for the sake of children and to grow old with me. Bhaga, Aryamā, Savitā and Puraṁdhi have given you to me to make me a householder. The seed of the woman which has been made auspicious by Pūṣaṇa, that seed man will impregnate. Whose thighs are spread, her organs are beaten by the male organ. Soma gave her to *gandharva*, *gandharva* to Agni. For the sake of wealth and children Agni has given her to me. Soma knew her first and then *gandharva* knew her. *Gandhrva* gave her to Agni and Agni gave her to me, her husband".

ततो गाथा वाचयति सरस्वति प्रेदमवेत्यनुवाकमुभावित्येके यदि पृथक्तंत्रम् ॥ उभावित्येके ॥१९॥

Then songs are sung with imploring "Sarasvatī makes her fit" and *anuvāka*.

प्रदक्षिणमग्निमानीय तत्रैवोपवेश्य संस्थापयेत् ॥२०॥
She is made to go around the fire and made to sit down.

एककर्मणि तन्त्रे उत्तरेणाग्निं प्रत्येत्य ततो विवाहः ॥२१॥
When a single ritual is to be performed, begin on the northern side of the fire. Marriage is different from this.

य इमे द्यावापृथिवीत्यादय उद्वाहहोमा जयप्रभृतयश्च नैककर्मणि तन्त्रे स्विष्टकृदाज्यभागौ च ॥२२॥
If beginning with heaven and earth, marriage, Jayādi and Sviṣṭakṛt *homa*s are carried out. These are not conducted with Ekakarmaṇi Tantra.

पश्चादग्नेर्दर्भेषु सा त्वमसीति वाचयति सा त्वमस्यमोऽहममोऽहमस्मि सा त्वं। ता एहि विववाहवै पुंसे पुत्राय कर्तवे। रायस्पोषाय सुप्रजास्त्वाय सुवीर्याय ॥२३॥
To the west of the fire, he is made to recite: "You are that (Goddess), I am this (God). Let us get married for begetting children. For the sake of wealth, good children and heroes."

अग्निमभिदक्षिणमानीयेह्यश्मानमातिष्ठाश्मेव त्वं स्थिरो भव। कृण्वन्तु विश्वेदेवा आयुष्टे शरदः शतमिति दक्षिणेन पदाश्मानमास्थापयत्यातिष्ठेममश्मानमश्मेव त्वं स्थिरा भव। प्रमृणीहि दुवस्यवः सहस्व पृतन्यत इति ॥२४॥
On the southern side of the fire a stone is kept saying, "be firm like a stone". Let Viśvadeva give you long life to see hundred autumns. He keeps her right foot on the stone and says: "Stand on this stone and be firm like it. Cause death to poverty and defeat enemies."

आज्यस्याञ्जलावुपस्तीर्येदं हविरित्यभिमृश्याथास्यै शमीलाजानावपति भ्राता ब्रह्मचारी वा ॥२५॥
Smear butter on her joined hands, "This is *havis* and touch it", and then her brother or a *brahmacārī* will pour fried grains on them.

तानविच्छिन्दती जुहोत्यर्यमणं नु देवमिति । अर्यमणं नु देवं कन्या अग्निमयक्षत । सोऽस्मान्देवो अर्यमा प्रेतो मुञ्चातु मामुष्य गृहेभ्यः स्वाहाः ॥२६॥

She offers the grains part by part to the fire. She is making offerings to Aryamā, "Aryamā release her from the fetters of her parents' house".

अग्निर्मा जनिमानिति वाचयति । आग्निर्मा जनिमाननया जनिमन्तं करोतु जीवपत्निर्भूयासम् ॥२७॥

"Agni is our creator" is recited. "O Agni! make this creation of yours live long as a wife."

इयं नारीति सर्वत्रानुषजति । इयं नार्यपब्रूते तोक्मान्यावपन्तिका । दीर्घायुरस्तु ज्ञातयो ममेति ॥२८॥

"This woman", is repeated everywhere. Make her a follower of her husband's family. Let our relations live long.

एवं द्विरुत्तरम् ॥२९॥

Similarly twice.

पर्ययणे पर्ययणे लाजाहोमो यजमानं चाश्मानं चास्थापयति गन्धर्वं पतिवेदनमिति ॥३०॥

Going round the fire twice, Lājā *homa* and Aśmarohaṇa are repeated.

गन्धर्वं पतिदेवनं कन्या अग्निमयक्षत । सोऽस्मान्देवो गन्धर्वः प्रेतो मुञ्चातु मामुष्य गृहेभ्यः स्वाहा ॥३१॥

Gandharva is like a god husband. I am offering oblations to *gandharva* through the fire. "O *gandharva* release her from the fetters of her parents' house."

सोमो मा ज्ञातिमानिति वाचयति । सोमो मा ज्ञातिमाननया ज्ञातिमन्तं करोतु जीवपत्निर्भूयासम् ॥३२॥

"Soma is our relation" is recited. "O Soma, her relation, make her a long living wife."

त्र्यम्बकं यजामहे इति । त्र्यम्बकं यजामहे सुगन्धिं पतिपोषणम् । उर्वारुकमिव बन्धनान्मृत्योर्मुक्षीय मामुष्य गृहेभ्यः स्वाहा ॥३३॥

Homa is carried out for Tryambaka. "Tryambaka I worship for the sake of taking care of the husband. Like a cucumber, release her from the bondage and fetters of her parents' house."

पूषा मा पशुमानिति वाचयति । पूषा मा पशुमाननया पशुमन्तं करोतु जीवपत्नीर्भूयासम् ॥३४॥
"Pūṣaṇa is like our cattle" is recited. "O Pūṣaṇa! make this woman a long-living wife."

शिष्टान्स्विष्टकृते जुहोति शूर्पेण कर्ता ॥३५॥
With the winnowing basket, the *purohita* offers Sviṣṭakṛt *homa*.

वरो दक्षिणा ॥३६॥
The groom will offer gifts.

तूष्णीं हस्तौ विमुच्य वि ते मुञ्चामिति सन्नहनम् ॥३७॥
Silently with his hands he releases her girdle of grass saying, "I release you".

उत्तरतोऽग्नेर्दर्भेषु प्राचीं प्रक्रामयत्येकमिषे द्वे ऊर्जे त्रीणि रायस्पोषाय चत्वारि मयोभवाय पञ्च प्रजाभ्यः षड्तुभ्यो दीर्घायुत्वाय सप्तमं सखा सप्तपदा भव । सुमृडीका सरस्वति मा ते व्योम सन्दृशि ॥ विष्णुस्त्वान्वेत्यनुषङ्गः ॥३८॥
To the northern side of the fire and east of the *darbha* grass, he makes her take seven steps with the *mantra*: "First step for sap, second for energy, third for wealth, fourth for happiness, fifth for children, sixth for seasons and long life, seventh for friendship." "Gracious Sarasvatī, do not take us to your heaven." At the end of each step, "Let Viṣṇu take you along" is recited.

तच्चक्षुरित्यादित्यमुपस्थापयति ॥३९॥
With the *mantra*, "Sūrya is rising in the east" he makes her sit down.

अस्तमितेऽग्निम् ॥४०॥

At sunset, establish the household fire.

जीवन्तीं ध्रुवं स्वस्त्यात्रेयं दर्शयत्यरुन्धतीं च । एतेषामेकैकं पश्यसित्याह । पश्यामिति प्रत्याह ॥४१॥

Show the living bride Dhruva, Svasti, Ātreya and Arundhatī. Show the stars one by one saying look at the star. She responds with "I see".

सुमङ्गलीरियं वधूरिमां समेत पश्यत । सौभाग्यमस्यै दत्त्वायाथास्तं विपरेतनेति वीक्षितानानुमन्त्रयते ॥४२॥

He addresses the onlookers before they go home with the verse, "This woman wears auspicious ornaments; come up to her and look at her; having brought luck to her, go back to your houses."

उदुत्तममिति प्रागुदीचीमावसथं यतीमनुमन्त्रयते यतो वा स्यात् । उदुत्तममरोहन्ती व्यस्यन्ती पृतन्यतः । मूर्धानं पत्यारोह प्रजया च विराड्भव ॥ इमां त्वमिन्द्र मीढ्वः सुपुत्रां सुभगां कृणु । दशास्यां पुत्रानां धेहि पतिमेकादशं कृधि ॥ सम्राज्ञी श्वशुरे भव सम्राज्ञी श्वश्र्वां भव । ननान्दरि सम्राज्ञी भव सम्राज्ञी अधि देवृषु ॥ स्नुषाणां श्वशुराणां च प्रजायाश्च धनस्य च । पतिनां देवराणां च सजातानां विराड्भवेति ॥४३॥

With chanting four times the *mantra* "with excellence" he takes her in the north-east direction to the place where they will live. "With excellence she rides and destroys enemies. Go to his top for the sake of children and rule. O Indra, make this woman have good children and fortunate. Give her ten children and make her husband the eleventh. Rule over your father-in-law, rule over your mother-in-law. Rule over your sisters-in-law and rule over your brothers-in-law. Rule over daughters-in-law, children and money. Be a queen over your husband and his relations."

षड्विंशी काण्डिका (Twenty-sixth Chapter)

पुण्याहे युंक्ते । योगे योग इति युनक्ति ॥१॥

When the bride goes to her husband's house on an auspicious day, the chariot is readied with "*yoge yoga*" *mantra*.

अङ्कन्यङ्का अभितो रथं ये ध्वान्ता वाताग्रमभि ये संपतन्ति । दूरहेतिः पतत्रिणीवाजिनीवांस्ते नोऽग्नयः प्रपयः पारयन्त्विति चक्रे अनुमन्त्रयते ॥२॥

With the verse, "The two curves, the two bows on both sides of the chariot, which move forward along the rushing wind, the far-darting one, the winged one, which drives swift mares, may these fires, the protectors protect us", he addresses the wheels of the chariot.

खे रथस्य खेऽनसः खे युगस्य च तर्मसु । खे अक्षस्य स्वे अवधामीति युगतर्मसु शमीशाखामवदधाति ॥३॥

In the hole of the chariot, in the hole of the cart, in the hole of the yoke, in the hole of the axle, he places the yoke pins saying, "do not kill".

सुकीशुकं शल्मलिं विश्वरूपं हिरण्यवर्णं सुवृतं सुचक्रम् । आरोह सूर्ये अमृतस्य योनिं स्योनं पत्ये वहतुं कृणुष्वेत्यारोपयते ॥४॥

With the verse, "Well adorned with *kiṁśuka* flowers, of *śālmali* wood, of various forms, gold coloured, running well, having good wheels, O Sūrya, mount this car, the world of *amṛta;* make the bridal procession agreeable for the husband" he makes her mount the chariot.

मा विदन्परिपन्थिनः सुमंगलीरिति च प्रवाहयते ॥५॥

"Do not put obstacles in the way of the chariot. A married woman is being carried."

संकाशया विवहतं ब्रह्मणा गृहैरघोरेण चक्षुषा मैत्रेण । पर्याणद्धं विश्वरूपं यदस्याः स्योनं पतिभ्यः सविता कृणोतु तदिति वधूसंगमे ॥ ६॥

Look at this married couple with unevil eyes and friendship. Let Savitā, the Viśvarūpa during his travel, make her husband happy when he meets his bride.

ये पथीनामिति चतुष्पथेषु जपतीमे चत्वार इति च ॥७॥

He chants the *mantra*, "you roads", at crossroads.

ये श्मशानेष्विति श्मशानेषु ॥८॥

He chants the *mantra*, "you cemeteries", at cemeteries.

ये वनोष्विति महावनं महावृक्षं च दृष्ट्वा जपति ॥९॥
He chants the *mantra,* "you trees", when he sees forests or big trees.

इह रडिरिति क्रूरं दृष्ट्वा ॥१०॥
He chants the *mantra,* "here is sport", when he sees wild beasts.

नमो अस्तु सर्पेभ्य इति सर्पान् ॥११॥
He chants the *mantra,* "I salute you" when he sees snakes.

ये तीर्थानीति तीर्थे ता मन्दमानेति च ॥१२॥
He chants the *mantra,* "You water bodies, flow slowly", at lakes, etc.

सप्तविंशी काण्डिका (Twenty-seventh Chapter)

शन्न इति नदीं तरति ॥१॥
Saying "do us good", he crosses the river.

य ऋत इति रथाङ्गे ऽवशीर्णे । य ऋते चिदभिश्रिषः पुरा जत्रुभ्य आतृदः । संधाता सन्धिं मघवा पुरूवसुर्निष्कर्ताविह्रुतं पुनरिति ॥२॥
If any part of the chariot is afflicted, he worships Indrī, Bṛhatī, etc.

अपराह्णेऽधिवृक्षसूर्ये गृहानुपयायोर्जं बिभ्रतीति गृहान्प्रतिदृश्य जपति । ऊर्जं बिभ्रति वसुवनिः सुमेधा गृहनागां मोदमाना सुवर्चाः । अघोरेण चक्ष्युषाहं मैत्रेण गृहाणां पश्यन्ती वय उत्तिरामि ॥ गृहाणामायुः प्र वयं तिराम गृहा अस्माकं प्रतिरन्त्वायुः ॥ गृहानहं सुमनसः प्रपद्ये वीरघ्नी वीरपतिः सुशेवा । इरां वहतो घृतमुक्षमाणांस्तेष्वहं सुमनाः संविशामि ॥ येषां मध्ये ऽधिप्रवसन्नेति सौमनसं बहु । गृहानुपह्वयामहे ते नो जानन्तु जानतः ॥ सूनृतावन्तः स्वधावन्त इरावन्तो ह सामदाः । अक्षुध्या अतृष्या गृहा मास्मद्बिभेतन ॥ उपहूता इह गाव उपहूता अजावयः । अथो अन्नस्य कीलाल उपहूतो गृहेषु मे ॥ उपहूता भूरिधनाः सखायः साधुसंमदाः । अरिष्टाः सर्वपुरुषा गृहा नः सन्तु सर्वदेति ॥३॥
In the afternoon, if they see sunbeams through trees, it is time to go to the house. She recites: "Bearing and nourishing food, bringing wealth and grains, beautiful with a good

mind, I have come home. Looking with an unveil eye and with friendliness, I see the house. Let the goddesses guarding the house increase our longevity. I enter the house with a happy mind of my husband who is heroic and well endowed. I will make food and ghee flow in the house so that we and other householders can live happily. It is with happiness I travel in their midst. O house, I beseech you to possess truthfulness, *pitṛ-yajñas*, food and peace and be devoid of famine and thirst and do not fear me. I have handled cows and sheep. I have also handled food related matters. I have also dealt with friends who have lots of money." Let our house always be rid of ill fortune and let all men live happily in it.

अष्टाविंशी काण्डिका (Twenty-eighth Chapter)

उलपराजीं स्तृणात्याशयनीयात् ॥१॥
Ulapa grass is strewn up to the bedroom.

तया प्रविशति ॥२॥
Then they enter.

अध्याहिताग्निं सोदकं सौषधमावसथं प्रतिपद्यते ॥३॥
Then they establish the *āhitāgni*, water vessel, herbs, etc. required for *pāka-yajñas*.

रोहिण्या मूलेन वा यद्वा पुण्योक्तमपरेणाग्निमानडुहे रोहिते चर्मण्युपवेस्यापिवा दर्भेष्वेव जयप्रभृतिभिर्हुत्वाग्निरैतु प्रथम ति च । अग्निरैतु प्रथमो देवतानां सो ऽस्याः प्रजां मुञ्चतु मृत्युपाशात् । अरिक्तोपस्था जीवितामस्तु माता पौत्रमानन्दमभिविबुध्यतामियं स्वाहा ॥ मा ते गृहे निशि घोर उत्थादन्यत्र त्वद्रुत्यः संविशन्तु । जीवपुत्रा पतिलोके विराज पश्यन्ती प्रजां सुमनस्यमानां स्वाहा ॥ मा ते कुमारः स्तनधः प्रमायि मा त्वं विकेश्युर आवधिष्टाः । स्तनं धयन्तं सविताभिरक्षत्वा वाससः परिधानाद्बृहस्पतिर्विश्वे देता अभिरक्षन्तु नित्यं स्वाहा ॥ अग्ने प्रायश्चित्ते त्वं देवानां प्रायश्चित्तिरसि यास्यां भृशा तनूस्तामस्या नाशया स्वाहा ॥ वायो प्रायश्चित्ते ॥ सूर्य प्रायश्चित्ते ॥ चन्द्र प्रायश्चित्ते ॥ विष्णो प्रायश्चित्ते ॥ विष्णो प्रायश्चित्ते ॥ चन्द्र प्रायश्चित्ते ॥ सूर्य प्रायश्चित्ते ॥ वायो प्रायश्चित्ते ॥ अग्ने प्रायश्चित्ते त्वं देवानां प्रायश्चित्तिरसि

यास्यां भृशा तनूस्तामस्या नाशया स्वाहा ॥ त्र्यायुषं जमदग्नेः कश्यपस्य त्र्यायुषं यद्देवानां त्र्यायुषं तन्मे अस्तु त्र्यायुषमिति ॥४॥

In the afternoon, under Rohiṇī, Mūlā and any other auspicious star, she is made to sit on a red bull skin strewn with *darbha*, Jayādi *homa*s are conducted with "Agni is the first". "Agni is the first among gods, let him release this woman's children from the fetters of death. Let her generative organs be alive for her to enjoy motherhood, *svāhā*! Let there be no evil happenings in the night in this house, *svāhā*! Let her see her children enjoy life in her husband's world, *svāhā*! Let her son not be starved of breast milk, let her not be made to be without hair (widow). Let Savitā protect her breast milk, let Bṛhaspati protect her clothes and Viśvedevās protect her constantly, *svāhā*! Agni expiation. You are the expiation of gods; destroy the violence in this woman's body, *svāhā*! Vāyu expiation. Sūrya expiation. Candra expiation. Viṣṇu expiation. Viṣṇu expiation. Candra expiation. Sūrya expiation. Vāyu expiation. Agni expiation, you are the expiation of gods destroy the violence in this woman's body, *svāhā*! Let *trayāyuṣaṁ* of Jamadagni, Kaśyapa, *deva*s be in her. Fifteen oblations are offered.

आज्यस्यैकदेशे दध्यासिच्य दधिक्राव्ण इति त्रिर्दधि भक्षयित्वा माणवकायोत्सङ्ग इढामग्न इति फलानि प्रददाति ॥५॥

After sacrifice sprinkling curds in one place, thrice eating curds saying *dadhikrāvṇa*, sitting with his wife he offers fruits to a youngster saying that this is for Iḍā.

एकोनत्रिंशी काण्डिका (Twenty-ninth Chapter)

तूष्णीमुपचरितं स्थालीपाकं श्रपयित्वा तस्याग्निमिष्ट्वा प्रजापतिं च शेषं प्राश्नीतः । अन्नमेव विवननमन्नं संवननं स्मृतम् ॥ अन्नं पशूनां प्राणोऽन्नं ज्येष्ठं भिषक् स्मृतम् ॥ अन्नमयेन मणिना प्राणसूत्रेण पृश्निना । सिनोमि सत्यग्रन्थिना हृदयं च मनश्च ते । सह वाचा मनो अस्तु सह चित्तं सह व्रतम् ॥ चक्रमिवानडुहः सूर्यं च मा चान्येषु मनः कृथाः । चाक्रवाकं संवननं मम चामुष्याश्च भूयादिति ॥१॥

Silently he makes portions of the *sthālīpāka*, offers part of it in the fire to Prajāpati and they eat the rest. "Smṛti says cooked rice will bring different minds together. Smṛti says cooked rice is the life of cattle and superior medicine. Cooked rice is the life thread of Pṛṣni (aquatic plant). I will cleanse your heart and mind through truth. Let your talk, mind and intelligence and *vrata* be with me. Be like the bull which is the wheel of Sūrya's chariot, do not think of anyone else. Like the concord of *cakravāka* birds let us be concordant."

Vaikhānasa Smārta Sūtra

Vaikhānasa Smārta Sūtra is the name of the text dealing with *saṁskāras* found in Gṛhya-Sūtras of other branches. It belongs to the Aukheya branch coming under Taittirīya branch of *Kṛṣṇa Yajurveda*. Some scholars believe that it is the latest of Gṛhya-Sūtras of *Kṛṣṇa Yajurveda*. Mahādeva has written a commentary on *Vaikhānasa Smārta Sūtra*. The following is the text of the *Vaikhānasa Smārta Sūtra* which deals with *vivāha saṁskāra*:

तृतीयः प्रश्नः (Third Chapter)
प्रथमः खण्डः (First Section)

अथातः पाणिग्रहणमष्टौ विवाहा भवन्ति ब्राह्मो दैवः प्राजपत्य आर्ष आसुरो गान्धर्वो राक्षसः पैशाच इति ॥ यदभिरूपं वृत्तवयः संपन्नमाहूयार्हयित्वा कन्यालंकृता दास्यते स ब्राह्म इति गीयते ॥ यदृत्विजो यज्ञस्यात्मनोऽलंकृत्य कन्यां प्रतिपादयति स दैवो ॥ युगपद्धर्मानुवार्तनौ स्यातामिति वाचानुमान्याग्निकार्यं स्वयं कृत्वा यत्कन्यामर्हयित्वा दद्यात्स प्राजापत्यो भवति ॥ यद्गोमिथुनेनैकेन द्वाभ्यां वा कन्यां ददाति तमार्षमाचक्षते ॥ यत्कन्यामाभरणमारोप्य शक्त्या बन्धुभ्यो धनं दत्त्वाहरते तमासुरमामनन्ति ॥ कामयोगो यदुभयोः स गान्धर्वः ॥ प्रसह्य यत्कन्याहरणं स राक्षसः ॥ सुप्तां प्रमत्तां वा रहसि यद्गच्छति स पैशाचो भवतीत्येतेषां प्रथमे चत्वारस्तोयप्रदानपूर्वकाः शस्ता ब्राह्मणस्य नेतरे जघन्या ॥ यस्मात्त्रीन्पूर्वांस्त्रीनपरानार्षीजातः षट् पूर्वान्षडपरान्प्राजापत्येनोढाया जातः सप्त पूर्वान्सप्तापरान्दैवीसुतो दश पूर्वान्दशापरानात्मानं चैकविंशतिकं ब्राह्मीपुत्रः पावयेदिति ॥१॥

Pāṇigrahaṇa (marriage) is of eight types: Brāhma, Daiva, Prājāpatya, Ārṣa, Āsura, Gāndharva, Rākṣasa and Paiśāca. When a well-adorned bride is given away in marriage to a worthy bridegroom invited by her father, it is called Brāhma wedding. When a well-adorned bride is given away in marriage by her father to a priest who has conducted a *yajña* as sacrificial fee, it is called Daiva marriage. When a worthy bridegroom seeks her hand in marriage for the sake of carrying out religious duties together, it is called Prājāpatya marriage. When the bride is given away in marriage to a groom who has given a cow and a bull, it is called Ārṣa marriage. When the groom puts ornaments in the bride and pays her relatives according to his ability, the marriage is called Āsura. Marriage by mutual consent is called Gāndharva marriage. When the girl is forcibly abducted for marriage, it is called Rākṣasa marriage. When a girl is seduced when she is asleep or drugged, it is called Paiśāca marriage. Out of these the first four preceded by a gift of water are approved for a brāhmaṇa. Not the other four. For a woman married as per Ārṣa marriage, the birth of a son will purify three ancestors and three descendants. As per Prājāpatya, the birth of a son will purify six ancestors and six descendants. As per Daiva, the birth of a son will purify seven ancestors and seven descendants. As per Brāhma, the birth of a son will purify ten ancestors and ten descendants.

द्वितीयः खण्डः (Second Section)

मातुरसपिण्डां पितुरसमानऋषिगोत्रजातां लक्षणसंपन्नां नग्निकां कन्यां वरयित्वा पञ्चाहेषु कुलस्य परिशुद्धै सपिण्डैः श्रोचियैः सह भूतं भुञ्जीत यस्मात्स पूतो भवतीति विज्ञायते ॥ कनिक्रदादिना कन्यागृह गत्वा प्र सु ग्मन्तेति तामीक्षित्वाभ्रातृघ्नीमिति तयेक्ष्यमाणो गुरुणाग्निमुखे कृते कन्याप्रदो वरगोचनाम शर्मान्तं तथैनामस्य सहधर्मचारिणी भवतीति ब्राह्मे विवाहे "धर्मप्रजासंपत्त्यर्थं यज्ञापत्त्यर्थं ब्रह्मदेवर्षिपितृतृप्त्यर्थं प्रजासहत्वकर्मभ्यो ददामीत्युदकेन" तां दद्यात् ॥ तां प्रजापतिः स्त्रियामित्युदकेन हरते वस्त्रगन्धाभरणादीनि संमृत्य कनिक्रदादिना कन्यागृहं सह बान्धवैर्गत्वा तेज आयुः श्रियामिति वस्त्रादिनालंकृत्य प्रजापतिः सोममिति तथाभरणमारोप्याददीतेत्येके ॥२॥

Having chosen a girl who is not a *sapiṇḍa* of the mother and not of the same *gotra* and *ṛṣi* of the father, who is a maiden with good features, he should, during five days, have proper food with his relations and learned brāhmaṇas. It is said that his family will be purified. Chanting *kanikradāt* hymn, he goes to the girl's house. He looks at her chanting the *mantras*, "Indra sends his fast horses", "Her, not brother slaying", etc. When the *guru* has conducted the *agnimukha*, the one who gives her away should recite the name of the groom ending with *śarma* and say, "I give this girl (name) for duty, progeny and prosperity: for success in sacrifices, for satisfying Brahmadeva, *ṛṣis*, the fathers in order that they may get offspring and fulfil their religious duties. He conducts the Brāhma type of marriage having poured water into the hands of the groom. He accepts her saying, "Prajāpati did put glory in women". According to some teachers, he should collect garments, perfumes, ornaments, etc. go to her house with his relations, should adorn her while chanting, "Lustre, long life, beauty, wealth, etc." He should put ornaments on her with the *mantra*, "Prajāpati created Soma, etc."

ततः सह स्नाताया वध्वा नववस्त्रालंकारायाः पुण्याहान्ते पाणिं गृहीत्वा सुमङ्गलरीयं वधूरित्यग्निशालामागत्य प्राङ्मुखमासयित्वा तस्यै शुद्धाम्बरवेषः कूर्चं ददाति॥ ततः परिसीर्याग्निरैत्विमामग्निस्त्रायतां मा ते गृहे द्योस्ते पृष्ठमप्रजस्तां देवकृतमिति पञ्चवारुणान्तं प्रधानाञ्जुहुयात् ॥ अग्नेपरस्यामास्तीर्णेषु दर्भेष्वश्मानमातिष्ठेति वध्वाः पादाङ्गुष्ठेन दक्षिणेन स्पर्शयति प्रत्यङ्मुख इति पाणिग्रहणं सरस्वतीति निसर्गमघोरचक्षुरित्यासनं च कृत्वेमांल्लाजानित्यभिघार्येयं नारिति तस्या लाजाञ्जलिना जुहोत्युदायुषेत्युत्तिष्ठति ॥ प्रत्यङ्मुख इति वधूमुखेक्षणं सरस्वतीति पाणिग्रहणमघोरचक्षुरिति विसर्गमिमांल्लाजानिति लाजपूरणमियं नारीति होममुदायुषेत्यग्निप्रणामं कुर्यादित्येके ॥३॥

Then after the *puṇyāha vācana*, having bathed together, and the bride is adorned with new garments, he holds her hand with the *mantra*, "Auspicious garments does this woman wear, etc." and leads her to the altar, himself dressed in white, he makes her sit down facing east and gives her *kūrca* grass. Then having strewn grass around the fire, he offers oblations to the fire with the *mantras*, "may Agni come here, the first of Gods", "may Agni *gārhaptya* protect this woman", "may no noise arise at night in your house", "may she be protected from childlessness, death of sons, etc." and closes with five Varuṇa *mantras*. A stone will be placed to the west of the fire on *darbha* grass, he makes her stand on it, "tread on this stone" he touches her feet with right thumb: Standing opposite to her, he holds her hand, saying, "Sarasvatī promote this union", "I seize your hand", he sits down chanting the *mantra*, "be not of evil eye", and he pours fried grains mixed with butter into her joined hands. According to some teachers, facing the west is for looking at her bride: With the *mantra*, "Sarasvatī", he should seize her hand and with "Be not of evil eye", he should let it go. He pours fried grain into her hands with the *mantra*, "this grain I pour", and she pours the grains into the fire with the *mantra*, "this woman, etc.".

विश्वा उत त्वयेत्यग्निं प्रदक्षिणं कृत्वातिगाहेमहि द्विष इत्यासित्वा त्रिधैवं लाजहोमं जुहुयात्ततो मूलहोमान्तेऽग्निं पतिघ्न्यन्तं वायुं निन्दतान्तमादित्यं घोरान्तं गन्धर्वं यशोघ्न्यन्तं वायुं चन्द्रं पुत्रघ्न्यन्तं हुत्वा व्याहृतिः ॥ प्रासावीतित्येन्तैश्चतुर्भिः प्रवाहणं कृत्वा पुनः परिस्तीर्य स्विष्टकृन्मिन्दाहुती विच्छिन्नमृद्धिसप्तसमिद्व्याहृतीश्च जुहुयात् ॥ अग्नेरपरस्यामा-स्तीर्योदगग्रान्सप्त बर्हिषो वध्वा सह दक्षिणेन पादेनैकमिषे विष्णुरिति द्वे ऊर्जे इति त्रीणि व्रतायेति चत्वारिति पञ्च पशुभ्य इति षड्रायस्पोषायेति सप्त सप्तभ्य इति तान्पर्यायेणाक्रम्य गत्वा सखेति निवर्तेत ॥ मम हृदय इति तस्या हृदयमभिमृशति ॥ प्रोक्षणैः प्रोक्ष्य पुण्याहं स्वस्तिघोषेणारुन्धतीन्द्राण्यदितिः श्रीरिवेति वध्वा मनुः प्रजापतिः पुरुषोत्तमो महेन्द्र इवेति वरस्य च चत्वारि स्तोमान्यरोपयेयुरिति पाणिग्रहणं ध्रुवदर्शनान्तमित्येके ॥ ततः प्रभ्रुति गार्हस्थ्यं धर्ममनुतिष्ठतिति विज्ञायते ॥४॥
With the *mantra*, "like a stream of water would submerge", having gone round the fire and set himself down with the *mantra*, "will find our way through hostile powers", he performs sacrifice with fried grains in three parts. Then at the end of the Mūla *homa*, he offers ghee into Agni with the *mantras* containing the words, "causing death of husband", to Vāyu with, "blameful", to Āditya with, "terrible", to *gandharva* with, "destroying fame", to Candra with, "causing death of sons" Then he follows with *vyāhṛtis*. Having effected the dismissal with the *mantras* which are

changed into the words, "you have allowed", he again strews *darbha* grass around the fire and performs oblations to Agni Sviṣṭakṛt, the two *mindāhutis*, the *vichinnāhutis*, the *ṛddhi-āhutis*, the seven fuel sticks and the *vyāhṛtis*. He strews seven northward pointed grass blades, treads with the right foot on these with his bride, each step with the *mantras*, "First step for sap, second for energy, third for vows, fourth for comfort, fifth for cattle, sixth for welfare, seven for seven sacrifices". At the end of each step, he says "Let Viṣṇu take you". After the seventh step, he says, "With seven steps, be my friend for life". He touches her heart with the *mantra*, "let your heart dwell in my heart". After the *purohitas* have sprinkled the place and declared *puṇyāham* and *svasti*, the relations bless the couple with chants to the bride, "be faithful to your husband as Arundhatī, be lucky like Indrāṇī, be rich in sons as Aditi, be blessed as Śrī (Lakṣmī)" and to the husband, "be of great authority as Manu, be rich in progeny as Prajāpati, be invincible as Puruṣottama, be perfect as Mahendra". This is the seizing the hand (*pāṇigrahaṇa*, the principal act of marriage). It ends with showing the polar star, Dhruva, according to some. So begins the duties of the householder, it is declared.

अथ चतुर्थीवासो ॥ वैवाहिकाग्निं वध्वा सहादाय संप्रवाहारयन्विति वधूं समं वध्वेत्यग्निं संशस्ति दक्षिणं पादमग्रेऽतिहर देहलिं माधिष्ठा इत्यावसथे प्रविश्य प्राच्यामर्ध समादधीताग्नेरपरस्यामानुडुहं चर्म लोहितं कृष्णाजिनं वा प्राचीनग्रीवमुत्तरलोमास्तृणाति ॥ तत्र प्राङ्मुखमुदङ्मुखं वा वधूमुपवेश्य पतिरिह गावः प्रजायध्वमिति पश्चान्निषीदेतां ॥ ज्योतिषां दर्शनाद्वाचंयमावन्यतरानुपेतावासाताम् ॥ उदिते नक्षत्रे प्राचीमुदीचीं वा देवीः षडुर्वीरिति दिशमुपस्थाय मा हास्महि प्रजयेति चन्द्रं सप्तर्षय इति सप्तर्षीकृत्तिका नक्षत्राण्यरुन्धतीं च ध्रुवक्षितिरिति ध्रुवं च दृष्ट्वोपतिष्ठेयातां मनोज्ञं तया सह संभाय्याथाग्नेयः स्थालीपाकः ॥ प्रजा स्थालीमिति स्थालीमभिमृश्याग्नये जुष्टं निर्वपामीति स्थाल्यां तण्डुलान्निर्वाप्य वाचस्पतये पवस्वेति वध्वा चरुं श्रपयत्यभिघार्योद्गृहस्य परिस्तीर्याग्निमुपसमाधाय हव्यवाहमिति स्विष्टकृता यजेन ॥ हुत शेषेण श्रोत्रियं ब्राह्मणं तर्पयित्वा तस्मा ऋषभं दत्त्वानृणो भवतीति विज्ञायते ॥५॥

Now, here are the ceremonies of the fourth day. Having

taken his wife to his house along with the *vivāhāgni* with the *mantras*, "O gods, let her be taken away", and "let the fire be taken with the wife", he tells her, "cross the threshold with your right foot first, do not stand on the threshold". Entering the house, he should establish the fire in the eastern half. To the west, a red bull's hide or the hide of a black antelope is spread out with its neck to the east and hairy side on top. He asks his wife to sit on it, facing the east or the north and he sits behind her with the *mantra*, "here, O cows, multiply yourselves". They sit until stars appear, restraining their speech and not touching one another. When star has appeared, they should worship with the *mantra*, "you six divine spaces", the eastern or northern direction: "May we not lose offspring", the moon: "Since the seven *ṛṣis*", the *saptaṛṣi maṇḍala*, the *nakṣatras*, Arundhatī, "Firm dwelling, firm origin", the polar star when they appear. Having a pleasant conversation, they return indoors. *Sthālīpāka* is prepared for Agni. Having touched the earthen pot with the *mantra*, "I touch the earthen pot of progeny, this *sthālī* full of nectar", he pours unhusked rice into the pot and with the *mantra*, "Vācaspate has clarified", he has the food cooked by his wife. Having sprinkled it with ghee, and having removed it from the fire in the northern direction, and having strewn grass around the fire and sticks of wood laid on it, he chants the *mantra*, "let us invoke Agni Sviṣṭakṛt, who conveys the sacrifice", etc. as invocatory verse and sacrifices a part of the food with the *mantra* addressed to Agni Sviṣṭakṛt. With the remainder of the food, he feeds a *śrotriya* brāhmaṇa and when he has presented a bull to him, he is free from all debt, it is said.

अत ऊर्ध्वं पर्वणि स्थालीपाकेन यजेत ॥ नित्यं यवैर्व्रीहिभिर्वा हस्तेन सूर्याय स्वाहा प्रजापतये स्वाहेति प्रातराहुती अग्नये स्वाहा प्रजापतये स्वाहेति सायमाहुतो जुहुयादग्न्यन्तरसंसर्गेऽनुगते वा पत्नौ कृच्छ्रं चरति ॥ श्रोत्रियागारान्मथित्वा वाग्निमादाय पुनरौपासनमादधीतोदक्याशुच्यादिसंसर्गे च विधानं यज्ञप्रायश्चित्ते वक्ष्यामो ॥ वियोगे पक्षस्योपावरोहेति समिधं

यावत्कृष्णं तावत्तप्त्वा समारोप्य गच्छेदहरहस्तां प्रज्वाल्य हुत्वा तथान्यां समिधं निदधाति ॥६॥

From that time onwards, he should perform a Sthālīpāka *homa* on full and new moon days. Constantly, he should offer with his hand, rice or barley in the morning two oblations: "For Sūrya, *svāhā*! For Prajāpati, *svāhā*!" In the evening: "For Agni, *svāhā*! For Prajāpati, *svāhā*!" If the fire has come into contact with any other fire or if it has been extinguished, his wife should perform *kṛchram*. He should take the fire from the house of a *śrotriya* or produce a new fire by attrition and establish again his fire for domestic worship. If the woman is in her menstrual period or if an impure animal contacts the fire, the rule for atonement is explained in Śrauta rites. In case of separation from his dwelling, he should, with the *mantra*, "descend, O Jātavedas", heat a fuel stick till it becomes black and make the fire ascend the stick and take it with him on his journey. Day after day, he should set fire to the stick and perform the daily sacrifices and reserve in the same way another stick of fuel for future use.

5

Gṛhya-Sūtras of Sāmaveda and Atharvaveda

THE Gṛhya-Sūtras belonging to *Sāmaveda* available presently are four, namely, Gobhila, Khadira, Jaiminīya and Kauthuma and that of *Atharvaveda* is one, namely, Kauśika.

Gobhila Gṛhya-Sūtra

Gobhila Gṛhya-Sūtra belongs to the Kauthuma branch of *Sāmaveda*. The Gṛhya-Sūtra presupposes the existence of a collection of *mantras* in what is known as Mantra Brāhmaṇa of *Sāmaveda*. Bhaṭṭa Nārāyaṇa has written a commentary on the *Gobhila Gṛhya-Sūtra*. The following is the text of *Gobhila Gṛhya-Sūtra* which deals with *vivāha saṁskāra*.

द्वितीयः प्रपाठकः (Second Chapter)
प्रथमा कण्डिका (First Section)

पुण्ये नक्षत्रे दारान् कुर्वीत ॥१॥
Under a propitious star, let him take a wife.

लक्षणप्रशस्तान् कुशलेन ॥२॥
Who should possess good qualities.

तदलाभे पिण्डान् ॥३॥
If he is unable to find one, he should make earth clods.

वेद्याः सीताया ह्रदाद्गोष्ठाच्चतुष्पथादादेवनादादहनादीरणात् ॥४॥
From an altar, a furrow, a pool, a cowshed, a place where four roads meet, a gambling place, a cemetery and from sterile soil.

सर्वेभ्यः सम्भार्य्यन्नवमम् ॥५॥
A ninth one a mix of all.

समान् कृतलक्षणान् ॥६॥
Make them equal and marked.

पाणावाधाय कुमार्या उपनामयेद् "ऋतमेव प्रथममृतं नात्येति कश्चनर्त्त इयं पृथिवी श्रिता सर्वमिदमसौ भूयात्" इति । तस्या नाम गृहित्वैषामन्यतमं गृहणेति ब्रूयात् ॥७॥
Taking the lumps in his hands he should offer them to a girl chanting, "Right alone is the first; which nobody oversteps; on right this earth is founded. May so named become this universe!" He should pronounce her name and say, "Take one of these".

पूर्वेषाञ्चतुर्णां गृह्णन्तीमुपयच्छेत् ॥८॥
If she takes one of the first four, he should marry her.

सम्भार्यमपीत्येके ॥९॥
According to some, if she takes the mixed one also.

क्लीतकैर्यवैर्माषैर्वाऽऽप्लुतां सुहृत्सुरोत्तमेन सशरीरां त्रिर्मूर्द्धन्यभिषीञ्चेत् "कामदेव ते नाम मदो नामासी"ति । "समानयामुमि"ति पतिनाम गृह्णीयात् ॥ स्वाहाकारान्ताभिरुपस्थमुत्तराभ्यां प्लावयेत् ॥१०॥
After she has been washed with *klītaka* (paste of sweet root), barley and beans, a friend should sprinkle her three times at her head, so that her whole body becomes wet, with *surā* of first quality, with the *mantra*, "Kāma, I know your name. Intoxication you are by name", "Bring here so named", he should pronounce his name. The *mantras* should have *svāhā* at the end. With the two following verses, her private parts should be washed.

ज्ञातिकर्म्मैतत् ॥११॥
That is to be done by her female relatives.

पाणिग्रहणे पुरस्ताच्छालाया अग्निरुपसमाहितो भवति ॥१२॥
At the wedding fire has to be established in the *agniśāla* to the east.

अथ जन्यानामेको ध्रुवाणामपां कलशं पूरयित्वा सहोदकुम्भः प्रावृतो बाग्यतोऽग्रेणाऽग्निं परिक्रम्य दक्षिणत उदङ्मुखोऽवतिष्ठते ॥१३॥

Then one of the relatives of the bride fills a vessel with water from a source which does not dry in summer and having walked around with the pot in front silently wrapped in his robe, stations himself to the south of the fire facing the north.

प्राजनेनान्यः ॥१४॥

Another person with a stick to control cattle walks in the same way and stations himself in the same place.

शमीपलाशमिश्रांश्च लाजांश्चतुरञ्जलिमात्रान् सूर्पेणोपसादयन्ति पश्चादग्नेः ॥१५॥

They place roasted grain mixed with *śamī* leaves to the amount of four handfuls, in a winnowing basket behind the fire.

दृषत्पुत्रञ्च ॥१६॥

And an upper millstone.

अथ यस्याः पाणिं ग्रहीष्यन्भवति सशिरस्का साऽऽप्लुता भवति ॥१७॥

Now the girl he is going to wed should be bathed including her head.

अहतेन वसनेन पतिः परिदध्यात् "या अकृन्तन्" इत्येतयर्च्चा । "परिधत्त धत्त वाससे"–ति च ॥१८॥

He should put on her new (unwashed) clothes with the *mantra*, "they who spin" and "put on her, dress her".

प्रावृतां तां यज्ञोपवीतिनीमभ्युदानयञ्जपेत् "सोमोऽददद् गन्धर्वाये"ति ॥१९॥

He should lead her who is wearing her upper garment like a sacred thread to the fire and chant, "Soma gave her to *gandharva*", etc.

पश्चादग्नेः संव्वोष्टितङ्कटमेवं जातीयं वाऽन्यत्पदा प्रवर्त्तयन्तीं वाचयेत् "प्र मे पति या नः पन्थाः कल्पताम्" इति ॥२०॥

While she to the west of the fire, pushes forward with her foot a coir cot or something similar, he should make her chant, "may the way which my husband takes be open to me".

स्वयञ्जपेदजपन्त्यां प्रास्या इति ॥२१॥
If she, out of shyness is not able to chant, let him chant with "to me" replaced by to her.

बर्हिषोऽन्तं कटान्तं प्रापयेत् ॥२२॥
Let her push the coir mat to the edge of the fire.

पूर्वे कटान्ते दक्षिणतः पाणिग्रहस्योपविशति ॥२३॥
On the east of the coir mat, she sits down to the right of the bridegroom.

दक्षिणेन पाणिना दक्षिणमंसमन्वारब्धायाः षडाज्याहुतीर्जुहोति । "अग्निरेतु प्रथमः" इत्येतन्प्रभृतिभिः ॥२४॥
While she touches his right shoulder with her right hand, he sacrifices six oblations of *ājya* with the *mantra*, "Agni is the first".

महाव्याहृतिभिश्च पृथक् ॥२५॥
With the *mahāvyāhṛtis* one by one.

समस्ताभिश्चतुर्थीम् ॥२६॥
And all together.

द्वितीया कण्डिका (Second Section)

हुत्वोपोत्तिष्ठतः ॥१॥
After the sacrifice they both arise.

अनुपृष्ठं पतिः परिक्रम्य दक्षिणत उदङ्मुखोऽवतिष्ठते वध्वञ्जलिङ् गृहीत्वा ॥२॥
The husband passes behind her back, stations himself to the south, with his face turned to the north seizes the wife's joined hands.

पूर्वा माता लाजानादाय भ्राता वा वधूमाक्रामयेदश्मानं दक्षिणेन प्रपदेन ॥३॥
Standing to the east her mother or her brother, having taken the roasted grain, should make the bride tread on the stone with the tip of her right foot.

पाणिग्राहो जपति "इममश्मानमारोहे"ति ॥४॥
The bridegroom chants, "tread on this stone".

सकृत्संगृहीतं लाजानामञ्जलिं भ्राता वध्वञ्जलावावपति ॥५॥
Her brother filling once his joined hands with roasted grain, pours it into her joined hands.

तंसोपस्तीर्णाऽभिघारितमग्नौ जुहोत्यविच्छिन्दत्यञ्जलिं "इयन्नार्युपब्रूते" इति ॥६॥
After *ājya* has been spread under and poured over the fried grain, she sacrifices that in the fire without opening her joined hands with the verse, "This woman says".

"अर्यमणन्नु देवं" "पूषणमि"–त्युत्तरयोः ॥७॥
"The God Aryamā", "Pūṣaṇa" are repeated at the two following oblations of fried grains.

हुते पतिर्यथेतं परिक्रम्य प्रदक्षिणमग्निं परिणयति मन्त्रवान्वाब्राह्मणः "कन्यला पितृभ्य" इति ॥८॥
After the sacrifice the husband, passing behind her back returns the same way and leads her around the fire so that their right sides are turned towards it, or a brāhmaṇa well versed in the *mantra*s does the same with the *mantra*, "the maid from the fathers".

परिणीता तथैवाऽवतिष्ठते, तथा क्रामति, तथा जपति, तथाऽऽवपति, तथा जुहोति ॥९॥
After she has been led around, she stands as before, as before treads on the stone, and he murmurs the *mantra*s as before and her brother pours the fried grains as before into her hands and she sacrifices as before.

एवं त्रिः ॥१०॥
In the same way, thrice.

शूर्पेण शेषमग्नावोप्य प्रागुदीचीमभ्युत्क्रामयन्ति — "एकमिषे" इति ॥११॥
After she has poured the remainder of the fried grains into the fire, they make her step forward in the north-easterly direction with the *mantra*, "First step for sap".

दक्षिणेन प्रक्रम्य सव्येनानुक्रामेत् ॥१२॥
She should step forward with her right leg and then the left.

"मा सव्येन दक्षिणमतिक्रामे"ति ब्रूयात् ॥१३॥
He should say to her "Do not put your left foot before the right foot".

ईक्षकान्प्रतिमन्त्रयेत "सुमङ्गलीरियं वधूरि"-ति ॥१४॥
He should address the onlookers with the *mantra*, "auspicious ornaments this woman wears".

अपरेणाग्निमौदकोऽनुसंव्रज्य पाणिग्राहं मूर्द्धदेशेऽवासिञ्चति । तथेतरां "समञ्जन्त्वे" तयर्च्चा ॥१५॥
To the west of the fire the water carrier follows and sprinkles the groom on the forehead and also the bride. The bridegroom chants, "may the Viśvedevās anoint".

अवसिक्तायाः सव्येन पाणिनाऽञ्जलिमुपोद्गृह्य दक्षिणेन पाणिना दक्षिणम्पाणिंसाङ्गुष्ठमुत्तानङ्गृहीच्चैताः षट् पाणिग्रहणीया जपति "गृभ्णामि ते" इति ॥१६॥
After she has been sprinkled, he puts up her joined hands with his left hand, seizes with his right hand her right hand with the thumb, her hand being turned with the palm upwards, and murmurs these six verses referring to the holding of her hand, "I seize your hand".

समाप्तासूद्वहन्ति ॥१७॥
When these are finished they carry her away.

तृतीया कण्डिका (Third Section)

प्रागुदीच्यान्दिशि यद्ब्राह्मणकुलमभिरूपम् ॥१॥
To the house of a brāhmaṇa which is situated in the north-east.

अत्राग्निरुपसमाहितो भवति ॥२॥
There the wood has been put on the nuptial fire.

अपरेणाऽग्निमानडुहं रोहितञ्चर्म्म प्राग्ग्रीवमुत्तरलोमास्तीर्णम्भवति ॥३॥
To the west of the fire a red bull's hide has been spread out with the neck to the east and with the hair outside.

तस्मिन्नेनां वाग्यतामुपवेशयन्ति ॥४॥
On that they make her, who has to be silent, sit down.

सा खल्वास्त एवानक्षत्रदर्शनात् ॥५॥
She remains sitting there until the stars appear.

प्रोक्ते नक्षत्रे षडाज्याहुतिर्जुहोति "रेखासन्धिष्वे" — तत्प्रभृतिभिः ॥६॥
When somebody says that stars have appeared, he sacrifices six oblations of *ājya* with verses commencing with, "in the junctions of the lines".

आहुतेराहुतेस्तु सम्पातं मूर्द्धनि वध्वा अवनयेत् ॥७॥
The remnants of each oblation he should sprinkle over her head.

हुत्वोपोत्थायोपनिष्क्रम्य ध्रुवन्दर्शयति ॥८॥
After the sacrifice, they arise, go out and he shows her the pole star.

"ध्रुवमसि ध्रुवाहं पतिकुले भूयासममुष्यासावि"ति पतिनाम गृह्णीयादात्मनश्च ॥९॥
"Firm are you, may I (name) become firm in the house of my husband (name)."

अरुन्धतीश्च ॥१०॥
He shows her Arundhatī also.

"अरुन्धत्यसि–रुद्धाहमस्मी"त्येवमेव ॥११॥
"I (name) am held fast". She says as above.

अथैनामनुमन्त्रयते — "ध्रुवा द्यौरि" — त्येतयर्च्चा ॥१२॥
He then addresses her with the *mantra*, "firm is the sky".

अनुमन्त्रिता गुरुं गोत्रेणाभिवादयते ॥१३॥
After she has been addressed, she respectfully calls her *guru* (husband) by his *gotra* name.

सोऽस्या वाग्विसर्गः ॥१४॥
Thus she breaks her silence.

तावुभौ तत्प्रभृति त्रिरात्रमक्षारलवणाशिनौ ब्रह्मचारिणौ भूमौ सह शयीयाताम् ॥१५॥

From that time for three nights the couple should avoid eating saline or pungent food, should sleep on the floor and should avoid intercourse.

अत्रार्घ्यमित्याहुः ॥१६॥

Some say that here the groom should be offered *arghya* reception.

आगतेष्वित्येके ॥१७॥

Some say that this reception should be offered at the time of their arrival.

हविष्यमन्नम्प्रथमं परिजपितम्भुञ्जीत ॥१८॥

He should eat the first food which is *haviṣya* food after chanting *mantras*.

श्वेभूते वा शमशनीयं स्थालीपाकं कुर्वीत ॥१९॥

Or he should prepare on the next day cooked food which they eat together.

तस्या देवता अग्निः प्रजापतिविश्वेदेवा अनुमतिरिति ॥२०॥

The deities to whom it belongs are Agni, Prajāpati, the Viśvedevās and Anumatī.

उद्धृत्य स्थालीपाकं व्यूह्यौकदेशं पाणिनाऽभिमृशेत् "अन्नप्राशेन मणिना" —ति ॥२१॥

Having taken out the vessel and having spread it out, he should touch part of it with his hand uttering, "with the tie of the food, the jewel".

भुक्त्वोच्छिष्टं वध्वे प्रदाय यथार्थम् ॥२२॥

After he has eaten and given the rest to his wife, they may do what they like.

गौर्दक्षिणा ॥२३॥

A cow is the sacrificial fee.

चतुर्थी कण्डिका (Fourth Section)

यानमारोहन्त्यामेतां "सुकिंशुकं शल्मलिमि"त्येतामृचं जपेत् ॥१॥
When she mounts the chariot, let him utter the *mantra*, "adorned with *kiṁśuka* flowers, of *śālmali* wood".

अध्वनि चतुष्पथान्प्रतिमन्त्रयेत नदीश्च विषमाणि च महावृक्षान्श्मशानञ्च "मा विदन्परिपन्थिन" इति ॥२॥
On the way when they encounter crossroads, rivers, uneven soil, big trees and burial grounds, he should chant, "may no way layers meet us".

अक्षभङ्गे नद्धविमोक्षे यानविपर्यासेऽन्यासु चापत्सु यमेवाग्निं हरन्ति तमेवोपसमाधाय व्याहृतिभिर्हुत्वाऽन्यद्द्रव्यमाहृत्य "य ऋते चिदभिश्रैष" इत्याज्यशेपेणाऽभ्यञ्जेत् ॥३॥
If the axle breaks or something that is bound gets loose, or if the chariot overturns, or if some other accident happens, they should put wood on the fire which they carry, should make oblations with the *vyāhṛti*s, should procure a new piece instead of the damaged one and besmear it with the remnants of the *ājya* with the verse, "he who without binding".

वामदेव्यङ्गीत्वाऽऽरोहेत् ॥४॥
Having sung Vāmadevya, they should mount again.

प्राप्तेषु वामदेव्यम् ॥५॥
When they have arrived, the Vāmadevya has to be sung again.

गृहागतां पतिपुत्रशीलसम्पन्ना ब्राह्मण्योऽवरोऽप्यानडुहे चर्म्मण्युपवेशयन्ति "इह गावः प्रजायध्वम्" इति ॥६॥
After they have reached the house, brāhmaṇa women of good character, whose husbands and sons are living, make her descend and make her sit down on a bull's hide with the verse, "here, you cows, bring forth calves".

तस्याः कुमारमुपस्थ आदध्युः ॥७॥
They should place a boy in her lap.

तस्मै शकलोटानञ्जलावावेपयुः ॥८॥
Into the joined hands of the boy, they should keep a clay toy.

फलानि वा ॥९॥
And fruits.

उत्थाप्य कुमारं ध्रुवा आज्याहुतीर्जुहोत्यष्टा — "विहधृतिरि" — ति ॥१०॥
After she has made the boy rise, she sacrifices the eight *ājya* oblations with the verse, "here is steadiness".

समाप्तासु समिधमाधाय यथावयसं गुरून्गोत्रेणाऽभिवाद्य यथार्थम् ॥११॥
When she has finished oblations, she puts a piece of wood on the fire and respectfully salutes the *gurus*, according to seniority with their *gotra* names. Then they may do what they like.

पञ्चमी कण्डिका (Fifth Section)

अथातश्चतुर्थीकर्म ॥१॥
Now follow the ceremonies of the fourth day.

अग्निमुपसमाधाय प्रायश्चित्ताज्याहुतीर्जुहोति "अग्ने प्रायश्चित्त" इति चतुः ॥२॥
Having put wood on the fire, he sacrifices four times with expiatory *ājya* oblations with the *mantra*, "Agni! You are expiation".

अग्नेः स्थाने वायुचन्द्रसूर्य्याः ॥३॥
With the same formula, putting instead of Agni, Vāyu, Candra and Sūrya.

समस्य पञ्चमी बहुवदूह्य ॥४॥
A fifth oblation together, changing the singular to plural.

आहुतेराहुतेश्च सम्पतमुदपात्रेऽवनयेत् ॥५॥
The remnants of each oblation, he should pour into a water pot.

तेनैनाँ सकेशनखामम्यज्य ह्रासयित्वाऽऽप्लावयन्ति ॥६॥
With that they besmear her body including her hair and nails, remove that water by rubbing and wash her.

ऊर्ध्वंत्रिरात्रात्सम्भव इत्येके ॥७॥

After three nights have passed, they should cohabit, according to some.

यदुर्त्तुमतीभवत्युपरतशोणिता तदा सम्भवकालः ॥८॥

When she has had her monthly period and the blood has ceased to flow, that is the time for cohabiting.

दक्षिणेन पाणिनोपस्थमभिमृशेत् । "विश्णुर्योनि कल्पयत्वे" — तयर्च्चा । "गर्भन्देहि सिनीवाली" — ति च ॥९॥

With his right hand he should touch her secret parts with the verse, "may Viṣṇu make your womb ready" and with "give conception, Sinīvālī".

समाप्यर्च्चौ सम्भवतः ॥१०॥

When the verses are finished, they co-habit.

Khādira Gṛhya-Sūtra

Khādira Gṛhya-Sūtra belongs to the Drāhyāyana branch of *Sāmaveda* and is also known as *Drāhyāyana Gṛhya-Sūtra*. It resembles *Gobhila Gṛhya-Sūtra* closely. A commentary has been written on *Khādira Gṛhya-Sūtra* by Rudraskanda. The following is the text of *Khādira Gṛhya-Sūtra* which deals with *vivāha saṁskāra*.

प्रथमः पटलः (First Chapter)
तृतीयः खण्डः (Third Section)

ब्रह्मचारी वेदमधीत्योपन्याहृत्य गुरवेऽनुज्ञातो दारान् कुर्वीत ॥१॥

The *brahmacārī*, after having studied Vedas and Vedāṅgas and having paid *dakṣiṇā* to his *guru*, should with the blessing of his *guru* seek a bride.

आप्लवनं च ॥२॥

He should also take the ritual bath.

तयोराप्लवनं पूर्वम् ॥३॥

Of these two, bath comes first.

मन्त्राभिवादात्तु पाणिग्रहणस्य पूर्वं व्याख्यातन् ॥४॥
As marriage is treated first in the collection of *mantras*, it is explained first here.

ब्राह्मणस्महोदकुम्भः प्रावृतो वाग्यतोऽग्रेणाग्निंगत्वोदङ्मुखस्तिष्ठेत् ॥५॥
A brāhmaṇa with a water pot, wrapped in his robe, keeping silence should step in front of the fire and should stand with his face to the north.

स्नातामहतेनाच्छाद्य या अकृन्तन्नित्यानीयमानायां पाणिग्राहो जपेत् सोमोऽददिति ॥६॥
After the bride has bathed, he should dress her in a garment which is not washed (new) with the verse, "they who spin". While she is led up to him, the bridegroom should murmur, "Soma gave her to . . .".

पाणिग्राहस्य दक्षिणत उपवेशयेत् ॥७॥
One who leads her should make her sit down to the south of the bridegroom.

अन्वारब्धायां स्रुवेणोपघातं महाव्याहृतिभिराज्यं जुहुयात् ॥८॥
When she touches him, he should make oblations of *ājya* with the *Sruva*, picking out portions of it with the *mahā-vyāhṛtis*.

समस्ताभिश्चतुर्थीम् ॥९॥
The fourth with the *mahā-vyāhṛtis* together.

एवं चौलोपनयनगोदानेषु ॥१०॥
The same at the ceremonies of *caula*, *upanayana* and *keśānta*.

अग्निरेतु प्रथम इति षड्भिश्च पाणिग्रहणे ॥११॥
And at thc marriage, he makes oblations with the six verses, "Agni is the first".

नाज्यभागौ न स्विष्टकृदाज्याहुतिष्वनादेशे ॥१२॥
Unless a special rule is given, the two *ājya* portions and the *sviṣṭakṛt* oblations are not offered.

सर्वत्रोपरिष्टान्महाव्याहृतिभिः ॥१३॥
After each chief oblation, he should always make oblations with the *mahā-vyāhṛtis*.

प्राजापत्याय च ॥१४॥
And the verse sacred to Prajāpati.

प्रायश्चित्तं जुहुयात् ॥१५॥
He should make an expiatory oblation.

हुत्वोपोत्तिष्ठतः ॥१६॥
After the sacrifice, they both rise.

अनुपृष्ठंगत्वा दक्षिणतोऽवस्थाय वध्वञ्जलिं गृह्णीयात् ॥१७॥
He should go round behind her, stand to the south and seize the bride's hand.

पूर्वा माता शमीपलाशमिश्रान् लाजाञ्छूर्पे कृत्वा ॥१८॥
Her mother who has, towards the east, put fried grain mixed with *śamī* leaves into a winnowing basket,

पश्चादग्नेर्दृषत्पुत्रमाक्रमतेद्वधूं दक्षिणेन प्रपदेन इममश्मानमिति ॥१९॥
He should make her tread with the tip of her right foot on an upper millstone, to the west of the fire with the verse, "On this stone".

सकृदगृहीतमञ्जलिं लाजानां वध्वञ्जलावावपेत् भ्राता ॥२०॥
Her brother filling once his joined hands with fried grain, should pour it into the bride's joined hands.

सुहृदा कश्चित् ॥२१॥
Or some friend instead of the brother.

तं साऽग्नौ जुहुयादविच्छिद्याञ्जलिं "इयं नारीति" ॥२२॥
That she should sacrifice over the fire without opening her joined hands with the verse, which the groom repeats, "this woman".

अर्यमणं पूषणमित्युत्तरयोः ॥२३॥
"Aryamā" and "Pūṣaṇa" are repeated at the two following oblations of fried grains.

हुते तेनैव गत्वा प्रदक्षिणमग्निं परिणयेत् "कन्यला पितृभ्य" इति ॥२४॥
After the sacrifice, he should go back in the same way and should lead her round the fire with the *śloka*, "This maid from the fathers".

अवस्थानप्रभृत्येवं त्रिः ॥२५॥
From the time of standing to the south, these rights are repeated thrice.

शूर्पेण शिष्टानग्नावोप्य प्रागुदीचीमुत्क्रमयेत् "एकमिष" इति ॥२६॥
After she has poured the remnants of the fried grain into the fire, he should make her step forward in the north-eastern direction with the *mantra*, "For sap with one step . . . ".

ईक्षकावेक्षणरथारोहणदुर्गानुमत्रणान्यभिरूपाभिः ॥२७॥
Looking on at the guests, mounting the chariot, at the places which are difficult to pass, the suitable *mantra*s should be recited.

अपरेणाग्निमौदको गत्वा पाणिग्राहं मूर्धन्यवसिञ्चेत् ॥२८॥
Walking forward behind the fire, the water carrier should besprinkle the bridegroom with water on his forehead.

वधूं च ॥२९॥
Also the bride.

समञ्जन्त्वित्यसिक्तः ॥३०॥
When he has been besprinkled, he should recite the verse, "may the Viśvedevās anoint".

दक्षिणं पाणिं साङ्गुष्ठं गृह्णियात् "गृभ्णामि ते" इति षड्भिः ॥३१॥
He should seize her right hand together with the thumb with the six verses, "I seize your hand".

चतुर्थः खण्डः (Fourth Chapter)

प्रागुदीचीमुद्वहेत् ॥१॥
He should carry her in a north-eastern direction.

ब्राह्मणकुलेऽग्निमुपसमाधाय पश्चादग्नेर्लोहितं चर्मानडुहमुत्तरलोम प्राग्ग्रीवमास्तीर्य वाग्यतामुपवेशयेत् ॥२॥
In a brāhmaṇa's house he should establish the nuptial fire, should spread out to the west of the fire a red bull's hide with the hair outside and with the neck to the east and should make her to sit down on it keeping silence.

प्रोक्ते नक्षत्रेऽन्वारब्धायां स्रुवेणोपघातं जुहुयात् षड्भिर्लेखाप्रभृति-भिस्सम्पातानवनयन् मूर्धानि वध्वाः ॥३॥
When someone says that stars have appeared, he should while she touches him, make *ājya* oblations with the *sruva*, picking out portions of it with the six verses commencing with, "in the lines".

प्रदक्षिणमग्निं परिक्रम्य धृवं दर्शयति ध्रुवाद्यौरिति ॥४॥
After they have gone around the fire, he shows her the polar star with the verse, "firm is the sky".

अभिवाद्य गुरून् गोत्रेण विसृजेद्वाचम् ॥५॥
She should break her silence by respectfully calling her *guru*'s names by their *gotra*.

गौर्दक्षिणा ॥६॥
A cow is given as the sacrificial fee.

अत्रार्घ्यम् ॥७॥
Here the *arghya* ceremony should be performed.

आगतेष्वित्येके ॥८॥
According to some, when they have arrived.

त्रिरात्रं क्षारलवणे दुग्धमिति वर्जयानौ सह शय्यानां ब्रह्मचारिणौ ॥९॥
Through a period of three nights, they should avoid eating salty food and milk, and sleep together without engaging in intercourse.

हविष्यमन्नं परिजप्यान्नपाशेनेत्यसाविति वध्वा नाम ब्रूयात् ॥१०॥
Having chanted over the cooked food for sacrifice the verse, "with the tie of the food", he should pronounce the name of his wife.

भुक्त्वोच्छिष्टं वध्वै दद्यात् ॥११॥
After he has eaten, he should give the remnants to his wife.

ऊर्ध्वं त्रिरात्राच्चतसृभिराज्यं जुहुयात् अग्ने प्रायश्चित्तिरिति समस्तपञ्चमी सम्पातनवनयन्नुदपात्रे ॥१२॥
After three nights, he should make oblations with the four verses, "Agni you are the expiation" and then a fifth combining the names of four gods invoked in those verses. The remnants of the water pot, he should pour into a water pot.

तेनैनां सकेशनखामाप्लावयेत् ॥१३॥
With that they besmear her body including her hair and nails.

ततो यथार्थं स्यात् ॥१४॥
Thereafter, he should behave as required by circumstances.

ऋतुकाले दक्षिणेन पाणिनोपस्थमालभेद्विष्णुर्योनिं कल्पयत्विति समाप्तायाम् ॥१५॥
At the time of her courses he should touch with his right hand her secret parts with the verse, "may Viṣṇu make your womb ready".

पञ्चमः खण्डः (Fifth Section)

यस्मिनग्नौ पाणिं गृह्णियात्स गृह्यः ॥१॥
The fire used at the wedding is kept as his domestic fire.

Jaimini Gṛhya-Sūtra

Jaimini Gṛhya-Sūtra belongs to the Jaimini branch of *Sāmaveda.* A commentary has been written on *Jaimini Gṛhya-Sūtra* by Srinivasa. It bears resemblance to other Gṛhya-Sūtras of

Sāmaveda, namely, Gobhila and Khādira. The following is the text of *Jaimini Gṛhya-Sūtra* which deals with *vivāha saṁskāra.*

पूर्वम् (Beforehand)

स्नात्वा मातापितरौ परिचरेत्तदधीनः स्यात्ताभ्यामनुज्ञातो जायां विन्देतानग्निकां समानजातीयामसगोत्रां मातुरसपिण्डां ज्यायसः कनीयसीं दूतमनुमन्त्रयते "ऽनृक्षरा ऋजवः सन्तु पन्था एभिः सखायो यन्ति नो वरेयम् । समर्यमा सं भगो नोऽनुनीयात्सं जास्पत्यं सुयममस्तु देवा" इति ॥

After having taken the ritual bath (*samāvartana*), he should return to his parents and look after them. With their permission, he should take a bride who has reached the age of puberty, of the same caste, of a different *gotra* from his, who should not be *sapiṇḍa* (not related to his mother to the seventh degree) and one who is younger than him. "Let the paths that our friends travel for the wooing be thornless and smooth. Let Aryamā and Bhaga lead us: O gods! Let the union of husband and wife be successful."

पाणिग्रहणेऽग्निमाह्रियमाणमनुमन्त्रयते "ऽग्निरैतु प्रथमो देवतानां सोऽस्यै प्रजां मुञ्चतु मृत्युपाशात् । तदयं राजा वरुणोऽनुमन्यतां यथेयं स्त्री पौत्रमधं न रोदादि"ति प्रज्वलितमुपतिष्ठत इमामग्निस्त्रायतां गार्हपत्यः प्रजामस्यै नयतु दीर्घमायुः । अशून्योपस्था जीवतामस्तु माता पौत्रमानन्दमभि प्रबुध्यतामियमिति पुरस्तादग्नेर्ब्राह्मणो वाग्यतः प्रत्यङ्मुख उदकुम्भं धारयंस्तिष्ठेद्दक्षिणतोऽग्नेः शमीपलाशमिश्रान्लाजाञ्छूर्पे माता धारयेन्मातुरभावे तन्मात्री प्रत्यगग्नेरेरकां तेजनीं वान्यद्वैवंजातीयं संवेष्ट्य निदध्याद्यथा प्रसार्यमाणं पश्चार्धं बर्हिषः प्राप्नोत्यथास्यै वाससी प्रोक्ष्यानुमन्त्र्य ददाति या अकृन्तन्नवयन्या अतन्वत याश्च देवीरन्तामभितोऽददन्त । तास्त्वा देवीर्जरसा संव्ययन्त्वायुष्मतीदं परिधत्स्व वास इति तां ब्रूयादिमामेरकां दक्षिणेन पादेनाभिजहीति प्र मे पतियानः पन्थाः कल्पतामित्यजपत्यां स्वयं जपेत्प्रास्या इति दक्षिणत एरकायां भार्यामुपवेश्योत्तरतः पतिरुभावन्वारभेयातां स्वयमुच्चै-र्जुहुयाज्जायायामन्वारब्धायां महाव्याहृतिभिर्हुत्वा या तिरश्चीति सप्तभिर्जुहोति संपातं प्रथमया मूर्धन्यासिञ्चेद्या तिरश्ची निपद्यसेऽहं विधरणी इति । तां त्वा घृतस्य धारया संराधा राधायामसि संराधायै स्वाहा ॥ मा ते गृहे निशि घोष उत्थादन्यत्र त्वद्रुदत्यः संविशन्तु । मा त्वं विकेश्युर आवधिष्ठा जीवपत्नी पतिलोके विराज प्रजां पश्यन्ती सुमनस्यमाना स्वाहा ॥ अन्वद्य नोऽनुमतिर्यज्ञं देवेषु मन्यताम् । अग्निश्च हव्यवाहनस्तत्करोतु समृध्यतां

स्वाहा ॥ द्यौस्ते पृष्ठं रक्षतु वायुरूरू अश्विनौ च स्तनं धयतस्ते पुत्रान्सविताभिरक्षतु । आ वाससः परिधानाद्बृहस्पतिर्विश्वे देवा अभिरक्षन्तु पश्चात्स्वाहा ॥ अप्रजस्तां पौत्रमृत्युं पाप्मानमुत वाघम् । शीर्ष्णः स्रजमिवोन्मुच्य द्विषद्भ्य प्रतिमुञ्चामि पाशं स्वाहा ॥ यानि कानि च पापानि सर्वाङ्गेषु तवाभवन् । पूर्णाहुतिभिराज्यस्य सर्वाणि तान्यशीशमं स्वाहा ॥ प्रजापत इत्येका ॥२०॥

At the time of *pāṇigrahaṇa* (holding of hands) during the wedding, he speaks the verse: "May Agni come here the first of the gods; may he release this bride from the clutches of death. May the King Varuṇa grant that this woman shall not weep over distress caused by sons." He stands before the fire that has been kindled, looking at it he addresses it with the verse: "May Agni *gārhapatya* protect this woman, may he lead her offspring to long life. With fertile womb may she be the mother of living children; may she experience delight in her children." In front of the fire, a brāhmaṇa restraining his speech should stand turned to the west holding a vessel filled with water. To the south of the fire the mother of the bride should stand holding in a winnowing basket roasted grain mixed with *śamī* leaves (in the absence of the mother any female person can replace her, i.e. the mother's sister or the mother's mother). To the west of the fire he should put down a mat of *eraka* reed or a bundle of grass or something else of the kind, so that after having rolled it up when at the moment the bride and groom are going to sit on it, it is spread out to touch the western part of the grass strewn around the fire. He gives her two garments after having sprinkled them and having spoken over them the verse: "The goddesses who spun, who wove, who spread out and who drew the ends of the sides, may these goddesses clothe you with long life. Put on these garments living long."

अथास्या दक्षिणेन पाणिना दक्षिणं पाणिं गृह्णाति प्रहस्तं पुंस अङ्गुली स्त्रियः साङ्गुष्ठं मिथुनकामो गृह्णामि ते सौभगत्वाय हस्तं मया पत्या जरदष्टिर्यथासत् । भगोऽर्यमा सविता पुरन्धिर्मह्यं त्वादुर्गार्हपत्याय देवाः ॥ सोमोऽददद्गन्धर्वाय गन्धर्वोऽददग्नये । सोमः प्रथमो विविदे गन्धर्वो विविद

उत्तरः । तृतीयोऽग्निष्टे पतिस्तुरीयोऽहं मनुष्यजा इत्युपनयनवृताश्मान-मधिष्ठापयेत्स्त्रीवत् उत्तरपुरस्तादग्नेर्भार्यया संप्रेक्ष्यमाणो जपत्यघोरचक्षुरपतिघ्नी म एधि शिवा पतिभ्यः सुमनाः सुवर्चाः । जीवसूर्देवकामा स्योना शं नो भव द्विपदे शं चतुष्पदे ॥ आ नः प्रजां जनयतु प्रजापतिराजरसाय समनक्त्वर्यमा । अदुर्मङ्गलीः पतिलोकमाविश शं न एधि द्विपदे शं चतुष्पदे ॥ तां पूषच्छिवतमामेरयस्व यस्यां बीजं मनुष्या वपन्ति । या न ऊरु उशति विस्रयातै यस्यामुशन्तः प्रहरेम शेफम् ॥ अमोऽहमस्मि सा त्वं सामाहमस्म्यृक्त्वं मनोऽहमस्मि वाक्त्वं द्यौरहं पृथिवी त्वं तावेहि संभवाव सह रेतो दधावहै पुंसे पुत्राय वेत्तवै मामनुव्रता भव सहशय्या मया भवासावित्यथास्या नाम गृहीत्वाग्निं परिक्रमेयातामीर्त्वमस्यूर्के माता नाम सा मामोहि सह प्रजया सह रायस्पोषेति तस्यां प्रत्यव्रजितायां भ्रातान्यो वा सुहृदभिघारितान्लाजाच्छूर्पादञ्जलिनोपघातमञ्जलावावपेदुपस्तीर्णाभि-घारितान्कृत्वा तानिरग्नौ जुहुयात्कन्यलेयं नार्यर्यम्णमिति कन्यला पितृभ्यः पतिलोकं यतीयमव दीक्षामयक्षत स्वाहा ॥ इयं नार्युपब्रूतेऽग्नौ लाजान्वपन्ती । दीर्घायुरस्तु मे पतिरेधन्तां ज्ञातयो मम स्वाहा ॥ अर्यम्णं नु देवं कन्याग्निमयक्षत । स इमां देवो अर्यमा प्रेतो मुञ्चातु मामुतः स्वाहेति होमान्तेषु जपति वतुर्विश्वा उत त्वया वयं धारा उदन्या इव । अतिगाहेमहि द्विष इति तूष्णीं धारिका कामायावपेच्चतुर्थं दक्षिणं शूर्पपुटं काम इत्याचक्षत उत्तरपुरस्तादग्नेः सप्त पदान्यभ्युत्क्रमयेदेकमिष इति प्रतिमन्त्रमेकमिषे विष्णुस्त्वान्वेतु । द्वे ऊर्जे विष्णुस्त्वान्वेतु । त्रीणि रायस्पोषाय विष्णुस्त्वान्वेतु । चत्वारि मयोभवाय विष्णुस्त्वान्वेतु । पञ्च प्रजाभ्यो विष्णुस्त्वान्वेतु । षड्ऋतुभ्यो विष्णुस्त्वान्वेतु । सखा सप्तपदी भवेति सप्तमे प्राचीमवस्थाप्योदकुम्भेन मार्जयेरन्नापोहिष्ठीयाभिस्तिसृभिः प्रेक्षकाननुमन्त्रयते सुमङ्गलीरियं वधूरिमां समेत पश्यत । सौभाग्यमस्यै दत्त्वायाथास्तं विपरेतनेति प्रेक्षयेद्ध्रुवमरुन्धतीं सप्त ऋषीन्पश्यानीति प्रतिजानानां ध्रुवोऽसीति ध्रुवमुपतिष्ठते ध्रुवोऽसि ध्रुवाहं पतिकुले भूयासममुष्येति पतिनाम गृह्णीयादसावित्यात्मनोऽरुन्धतीमरुन्धत्यरुद्धाहं पत्या भूयासममुनेति पतिनाम गृह्णीयादसावित्यात्मनः ॥२१॥

Now he seizes with his right hand her right hand, if he wishes male children, her open hand with the fingers extended, if he wishes female children, her fingers only, if he wishes both her hand together with the thumb with the *śloka*, "I seize your hand so that we may be blessed with good fortune that with me as your husband you may live to old age. The gods Bhaga, Aryamā, Savitā and Puraṁdhi have given you to me so that we may rule the house." "Soma gave her to *gandharva*, *gandharva* to Agni. Soma looked after you first, then *gandharva* and then Agni. Agni gave her to man (I), the fourth one". Then he makes her stand on a stone as before changing the masculine to feminine gender. With her on the north-eastern part of the fire, he chants, "Do not cast an evil eye bringing death to me your husband. Bring luck to cattle, be with good mind and with luster. Give birth to children, love the gods and be friendly. Bring luck to our two- and four-footed ones." "May Prajāpati give us progeny, may Aryamā unite us to reach old age, enter without ill omen, the world of your husband. Bring luck to our two- and four-footed ones. Lead her, O Pūṣaṇa to us the highly blessed one into whom men pour their sperm. Her who may willingly part her thighs into whom we may willingly introduce the male organ. I am this, you are that. I am the song, you are the verse, I am the mind, you are the word, I am the heaven, you are the earth. Come let us get together and generate children. Be devoted to me, share our bed, you (her name)." Then the pair should walk around the fire when he murmurs, "you are food, strength by name is your mother; come to me with children, with wealth".

After the circumambulation her brother or a friend of hers should pour with his joined hands out of the winnowing basket into her joined hands roasted grain sprinkled with ghee, "picking out" again and again. Having spread under and poured over the roasted grain some ghee, she should sacrifice it in the fire with the three verses: "This young girl going from her parents to the world of her husband, has sacrificed away her *dīkṣā, svāhā*!" This woman, strewing grains into the fire, prays: "May my husband live long, may my relations be prosperous, *svāhā*!" To the God Aryamā the girl has sacrificed, to Agni: may he, loosen her from here and not from there, *svāhā*! After each oblation he mutters, four times the verse, "may we find our way with you through all hostile powers, as through streams of water". Without *mantra* the person who holds the roasted grain (mother, etc.) should pour out as a fourth oblation the rest of the grain for obtaining a special wish (on which the bride has to fix her thought). The right neb of the winnowing basket they call the wish.

On the north-eastern part of the fire, he makes her take seven steps, each one with the following *mantra*: "One for sap; may Viṣṇu lead you. Two for juice; may Viṣṇu lead you. Three for prosperity; may Viṣṇu lead you. Four for comfort; may Viṣṇu lead you. Five for progeny; may Viṣṇu lead you. Six for the seasons; may Viṣṇu lead you. Be a friend of seven steps."

At the seventh step, having made her to stand facing east, they should sprinkle her with water with the three verses beginning: "you waters are beneficent". He addresses the guests with the verse: "She is adorned with auspicious ornaments. Come up to her and behold her. Having brought luck to her, go back to your houses."

Then he should make her look at the pole star Dhruva, the star Arundhatī of the *sapta ṛṣi maṇḍala*, when she declares: "Let me see the stars". She addresses Dhruva: You are the pole star (Dhruva), may I become firm in the house of my husband (his name) and at the end of the *mantra*, her own name." Looking at Arundhatī she chants: "Arundhatī, may I be held fast by my husband (his name) and then uttering her own name."

पूषा त्वेत इति प्रस्थितामनुमन्त्रयते पूषा त्वेतो नयतु हस्तगृह्याश्विनौ त्वा प्रवहतां रथेन । गृहान्गच्छ गृहपत्नी यथासो वशिनी त्वं विदथमावदासीति स्वं कुलं प्राप्तां कल्याणशीलाः कल्याणप्रजाः समवजीर्णाः प्रत्यवरोपयन्तीह प्रियं प्रजया ते समृध्यतामस्मिन्गृहे गार्हपत्याय जागृहि । एना पत्या तन्वं संसृजस्वाथाजीव्री विदथमावदासीति प्रत्यवरोप्यानडुहे चर्मण्युत्तर-लोमन्युपवेशयोदिह गावो निषीदन्त्विहाश्वा इह पुरुषाः । इहो सहस्रदक्षिणोऽभि पूषा निषीदत्विति कुमारमुपस्थ आधाय शकलोटानावपेत्फलानि वोत्थाप्य कुमारमन्वारब्धायां जुहुयादिह धृतिरित्यष्टाभिः स्वाहाकारान्तैरिह धृतिरिह स्वधृतिरिह रन्तिरिह रमस्व । मयि धृतिर्मयि स्वधृतिर्मयि रमो मयि रमस्वेति त्रिरात्रमक्षारालवणाशिनौ ब्रह्मचारिणावधः संवेशिनावसंवर्तमानौ सह शयातामूर्ध्वं त्रिरात्रात्संभवो निशायां जायापतिकर्मण्यं प्रायश्चित्तीर्जुहुयादग्ने प्रायश्चित्ते त्वं देवानां प्रायश्चित्तिरसि ब्राह्मणस्त्वा नाथकाम उपधावामि यास्यै प्रजाघ्नी

तनूस्तामस्या अपजहि स्वाहा । वायो प्रायश्चित्ते त्वं देवानां प्रायश्चित्तिरसि ब्राह्मणस्त्वा नाथकाम उपधावामि यास्यै पतिघ्नी तनूस्तामस्या अपजहि स्वाहा । चन्द्र प्रायश्चित्ते त्वं देवानां प्रायश्चित्तिरसि ब्राह्मणस्त्वा नाथकाम उपधावामि यास्यै गृहघ्नी तनूस्तामस्या अपजहि स्वाहा । अग्ने वायो सूर्य चन्द्र प्रायश्चित्तयो यूयं देवानां प्रायश्चित्तय स्थ ब्राह्मणो वो नाथकाम उपधावामि यास्यै यशोघ्नी तनूस्तामस्या अपहत स्वाहेति स्थालीपाकादग्निं प्रजापतिं चेष्ट्वा संपातांश्चमस आनीय स्त्रोतांस्याङ्क्ष्वेत्येनां ब्रूयान्नाभिं प्रथमं ततो यान्यूर्ध्वं ततो यान्यर्वाञ्च्यूर्ध्वमर्धरात्रात्संवेशनं विष्णुर्योनिं कल्पयत्वित्येन तृचेन विष्णुर्योनिं कल्पयतु त्वष्टा रूपाणि पिंशतु । आसिञ्चतु प्रजापतिर्धाता गर्भं दधातु ते ॥ गर्भं धेहि सिनीवालि सरस्वति । गर्भं ते अश्विनौ देवावाधत्तां पुष्करस्रजौ ॥ हिरण्ययी अरणी यं निर्मन्थतामश्विनौ । तं ते गर्भं दधाम्यहं दशमे मासि सूतवा इत्यृतावृतवेवमेव संवेशने हुत्वाचार्याय गां दद्याददर्शने ब्राह्मणेभ्यो गां दद्यात् ॥२२॥

When she departs to the house of her husband, he speaks over her the verse: "May Pūṣaṇa lead you there grasping your hand; may Aśvins carry you forth in a chariot; go to the house, that you may become a housewife; with control you shall speak into the council." When she has reached her husband's house, some women of good disposition who possess beautiful progeny and have reached old age with their husbands, make her descend with the *mantra*: "May this succeed for you by progeny who are dear to you. Watch over this house as a *gṛhiṇī*. Unite yourself with this husband. Then being not deficient, you shall speak to the gathering."

Then he makes her sit on a bull's hide with the hairy side turned upwards with the verse. "Here may cows sit down, here horses, here men. Here may also Pūṣaṇa with 1,000 sacrificial gifts sit down." Having placed a boy in her lap he should give sweets or fruits to the boy while the wife holds on to him from behind, he should sacrifice with the following eight *mantras* each concluding with *svāhā*! "Here is steadiness. Here is independent steadiness. Here is delight. In me the steadiness. In me the joy. In me rejoice."

During a period of three days and nights, they should abstain from saline or pungent food and from intercourse, sleeping on the ground and lying together without approaching one another. After the lapse three days, they should cohabit. In the night begins the ritual work of the pair. He should sacrifice the expiatory oblations with the formulae: "Expiatory Agni! You are the expiation of the gods. I, a brāhmaṇa, entreat you, desirous of protection. The substance which dwells in her that brings death to progeny, remove from her, *svāhā*! Expiatory Vāyu! You are the expiation of the gods. I, a brāhmaṇa, entreat you, desirous of protection. The substance that dwells in her that brings death to the cattle, remove from her, *svāhā*! Expiatory Sūrya! You are the expiation of the gods. I, a brāhmaṇa, entreat you, desirous of protection. The substance that dwells in her that brings death to the husband, remove from her, *svāhā*! Expiatory Candra! You are the expiation of the gods. I, a brāhmaṇa, entreat you, desirous of protection. The substance, which dwells in her which brings destruction to the house, remove from her, *svāhā*! Expiatory Agni, Vāyu, Sūrya, Candra, you are the expiation of the gods. I, a brāhmaṇa, entreat you, desirous of protection. The substance, which dwells in her that brings destruction to fame remove from her, *svāhā*!"

Having sacrificed from a *sthālīpāka* to Agni and Prajāpati and having poured together into a wooden vessel the remnants of each oblation, he should address her with the words: "Anoint your vital canals". First she anoints the navel, then the organs of sense which are above and then those beneath the navel. After three days have passed, the cohabitation takes place after the husband has chanted the following verses: "May Viṣṇu make the womb ready; may Tvaṣṭā frame the shape of the child; may Prajāpati pour forth the sperm; may Dhātṛ give you conception — give conception, Sinīvālī; give conception, Sarasvatī; may the two Aśvins, the gods wreathed with lotus, give conception to you. The embryo, which the Aśvins with golden fire drill produce, that embryo I put into you for giving birth in the tenth month."

The cohabitation takes place in this manner after each menstrual period. After the burnt oblations he should give a cow to the teacher. In default of a teacher, he should give the cows to some brāhmaṇas.

Kauśika Gṛhya-Sūtra

Kauśika Gṛhya-Sūtra is the only extant text of *Atharvaveda*. Darila has written a commentary on *Kauśika Gṛhya-Sūtra* and Keśava has written a *paddhati*. The following is the text of *Kauśika Gṛhya-Sūtra* which deals with *vivāha saṁskāra*.

दशमः अध्यायः (Tenth Chapter)
प्रथमा काण्डिका (First Section)

अथ विवाहः ॥१॥
We will now study *vivāha saṁskāra*.

ऊर्ध्वं कार्त्तिक्या आ वैशाख्याः ॥२॥
The period from the month of Kārttika to Vaiśākha is suitable for marriages.

यथाकामि वा ॥३॥
You can conduct marriages whenever you wish.

चित्रापक्षं तु वर्जयेत् ॥४॥
Do not conduct marriages under Citrā *pakṣa*.

मघासु हन्यन्ते गावः फल्गुनीषु व्युह्यत इति विज्ञायते मङ्गलं च ॥५॥
Cows are killed in the month of Māgha and the bride is taken away in the month of Phālguna.

सत्येनोत्तभिता पूर्वापरमित्युपदधीत ॥६॥
With the *mantras*, "from truth is established earth" and "these two go after one another by magic", oblations are offered.

पतिवेदनं च ॥७॥
With the *mantra*, "let Agni come", the bride is given food mixed with sesame.

युवं भगमिति संभलं सानुचरं प्रहिणोति ॥८॥

With the *mantra*, "you two bring together", the wooer is sent with companions.

ब्रह्मणस्पत इति ब्रह्मणम् ॥९॥

With the *mantra*, "let the lord of brāhmaṇas", let the wooer go and describe the virtues of the bride to the groom.

तद्विवृहाच्छङ्कमानो निशि कुमारीकुलाद्वलीकान्यादीप्य ॥१०॥

If Brahmā is afraid of the dark in the night, light a lamp in the bride's house.

देवा अग्र इति पञ्चभिः सकृत्पूल्यान्यावापयति ॥११॥

With the *mantra*, "O Agni god", offer five oblations with single corn stem.

अनृक्षरा इति कुमरीपालं प्रहिणोति ॥१२॥

The wooers are sent with the *mantra*, "Let the path be smooth and thornless".

उदाहारस्य प्रतिहितेषुस्यतो जघनतो ब्रह्मा ॥१३॥

In the front of the water carrier will be men carrying bows and arrows and at the back *ācārya*s.

यो अनिध्म इत्यप्सु लोगं प्रविद्यति ॥१४॥

When they reach a water body, they recite, "One who shines in the water without fuel".

इदमहमित्यपोह्य ॥१५॥

With the *mantra*, "this I remove", water is filled in the vessel.

यो भद्र इत्यन्वीपमुदच्य ॥१६॥

The *mantra*, "that which is excellent", is also recited.

आस्यै ब्राह्मणा इति प्रयच्छति ॥१७॥

With the *mantra*, "let brāhmaṇa take for her", the vessel is given to the water carrier.

आव्रजतामग्रतो ब्रह्मा जघनतोऽधिज्यधन्वा ॥१८॥
During the journey, the *ācārya*s will be ahead and the archers at the back.

बाह्यतः प्रक्षोदुम्बरस्योत्तरतोऽग्रे शाखायामासजति ॥१९॥
When they reach home, the fire is brought out, the water vessel is kept to the north of the fire on branches of *udumbara* tree.

तेनोदकार्थान्कुर्वन्ति ॥२०॥
With this the rituals with water are carried out.

ततश्चान्वासेचनमन्येन ॥२१॥
If the water in the vessel is at a low level, sprinkle with other water.

अन्तरुपातीत्यार्यमणमिति जुहोति ॥२२॥
Oblations are offered to Aryamā.

प्र त्वा मुञ्चामीति वेष्टं विचृतति ॥२३॥
With the *mantra*, "I release you", he ties her in braids.

उशतीरित्येतया त्रिराधापयति ॥२४॥
With the *mantra*, "eager is the girl", she is made to stand.

सप्तभिरुष्णाः संपातवतीः करोति ॥२५॥
With seven *mantra*s, she is bathed with warm water.

यदासन्द्यामिति पूर्वयोरुत्तरस्यां स्रत्त्यां तिष्ठन्तीमाप्लावयति ॥२६॥
With the *mantra*, "What is done in the seat earlier", she is bathed over her head standing up.

यच्च वर्चो यथा सिन्धुरित्युत्क्रान्तामन्येनावसिञ्चति ॥२७॥
With the *mantra*, "where there is lustre", cold water is sprinkled where she is standing to bathe.

द्वितीया काण्डिका (Second Chapter)

यद्दुष्कृतमिति वाससाङ्गानि प्रमृज्य कुमारीपालाय प्रयच्छति ॥१॥

With the *mantra*, "What ill deed", the dress for covering the bride is given to her guardian.

तुम्बरदण्डेन प्रतिपाद्य निर्व्रजेत् ॥२॥

Having given the clothes with a staff of *tumbara* wood, he moves away.

तद्वन आसजति ॥३॥

The bride will go to the forest and throw away the staff.

या अकृन्तंस्त्वष्टा वास इत्यहतेनाछादयति ॥४॥

With the *mantras*, "those who spun the cloth", "Tvaṣṭā gave this cloth", her dresses are bound with the sacred thread.

कृत्रिम इति शतदंतैषीकेण कङ्कतेन सकृत्प्रलिख्य ॥५॥

With the *mantra*, "the artificial hundred-toothed comb", her hair is combed with a hundred-toothed comb.

कृतयाममित्यवसृजति ॥६॥

With the *mantra*, "the work is done", the comb is disposed off.

आशासाना सं त्वा नह्यामीत्युभयतः पाशेन योक्तेन संनह्यति ॥७॥

With the *mantra*, "hoping for", she is bound by a girdle.

इयं वीरुदिति मदुघमणिं लाक्षारक्तेन सूत्रेण विग्रथ्यामिकायां बध्नाति ॥८॥

With the *mantra*, "this creeper", a thread coloured red with *lakṣa* dye and strung with *madugha* beads is tied on her ring finger.

अन्ततो ह मणिर्भवति बाह्यो ग्रन्थिः ॥९॥

At the end, let there be a bead outside.

भगस्त्वेत इति हस्तेगृह्य निर्णयति ॥१०॥

With the *mantra*, "Bhaga has grasped your hand", the teacher takes the bride outside the Kautaka house.

शाखायां युगमाधाया दक्षिणतोऽन्यो धारयति ॥११॥
The yoke of the chariot is brought and borne by other men to the south.

दक्षिणस्यां युगधुर्युत्तरस्मिन्युगतर्ह्मनि दर्भेण विग्रथ्य शं न इति ललाटे हिरण्यं संस्तभ्य जपति ॥१२॥
On the right side of the yoke, *darbha* grass and gold are kept on her forehead through the holes of the yoke and oblations are offered with the *mantra*, "Weal be to you".

तर्ह्म समयावसिञ्चति ॥१३॥
At that time water is sprinkled.

उपगृह्योत्तरतोऽग्नेरङ्गादिति निनयति ॥१४॥
Having brought the water from the north of the fire, she is sprinkled with the *mantra*, "away from every limb".

स्योनमिति शकृत्पिण्डऽश्मानं निदधाति ॥१५॥
With the *mantra*, "I keep this stone", he keeps a stone on a base of cow dung.

तमा तिष्ठेत्यास्थाप्य ॥१६॥
He makes her stand on it.

इयं नारीति ध्रुवां तिष्ठन्ती पूल्यान्यावापयति ॥१७॥
With the *mantra*, "this woman", she stands on it and offers roasted grains.

त्रिराविछिन्दतीं चतुर्थीं कामाय ॥१८॥
The bride's father, reciting the names and *gotra*s four times, offers *kanyādāna*.

येनाग्निरिति पाणिं ग्राहयति ॥१९॥
He holds her hand with the five *mantra*s beginning with, "that Agni who has grasped your hand".

अर्यम्ण इत्यग्निं त्रिः परिणयति ॥२०॥
With the *mantra*, "let her go round the fire of Aryamā", she is taken round the fire thrice.

सप्त मर्यादा इत्युत्तरतोऽग्नेः सप्त लेखा लिखति प्राच्यः ॥२१॥
With the *mantra*, "seven boundaries", he draws seven lines towards the east on the northern side of the fire.

तासु पदान्युत्क्रामयति ॥२२॥
He makes her take steps on them.

इषे त्वा सुमङ्गलि प्रजावति सुसीम इति प्रथमम् ॥२३॥
The first step for sap for you the *sumaṅgalī* the child-bearer.

ऊर्जे त्वा रायस्पोषाय त्वा सौभाग्याय त्वा साम्राज्याय त्वा संपदे त्वा जीवातवे त्वा सुमङ्गलि प्रजावति सुसीम इति सप्तमं सखा सप्तपदी भवेति ॥२४॥
Second for energy, third for wealth, fourth for fortune, fifth for kingdom. Sixth for long life. You a *sumaṅgalī* and child-bearer become my friend for life.

आ रोह तल्पं भगस्ततक्षेति तल्प उपवेशयति ॥२५॥
He makes her sit on the bed with the *mantra*, "mount on it" and "Bhaga has fashioned".

उपविष्ठायाः सुहृत्पादौ प्रक्षालयति ॥२६॥
The feet of the bride sitting on the bed are washed by her friends.

प्रक्षाल्यमानवनुमन्त्रयते ॥ इमौ पदौ सुभगौ सौभाग्याय कृणुतां नो अघाय। प्रक्षल्यमानौ सुभगौ सुपत्न्याः प्रजां पशून्दीर्घमायुश्च धत्तामिति ॥२७॥
When the feet are being washed he chants: "Let her feet make her fortunate and happy and not sinful. Let them give me a happy wife with children, cattle and long life."

अहं वि ष्यामि प्र त्वा मुञ्चामीति योक्त्रं विचृतति ॥२८॥
With the *mantra*, "I release you", he unties the girdle from her.

अपरस्मिन्भृत्याः संरभन्ते ॥२९॥
During this time her female friends prevent him from untying.

ये जयन्ति ते बलीयांस एव मन्यन्ते ॥३०॥
Who wins will be considered stronger.

ब्रहस्पतिनेति सर्वसुरभिचूर्णान्यृचर्चा काम्पीलपलाशेन मूर्ध्न्यावपति ॥३१॥
With the five *mantras*, "released by Bṛhaspati", etc. her friends besmear her with scented potions using *kāmpila* leaves.

उद्यछध्वं भगस्ततक्षाभ्रातृघ्नोमित्येकैकयोत्थापयति ॥३२॥
With the *mantras*, "raise your weapons" and "Bhaga has delivered" and "not brother slaying", he raises one or two by their head.

प्रति तिष्ठेति प्रतिष्ठापयति ॥३३॥
With the *mantra*, "stand firm", he makes her stand up.

तृतीया काण्डिका (Third Chapter)

सुकिंशुकं रुक्मप्रस्तरणमिति यानमारोहयति ॥१॥
With the *mantra*, "let the chariot well adorned with *kiṁśuka* flowers take her", he makes her mount the chariot.

एमं पन्थां ब्रह्मामरमित्यग्रतो ब्रह्मा प्रपद्यते ॥२॥
With the *mantras*, "we have started on this road" and "let Brahmā be yoked after", they proceed on the journey with the *purohita* travelling in front.

मा विदन्ननृक्षरा अध्वानमित्युक्तम् ॥३॥
Chanting "let not the waylayers find them" and "let the path be smooth and thornless", they leave.

येदं पूर्वेति तेनान्यस्यामूढायां वाधूयस्य दशां चतुष्पथे दक्षिणौरभितिष्ठति ॥४॥
If on the way they encounter another married couple, they stand at the crossroads with the cloth held by the border to the south of the crossroads.

स चेदुभयोः शुभकामो भवति सूर्यायै देवेभ्य इत्येतामृचं जपति ॥५॥
He worships Sūrya and other gods with the *mantra*, "Let good things happen to both".

समृच्छत स्वपथोऽनवयन्तः सुसीमकामावुभे विराजावुभे सुप्रजसावित्यातिक्रमयतीऽन्तरा ब्रह्माणम् ॥६॥

He instructs the brāhmaṇa for the sake of reaching the end of the journey, with success with children to chant the following.

य ऋते चेदभिश्रिष इति यानं संप्रोक्ष्य विनिष्कारयति ॥७॥

"He who without a clamp joins." And after sprinkling water over the chariot, they proceed.

सा मन्दसानेति तीर्थे लोग प्रविध्यति ॥८॥

When they encounter water bodies, they chant, "she with a happy mind" and through a handful of mud.

इदं सु म इति महावृक्षेषु जपति ॥९॥

When they see big trees, they chant, "now you hear me O men".

सुमङ्गलीरिति वध्वीक्षीः प्रति जपति ॥१०॥

When another woman sees the bride, they chant, "*sumaṅgalī*".

या ओषधय इति मन्त्रोक्तेषु ॥११॥

At different places (fields, forest, rivers, etc.) they chant, "you herbs".

ये पितर इति श्मशानेषु ॥१२॥

At a cemetery, he chants, "the forefathers who have come".

प्र बुध्यस्वेति सुप्तां प्रबोधयेत् ॥१३॥

He addresses her who is sleeping, "continue to be awake".

सं काशयामीति गृहसंकाशे जपति ॥१४॥

When they near his house, he chants, "I will make them who look at the bridal chariot with a good eye".

उद्व ऊर्मिरिति यानं संप्रोक्ष्य विमोचयति ॥१५॥

When they reach he chants, "let your wave smite up the pegs" and after sprinkling the chariot, releases the yoke.

उत्तिष्ठेत इति पत्नी शालां संप्रोक्षति ॥१६॥
With the *mantra*, "stand up here", he makes her sprinkle the ground.

स्योनमिति दक्षिणतो वलीकानां शकृत्पिण्डेऽश्मानं निदधाति ॥१७॥
With the *mantra*, "I place upon the earth this stone". He places a stone on a lump of *gobara* from a bull.

तस्योपरि मध्यमपलाशे सर्पिष चत्वारि दूर्वाग्राणि ॥१८॥
On that in the middle *palāśa* leaves holding butter, her friends will go round the fire four times.

तमा तिष्ठेत्यास्थाप्य ॥१९॥
With the *mantra*, "you stand", she is made to stand on the stone.

सुमङ्गली प्रतरणिह प्रियं मा हिंसिष्टं ब्रह्मापरमिति प्रत्यृचं प्रपादयति ॥२०॥
With the *mantras*, "with good fortune you enter", "what you desire", and "let no one harm her", he makes her go round the fire.

सुहृत्पूर्णकंसेन प्रतिपादयति ॥२१॥
Her friends will go round the fire with brass vessels filled.

अघोरचक्षुरित्यग्निं त्रिः परिणयति ॥२२॥
With the *mantra*, "not with an evil eye", they go around the fire thrice.

यदा गार्हपत्यं सूर्यायै देवेभ्य इति मन्त्रोक्तेभ्यो नमस्कुर्वतीमनुमन्त्रयते ॥२३॥
She worships with chanting of *mantras*, "when she worships the household fire" and "to Surya and gods".

चतुर्थी काण्डिका (Fourth Chapter)

शर्म वर्मेति रोहितचर्माहरन्तम् ॥१॥
Bring a red skin reciting the *mantra*, "for her protection".

चर्म चोपस्तृणीथनेत्युपस्तृणन्तम् ॥२॥
With the *mantra*, "the skin that you spread", it is spread.

यं बलबजमिति बल्बजं न्यस्यन्तम् ॥३॥
With the *mantra*, "that *balbaja* grass", he brings the grass.

उप स्तृणीहीत्युपस्तृणान्तम् ॥४॥
With the *mantra*, "that which spreads", he spreads the grass on the skin.

तदा रोहतु इत्यारोहयति ॥५॥
Saying mount the skin, he makes her mount the skin.

तत्रोपविश्येत्युपवेशयति ॥६॥
Saying sit on that, he makes her sit on the skin.

दक्षिणोत्तरमुपस्थं कुरुते ॥७॥
She is made to sit in a north–south direction.

सुज्येष्ठ इति कल्याणनामानं ब्राह्मणायनमुपस्थ उपवेशयति ॥८॥
With the *mantra*, "let your first son be a good lead for other children", a brāhmaṇa boy with a good name is made to sit in her lap.

वि तिष्ठन्तानामानं प्रमदनं प्रमायोत्थापयति ॥९॥
With the *mantra*, "let good children, etc. come from you", the boy is given fruits, sweets and made to get up.

तेन भूतेन तुभ्यमग्रे शुम्भनी अग्निर्जनविन्मह्यं जायामिमामदात्सोमो वसुविन्मह्यं जायामिमामदात्पूषा जातिविन्मह्यं जायामिमामदादिन्द्रः सहीयान्मह्यं जायामिमामदादग्नये जनविदे स्वाहा सोमाय वसुविदे स्वाहा पूष्णे जातिविदे स्वाहेन्द्राय सहीयसे स्वाहेत्यागछतः ॥१०॥
With the *mantra*, "by the elements" and five *mantras* beginning with "first to you" and "beautiful you are", he offers oblations saying: "From Agni she is given to me, from Soma she is given to me, from Pūṣaṇa she is given to me, from Indra she is given to me, to Agni the knower, *svāhā*! To Soma the knower, *svāhā*! To Soma and Vasu, *svāhā*! He welcomes her.

सविता प्रसवानामिति मूर्ध्नोः संपातानानयति ॥११॥
With the *sūkta*, "sun the god of births", he offers oblations and with remnants smears her head.

उदपात्र उत्तरान् ॥१२॥
He keeps the water vessel to the north.

शुम्भन्याञ्जल्योर्निनयति ॥१३॥
With the *mantra*, "beautiful you are", he pours water in her joined hands.

तेन भूतेनेति समश्नम् ॥१४॥
With the *mantra*, "by the elements, etc.", they eat together.

रसानाशयति स्थालीपाकं च ॥१५॥
They partake liquids and cooked food.

यवानामाज्यमिश्रणां पूर्णाञ्जलिं जुहोति ॥१६॥
With barley mixed with butter, they offer a handful and worship.

पञ्चमी काण्डिका (Fifth Chapter)

सप्त मर्यादा इति तिसृणां प्रातरावपते ॥१॥
With the *mantra*, "seven boundaries did the poets establish", he sacrifices in the morning with rice grain and barley in the marriage fire.

अक्ष्यो नाविति समाञ्जाते ॥२॥
With the *mantra*, "our eyes", they apply collyrium around each other's eyes.

महीमू ष्विति तल्पमालम्भयति ॥३॥
With the *mantra*, "we seek the help of the great mother", they touch the bed.

आ रोह तल्पमित्यारोहयति ॥४॥
Saying mount the bed, he makes her mount the bed.

तत्रोपविश्येत्युपवेशयति ॥५॥

Saying sit on the bed, he makes her sit on the bed.

देवा अग्र इति संवेशयति ॥६॥

With the *mantra*, "Gods in the beginning", they embrace each other.

अभि त्वेत्यभिछादयति ॥७॥

With the *sūkta*, "you of Manu's lineage", they remove their clothes.

सं पितराविति समावेशयति ॥८॥

With the *mantra*, "you two to be parents", they have intercourse.

इहेमाविति त्रिः संनुदति ॥९॥

With the *mantra*, "here O Indra", the groom holds the bride's neck thrice.

मधुघमणिमौक्षेऽपनीयेयं वीरुदमोऽहमिति संस्पृशतः ॥१०॥

With scented necklaces of *madhuga* beads, he recites, "I am this, you are that", and they touch each other's necklaces.

ब्रह्म जज्ञानमित्यङ्गुष्ठेन व्यचस्करोति ॥११॥

With the *mantra*, "the *Brahman* who was born of the old", he touches her genital organ with his thumb.

स्योनाद्योनेरित्युत्थापयति ॥१२॥

With the *mantra*, "awaking out of a *yoni*", they raise from the bed.

परिधापनीयाभ्यामहतेनाछादयति ॥१३॥

After washing themselves, with the *mantra*, "who has spun", both of them wear new clothes.

बृहस्पतिरिति शष्पेणाभिघार्य व्रीहियवाभ्यामभिनिधाय दर्भपिञ्जूल्या सीमन्तं विचृतति ॥१४॥

With the *mantra*, "Bṛhaspati" he sprinkles with young blades of grass, offers rice grains and barley and with *darbha* grass parts her hair.

शणशाकलेन परिवेष्ट्य तिस्रो रात्रीः प्रति सुप्तास्ते ॥१५॥
Tying her hair with hemp thread, they sleep for three nights.

अनुवाकाभ्यामन्वारब्धाभ्यामुपदधीत ॥१६॥
With *anuvāka*s and *mantra,* "by truth is established", he sacrifices with rice grains, barley, etc. as expiation.

इहेदसाथेत्येतया शुल्कमपाकृत्य ॥१७॥
With the *mantra,* "may you be here", he keeps ready the bride fee.

द्वाभ्यां निवर्तयतीह मम राध्यतामत्र तवेति ॥१८॥
I am giving this money for you, he says twice and gives.

यथा वा मन्यन्ते ॥१९॥
Or he does as he wishes.

परा देहीति वाधूयं ददतमनुमन्त्रयते ॥२०॥
With the *mantra,* "give back", he gives her dresses.

देवैर्दत्तमिति प्रतिगृह्णाति ॥२१॥
Saying "this is god given", she receives the dresses.

अपास्मत्तम इति स्थाणावासाजति ॥२२॥
With the *mantra,* "let the darkness be away from us", he puts the dress on her.

यावतीः कृत्या इति व्रजेत् ॥२३॥
With the *mantra,* "how many evil things are in these garments", he takes away the dress.

या मे प्रियतमेति वृक्षं प्रतिछादयति ॥२४॥
With the *mantra,* "she who is my beloved", he throws the dress on a tree.

शुम्भन्याप्लुत्य ॥२५॥
With the *mantra*, "beautiful you are" all of them bathe.

ये अन्ता इत्याछादयति ॥२६॥
With the *mantra*, "what ends", he dresses the bride.

नवं वसान इत्याव्रजति ॥२७॥
With the *mantra*, "newly-dressed I am", he clothes himself.

पूर्वापरं यत्र नाधिगछेद्ब्रह्मापरमिति कुर्यात् ॥२८॥
If offerings have been made earlier, he chants the *mantra*, "let Brahmā be yoked after".

गौर्दक्षिणा प्रतीवाहः ॥२९॥
The *purohita* is given a cow as *dakṣiṇā*.

जीवं रुदन्ति यदीमे केशिन इति जुहोति ॥३०॥
With the *mantra*, "they bewail the living one", he offers oblations if her relations or crying.

एष सौर्यो विवाहः ॥३१॥
This is Saurya marriage.

ब्रह्मापरमिति ब्राह्म्यः ॥३२॥
With the *mantra*, "Brahmā is yoked", it is called Brāhma *vivāha*.

आवृतः प्राजापत्याः प्राजापत्याः ॥३३॥
If the marriage is conducted without *mantras*, it is called Prājāpatya, as in the case of śūdras.

6

Types of Rituals

Every part of the marriage ceremony is marked by a specific ritual to be performed described in Gr̥hya-Sūtras. Beginning with negotiations to select the bride and the groom to consummation of the marriage, elaborate rituals have been prescribed by Gr̥hya-Sūtras. There is variation in the type and order of performance of the rituals in different Gr̥hya-Sūtras. The following passages describe the types of major rituals and their significance. *Mantras* shown are only indicative as there are variations in the content, order and time of chanting them in various Gr̥hya-Sūtras.

Negotiations

The tradition was that negotiators were sent to the bride's family to discuss the possibility of an alliance. They were sent with the following *mantra* to facilitate a smooth journey:

अनृक्षरा ऋजवः सन्तु पन्था येभिः सखायो यन्ति नो वरेयम् ।
समर्यमा सम्भगो नो निनीयात् सं जास्पत्यं सुयममस्तु देवाः ॥

Let the path of the wooers be thornless and smooth. Let Aryamā and Bhaga lead them and let the alliance happen smoothly, O gods!

प्र सु ग्मन्ता धियसानस्य सक्षणि वरेभिर्वराँ अभि षु प्रसीदतः ।
अस्माकमिन्द्र उभयं जुजोषिति यत्सोम्यस्यान्धसो बुबोधिति ॥

Indra sends his fast running horses to the service of the *yajamāna* expectant of his coming. Indra is satisfied by the sacrifices and food offered to him when he tastes the Soma-laced food.

Vāgdāna

This ritual is performed to confirm that the groom's and the bride's family have agreed upon the alliance and give each other assurances to that effect. As per Śāṅkhāyana, a vessel filled with water, flowers, *akṣata*, barley, fruits and gold is touched by the bride's and groom's people as a sign of acceptance while the following *mantra*s are chanted:

अनाधृष्टमस्यानाधृष्ट्य देवानामोजाऽनभिशस्त्यभिशस्तिपा ।
अनभिशस्तेयऽन्यमञ्जसा सत्यमुपगेषं सुविते मा धाः ॥

Undisturbed are you, the undisturbable vigour of the gods, not cursed, protecting against a curse, unexposed to a curse. May I straightaway attain the truth. Put me into prosperity.

आ नः प्रजां जनयतु प्रजापतिराजरसाय समनक्त्वर्यमा ।
अदुर्मङ्गलीः पतिलोकमा विश शं नो भव द्विपदे शं चतुष्पदे ॥

May Prajāpati grant us offspring, May Aryamā unite us till old age; free from evil omens enter your husband's home, bring prosperity to our bipeds and quadrupeds.

Madhuparka

Madhuparka is the mixture of curd, ghee and honey which is offered to any honoured guest. The bridegroom is welcomed with *madhuparka* when he arrives for the marriage, which used to be held in the bride's house. The bridegroom is made to sit and his feet are washed by the parents of the bride.

आपः पादावनेजनीर्द्विषन्तं नाशयन्तु मे ।
अस्मिन् कुले ब्रह्मवर्चस्यानि ॥

Let the waters that flow over my feet destroy my enemies. Let me attain the lustre of my pedigree.

यन्मधुनो मधव्यस्य परमस्यान्नाद्यस्य परममन्नाद्यं रूपम् ।
तेनाहं मधुनो मधव्यस्य परमस्यान्नाद्यस्य परमोऽन्नाद्यो मधव्यो भूयासम् ॥

O celestial beings! The luscious sweetness which lights up the body despite all passage of time and circumstance;

which is the quintessence of all primary juices and which will be the cause of my sweetness.

Maṇḍapākaraṇa

The *paṇḍāla* where the marriage is conducted is erected outside the house as per prescribed norms with the altar built keeping proper orientation in mind. All the materials necessary for conducting the marriage, such as *darbha* grass, brass vessels, water, flowers, *śamī* leaves, roasted grain, gold pieces and mill stone are kept in the *maṇḍapa* or *paṇḍāla*. Limits are sets for the altar using *paridhis* (yoke pins). The marriage fire is expected to be started by attrition. The floor of the *maṇḍapa* is coated with cow dung. Suitable *vistāras* (seats) are readied and kept in assigned places. The place is sanctified by *puṇyāha vācana*.

Snāpana, Paridhāpana and Saṁnahana

This ritual concerns the ritual bathing of the bride, clothing her in new dress and tying a girdle made of *darbha* grass around her waist.

हिरण्यवर्णाः शुचयः पावका यासु जातः कश्यपो यास्विन्द्रः ।
अग्निं या गर्भं दधिरे विरूपास्ता न आपः शं स्योना भवन्तु ॥

Let the golden-coloured waters pure, holy with various forms from whom came Kaśyapa and Indra, who bear Agni in the form of an embryo, be the harbingers of happiness and peace for us.

रैभ्यासीदनुदेयी नाराशंसी न्योचनी ।
सूर्याय भद्रमिद्वासो गाथयैति परिष्कृतम् ॥

Raibhi was her happy companion; Nārāśaṁsī was her slave; Sūryā's good dress wraps her through the song.

जरां गच्छ परिधत्स्व वासो भवाकृष्टीनामभिशस्तिपावा ।
शतं च जीव शरदः सुवर्च्चा रायश्च पोषमुपसंव्ययस्व ॥

Live to old age; put on the garment; be a protectress of people against imprecation; live to see hundred autumns; clothe yourself in wealth and children, and blessed with life; wear this garment.

या अकृन्तन्नवयन् याश्च तन्निरे या देवीरन्तां अभितोऽददन्त ।
तास्त्या जरसे सव्ययन्त्वायुष्मतीदं परिधत्स्व वासः ॥

Let the goddesses who spun, wove and stretched the ends of this dress wrap you in it for long life. Let the long-lived ones put this dress on you.

परिधत धत्त वाससैनां शतायुषी कृणुत दीर्घमायुः ।
बृहस्पतिः प्रायच्छद्वास एतत् सौभाग्यं राज्ञे परिधतवा ॥

Put this dress on her who will live hundred years: Bṛhaspati has decidedly given this dress to King Soma to wear.

Pratisāra Bandhana

Also called *kautuka* or *baddha kautaka*, this ritual calls for tying an amulet with a string on the hand of the bride, while the following *mantra* is chanted:

यथेय शचीं वावातां सुपुत्रां च यथाऽदितिं ।
अविधवां चापालामेवं त्वामिह रक्षातादिममिति ॥

As this has protected Śacī, the beloved one, Aditi, the mother of noble sons, and Apālā, who was free from widowhood, may it protect you.

Paraspara Samīkṣaṇa

The bride and groom look at each other in this ritual. Sometimes, a piece of cloth is held between them and removed at the astrologically right time while *mantra*s are being chanted.

अघोरचक्षुरपतिध्न्ये धि शिवा पशुभ्यः सुमना सुवर्चाः ।
वीरसूर्देवकामा स्योना शं नो भव द्विपदे शं चतुष्पदे ॥

Look at your husband with no angry eye, be tender to animals, be amiable, be virtuous; be mother to heroic sons, be devoted to gods, bestow happiness and bring happiness to our bipeds and quadrupeds.

अभ्रातृघ्नीं वरुणापतिघ्नीं बृहस्पते ।
इन्द्रापुत्रघ्नीं लक्ष्म्यं तामस्यै सवितस्सुव ॥

One who is not brother slaying, O Varuṇa, not husband slaying, O Bṛhaspati, One who will possess children O Indra, One who is Lakṣmī, bring her to us, O Savitā.

Mekhalā or Yoktra Bandhana

In some Gṛhya-Sūtras, this ceremony is featured wherein the groom places a round piece of *darbha* network on the bride's head. On that he places a right yoke hole. On this hole he lays a piece of gold, and washes her so that the water runs over that gold and through the yoke hole. Then, he causes her to dress in a fresh garment and he girds her with a rope (*mekhalā*).

आशासाना सौमनसं प्रजाँ सौभाग्यं तनूम् ।
अग्नेरनुव्रता भूत्वा सं नह्ये सुकृताय कम् ॥

I pray for a happy mind, children, wealth and prosperity. I follow Agni and for good deeds to be done and I tie myself with happiness.

Later, after *aśmārohaṇa* he releases the girdle with the following *mantra*:

प्र त्वा मुञ्चामि वरुणस्य पाशाद्येन त्वाबध्नात्सविता सुकेतः ।
धातुश्च योनौ सुकृतस्य लोके स्योनं ते सह पत्या करोमि ॥

I set you free from Varuṇa's noose which the adorable Savitā had bound you. In place of sacrifice in the world of good deeds, I unite you, unharmed with your husband.

Kanyādāna

In this ritual, the father of the bride gives away the bride to the groom and elicits assurances from him that he would be faithful to her. The name, *gotra* and parentage of the bride are uttered while being gifted away. The bride is dressed in new clothes and decorated with ornaments suitably.

> कन्यां कनकसंपन्नां कनकाभरणैर्युताम् ।
> दास्यामि विष्णवे तुभ्यं ब्रह्मलोकजिगीषया ॥
>
> This bride who is decorated with gold ornaments and who is endowed with golden qualities, I give to you in the name of Viṣṇu for the sake of attaining *brahmaloka*.
>
> विश्वंभरः सर्वभूताः साक्षिण्यः सर्वदेवताः ।
> इमां कन्यां प्रदास्यामि पितॄणां तारणाय च ॥
>
> With the all-pervading God, all the elements and all the goddesses as witnesses, I give this bride to you for the sake of pleasing (liberating) our ancestors.
>
> धर्मप्रजासम्पत्त्यर्थं यज्ञापत्त्यर्थं ब्रह्मदेवर्षितृप्त्यर्थं
> प्रजासहत्वकर्मभ्यो ददामि ॥
>
> For the sake of *dharma*, children, wealth, for carrying out *yajñas*, to please gods and manes and for carrying out rituals as children I give this bride.
>
> धर्मे च अर्थे च कामे च नाति चरामि ॥
>
> The groom while accepting the bride promises not to go against her wishes in the matter of *dharma*, money and desires.

Vivāha Homas

Agni is established sometimes by attrition in the altar and a number of *homas* are conducted. These include Ājya, Jayā, Abhyātāna, Raṣṭrabhṛt, Sviṣṭakṛt and Aupāsanā and other *homas*. The order and number of *homas* vary from *sūtrakāra* to *sūtrakāra*.

आज्य होमः (Ājya Homa)

> अग्निरैतु प्रथमो देवतानाम् सोऽस्यै प्रजां मुञ्चतु मृत्युपाशात् । तदयं राजा वरुणोऽनुमन्यतां यथेयम् स्त्री पौत्रमघं न रोदात् । इमामग्निस्त्रायतां गार्हपत्यः प्रजामस्यै नयतु दीर्घमायुः । अशून्योपस्था जीवतामस्तु माता

पौत्रमानन्दमभिविबुध्यामियम् । मा ते गृहे निशि घोष उत्थादन्यत्र त्वद्रुदत्यस्संविशन्तु । मा त्वं विकेश्युर अवधिष्टा जीवपत्नी पतिलोके विराज पश्यन्ती प्रजां सुमनस्यमानां ॥ स्वस्ति नो अग्ने दिव आपृथिव्या विश्वानि धेह्ययथा यजत्र । यदस्यां महि दिवि जातं प्रशस्तं तदस्मासु द्रविणं धेहि चित्रम् । सुगन्न पन्थां प्रदिशन्न एहि ज्योतिष्मद्धेह्यजरन्न आयुः । अपैतु मृत्युरमृतश्च आगाद्वैवस्वतो नो अभयं कृणोतु ॥

May Agni come here, the first of gods. May he release the offspring of this wife from the fetters of death. May this king Varuṇa grant that this wife may not weep over distress caused through her sons, *svāhā*. May Agni Gārhapatya protect this woman. May he lead her offspring to old age. With fertile womb, may she be the mother of living children. May she experience delight in her sons. Let there be no noise in your house in the night, let women who cry and demoness go to some other place. Do not be a woman without hair (widow), shine in your husband's house with a living husband with a pleasant mind and seeing children. Make, Agni, all ways of heaven and earth blissful to us, O you who are worthy of sacrifices. What is great born on this earth and praised, in heaven, that bestow on us, rich treasures, *svāhā*.

जया होमः (Jayā Homa)

चित्तं च चित्तिश्चाकूतं चाकूतिश्च विज्ञातं च विज्ञानं च मनश्च शक्वरिश्च दर्शश्च पूर्णमासश्च बृहच्च रथन्तरं च प्रजापतिर्जयानिन्द्राय वृष्णे प्रायच्छदुग्रः पृतनाज्येषु तस्मै विशः समनमन्त सर्वाः स उग्रः स हि हव्यो बभूव देवासुराः संयत्ता आसन्त्स इन्द्रः प्रजापतिमुपधावतस्मा एताञ्जायान्प्रायत्ता-नजुहोत्ततो वै देवा असुरानजयन्यदजयन्तञ्जयानां जयत्वँ स्पर्धमानेनैते होतव्या जयत्येव ताम्पृतनाम् ॥

Sentience and the sentient, the substance of intent and intent, the basis of learning and learning, the mind, the sensory organs, the rituals of Darśa and Pūrṇamāsa, the *sāmas* of Bṛuhut and Rathantara, were all given to Indra, the one who causes rain by Prajāpati. People who were engaged in battling enemies received these as worthy of offering as *havya*. *Devas* and *asuras* were fighting each other. Indra and

Prajāpati went there speedily and gave these Jayā *mantras* to *devas*. *Devas* having carried out these Jayā *homas* were able to defeat the *asuras*. Those engaged in contests will emerge victorious if Jayā *homas* are carried out and opponents will be defeated.

अभ्यातान होमः (Abhyātāna Homa)

अग्निर्भूतानामधिपतिः स माऽवत्विन्द्रो ज्येष्ठानां, यमः पृथिव्या, वायुरन्तरिक्षस्य, सूर्यो दिवश्चन्द्रमा नक्षत्राणां, बृहस्पतिर्ब्रह्मणे, मित्रः सत्यानां, वरुणोऽपाम्, समुद्रः स्रोत्यानामन्नटम् साम्राज्यानामधिपति तन्मावतु, सोम ओषधीनां, सविता प्रसवानाम्, रुद्रः पशूनां, त्वष्टा रूपाणां, विष्णुः पर्वतानां, मरुतो गणानामधिपतयस्ते मावन्तु पितरः पितामहाः परेवरे ततास्ततामहाः । इह मावन्त्वस्मिन्ब्रह्मण्यस्मिन् क्षत्रेऽस्यामाशिष्यस्यां पुरोधायामास्मिन्कर्मण्यस्यां देवहूत्याम् ॥

May Agni, the first among lords, protect me. May Indra, the lord of the elders, Yama of the earth, Vāyu of the air, Sun of the heaven, Moon of the *nakṣatras*, Bṛhaspati of the *Brahman*, Mitra of the truth, Varuṇa of the waters, the sea, of the rivers, food, the lord of royalty, protect me. May Soma of the herbs, Sāvitrī of impulses, Rudra of cattle, Tvaṣṭā of forms, Viṣṇu of mountains, Marut the lord of the hosts protect me. May the fathers, the grandfathers, the former, the later protect me in the power of holiness, in this worldly power, in this prayer, in this purohitship, in this invocation of the gods, *svāhā*.

राष्ट्रभृत् होमः (Rāṣṭrabhṛt Homa)

ऋताषाड़तधामाग्निर्गन्धर्वस्तस्यौषधयोऽप्सरस ऊर्जो नाम स इदं ब्रह्म क्षत्रम्पातु त इदम्ब्रह्म क्षत्रम्पातु तस्मै स्वाहा ताभ्यः स्वाहा संहितो विश्वसामा सूर्यो गन्धर्वस्तस्य मरीचयोऽप्सरस आयुवः सुषुम्नः सूर्यरश्मिचन्द्रमा गन्धर्वस्तस्य नक्षत्रायणयप्सरसो बेकुरयो भुज्युः सुपर्णो यज्ञो गन्धर्वस्तस्य दक्षिणा अप्सरसः स्तवाः प्रजापतिर्विश्वकर्मा मनो गन्धर्वस्तस्यक्सामान्यप्सरसो वह्नय इषिरो विश्वव्यचा वातो गन्धर्वस्तस्यापोऽप्सरसो मुदा भुवनस्य पते यस्य न उपरि गहा इह च । परमेष्ठ्याधिपतिर्मृत्युगन्धर्वस्तस्य विश्वमप्सरसो भुवः सुक्षितिः सुभूतिर्भद्रकृत्सुवर्वान्पर्जन्यो गन्धर्वस्तस्य विद्युतोऽप्सरसो रुचो दूरेहतिरमृडयो

मृत्युर्गब्धर्वस्तस्य प्रजा अप्सरसो भीरुव श्चारुः कृपणकाशी कामो गन्धर्वस्तस्याधयोऽप्सरसः शोवयन्तीर्नाम स इदम्ब्रह्म क्षत्रम्पातु ता इदम्ब्रह्म क्षत्रम्पातु तस्मै स्वाहा ताभ्यः स्वाहा स नो भुवनस्य पते यस्य त उपरि गृहा इह च। उरु ब्रह्मणेऽस्मै क्षत्राय महि शर्म यच्छ ॥

Let the *gandharva* who is bearing the responsibility for various *yajña*s being carried out in this *brahmakṣetra* and who in his own form and in the form of Agni protect this sacrificial rite. Agni in *gandharva* form, *svāhā*! Let the *apsaras*es who assume the form of Herbs which give strength to innumerable lives who are part of this Agni in *gandharva* form and who protect this *yajña*, to them *svāhā*! The one who lives in Candra, Agni, Eyes through his rays, one who decides the life limits of the universe, the *gandharva* called Sūrya who with the *apsaras*es in the form of rays will protect this *yajña*, *svāhā*! One who gives intense happiness in the form of sunrays, the *gandharva* with dear wives in the form of stars called Bekuraya will protect this *yajña* along with the *apsaras*es, *svāhā*! One who protects the Universe, who transits high in the heaven, who takes the form of the *yajña*, the *gandharva* with his wives who are called Stavā in the form *apsaras*es in Dakṣiṇa form will protect this *yajña*, *svāhā*! The one who is the creator of the universe, the *gandharva* who protects it with his wives called Vahni, the *apsaras*es Ṛg, Yajur, Sāma will protect this *yajña*, *svāhā*! The *gandharva* called Vāta who is forever moving, the one is in the body in the form of five *prāṇa*s with his wives called Mudā along with *apsaras* called Abrūpa will protect this *yajña*, *svāhā*! O the lord of the Universe, whose presence shines in the high and low regions, in heaven, sky and earth, please give us endless wealth, valiant sons, year-long food and grant us happiness, *svāhā*! The *gandharva* who controls the entire Universe, the one who occupies the highest position, with the form of death, protect this *yajña* with your wives Bhuvā and Apsaras, *svāhā*! Let the *gandharva* who is exalted who blesses people on earth with surprising bounties, the *gandharva* called Parjanya who lives in heaven with his wives Ṛcā and Apsaras in the form of lightning protect this *yajña, svāhā*! The *gandharva* called Mṛtyu who can use weapons from afar, who takes away the happiness of living beings, who along with wives called Bhīruva and Apsaras will protect this *yajña, svāhā*! Let the *gandharva* called Kāma who is stingy in issues with his wives called Śocayantī along with apsaras called Ādhi protect this *yajña, svāhā*! O Lord of the Universe, whose position in the heaven and earth, who is called Tridhāma, please grant us worthy, strong and successful happiness and bless us, *svāhā*!

सोमः प्रथमो विविदे गन्धर्वो विविद उत्तरः ।
तृतीयो अग्निष्टे पतिस्तुरीयस्ते मनुष्यजाः ॥

Soma was the first, *gandharva* came next Agni was the third and the fourth was man.

सोमोऽददद्गन्धर्वाय गन्धर्वोऽदददग्नये ।
रयिं च पुत्रांश्चा दादग्निर्मह्यमथो इमाम् ॥

Soma gave her to *gandharva, gandharva* to Agni
For the sake of wealth and sons Agni gave her to me.

सोमाय जनिविदे स्वाहा ।
गन्धर्वाय जनिविदे स्वाहा ।
अग्नये जनिविदे स्वाहा ।

To Soma who gave me my wife, *svāhā*!
To *gandharva* who gave me my wife, *svāhā*!
To Agni who gave me my wife, *svāhā*!

कन्यला पितृभ्यो यती पतिलोकमव दक्षिणमदास्थ स्वाहा ।
कन्या उत त्वया वयं धारा उदन्या इवातिगहेमहि द्विशः ॥

The bride brought into the world by her father is entering her husband's home
With the bride we will wash away our enemies like a torrent of water.

Pāṇigrahaṇa

This is a very important ritual and one of the earliest, connected with marriage having been mentioned in *R̥gveda*. It denotes the holding of the bride's hand by the groom and saying that she is God's gift to him to become a householder, beget progeny and live up to old age with her. The following *mantra* is chanted by the bridegroom during *pāṇigrahaṇa*.

गृभ्णामि ते सौभगत्वाय हस्तं मया पत्या जरदष्टिर्यथासः ।
भगो अर्यमा सविता पुरंधिर्मह्यं त्वादुर्गार्हपत्याय देवाः ॥

I hold your fortunate hand so that we grow to a live along life together. Bhaga, Aryamā, Savitā and Puraṁdhi have gifted you to me so that I may become a householder.

अमोऽहमस्मि सा त्वं सा त्वमस्यमोऽहम् ।
सामाहमस्मि ऋक्त्वं द्यौरहं पृथिवी त्वं ।
तावेहि विवहावहै सह रेतो दधावहै ।
प्रजां प्रजनयावहै पुत्रान् विन्द्यावहै ।
पुंसे पुत्राय कर्तवे रायस्पोषय सुप्रजस्त्वाय सुवीर्याय ॥

बहून् ते सन्तु जरदष्टयः संप्रियौ रोचिष्णु सुमनस्यमनु ।
पश्येम शरदः शतं जीवेम शरदः शतं श्रुणुयाम शरदः शतम् ॥

I am this (God), you are her (Goddess), you are her, I am this; I am the song, you are the lyric; I am the heaven, you are the earth; let us beget children, let us produce sons; let us come together for the sake of wealth, heroic sons who will live to old age, happy and with good minds; let us see hundred autumns.

Lājā Homa

This is a ritual performed by the bride wherein she offers roasted rice grains to gods and seeks long life for her husband and fertility for her to beget issues. Sometimes, the brother of the bride offers the grains to the fire.

इयं नार्युपब्रूतेऽग्नौ लाजानावपन्तिका ।

दीर्घायुरस्तु मे पतिर्जीवातु शरदश्शतं ॥

This woman is offering roasted grains to Agni. She prays: "Let my husband be long living and let him live to see hundred autumns."

इमाँल्लाजानावपाम्यग्नौ समृद्धिकरणं तव ।
मम तुभ्य च संवननंतदग्निरनुमन्यतामियम् ॥

I offer this roasted grain to Agni for the sake of your prosperity. I pray to Agni for concord between you and me.

Agni Pariṇayana

This is an important ritual as they go round the fire a number of times during the marriage. As Agni is considered to be the God through whom other gods are propitiated, he becomes an important part of the ceremony. Also, he is considered to be a witness to the ceremony (*agni sākṣī*). Some *sūtrakāra*s prescribe the following *mantra* to be chanted during Agni Pariṇayana:

अमोऽहमस्मि सा त्वं सा त्वमस्यमोऽहम् ।
सामाहमस्मि ऋक्त्वं द्यौरहं पृथिवी त्वं ।
तावेहि विवहावहै सह रेतो दधावहै ।
प्रजां प्रजनयावहै पुत्रान् विन्द्यावहै ।
पुंसे पुत्राय कर्तवे रायस्पोषय सुप्रजस्त्वाय सुवीर्याय ॥

बहून् ते सन्तु जरदष्टयः संप्रियौ रोचिष्णु सुमनस्यमनु ।
पश्येम शरदः शतं जीवेम शरदः शतं श्रृणुयाम शरदः शतम् ॥

I am this (God), you are her (Goddess), you are her, I am this; I am the song, you are the lyric; I am the heaven, you are the earth; let us beget children, let us produce sons; let us come together for the sake of wealth, heroic sons who will live to old age, happy and with good minds; let us live to see hundred autumns.

Aśmārohaṇa

Here the groom keeps a stone and makes her stand on it while chanting *mantras* which ask her to be firm like a stone and be prepared to face vicissitudes and enemies successfully in her married life.

स्योनं ध्रुवं प्रजायै धारयामि ते अश्मानं देव्याः पृथिव्या उपस्थे ।
तम तिष्ठानुमाद्या सुवर्चा दीर्घं त आयुः सविता कृणोतु ॥

I place upon the lap of the earth, an auspicious and firm stone for you for the sake of progeny. Stand on it, greeted with joy, may Savitā give you long life.

आतिष्ठेममश्मानमश्मेव त्वं स्थिरा भव ।
अभितिष्ठ पृतन्यतस्सहस्व पृतनायतः ॥

May you step on this stone and be strong and unshakeable like it. May you face the challenges in life and may you withstand all adversities and enemies.

Saptapadī

This is also a prominent part of the marriage ceremony where the groom and the bride take seven steps together with each step meant to give a particular benefit such as sap, energy and wealth, etc. At the end of seven steps, the groom asks the bride to be his friend for life. The direction in which they should walk is specified in the Sūtras. The words of the *mantras* change in the Sūtras of *Ṛgveda*.

१. एकमिषे विष्णुस्त्वान्वेतु ।
२. द्वे ऊर्जे विष्णुस्त्वान्वेतु ।
३. त्रीणि व्रताय विष्णुस्त्वान्वेतु ।
४. चत्वारि मायोभवाय विष्णुस्त्वान्वेतु ।
५. पञ्च पशुभ्यो विष्णुस्त्वान्वेतु ।
६. षड़ृतुभ्यो विष्णुस्त्वान्वेतु ।
७. सप्त सप्तभ्यो होत्राभ्यो विष्णुस्त्वान्वेतु ।
सखा सप्तपदा भव सखायौ सप्तपदा बभूव ।

1. First step for sap or food

2. Second step for strength
3. Third step for vows (*vrata*)
4. Fourth step for happiness
5. Fifth step for cattle (wealth)
6. Sixth step for all seasons
7. Seventh step for *hotra* (sacrificial rites)

At the end, the bridegroom says "be my friend for life".

Journey of the Bride to Husband's Home

Most of the Gṛhya-Sūtras have written elaborately on taking the newly-married couple to the bridegroom's house. There are rituals for preparing the chariot, setting the yoke, etc. *Mantra*s to be chanted on the way when different places are encountered such as crossroads, water bodies and cemeteries, etc. are prescribed. The rituals to be performed if there is a breakdown are specified.

खे रथस्य खेऽनसः खे युगस्य शतक्रतो ।
अपालमिन्द्र त्रिष्पूत्व्यकृणोः सूर्यत्वचम् ॥

In the hole of the chariot, in the hole of the yoke Indra of hundred activities who thrice purified Apāla and made her sun-skinned.

सुकिँशुकँ शल्मलिं विश्वरूपँ हिरण्यवर्णँ सुधुरँ सुचक्रम् ।
आरोह सूर्ये अमृतस्य लोकं स्योनं पत्ये वहतुं कृणुष्व ॥

Ascend Sūrye (Bride) this chariot of Śalmali wood decorated with *kiṁśuka* flowers, of multiform, well covered, with good wheels and of the immortal world. Make this journey with your husband a pleasant one.

सम्राज्ञी स्वशुरे भव सम्राज्ञी स्वश्र्वां भव ।
ननान्दरि सम्राज्ञी भव सम्राज्ञी अधि देवृषु ॥

Be a queen over your father-in-law and your mother-in-law Be a queen over your sisters-in-law and your brothers-in law.

नीललोहितं भवति कृत्यासक्तिर्व्यज्यते ।
एधन्ते अस्या ज्ञातयः पतिर्बन्धेषु बध्यते ॥

The colour of the evil witch Kṛtya is Blue Red. She is driven away.
The Bride's relations prosper and her husband is bound in familial bonds.

सत्येनोत्तभिता भूमिस्सूर्येणोत्तभिता द्यौः ।
ऋतेनादित्यास्तिष्ठन्ति दिवि सोमो अधि श्रितः ॥

Earth is established by truth. Sky is upheld by the Sun. Adityas are supported by Righteousness. Soma is set upon in the sky.

युञ्जन्ति ब्रध्नमरुषं चरन्तं परि तस्थुषः ।
रोचन्ते रोचिना दिवि ॥

Indra is present in the form of the Sun in heaven,
in the form of non-violent Agni on earth and
in the form of Vāyu in space.
All living beings in the three worlds consider him God. The same Indra is shining in the sky in the form of *nakṣatras*.

योगे योगे तवस्तरं वाजेवाजे हवामहे ।
सखाय इन्द्रमूतये ॥

In all our good deeds, we invoke Lord Indra who is mighty and who has defeated enemies repeatedly. We consider him our friend.

उदुत्तरमारोहन्ती व्यस्यन्ती पृतन्यतः ।
मूर्धानं पत्युरा रोह प्रजया च विराड्भव ॥

O Bride! You are ascending into a good household.
Getting rid of enemies, enter your husband's head.
With children lead a splendid life.

ये वध्वश्चन्द्रं वहतुं यक्ष्मा यन्ति जनाँ अनु ।
पुनस्तान्यज्ञिया देवा नयन्तु यत आगताः ॥

May the adorable gods drive back the diseases

Which come from the people who follow the bride's
Golden car, to the places where they came from.

Gṛha-Praveśa

This ritual is to be carried out when the bride enters her husband's house for the first time. It details the *homa*s to be carried out. At her husband's house she is made to sit on a hide of a bull while *mantra*s are chanted. A boy is placed in her lap. This seems to be a fertility rite.

शर्म वर्मेदमा भरास्यै नार्या उपस्तिरे ।
सिनीवालि जायतामियं भगस्य सुमतावसत् ॥

O Sinīvāli, ensure this woman's protection and defence
Let her have children and be in Bhaga's favour.

गृहानहं सुमनसः प्रापद्ये वीरं वीरवतः सुशेवा ।
इरां वहन्ती घृतमुक्षमाणास्तेष्वहँ सुमनाः संवसामः ॥

I enter this house with a pleasant mind where happy and valiant people live.
I will produce heroic sons. In this house where milk flows and ghee is dripping
I will live happily.

इह गावः प्र जायध्वमिहमश्वा इह पुरुषाः ।
इहो सहस्रदक्षिणो रायस्पोषो निषीदतु ॥

Let cows sit here, the bride here, horses here, men here
Here let thousand offerings and wealth sit.

Dhruva-Arundhatī Darśana

In the evening of the day she enters her husband's house, after sunset, she is shown the pole star, Dhruva, and told that she should be constant like the star. The star Arundhatī is also shown to her as Arundhatī as the wife of Vasiṣṭha is the embodiment of faithfulness. Some Gṛhya-Sūtras also include the showing of the *saptarṣi maṇḍala* to the newly-wedded wife.

ध्रुवोऽसि ध्रुवक्षितिर्ध्रुवमसि ध्रुवतस्स्थितम् ।
त्वं नक्षत्राणां मेथ्यसि स मा पाहि पृतन्यतः ॥

You are Dhruva, the firm one. The firm one are you, standing on the side of firmness.
You are the pillar of the stars; protect me against my enemies.

सप्त ऋषयः प्रथमां कृत्तिकानामरुन्धतीं यद्ध्रुवतां ह नित्युः ।
षट्कृत्तिका मुख्ययोगं वहन्तीयमस्माकमेधत्वष्टम्यरुन्धती ॥

The seven *ṛṣi*s who have led to firmness she, Arundhatī, who stands first among the six Kṛttikās: May she the eighth one, who leads the conjunction of the moon with the six Kṛttikās, the first among conjunctions shine upon us!

Trirātra Vrata

The couple observe three nights of this *vrata* during which time they are expected to sleep on the floor, be celibate and eat bland food. A staff coated with sandal paste is kept between them when they lie down.

Caturthī Karma

On the fourth night, this ritual is carried out with the indicated *mantra*s being chanted. Consummation of marriage takes place after the ritual. There are *mantra*s to be chanted prior to consummation.

अग्ने व्रतपते उपयमनं व्रतं चरिष्यामि तच्छकेयम् तन्मे राध्यताम् ।
वायो व्रतपत आदित्य व्रतपते व्रतानां व्रतपते उपयमनं व्रतं चरिष्यामि तन्मे राध्यताम् ॥

I carry out this marriage *vrata* for Agni, lord of *vrata*s and satisfy him and worship him. I carry out this marriage *vrata* for Vāyu and Āditya who are lords of *vrata*s and satisfy them and worship them.

प्रायश्चित्त होमः (Expiation Homa)

अग्ने प्रायश्चित्ते त्वं प्रायश्चित्तिरसि ब्राह्मणस्त्वा नाथकाम उपधावामि यास्यै

घोरा तनूस्तामितो नाशय स्वाहा ॥ वायो प्रायश्चित्ते त्वं प्रायश्चित्तिरसि ब्राह्मणस्त्वा नाथकाम उपधावामि यास्यै निन्दिता तनूस्तामितो नाशय स्वाहा ॥ आदित्य प्रायश्चित्ते त्वं प्रायश्चित्तिरसि ब्राह्मणस्त्वा नाथकाम उपधावामि यास्यै पतिघ्नी तनूस्तामितो नाशय स्वाहा ॥ आदित्य प्रायश्चित्ते वायो प्रायश्चित्तेग्ने प्रायश्चित्तेग्ने प्रायश्चित्ते वायो प्रायश्चित्त आदित्य प्रायश्चित्ते ॥ इति ॥

Agni! Expiation! You are expiation. I, the brāhmaṇa, entreat you desirous of protection. What is terrible in her drive that away from her, *svāhā*! "Vāyu! Expiation! You are expiation. I, the brāhmaṇa, entreat you desirous of protection. What is blameful in her drive that away from her", *svāhā*! "Āditya! Expiation! You are expiation. I, the brāhmaṇa, entreat you desirous of protection. What dwells in her that is death-bringing to her, drive that away from her, *svāhā*! Āditya! Expiation! Vāyu Expiation! Agni Expiation! Agni Expiation! Vāyu Expiation! Āditya Expiation!"

विष्णुर्योनिं कल्पयतु त्वष्टा रूपाणि पिंशतु ॥ आसिञ्चतु प्रजापतिधाता गर्भं दधातु ते ॥ गर्भं देहि सिनीवालि गर्भं देहि सरस्वति । गर्भं ते अश्विनावुभावाधत्तां पुष्करस्रजौ । हिरण्ययी अरणीं यं निर्मन्थतो अश्विना । तं ते गर्भं हवामहे दशमास्याय सूतवे ॥ यथाग्निगर्भा पृथिवी द्यौर्यथेन्द्रेण गर्भणी । वायुर्यथा दिशां गर्भ एवं दधामि ते ॥ यस्य योनिं प्रति रेतो गृहाण पुमान्पुत्रो जायतां गर्भो अन्तः । तं माता दश मासो बिभर्तु स जायतां वीरतमः स्वानाम् ॥ आ ते गर्भो योनिमेतु पुमान्बाण इवेषुधिम् । आ वीरो अत्र जायतां पुत्रस्ते दशमास्यः ॥ करोमि ते प्रजापत्यमा गर्भो योनिमेतु ते । अनूनः पूर्णो जायतामनन्धोऽश्लोणोपिशाचधीरः ॥ यानि प्रभूणि वीर्याण्यृषभा जनयन्तु नः । तैस्त्वं गर्भिणी भव स जायतां वीरतमः स्वानाम् ॥ यो वशायां गर्भो यश्च वेहतीन्द्रस्तं निदधे वनस्पतौ । तेन त्वं गर्भिणी भव सा प्रसूर्धेनुगा भव ॥ सं नाम्नः ॥ चाक्रवाकम् ॥ इति च ॥

May Viṣṇu make your womb ready; may Tvaṣṭā frame the shape of the child; may Prajāpati pour forth the sperm; may Dhātrī give you conception! "Give conception, Sinīvāli; give conception, Sarasvatī! May the two Aśvins, wreathed in flowers give conception to you". "The embryo, which the two Aśvins produce with their golden kindling-sticks, that embryo we call into your womb, that you may give birth to it in ten months." "As the earth is pregnant with Agni, as the heaven is with Indra pregnant, as Vāyu dwells in the womb of the regions, thus I place an embryo into your womb." "Open your womb; take in the sperm; may a male child, an embryo be begotten in the womb. The mother bears him ten months; may he be born, the most valiant of the kin." "May a male embryo enter your womb as an arrow the quiver; may a man be born here, your son after ten months". "I do with you that which is sacred to Prajāpati; may an embryo enter your womb; may a child be born without deficiency, with all its limbs, not blind, not lame, not sucked out by *piśācas*." "By the superior powers which the bulls shall produce for us, thereby you become pregnant; may he be born, the most valiant of his kin." "Indra has laid down in the tree the embryo of the sterile cow and of the cow that prematurely produces; thereby you become pregnant; be a well-breeding cow". And with the two *mantras*, "United are our names" and "The concord of the *cakravāka* birds".

Aupāsana Homa

The fire lit at the marriage ceremony is carried to the husband's house and established there. This fire is expected to be burning constantly and is called the *gṛhyāgni*. The couple is expected to perform all household rituals together from then on using the fire established. Aupāsana *homa* is to be performed daily in the morning and evening.

7

Comparative Study

THIS chapter attempts to list rituals as they appear in each Gṛhya-Sūtra and highlight the differences and carry out a comparative study of *vivāha saṁskāra* as depicted in the available Gṛhya-Sūtras.

Number and Types of Rituals in Each Gṛhya-Sūtra

Apart from the rituals, other aspects such as suitable time for marriage, forms of marriage, etc. are also analysed for variations. Translated parts of each *sūtra* dealing with a particular ritual from all the Gṛhya-Sūtras have been presented for comparison.

SUITABLE TIME FOR MARRIAGE

Generally, it is stated that the period of waxing moon during the northern movement of the sun, under an auspicious star, is the best for conducting marriages. However, opinions vary as can be seen hereunder.

Aśvalāyana: During the northern course of the sun, in the period of the waxing moon (*śukla pakṣa*), under an auspicious *nakṣatra*, the *saṁskāra*s of *caulakarma*, *upanayana*, *godāna* (*keśānta*) and *vivāha* can be performed. However, some people opine that marriage can be conducted at all times.

Śāṅkhāyana: During the northern course of the sun, in *śukla pakṣa*, on an auspicious day, he shall seize the hand of a girl (marry her).

Kauṣītaki: During the northern course of the sun, in *śukla pakṣa*, on an auspicious day he shall seize the hand of a girl (marry her), one who has good qualities.

Pāraskara: Marriages are to be conducted during the northern course of the sun, in *śukla pakṣa*, on an auspicious day. Under the three stars which begin with the three Uttaras (1. Uttara Phālgunī, Hastā, Citrā; 2. Uttarāṣāḍha, Śravaṇā, Dhaniṣṭhā; 3. Uttarabhādra, Revatī, Aśvinī). Or under Svāti, Mr̥gaśirā and Rohiṇī.

Āpastamba: All seasons are fit for marriage except for two months of winter and the last month of summer. These are Māgha, Phālguna and Āṣāḍha. All *nakṣatra*s which are said to be pure are fit for marriage. A father who wishes his daughter to be dear to her husband should give her in marriage under the Niṣṭya (Svāti) *nakṣatra*.

Hiraṇyakeśi: Whatever he intends to do (marry, etc.), he should do on an auspicious day only, during the five times of the day, namely, morning, forenoon, midday, afternoon or in the evening.

Baudhāyana: During the northern course of the sun, during the period of the rising moon under an auspicious *nakṣatra*, two brāhmaṇas are sent to look for a bride. All months are suitable for marriages. Some say the months of Śuci (Āṣāḍha), Tapas (Māgha) and Tapasyā (Phālguna) are to be avoided. Rohiṇī, Mr̥gaśirā, Uttara Phālgunī and Svāti are auspicious stars for marriage. If other stars have been declared auspicious, then before the *puṇyāha vācana*, let two brāhmaṇas be fed.

Vārāha: Let him marry under the stars Kr̥ttikā, Svāti and Pūrva (Āṣāḍha, Bhādrapada, Phālgunī). Mr̥gaśirā, Rohiṇī, Śravaṇa, Dhaniṣṭhā and the stars beginning with Uttara (Āṣāḍha, Bhādrapada, Phālgunī) are auspicious for marriage.

Mānava: Let him seek a bride under the *nakṣatra*s Kr̥ttikā, Svāti, Pūrva-Phālgunī, Purvāṣāḍha and Pūrva-Bhādrapada. Get married under Rohiṇī, Mṛgaśirā, Śravaṇa, Śraviṣṭhā (Dhaniṣṭhā) or the three Uttara *nakṣatras* (Phālgunī, Āṣāḍha, Bhādrapada) which are considered auspicious for marriage.

***Agniveśya*:** During *śukla pakṣa*, under an auspicious star, having built a decorated *maṇḍapa*, having conducted the premarital ceremony (tying a marriage thread on the hand, etc.) with auspiciousness and happiness, he walks to the bride's house, and holding the *madhuparka* vessel, gathering good quality material required such as fried grains, the stone, new clothes, he prepares the dresses for *brahmapraveśa*, etc.

***Bhāradvāja*:** Get married in the northern movement of the sun. The period belongs to gods and is fit for good rituals. *Dakṣiṇāyana* is said to belong to the manes and therefore is suitable for rituals involving manes. *Śukla pakṣa* belongs to *devas* and is suitable for rituals involving *devas* including marriage. *Kṛṣṇa pakṣa* belongs to the manes and therefore is suitable for rituals involving manes including marriage. Forenoon belongs to the gods and therefore is suitable for rituals involving gods including marriage. The midday is said to belong to *ṛṣis* and is therefore suitable for all auspicious ceremonies including marriage. The afternoon is said to belong to the manes and therefore is suitable for rituals involving manes including marriage. Afternoon is said to belong to Bhaga and is suitable for marriage. Under an auspicious star it is good to conduct the marriage. Some *ācāryas* say that a bride who has been chosen under Invakā (Mṛgaśirā) star will bring happiness to the bridegroom with her family. Marriage is performed in Māgha and the bride is taken to her husband's house in Phālguna. One who treats the daughter as a favourite should give her away under Svāti *nakṣatra*. She will become dear to her husband and will not return to her father's house, it is said.

***Kāṭhaka*:** Marry under Kṛttikā, Svāti and stars beginning with Pūrva (Pūrva-Phālgunī, Pūrvāṣāḍha, Pūrvabhādra). Get a bride during the northern course of the sun. During the *śukla pakṣa* on an auspicious day, on a spread of *darbha* grass, the parents of the bride sit facing west and the groom facing east.

***Vaikhānasa*:** There is no specific mention of a suitable time for marriages in *Vaikhānasa Smārta-Sūtra*.

***Gobhila*:** Under a propitious star, let him take a wife.

***Khādira*:** There is no specific mention of a suitable time for marriages in *Khādira Gr̥hya-Sūtra*.

***Jaimini*:** There is no specific mention of a suitable time for marriages in *Jaimini Gr̥hya-Sūtra*.

***Kauśika*:** The period from the month of Kārttika to Vaiśākha is suitable for marriages. You can conduct marriages whenever you wish. Do not conduct marriages under *citra pakṣa*.

QUALITIES OF BRIDE AND GROOM

Many of the Gr̥hya-Sūtras list the method to select a bride and the qualities of the bride and the groom.

***Āśvalāyana*:** Let him examine the family of the bride or groom, as it has been said before, "those who are from the father's side or from the mother's side". The father should give the girl to an intelligent groom. Let him marry a girl who is endowed with intelligence, beauty, moral conduct and one who is free from disease. It is difficult to discern the qualities. Let him prepare eight lumps of earth and recite over the lumps the *mantra*:

> In the beginning, right was established. On the right, truth is founded. For what purpose the girl is born, may she attain that here. What is true may be seen here.

Then let him tell her to pick one of the lumps. If the girl chooses the lump from a field that produces two crops a year, he may know that her offspring will be rich in food. If from a cow stable, they will be rich in cattle. If from a Vedic altar, they will be rich in holy lustre. If from a pool which does not dry up, they will be rich in everything. If from a gambling place, they will be addicted to gambling. If from a place where four roads meet, they will be wandering in different directions. If from a barren ground, they will be poor. If she chooses the lump from a burial ground, she will cause the death of her husband.

***Śāṅkhāyana*:** A bride who has good qualities. Whose limbs are proportionate. Whose hair is smooth. Who should have at her neck two curls turned to the right. He shall know that such a girl will give birth to six manly children.

***Kauṣītaki*:** A bride whose limbs are proportionate, whose hair is smooth. Who should have at her neck two curls turned to the right, he shall know that such a girl will give birth to six manly children.

***Pāraskara*:** There is no specific mention of the qualities of the bride and the groom in *Pāraskara Gṛhya-Sūtra*.

***Āpastamba*:** Let the wooer avoid a girl who sleeps, or cries or one who has left home. And let him avoid one who has been given to another, and who is guarded by her relations, one who has a wicked look, one who is built like a bull, a bald-headed girl, one whose skin is like a frog's, a girl who has gone over to another family, a girl given to many sensual pleasures, one who has too many friends, one who has a fine younger sister, or whose age is too near that of the bridegroom. Girls who have names of *nakṣatra*s, rivers or trees are to be avoided. All girls whose names have *r* or *l* as the last but one letter are to be avoided. If possible, he should place the following objects hidden before the girl and say to her, "touch". Different kinds of seeds mixed together, loose earth from an altar, a field, cow dung and an earth clod from a cemetery. If she touches one of the former objects, it portends prosperity accordingly. The last is regarded as objectionable. Let him marry a girl of good family and character with auspicious characteristics and of good health. Good family, a good character, auspicious characteristics, learning and good health are the accomplishments of a bridegroom. A girl, who is pleasing to his mind and his eyes, will bring happiness to him. Let him disregard other things, according to some.

***Hiraṇyakeśi*:** He should take a wife belonging to the same caste, a maiden who is a virgin belonging to a different *gotra*.

***Baudhāyana*:** There is no specific mention of the qualities of the bride and the groom in *Baudhāyana Gṛhya-Sūtra*.

***Vārāha*:** Let the groom who has controlled anger and is happy choose a queenly bride who is not in any other's possession and one who is young. Let her be from a different *gotra* from his. Let her be a seven times removed from his father and five times from his mother as a relative. The bride's father will look at the following aspects of the groom: money, looks, education, intelligence and family. If all five qualities are not present, he can overlook money. Second, he can overlook looks, third, education if he is intelligent and from a good family. Let her be one who does not have relation with another, of another *gotra*, a virgin. To find out her goodness do the following. Get four mud lumps. From a ploughed field, altar, cowshed and cemetery. From these, ask her to take one. If she takes the lump from the cemetery, do not choose her. Choose one who is not associated with unethical values. Marry as per Brāhma or Ārṣa form of wedding.

***Mānava*:** There are five characteristics for marriage. Wealth, beauty, knowledge, intellect and relationship. If one has to be given up, let him leave out wealth, if two let him leave out beauty, if three let him leave out knowledge. There is a dispute about intellect and relationship. He should marry a girl of a good family, who is a virgin, who belongs to the same caste, who is not of the same *gotra*, who is yet to reach puberty. To know (test) her. He should take eight clods of earth, from a ploughed field, from an altar, from a *darbha* grass field, from cow dung, from below a fruit-bearing tree, from a cemetery, from a road and from saline soil. Having put them in a temple, he makes her pick one of them. If the clod taken is from the cemetery, road or the saline soil, he should not marry her.

***Agniveśya*:** With the advice of the *guru*, "do not break your lineage" he chooses a bride who has all limbs in order, pleasing to look at, younger, unmarried who is not of the same *gotra*, not *sapiṇḍa* from mother's side, not committed to a household, he walks to the house of the bride and having partaken *madhuparka*, one who is not named after a *nakṣatra*, river or tree.

***Bhāradvāja*:** There are four aspects in choosing a bride: wealth, beauty, intelligence and relations. If you cannot find all the aspects, you can leave out wealth. Similarly beauty, intelligence and relations are accepted. Some say that relations also can be ignored. Who can live with someone who is not intelligent? It is said that one does choose a girl for money alone. The main purpose is to beget children. It is enough if the girl is with features which will help beget good children. Do not marry a girl who is sleeping when you visit or one who goes out. Get four lumps of mud prepared, one from an altar, one from a cowshed, one from a ploughed field and one from a cemetery and ask her to choose one. If she chooses the lump from the altar, she will give birth to a son who will be a teacher, one who carries out frequent *homa*s, etc. If she chooses the one from the cowshed, they will be rich in cattle. If she chooses from the lump from a ploughed field, they will have a lot of fields. If she chooses the one from a cemetery, there will be misery due to burning, etc. Do not marry if she chooses the one from the cemetery. Then there are many features of a bride. The *śloka* on features says:

> The one whom the mind likes which fixes one's eyes on her,
> marry her as a Lakṣmī, what other knowledge is required?

***Kāṭhaka*:** Examine the features of the bride (before selection).

Select from her background or using lumps of mud. Make nine lumps of mud, eight from an altar, a ploughed field, a reservoir, a cowshed, a gambling den, a cemetery, crossroads, an arid place and the ninth one made from the mixture of all the above. Chanting the *mantra*, keep the lumps on the floor and make them all similar. Taking her name, decorating them all round, ask her to give a name and pick one of the lumps. Earlier all the lumps would be kept in a square. Some say mix them all together.

***Vaikhānasa*:** Having chosen a girl who is not a *sapiṇḍa* of the mother and not of the same *gotra* and *ṛṣi* of the father, who is a maiden with good features, he should during five days, have proper food with his relations and learned brāhmaṇas. It is said that his family will be purified.

***Gobhila*:** One who should possess good qualities. If he is unable to find one, he should make earth clods. From an altar, a furrow, a pool, a cowshed, a place where four roads meet, a gambling place, a cemetery and from sterile soil. A ninth one a mix of all. Make them equal and marked. Taking the lumps in his hands he should offer them to a girl chanting:

> Right alone is the first; which nobody oversteps; on right this earth is founded. May so named become this universe!

He should pronounce her name and say, "take one of these". If she takes one of the first four, he should marry her. According to some, if she takes the mixed one also.

***Khādira*:** There is no specific mention of the qualities of the bride and the groom in *Khadira Gṛhya-Sūtra*.

***Jaimini*:** He should take a bride who has reached the age of puberty, of the same caste, of a different *gotra* from his, who should not be a *sapiṇḍa* (not related to his mother to the seventh degree) and one who is younger to him.

***Kauśika*:** There is no specific mention of the qualities of the bride and the groom in *Kauśika Gṛhya-Sūtra*.

FORMS OF MARRIAGE

Generally, eight types of marriages have been described in Sūtras and other texts. The following description shows the forms of marriage in each Gṛhya-Sūtra.

Aśvalāyana: The father may give away the daughter adorned with ornaments to the bridegroom with a libation of water. Such a marriage is called Brāhma-Vivāha. A son born of this union will purify twelve descendants and twelve ancestors on both sides. He may give her away to an officiating priest having adorned her with jewels while a sacrifice with three Śrauta fires is going on. Such a marriage is called a Daiva-Vivāha. A son from this marriage will bring purification to ten descendants and ten ancestors on both sides. If the bride and the groom observe the nuptial rites (dhārmic) together, the marriage is called Prājāpatya-Vivāha. A son born of such a marriage will purify eight descendants and eight ancestors from both sides. If the father receives a bull and a cow from the groom for giving away the bride, such a marriage is called Ārṣa. A son from this marriage purifies seven descendants and seven ancestors on both sides. If the bride and groom marry after mutual agreement, the marriage is called Gāndharva-Vivāha. If the groom marries the girl after having satisfied her father with money, such a marriage is called Āsura. If the groom carries off the bride while her people are asleep or inattentive, the marriage is called Paiśāca. If he carries off the girl after killing her relatives and while she and relatives weep, the marriage is called Rākṣasa.

Śāṅkhāyana: There is no mention of the forms of marriage in *Śāṅkhāyana Gṛhya-Sūtra*.

Kauṣītaki: There is no mention of the forms of marriage in *Kauṣītaki Gṛhya-Sūtra*.

Pāraskara: There is no mention of the forms of marriage in *Pāraskara Gṛhya-Sūtra*.

***Āpastamba*:** There is no mention of the forms of marriage in *Āpastamba Gṛhya-Sūtra.*

***Hiraṇyakeśi*:** There is no mention of the forms of marriage in *Hiraṇyakeśi Gṛhya-Sūtra.*

***Baudhāyana*:** There is no mention of the forms of marriage in *Baudhāyana Gṛhya-Sūtra.*

***Vārāha*:** Choose one who is not associated with unethical values. Marry as per Brāhma or Ārṣa form of wedding.

***Mānava*:** Choose one who is not associated with unethical values. Marry as per Brāhma or Ārṣa form of wedding.

***Agniveśya*:** There is no mention of the forms of marriage in *Agniveśya Gṛhya-Sūtra.*

***Bhāradvāja*:** There is no mention of the forms of marriage in *Bhāradvāja Gṛhya-Sūtra.*

***Kāṭhaka*:** We will study the procedures as per Brāhma and other types of marriages. During the *śukla pakṣa* on an auspicious day, on a spread of *darbha* grass, the parents of the bride sit facing west and the groom facing east. In the centre to the east, *darbha* grass is spread, and water and rice grains are kept, and *purohitas* sitting to the south will conduct the marriage. The *purohitas* ask the father of the bride to say, "I offer my daughter" thrice, and groom says "I will accept" thrice. "This giving is true and equal" say the *purohitas*. They ask the parents of the groom to observe. Now, the giving of bride price in the case of Āsura type of marriage. Gold is given by the groom's father. Groom's father gives the gold saying, "For the sake of children". The bride's father receives saying for the sake of wealth. Keeping the gold in a brass vessel, it is touched four times chanting, "golden coloured".

***Vaikhānasa*:** *Pāṇigrahaṇa* or marriage is of eight types. Brāhma, Daiva, Prājāpatya, Ārṣa, Āsura, Gāndharva, Rākṣasa and Paiśāca. When a bride well adorned is given away in marriage to a worthy bridegroom invited by her father, it is called Brāhma wedding. When a well-adorned bride is given away in marriage by her father to a priest who has conducted a *yajña* as sacrificial fee, it is called Daiva marriage. When a worthy bridegroom seeks her hand in marriage for the sake of carrying out religious duties together, it is called Prājāpatya marriage. When the bride is given away in marriage to a groom who has given a cow and a bull, it is called Ārṣa marriage. When the groom puts ornaments on the bride and pays her relatives according to his ability, the marriage is called Āsura. Marriage by mutual consent is called Gāndharva marriage. When the girl is forcibly abducted for marriage, it is called Rākṣasa marriage. When a girl is seduced when she is asleep or drugged, it is called Paiśāca marriage. Out of these the first four preceded by a gift of water are approved for a brāhmaṇa. Not the other four. For a woman married as per Ārṣa marriage, the birth of a son will purify three ancestors and three descendents. As per Prājāpatya, the birth of a son will purify six ancestors and six descendants. As per Daiva, the birth of a son will purify seven ancestors and seven descendants. As per Brāhma, the birth of a son will purify ten ancestors and ten descendants.

Gobhila: There is no mention of the forms of marriage in *Gobhila Gṛhya-Sūtra*.

Khādira: There is no mention of the forms of marriage in *Khādira Gṛhya-Sūtra*.

Jaimini: There is no mention of the forms of marriage in *Jaimini Gṛhya-Sūtra*.

Kauśika: There is no mention of the forms of marriage in *Kauśika Gṛhya-Sūtra*.

VĀGDĀNA OR VĀṄNIŚCAYA

This is a ritual to confirm acceptance of the alliance by the groom's and bride's families.

***Aśvalāyana*:** There is no mention of *vāgdāna* in *Aśvalāyana Gṛhya-Sūtra.*

***Śāṅkhāyana*:** When both sides have agreed, let them touch a vessel into which have been put flowers, *akṣata*, barley, fruits and gold, and let them recite the *mantra*:

> Undisturbed are you, the undisturbable vigour of the gods,
> not cursed, protecting against a curse, unexposed to a curse.
> May I straightaway attain the truth. Put me into prosperity.

With the verse, "let offspring be produced", the *ācārya* of the girl's family standing up places the vessel on girl's head pronouncing:

> Offspring I give into you, cattle I give into you, splendour and holy lustre, I put into you.

***Kauṣītaki*:** When both sides have agreed, let them touch a vessel into which have been put flowers, *akṣata*, barley, fruits and gold, and let them recite the *mantra*:

> Undisturbed are you, the undisturbable vigour of the gods,
> not cursed, protecting against a curse, unexposed to a curse.
> May I straightaway attain the truth. Put me into prosperity.

With the verse, "let offspring be produced", the *ācārya* of the girl's family standing up places the vessel on the girl's head pronouncing:

> Offspring I give into you, cattle I give into you, splendour and holy lustre, I put into you.

***Pāraskara*:** There is no mention of *vāgdāna* in *Pāraskara Gṛhya-Sūtra.*

***Āpastamba*:** There is no mention of *vāgdāna* in *Āpastamba Gṛhya-Sūtra.*

***Hiraṇyakeśi*:** There is no mention of *vāgdāna* in *Hiraṇyakeśi Gṛhya-Sūtra.*

***Baudhāyana*:** There is no mention of *vāgdāna* in *Baudhāyana Gṛhya-Sūtra.*

Vārāha: Lumps of cow dung are prepared with two being held by the bride's parents and two by the bride. Let the parents of the bride declare, "no money". The groom's parents say, "will I give". Thrice holding the lumps. The lumps are then broken up. This kind of practice is called *trirānanda* by the people of Magadha.

Mānava: To the west of the fire arrange four seats. On these they sit down: on the eastern side with his face to the west, the giver (father of the bride); on the western side with his face to the east, the receiver (bridegroom); to the north of the giver with her face to the west, the bride; to the south with his face to the north, the *purohita*. Having strewn *darbha* grass with their ends pointing east in the middle, having filled a brass vessel filled with *akṣata* water, a *sumaṅgalī* gives the vessel to the groom. In that gold pieces are kept. He announces eight auspicious things. When the auspicious things have been announced, the father or the brother of the bride should give her away, if she marries according to the Brāhma form of marriage, saying the words: "I give" thrice and the receiver accepts with the words: "I accept" thrice. The giver gives handful of gold pieces with the words "For the sake of wealth" and the receiver gives them back with the words "for the sake of children".

Agniveśya: There is no mention of *vāgdāna* in *Agniveśya Gṛhya-Sūtra*.

Bharadvaja: There is no mention of *vāgdāna* in *Bhāradvāja Gṛhya-Sūtra*.

Kāṭhaka: There is no mention of *vāgdāna* in *Kāṭhaka Gṛhya-Sūtra*.

Vaikhānasa: There is no mention of *vāgdāna* in *Vaikhānasa Gṛhya-Sūtra*.

Gobhila: There is no mention of *vāgdāna* in *Gobhila Gṛhya-Sūtra*.

Khādira: There is no mention of *vāgdāna* in *Khādira Gṛhya-Sūtra*.

Jaimini: There is no mention of *vāgdāna* in *Jaimini Gṛhya-Sūtra*.

Kauśika: There is no mention of *vāgdāna* in *Kauśika Gṛhya-Sūtra*.

KANYĀDĀNA

This is the ritual where the father of the bride gifts his daughter in marriage to the bridegroom. It does not appear in all the Gṛhya-Sūtras, probably because it was said that the bride is gods' gift to the groom.

Āśvalāyana: The father may give away the daughter adorned with ornaments to the bridegroom with a libation of water. He may give her away to an officiating priest having adorned her with jewels while a sacrifice with three Śrauta fires are going on. If the father receives a bull and a cow from the groom for giving away the bride, such a marriage is called Ārṣa.

Śāṅkhāyana: There is no mention of *kanyādāna* in *Śāṅkhāyana Gṛhya-Sūtra*.

Kauṣītaki: There is no mention of *kanyādāna* in *Kauṣītaki Gṛhya-Sūtra*.

Pāraskara: Then the bride and groom are made to face each other with the verse:

> Let Viśvedevās and let waters unite these hearts. May Mātariśvan and Deṣṭrī bring us together.

The bridegroom holds the hand of the bride who has been given away by her father and leaves with the verse:

> When you wander far away in your mind like the wind, let the golden-winged Vaikarṇa make you heart live in me.

Āpastamba: There is no mention of *kanyādāna* in *Āpastamba Gṛhya-Sūtra*.

Hiraṇyakeśi: There is no mention of *kanyādāna* in *Hiraṇyakeśi Gṛhya-Sūtra*.

***Baudhāyana*:** Where the bride is given away with offerings, there is no need for further offerings for the groom. Let the bridegroom accept these with six *mantra*s beginning with, "Prajāpati is women's fame".

***Vārāha*:** There is no mention of *kanyādāna* in *Vārāha Gṛhya-Sūtra*.

***Mānava*:** When the auspicious things have been announced, the father or the brother of the bride should give her away, if she marries according to the Brāhma form of marriage, saying the words: "I give" thrice and the receiver accepts with the words "I accept" thrice. The giver gives handful of gold pieces with the words "for the sake of wealth" and the receiver gives them back with the words "for the sake of children". Having repeated four times, he gives her away. After having accepted the girl with the Savitra verse, he says "to Prajāpati", etc.

> Who has given this to whom? Love has given it to love. Love is the giver and love is the receiver; for love I accept you.

***Agniveśya*:** During this time, the bride after tying a marriage thread on her hand is led after the wearing of the sacred thread and sipping water from the north-west of the fire and made to stand at the south-east of the fire; the bridegroom goes from the north-east of the fire and stands in the west opposite the bride and with the *pavitra* water recites the *vyāhṛtis* and murmurs, "Prajāpati of the women" six times; to the south of these, facing north, the bride's parents say "we give this (name) of . . . *gotra* to you for the sake of progeny and receive the *strīdhana*".

***Bhāradvāja*:** One who treats the daughter as a favourite should give her away under Svāti *nakṣatra*.

***Kāṭhaka*:** The *purohitas* ask the father of the bride to say, "I offer my daughter" thrice, and groom says "I will accept" thrice. "This giving is true and equal" say the *purohitas*. They ask the parents of the groom to observe.

***Vaikhānasa*:** When the *guru* has conducted the *agnimukha*, the one who gives her away should recite the name of the groom ending with Śarma and say, "I give this girl (name) for duty, progeny and prosperity: for success in sacrifices, for satisfying, Brahmadeva, *ṛṣis*, the fathers in order that they may get offspring and fulfil their religious duties".

***Gobhila*:** There is no mention of *kanyādāna* in *Gobhila Gṛhya-Sūtra*.

***Khādira*:** There is no mention of *kanyādāna* in *Khādira Gṛhya-Sūtra*.

***Jaimini*:** There is no mention of *kanyādāna* in *Jaimini Gṛhya-Sūtra*.

***Kauśika*:** There is no mention of *kanyādāna* in *Kauśika Gṛhya-Sūtra*.

BATHING AND DRESSING OF THE BRIDE

***Aśvalāyana*:** There is no mention of bathing and dressing of the bride in *Āśvalāyana Gṛhya-Sūtra*.

***Śāṅkhāyana*:** They make her wear a new garment which has not yet been washed. On that night when the night is gone, they wash the girl up to her head with water made fragrant by herbs, fruits and scents. With their permission, he then gives her the garment with the *mantra*, "*raibhyasi . . .*".

***Kauṣītaki*:** When the bride is to be carried away to the groom's house that night, or on the next or on the third night, on that night when the night is gone, they wash the girl up to her head with water made fragrant by herbs, fruits and scents. They make her wear a new garment which has not yet been washed. With their permission, he then gives her the garment with the *mantra*, "*raibyasi . . .*". And the *mantra*, "these dresses".

***Pāraskara*:** He makes her put on the garment with the verse:

> Live to old age, be a saviour of the family against curses.

> Live 100 years virtuously, clothe yourself in wealth and children, put on this garment being blessed.

Then the upper garment:

> May the goddesses who spun, wove and spread the garment and who drew out the threads on both sides, let the goddesses clothe you for a long life. Blessed with life, put on this garment.

Āpastamba: With the next *mantra*, he places a round piece of *darbha* network on her head. On that, with the next verse he places a right yoke hole. On this hole he lays with the next verse a piece of gold, and washes her with the next five verses, so that the water runs over that gold and through the yoke hole. With the next verse, he causes her to dress in a fresh garment and with the next, he girds her with a rope.

Hiraṇyakeśi: Having put wood on the fire, set the limits and performed the preparatory rites, he looks at the bride who is led to him with the verse:

> Auspicious ornaments does this woman wear. Look at her and having brought luck to her, go back to your houses.

Baudhāyana: Having smeared sesame seeds with a mix of flowers, fruits, *akṣata*, offering a mix of curds and rice, having knelt with the right knee on the ground, worn the sacred thread (on the left), having chanted the verse, "for goddess Iḍā" he makes the brāhmaṇas say, "let *nāndimukha* ancestors be pleased" and "today is the marriage" and having fed the brāhmaṇas with cooked rice, he makes them to recite thrice, "Puṇyāham, Svasti and Ṛddhi", he takes bath and wears new (unwashed) clothes, wears garland with sandal paste on it, he goes to the bride's place as a guest and worshipper; he looks at the bride who has bathed and worn new clothes and garland with the *mantra*:

> Her, not brother-slaying, O Varuṇa, not husband-slaying,

O Bṛhaspati; O Indra, not children-slaying, she who is Lakṣmī, bring her to us O Savitā.

Vārāha: Give clothes which bring pleasure to her and to her parents. First to her parents and then to her. Now dressing up is done. "You are the decoration. May I be adequate for everyone." With the *mantra*, "satiate my *prāṇa* and *apāna*, satiate my *samāna* and *vyāna*, satiate my *udāna* and beauty, may I become splendid of face, may I come to hear well with my ears", she touches herself and takes new dresses smeared with sandal paste. With the verses, "I shall put on glory, I shall wear this garment for the sake of long life. May we live to old age and see hundred autumns" she wears the garment after sacrificing chanting *vyāhṛtis* with barley, rice husk, etc. Now they say that the bride having fasted, bathed including her head, clothed in new clothes will be asked to sit on the spread grass near the fire, arrange the selected musical instruments and Sviṣṭakṛt sacrifice will be carried out.

Mānava: Now she puts on a garment with the words, "you are an ornament: may I be adequate for everyone". With the verses, "satiate my *prāṇa* and *apāna*, satiate my *samāna* and *vyāna*, satiate my *udāna* and beauty; may I come to see well with my eyes, may I become splendid of face, may I hear well with my ears", she touches respective parts of her body. Now the scented dresses are readied. With the verses, "I shall put on glory, I shall wear this for long life; may I attain old age, may we live to see hundred autumns; I shall wrap myself up in increasing wealth; with glory to me, heaven and earth, Indra and Bṛhaspati; may glory and good fortune not be lost to me, may glory not be lost", she puts on the garment.

Agniveśya: There is no mention of bathing and dressing of the bride in *Agniveśya Gṛhya-Sūtra.*

Bhāradvāja: After the *madhuparka*, she is brought by her relatives for ritual bathing. After she has bathed, she is given new clothes. These will have the blessing of the goddess for long life. She is made to wear the new clothes by her relations saying that she will live 100 years. They bless her saying:

> You will live to see hundred autumns with luster, wealth and well-being.

After she is dressed, Svasti is recited and she is blessed: "Live to see a hundred autumns."

***Kāṭhaka*:** With the *mantra*, "*godanika*" the bride is decorated and made to sit on a seat with four legs. On the opposite side will be four *sumaṅgalī*s. On the left her mother and on the right her father. In the front, her *guru* who will conduct the marriage as the seventh. The bride is bathed and made to wear new clothes and oblations are offered with cooked food to Indra, Kāma, Bhaga, Hriya, Śrī, Puṣṭi, Viśvavasavas, king of *gandharvas*, *svāhā*!.

***Vaikhānasa*:** According to some teachers, he should collect garments, perfumes, ornaments, etc. go to her house with his relations, should adorn her while chanting, "lustre, long life, beauty, wealth, etc.". He should put ornaments on her with the *mantra*: "Prajāpati created Soma, etc." Then after the *puṇyāha vācana*, having bathed together, and the bride is adorned with new garments, he holds her hand with the *mantra*: "Auspicious garments does this woman wear, etc."

***Gobhila*:** Now the girl he is going to wed should be bathed including her head. He should put on her new (unwashed) clothes with the *mantra*, "they who spin" and "put on her, dress her". He should lead her who is wearing her upper garment like a sacred thread to the fire and chant, "Soma gave her to *gandharva*", etc.

***Khādira*:** After the bride has bathed, he should dress her in a garment which is not washed (new) with the verse, "they who spin". While she is led up to him, the bridegroom should murmur, "Soma gave her".

Jaimini: He gives her two garments after having sprinkled them and having spoken over them the verse:

> The goddesses who spun, who wove, who spread out and who drew the ends of the sides, may these goddesses clothe you with long life. Put on these garments for living long.

Kauśika: With seven *mantra*s, she is bathed with warm water. With the *mantra*, "what is done in the seat earlier", she is bathed over her head standing up. With the *mantra*, "where there is lustre", cold water is sprinkled where she was standing to bathe. With the *mantra*, "what ill deed", the dress for covering the bride is given to her guardian. Having given the clothes with a staff of *tumbara* wood, he moves away. With the *mantra*s, "those who spun the cloth", "Tvaṣṭā gave this cloth", her dresses are bound with the sacred thread. With the *mantra*, "the artificial hundred-toothed comb", her hair is combed with a hundred-toothed comb.

PĀṆIGRAHAṆA

This is probably the earliest marriage ritual specified as it appears in *Ṛgveda*. It means holding of the bride's hand by the bridegroom and saying that she has been gifted to him by gods so that he could become a householder and grow to old age with her.

Āśvalāyana: Having placed to the west of the fire a stone and a water pot to the north-east, he should sacrifice while she takes hold of him. Standing with his face to the west, while she is sitting with her face to the east, he should with the *mantra* "I seize your hand for the sake of happiness" seize her thumb if he desires that only male issues be born to him. Other fingers, if he is desirous of female children. If he desires both male and female children, he should seize her hand on the hair-side together with the thumb.

Śāṅkhāyana: With these words "I seize your hand for the sake of happiness" the bridegroom seizes with his right hand her right hand with the thumb, both hands being turned with the palms turned upwards, he standing while she is sitting, with his face to the west while her face is to the east.

Kauṣītaki: After reciting "come, joyful one" and "I seize your hand for the sake of happiness", the bridegroom seizes with his right hand her right hand with the thumb, both hands being turned with the palms turned upwards, standing while she is sitting, with his face to the west while her face is to the east.

Pāraskara: He then seizes her right hand together with the thumb with the verse:

> I seize your hand for the sake of happiness, that you may live to an old age with me, your husband. Bhaga, Aryamā, Savitā, Puraṁdhi have given you to me so that we may rule our house.

Āpastamba: Then he should take with his right hand palm down, her right hand which she holds palm up. If he wishes that only daughters may be born to him, he should seize only the fingers without the thumb. If he wishes that only sons may be born to him, the thumb. He takes her hand so as just to touch her thumb and the hairs on her hand. With the four verses, "I seize your hand".

Hiraṇyakeśi: Facing the east, while she faces the west or facing the west while she faces the east, he should seize her hand. If he desires to have male children, he should seize her thumb; If he desires female children, her other fingers; if he desires both male and female children, let him seize the thumb together with the other fingers with the hairs on the hand on the top. He should recite the two *mantras*:

> Sarasvatī! Promote this undertaking, O, gracious one, rich in studs, you whom we sing first of all that is.
>
> I seize your hand that we may be blessed with offspring, that you may live to old age with me, your husband. Bhaga,

> Aryamā, Savitā, Puraṁdhi have given you to me that I may become a householder with you.

***Baudhāyana*:** Now he takes her right hand with his right hand with the thumb and the hairy outer portion with the *mantra*,

> I take your hand in mine so that we may live up to old age. The gods Bhaga, Aryamā, Savitā and Puraṁdhi have given you to me so that I may become a householder.

***Vārāha*:** I hold your blessed hand so that you will be my wife till old age. The gods, Bhaga, Aryamā, Savitā and Puraṁdhi have gifted you to me so that I may become a householder. From above the gods are uttering their blessings.

***Mānava*:** By the impulse of god Savitṛ, with the arms of the two Aśvins, with Pūṣaṇa's hands, I seize your hand (her name) while her face is turned eastward and his westward, while he is standing upright and she is sitting, her right hand upwards and his downwards, her hand which is not empty, with his hand which is not empty. After seizing her hand he chants:

> In the same manner in which Indra, Savitṛ, Varuṇa and Bhaga have seized her hand, I seize your hand for the sake of happiness, in order that you may live to old age with me your husband. Bhaga, Aryamā, Savitṛ and Puraṁdhi, the gods, have given you to me for making me a householder.

***Agniveśya*:** Then he holds her right hand with his right hand including the thumb and with the hairs on the hand, with the verse, "You belong to gods". Then he makes her raise with the verse, "Bhaga, Aryamā, etc." five times.

***Bhāradvāja*:** Then he holds her right hand with his right hand including the thumb and the back of the hand with hairs saying:

> You belong to the god, Savitā's womb, the two Aśvins' shoulders and Pūṣaṇa's hands.
>
> I hold your hand in mine for good fortune and grow old as your husband. Bhaga, Aryamā, Savitā and Puraṁdhi have given you to be my wife.

***Kāṭhaka*:** He holds her right hand with the thumb upwards, not left with left hand. He chants four times:

> I hold your hands for the sake of children and to grow old with me. Bhaga, Aryamā, Savitā and Puraṁdhi have given you to me to make me a householder.

***Vaikhānasa*:** Standing opposite to her, he holds her hand, saying, "Sarasvatī promote this union", "I seize your hand", he sits down chanting the *mantra*, "be not of evil eye", and he pours fried grains mixed with butter into her joined hands. This is the seizing the hand (*pāṇigrahaṇa*, the principal act of marriage).

***Gobhila*:** After she has been besprinkled, he puts up her joined hands with his left hand, seizes with his right hand her right hand with the thumb, her hand being turned with the palm upwards, and murmurs these six verses referring to the holding of her hand, "I seize your hand".

***Khādira*:** He should seize her right hand together with the thumb with the six verses, "I seize your hand".

***Jaimini*:** Now he seizes with his right hand her right hand. If he wishes male children, her open hand with the fingers extended, if he wishes female children, her fingers only, if he wishes both her hand together with the thumb with the *śloka*:

> I seize your hand so that we may be blessed with good fortune that with me as your husband you may live to old age. The gods Bhaga, Aryamā, Savitā and Puraṁdhi have given you to me so that we may rule the house.

***Kauśika*:** He holds her hand with the five *mantras* beginning with, "that Agni who has grasped your hand".

SAPTAPADĪ

This ritual wherein the couple take seven steps together is included in all the Gṛhya-Sūtras. There are variations in the words of the *ślokas* chanted as described in Chap. 8.

Āśvalāyana: He then makes her walk seven steps in the north-eastern direction with the following *mantra*:

> One step for sap, two for energy, three for wealth, four for prosperity, five for offspring, six for seasons and be a friend with seven steps. So be devoted to me. Let us beget many sons who may reach old age.

Śāṅkhāyana: They are made to take seven steps in the north-eastern direction. For sap with one step, for energy with two steps, for prosperity with three steps, for comfort with four steps, for cattle with five steps, for the seasons with six steps. Be a friend with seven steps. *Ācārya* sprinkles those feet with water.

Kauṣītaki: He makes her take seven steps. For sap with one step, for energy with two steps, for prosperity with three steps, for comfort with four steps, for cattle with five steps, for the seasons with six steps. Be a friend with seven steps. With each they follow with "let Viṣṇu carry you forward".

Pāraskara: Then he makes her step forward in the northern direction seven steps with the words:

> One for sap, two for energy, three for prosperity, four for comfort, five for cattle, six for seasons. Be a friend with me with the seventh step, be one with me.

The words, "may Viṣṇu lead you" are added after each step.

Āpastamba: He then makes her step forward with her right foot, to the north of the fire, in an easterly or northerly direction, with the *mantra*, "One step for sap . . .". At her seventh step, he murmurs, "be a friend".

Hiraṇyakeśi: To the west of the fire, he makes her step forward in an easterly or northerly direction the steps of Viṣṇu. He says to her:

> Step forward with the right foot and follow with the left. Do not put the left before the right.

One step for sap, may Viṣṇu lead you; second step for energy, may Viṣṇu lead you; third step for vows, may Viṣṇu lead you; fourth step for comfort, may Viṣṇu lead you; fifth step for cattle, may Viṣṇu lead you; sixth step for prosperity, may Viṣṇu lead you; seventh step for rituals, may Viṣṇu lead you. After the seventh step, he murmurs;

> With seven steps, we have become friends. May we attain your friendship. May I not be separated from your friendship. May you not be separated from my friendship.

Baudhāyana: Then he makes her step forward with the *mantra*:

> First step for sap, let Viṣṇu take you along. Second step for energy, let Viṣṇu take you along. Third step for *vrata*s, let Viṣṇu take you along. Fourth step for happiness, let Viṣṇu take you along. Fifth step for cattle, let Viṣṇu take you along. Sixth step for wealth, let Viṣṇu take you along. Seventh step for friendship and for sacrifices, let Viṣṇu take you along.

With the seventh step taken he says:

> We will become friends, you are the woman by my side, my companion.

Vārāha: Then he makes her take seven steps to the east — first step for sap, let Viṣṇu lead you; second step for energy, let Viṣṇu lead you; third step for wealth, let Viṣṇu lead you; fourth step for health, let Viṣṇu lead you; fifth step for children, let Viṣṇu lead you; sixth step for seasons, let Viṣṇu lead you; seventh step for riuals, let Viṣṇu lead you, let them repeat following the first one. He says "be my friend with the seventh step, let me go as your friend, do not harm me". The seventh step will look after her.

Mānava: Then he makes her take seven steps in the eastern direction.

> First step for sap, second for energy, third for offspring, fourth for prosperity, fifth for welfare, sixth for the seasons, be a friend with the seventh step.

Be very gracious Sarasvatī! May we not be removed from your sight. With each step, he subjoins the words, "let Viṣṇu lead you".

Agniveśya: Then to west of the fire, he makes her take steps with the *mantra*, "first step for sap, let Viṣṇu carry you". He makes her step with her right foot first and finish with the left foot. Similarly, they take seven steps. They will cross the boundaries of Agni. With the seventh step, he chants, "with the seventh step let us become friends".

Bhāradvāja: He makes her take seven steps with, "first step for sap, second for energy, third for *vrata*s, fourth for happiness, fifth for cattle, sixth for wealth, seventh for rituals". At each step, "let Viṣṇu lead you" is recited. At the end of the seventh step he says, "be my friend, let us be friends for life".

Kāṭhaka: To the northern side of the fire and east of the *darbha* grass, he makes her take seven steps with the *mantra*:

> First step for sap, second for energy, third for wealth, fourth for happiness, fifth for children, sixth for seasons and long life, seventh for friendship.

Gracious Sarasvatī, do not take us to your heaven. At the end of each step, "let Viṣṇu take you along" is recited.

Vaikhānasa: He strews seven northward pointed grass blades, treads with the right foot on these with his bride, each step with the *mantra*s:

> First step for sap, second for energy, third for vows, fourth for comfort, fifth for cattle, sixth for welfare, seventh for seven sacrifices.

At the end of each step, he says "let Viṣṇu take you". After the seventh step, he says, "with seven steps, be my friend for life".

Gobhila: After she has poured the remainder of the fried grains into the fire, they make her step forward in the north-easterly direction with the *mantra*, "first step for sap". She should step forward with her right and then the left. He should say to her "do not put your left foot before the right foot".

***Khādira*:** After she has poured the remnants of the fried grain into the fire, he should make her step forward in the north-eastern direction with the *mantra*, "for sap with one step . . .".

***Jaimini*:** On the north-eastern part of the fire, he makes her take seven steps, each one with the following *mantra*:

> One for sap; may Viṣṇu lead you. Two for juice; may Viṣṇu lead you. Three for prosperity; may Viṣṇu lead you. Four for comfort; may Viṣṇu lead you. Five for progeny; may Viṣṇu lead you. Six for the seasons; may Viṣṇu lead you. Be a friend of seven steps.

***Kauśika*:** With the *mantra*, "seven boundaries" he draws seven lines towards the east on the northern side of the fire. He makes her take steps on them. The first step for sap for you the *sumaṅgalī* the child-bearer. Second for energy, third for wealth, fourth for fortune, fifth for kingdom. Sixth for long life. With seventh, he says, "you, a *sumaṅgalī* and child-bearer, become my friend for life.

AŚMĀROHAṆA

In this ritual, the bride is made to stand on a mill stone while the husband chants:

> Stand on this stone and be firm like it to face all adversities and destroy enemies.

***Āśvalāyana*:** Each time after he has taken her around the fire, he makes her tread on a stone reciting the *mantra*:

> Ascend this stone; be firm like a stone. Overcome enemies, tread the enemies down.

***Śāṅkhāyana*:** He makes her tread on the stone with her right foot with the verse:

Come tread on the stone;
Be firm like a stone;
Tread the foes down;
Overcome your enemies.

Kauṣītaki: After a stone is placed towards the northern direction, he makes her rise with the verse, "come, joyful one". He makes her tread on the stone with her right foot with the verse:

Come tread on the stone;
Be firm like a stone;
Tread the foes down;
Overcome the enemies.

Pāraskara: He then makes her thread on a stone, to the north of the fire, with her right foot while reciting the verse:

Tread on this stone;
Be firm like a stone,
Tread the foes down;
Turn away enemies.

Āpastamba: He then makes her, to the north of the fire, to tread with her right foot on a stone with the *mantra*, "tread . . . ".

Hiraṇyakeśi: After he has sacrificed with the verses, "this O Varuṇa", "for this I entreat you", "you Agni", "thus you Agni", "you Agni are quick", "Prajapati"— he makes her tread on a stone with the verse:

Tread on this stone; like a stone be firm. Destroy those who seek to do you harm; overcome your enemies.

Baudhayāna: Then he makes her stand up to the north of the fire and puts her right leg on the stone and makes her stand with the *mantra*:

Stand on this stone and be firm like it. Stand up to your enemies and destroy your ill wishers.

Vārāha: To the west of the fire on *darbha* grass, he places a stone. He says:

> Stand on the stone so that you become as firm as the stone. Let the gods make you live to see hundred autumns.

Mānava: After going round the fire, he makes them both step onto a stone with their right feet with the verse:

> Come step you both on this stone; be firm like a stone; let the gods make you live to see hundred autumns.

With the verse:

> In the same way that Indra together with Indrāṇī descended from the Gandhamādana, likewise you must descend from this stone together with your wife.
>
> Mount together so that she will have long life with children.

They are made to mount the stone twice.

Agniveśya: Keeping a stone on the northern half of the *paridhi*, he makes her stand on it with her right foot with the verse, "stand on this stone, etc.".

Bhāradvāja: Then he makes her stand on a stone saying, "be unmoving like the stone: cause death to the evil minded and face enemies with strength".

Kāṭhaka: On the southern side of the fire a stone is kept saying, "be firm like a stone". Let Viśvedevā give you long life to see hundred autumns. He keeps her right foot on the stone and says: "Stand on this stone and be firm like it. Cause death to poverty and defeat enemies."

Vaikhānasa: A stone will be placed to the west of the fire on *darbha* grass, he makes her stand on it, "tread on this stone" he touches her feet with right thumb.

Gobhila: Standing to the east her mother or her brother, having taken the roasted grain, should make the bride tread on the stone with the tip of her right foot. The bridegroom chants, "tread on this stone".

Khādira: Should make her tread with the tip of her right foot on an upper millstone, to the west of the fire with the verse, "on this stone".

Jaimini: Then he makes her stand on a stone as before changing the masculine to feminine gender.

Kauśika: With the *mantra*, "I keep this stone" he keeps a stone on a base of cow dung. He makes her stand on it.

LĀJĀ HOMA

This ritual is performed by the bride, seeking longevity for her husband. Many Gṛhya-Sūtras suggest that her brother should assist her in this ritual.

Āśvalāyana: Having spread butter over the hands of the bride, her brother or a substitute should pour fried grain twice over her joined hands. "For God Aryamā the girls have offered oblations to Agni. May he, God Aryamā release her from this and not that place. For God Varuṇa, the girls have offered oblations to Agni. May he, God Varuṇa release her from this and not that place. For God Pūṣaṇa, the girls have offered oblations to Agni. May he, God Puṣaṇa release her from this and not that place." With these verses she should offer fried grain without opening her hand as if she did so with a spoon (*śṛk*). Without being taken around the fire, she offers grain from the basket towards herself, silently a fourth time. Some lead the bride around each time after the fried grain has been poured out. Thus the last two oblations do not immediately succeed each other.

Śāṅkhāyana: Her father or brother pours out fried grain mixed with *śamī* leaves into her joined hands. Then spreading under and sprinkling over the grains and second sprinkling with *ājya*. She sacrifices the grains. "This woman, offering grains, prays thus, may I bring bliss to may relations; may my husband live long, *svāhā*" — while her husband recites this, she sacrifices standing.

Kauṣītaki: Her father or brother pours out fried grain mixed with *śamī* leaves into her joined hands. Then spreading under and sprinkling over the grains and second sprinkling with *ājya*. She sacrifices the grains. "This woman, offering grains, prays thus, may I bring bliss to my relations; may my husband live long, *svāhā*", this she sacrifices standing, while her husband recites.

***Pāraskara*:** The girl's brother pours out of his joined hands into her joined hands fried grains (*lājā*) mixed with *śamī* leaves. This she sacrifices with firmly joined hands, standing while the verses are being recited:

> To the God Aryamā the girls have made sacrifice to Agni. May he, God Aryamā, loosen us from here and not from the husband, *svāhā*.

This woman strewing grains, prays thus:

> May my husband live long. May my relations be prosperous, *svāhā*.
>
> These grains I throw into the fire: may this bring prosperity to you and may it unite me with you. May Agni grant us that, *svāhā*.

***Āpastamba*:** Having "spread under" *ājya* into her joined hands, he pours roasted grains twice into her hands and sprinkles *ājya* over it. Some say her brother pours the grains into her hands. Sacrifices with the verse, "this woman".

***Hiraṇyakeśi*:** After he has made her sit down in her proper place, and sprinkled *ājya* into her joined hands, he twice pours fried grains into them with the verse:

> This grain I pour into your hands; may it bring prosperity to me and may it unite us. May Agni grant us that.

After he has sprinkled *ājya* over the grains in her hands, he sacrifices holding her hands with the verse, "this woman strewing the grains into the fire". She prays thus, "may my husband live long; may my relations be prosperous, *svāhā*!" Having made her rise with the verse, "up with life" and having circumambulated the fire with the verse, "may we find our way with you through all hostile powers as though streams of water" — he pours fried grain into her hands and sacrifices as before. Having circumambulated a second time, he pours fried grain into her hands and she sacrifices, as before.

Baudhāyana: Then joining her hands together, her brother pours fried grains into them. She offers the fried grains to the fire with the *mantra*, "this woman is offering fried grains to Agni", saying, "let my husband have a long life and live to see hundred autumns, *svāhā*!" Then he makes her go around the fire with the verse:

> The gods have brought Sūrya's chariot to take you round the fire. Agni, again gives the husband a wife with children.

As he pours the fried grains, she offers oblations. Again he makes her go around the fire with the verse:

> Agni, give again the wife with long life with luster. Let her live long with her husband and see hundred autumns.

As he pours the fried grains, she offers oblations.

Vārāha: The material for Lājā Homa may be carried by her brother or a *brahmacārī* to the south of the fire. The fried grains mixed with *śamī* leaves are carried in a basket to the south (of the fire) by the mother or any *sumaṅgalī*. With the "Brāhmaṇa" *mantra*, the *ājya* is cleaned and kindling the fire with wood, holding part of the *ājya*, it is sacrificed.

Mānava: Having placed the grain to the west of the fire, having mixed it with *śamī* leaves, having divided it in the winnowing basket into four equal parts, and having to the east of the fire handed over the winnowing basket, he gives it back to the *lājādhārī*. The bride's brother or a *brahmacārī* scatters the grain with his two hands joined together into their hands. They offer the residue of the spreadings and the pouring together without opening their hands with the verses: "To God Aryamā the girls have sacrificed and to Agni; may he, God Aryamā, set us free from here (father's house) but not from there (husband's house), *svāhā*!" "For you in the beginning they have carried round Sūrya in the bridal procession; may you give back, Agni, to the husbands their wives together with offspring — Agni has given back the wife with long life and splendour; he who is her husband, may he live a long life time, a hundred autumns; this woman who is strewing fried grains into the fire prays thus; may my husband live a long time; may my relationship be prosperous." Similarly, she offers to God Pūṣaṇa and God Varuṇa.

***Agniveśya*:** Then he makes her join her hands together and pours fried grains in them twice with the verse, "I pour fried grains in these". Gathering the *darvi* spoons, he chants, "I am gathering because of Bhaga". Then he sacrifices with the verse, "this woman".

***Bhāradvāja*:** Then her brother pours fried grains into her holded hands and mixed with ghee, she offers the grains to Agni. "Let my husband live long, let my relations flourish. I join you with happiness like rice gruel is mixed with *surā*." Then he recites: "I offer fried grains for the sake of prosperity. Let me be one with you with the blessings of Agni."

***Kāṭhaka*:** Smear butter on her joined hands, this is *havis* and touch it, and then her brother or a *brahmacārī* will pour fried grains in them. She offers the grains part by part to the fire. She is making offerings to Aryamā:

> Aryamā release her from the fetters of her parents' house.
> "Agni is our creator" is recited. O Agni make this creation
> of yours live long as a wife.

"This woman" is repeated everywhere. "Make her a follower of her husband's family. Let our relations live long." Similarly twice. Going round the fire twice, Lājā Homa and Aśmarohaṇa are repeated.

Vaikhānasa: "Be not of evil eye" and he pours fried grains mixed with butter into her joined hands. According to some teachers, facing the west is for looking at the bride. With the *mantra*, "Saraswatī" he should seize her hand and with "be not of evil eye", he should let it go. He pours fried grain into her hands with the *mantra*, "this grain I pour", and she pours the grains into the fire with the *mantra*, "this woman, etc."

Gobhila: Standing to the east her mother or her brother, having taken the roasted grain, should make the bride tread on the stone with the tip of her right foot. The bridegroom chants, "tread on this stone". Her brother filling once his joined hands with roasted grains, pours it into her joined hands. After *ājya* has been spread under and poured over the fried grain, she sacrifices that in the fire without opening her joined hands with the verse, "this woman says". After she has been led around, she stands as before, as before treads on the stone, and he murmurs the *mantra*s as before and her brother pours the fried grains as before into her hands and she sacrifices as before. In the same way, thrice. After she has poured the remainder of the fried grains into the fire, they make her step forward in the north-easterly direction with the *mantra*, "first step for sap".

Khādira: Her brother filling once his joined hands with fried grain, should pour it into the bride's joined hands. Or some friend instead of the brother. That, she should sacrifice over the fire without opening her joined hands with the verse, which the groom repeats, "this woman".

Jaimini: After the circumambulation her brother or a friend of hers should pour with his joined hands out of the winnowing basket into her joined hands roasted grain sprinkled with ghee, "picking out" again and again. Having spread under and poured over the roasted grain some ghee, she should sacrifice it in the fire with the three verses: "This young girl going from her parents to the world of her husband, has sacrificed away her *dīkṣā, svāhā*!" This woman, strewing grains into the fire, prays: "May my husband live long, may my relations be prosperous, *svāhā*!" "To the God Aryamā the girl has sacrificed, to Agni; may he, loosen her from here and not there, *svāhā*!" After each oblation he mutters, four times the verse:

> May we find our way with you through all hostile powers, as though streams of water.

Without *mantra* the person who holds the roasted grain (mother, etc.) should pour out as a fourth oblation the rest of the grain for obtaining a special wish (on which the bride has to fix her thought).

Kauśika: With the *mantra*, "I keep this stone" he keeps a stone on a base of cow dung. He makes her stand on it. With the *mantra*, "this woman", she stands on it and offers scattered grains.

AGNI PARIṆĀYANA

Going around the sacrificial fire is an essential part of the marriage ceremony. This is done a number of times in the performance of various parts of the ceremony.

Aśvalāyana: He should lead her round the nuptial fire and the water pot thrice. He should recite the *mantra*:

> This am I (God), that are you. That are you (Goddess), this I am. I am the heaven, you are the earth. I am the song, you are the words. Come let us marry. Let us beget offspring. Loving, bright and with good minds may we live to see a hundred autumns.

Śāṅkhāyana: He then leads her around the fire.

Kauṣītaki: He then leads her around the fire. With the same *mantra*, gives her a second garment.

Pāraskara: According to some, after leading the bride around the fire (giving the garment, etc.).

Āpastamba: Having gone around the fire so that their right sides are towards it, they sit down in their former position and while she takes hold of him, he offers the oblations with the *mantra*, "to Soma who gave me my wife, *svāhā*!", one oblation with each *mantra*.

Hiraṇyakeśi: Having made her rise with the verse, "up with life", and having circumambulated the fire with the verse, "may we find our way with you through all hostile powers as though streams of water", he pours fried grain into her hands and sacrifices as before.

Baudhāyana: Then he makes her go around the fire with the verse:

> The gods have brought Sūrya's chariot to take you around the fire. Agni, again give the husband a wife with children.

Vārāha: They go around the fire.

Mānava: After going around the fire, he makes them both step onto a stone with their right feet with the verse:

> Come step you both on this stone; be firm like a stone; may all the gods life to live a hundred autumns.

Agniveśya: With the verse, "The gods have brought Sūrya's chariot for us to go together", they go round the fire.

Bhāradvāja: He takes her around the fire saying:

> We will be like the flow which submerges everything, we will suppress our enemies in your company.

Kāṭhaka: Going around the fire twice, Lājā Homa and Aśmarohaṇa are repeated.

Vaikhānasa: With the *mantra*, "like a stream of water would submerge", having gone around the fire and set himself down with the *mantra*, "will find our way through hostile powers", he performs sacrifice with fried grains in three parts.

***Gobhila*:** After the sacrifice the husband, passing behind her back returns the same way and leads her around the fire so that their right sides are turned towards it, or a brāhmaṇa well versed in the *mantra*s does the same with the *mantra*, "the maid from the fathers".

***Khādira*:** After the sacrifice, he should go back in the same way and should lead her around the fire with the *śloka*, "This maid from the fathers".

***Jaimini*:** Then the pair should walk around the fire when he murmurs:

> You are food, strength by name is your mother; come to me with children, with wealth.

***Kauśika*:** With the *mantra*, "let her go around the fire of Aryamā", she is taken round the fire thrice.

GṚHA-PRAVEŚA

Many rituals are performed when the newly married enters her husband's home. *Homa*s are conducted and fertility rites are performed.

***Aśvalāyana*:** He should set up the nuptial fire in the house and then spread to the west of it a hide of a bull with its neck to the east and with the hair on top. He should offer oblations to the fire while she sits on the hide and takes hold of him with the four verses, "may Prajāpati create offsprings to us", and after each verse offer oblations. And with the verse, "may all Gods unite", he partakes curds and offers a portion to her, or he besmears their two hearts with the rest of the *ājya*.

***Śāṅkhāyana*:** The seven verses, "here may delight", when she has reached the house omitting the verses already recited. A bull's hide — this has been declared. On that hide he makes her sit down and sacrifices while she takes hold of him with four oblations. "With God Agni, with the earth world of worlds, with *Ṛgveda* of the Vedas: therewith I appease you, *svāhā*!" "With God Vāyu, with the sky world of worlds, with *Yajurveda* of the Vedas; therewith I appease you, *svāhā*!" "With God Sūrya, with the heaven of the worlds, with the *Sāmaveda* of the Vedas, therewith I appease you, *svāhā*!" "With God Candra, with the cardinal world of the worlds, with the *Brahmaveda* of the Vedas, therewith I appease you, *svāhā*!" "Bhūḥ, what harm dwells in you, bringing death to your husband, death to your husband's brother, that I make death-bringing to your paramour, *svāhā*!", thus the first may be joined with the first, the second with the second and the third with the third, the fourth with all the three (*vyāhṛtis*) together. "With no evil eye", let him smear *ājya* on his eyes. Bridegroom having touched the ends of her hair with the three verses, "how may us the resplendent one . . .". And having recited the four verses, "and those divine medicines", ending with *svāhā*, he pours out the remainder on her head. Here some place a boy of good birth on both sides, on her lap, with the verse, "into your womb". Or also silently. Into the boy's joined hands, the bridegroom gives fruits and asks the brāhmaṇas to recite *puṇyāham*. Thus she becomes the mother of male children. With the rest of the hymn, "stay you both here", they make them enter the house. With the verse, "I praise *dadhikrāvṇa*", let them drink curds together.

***Kauṣītaki*:** The seven verses, "here may delight", when she has reached the house. Omitting the verses already recited. After reaching the house, he makes her sit on a bull's hide and after strewing *kuśa* grass he sacrifices:

> With God Agni, with the earth world of worlds, with *Ṛgveda* of the Vedas; therewith I appease you, *svāhā*!
>
> With God Vāyu, with the sky world of worlds, with *Yajurveda* of the Vedas; therewith I appease you, *svāhā*!

With God Sūrya, with the heaven of the worlds, with the *Sāmaveda* of the Vedas; therewith I appease you, *svāhā*!

With God Candra, with the cardinal world of the worlds, with the *brahmaveda* of the Vedas, therewith I appease you, *svāhā*!

Bhūḥ, what harm dwells in you, bringing death to your husband, death to your husband's brother, that I make death-bringing to your paramour, *svāhā*!

Thus the second *vyāhṛti* may be joined with the second. And the third with the third. The fourth with all the three (*vyāhṛtis*) together. "With no evil eye", let him smear *ājya* on his eyes. The bridegroom having touched the ends of her hair with the three verses, "how may us the resplendent one . . .". And having recited the four verses, "and those divine medicines", ending with *svāhā*, he pours out the remainder on her head. Here some place a boy of good birth on both sides, on her lap, with the verse, "into your womb", or also silently. Into the boy's joined hands, the bridegroom gives fruits and asks the brāhmaṇas to recite *puṇyāham*. "Become the mother of male children."

Pāraskara: A strong man lifts her up from the ground and sets her down on a red bull's hide in an eastern or northern direction with the words:

Here may the cows sit down, here the horses, here the men. Here may sacrifice with a thousand gifts, here may Pūṣaṇa sit down.

Do what the village people tell them what should be done.

Āpastamba: With the next verse, he shows her the house. Having, with the next verse, spread out in the centre of the house a red bull's skin with the neck to the east and hair on top, he makes her recite the verse, while he makes her enter the house with her right foot. And she does not stand on the threshold. In the north-east part of the house the ceremonies from the putting of wood on the fire to the *ājyabhāga* oblations are performed and while she takes hold of him, he offers oblations with the *mantras*. Then, he starts the *jayādi* oblations and performs rites down to sprinkling of water around the fire. Then they sit down on the skin with the verse, the bridegroom to the north. He then places with the verse, "the son of a wife who has only sons and whose children are alive" in her lap, gives fruit to the child with the next *mantra*.

***Hiraṇyakeśi*:** When they reach his house, he says to her:

> Cross the threshold with your right foot first; do not stand on the threshold.

In the eastern part of the hall, he keeps the fire and puts wood on it. To the west of the fire, he spreads a red bull's skin with the neck to the east and with the hair outside. On that skin they both sit down facing east or north. The wife sits behind her husband with the verse:

> Here may the cows sit down, here the horses, here the men.
> Here may Pūṣaṇa also with a thousand gifts.

***Baudhāyana*:** Now having brought his wife, he enters his house:

> Bring into the house your good mind and enter for the sake of brave children.

Then he makes her sit on a bull's hide:

> May the men, children and horses born here in abundance and the cows may grow their clan. Let the one who provides the thousand contributions and wealth be enshrined here.

Here his confidants throw water and *akṣata*.

***Vārāha*:** He leads her to the house. "I enter the house with a good mind, which is the house of heroes and well endowed. I bring cooked rice, ghee with which we will reside with a good mind." Let her sit on the bull's hide. On her lap place a boy whose parents are living. Give rice and fruits in his hands.

Mānava: At twilight the next day, he takes her inside the house. He strews *ulapa* grass from the cowshed continuously from the chariot to the house. With the verse, "to whichever house the traveller returns from a journey, where there is comfort, that house we invoke; may it know us as we approach", he walks over the grass layer towards the house with his bride following:

> I enter the house which is pleasant, which is full of heroes, with my endowed husband, I bring food to the house which drips with ghee, kindly disposed.

She enters the house which has the fire kindled, water and plants are ready under the stars, Rohiṇī or Mūlā or whichever is said to be auspicious. To the west of the fire, he makes the bride to sit down upon a red bull skin of which the neck is turned eastward, on the hairy side after having strewn it with *darbha* grass or he makes her sit on *darbha* grass only. Then he makes a *brahmacārī* to sit in her lap with the verse:

> Through Soma are the Ādityas strong, through Soma the earth is great; he, Soma is put in the lap of these *nakṣatras*.

Agniveśya: Then to the west of the fire with face turned to the north, they see the *saptarṣi maṇḍala* with the *mantra*, "seven *ṛṣis* with Kṛttikā being first". At the right time, having brought the *aupāsana* fire in a vessel, the people present bless the couple. They then walk to the cowshed. Then he takes her right hand in his right hand, he touches the southern door with the *mantra*, "let the two-footed and four-footed prosper". Similarly, with the northern door. Entering the house, they make her sit on a bull's hide with the hair on the upper side, "here cows are not allowed". The couple enter into conversation with the relations.

Bhāradvāja: Then after she enters the house, she is made to sit on a red skin of a bull. Here men gift her cows. Here Pūṣaṇa will grant her a thousand gifts. Then he makes her offer sacrifice to Agni with *sthālīpāka*. Then from the *sthālīpāka* taking the remainder of cooked food, he worships, "to Agni, *svāhā*! To Agni and to the one with Agni, *svāhā*! To Agni and the one who gave the cooked rice, *svāhā*! To Sviṣṭakṛt, *svāhā*!" To the eternal fire, he offers rice grains, barley saying "To Agni, *svāhā*!", in the morning and evening, first to Agni and then to Prajāpati. Some say it is equivalent to offer oblations to the Sun goddesses first in the morning.

***Kāṭhaka*:** In the afternoon, if they see sunbeams through trees, it is time to go to the house. She recites: "Bearing and nourishing food, bringing wealth and grains, beautiful with a good mind, I have come home. Looking with an unevil eye and with friendliness, I see the house. Let the goddesses guarding the house increase our longevity. I enter the house with a happy mind of my husband who is heroic and well endowed. I will make food and ghee flow in the house so that we and other householders can live happily. It is with happiness I travel in their midst. O house, I beseech you to possess truthfulness, *pitṛ-yajña*s, food and peace, and be devoid of famine and thirst, and do not fear me. I have handled cows and sheep. I have also handled food-related matters. I have also dealt with friends who have lots of money. Let our house always be rid of ill fortune and let all men live happily in it." *Ulapa* grass is strewn up to the bedroom. Then they enter. Then they establish the *āhitāgni*, water vessel, herbs, etc. required for *pāka-yajña*s. In the afternoon, under Rohiṇī, Mūlā and any other auspicious star, she is made to sit on a red bull skin strewn with *darbha*, *jayādi homa*s are conducted with "Agni is the first". After sacrifice, sprinkling curds in one place, thrice eating curds saying *dadhikrāvṇa*, sitting with his wife he offers fruits to a youngster saying that this is for Iḍā.

***Vaikhānasa*:** Now. Here are the ceremonies of the fourth day. Having taken his wife to his house along with the *vivāhāgni* with the *mantra*s, "O gods, let her be taken away", and "let the fire be taken with the wife", he tells her, "cross the threshold with your right foot first, do not stand on the threshold". Entering the house, he should establish the fire in the eastern half. To the west, a red bull's hide or the hide of a black antelope is spread out with its neck to the east and hairy side on top. He asks his wife to sit on it, facing the east or the north and he sits behind her with the *mantra*, "here, O cows, multiply yourselves".

Gobhila: After they have reached the house, brāhmaṇa women of good character whose husbands and sons are living make her descend and make her sit down on a bull's hide with the verse, "here, you cows, bring forth calves". They should place a boy in her lap. Into the joined hands of the boy, they should keep a clay toy. And fruits. After she has made the boy rise, she sacrifices the eight *ājya* oblations with the verse, "here is steadiness". When she has finished, she puts a piece of wood on the fire and respectfully salutes the *gurus*, according to seniority with their *gotra* names. Then they may do what they like.

Khādira: In a brāhmaṇa's house he should establish the nuptial fire, should spread out to the west of the fire a red bull's hide with the hair outside and with the neck to the east and should make her to sit down on it keeping silent.

Jaimini: When she departs to the house of her husband, he speaks over her the verse:

May Pūṣaṇa lead you there grasping your hand;
May Aśvins carry you forth in a chariot;
Go to the house, that you may become a house wife;
With control you shall speak into the council.

When she has reached her husband's house, some women of good disposition who possess beautiful progeny and have reached old age with their husbands, make her descend with the *mantra*,

> May here succeed for you by progeny who are dear to you. Watch over this house as a *gṛhiṇī*. Unite yourself with this husband. Then being not deficient, you shall speak to the gathering.

Then he makes her sit on a bull's hide with the hairy side turned upwards with the verse:

> Here may cows sit down, here horses, here men. Here may also Pūṣaṇa with a thousand sacrificial gifts sit down.

Having placed a boy in her lap he should give sweets or fruits to the boy while the wife holds on to him from behind, he should sacrifice with the following six *mantras* each concluding with *svāhā*!

> Here is steadiness. Here is independent steadiness. Here is delight. In me the steadiness. In me the joy. In me rejoice.

Kauśika: When they reach he chants, "let your wave smite up the pegs" and after sprinkling the chariot, releases the yoke. With the *mantra,* "stand up here", he makes her sprinkle the ground. With the *mantra,* "I place upon the earth this stone". He places a stone on a lump of gobar from a bull. On that in the middle *palāśa* leaves holding butter, her friends will go round the fire four times. With the *mantra,* "you stand", she is made to stand on the stone. With the *mantras*, "with good fortune you enter", "what you desire", and "let no one harm her", he makes her go around the fire. Her friends will go around the fire with brass vessels filled. With the *mantra,* "not with an evil eye", they go around the fire thrice. She worships with chanting of *mantras*, "when she worships the household fire", and "to Sūrya and gods". Bring a red skin reciting the *mantra,* "for her protection". With the *mantra,* "the skin that you spread", it is spread. With the *mantra,* "that *balbaja* grass", he brings the grass. With the *mantra,* "that which spreads", he spreads the grass on the skin. Saying "mount the skin", he makes her mount the skin. Saying "sit on that", he makes her sit on the skin. She is made to sit in a north–south direction. With the *mantra*, "let your first son be a good lead for other children", a brāhmaṇa boy with a good name is made to sit in her lap. With the *mantra*, "let good children, etc. come from you", the boy is given fruits, sweets and made to get up.

DHRUVA–ARUNDHATĪ DARŚANA

On the night of the couple reaching the husband's home, the bride is shown the Pole Star, Dhruva and the star Arundhatī. Dhruva represents constancy and Arundhatī, being the wife of Vasiṣṭha represented as a binary star of the star Vasiṣṭha in the *saptarṣi maṇḍala*, represents faithfulness.

***Aśvalāyana*:** When she sees the star Dhruva, the star Arundhatī and the *saptarṣi maṇḍala*, let her break her silence and say, "may my husband live long and may I get children".

***Śāṅkhāyana*:** When she sees the star Dhruva, the star Arundhatī and the *saptarṣi maṇḍala*, let her break her silence and say, "may my husband live long and may I get children".

***Kauṣītaki*:** Let them sit silent, when the sun has set, until the polar star (Dhruva) appears. When the stars appear, he shows her Dhruva. With the verse, "be firm like Dhruva, prospering with me". She will say, "I see Dhruva, may I get offspring like Dhruva".

***Pāraskara*:** After sunset, he shows her the Dhruva star with the verse:

> Firm are you; I see you the firm one. Be firm with me, O thriving one.
>
> Bṛhaspati has given you to me; obtaining offspring through me, live a hundred autumns.

If she is not able to see (Dhruva), let her say, "I see, I see".

***Āpastamba*:** When the stars have appeared, he goes out of the house with her in an easterly or northerly direction and shows her the polar star and Arundhatī with the verses.

Hiraṇyakeśi: When the stars have appeared, he goes out of the house in an easterly or northerly direction and worships the four directions with the *mantra*, "you goddesses, you six wide ones". He worships the stars with the verse, "may we not be deprived of our offspring". He worships the *saptarṣi maṇḍala*:

> The seven *ṛṣi*s who have led to firmness she, Arundhatī, who stands first among the six Kṛttikās; let her be the eighth one, who leads the conjuction of the moon with the six Kṛttikās, the first among conjuctions shine upon us!

Then he worships Dhruva star with the *mantra*:

> Firm dwelling, firm origin. The firm one are you, standing on the side of firmness. You are the pillar of the stars; protect me against my enemies.

Baudhāyana: Then when they appear, they go out and she is shown the pole star and the Arundhatī star. "You are Dhruva, Dhruva's horizon, Dhruva's fixedness. You are the pole of the stars, protect me from enemies. The first among Kṛttikās established by the seven *ṛṣis*; that eighth one, Arundhatī, six Kṛttikās and Candra, be our guide."

Vārāha: You are the steady Dhruvapatnī. Let us all see the Dhruva star. They see Dhruva after Jayādi and Ājya *homa*s and then Sviṣṭakṛt *homa*.

Mānava: Then after having filled the boy's hands with a mixture of sesamum seeds, rice and fruits, he makes him stand up and he makes her look at the pole star, Dhruva and Arundhatī and the *saptarṣi maṇḍala*. He chants:

> Unshakeable, steadfast, a steadfast wife may she be, may we look steadfast all around; steadfast are the mountains, steadfast may this woman in the family of her husband.

Agniveśya: Then to the west of the fire with face turned to the north, they see the *saptarṣi maṇḍala* with the *mantra*, "seven *ṛṣis* with Kṛttikā being first". At the right time, having brought the *aupāsana* fire in a vessel, the people present bless the couple.

***Bhāradvāja*:** Then he shows her Dhruva, Arundhatī and other stars with the *anuvāka*: "I salute you Brahmā, Dhruva who is unmoving and firm; Dhruva you are the source of constancy. You are the pole of stars, protect us from enemies. The first star among Kṛttikās is Arundhatī whose steadfastness is eternal. Please make our relationship be similar."

***Kāṭhaka*:** Show the living bride Dhruva, Svasti, Ātreya and Arundhatī. Show the stars one by one saying look at the star. She responds with "I see".

***Vaikhānasa*:** It ends with showing the polar star, Dhruva, according to some.

***Gobhila*:** After the sacrifice, they arise, go out and he shows her the pole star. "Firm are you, may I (name) become firm in the house of my husband (name)." He shows her Arundhatī also. "I (name) am held fast." She says as above. He then addresses her with the *mantra*, "firm is the sky".

***Khādira*:** After they have gone around the fire, he shows her the polar star with the verse, "firm is the sky".

***Jaimini*:** Then he should make her look at the pole star Dhruva, the star Arundhatī of the *saptarṣi maṇḍala*, when she declares: "Let me see the stars." She addresses Dhruva, "You are the pole star (Dhruva). May I become firm in the house of my husband (his name)" and at the end of the *mantra*, her own name. Looking at Arundhatī she chants:

> Arundhati, may I be held fast by my husband (his name) and then uttering her own name.

***Kauśika*:** There is no mention of Dhruva–Arundhatī Darśana in *Kauśika Gṛhya-Sūtra*.

TRIRĀTRA VRATA

The newly-married couple is expected to observe this *vrata* after reaching the husband's home. Consummation of marriage will be after observing this *vrata* and after conducting *caturthī karma*.

***Āśvalāyana*:** From that time they should not eat saline food, they should be celibate, wear no ornaments and sleep on the floor. This they should observe for three nights or twelve nights. Or for one year according to some. A sage will be born to them.

***Śāṅkhāyana*:** For three nights let them be celibate. Let them sleep on the floor. Let them eat together cooked rice and curds with the three verses, "drink and satiate yourselves". Let them feed the nuptial fire, in the evening and morning with the words, "to Agni, *svāhā*, to Agni Sviṣṭakṛt, *svāhā*". "Let the two men Mitra and Varuṇa, let the two Aśvins, let Indra and Agni make a male grow in her, *svāhā*." Let them not travel out for ten days.

***Kauṣītaki*:** For three days they should sleep on the floor and eat food without spices and salt. Similarly during travel. Not eat together. Let there be no intercourse for one year, twelve nights or six nights.

***Pāraskara*:** Through a period of three nights they shall eat no saline food. They shall sleep on the floor. Through one year they shall refrain from intercourse, or for twelve nights, or six nights, or at least three nights.

***Āpastamba*:** From that day through three nights they should sleep on the floor, be chaste and avoid food with salt and spices. Between their sleeping places a staff is kept which is anointed with perfumes and wrapped round with a garment or thread.

***Hiraṇyakeśi*:** For a period of three nights they should eat no saline food, sleep on the floor, wear no ornaments and be chaste.

Baudhāyana: Both husband and wife observe celibacy and sleep on the floor. In between them, a staff smeared with sandal paste and tied with a cloth string around it, is made to stand with *pakka homa*.

Vārāha: Practise celibacy for one year. Or twelve nights or three nights or one night.

Mānava: Let them practise celibacy for one year, twelve nights, three nights or one night.

Agniveśya: The *trirātra vrata* is observed with celibacy, avoiding food with spices and salt and sleeping on the ground.

Bhāradvāja: For three nights they observe *vrata*, eating bland food, sleeping on the floor and practising celibacy.

Kāṭhaka: There is no mention of *trirātra vrata* in *Kāṭhaka Gṛhya-Sūtra*.

Vaikhānasa: Though there is no clear mention of *trirātra vrata* in *Vaikhānasa Gṛhya-Sūtra*, the following sentence implies it: "now here are the ceremonies of the fourth day."

Gobhila: Though there is no clear mention of *trirātra vrata* in *Gobhila Gṛhya-Sūtra*, the following sentence implies it: "now follow the ceremonies of the fourth day."

Khādira: After three nights, he should make oblations with the four verses, "Agni you are the expiation", and then a fifth combining the names of four gods invoked in those verses. The remnants of the water pot, he should pour into a water pot.

Jaimini: During a period of three days and nights, they should abstain from saline or pungent food and from intercourse, sleeping on the ground and lying together without approaching one another. After the lapse of three days, they should cohabit.

Kauśika: Tying her hair with hemp thread, they sleep for three nights.

CATURTHĪ KARMA

This ritual is performed at the end of the *trirātra vrata*. The marriage is consummated after the *caturthī karma*.

***Aśvalāyana*:** When he has fulfilled his vow, he should give the bridal dress to one who knows the Sūrya hymn. He should give food to brāhmaṇas. Then he should cause them to pronounce *svastivācanas*.

***Śāṅkhāyana*:** Now the rites of the fourth day. When three nights have elapsed, he makes offerings of cooked food. "Agni, you are expiation; you are the expiation of the gods. The substance that exists that brings death to her husband, drive that away from her." "Vāyu, you are expiation; you are the expiation of the gods. The substance that exists that brings sonlessness, drive that away from her." "Sūrya, you are expiation; you are the expiation of the gods. The substance that exists that brings destruction of cattle, drive that away from her." "To God Aryamā, the girls have made sacrifice to Agni; may he, God Aryamā, loosen her from this and not from that place." "To God Varuṇa, the girls have made sacrifice to Agni; may he, God Varuṇa, loosen her from this and not from that place." "To God Pūṣaṇa, the girls have made sacrifice to Agni; may he, God Pūṣaṇa, loosen her from this and not from that place." The seventh oblation with the verse, "to Prajāpati". The eighth oblation with the verse, "to Sviṣṭakṛt".

***Kauṣītaki*:** In *caturthī karma,* when three nights have elapsed, he makes offerings of cooked food. Milk and cooked food to be used in the *pāka-yajña*. "Agni, you are expiation; you are the expiation of the gods. The substance that exists that brings death to her husband, drive that away from her." "Vāyu, you are expiation; you are the expiation of the gods. The substance that exists that brings sonlessness, drive that away from her." "Sūrya, you are expiation; you are the expiation of the gods. The substance that exists that brings destruction of cattle, drive that away from her." "To God Aryamā, the girls have made sacrifice to Agni; may he, God Aryamā, loosen her from this and not from that place." "To God Varuṇa, the girls have made sacrifice to Agni; may he, God Varuṇa, loosen her from this and not from that place." "To God Pūṣaṇa, the girls have made sacrifice to Agni; may he, God Pūṣaṇa, loosen her from this and not from that place." The seventh oblation with the verse, "to Prajāpati". The eighth oblation with the verse, "to Sviṣṭakṛt".

***Pāraskara*:** In *caturthī karma*, when three nights have elapsed, he makes offerings of cooked food. Milk and cooked food to be used in the *pāka-yajña*. "Agni, you are expiation; you are the expiation of the gods. The substance that exists that brings death to her husband, drive that away from her." "Vāyu, you are expiation; you are the expiation of the gods. The substance that exists that brings sonlessness, drive that away from her." "Sūrya, you are expiation; you are the expiation of the gods. The substance that exists that brings destruction of cattle, drive that away from her." "To God Aryamā, the girls have made sacrifice to Agni; may he, God Aryamā, loosen her from this and not from that place." "To God Varuṇa, the girls have made sacrifice to Agni; may he, God Varuṇa, loosen her from this and not from that place." "To God Pūṣaṇa, the girls have made sacrifice to Agni; may he, God Pūṣaṇa, loosen her from this and not from that place." The seventh oblation with the verse, "to Prajāpati". The eighth oblation with the verse, "to Sviṣṭakṛt".

***Āpastamba*:** In the last part of the fourth night he takes the staff with the verses, washes it and puts it away; then the ceremonies from putting of wood on the fire down to *ājyabhāga* oblations are performed and while she takes hold of him, he sacrifices the oblations with the *mantra*s; then he starts the oblations beginning with Jayā *homa* and performs the rites down to the sprinkling of water around the fire. Then he makes her sit down to the west of the fire, facing the east and pours some *ājya* of the remains on her head with the three *vyāhṛtis* and the word *oṁ* as the fourth. Then they look at each other with the next two verses, according to the characteristics. With the next verse he applies the regions of their hearts with the remains of the *ājya*. Then he murmurs the next verses and should murmur the rest of the *anuvāka* when cohabiting with her.

Hiraṇyakeśi: In the fourth night, towards morning, he puts wood on the fire, performs regular ceremonies down to expiatory oblations and sacrifices nine expiatory oblations with the following *mantras*. "Agni! Expiation! You are expiation. I, the brāhmaṇa, entreat you desirous of protection. What is terrible in her drive that away from here, *svāhā*!" "Vāyu! Expiation! You are expiation. I, the brāhmaṇa, entreat you desirous of protection. What is blameful in her drive that away from here, *svāhā*!" "Āditya! Expiation! You are expiation. I, the brāhmaṇa, entreat you desirous of protection. What dwells in her that is death-bringing to her, drive that away from her, *svāhā*!" Āditya! Expiation! Vāyu! Expiation! Agni! Expiation! Agni! Expiation! Vāyu! Expiation! Āditya! Expiation!". Having sacrificed these oblations, he then pours the remainder as an oblation on her head with the *mantra*:

> Bhūḥ! I sacrifice fortune over you, *svāhā*! Bhuvaḥ! I sacrifice glory over you, *svāhā*! Suvaḥ! I sacrifice beauty over you. *svāhā*! *Bhūr bhuvaḥ suvaḥ*! I sacrifice brightness over you, *svāhā*!

There near the fire he places a water pot, walks around the fire and the water pot, makes her lie down to the west of the fire facing east or north and touches her *yoni* with the *mantra*:

> We touch you with five forked, auspicious, unhostile, thousandholdedly blessed, glorious hand that you may be rich in offspring!

He then cohabits with her with the *mantra*:

> United is our soul, united our hearts, united our navel, united our skin. I will bind you with the bond of love; that shall be unbreachable.

He then embraces her with the *mantra*:

> Be devoted to me; be my companion. What dwells in you that is death-bringing to your husband, that I make death-bringing to your paramours. Bring luck to me; be a sharp-cutting destroyer to your paramours.

He then seeks her mouth with his mouth, with the verses:

> Honey! Lo! Honey! This is honey! My tongue's speech is honey; in my mouth dwells the honey of the bee; on my teeth dwells concord.
>
> The magic charm of concord that belongs to *cakravāka* birds, that is brought out of the rivers, of which the divine *gandharva* is possessed, thereby we are concordant.

***Baudhāyana*:** On the fourth night after performing *pakka homa*, giving up the *vrata*, the staff is removed — "You have sprung up from the energy of the earth, *vanaspati* spread hundred branches. From you we will draw sap, energy and wealth and be happy with that." Then he gives the staff to the wife — "I will join you for the sake of children just like rice gruel is mixed with *surā*." The wife holds the staff and says, "I will become child bearing". Then she hands it over to her husband, "I will join you for the sake of children and cattle just like rice gruel is mixed with *surā*". He takes it from her — "I will be with children and cattle". Then they keep the staff with pillars and return inside. Then intercourse takes place.

***Vārāha*:** Observe similarly the *caturthī* with the *mantra*, "Hiraṇyagarbha". And worship with Jayādi, Ājya *homa*s followed by Sviṣṭakṛt *homa*. Now to her left he worships the knot tying her dress with the *mantra*, "Pūṣaṇa your knot, I loosen". Four *sumaṅgalī*s will undress her. Gold is given to them. Do not travel for one year. Or twelve nights, or three nights, or one night.

Mānava: Then he should give her the authority over the house. Having untied the yoke rope, they lie down together and in turn murmur the verses:

> I saw you observing in your mind what is born of *tapas*, what has come into existence from *tapas*.
>
> Granting here offspring and wealth, propagate yourself through offspring, O you, who are desirous of sons, I saw you while you were desiring in your mind, and praying for our own body, in the time proper for procreation.
>
> Approach me powerfully, young woman, propagate yourself through offspring, O you, who are desirous of sons.
>
> Prajāpati, may you be delighted in my body, and Tvaṣṭā and powerful Indra and other gods, accompanied by all gods and seasons.
>
> May we be the parents of many sons.
>
> I impregnated the plants, I impregnated all creatures.
>
> I begot offspring in the earth, I shall beget sons for women in future nights.

Prouncing the words, "may it bring forth", he touches her private parts. Prouncing the words, "may it beget", she touches his organ. At the word, "great", sperm is ejaculated.

Agniveśya: After finishing the *vrata* with "Agni! God of *vrata*s, I have done the *vrata*s". *Puṇyāham* will be read out, "Let this couple be fortunate and happy." "This couple will be", is said in return. He then touches her private parts, "with auspiciousness I touch you". He has intercourse, "with the shoulders of a bull". After the intercourse he chants, "let this *yoni* create the embryo".

Bhāradvāja: Then on the fourth night, he establishes the fire on the northern side of the hall and carries out Jayā, Abhyātāna and Rāṣṭrabhṛt *homas*. He carries out expiation of gods. "You are the expiation of the gods, our desires are met by you. What is in her that may kill her husband, cattle and wealth, destroy it. Vāyu, you are expiation, Āditya, you are expiation, Prajāpati, you are expiation. Destroy the evil in her body." Then silently he holds her and says:

> I am this (God), you are that (Goddess), heaven, I am, earth you are, I am the song, you are the lyric, let us get together, I give my sperm for begetting children. For the sake of good children, heroes, wealth and happiness.

Then he embraces, brings his face to her face, and breathes together with her. She reciprocates. Then sipping water, washing his hand, he touches her, "I touch you with auspicious hand, without enemity, happily for the sake of good children". If her dress is dirtied, she makes her do the *brāhmaṇa pratiṣiddha vratas*. Then on the fourth day, they bathe and wear different clothes and with the *anuvāka*, "my mind in yours", he makes intercourse with her.

***Kāṭhaka*:** There is no mention of *caturthī karma* in *Kāṭhaka Gṛhya-Sūtra*, but the procedure followed including *sthālīpāka* and other *homas* are mentioned.

***Vaikhānasa*:** Now, here are the ceremonies of the fourth day. Having taken his wife to his house along with the *vivāhāgni* with the *mantras*, "O Gods, let her be taken away", and "let the fire be taken with the wife", he tells her, "cross the threshold with your right foot first, do not stand on the threshold". Entering the house, he should establish the fire in the eastern half. To the west, a red bull's hide or the hide of a black antelope is spread out with its neck to the east and hairy side on top. He asks his wife to sit on it, facing the east or the north and he sits behind her with the *mantra*, "here, O cows, multiply yourselves". They sit until stars appear, restraining their speech and not touching one another. When the star has appeared, they should worship with the *mantra*, "you six divine spaces", the eastern or northern direction: "may we not lose offspring", the moon: "since the seven *ṛṣis*", the *saptarṣi maṇḍala*, the *nakṣatras*, Arundhatī, "firm dwelling, firm origin", the polar star when they appear. Having a pleasant conversation, they return indoors. *Sthālīpāka* is prepared for Agni. Having touched the earthen pot with the *mantra*, "I touch the earthen pot of progeny, this *sthālī* full of nectar", he pours unhusked rice into the pot and with the *mantra*, "Vācaspate has clarified", he has the food cooked by his wife. Having sprinkled it with ghee, and having removed it from the fire in the northern direction, and having strewn grass around the fire and sticks of wood laid on it, he chants the *mantra*, "let us invoke Agni Sviṣṭakṛt, who conveys the sacrifice", etc. as invocatory verse and sacrifices a part of the food with the *mantra* addressed to Agni Sviṣṭakṛt. With the remainder of the food, he feeds a *śrotriya* brāhmaṇa and when he has presented a bull to him, he is free from all debts, it is said.

Gobhila: Now follow the ceremonies of the fourth day. Having put wood on the fire, he sacrifices four times expiatory *ājya* oblations with the *mantra*, "Agni! You are expiation". With the same formula, putting instead of Agni, Vāyu, Candra and Sūrya. A fifth oblation together, changing the singular to plural. The remnants of each oblation, he should pour into a water pot. With that they besmear her body including her hair and nails, remove that water by rubbing and wash her.

Khādira: After three nights, he should make oblations with the four verses, "Agni you are the expiation", and then a fifth combining the names of four gods invoked in those verses. The remnants of the water pot, he should pour into a water pot. With that they besmear her body including her hair and nails. Thereafter, he should behave as required by circumstances.

***Jaimini*:** In the night begins the ritual of work of the pair. He should sacrifice the expiatory oblations with the formulae: "Expiatory Agni! You are the expiation of the gods. I, a brāhmaṇa, entreat you, desirous of protection. The substance which dwells in her that brings death to progeny, remove from her, *svāhā*! Expiatory Vāyu! You are the expiation of the gods. I, a brāhmaṇa, entreat you, desirous of protection. The substance that dwells in her that brings death to the cattle, remove from her, *svāhā*! Expiatory Sūrya! You are the expiation of the gods. I, a brāhmaṇa, entreat you, desirous of protection. The substance that dwells in her that brings death to the husband, remove from her, *svāhā*! Expiatory Candra! You are the expiation of the gods. I, a brāhmaṇa, entreat you, desirous of protection. The substance, which dwells in her which brings destruction to the house, remove from her, *svāhā*! Expiatory Agni, Vāyu, Sūrya, Candra, you are the expiation of the gods. I, a brāhmaṇa, entreat you, desirous of protection. The substance, which dwells in her that brings destruction to fame remove from her, *svāhā*!" Having sacrificed from a *sthālīpāka* to Agni and Prajāpati and having poured together into a wooden vessel the remnants of each oblation, he should address her with the words: "anoint your vital canals". First she anoints the navel, then the organs of sense which are above then those beneath the navel. After three days have passed, the cohabitation takes place after the husband has chanted the following verses:

May Viṣṇu make the womb ready;
May Tvaṣṭā frame the shape of the child;
May Prajāpati pour forth the sperm;
May Dhātṛ give you conception — give conception, Sinīvālī, give conception, Sarasvatī;
May the two Aśvins, the gods wreathed with lotus, give conception to you.
The embryo which the Aśvins with golden fire drill produce;
That embryo I put into you for giving birth in the tenth month.

Kauśika: There is no specific mention of *caturthī karma* in *Kauśika Gṛhya-Sūtra*.

Order of Vivāha Saṁskāra Rituals in each Gṛhya-Sūtra

The following depict the rituals in the order in which they appear in the texts:

Āśvalāyana: 1. Suitable time for marriage; 2. qualities of bride and groom; 3. forms of marriage; 4. *pāṇigrahaṇa*; 5. *agni pariṇayana*; 6. *aśmārohaṇa* — thrice; 7. *lājā homa* — twice; 8. *ājya homa*; 9. loosening of hair; 10. *saptapadī*; 11. Dhruva–Arundhatī *darśana*; 12. carrying the bride home; 13. gṛha-Praveśa; 14. domestic fire; 15. *trirātra vrata*; 16. *caturthī karma*; and 17. cohabitation.

Śāṅkhāyāna: 1. Suitable time for marriage; 2. qualities of bride and groom; 3. sending negotiators; 4. *vāgdāna*; 5. sending the bride to the groom's house; 6. *pratisāra bandhana*; 7. *pāṇigrahaṇa*; 8. *agni pariṇayana*; 9. *aśmārohaṇa*; 10. *lājā homa*; 11. *saptapadī*; 12. *mūrdhābhiṣeka*; 13. carrying the bride home; 14. sitting on a bull's hide; 15. placing a boy in her lap; 16. Dhruva–Arundhatī *darśana*; 17. *trirātra vrata*; 18. *caturthī karma*; 19. cohabitation; and 20. *sthālīpāka*.

Kauṣītaki: 1. Suitable time for marriage; 2. qualities of bride and groom; 3. sending negotiators; 4. *vāgdāna*; 5. sending the bride to the groom's house; 6. *pratisāra bandhana*; 7. *pāṇigrahaṇa*; 8. *agni pariṇayana*; 9. *aśmārohaṇa*; 10. *lājā homa*; 11. *saptapadī*; 12. *mūrdhābhiṣeka*; 13. carrying the bride home; 14. sitting on a bull's hide; 15. placing a boy in her lap; 16. Dhruva–Arundhatī *darśana*; 17. *trirātra vrata*; 18. *caturthī karma*; 19. cohabitation; and 20. *sthālīpāka homa*.

Pāraskara: 1. Suitable time for marriage; 2. qualities of bride and groom; 3. *kanyādāna*; 4. *samīkṣaṇam*; 5. *agni pariṇayana*; 6. *jayā, abhyātāna, raṣṭrabhṛt homas*; 7. *lājā homa*; 8. *pāṇigrahaṇa*;

9. *aśmārohaṇa*; 10. *agni pariṇayana*; 11. *saptapadī*; 12. touching her heart; 13. sitting on a bull's hide; 14. Dhruva–Arundhatī *darśana*; 15. *trirātra vrata*; 16. *caturthī karma*; 17. cohabitation; 18. *aupāsana homa*; and 19. *sthālīpāka homa*.

***Āpastamba*:** 1. Suitable time for marriage; 2. qualities of bride and groom; 3. *samīkṣaṇa*; 4. *pāṇigrahaṇa*; 5. *mūrdhābhiṣeka*; 6. *mekhalā bandhana*; 7. *saptapadī*; 8. *agni pariṇayana*; 9. *aśmārohaṇa*; 10. *lājā homa*; 11. *jayā* and other *homa*s; 12. sitting on a bull's hide; 13. placing a boy in her lap; 14. Dhruva–Arundhatī *darśana*; 15. *sthālīpāka*; 16. *baliharaṇa*; 17. *trirātra vrata*; 18. *caturthī karma*; and 19. cohabitation.

***Hiraṇyakeśi*:** 1. Suitable time for marriage; 2. *aśmārohaṇa*; 3. *pāṇigrahaṇa*; 4. *vivāha homa*; 5. *lājā homa*; 6. *agni pariṇayana*; 7. *jayā* and other *homa*s; 8. *saptapadī*; 9. touching her heart; 10. *gṛha-praveśa*; 11. sitting on a bull's hide; 12. Dhruva–Arundhatī *darśana*; 13. *sthālīpāka*; 14. *trirātra vrata*; 15. *caturthī karma*; and 16. cohabitation.

***Baudhāyana*:** 1. Sending negotiators; 2. suitable time for marriage; 3. *agni pariṇayana*; 4. *samīkṣaṇa*; 5. *saptapadī*; 6. washing the feet of the groom; 7. *madhuparka*; 8. touching her heart; 9. *pāṇigrahaṇa*; 10. *aśmārohaṇa*; 11. *agni pariṇayana*; 12. *lājā homa*; 13. *jayā, abhyātāna* and *raṣṭrabhṛt homa*s; 14. *gṛha-praveśa*; 15. sitting on a bull's hide; 16. Dhruva–Arundhatī *darśana*; 17. *trirātra vrata*; 18. *caturthī karma*; 19. cohabitation; 20. *sthālīpāka*; and 21. *nāpita karma*.

***Vārāha*:** 1. Qualities of the bride; 2. suitable time for marriage; 3. sending negotiators; 4. qualities of the groom; 5. *madhuparka*; 6. *mūrdhādhiṣeka*; 7. tying *mekhalā*; 8. *pāṇigrahana*; 9. *agni pariṇayana*; 10. *lājā homa*; 11. *vivāha homa*; 12. *aśmārohaṇa*; 13. *saptapadī*; 14. carrying the bride; 15. sitting on a bull's hide; 16. placing a boy on her lap; 17. Dhruva *darśana*; 18. *jayā, abhyātāna, raṣṭrabhṛt homas*; 19. *svisṭakṛt homa*; 20. *trirātra vrata*; 21. *caturthī karma*; and 22. cohabitation.

Mānava: 1. Suitable time for marriage; 2. qualities of bride; 3. *kanyādāna*; 4. *mūrdhābhiṣeka*; 5. *madhuparka*; 6. *vivāha homa*; 7. *samīkṣaṇa*; 8. *pāṇigrahaṇa*; 9. *amūhamasmi*; 10. *aśmārohaṇa*; 11. *lājā homa*; 12. *jayā, abhyātāna* and *rāṣṭrabhṛt homas*; 13. *saptapadī*; 14. parting of her hair; 15. carrying the bride; 16. sitting on a bull's hide; 17. placing a boy on her lap; 18. untying the *mekhalā*; 19. *trirātra vrata*; 20. *caturthī karma*; and 21. cohabitation.

Agniveśya: 1. Suitable time for marriage; 2. qualities of bride; 3. *vāgdāna*; 4. *kanyādāna*; 5. *jayā, abhyātāna, rāṣṭrabhṛt homas*; 6. *pāṇigrahaṇa*; 7. *lājā homa*; 8. *aśmārohaṇa*; 9. *agni pariṇayana*; 10. *vivāha homa*; 11. touching her heart; 12. *saptapadī*; 13. *gṛha-praveśa*; 14. sitting on a bull's hide; 15. *trirātra vrata*; 16. *caturthī karma*; and 17. cohabitation.

Bhāradvāja: 1. Qualities of the bride; 2. suitable time for marriage; 3. *madhuparka*; 4. *jayā, abhyātāna* and *rāṣṭrabhṛt homas*; 5. *pāṇigrahaṇa*; 6. *aśmārohaṇa*; 7. *agni pariṇāyana*; 8. *lājā homa*; 9. *saptapadī*; 10. touching her heart; 11. *mūrdhābhiṣeka*; 12. carrying the bride; 13. sitting on a red bull's hide; 14. *sthālīpāka*; 15. *aupāsana homa*; 16. Dhruva–Arundhatī *darśana*; 17. *trirātra vrata*; 18. *caturthī karma*; 19. *amūhamasmi*; and 20. cohabitation.

Kāṭhaka: 1. Suitable time for marriage; 2. qualities of bride; 3. *kanyādāna*; 4. *vivāha homa*; 5. music; 6. *puṇyāha vācana*; 7. *madhuparka*; 8. *jayā, abhyātāna* and *rāṣṭrabhṛt homas*; 9. *pāṇigrahaṇa*; 10. *agni pariṇayana*; 11. *amūhamasmi*; 12. *lājā homa*; 13. *aśmārohaṇa*; 14. *sviṣṭakṛt homa*; 15. *untying mekhalā*; 16. *saptapadī*; 17. Dhruva–Arundhatī *darśana*; 18. *mūrdhābhiṣeka*; 19. *gṛha-praveśa*; 20. sitting on a bull's hide; 21. placing a boy in her lap; and 22. *sthālīpāka*.

Vaikhānasa: 1. Forms of marriage; 2. *kanyādāna*; 3. *aśmārohaṇa*; 4. *pāṇigrahaṇa*; 5. *lājā homa*; 6. *saptapadī*; 7. touching her heart; 8. *trirātra vrata*; 9. *caturthī karma*; 10. sitting on a bull's hide; 11. Dhruva–Arundhatī *darśana*; 12. *sthālīpāka*; and 13. cohabitation.

***Gobhila*:** 1. Suitable time for marriage; 2. qualities of bride; 3. *aśmārohaṇa*; 4. *lājā homa*; 5. *agni pariṇayana*; 6. *saptapadī*; 7. *pāṇigrahaṇa*; 8. carrying the bride to a brāhmaṇa's house; 9. sitting on a bull's hide; 10. Dhruva *darśana*; 11. *trirātra vrata*; 12. *sthālīpāka*; 13. taking the bride to her husband's home; 14. sitting on a bull's hide; 15. placing a boy in her lap; 16. Arundhatī *darśana*; 17. *caturthī karma*; and 18. cohabitation.

***Khādira*:** 1. Suitable time for marriage; 2. *lājā homa*; 3. *agni pariṇayana*; 4. *saptapadī*; 5. *pāṇigrahaṇa*; 6. *aśmārohaṇa*; 7. carrying the bride to a brāhmaṇa's house; 8. sitting on a bull's hide; 9. Dhruva *darśana*; 10. *trirātra vrata*; 11. *sthālīpāka*; 12. taking the bride to her husband's home; 13. *caturthī karma*; and 14. cohabitation.

***Jaimini*:** 1. Suitable time for marriage; 2. qualities of bride; 3. sending negotiators; 4. *pāṇigrahaṇa*; 5. *aśmārohaṇa*; 6. *amūhamasmi*; 7. *agni pariṇayana*; 8. *lājā homa*; 9. *saptapadī*; 10. Dhruva–Arundhati *darśana*; 11. taking the bride to her husband's home; 12. *trirātra vrata*; 13. *sthālipāka*; 14. *caturthī karma*; and 15. cohabitation.

***Kauśika*:** 1. Suitable time for marriage; 2. qualities of bride; 3. sending negotiators; 4. bathing and dressing of the bride; 5. *mūrdhabhiṣeka*; 6. *aśmārohaṇa*; 7. *kanyādāna*; 8. *pāṇigrahaṇa*; 9. *saptapadī*; 10. untying the girdle; 11. taking the bride to her husband's home; 12. *gṛha-praveśa*; 13. sitting on a bull's hide; 14. placing a boy in her lap; 15. *sthālīpāka*; 16. *amūhamasmi*; and 17. cohabitation.

8

Vivāha Mantras

GṚHYA-SŪTRAS presuppose the existence of *mantra*s used in the rituals of *vivāha saṁskāra*. Most of the *mantra*s can be traced to *Ṛgveda* and *Atharvaveda*. However, there are many *mantra*s whose origins are not definitely known. A collection of *mantra*s used by the followers of Āpastamba has been brought out by M. Winternitz under the name *Mantra Pāṭha of Āpastambins*. *Mantra Brāhmaṇa* of *Sāmaveda* is generally associated with *Gobhila Gṛhya-Sūtra*. *Agnivesya Gṛhya-Sūtra* contains a list of *mantra*s as part of the text on *vivāha saṁskāra*. Major *mantra*s are listed hereunder. The sources of the *mantra*s have been indicated wherever available. *Mantra*s used in supplementary activities such as *saṁkalpa, nāndiśrāddha, puṇyāha vācana, navagraha pūjā*, etc. are not listed here.

*Mantra*s are recited at various parts of the marriage ceremony. However, there are variations in different Gṛhya-Sūtras of sections where a particular *mantra* is expected to be recited.

When the wooers are sent to the prospective bride's house, the following *mantra*s are recited:

अनृक्षरा ऋजवः सन्तु पन्था येभिः सखायो यन्ति नो वरेयम् ।
समर्यमा सम्भगो नो निनीयात् सं जास्पत्यं सुयममस्तु देवाः ॥
— *ṚV* X.85.23; *AV* XIV.1.34

प्र सु ग्मन्ता धियसानस्य सक्षणि वरेभिर्वराँ अभि षु प्रसीदतः ।
अस्माकमिन्द्र उभयं जुजोषिति यत्सोम्यस्यान्धसो बुबोधति ॥
— *ṚV* X.32.1

समाना व आकूतानि समाना हृदयानि वः ।
समानमस्तु वो मनो यथा वः सुसहासति ॥
— *ṚV* X.191.4

At the time of *vāgdāna:*

अनाधृष्टमस्यानाधृष्टय़ देवानामोजाऽनभिशस्त्यभिशस्तिपा ।
अनभिशस्तेयमञ्जसा सत्यमुपगेषं सुविते मा धा ॥
— *Sh.Sh.S* V.8.2

At the time of Madhuparka:

यन्मधुनो मधव्यं परममनाद्यं वीर्यम् ।
तेनाहं मधुनो मधव्येन परमेणान्नाद्येन वीर्येण परमोऽन्नादो मधुव्योऽसानि ॥
— *Ma.Pa* II.10.5

मधुगो मध्वगाहे जिह्वा मे मधुवादिनी ।
मुखे मे सारघं मधु दत्सु संवननं कृतम् ॥

मधु वाता ऋतायते मधु क्षरन्ति सिन्धवः । माध्वीर्नः सन्त्वोषधीः ॥
मधु नक्तमुतोषसो मधुमत् पार्थिवं रजः । मधु द्योरस्तु नः पिता ॥
मधुमान्नो वनस्पतिर्मधुमाँ अस्तु सूर्यः । माध्वीर्गावो भवन्तु नः ॥

When the bride is given new clothes to wear after bathing:

रैभ्यासीदनुदेयी नाराशंसी न्योचनी ।
सूर्याय भद्रमिद्वासो गाथयैति परिष्कृतम् ॥
— *ṚV* X.85.6; *AV* XIV.1.7

चित्तिर उपब्रह्मणं चक्षुरा अभ्यञ्जनम् ।
द्योर्भूमिः कोश आसीद् यदायात् सूर्या पतिम् ॥
— *ṚV* X.85.7; *AV* XIV.1.6

जरां गच्छ परिधत्स्व वासो भवाकृष्टीनामभिशस्तिपावा ।
शतं च जीव शरदः सुवर्च्चा रायश्च पोषमुपसंव्ययस्व ॥
— *AV* XIX.24.5

(सु is added after जरां, and गृष्टी instead of कृष्टी in *AV*.)

या अकृन्तन्नवयन् याश्च तन्निरे या देवीरन्तां अभितोऽददन्त ।
तास्त्वा जरसे सव्ययन्त्वायुष्मतीदं परिधत्स्व वासः ॥
— *AV* XIV.1.45

परिधत धत्त वाससैनां शतायुषी कृणुत दीर्घमायुः ।
बृहस्पतिः प्रायच्छद्वास एतत् सौभाग्यं राज्ञे परिधातवा ॥
— *AV* XIX.24.4; *MBr* I.1.6

समञ्जन्तु विश्वे देवाः समापो हृदयानि नौ ।
सं मातरिश्वा सं धाता समु देष्ट्री दधातु नौ ॥
— *Ṛ̥V* X.85.47

यथेय शचीं वावातां सुपुत्रां च यथाऽदितिम् ।
अविधवां चापालामेवं त्वामिह रक्षातादिममि ॥

रूपं रूपं प्रतिरूपो बभूव तदस्य रूपं प्रतिचक्षणाय ।
इन्द्रो मायाभिः पुरुरूप ईयते युक्ता ह्यस्य हरयः शता दश ॥
— *Ṛ̥V* VI.47.18; *AV* XIV.1.6

हिरण्यवर्णाः शुचयः पावका यासु जातः कश्यपो यास्विन्द्रः ।
अग्निं या गर्भं दधिरे विरूपास्ता न आपः शं स्योना भवन्तु ॥
— *AV* I.33.1

At the time of *parisāra bandhana* and before mounting the chariot:

नीललोहितं भवति कृत्यासक्तिर्व्यज्यते ।
एधन्ते अस्या ज्ञातयः पतिर्बन्धेषु बध्यते ॥
— *Ṛ̥V* X.85.28; *AV* XIV.1.26

At the time of *mekhalā bandhana*

अभ्रातृघ्नीं वरुणापतिघ्नीं बृहस्पते ।
इन्द्रापुत्रघ्नीं लक्ष्म्यं तामस्यै सवितस्सुव ॥
— *AV* XIV.1.62

अघोरचक्षुरपतिघ्न्ये धि शिवा पशुभ्यः सुमना सुवर्चाः ।
वीरसूर्देवकामा स्योना शं नो भव द्विपदे शं चतुष्पदे ॥
— *Ṛ̥V* X.85.44; *AV* XIV.2.17, 18

सं त्वा नह्यामि पयसा पृथिव्याः सं त्वा नह्याम्याद्भिरोषधीभिः ।
सं त्वा नह्यामि प्रजया धनेन सह संनद्धा सुनुहि भागधेयम् ॥
— *AV* XIV.2.70 (वाजमेमम् for भागधेयम्)

सोमः प्रथमो विविदे गन्धर्वो विविद उत्तरः ।
तृतीयो अग्निष्टे पतिस्तुरीयस्ते मनुष्यजाः ॥
— *Ṛ̥V* X.85.40

सोमोऽददद्गन्धर्वाय गन्धर्वोऽददग्नये ।
रयिं च पुत्रांश्चा दादग्निर्मह्यमथो इमाम् ॥
— *Ṛ̥V* X.85.41

सोमाय जनिविदे स्वाहा ।
गन्धर्वाय जनिविदे स्वाहा ।
अग्नये जनिविदे स्वाहा ।
— *M.Pā.* I.4.1-3

At the time of *pānigrahaṇa*

गृभ्णामि ते सौभगत्वाय हस्तं मया पत्या जरदष्टिर्यथासः ।
भगो अर्यमा सविता पुरंधिर्मह्यं त्वादुर्गार्हपत्याय देवाः ॥
— *ṚV* X.85.36; *AV* XIV.1.50

अमोऽहमस्मि सा त्वं सा त्वमस्यमोऽहम् ।
सामाहमस्मि ऋक्त्वं द्योरहं पृथिवी त्वं ।
तावेहि विवहावहै सह रेतो दधावहै ।
प्रजां प्रजनयावहै पुत्रान् विन्द्यावहै ।
पुंसे पुत्राय कर्तवे रायस्पोषय सुप्रजस्त्वाय सुवीर्याय ॥
बहून् ते सन्तु जरदष्टयः संप्रियौ रोचिष्णु सुमन्स्यमनु ।
पश्येम शरदः शतं जीवेम शरदः शतं श्रुणुयाम शरदः शतम् ॥
— *AV* XIV.2.71; *M.Pā.* I.3.14

सरस्वति प्रेदमव सुभगो वाजिनीवती ।
श्या त्वा विश्वस्य भूतस्य प्रजायामस्याग्रतः ।
यस्यां भूतं समभवद्यस्यां विश्वमिदं जगत् ।
तामध्य गाथां गास्यामि या स्त्रीणामुत्तमं यशः ॥
— *Anuvāka*

At the time of Aśmārohaṇa

स्योनं ध्रुवं प्रजायै धारयामि तेऽश्मानं देव्याः पृथिव्या उपस्थे ।
तमातिष्ठानुमाद्या सुवर्चा दीर्घं त आयुः सविता कृणोतु ॥
— *AV* XIV.1.47

आतिष्ठेममश्मानमश्मेव त्वं स्थिरा भव ।
अभितिष्ठ पृतन्यतस्सहस्व पृतनायतः ॥
— *Ma.Pā.* I.5.1

At the time of Lājā Homa

इयं नार्युपब्रूतेऽग्नौ लाजानावपन्तिका ।
दीर्घायुरस्तु मे पतिर्जीवातु शरदश्शतं ॥
— *AV* XIV.2.63 (पूल्या for लाजा)

At the time of *agni pariṇayana*

तुभ्यमग्ने पर्यवहन् सूर्यां वहतुना सह ।
पुनः पतिभ्यो जायां दा अग्ने प्रजया सह ॥

— *ṚV* X.85.38; AV XIV.2.1 (स नः for पुनः)

पुनः पत्नीमग्निरदादायुषा सह वर्चसा ।
दीर्घायुरस्या यः पतिस्स एतु शरदशतम् ॥

— *ṚV* X.85.39; *AV* XIV.2.2

At the time of journey to husband's house

खे रथस्य खेऽनसः खे युगस्य शतक्रतो ।
अपालमिन्द्र त्रिष्पूत्व्यकृणोः सूर्यत्वचम् ॥

— *ṚV* VIII.91.7; *AV* XIV.1.41

सुकिँशुकँ शल्मलिं विश्वरूपँ हिरण्यवर्णँ सुधुरँ सुचक्रम् ।
आरोह सूर्ये अमृतस्य लोकं स्योनं पत्ये वहतुं कृणुष्व ॥

— *ṚV* X.85.20; *AV* XIV.1.61
(वहतुं for शल्मलिं, पतिभ्यो for पत्ये, कृणु त्वम् for कृणुष्व)

मा विदन्परिपन्थिनो य आसीदन्ति दम्पती ।
सुगेभिर्दुर्गमतीतामप द्रान्त्वरातयः ॥

— *ṚV* X.85.32

ये वध्वश्चन्द्र वहतुं यक्ष्मा यन्ति जनादनु ।
पुनस्तान्यज्ञिया देवा नयन्तु यत आगताः ॥

— *ṚV* X.85.31

सुमङ्गलीरियं वधूरिमां समेत पश्यत ।
सौभाग्यामस्यै दत्वायाथास्तं विपरेतन ॥

— *ṚV* X.85.33; *AV* XIV.2.28 (दौर्भाग्यै for याथास्तं)

जीवां रुदन्ती विमयन्तो अध्वरे दीर्घामनुप्रसितिं दीधियुर्नरः ।
वामं पितृभ्यो य इदं समेरिरे मयः पतिभ्यो जनयः परिष्वजे ॥

— *ṚV* X.40.10; *AV* XIV.1.46
(नयत्यध्वरं for विमन्यतो अध्वरे, दीध्युर्नरः for दीधियुर्नरः)

At the time of *hṛdaya sparśa*

मम हृदये हृदयं ते अस्तु मम चित्तं चित्तेनान्वेहि ।
मम वाचमेकमना जुषस्व प्रजापतिष्ट्वा नियुनक्तु मह्यम् ॥

— *Ma.Br.* I.2.21

At the time of untying the *mekhalā* and *śikhā vimocana*

प्र त्वा मुञ्चामि वरुणस्य पाशाद् येन त्वाबध्नात् सविता सुशेवाः ।
ऋतस्य योनौ सुकृतस्य लोकेऽरिष्टां त्वा सह पत्या दधामि ॥

— *ṚV* X.85.24; *AV* XIV.1.19

(स्योनं ते अस्तु सहसंभलायै for अरिष्टां त्वा सह पत्या दधामि)

प्रेतो मुञ्चामि नामुतः सुबद्धाममुतस्करम् ।
यथेयमिन्द्रं मीढ्वः सुपुत्रा सुभगासति ॥

— *ṚV* X.85.25; *AV* XIV.1.18

At the time of *saptapadī*

एकमिषे विष्णुस्त्वान्वेतु ।
द्वे ऊर्जे विष्णुस्त्वान्वेतु ।
त्रीणि व्रताय विष्णुस्तान्वेतु ।
चत्वारि मायोभवाय विष्णुस्तान्वेतु ।
पञ्च पशुभ्यो विष्णुस्तान्वेतु ।
षड्रायस्पोषाय विष्णुस्तान्वेतु ।
सप्त सप्तभ्यो होत्राभ्यो विष्णुस्तान्वेतु ।
सखा सप्तपदा भव सखायौ सप्तपदा बभूव ॥

— *Tai.Br* III.7.7.11

(इष एकपद्यूर्जे द्विपदो रायस्पोषाय त्रिपदी मायोभव्याय चतुष्पदी प्रजाभ्यः पञ्चपद्युतुभ्यः षट्पदी सखा सप्तपदी भव सा मामनुव्रता भव । पुत्रान्विन्दावहै बहूँस्ते सन्तु जरदष्टयः)

आपो हि ष्ठा मयोभुवस्ता न ऊर्जे दधातन । महे रणाय चक्षसे ॥
यो वः शिवतमो रसस्तस्य भाजयतेह नः । उशतीरिव मातरः ॥
तस्मा अरं गमाम वो यस्य क्षयाय जिन्वथ । आपो जनयथा च नः ॥

— *ṚV* X.9.1, 2, 3; *AV* I.5.1-3

At the time of *gṛha-praveśa*

इह गावो निषिदन्त्विहाश्वा इह पूरुषाः ।
इहो सहस्रदक्षिणो यज्ञ इह पूषा निषीदतु ॥

— *Ma.Pā* I.9.1

आ नः प्रजां जनयतु प्रजापतिराजरसाय समनक्त्वर्यमा ।
अदुर्मङ्गलीः पतिलोकमा विश शं नो भव द्विपदे शं वतुष्पदे ॥

— *ṚV* X.85.43

इमां त्वमिन्द्र मीढ्वस्सुपुत्रां सुभगां कृणु ।
दशास्यां पुत्रानाधेहि पतिमेकादशं कृधि ॥
— *Ṛ̥V* X.85.44

सम्राज्ञी श्वशुरे भव सम्राज्ञी श्वश्र्वां भव ।
ननान्दरि सम्राज्ञी भव सम्राज्ञी अधि देवृषु ॥
— *Ṛ̥V* X.85.45

At the time of Dhruva Arundhatī Darśana

ध्रुवैधि पोष्या मयि मह्यं त्वादाद्बृहस्पतिः ।
मया पत्या प्रजावती सं जीव शरद शतम् ॥

At the time of *caturthī karma*

पुमाँसौ मित्रवरुणौ पुमाँसाविश्विनावुभौ ।
पुमानिन्द्रश्च सूर्यश्च पुमाँसं वर्ततां मयि पुनः ॥
— *Ma.Br* I.4.8

विष्णुर्योनिं कल्पयतु त्वष्टा रूपाणि पिंशतु ।
आसिञ्चतु प्रजापतिर्धाता गर्भं दधातु ते ॥
— *Ṛ̥V* X.184.1; *AV* V.25.5

गर्भं धेहि सिनीवालि गर्भं धेहि सरस्वति ।
गर्भं ते अश्विनौ देवावाधत्तां पुष्करस्रजा ॥
— *Ṛ̥V* X.184.2; *AV* V.25.4

हिरण्ययी अरुणी यं निर्मन्थतो अश्विना ।
तंते गर्भं दधाम्यहं दशमे मासि सूतवे ॥
— *Ṛ̥V* X.184.3

अग्ने प्रायश्चित्ते त्वं देवानां प्रायश्चित्तिरसि ब्राह्मणस्त्वा नाथकाम उपधावामि याऽस्यै पतिघ्नी तनूस्तामस्यै नाशय स्वाहा । वायो प्रायश्चित्ते त्वं देवानां प्रायश्चित्तिरसि ब्राह्मणस्त्वा नाथकाम उपधावामि याऽस्यै प्रजाघ्नी तनूस्तामस्यै नाशय स्वाहा । सूर्यं प्रायश्चित्ते त्वं देवानां प्रायश्चित्तिरसि ब्राह्मणस्त्वा नाथकाम उपधावामि याऽस्यैं पशुघ्नी तनूस्तामस्यै नाशय स्वाहा । चन्द्र प्रायश्चित्ते त्वं देवानां प्रायश्चित्तिरसि ब्राह्मणस्त्वा नाथकाम उपधावामि याऽस्यै गृहघ्नी तनूस्तामस्यै नाशय स्वाहा । गन्धर्व प्रायश्चित्ते त्वं देवानां प्रायश्चित्तिरसि ब्राह्मणस्त्वा नाथकाम उपधावामि प्रायश्चित्ते त्वं देवानां प्रायश्चित्तिरसि ब्राह्मणस्वा नाथकाम उपधावामि याऽस्यै यशोघ्नी तनूस्तामस्यै नाशय स्वाहेति ॥
— *Ma.Pā* I.10.3-6

At the time of Jāyā Homa

चित्तं च चित्तिश्चाकूतं चाकूतिश्च विज्ञातं च विज्ञानं च मनश्च शक्वरिर्श्च च दर्शश्च पूर्णमासश्च बृहच्च रथन्तरं च प्रजापतिर्जयानिन्द्राय वृष्णे प्रायच्छदुग्रः पृतनाज्येषु तस्मै विशः समनमन्त सर्वाः स उग्रः स हि हव्यो बभूव देवासुराः संयत्ता आसन्त्स इन्द्रः प्रजापतिमुपधावतस्मा एताञ्जायान्प्रायत्तानजुहोत्ततो वै देवा असुरानजयन्यदजयन्तञ्जयानां जयत्वँ स्पर्धमानेनैते होतव्या जयत्येव ताम्पृतनाम्

— *Tai.Sa* III.4.4

At the time of Abhyātāna Homa

अग्निर्भूतानामधिपतिः स माऽवत्विन्द्रो ज्येष्ठानां, यमः पृथिव्या, वायुरन्तरिक्षस्य, सूर्यो दिवश्चन्द्रमा नक्षत्राणां, बृहस्पतिब्रह्मणे, मित्रः सत्यानां, वरुणोऽपाम्, समुद्रः स्रोत्यानामन्नटम् साम्राज्यानामधिपति तन्मावतु, सोम ओषधीनां, सविता प्रसवानाम्, रुद्रः पशूनां, त्वष्टा रूपाणां, विष्णुः पर्वतानां, मरुतो गणानामधिपतयस्ते मावन्तु पितरः पितामहाः परेवरे ततास्ततामहाः । इह मावन्त्वस्मिन्ब्रह्मण्यस्मिन् क्षत्रेऽस्यामाशिष्यस्यां पुरोधायामास्मिन्कर्मण्यस्यां देवहूत्याम् ॥

— *Tai.Sa* III.4.5

At the time of Rāṣṭrabhṛt Homa

ऋताषाड़ृतधामाग्निर्गन्धर्वस्तस्यौषधयोऽप्सरस ऊर्जो नाम स इदं ब्रह्म क्षत्रम्पातु त इदम्ब्रह्म क्षत्रम्पातु तस्मै स्वाहा ताभ्यः स्वाहा संहितो विश्वसामा सूर्यो गन्धर्वस्तस्य मरीचयोऽप्सरस आयुवः सुषुम्नः सूर्यरश्मिचन्द्रमा गन्धर्वस्तस्य नक्षत्रायणयप्सरसो बेकुरयो भुज्युः सुपर्णो यज्ञो गन्धर्वस्तस्य दक्षिणा अप्सरसः स्तवाः प्रजापतिर्विश्वकर्मा मनो गन्धर्वस्तस्यक्सामान्यप्सरसो वह्नय इषिरो विश्वव्यचा वार्तो गन्धर्वस्तस्यापोऽप्सरसो मुदा भुवनस्य पते यस्य न उपरि गृहा इह च।

परमेष्ठ्याधिपतिर्मृत्युर्गन्धर्वस्तस्य विश्वमप्सरसो भुवः सुक्षितिः सुभूतिर्भद्रकृत्सुवर्वान्पर्जन्यो गन्धर्वस्तस्य विद्युतोऽप्सरसो रुचो दूरेहतिरमृडयो मृत्युर्गन्धर्वस्तस्य प्रजा अप्सरसो भीरुव श्चारुः कृपणकाशी कामो गन्धर्वस्तस्याधयोऽप्सरसः शोवयन्तीर्नाम स इदम्ब्रह्म क्षत्रम्पातु ता इदम्ब्रह्म क्षत्रम्पातु तस्मै स्वाहा ताभ्यः स्वाहा स नो भुवनस्य पते यस्य त उपरि गृहा इह च । उरु ब्रह्मणेऽस्मै क्षत्राय महि शर्म यच्छ ॥

— *Tai.Sa* III.4.7

At the time of Ājya Homa

अग्निरैतु प्रथमो देवतानाम् सोऽस्यै प्रजां मुञ्चतु मृत्युपाशात् । तदयं राजा वरुणोऽनुमन्यतां यथेयम् स्त्री पौत्रमघं न रोदात् । इमामग्निस्त्रायतां गार्हपत्यः प्रजामस्यै नयतु दीर्घमायुः अशून्योपस्था जीवतामस्तु माता पौत्रमानन्द-मभिविबुध्यामियम् । मा ते गृहे निशि घोष उत्थादन्यत्र त्वद्रुदत्यस्संविशन्तु । मा

त्वं विकेश्युर अवधिष्टा जीवपत्नी पतिलोके विराज पश्यन्ती प्रजां सुमनस्यमानां ॥ स्वस्ति नो अग्ने दिव आपृथिव्या विश्वानि धेह्ययथा यजत्र । यदस्यां महि दिवि जातं प्रशस्तं तदस्मासु द्रविणं धेहि चित्रम् । सुगन्न पन्थां प्रदिशन्न एहि ज्योतिष्मद्धेह्यजरन्न आयुः । अपैतु मृत्युरमृतश्च आगाद्वैवस्वतो नो अभयं कृणोतु ॥

Differences in Mantras

As there are differences in the order of rituals in different Gṛhya-Sūtras, there are variations in *mantras* also. The Annexure at the end of the book shows all the *vivāha mantras* as depicted in each Gṛhya-Sūtra. While each Gṛhya-Sūtra may contain common *mantras* and exclusives ones, variations are also found among the common *mantras*. The section of the Gṛhya-Sūtra where each *mantra* is recited is also shown in the Annexure. It can be seen that some of the *mantras* are recited at different parts of the marriage ritual in different Gṛhya-Sūtras. Some of the major *mantras* where variations occur are listed hereunder:

१. अनृक्षरा ऋजवः सन्तु पन्था येभिः सखायो यन्ति नो वरेयम् ।
समर्यमा सम्भगो नो निनीयात् सं जास्पत्यं सुयममस्तु देवाः ॥

(In *Jaimini Gṛhya-Sūtra,* येभिः becomes एभिः and निनीयात् becomes अनुनीयात्.)

२. यन्मधुनो मधव्यं परममनाद्यं वीर्यम् ।
तेनाहं मधुनो मधव्येन परमेणान्नाद्येन वीर्येण परमोऽन्नादो मधुव्योऽसानि ॥

(In *Pāraskara Gṛhya-Sūtra,* वीर्यम् is replaced by रूपम् and वीर्येण by रूपेण.) In *Kāṭhaka Gṛhya-Sūtra,* the following verse is used:

यन्मधुनो मधव्यस्य परमस्यान्नाद्यस्य परममन्नाद्यं रूपं ॥
तेनाहं मधुनो मधव्यस्य परमस्यान्नाद्यस्य परमोऽन्नादो मधव्यो भूयासम् ॥

३. जरां गच्छ परिधत्स्व वासो भवाकृष्टीनामभिशस्तिपावा ।
शतं च जीव शरदः सुवर्च्चा रायश्च पोषमुपसंव्ययस्व ॥

(In *Agniveśya Gṛhya-Sūtra* and in *Bhāradvāja Gṛhya-Sūtra,* गच्छ becomes गच्छासि.)

४. या अकृन्तन्नवयन् याश्च तत्निरे या देवीरन्तां अभितोऽददन्त ।
तास्त्वा जरसे सव्ययन्त्वायुष्मतीदं परिधत्स्व वासः ॥

In *Pāraskara Gṛhya-Sūtra*, the verse is:

या अकृन्तन्नवयँय्या अतन्वत याश्च देवीस्तन्तूनभिता ततन्थ ।
तास्त्वा देवीर्जरसे सव्ययस्वायुष्मतीदं परिधत्स्व वासः ॥

In *Mānava Gṛhya-Sūtra* and *Bhāradvāja Gṛhya-Sūtra*, the verse is:

या अकृन्तन्या अतन्वन्या अवाहरन् याश्चाग्नादेव्योऽन्तानभितोऽततनन्त ।
तास्त्वादेव्यो जरसे सँव्ययन्त्वायुष्मतीदं परिधत्स्व वासः ॥

In *Agniveśya Gṛhya-Sūtra* it is:

या अकृन्तन्नवयन् या अतन्वत याश्च देवीरन्तानभितोऽददन्त ।
तास्त्वा देवीर्जरसा संव्ययन्त्वायुष्मतीदं परिधत्स्व वासः ॥

In *Kāṭhaka Gṛhya-Sūtra* it is:

या अकृन्तन्या अवयन्या अतन्वत याश्च देवीरन्तां अभितोऽततन्थ ।
तास्त्वा देवीर्जरसा संव्ययन्त्वायुष्मतीदं परिधत्स्व वासः॥

In *Gobhila* and *Khādira Gṛhya-Sūtra*, the verse is:

या आकृन्तन्नवयन् या अतन्वत याश्च देव्योऽन्तानभितो ततन्थ ।
तास्त्वा देव्यो जरसे संव्ययन्त्वायुष्मतीदं परिधत्व वासः ॥

In *Kauśika Gṛhya-Sūtra* it is:

या अकृन्तन्नवयन् याश्च तत्निरे या देवीरन्तां अभितोऽददन्त ।
तास्त्या जरसे सव्ययन्त्वायुष्मतीदं परिधत्स्व वासः ॥

५. परिधत धत्त वाससैनां शतायुषी कृणुत दीर्घमायुः ।
बृहस्पतिः प्रायच्छद्वास एतत् सौभाग्यं राज्ञे परिधातवा ॥

In *Agnivesya Gṛhya-Sūtra* and in *Bhāradvāja Gṛhya-Sūtra*,

सौभाग्यं becomes सोमाय. In *Gobhila*, *Khādira*, *Jaimini* and *Kauśika Gṛhya-Sūtra*, the second line is शतं च जीव शरदः सुवर्चा वसूनिचार्ये विभृजासि जीवन् ॥

६. हिरण्यवर्णाः शुचयः पावका यासु जातः कश्यपो यास्विन्द्रः ।
अग्निं या गर्भं दधिरे विरूपास्ता न आपः शं स्योना भवन्तु ॥

In *Āpastamba* and *Hiraṇyakeśi Gṛhya-Sūtra*, the second line is

या अग्निं गर्भे दधिरे सुवर्णास्तास्त आपश्शँ स्योना भवन्तु ॥

७. नीललोहितं भवति कृत्यासक्तिर्व्यज्यते ।
एधन्ते अस्या ज्ञातयः पतिर्बन्धेषु बध्यते ॥

In *Pāraskara* and *Hiraṇyakeśi Gṛhya-Sūtra*, भवतः replaces भवति.

८. अघोरचक्षुरपतिघ्न्ये धि शिवा पशुभ्यः सुमना सुवर्चाः ।
वीरसूर्देवकामा स्योना शं नो भव द्विपदे शं चतुष्पदे ॥

In *Hiraṇyakeśi Gṛhya-Sūtra*, जीवसूर्वीरसूः replaces वीरसूर्देवकामा. In *Vārāha Gṛhya-Sūtra*, the verse is:

अघोरचक्षुरपतिघ्न्येधि । एहि शिवा पशुभ्यः सुमना सुवर्चाः ।
दीर्घायुपत्नी प्रजया स्वर्विदिन्द्रप्रणयीरुप नो वस्तुमेहि ॥

In *Jaimini Gṛhya-Sūtra*, वीरसर्जीवसूर्देवकामा replaces वीरसूर्देवकामा.

९. सुमङ्गलीरियं वधूरिमां समेत पश्यत ।
सौभाग्यामस्यै दत्वायाथास्तं विपरेतन ॥

In *Vārāha Gṛhya-Sūtra*, यथार्थँ replaces याथास्तं.

१०. गृभ्णामि ते सौभगत्वाय हस्तं मया पत्या जरदष्टिर्यथासः ।
भगो अर्यमा सविता पुरंधिर्मह्यं त्वादुर्गार्हपत्याय देवाः ॥

In *Āpastamba, Hiraṇyakeśi, Baudhāyana, Kāṭhaka Gṛhya-Sūtra*, सुप्रजस्त्वाय replaces सौभगत्वाय. In *Hiraṇyakeśi, Vārāha, Bhāradvāja Gṛhya-Sūtra* गृह्णामि replaces गृभ्णामि.

११. अमोऽहमस्मि सा त्वं सा त्वमस्यमोऽहम् । सामाहमस्मि ऋक्त्वं द्योरहं पृथिवी त्वं । तावेहि विवहावहै सह रेतो दधावहै । प्रजां प्रजनयावहै पुत्रान् विन्द्यावहै । पुंसे पुत्राय कर्तवे रायस्पोषय सुप्रजस्त्वाय सुवीर्याय ॥ बहून् ते सन्तु जरदष्टयः संप्रियौ रोचिष्णु सुमन्स्यमनु । पश्येम शरदः शतं जीवेम शरदः शतं श्रुणुयाम शरदः शतम् ॥

In *Aśvalāyana, Śāṅkhāyana Gṛhya-Sūtra*, the verse is:

अमोऽहमस्मि सा त्वं सा त्वमस्यमोऽहम् । द्योरहं पृथिवी त्वं सामाहमृक्त्वं तावेहि विवहावहै ।
प्रजां प्रजनयावहै संप्रियौ रोचिष्णू सुमनस्यमानौ जीवेव शरदः शतम् ॥

In *Kauṣītaki Gṛhya-Sūtra*, the third line is:

प्रजां प्रजनयावहै पुत्रान् विन्दावहै बहूस्ते सन्तु जरदष्टयः ॥

In *Pāraskara Gṛhya-Sūtra*, the verse is:

अमोऽहमस्मि सा त्वं सा त्वमस्यमोऽहम् । सामाहमस्मि ऋक्त्वं द्योरहं पृथिवी त्वं तावेहि विवहावहै । सह रेतो दधावहै प्रजां प्रजनयावहै पुत्रान् विन्द्यावहै ।

बहून् ते सन्तु जरदष्टयः संप्रियौ रोचिष्णु सुमन्स्यमनु । पश्येम शरदः शतं जीवेम शरदः शतं श्रुणुयाम शरदः शतम् ॥

In *Āpastamba Gṛhya-Sūtra*, the verse is:

सा त्वमस्यमूहममूहमस्मि सा त्वं द्योरहं पृथिवी त्वं रेतोऽहं रेतोभृत्त्वं मनोऽहमस्मि वाक्त्वँ सामाहमस्म्यृक्त्वँ सा मामनुव्रता भव पुँसे पुत्राय वेत्तवै श्रियै पुत्राय वेत्तवा एहि सूनृते ॥

In *Hiraṇyakeśi Gṛhya-Sūtra*, the verse is:

अमूहमस्मि सा त्वं द्यौरहं पृथिवी त्वं सामाहमृक्त्वं
तावेहि संभवाव सह रेतो दधावहै पुंसे पुत्राय वेत्तवै
रायस्पोषाय सुप्रजास्त्वाय सुवीर्याय ॥

In *Baudhāyana Gṛhya-Sūtra*, the verse is:

अमूहमस्मि सा त्वं द्योरहं पृथिवी त्वं रेतोऽहं रेतोभृत्त्वं मनोऽहमस्मि वाक्त्वं सामाहमस्मि ऋक्त्वं तावेहि सम्भवाव सह रेतो दधावहै पुंसे पुत्राय वेत्तवै रायस्पोषाय सुप्रजास्त्वाय सुवीर्याय ॥

In *Vārāha Gṛhya-Sūtra*, the verse is:

सा त्वमस्यमोऽहमोऽहमसि सा त्वम् । द्योरहं पृथिवी त्वं बृहदहं रथन्तरं त्वम् । रेतोऽहमस्मि रेतोधृक्त्वम् ॥ सामाहमस्मि ऋक्त्वं मनोऽहमस्मि वाक्त्वम् । सा मामनुव्रता भव सा मामनुप्रजायस्व ॥ प्रजाँ सृजावहा उभौ पुँसे पुत्राय कर्तवे । श्रियै पुत्राय वेथवेह सूनृते ॥

In *Mānava Gṛhya-Sūtra*, the verse is:

अमोह मस्मि सा त्वं सा त्वमस्यप्यमोहम् । द्योरहं पृथिवी त्वमृक् त्वमसि सामाऽहम् रेतोह मस्मि रेतो धत्तम् ॥ ता एव विवाहवहै पुँसे पुत्राय कर्त्तवे । श्रीये पुत्राय वेधवै ॥ रायस्पोषाय सुप्रस्त्वाय सुवीर्याय ॥

In *Agniveśya Gṛhya-Sūtra*, the verse is:

अमूहमस्मि सा त्वं सा त्वमस्यमूहं ऋगहमस्मि साम त्वं द्योरहं पृथिवी त्वम् ॥

In *Bhāradvāja Gṛhya-Sūtra*, the verse is:

अमूहमस्मि सा त्वं द्योरहं पृथिवी त्वं सामाहमृक्त्वं तावेहि संभवाव सह रेतो दधावहै पुंसे पुत्राय वेत्तवै रायस्पोषाय सुप्रजस्त्वाय सुवीर्याय ॥

In *Kāṭhaka Gṛhya-Sūtra*, the verse is:

सा त्वमस्यमोऽहममोऽहमस्मि सा त्वं । ता एहि विववाहवै पुंसे पुत्राय कर्तवे । रायस्पोषाय सुप्रजास्त्वाय सुवीर्याय ॥

In *Jaimini Gṛhya-Sūtra*, the verse is:

अमोऽहमस्मि सा त्वं सामाहमस्म्यृक्त्वं मनोऽहमस्मि वाक्त्वं द्योरहं पृथिवी त्वं तावेहि संभवाव सह रेतो दधावहै पुंसे पुत्राय वैत्तवै मामनुव्रता भव सहशय्या मया भवासाव ॥

In *Kauśika Gṛhya-Sūtra*, the verse is:

अमोऽहमस्मि सा त्वं सामाहमस्म्यृक् त्वं द्योरहं पृथिवी त्वं । ताविह सं भवाय प्रजामा जनयावहै ॥ जनियन्ति नावग्रवः पुत्रियन्ति सुदानवः । अरिष्टास् सचेवहि बृहते वाजसातये ॥

१२. आतिष्ठेममश्मानमश्मेव त्वं स्थिरा भव ।
अभितिष्ठ पृतन्यतस्सहस्व पृतनायतः ॥

In *Aśvalāyana Gṛhya-Sūtra*, the verse is:

आरोहाममश्मानमश्मेव त्वं स्थिरा भव ।
सहस्व पृतनायतोऽभितिष्ठ पृतन्यतः ॥

In *Śāṅkhāyana Gṛhya-Sūtra*, the verse is:

एह्यश्मानमातिष्ठाश्मेव त्वं स्थिरा भव ।
अभि तिष्ठ पृतन्यतः सहस्व पृतनायत ॥

In *Kauṣītaki Gṛhya-Sūtra*, the verse is:

एह्याश्मानमातिष्ठ । आरोहाश्मेव त्वं स्थिरा भव ।
अभितिष्ठ पृतन्यतः । सहस्व पृतनायतः ॥

In *Pāraskara Gṛhya-Sūtra*, the verse is:

आरोहममश्मानमश्मेव त्वं स्थिरा भव ।
अभितिष्ठ पृतन्यतोऽवबाधस्व प्रुतनायत ॥

In *Āpastamba* and *Baudhāyana Gṛhya-Sūtra*, the verse is:

आतिष्ठेममश्मानमश्मेव त्वं स्थिरा भव ।
अभितिष्ठ पृतन्यतस्सहस्व पृतनायतः ॥

In *Hiraṇyakeśi*, *Agniveśya* and *Bhāradvāja Gṛhya-Sūtra*, the verse is:

आतिष्ठेममश्मानमश्मेव त्वं स्थिरा भव ।
प्रमृणीहि दुरस्यून्सहस्व पृतनायतः ॥

In *Vārāha Gṛhya-Sūtra*, the verse is:

आतिष्ठेममश्मानमश्मेव त्वँ स्थिरा भव ।
कृण्वन्तु विश्वे देवा आयुष्टे शरदः शतम् ॥

In *Mānava Gṛhya-Sūtra*, the verse is:

एतमश्मानमातिष्ठतमश्मेव युवां स्थिरौ भवतम्
कृण्वन्तु विश्वे देवा आयुर्वां शरदः शतम् ॥

In *Kāṭhaka Gṛhya-Sūtra*, the verse is:

अश्मानमातिष्ठाश्मेव त्वं स्थिरो भव ।
कृण्वन्तु विश्वेदेवा आयुष्टे शरदः शतम् ।

आतिष्ठेममश्मानमश्मेव त्वं स्थिरा भव ।
प्रमृणीहि दुवस्यवः सहस्व पृतन्यतः ॥

In *Gobhila* and *Khādira Gṛhya-Sūtra*, the verse is:

इममश्मानारोहाश्मेव त्वं स्थिरा भव ।
द्विषन्तमप बाधदस्व मा च त्वं द्विषतामधः ॥

In *Kauśika Gṛhya-Sūtra*, the verse is:

स्योनं ध्रुवं प्रजायै धारयामि तेऽश्मानं देव्याः पृथिव्या उपस्थे ।
तमातिष्ठानुमाद्या सुवर्चा दीर्घं त आयुः सविता कृणोतु ॥

१३. इयं नार्युपब्रूतेऽग्नौ लाजानावपन्तिका ।
दीर्घायुरस्तु मे पतिर्जीवातु शरदश्शतं ॥

In *Śāṅkhāyana* and *Kauṣītaki Gṛhya-Sūtra*, the verse is:

इयं नार्युपब्रूतेऽग्नौ लाजानावपन्तिका ।
शिवा ज्ञातिभ्यो भूयासं चिरं जीवतु मे पतिः॥

In *Pāraskara Gṛhya-Sūtra*, the verse is:

इयं नार्युपब्रूते लाजानावपन्तिका ।
आयुष्मानस्तु मे पतिरेधन्तां ज्ञातयो मम स्वाहा ॥

In *Āpastamba Gṛhya-Sūtra*, the verse is:

इयं नार्युप ब्रूते कुल्यान्यावपन्तिका ।
दीर्घायुरस्तु मे पतिर्जीवातु शरदश्शतं ॥

In *Hiraṇyakeśi* and *Jaimini Gṛhya-Sūtra*, the verse is:

इयं नार्युपब्रूतेग्नौ लाजानावपन्ती ।
दीर्घायुरस्तु मे पतिरेधन्तां ज्ञातयो मम ॥

In *Baudhāyana* and *Agniveśya Gṛhya-Sūtra*, the verse is:

इयं नार्युपब्रूतेऽग्नौ लाजानावपन्ती ।
दीर्घायुरस्तु मे पतिर्जीवातु शरदश्शतम् ॥

In *Vārāha, Mānava, Bhāradvāja, Kāṭhaka* and *Agniveśya Gṛhya-Sūtra*, the verse is:

इयं नार्युपब्रूते लाजानावपन्तिका ।
दीर्घायुरस्तु मे पतिरेधान्तां ज्ञातयो मम ॥

In *Gobhila* and *Khādira Gṛhya-Sūtra*, the verse is:

इयं नार्यूपब्रूतेऽग्नौ लाजानापवन्ती ।
दीर्घायुरस्तु मे पतिः शतं वर्षाणि जीवतु ।
एधन्ताम् ज्ञातयो मम स्वाहा ॥

In *Kauśika Gṛhya-Sūtra*, the verse is:

इयं नार्युपब्रूते पूल्यान्यावपन्तिका ।
दीर्घायुरस्तु मे पतिर्जीवाति शरदः शतम् ॥

१४. खे रथस्य खेऽनसः खे युगस्य शतक्रतो ।
अपालमिन्द्र त्रिष्पूत्व्यकृणोः सूर्यत्वचम्॥

In *Āpastamba Gṛhya-Sūtra*, the verse is:

खेऽनसः खे रथः खे युगस्य शचीपते ।
अपालमिन्द्र त्रिः पूत्व्यकरत्सूर्यवर्चसम् ॥

In *Vārāha* and *Mānava Gṛhya-Sūtra*, the verse is:

खे रथस्य खेऽनसः खे युगस्य शतक्रतोः ।
अपालामिन्द्रस्त्रिः पूर्त्यवकृणोत्सूर्यत्वचसः ॥

In *Kāṭhaka Gṛhya-Sūtra*, the verse is:

खे रथस्य खेऽनसः खे युगस्य शतक्रतो ।
अपालामिन्द्रस्त्रिष्पूत्वा करोतु सूर्यवर्चसम् ॥

१५. सुकिँशुकँ शल्मलिं विश्वरूपँ हिरण्यवर्णँ सुधुरँ सुचक्रम् ।
आरोह सूर्ये अमृतस्य लोकं स्योनं पत्ये वहतुं कृणुष्व ॥

In *Āpastamba Gṛhya-Sūtra*, the verse is:

सुकिँशुकँ शल्मलिं विश्वरूपँ हिरण्यवर्णँ सुवृतँ सुचक्रम् ।
आरोह वध्वमृतस्य लोकं स्योनं पत्ये वहतुं कृणुष्व ॥

In *Vārāha Gṛhya-Sūtra*, the verse is:

सुकिँशुकँ शल्मलिं विश्वरूपँ हिरण्यवर्णँ सुधुरँ सुचक्रम् ।
आरोह सूर्ये अमृतस्य पन्थाँस्तेन याहि गृहान्स्वस्ति ॥

In *Gobhila* and *Khādira Gṛhya-Sūtra*, the verse is:

सुकिँशुकं शल्मलिं विश्वरूपं सुवर्णवर्णँ सुकृतँ सुचक्रम् ।
आरोह सूर्ये अमृतस्य नाभिँ स्योनं पत्ये वहतुं कृणुष्व ॥

In *Kauśika Gṛhya-Sūtra*, the verse is:

सुकिंशुकं वहतुं विश्वरूपं हिरण्यवर्णं सुवृतं सुचक्रम् ।
आरोह सूर्ये अमृतस्य लोकं स्योनं पतिभ्यो वहतुं कृणु त्वम् ॥

१६. मम हृदये हृदयं ते अस्तु मम चित्तं चित्तेनान्वेहि ।
मम वाचमेकमना जुषस्व प्रजापतिष्ट्वा नियुनक्तु मह्यम् ॥

In *Pāraskara Gṛhya-Sūtra*, the verse is:

मम व्रते ते हृदयम् दधामि मम चित्तमनुचित्तं ते अस्तु ।
मम वाचमेकमना जुषस्व प्रजापतिष्ट्वा नियुनक्तु मह्यम् ॥

In *Baudhāyana Gṛhya-Sūtra*, the verse is:

मम हृदये हृदयं ते अस्तु मम चित्ते चित्तमस्तु ते ।
मम वाचकमेकमनाः शृणु मामेवानुव्रता सहचर्या मया भव ॥

In *Agnivesya Gṛhya-Sūtra*, the verse is:

मम हृदये हृदयं ते अस्तु । मम चित्ते चित्तमस्तु ते ।
मम वाचमेकमनाः श्रुणु । मामेवानुव्रता सहचर्या मया भव ॥

In *Bhāradvāja Gṛhya-Sūtra*, the verse is:

मम हृदये हृदयं ते अस्तु मम चित्ते चित्तमस्तु ते ।
मम वाचमेकमना शृणु मामेवानुव्रता भव सहचर्या मया भव ॥

In *Khādira Gṛhya-Sūtra*, the verse is:

मम व्रते ते दयं दधातु मम चित्तमनु चित्तं ते अस्तु ।
मम वाचमेकमना जुषस्व बृहस्पतिस्त्वा नियुनक्तु मह्यम् ॥

In *Jaimini Gṛhya-Sūtra*, the verse is:

मम व्रते ते दयं दधातु मम चित्तमनु चित्तं ते अस्तु ।
मम वाचमेकमना जुषस्व बृहस्पतिस्त्वा नियुनक्तु मह्यम् ॥

१७. प्र त्वा मुञ्चामि वरुणस्य पाशाद् येन त्वाबध्नात् सविता सुशेवाः ।
ऋतस्य योनौ सुकृतस्य लोकेऽरिष्टां त्वा सह पत्या दधामि ॥

In *Āpastamba Gṛhya-Sūtra*, the verse is:

प्र त्वा मुञ्चामि वरुणस्य पाशाद् येन त्वाबध्नात् सविता सुकेतः ।
धातुश्च योनौ सुकृतस्य लोके स्योनं ते सह पत्या कृणोमि ॥

In *Baudhāyana Gṛhya-Sūtra*, the verse is:

प्रेतो मुञ्चाति नामुतस्सुबद्धाममुतस्करत् ।
यथेयमिन्द्रमीढ्वस्सुपुत्रा सुभगा सती ॥

In *Vārāha Gṛhya-Sūtra,* the verse is:

प्र त्वा मुञ्चातु वरुणस्य पाशाद्येन त्वाबध्नात्सविता सुशेवः ।
धातुश्च योनौ सुकृतस्य लोके हृष्टा सँ सह पात्या भूयासम् ॥

In *Kāṭhaka Gṛhya-Sūtra,* the verse is:

प्रेतो मुञ्चातु मामुतः सुबद्धाममृतस्करम् ।
यथेयमिंद्र मीढ्वः सुपुत्रा सुभगासति ॥

१८. एकमिषे विष्णुस्त्वान्वेतु । द्वे ऊर्जे विष्णुस्त्वान्वेतु । त्रीणि व्रताय विष्णुस्तान्वेतु । चत्वारि मायोभवाय विष्णुस्तान्वेतु । पञ्च पशुभ्यो विष्णुस्तान्वेतु । षड्रायस्पोषाय विष्णुस्तान्वेतु । सप्त सप्तभ्यो होत्राभ्यो विष्णुस्तान्वेतु । सखा सप्तपदा भव सखायौ सप्तपदा बभूव ॥

In *Aśvalayana* and *Śāṅkhāyana Gṛhya-Sūtra,* the verse is:

इष एकपद्यूर्जे द्विपदी रायस्पोषाय त्रिपदी मायोभव्याय चतुष्पदी प्रजाभ्यः पञ्चपद्यृतुभ्यः षट्पदी सखा सप्तपदी भव सा मामनुव्रता भव । पुत्रान्विन्दावहै बहूँस्ते सन्तु जरदष्टयः ॥

In *Kauṣītaki Gṛhya-Sūtra,* the verse is:

इष एकपदी । विष्णुस्त्वा नयतु । ऊर्जे द्विपदी । विष्णुस्त्वा नयतु । रायस्पोषाय त्रिपदी । विष्णुस्त्वा नयतु । मायो भव्याय चतुष्पदी । विष्णुस्त्वा नयतु । प्रजाभ्यः पञ्चपदी । विष्णुस्त्वा नयतु । विष्णुस्त्वा नयतु । ऋतुभ्यः षट्पदी । विष्णुस्त्वा नयतु । "सखा सप्तपदी भव" इति । विष्णुस्त्वा नयतु ॥

In *Pāraskara Gṛhya-Sūtra,* the verse is:

एकमिषे विष्णुस्त्वान्नयतु । द्वे ऊर्जे विष्णुस्त्वान्नयतु । त्रीणि रायस्पोषाय विष्णुस्त्वान्नयतु । चत्वारि मायोभवाय विष्णुस्त्वान्नयतु । पञ्च पशुभ्यः विष्णुस्त्वान्नयतु । षड् ऋतुभ्यः विष्णुस्त्वान्नयतु । सखे सप्तपदा भव सा मामनुव्रता भव ॥

In *Āpastamba Gṛhya-Sūtra,* the verse is:

एकमिषे विष्णुस्त्वान्वेतु । द्वे ऊर्जे विष्णुस्त्वान्वेतु । त्रीणि व्रताय विष्णुस्तान्वेतु । चत्वारि मायोभवाय विष्णुस्तान्वेतु । पञ्च पशुभ्यो विष्णुस्तान्वेतु । षड्तुभ्यो विष्णुस्तान्वेतु । सप्त सप्तभ्यो होत्राभ्यो विष्णुस्तान्वेतु । सखा सप्तपदा भव सखायौ सप्तपदा बभूव । सख्यं ते गमेयँ सख्यात्ते मा योषं सख्यान्मे मा योष्ठाः । समयाव सं कल्पावहै संप्रियौ रोचिष्णू
सुमनस्यमानौ । इषमूर्जमभि संवसानौ । सं नो मनाँसि सं व्रता समु चित्तान्या करम् ॥

In *Hiraṇyakeśi Gṛhya-Sūtra*, the verse is:

एकमिषे विष्णुस्त्वान्वेतु । द्वे ऊर्जे विष्णुस्त्वान्वेतु । त्रीणि व्रताय विष्णुस्तान्वेतु । चत्वारि मायोभवाय विष्णुस्तान्वेतु । पञ्च पशुभ्यो विष्णुस्तान्वेतु । षड्रायस्पोषाय विष्णुस्तान्वेतु । सप्त सप्तभ्यो होत्राभ्यो विष्णुस्तान्वेतु ॥ सखायौ सप्तपदाबभूव सख्यं ते गमेयं सख्यात्रे मा योषं सख्यान्मे मा योष्ठाः ॥

In *Baudhāyana Gṛhya-Sūtra*, the verse is:

एकमिषे विष्णुस्त्वाऽन्वेतु । द्वे ऊर्जे विष्णुस्त्वाऽन्वेतु । त्रीणि व्रताय विष्णुस्त्वाऽन्वेतु । चत्वारि मायोभवाय विष्णुस्त्वाऽन्वेतु । पञ्च पशुभ्यो विष्णुस्त्वाऽन्वेतु । षड्रायस्पोषाय विष्णुस्त्वाऽन्वेतु । सप्त सप्तभ्यो होत्राभ्यो विष्णुस्त्वाऽन्वेतु ॥ सखायस्सप्तपदा अभुम सव्यं ते गमेयं सख्याते मा योषं मा योष्ठाः ॥

In *Vārāha Gṛhya-Sūtra*, the verse is:

एकमिषे विष्णुस्त्वां नयतु । द्वे ऊर्जे । त्रीणि रायस्पोषाय । चत्वारि मायोभवाय । पञ्च प्रजाभ्यः । षड्तुभ्यः । सप्त सप्तभ्यो होत्राभ्यः ॥ सखी सप्तपदी भव सख्यं ते गमेयँ सख्यात्ते मा रिषिम् ॥

In *Mānava Gṛhya-Sūtra*, the verse is:

एकमिषे द्वे ऊर्जे त्रीणि प्रजाभ्यश्चत्वारि रायस्पोषाय पञ्च भवाय षड्तुभ्यः । सखा सप्तदीभव सुमृडीका सरस्वती । सा ते व्योम संदृशी । विष्णुस्त्वा मुन्नयत्विति सर्वत्रानुषजति ॥

In *Agniveśya Gṛhya-Sūtra*, the verse is:

एकमिषे विष्णुस्त्वान्वेतु द्वे ऊर्जे विष्णुस्त्वान्वेतु त्रीणि व्रताय विष्णुस्त्वान्वेतु चत्वारि मायोभवाय विष्णुस्त्वान्वेतु पञ्च पशुभ्यो विष्णुस्त्वान्वेतु षड् रायस्पोषाय विष्णुस्त्वान्वेतु सप्त सप्तभ्यो होत्राभ्यो विष्णुस्त्वान्वेतु । सखायौ सप्तपदाबभूव सख्यं ते गमेयं सख्यात्ते मा योषं सख्यान्मे मा योष्ठाः ॥

In *Bhāradvāja Gṛhya-Sūtra*, the verse is:

एकमिषे विष्णुस्त्वान्वेतु द्वे ऊर्जे विष्णुस्त्वान्वेतु त्रीणि व्रताय विष्णुस्त्वान्वेतु चत्वारि मायोभवाय विष्णुस्त्वान्वेतु पञ्च पशुभ्यो विष्णुस्त्वान्वेतु षड्रायस्पोषाय विष्णुस्त्वान्वेतु सप्त सप्तभ्यो होत्राभ्यो विष्णुस्त्वान्वेतु ॥ सखा सप्तपदा भव सखायौ सप्तपदाबभूव । सख्यं ते गमेयं सख्यात्ते मा योषं सख्यान्मे मायोष्ठा ॥

In *Kāṭhaka Gṛhya-Sūtra*, the verse is:

एकमिषे द्वे ऊर्जे त्रीणि रायस्पोषाय चत्वारि मयोभवाय पञ्च प्रजाभ्यः षड्तुभ्यो दीर्घायुत्वाय सप्तमं सखा सप्तपदा भव । सुमृडीका सरस्वति मा ते व्योम सन्दृशि ॥ विष्णुस्त्वान्वेत्यनुषङ्गः ॥

In *Vaikhānasa Gṛhya-Sūtra*, the verse is:

एकमिषे विष्णुरिति द्वे ऊर्जे इति त्रीणि व्रतायेति चत्वारिति पञ्च पशुभ्य इति षड्रायस्पोषायेति सप्त सप्तभ्य इति तान्पर्यायेणाक्रम्य गत्वा सखेति निवर्तेत ॥

In *Gobhila* and *Khādira Gṛhya-Sūtra*, the verse is:

एकं इषे विष्णुस्त्वा नयतु । द्वे ऊर्जे विष्णुस्त्वा नयतु । त्रीणि व्रताय विष्णुस्त्वा नयतु । चत्वारि मायोभवाय विष्णुस्त्वा नयतु । पञ्च पशुभ्यो विष्णुस्त्वा नयतु । षड्रायस्पोषाय विष्णुस्त्वा नयतु । सप्त सप्तभ्यो होत्राभ्यो विष्णुस्त्वा नयतु । सखा सप्तपदी भव सख्यं ते गमेयँ सख्यं ते मा योषाः सख्यं ते मा योष्ठाः ॥

In *Jaimini Gṛhya-Sūtra*, the verse is:

एकमिषे विष्णुस्त्वान्वेतु । द्वे ऊर्जे विष्णुस्त्वान्वेतु । त्रीणि रायस्पोषाय विष्णुस्त्वान्वेतु । चत्वारि मयोभवाय विष्णुस्त्वान्वेतु । पञ्च प्रजाभ्यो विष्णुस्त्वान्वेतु । षड्तुभ्यो विष्णुस्त्वान्वेतु । सखा सप्तपदी भव ॥

In *Kauśika Gṛhya-Sūtra*, the verse is:

सप्तमर्यादाः कवयस्ततक्षुस्तासामिदेकामभ्यं हुरो गात् । आयोर्ह स्कम्भ उपमस्य नीडे पथां विसर्गे धरुणेषु तस्थौ ॥ इषे त्वा सुमङ्गलि प्रजावति सुसीम । ऊर्जे त्वा रायस्पोषाय त्वा सौभाग्याय त्वा साम्राज्याय त्वा संपदे त्वा जीवातवे त्वा सुमङ्गलि प्रजावति सुसीम इति सप्तमं सखा सप्तपदी भव ॥

१९. इह गावो निषिदन्त्विहाश्वा इह पूरुषाः ।
इहो सहस्रदक्षिणो यज्ञ इह पूषा निषीदतु ॥

In *Āpastamba* and *Baudhāyana Gṛhya-Sūtra*, the verse is:

इह गावः प्र जायध्वमिहाश्वा इह पुरुषाः ।
इहो सहस्रदक्षिणो रायस्पोषो निषीदतु ॥

In *Agniveśya Gṛhya-Sūtra*, the verse is:

इह गावो निषीदन्त्विहाश्वा इह पुरुषाः ।
इहो सहस्रदक्षिणो अधिपूषा निषीदतु ॥

In *Bhāradvāja Gṛhya-Sūtra*, the verse is:

इह गावो निषीदन्त्विहाश्वा इह पुरुषाः ।
इहो सहस्रदक्षिणोऽभि पूषा निषीदत्व ॥

In *Vaikhānasa Gṛhya-Sūtra*, the verse is:

इह गावो निषीदन्त्वहाश्वा इह पुरुषाः ।
इहो सहस्रदक्षिणो अपि पूषा निषीदतु ॥

In *Gobhila, Khādira* and *Jaimini Gṛhya-Sūtra*, the verse is:

इह गावः प्रजायध्वमिहाश्वा इह पूरूषाः ।
इहो सहस्रदक्षिणोऽपि पूषा निषीदतु ॥

२०. इमां त्वमिन्द्र मीढ्वस्सुपुत्रां सुभगां कृणु ।
दशास्यां पुत्रानाधेहि पतिमेकादशं कृधि ॥

In *Āśvalāyana Gṛhya-Sūtra*, the verse is:

इमां त्वमिन्द्र मीढ्वस्सुपुत्रां सुभगां कुरु ।
दशाभ्यां पुत्रानाधेहि पतिमेकादशं कृधि ॥

२१. ध्रुवैधि पोष्या मयि मह्यं त्वादाद्बृहस्पतिः ।
मया पत्या प्रजावती सं जीव शरद शतम् ॥

In *Pāraskara Gṛhya-Sūtra*, the verse is:

ध्रुवमसि ध्रुवं त्वा पश्यामि ध्रुवैधि पोष्ये मयि ।
मह्यं त्वाऽदाद् बृहस्पतिर्मया पत्या प्रजावती संजीव शरदः शतम् ॥

In *Āpastamba, Hiraṇyakeśi, Baudhāyana, Bhāradvāja* and *Vaikhānasa Gṛhya-Sūtra*, the verse is:

ध्रुवक्षितिर्ध्रुवयोनिर्ध्रुवमसि ध्रुवत स्थितम् ।
त्वं नक्षत्राणां मेथ्यसि स मा पाहि पृतन्यतः ॥

In *Vārāha* and *Mānava Gṛhya-Sūtra*, the verse is:

अच्युता ध्रुवा ध्रुवपत्नी ध्रुवं पश्येम सर्वतः ।
ध्रुवासः पर्वता इमे ध्रुवा स्त्री पतिकुलेयम् ॥

In *Agniveśya Gṛhya-Sūtra*, the verse is:

ध्रुवं नमस्यामि मनसा ध्रुवेण ध्रुवं नो सख्यं दीर्घमायुश्च भुयात् ।
अद्रुग्धावस्मिंश्च परे च लोके ध्रुवं प्रविष्टौ स्याम शरणं सुखातौ ।
शन्न एधि द्विपदे शं चतुष्पदे ॥

In *Gobhila, Khādira* and *Jaimini Gṛhya-Sūtra*, the verse is:

ध्रुवा द्योर्ध्रुवा पृथिवी ध्रुवं विश्वमिदं जगत् ।
ध्रुवासः पर्वता इमे ध्रुवा स्त्री पतिकुले इयम् ॥

9

Summary

IT becomes clear from the study that *vivāha* (marriage) was a highly ritualistic ceremony. Marriage was considered to be a religious duty for fulfilling the requirements of *gr̥hasthāśrama*. Marriages involved the families of the bride and the groom and generally were arranged keeping in mind the caste, *gotra*, qualities of the bride and groom in mind. While specifying the qualities of the bride, rituals were also used to select the bride. There was recognition of the social realities of the times in that classification of different types of marriages was required to be established. Gr̥hya-Sūtras specified eight different forms of marriage. Auspicious times were prescribed for conducting the marriage, with certain periods declared unsuitable. Recognition of existing traditions and customs in each area was considered important. In fact, in *Āpastamba Gr̥hya-Sūtra*, one is requested to take the opininon of the old ladies of the locality to learn about the customs and traditions of that area. There were differences among the followers of various branches of the four Vedas though the underlying rituals were very similar.

Beginning with sending negotiators to the house of the bride, the rituals mainly consisted of selection of the bride, fixing an auspicious time, *vagdana, madhuparka* reception to the bridegroom, setting up the *maṇḍapa*, bathing and dressing up of the bride, *ājya homas*, *pāṇigrahaṇa*, *aśmārohaṇa*, *agni pariṇayana*, *saptapadī*, *lājā homa*, journey to the husband's home, *gr̥ha-praveśa*, fertility rites, *trirātra vrata, caturthī karma* and consummation of the marriage. Other rituals such as *mekhalā bandhana*, *mūrdhābhiṣeka, hṛdaya-sparśa,* etc. were included in some of the Gṛhya-Sūtras.

It was the practice of the times to conduct each ceremony by invoking the blessings of gods through *homa*s and by offering sacrifices. Specifications were laid down for conducting every part of the ceremony with materials to be used, the cardinal directions, etc. minutely detailed. Water and fire were essential parts of the ceremonies. Importance of bathing as means of purification was stressed. Types of grass, wood, offerings, etc. to be used were specified. Wearing of fresh clothes was emphasized.

The *mantra*s used at each section were highly significant. Gods were invoked to make the marriage a success so that the couple would live happily for hundred autumns blessed with valiant sons, wealth and health. *Mantra*s also urged that evil forces be destroyed. The bride was considered to be a gift of the gods in order that the groom would become a house holder and live up to old age with her. She was required to be his companion in performing religious duties in *gṛhasthāśrama.* The fire started at the wedding was expected to be carried home and used for performing rituals in their life. *Mantra*s were recited to seek blessings for the coming together of the two minds and hearts and to live in concord as a couple. At the end of *saptapadī,* the groom requests her to be his friend for life. The bride performs *lājā homa* for the longevity of her husband's life. The journey to the husband's home is carried out reciting various *mantra*s to ward off evil, overcome obstacles. Passersby are requested to bless the couple. Fertility rites such as making her sit on a bull's hide and placing a boy in her lap were carried out. Consummation of the marriage was carried out after observing *trirātra vrata* and conducting *caturthī karma* during which expiation offerings were made.

The rituals became more and more complex as time went by and divisions of branches took place. From the simple rituals mentioned in *Ṛgveda*, there were changes mentioned in *Atharvaveda*. Each branch of the four Vedas, though following the original rituals, added on more and more rituals. Sociological and geographical influences resulted in additions, modifications and changes in the order of rituals. It appears that traditions and customs changed from place to place and this reflected in the contents of the Gṛhya-Sūtras. It is also possible that the Sūtras were interpreted differently by different commentary writers resulting in divergence.

Other Sources for References on Vivāha

Pariśiṣṭas, *prayogas*, *paddhatis* and *kārikās* were written by various authors based on Gṛhya-Sūtras. These explained Sūtras with reference to the contexts and practices prevailing in their geographical locations. Many of the Gṛhya-Sūtras have more than one commentary writer. In fact, it is difficult to understand the rituals as mentioned in Gṛhya-Sūtras without the help of these supplementary texts.

Apart from Gṛhya-Sūtras which deal with *smārta saṁskāras* in detail, the marriage ceremony has been mentioned in Śrauta-Sūtras, Dharma-Sūtras, Smṛtis, Purāṇas, *Mahābhārata*, *Rāmāyaṇa*, Kāvyas, Nāṭakas, *Kāma-Sūtra*, etc. Śrauta-Sūtras contain some of the rituals adopted for Smārta-Sūtras such as *vivāha saṁskāra*. Dharma-Sūtras which closely followed Gṛhya-Sūtras refer to the marriage ceremony. Smṛtis which were written in a period subsequent to that of Gṛhya-Sūtras, made further additions and modifications. Smṛtis brought in many changes to the *vivāha* rituals as they dealt more with social (*smārta*) aspects of *saṁskāras* rather than the Vedic (*śrauta*) aspects. Manu, Yājñavalkya, Parāśara and others have dealt with marriage rituals in detail in their Smṛtis. It appears that child marriages which were not mentioned in Gṛhya-Sūtras, began to be observed during and after the Smṛti period. Purāṇas describe marriages of various gods and goddesses.

Mahābhārata describes the various marriages of Kṛṣṇa and marriages of other characters such as Arjuna. *Rāmāyaṇa* describes the *svayaṁvara* of Sītā with Rāma. *Kāma-Sūtra* of Vātsyāyana describes the marriage ceremony in detail.

Kālidāsa's *Abhijñāna-Śākuntalam* describes the Gāndharva form of marriage of Śakuntalā with Duṣyanta. His *Raghuvaṁśa* also describes the various steps which form part of the marriage ceremony. Marriages of Nala with Damayantī and other famous literary personalities are found in Kāvyas and Nāṭakas. *Mitākṣarā*, a commentary on *Yājñavalkya Smṛti* written by Vijñāneśvara and considered to be authoritative on law contains much material on marriage. Medhātithi, a commentator on *Manu Smṛti* also refers to *vivāha saṁskāra* in his work. Similarly, *Dāyabhāga*, a law book written by Jīmūtavāhana refers to the question of inheritance after marriage.

Saṁskāra Ratnamālā and *Saṁskāra Prakāśa* describe *vivāha saṁskāra* in detail along with other *saṁskāras*. These are based on particular Gṛhya-Sūtras. *Satyārtha Prakāśa* of Dayananda Sarasvati gives a modified and simplified version of the marriage ceremony.

Importance of Commentaries

As mentioned earlier, Gṛhya-Sūtras like all Kalpa-Sūtras are in the form of aphorisms, perhaps to facilitate memorizing them easily. It is difficult to comprehend all that was meant to be conveyed in the Sūtras by reading them and grammatically analysing them. It becomes important to understand the contexts under which the Sūtras were written. The role of commentaries, therefore, becomes extremely important in getting at and understanding the rituals referred to in the Sūtras in a comprehensive manner. All the Gṛhya-Sūtras have commentaries written on them, sometimes by more than one commentator. The commentators, with the knowledge of the social, scriptural and traditional background of the rituals were in a position to expand and explain the Sūtras as they were meant to be.

The following is a list of Gṛhya-Sūtras and their commentators:

Gṛhya-Sūtras	*Commentary Writers*
Āśvalāyana	Devatrāta Devasvāmin and Naidhruva Nārāyaṇa. *Pariśiṣṭa* and *Kārikā* by Kumārila Bhaṭṭa
Śāṅkhāyana	Nārāyaṇa, *paddhati* by Rāmacandra; *saṁgraha* by Vāsudeva
Kauṣītaki	Bhavatrāta
Pāraskara	Harihara, Gadādhara and Jayarāma
Āpastamba	Haradatta, Sudarśanācārya and Kapardisvāmin
Hiraṇyakeśin	Matridatta
Baudhāyana	Bhāvasvāmi and Govindasvāmi (Dharma-Sūtra)
Vārāha	*Paddhatis* by Gaṅgādhara and Vasiṣṭha
Mānava	Aṣṭāvakra
Agniveśya	Not known
Bhāradvāja	Not known
Kāṭhaka	Devapāla
Vaikhānasa	Mahādeva
Gobhila	Bhatta Nārayaṇa
Khādira	Rudraskanda
Jaimini	Śrīnivāsa
Kauśika	Dārila, *paddhati* by Keśava

Based on the commentaries, *prayogas*, *paddhatis*, *kārikās*, etc. were written which detailed the various steps to be taken in conducting the rituals. Supplementary rituals such as Gaṇapati-Pūjā, Nāndī-Śrāddha, Navagraha-Pūjā, Puṇyāha-Vācana, etc. were also elaborated in these texts.

Further Evolution from Gṛhya-Sūtras

As time went by, changes took place in the way the marriage ceremony was conducted. Sociological and geographical factors brought in changes which varied from region to region. Some of the original rituals were abandoned and others were added. Some of the features that form part of marriages these days are as under.

BĀRĀT AND JANAVĀSAM

The bridegroom arrives on a horse with a band of musicians playing songs. This is common in north Indian communities. Janavāsam or Vara-Pūjā practised in south Indian communities features the bridegroom being taken around in a decorated car to the marriage venue.

KĀŚĪ YĀTRĀ

The bridegroom after the completion of Vedic studies, says he wishes to go to Vārāṇasī to interact with the scholars there. He is prevented from going there by the father of the bride who offers the hand of his daughter in marriage. The bridegroom is expected to carry an umbrella, walking stick, etc. during this essentially social, fun-filled ritual.

OOÑJAL (SWING)

Popular in Tamil Nadu, this ritual has the bride and the groom sitting on a decorated swing and *sumaṅgalī* women warding off the evil eye falling on them. This ritual is performed before the main ceremony.

ANTARPAṬA

This is part of the *paraspara samīkṣaṇam* where the bride and the groom stand opposite each other with a cloth separating them. The cloth is removed at the appropriate time and the couple pour *akṣata* over each other's head. In some communities, the bride is brought in a basket by her maternal uncle before this event.

MĀṄGALYA DHĀRAṆA

This ritual is not mentioned in any of the Gṛhya-Sūtras and is supposed to have been adopted from tribal customs. A *thāli* (yellow string) is tied by the groom around the neck of the bride with three knots saying that he is tying it for good fortune and long life with the bride. This ritual is considered extremely important especially in south India and the *thāli* has become a symbol of marriage.

There are many other rituals added on in various regions. A lot of singing and dancing goes on in north Indian marriages. Some of the features are also being abandoned. With the improvement in transport, the journey to the bridegroom's house has become less hazardous and many of the *mantra*s to be recited during the journey have been given up. With social norms changing, rituals such as *trirātra vrata* and *caturthī karma* are also being abandoned.

However, the basic rituals as elaborated in the Gṛhya-Sūtras are still being practised wherever Hindu weddings are being conducted.

Conclusion

AT the end, I would like to state that it has been a very rewarding experience to collect material, study the contents and arrive at the stage of concluding the book. When I began the project, I had no idea of the effort needed to bring together original texts and translations available on the subject. I was also unaware of the relevance of the texts in understanding the social and historical aspects of the way ancient Hindus lived. It has been a gratifying experience to delve into works such as Gṛhya-Sūtras which are indeed a valuable source in understanding the society and its value systems of the people in Vedic India.

The material of Gṛhya-Sūtras has been researched and edited by eminent scholars, both Indian and Western from available palm-leaf manuscripts in a number of languages such as Sanskrit written in different scripts, Grantha, Telugu, Malayalam and others. Scholars have studied the various manuscripts available on each Gṛhya-Sūtra, corrected mistakes by comparison and scholarship and have brought out critical editions. Supplementary texts such as commentaries, *prayogas*, *paddhatis*, *pariśiṣṭas*, *saṁgrahas*, *kārikās*, etc. have been studied in detail. Translations have been brought out in German, French, English and in various Indian languages. The various Oriental Research Institutes and other committed organizations in India are carrying out remarkable work in preserving the manuscripts and the heritage they represent.

It is evident that rituals played an important part in the

lives of people of the Vedic age. A highly-evolved system of concepts and practices guided people to live life in a disciplined manner. The importance of the *āśramas* and *puruṣārthas* cannot be overemphasized. The concept of *āśramas* recognized the practical and spiritual aspects of a person's life and the concept of *puruṣārthas* set the moral standard for living it. Accepting the fallible nature of humans and the existence of superhuman entities both good and evil, practices were evolved to seek benefits as well as ward off evil occurrences at every stage in a person's life. *Saṁskāras* showed the way to lead a life according to these practices in a detailed manner.

Vedas are considered to be the source of all spiritual and ethical concepts. The concept of Vedas being *apauruṣeya* and *anādi* lent a religious and spiritual authority to the practices that emerged out of the Vedas. *Vivāha saṁskāra* was considered the most important of the *smārta saṁskāras*. Marriage was considered to be a religious duty and not just fulfilment of biological needs. It is remarkable that elaborate rituals to be practised evolved with the underlying stress on *dharma* (righteousness) based on the Vedas. Every aspect of *vivāha saṁskāra* has been considered and rituals are prescribed for it. The main purpose of the rituals appear to be to seek a happy marriage blessed with longevity, good children, wealth, health and fulfilment of religious obligations. It is remarkable that the rituals are generally in favour of the bride with the groom expected to adhere to dhārmic practices in order to ensure that she does not suffer. There is no indication of subjugation of the wife to the husband or vice versa. It is emphasized that they are equals and friends for life with no suggestion of one dominating the other. The rituals also seek the destruction of evil forces so that untimely death does not occur.

Every aspect of the marriage ceremony has been dealt with in the Gṛhya-Sūtras. From the negotiations to agree upon an alliance, qualities of the bride and the groom, the reception to the groom, the purification ceremony, wearing of new clothes, travel to entering the husband's home, etc. are described in detail. The main rituals to ensure the success of the marriage such as *pāṇigrahaṇa*, *aśmārohaṇa*, *saptapadī*, *lājā homa*, *agni pariṇayana*, *vivāha homa*s are detailed in all the Gṛhya-Sūtras. *Gṛha-praveśa*, Dhruva–Arundhatī *darśana*, fertility rites, *tri-rātra vrata*, expiation rites, *caturthī karma* and the consummation of marriage are elaborately dealt with.

One can conclude that society was well developed during the Vedic age with ethics, religious practices and disciplined living having been laid down for people to follow. Apart from evolving rituals based on dhārmic values, people also realized that there was a force guiding human life and that they were not entirely in charge of their destinies. While religion entreated each person to achieve perfection, offerings and sacrifices also were recommended to propitiate gods to achieve worldly ends.

The highly meaningful *mantra*s used in the marriage ceremony testify the values placed on family life, togetherness, importance of children and leading a life of longevity, responsibility and religious activities. It is indeed the values behind the rituals that have ensured their survival over centuries. The basic rituals are observed even today all over India during the Hindu marriage ceremony.

Appendix A

Vivāha Mantras as Depicted in Gṛhya-Sūtras

VIVĀHA *mantras* as they have been depicted in Gṛhya-Sūtras are listed hereunder. Some of the Gṛhya-Sūtras include the entire *mantra* whereas others give just the beginning words. *Mantras* have been shown in their entirety in this section. Differences can be seen in many of the *mantras* in the different texts. *Mantras* have been in the order of their appearance with chapter and section markings for easy reference. Only those *mantras* which find reference in the Gṛhya-Sūtra texts have been included.

आश्वलायन गृह्यसूत्र विवाह मन्त्राः

१.४.४. अग्न आयूंषि पवस आ सुवोर्जमिषं च नः । आ रे बाधस्व दुच्छुताम् ॥
अग्निऋर्षिः पवमानः पाञ्चजन्य पुरोहितः । तमीमहे महागयम् ॥
अग्ने पवस्व स्वपा अस्मे वर्चः सुवीर्यम् । दधद्रयिं मयि पोषम् ॥

१.४.७. त्वमर्यमा भवसि यत्कनीनां नाम स्वधावन्गुह्यं बिर्भषि ।
अञ्जन्ति मित्रं सुधितं न गोभिर्यद्दम्पती समनसा कृणोषि ॥

१.५.५. ऋतमग्रे प्रथमं जज्ञे ऋते सत्यं प्रतिष्ठितम् ।
यदियं कुमार्यभिजाता तदियमिह प्रतिपद्यतां यत् सत्यं तद् दृश्यताम् ॥

१.७.३. गृभ्णामि ते सौभगत्वाय हस्तं मया पत्या जरदष्टिर्यथासः ।
भगो अर्यमा सविता पुरंधिर्मह्यं त्वादुर्गार्हपत्याय देवाः ॥

१.७.६. अमोऽहमस्मि सा त्वं सा त्वमस्यमोऽहम् ।
द्योरहं पृथिवी त्वं सामाहमृक्त्वं तावेहि विवहावहै ।
प्रजां प्रजनयावहै संप्रियौ रोचिष्णू सुमनस्यमानौ जीवेव शरदः शतम् ॥

१.७.७. आरोहाश्मेव त्वं स्थिरा भव ।
सहस्व पृतनायतोऽभितिष्ठ पृतन्यतः ॥

१.७.८. इयं नार्युपब्रूतेऽग्नौ लाजानावपन्तिका ।
दीर्घायुरस्तु मे पतिर्जीवातु शरदश्शतम् ॥

१.७.१३. अर्यमणं नु देवं कन्या अग्निमयक्षत ।
स इमां देवोऽर्यमा प्रेतो मुञ्चातु नामुतः स्वाहा ॥

वरुणं नु देवं कन्या अग्निमयक्षत ।
स इमां देवोऽर्यमा प्रेतो मुञ्चातु नामुतः स्वाहा ॥

पूषणं नु देवं कन्या अग्निमयक्षत ।
स इमां देवोऽर्यमा प्रेतो मुञ्चातु नामुतः स्वाहा ॥

१.७.१७. प्र त्वा मुञ्चामि वरुणस्य पाशाद् येन त्वाबध्नात् सविता सुशेवः ।
ऋतस्य योनौ सुकृतस्य लोकेऽरिष्टां त्वा सह पत्या दधामि ॥

१.७.१९. इष एकपद्यूर्जे द्विपदी रायस्पोषाय त्रिपदी मायोभव्याय चतुष्पदी प्रजाभ्यः पञ्चपद्यृतुभ्यः षट्पदी सखा सप्तपदी भव सा मामनुव्रता भव । पुत्रान्विन्दावहै बहूँस्ते सन्तु जरदष्टयः ॥

१.७.२२. ध्रुवं पश्यामि प्रजां विन्देय ॥ जीवपत्नीं प्रजां विन्देय ॥

१.८.१. पूषा त्वेतो नयतु हस्तगृह्याश्विना त्वा प्रवहतां रथेन ।
गृहान् गच्छ गृहपत्नी यथासो वशिनी त्वं विदथमा वदासि ॥

१.८.२. अश्मन्वती रीयते सं रभध्वमुतिष्ठत प्र तरता सखायः ।
अत्रा जहाम ये असन्शेवाः शिवान् वयमुत्तरेमभि वाजान् ॥

१.८.४. जीवां रुदन्ती विमयन्तो अध्वरे दीर्घामनुप्रसितिं दीधियुर्नरः ।
वामं पितृभ्यो य इदं समेरिरे मयः पतिभ्यो जनयः परिष्वज ॥

१.८.६. मा विदन्परिपन्थिनो य आसीदन्ति दम्पती ।
सुगेभिर्दुर्गमतीतामप द्रान्त्वरातयः ॥

१.८.७. सुमङ्गलीरियं वधूरिमां समेत पश्यत ।
सौभाग्यमस्यै दत्वायाथास्तं विपरेतन ॥

१.८.८. इह प्रियं प्रजया ते समृध्यतामस्मिन् गृहे गार्हपत्याय जागृहि ।
एना पत्या तन्वं सं सृजस्वाधा जिव्री विदथमा वदाथः ॥

१.८.९. आ नः प्रजां जनयतु प्रजापतिराजरसाय समनक्त्वर्यमा ।
अदुर्मङ्गलीः पतिलोकमा विश शं नो भव द्विपदे शं चतुष्पदे ॥

अघोरचक्षुरपतिघ्न्ये धि शिवा पशुभ्यः सुमना सुवर्चाः ।
वीरसूर्देवकामा स्योना शं नो भव द्विपदे शं चतुष्पदे ॥

इमां त्वमिन्द्र मीढ्वस्सुपुत्रां सुभगां कुरु ।
दशाभ्यां पुत्रानाधेहि पतिमेकादशं कृधि ॥

सम्राज्ञी श्वशुरे भव सम्राज्ञी श्वश्र्वां भव ।
ननान्दरि सम्राज्ञी भव सम्राज्ञी अधि देवृषु ॥

समञ्जन्तु विश्वे देवाः समापो हृदयानि नौ ।
सं मातरिश्वा सं धाता समु देष्ट्री दधातु नौ ॥

शाङ्खायन गृह्यसूत्र विवाह मन्त्राः

१.६.१. अनृक्षरा ऋजवः सन्तु पन्था येभिः सखायो यन्ति नो वरेयम् ।
समर्यमा सम्भगो नो निनीयात् सं जास्पत्यं सुयममस्तु देवाः ॥

१.६.५. अनाधृष्टमस्यानाधृष्टय देवानामोजाऽनभिशस्त्यभिशस्तिपा
अनभिशस्तेयमञ्जसा सत्यमुपगेषं सुविते मा धा ॥

१.५.६. आ नः प्रजां जनयतु प्रजापतिराजरसाय समनक्त्वर्यमा ।
अदुर्मङ्गलीः पतिलोकमा विश शं नो भव द्विपदे शं चतुष्पदे ॥
प्रजां त्वयि दधामि, पशूँस्त्वयि दधामि, तेजो ब्रह्मवर्चसं त्वयि दधामि ॥

१.७.९. अग्निं प्रणयामि मनसा शिवेनायमस्तु संगमतो बहूनाम् ।
मा नो हिंसीः स्थविरं मा कुमारं शं नो भव द्विपदे शं चतुष्पदे ॥

१.८.२१. सवितुष्ठ्वा प्रसव उत्पुनाम्यच्छिद्रेण पवित्रेण वसोः सूर्यस्य रश्मिभिः ॥

१.९.९. अग्निर्जनिता स मेऽमू जायां ददातु स्वाहा ॥ सोमो जनिमान्त्स माऽमुया जनिमन्तं करोतु स्वाहा ॥ पूषा ज्ञातिमानन्त्स माऽमुष्यै पित्रा मात्रा भ्रातृभिर्ज्ञातिमन्तं करोतु स्वाहा ॥

१.१०.७. हुतोऽग्निहोत्रहोमेनाऽहुतो बलिकर्मणा ।
प्रहुतः पितृकर्मणा प्राशीतो ब्राह्मणे हुतः ॥

१.१०.८. अनूर्ध्वज्ञु व्यूळजानुर्जुहुयात् सर्वदा हविः ।
न हि बाह्यहुतं देवाः प्रतिगृह्णन्ति कर्हिचित् ॥

१.१०.९. रौद्रं तु राक्षसं पित्र्यमासुरं चाऽऽभिचारिकम् ।
उक्त्वा मन्त्रं स्पृशेदप आलभ्यात्मानमेव च ॥

१.१२.३. रैभ्यासीदनुदेयी नाराशंसी न्योचनी ।
सूर्याय भद्रमिद्वासो गाथयैति परिष्कृतम् ॥

१.१२.४. चित्तिर उपब्रह्मणं चक्षुरा अभ्यञ्जनम् ।
द्यौर्भूमिः कोश आसीद् यदायात् सूर्या पतिम् ॥

१.१२.५. समञ्जन्तु विश्वे देवाः समापो हृदयानि नौ ।
सं मातरिश्वा सं धाता समु देष्ट्री दधातु नौ ॥

१.१२.६. यथेय शचीं वावातां सुपुत्रां च यथाऽदितिं ।
अविधवां चापालामेवं त्वामिह रक्षातादिममि ॥

१.१२.७. रूपं रूपं प्रतिरूपो बभूव तदस्य रूपं प्रतिचक्षणाय ।
इन्द्रो मायाभिः पुरुरूप ईयते युक्ता ह्यस्य हरयः शता दश ॥

१.१२.८. नीललोहितं भवति कृत्यासक्तिर्व्यज्यते ।
एधन्ते अस्या ज्ञातयः पतिर्बन्धेषु बध्यते ॥

१.१२.९. मधुमतीरोषधीर्द्याव आपो मधुमन्नो भवत्वन्तरिक्षम् ।
क्षेत्रस्य पतिर्मधुमान् नो अस्त्वरिष्यन्तो अन्वेनं चरेम ॥

१.१३.१. सम्राज्ञी श्वशुरे भव सम्राज्ञी श्वश्वां भव ।
ननान्दरि सम्राज्ञी भव सम्राज्ञी अधि देवृषु ॥

१.१३.२. गृभ्णामि ते सौभगत्वाय हस्तं मया पत्या जरदष्टिर्यथासः ।
भगो अर्यमा सविता पुरंधिर्मह्यं त्वादुर्गार्हपत्याय देवाः ॥

१.१३.४. अमोऽहमस्मि सा त्वं सा त्वमस्यमोऽहम् ।
द्यौरहं पृथिवी त्वं सामाहमृक्त्वं तावेहि विवहावहै ।
प्रजां प्रजनयावहै संप्रियौ रोचिष्णू सुमनस्यमानौ जीवेव शरदः शतम् ॥

१.१३.१२. एह्यश्मानमातिष्ठाश्मेव त्वं स्थिरा भव ।
अभि तिष्ठ पृतन्यतः सहस्व पृतनायत ॥

१.१४.१. इयं नार्युपब्रूतेऽग्नौ लाजानावपन्तिका ।
शिवा ज्ञातिभ्यो भूयासं चिरं जीवतु मे पतिः ॥

१.१४.६. इष एकपद्यूर्जे द्विपदी रायस्पोषाय त्रिपदी मायोभव्याय चतुष्पदी प्रजाभ्यः
पञ्चपद्यृतुभ्यः षट्पदी सखा सप्तपदी भव सा मामनुव्रता भव । पुत्रान्विन्दावहै
बहूँस्ते सन्तु जरदष्टयः ॥

१.१४.८. आपो हि ष्ठा मयोभुवस्ता न ऊर्जे दधातन । महे रणाय चक्षसे ॥
यो वः शिवतमो रसस्तस्य भाजयतेह नः । उशतीरिव मातरः ॥
तस्मा अरं गमाम वो यस्य क्षयाय जिन्वथ । आपो जनयथा च नः ॥

१.१५.१. प्र त्वा मुञ्चामि वरुणस्य पाशाद् येन त्वाबध्नात् सविता सुशेवः ।
ऋतस्य योनौ सुकृतस्य लोकेऽरिष्टां त्वा सह पत्या दधामि ॥

१.१५.२. जीवां रुदन्ती विमयन्तो अध्वरे दीर्घामनुप्रसितिं दीधियुर्नरः ।
वामं पितृभ्यो य इदं समेरिरे मयः पतिभ्यो जनयः परिष्वज ॥

१.१५.३. अक्षन्नमीमदन्त ह्यव प्रिया अधूषत ।
अस्तोषत स्वभानवो विप्रा नविष्ठया मती योजा न्विन्द्र ते हरि ॥

१.१५.४. शुची ते चक्रे यात्या व्यानो अक्ष आहतः ।
अनो मनस्मयं सूर्यरोहत्प्रयती पतिम् ॥

द्वे ते चक्रे सूर्ये ब्रह्माण ऋतुथा विदुः ।
अथैकं चक्रं यद्गुहा तदद्धाताय इद्विदुः ॥

१.१५.६. खे रथस्य खेऽनसः खे युगस्य शतक्रतो ।
अपालमिन्द्र त्रिष्पूत्व्यकृणोः सूर्यत्वचम् ॥

१.१५.८. युक्तस्ते अस्तु दक्षिण उत सव्यः शतक्रतो ।
तेन जायामुप प्रियां मन्दानो याह्यन्धसो योजा न्विन्द्र ते हरी ॥
युनज्मि ते ब्रह्मणा केशिना हरी उप प्र याहि दधिषे गभस्त्योः ॥
उत् त्वा सुतासो रभसा अमन्दिषुः पूषण्वान् वज्रिन्त्समु पत्न्यामदः ॥
शुक्रावनड्वाहावास्तां यदयात्सूर्या गृहम् ॥

१.१५.१०. अभि व्ययस्व खदिरस्य सारमोजो धेहि स्पन्दने शिंशपायाम् ।
अक्ष वीडो वीडित वीडयस्व मा यामादस्मादव जीहिपो नः ॥

१.१५.११. त्यं चिदश्वं न वाजिनमरेणवो यमत्नत ।
दृळ्हं ग्रन्थिं न वि ष्यतमत्रिं यविष्ठमा रजः ॥

१.१५.१२. स्वस्ति नो मिमीतामश्विना भगः स्वस्ति देव्यदितदितिरनर्वणः ।
स्वस्ति पूषा असुरो दधातु नह् स्वस्ति द्यावापृथिवी सुचेतुना ॥

स्वस्तये वायुमुप ब्रवामहे सोम स्वस्ति भुवनस्य यस्पतिः ।
ब्रहस्पतिं सर्वगणं स्वस्तये स्वस्तय आदित्यासो भवन्तु नः ॥

विश्वे देवा नो अद्या स्वस्तये वैश्वानरो वसुरग्निः स्वस्तये ।
देवा अवन्त्वृभवः स्वस्तये स्वस्ति नो रुद्रः प्रात्वंहसः ॥

स्वस्ति मित्रवरुणा स्वस्ति पथ्ये रेवति ।
स्वस्ति न इन्द्रश्चाग्निश्च स्वस्ति नो अदिते कृधि ॥

स्वस्ति पन्थमनु चरेम सूर्याचन्द्रमसाविव ।
पुनर्ददताघ्नता जानता सं गमेमहि ॥

१.१५.१३. सुकिँ शुकँ शल्मलिं विश्वरूपँ हिरण्यवर्णँ सुधुरँ सुचक्रम् ।
आरोह सूर्ये अमृतस्य लोकं स्योनं पत्ये वहतुं कृणुष्व ॥

१.१५.१४. मा विदन्परिपन्थिनो य आसीदन्ति दम्पती ।
सुगेभिर्दुर्गमतीतामप द्रान्त्वरातयः ॥

१.१५.१५. ये वध्वश्चन्द्र वहतुं यक्ष्मा यन्ति जनादनु ।
पुनस्तान्यज्ञिया देवा नयन्तु यत आगताः ॥

१.१५.१६. वनस्पते शतवल्शो वि रोह सहस्रवल्शा वि वयं रुहेम ।
यं त्वामयं स्वधितिस्तेजमानः प्रणिनाय महते सौभगाय ॥

१.१५.१७. सुत्रमाणं पृथिवीं द्यामनेहसं सुशर्माणमदितिं सुप्रणीतिम् ।
दैवीं नाविं स्वरित्रामनागसमस्रवन्तीमा रुहेमा स्वस्तये ॥

१.१५.१८. अश्मवन्ती रीयते सं रभध्वमुतिष्ठत प्र तरता सखायः ।
अत्रा जहाम ये असन्नशेवाः शिवान्वयमुत्तरेमाभि वाजान् ॥

१.१५.२०. उद्व ऊर्मिः शम्या हनत्वापो योक्त्राणि मुञ्चत ।
मादुष्कृतौ व्येनसाऽघ्न्यौ शूनमारताम् ॥

१.१५.२२. इह प्रियं प्रजाया ते समृध्यतामस्मिन् गृहे गार्हपत्याय जागृहि ।
एना पत्या तन्वं सं सृजस्वाधा जिव्री विदथमा वदाथः ॥

परा देहि शामुल्ये ब्रह्माभ्यो वि भजा वसु ।
कृत्येषा पद्वती भूत्व्या जाया विशते पतिम् ॥

अश्रिरा तनूर्भवति रुशति पापयामुया ।
पतिर्यद्वध्वो वाससा स्वमङ्गमभिधित्सते ॥

सुमङ्गलीरियं वधूरिमां समेत पश्यत ।
सौभाग्यमस्यै दत्त्वायाथास्तं विपरेतन ॥

१.१६.३. अग्निना देवेन पृथिवीलोकेन लोकानामृग्वेदेन वेदानां त्वा शमयाम्यसौ
स्वाहा । वायुना देवेनान्तरिक्षेण लोकेन लोकानां यजुर्वेदेन वेदानां तेन त्वा
शमयाम्यसौ स्वाहा । सूर्येन देवेन दिवो लोकेन लोकानां सामवेदेन वेदानां
तेन त्वा शमयाम्यसौ स्वाहा । चन्द्रेण देवेन दिशां लोकेन लोकानां ब्रह्मवेदेन
वेदानां तेन त्वा शमयाम्यसौ स्वाहा ॥

१.१६.४. भूर्या ते पतिघ्न्यलक्ष्मी देवरघ्नी जारघ्नी तां करोमि तेऽसौ ॥

१.१६.५. अघोरचक्षुरपतिघ्न्ये धि शिवा पशुभ्यः सुमना सुवर्चाः ।
वीरसूर्देवकामा स्योना शं नो भव द्विपदे शं चतुष्पदे ॥

१.१६.६. कया नश्चित्र आ भुव दूती सदावृधः सखा । कया शचिष्ठया वृता ॥
कस्त्वा सत्यो मदानां मंहिष्ठो मत्सदन्धसः । दृळहा चिदारुजे वसु ॥
अभी षु णः सखीनामविता जरितृणाम् । शतं भवास्यूतिभिः ॥

१.१६.७. उता त्या दैव्या भिषजा शं नः करतो अश्विना ।
युयुयातमितो रपो अप स्रिधः ॥

१.१६.८. आ ते योनिं गर्भं एतु पुमान् बाण इवेषुधिम् ।
आ वीरो अत्र जायतां पुत्रस्ते दशमास्यः ॥

१.१६.१२. इहैव स्तं मा वि यौष्टं विश्वमायुर्व्यश्नुतम् ।
क्रीळन्तौ पुत्रैर्नप्तृभिर्मोदमानौ स्वे गृहे ॥

१.१७.१. दधिक्राण्वो अकारिषं जिष्णोरश्वस्य वाजिनः ।
सुरभि नो मुखा करत् प्र ण आयूंषि तारिषत् ॥

१.१७.३. ध्रुवैधि पोष्या मयि मह्यं त्वादाद्बृहस्पतिः ।
मया पत्या प्रजावती सं जीव शरद शतम् ॥

१.१७.४. ध्रुवं पश्यामि प्रजां विन्देय ॥

१.१७.७. पिबतं च तृप्णुतं चा च गच्छतं प्रजां च धत्तं च द्रविणं च धत्तम् ।
सजोषसा उषसा सूर्येण चोर्जं नो धत्तमश्विना ॥

जयतं च प्र स्तुतं च प्र चावतं । प्रजां च धत्तं च द्रविणं च धत्तम् ।
सजोषसा उषसा सूर्येण चोर्जं नो धत्तमश्विना ॥

हतं च शत्रून् यततं च मित्रिणः प्रजां च धत्तं च द्रविणं च धत्तम् ।
सजोषसा उषसा सूर्येण चोर्जं नो धत्तमश्विना ॥

१.१८.३. अग्ने प्रायश्चित्तिरसि त्वं देवानां प्रायश्चित्तिरसि ।
यास्याः पतिघ्नी तनूस्तामस्या अप जहि ।

वायो प्रायश्चित्तिरसि त्वं देवानां प्रायश्चित्तिरसि ।
यास्याः अपुत्रिया तनूस्तामस्या अप जहि ।

सूर्यं प्रायश्चित्तिरसि त्वं देवानां प्रायश्चित्तिरसि ।
यास्याः अपशव्या तनूस्तामस्या अप जहि ।

अर्यमणं नु देवं कन्या अग्निमयक्षत ।
सोमां देवो अर्य्यमा प्रेतो मुञ्चातु मामुतः ॥

वरुणं नु देवं कन्या अग्निमयक्षत ।
सोमां देवो वरुण प्रेतो मुञ्चातु मामुतः ॥

पूषणं तु देवं कन्या अग्निमयक्षत ।
सोमां देवः पूषा प्रेतो मुञ्चातु मामुतः ॥

कौषीतकि गृह्यसूत्र विवाह मन्त्राः

१.२.१. अनृक्षरा ऋजवः सन्तु पन्था येभिः सखायो यन्ति नो वरेयम् ।
समर्यमा सम्भगो नो निनीयात् सं जास्पत्यं सुयममस्तु देवाः ॥

१.२.३. अनाधृष्टमस्यानाधृष्टयं देवानामोजाऽनभिशस्त्यभिशस्तिपा अनभिशस्तेयमञ्जसा
सत्यमुपगेषं सुविते मा धाः ॥

आ नः प्रजां जनयतु प्रजापतिराजरसाय समनक्त्वर्यमा ।
अदुर्मङ्गलीः पतिलोकमा विश शं नो भव द्विपदे शं चतुष्पदे ॥

प्रजास्त्वयि दधामि । पशूंस्त्वयि दधामि । तेजो ब्रह्मवर्चस्यं त्वयि दधामि ।

१.३.२. अग्निं दधामि मनसा शिवेनायमस्तु संगमतो बहूनाम् ।
मा नो हिंसीः स्थविरं मा कुमारं शं नो भव द्विपदे शं चतुष्पदे ॥

१.४.५. सवितुष्ट्वा प्रसव उत्पुनाम्यच्छिद्रेण पवित्रेण वसोः सूर्यस्य रश्मिभिः ॥

१.५.२६. अग्निर्जनिना स मेऽमूं जायां ददातु स्वाहा । सोमो जनिमान् स मामुया जनिमन्तं करोतु स्वाहा । पूषा ज्ञातिमान् स मामुष्यै पित्रा मात्रा भ्रातृभिर्ज्ञातिमन्तं करोतु स्वाहा ॥

१.६.७. हुतोऽग्निहोत्रहोमेनाऽहुतो बलिकर्मणा ।
प्रहुतः पितृकर्मणा प्राशीतो ब्राह्मणे हुतः ॥

अनूर्ध्वज्ञु र्व्यूळजानुर्जुहुयात् सर्वदा हविः ।
न हि बाह्यहुतं देवाः प्रतिगृह्णन्ति कर्हिचित् ॥

रौद्रं तु राक्षसं पित्र्यमासुरं चाऽऽभिचारिकम् ।
उक्त्वा मन्त्रं स्पृशेदप आलभ्यात्मानमेव च ॥

१.८.२. रैभ्यासीदनुदेयी नाराशंसी न्योचनी ।
सूर्याय भद्रमिद्वासो गाथयैति परिष्कृतम् ॥

१.८.३. युवं वस्त्राणि पीयसा वसाथे युवोरच्छिद्रा मन्तवो ह सर्गाः ।
अवातिरतमनृतानि विश्व ऋतेन मित्रावरुणा सचेथे ॥

१.८.४. चित्तिरा उपबर्हणं चक्षुरा अभ्यञ्जनम् ।
द्योर्भूमिः कोश आसीद् यदवत् सूर्या पतिम् ॥

१.८.५. समञ्जन्तु विश्वे देवाः समापो हृदयानि नौ ।
सं मातरिश्वा सं धाता समु देष्ट्री दधातु नौ ॥

१.८.६. यथेयं शचीं वावातां सुपुत्रां च यथादितिम् ।
अविधवां चापालामेवं त्वमिह रक्षत ॥

१.८.७. रूपं रूपं प्रतिरूपो बभूव तदस्य रूपं प्रतिचक्षणाय ।
इन्द्रो मायाभिः पुरुरूप ईयते युक्ता ह्यस्य हरयः शता दश ॥

१.८.८. नीललोहितं भवति कृत्यासक्तिर्व्यज्यते ।
एधन्ते अस्या ज्ञातयः पतिर्बन्धेषु बध्यते ॥

१.८.९. मधुमतीरोषधीर्द्याव आपो मधुमन्नो भवत्वन्तरिक्षम् ।
क्षेत्रस्य पतिर्मधुमान् नो अस्त्वरिष्यन्तो अन्वेनं चरेम ॥

१.८.१३. ब्रहस्पतये त्वा मह्यं वरुणो ददातु । सोऽमृतत्वमशीय ।
त्वद्राष्ट्र्योरधिमयो मह्यं प्रतिगृह्णते ॥

१.८.१४. सम्राज्ञी श्वशुरे भव सम्राज्ञी श्वश्र्वां भव ।
ननान्दरि सम्राज्ञी भव सम्राज्ञी अधि देवृषु ॥

१.८.१७. गृभ्णामि ते सौभगत्वाय हस्तं मया पत्या जरदष्टिर्यथासः ।
भगो अर्यमा सविता पुरंधिर्मह्यं त्वादुर्गार्हपत्याय देवाः ॥

१.८.१८. अमोऽहमस्मि सा त्वं सा त्वमस्यमोऽहम् ।

द्योरहं पृथिवी त्वं सामाहमृक्त्वं तावेहि विवहावहै ।
प्रजां प्रजनयावहै पुत्रान् विन्दावहै बहूस्ते सन्तु जरदष्टयः ॥

१.८.२०. एह्याश्मानमातिष्ठ । आरोहाश्मेव त्वं स्थिरा भव ।
अभितिष्ठ पृतन्यतः । सहस्व पृतनायतः ॥
विश्वा उत त्वया वयं धारा उदन्या इव । अतिगाहेमहि द्विषः ॥

१.८.२३. इयं नार्युपब्रूतेऽग्नौ लाजानावपन्तिका ।
शिवा ज्ञातिभ्यो भूयासं चिरं जीवतु मे पतिः ॥

१.८.२८. इष एकपदी । विष्णुस्त्वा नयतु । ऊर्जे द्विपदी । विष्णुस्त्वा नयतु । रायस्पोषाय त्रिपदी । विष्णुस्त्वा नयतु । मायो भव्याय चतुष्पदी । विष्णुस्त्वा नयतु । प्रजाभ्यः पञ्चपदी । विष्णुस्त्वा नयतु । ऋतुभ्यः षट्पदी । विष्णुस्त्वा नयतु । सखा सप्तपदी भव इति । विष्णुस्त्वा नयतु ॥

१.८.२९. आपो हि ष्ठा मयोभुवस्ता न ऊर्जे दधातन । महे रणाय चक्षसे ॥
यो वः शिवतमो रसस्तस्य भाजयतेह नः । उशतीरिव मातरः ॥
तस्मा अरं गमाम वो यस्य क्षयाय जिन्वथ । आपो जनयथा च नः ॥

१.९.१. प्र त्वा मुञ्चामि वरुणस्य पाशाद् येन त्वाबध्नात् सविता सुशेवः ।
ऋतस्य योनौ सुकृतस्य लोकेऽरिष्टां त्वा सह पत्या दधामि ॥

१.९.२. जीवां रुदन्ती विमयन्तो अध्वरे दीर्घामनुप्रसितिं दीधियुर्नरः ।
वामं पितृभ्यो य इदं समेरिरे मयः पतिभ्यो जनयः परिष्वजे ॥

१.९.३. अभि व्ययस्व खादिरस्य सारमोजो धेहि स्पन्दने शिंशपायाम् ।
अक्ष वीडो वीडित वीडयस्व मा यामादस्मादव जीहपो नः ॥

१.९.४. शुची ते चक्रे यात्वा व्यानो अक्ष आहतः ।
अनो मनस्मयं सूर्याऽऽरोहत् प्रयती पतिम् ॥

द्वे ते चक्रे सूर्ये ब्रह्मणा ऋतुथा विदुः ।
अथैकं चक्रं यद्गुहा तदद्धातय इद्विदुः ॥

१.९.७. खे रथस्य खेऽनसः खे युगस्य शतक्रतो ।
अपालमिन्द्र त्रिष्पूत्व्यकृणोः सूर्यत्वचम् ॥

युक्तस्ते अस्तु दक्षिण उत सव्यः शतक्रतो ।
तेन जायामुप प्रियां मन्दानो याह्यान्धसो योजा न्विन्द्र ते हरी ॥

१.९.८ सुकिँशुकँ शल्मलिं विश्वरूपँ हिरण्यवर्णँ सुधुरँ सुचक्रम् ।
आरोह सूर्ये अमृतस्य लोकं स्योनं पत्ये वहतुं कृणुष्व ॥

१.९.१०. मा विदन्परिपन्थिनो य आसीदन्ति दम्पती ।
सुगेभिर्दुर्गमतीतामप द्रान्त्वरातयः ॥

१.९.११. ये वध्वश्चन्द्र वहतुं यक्ष्मा यन्ति जनादनु ।
पुनस्तान्यज्ञिया देवा नयन्तु यत आगताः ॥

१.९.१७. इह प्रियं प्रजाया ते समृध्यतामस्मिन् गृहे गार्हपत्याय जागृहि ।
एना पत्या तन्वं सं सृजस्वाधा जिव्री विदथमा वदाथः ॥

परा देहि शामुल्यं ब्रह्माभ्यो वि भजा वसु ।
कृत्येषा पद्वती भूत्वा जाया विशते पतिम् ॥

अश्रिरा तनूर्भवति रुशति पापयामुया ।
पतिर्यद्वध्वो वाससा स्वमङ्गमभिधित्सते ॥

सुमङ्गलीरियं वधूरिमां समेत पश्यत ।
सौभाग्यमस्यै दत्त्वायाथास्तं विपरेतन ॥

इमां त्वमिन्द्र मीढ्वस्सुपुत्रां सुभगां कुरु ।
दशाभ्यां पुत्रानाधेहि पतिमेकादशं कृधि ॥

१.१०.१. अग्निना देवेन पृथिवीलोकेन लोकानामृग्वेदेन वेदानां त्वा शमयाम्यसौ
स्वाहा । वायुना देवेनान्तरिक्षेण लोकेन लोकानां यजुर्वेदेन वेदानां तेन त्वा
शमयाम्यसौ स्वाहा । सूर्येन देवेन दिवो लोकेन लोकानां सामवेदेन वेदानां
तेन त्वा शमयाम्यसौ स्वाहा । चन्द्रेण देवेन दिशां लोकेन लोकानां ब्रह्मदेवेन
वेदानां तेन त्वा शमयाम्यसौ स्वाहा ॥

१.१०.२. भूर्या ते पतिघ्न्यलक्ष्मी देवरघ्नी जारघ्नी तां करोमि तेऽसौ ॥

१.१०.६. अघोरचक्षुरपतिध्न्ये धि शिवा पशुभ्यः सुमना सुवर्चाः ।
वीरसूर्देवकामा स्योना शं नो भव द्विपदे शं चतुष्पदे ॥

कया नश्चित्र आभुवदूती सदावृधः सखा । कया शचिष्ठया वृता ॥
कस्त्वा सत्यो मदानां मंहिष्ठो मत्सदन्धसः । दृळ्हा चिदारुजे वसु ॥

अभी षु णः सखीनामविता जरितृणाम् । शतं भवास्यूतिभिः ॥
उता त्या दैव्या भिषजा शं नः करतो अश्विना ।
युयुयातमितो रपो अप स्रिधः ॥

१.१०.१३. ध्रुवैधि पोष्या मयि मह्यं त्वादाद्बृहस्पतिः ।
मया पत्या प्रजावती सं जीव शरद शतम् ॥
ध्रुवं पश्यामि प्रजां विन्देय ॥

१.१०.१४. दधिक्राण्वो अकारिषं जिष्णोरश्वस्य वाजिनः ।
सुरभि नो मुखा करत् प्र ण आयूंषि तारिषत् ॥

१.१०.२४. पुमांसौ मित्रावरुणौ पुमांसावश्विनावुभौ ।
पुमानिन्द्रश्चाग्निश्च पुमांसं वर्धतां मयि पुनः ॥

१.११.४. अग्ने प्रायश्चित्तिरसि त्वं देवानां प्रायश्चित्तिरसि ।
यास्याः पतिघ्नी तनूस्तामस्या अप जहि ।

वायो प्रायश्चित्तिरसि त्वं देवानां प्रायश्चित्तिरसि ।
यास्याः अपुत्रिया तनूस्तामस्या अप जहि ।

सूर्य प्रायश्चित्तिरसि त्वं देवानां प्रायश्चित्तिरसि ।
यास्याः अपशव्या तनूस्तामस्या अप जहि ।

अर्यमणं नु देवं कन्या अग्निमयक्षत ।
सोमां देवो अर्य्यमा प्रेतो मुञ्चातु मामुतः ॥

वरुणं नु देवं कन्या अग्निमयक्षत ।

सोमां देवो वरुण प्रेतो मुञ्चातु मामुतः ॥
पूषणं तु देवं कन्या अग्निमयक्षत ।
सोमां देवः पूषा प्रेतो मुञ्चातु मामुतः ॥

पारस्कर गृह्यसूत्र विवाह मन्त्राः

१.४.१३. जरां गच्छ परिधत्स्व वासो भवाकृष्टीनामभिशस्तिपावा ।
शतं च जीव शरदः सुवर्च्चा रयिं च पुत्राननुसंव्ययस्व ॥

१.४.१४. या अकृन्तन्नवयँय्या अतन्वत याश्च देवीस्तन्तूनभिता ततन्थ ।
तास्त्वा देवीर्जरसे सव्ययस्वायुष्मतीदं परिधत्स्व वासः ॥

१.४.१५. समञ्जन्तु विश्वे देवाः समापो हृदयानि नौ ।
सम्मातरिश्वा सन्धाता समु देष्ट्री दधातु नौ ॥

१.४.१६. यदौषि मनसा दुरं दिशोऽनु पवमानो वा ।
हिरण्यपर्णो वैकर्णः स त्वा मन्मनसां करोत्वित्यसौ ॥

१.४.१७. अघोरचक्षुरपतिघ्न्येधि शिवा पशुभ्यः सुमनाः सुवर्च्चाः ।
वीरसूर्देवकामा स्योना शन्नो भव द्विपदे शं चतुष्पदे ॥

सोमः प्रथमो विविदे गन्धर्वो विविद उत्तरः ।
तृतीयोग्निष्टे प्रतिस्तुरीयस्ते मनुष्यजाः ॥

सोमोऽददद् गन्धर्वाय, गन्धर्वोददद्ग्नये ।
रयिं च पुत्रांश्चादादग्निर्मह्यमथो इमाम् ॥

सा नः पूषा शिवतमामैरय सा न ऊरू उशती विहर ।
यस्यामुशन्त प्रहराम शेपं यस्यामु कामा बहवोनिविष्ट्या ॥

१.५.९. चित्तं च चित्तिश्चाकूतं चाकूतिश्च विज्ञातं च विज्ञातिश्च मनश्च शक्वरीश्च दर्शश्च पौर्णमासं च बृहच्च रथन्तरं च । प्रजापतिर्जयानिन्द्राय वृष्णे प्रायच्छदुग्रः पृतनाजयेषु । तस्मै विशः समनमन्त सर्वाः स उग्रः स इहव्यो बभूव स्वाहा ॥

१.५.१०. अग्निर्भूतानामधिपतिः स माऽवत्विन्द्रो ज्येष्ठानां, यमः पृथिव्या, वायुरन्तरिक्षस्य, सूर्यो दिवश्चन्द्रमा नक्षत्राणां, बृहस्पतिब्रह्मणे, मित्रः सत्यानां, वरुणोऽपाम्, समुद्रः स्रोत्यानामन्नटम् साम्राज्यानामधिपति तन्मावतु, सोम ओषधीनां, सविता प्रसवानाम्, रुद्रः पशूनां, त्वष्टा रूपाणां, विष्णुः पर्वतानां, मरुतो गणानामधिपतयस्ते मावन्तु पितरः पितामहाः परेवरे ततास्ततामहाः । इह मावन्त्वस्मिन्ब्रह्मण्यस्मिन् क्षत्रेऽस्यामाशिष्यस्यां पुरोधायामास्मिन्कर्मण्यस्यां दवेहूत्याम् स्वाहा ॥

१.५.११. अग्निरैतु प्रथमो देवतानाम् सोऽस्यै प्रजां मुञ्चतु मृत्युपाशात् । तदयं राजा वरुणोऽनुमन्यतां यथेयां स्त्री पौत्रमघं न रोदात्स्वाहा । इमामग्निस्त्रायतां गार्हपत्यः प्रजामस्यै नयतु दीर्घमायुः । अशून्योपस्था जीवतामस्तु माता पौत्रमानन्दमभिविबुध्यामियाम् स्वाहा । स्वस्ति नो अग्ने दिव आपृथिव्या विश्वानि धेह्ययथा यजत्र । यदस्यां महि दिवि जातं प्रशस्तं तदस्मासु द्रविणं धेहि चित्रम् स्वाहा । सुगन्न पन्था प्रदिशन्न एहि ज्योतिष्मद्धेह्यजरन्न आयुः । अपैतु मृत्युरमृतश्च आगाद्वैवस्वतो नो अभयं कृणोतु स्वाहा ॥

१.६.२. अर्यमणं देवं कन्याऽग्निमवक्षत ।
स नो अर्यमा देवः प्रेतो मुञ्चतु मा पतेः स्वाहा ॥

इयं नार्युपब्रूते लाजानावपन्तिका ।
आयुष्मानस्तु मे पतिरेधन्तां ज्ञातयो मम स्वाहा ॥

इमाँल्लाजानावपाम्यग्नौ समृद्धिकरणं तव ।
मम तुभ्य च संवननं तदग्निरनुमन्यतामियम् स्वाहा ॥

१.६.३. गृभ्णामि ते सौभगत्वाय हस्तं मया पत्या जरदष्टिर्यथाऽऽसः ।
भगोऽऽर्यमा सविता पुरन्धिर्मह्यं त्वाऽदुर्गार्हपत्याय देवाः ॥

अमोऽहमस्मि सा त्वं सा त्वमस्यमोऽहम् । सामाहमस्मि ऋक्त्वं द्यौरहं पृथिवी त्वं तावेहि विवहावहै । सह रेतो दधावहै प्रजां प्रजनयावहै पुत्रान् विन्द्यावहै । बहून् ते सन्तु जरदष्टयः संप्रियौ रोचिष्णु सुमनस्यमनु । पश्येम शरदः शतं जीवेम शरदः शतं श्रुणुयाम शरदः शतम् ॥

१.७.१. आरोहममश्मानमश्मेव त्वं स्थिरा भव ।
अभितिष्ठ पृतन्यतोऽवबाधस्व पृतनायत ॥

१.७.२. सरस्वति प्रेदमव सुभगो वाजिनीवती । या त्वा विश्वस्य भूतस्य
प्रजायामस्याग्रतः। यस्यां भूतं समभवद्यस्यां विश्वमिदं जगत् । तामध्य
गाथां गास्यामि या स्त्रीणामुत्तमं यश ॥

१.७.३. तुभ्यमग्रे पर्यवहन्सूर्यां वहतु ना सह ।
पुनः पतिभ्यो जायां दाग्ने प्रजया सह ॥

१.८.१ एकमिषे विष्णुस्त्वान्नयतु । द्वे ऊर्जे विष्णुस्त्वान्नयतु । त्रीणि रायस्पोषाय
विष्णुस्त्वान्नयतु । चत्वारि मायोभवाय विष्णुस्त्वान्नयतु । पञ्च पशुभ्यः
विष्णुस्त्वान्नयतु । षड् ऋतुभ्यः विष्णुस्त्वान्नयतु । सखे सप्तपदा भव सा
मामनुव्रता भव ॥

१.८.५. आपः शिवाः शिवतमाः शान्ताः ।
शान्ततमास्तास्ते कृण्वन्तु भेषजम् ॥

१.८.६. आपो हि ष्ठा मयोभुवस्ता न ऊर्जे दधातन । महे रणाय चक्षसे ॥

यो वः शिवतमो रसस्तस्य भाजयतेह नः । उशतीरिव मातरः ॥

तस्मा अरं गमाम वो यस्य क्षयाय जिन्वथ । आपो जनयथा च नः ॥

१.८.७. तच्छक्षुर्वेवहितं पुरस्ताच्छुक्रमच्चुरत् ।
पश्येम शरदः शतं जीवेम शरदः शतं श्रुणुयाम शरदः शतं प्रबवाम शरदः
शतं शतमदीनाः स्याम शरदः शतं भूयश्च शरदः शतात् ॥

१.८.८. मम व्रते ते हृदयम् दधामि मम चित्तमनुचित्तं ते अस्तु ।
मम वाचमेकमना जुषस्व प्रजापतिष्ट्वा नियुनक्तु मह्यम् ॥

१.८.९ सुमङ्गलीरियं वधूरिमाम् समेत पश्यत ।
सौभाग्यमस्यै दत्त्वा यथाऽस्तं विपरेतन ॥

१.८.१०. इह गावो निषिदन्त्विहाश्वा इह पूरुषाः ।
इहो सहस्रदक्षिणो यज्ञ इह पूषा निषीदतु ॥

१.८.१९. ध्रुवमसि ध्रुवं त्वा पश्यामि ध्रुवैधि पोष्ये मयि ।
मह्यं त्वाऽदाद् बृहस्पतिर्मया पत्या प्रजावती संजीव शरदः शतम् ॥

१.९.६. पुमाँसौ मित्रवरुणौ पुमाँसाविश्विनावुभौ ।
पुमानिन्द्रश्च सूर्यश्च पुमाँसं वर्ततां मयि पुनः ॥

१.११.२. अग्ने प्रायश्चित्ते त्वं देवानां प्रायश्चित्तिरसि ब्राह्मणस्त्वा नाथकाम उपधावामि याऽस्यै पतिघ्नी तनूस्तामस्यै नाशय स्वाहा । वायो प्रायश्चित्ते त्वं देवानां प्रायश्चित्तिरसि ब्राह्मणस्त्वा नाथकाम उपधावामि याऽस्यै प्रजाघ्नी तनूस्तामस्यै नाशय स्वाहा । सूर्य प्रायश्चित्ते त्वं देवानां प्रायश्चित्तिरसि ब्राह्मणस्त्वा नाथकाम उपधावामि याऽस्यै पशुघ्नी तनूस्तामस्यै नाशय स्वाहा । चन्द्र प्रायश्चित्ते त्वं देवानां प्रायश्चित्तिरसि ब्राह्मणस्त्वा नाथकाम उपधावामि याऽस्यै गृहघ्नी तनूस्तामस्यै नाशय स्वाहा । गन्धर्व प्रायश्चित्ते त्वं देवानां प्रायश्चित्तिरसि ब्राह्मणस्त्वा नाथकाम उपधावामि प्रायश्चित्ते त्वं देवानां प्रायश्चित्तिरसि ब्राह्मणस्त्वा नाथकाम उपधावामि याऽस्यै यशोघ्नी तनूस्तामस्यै नाशय स्वाहेति ॥

१.११.४. या ते पतिघ्नी प्रजाघ्नी पशुघ्नी गृहघ्नी यशोघ्नी निन्दिता तनूर्जारघ्नीं तत एनां करोमि सा जीर्य त्वं मया सह ॥

१.११.५. प्राणैस्ते प्राणान्त्संदधाम्यस्थिभिरस्थीनि माँसैर्माँसानि त्वचा त्वचम् ॥

आपस्तम्ब गृह्यसूत्र विवाह मन्त्राः

२.४.२. प्र सु ग्मन्ता धियसानस्य सक्षणि वरेभिर्वराँ अभि षु प्रसीदतः ।
अस्माकमिन्द्र उभयं जुजोषिति यत्सोम्यस्यान्धसो बुबोधिति ॥

अनृक्षरा ऋजवः सन्तु पन्था येभिः सखायो यन्ति नो वरेयम् ।
समर्यमा सम्भगो नो निनीयात् सं जास्पत्यं सुयममस्तु देवाः ॥

२.४.३. अभ्रातृघ्नीं वरुणापतिघ्नीं बृहस्पते ।
इन्द्रापुत्रघ्नीं लक्ष्म्यं तामस्यै सवितस्सुव ॥

२.४.४. अघोरचक्षुरपतिघ्न्ये धि शिवा पशुभ्यः सुमना सुवर्चाः ।
वीरसूर्देवकामा स्योना शं नो भव द्विपदे शं चतुष्पदे ॥

२.४.५. इदमहं या त्वयिं पतिघ्न्यलक्ष्मिस्तां निर्दिशामि ॥

२.४.६. जीवां रुदन्ती विमयन्तो अध्वरे दीर्घामनुप्रसितिं दीधियुर्नरः ।
वामं पितृभ्यो य इदं समेरिरे मयः पतिभ्यो जनयः परिष्वजे ॥

२.४.७. व्युक्षत्क्रूरमुदचन्त्वाप आस्यै ब्राह्मणा स्नपनँ हरन्तु ।
अवीरघ्नीरुदचन्त्वापः ॥

२.४.८. अर्यम्णो अग्निं परिं यन्तु क्षिप्रं प्रतीक्षान्ताँ श्वश्रुवो देवराश्च ॥

खेऽनसः खे रथः खे युगस्य शचीपते ।
अपालमिन्द्र त्रिः पूत्व्यकरत्सूर्यवर्चसम् ॥

शं ते हिरण्यँ समु शन्त्वापश्शं ते मेथी भवतु शं युगस्य तृत्म ।
शं त आपश्शतपवित्रा भवन्त्वथा पत्या तन्वँ सँ सृजस्व ॥

हिरण्यवर्णाः शुचयः पावकाः प्र चक्रमुर्हित्वावद्यमापः ।
शतं पवित्रा वितता ह्यासु ताभिष्ट्वा देवस्सविता पुनातु ॥

हिरण्यवर्णाः शुचयः पावका यासु जातः कश्यपो यास्विग्निः ।
या अग्निं गर्भे दधिरे सुवर्णास्तास्त आपश्शँ स्योना भवन्तु ॥

यासाँ राजा वरुणो याति मध्ये सत्यानृते अवपश्यञ्जनानाम् ।
या अग्निं गर्भे दधिरे सुवर्णास्तास्त आपश्शँ स्योना भवन्तु ॥

यासाँ देवा दिवि कृण्वन्ति भक्ष्यं या अन्तरिक्षे बहुधा निविष्टाः ।
या अग्निं गर्भे दधिरे सुवर्णास्तास्त आपश्शँ स्योना भवन्तु ॥

शिवेन त्वा चक्षुषा पश्यन्त्वापश्शिवयां तन्वोपं स्पृशन्तु त्वचं ते ।
घृतश्चुतश्शुचयो याः पावकास्तास्त अपश्शँ स्योना भवन्तु ॥

परि त्वा गिर्वणो गिर इमा भवन्तु विश्वतः ।
वृद्ध्वायुमनु वृद्धयो जुष्टा भवन्तु जुष्टयः ॥

आशासाना सौमनसं प्रजाँ प्रजाँ सौभाग्यं तनूम् ।
अग्नेरनुव्रता भूत्वा सं नह्ये सुकृताय कम् ॥

२.४.९. पूषा त्वेतो नयतु हस्तगृह्याश्विनौ त्वा प्र वहतां रथेन ।
गृहान्गच्छ गृहपत्नी यथासो वशिनी त्वं विदथमा वदासि ॥

२.४.१०. सोमः प्रथमो विविदे गन्धर्वो विविद उत्तरः ।
तृतीयो अग्निष्टे पतिस्तुरीयस्ते मनुष्यजाः ॥

सोमो ददद्गन्धर्वाय गन्धर्वो दददग्नये ।
रयिं च पुत्राँश्चादादग्निर्मह्यमथो इमाम् ॥

२.४.१४. गृभ्णामि ते सुप्रजस्त्वाय हस्तं मया पत्या जरदष्टिर्यथासः ।
भगो अर्यमा सविता पुरन्धिर्मह्यं त्वादुर्गार्हपत्याय देवाः ॥

ते ह पूर्वे जनासो यत्र पूर्ववतो हिताः ।
मूर्धन्वान्यत्र सौभ्रवः पूर्वो देवेभ्य आतपत् ॥

सरस्वति प्रेदमव सुभगे वाजीनीवति ।
तां त्वा विश्वस्य भूतस्य प्र गायामस्यग्रतः ॥

य एतिं प्रदिशस्सर्वा दिशोऽनु पवमानः ।
हिरण्यहस्त एरम्मस्स त्वा मन्मनसं कृणोतु ॥

२.४.१५. एकमिषे विष्णुस्त्वान्वेतु । द्वे ऊर्जे विष्णुस्त्वान्वेतु । त्रीणि व्रताय विष्णुस्तान्वेतु ।
चत्वारि मायोभवाय विष्णुस्तान्वेतु । पञ्च पशुभ्यो विष्णुस्तान्वेतु । षड्तुभ्यो
विष्णुस्तान्वेतु । सप्त सप्तभ्यो होत्राभ्यो विष्णुस्तान्वेतु ।

२.४.१६. सखा सप्तपदा भव सखायौ सप्तपदा बभूव । सख्यं ते गमेयँ सख्यात्ते मा
योषं सख्यान्मे मा योष्ठाः । समयाव सं कल्पावहै संप्रियौ रोचिष्णू
सुमनस्यमानौ । इषमूर्जमभि संवसानौ । सं नो मनाँसि सं व्रता सामु
चित्तान्या करम् । सा त्वमस्यमूहममूहमस्मि सा त्वं द्यौरहं पृथिवी त्वं
रेतोऽहं रेतोभृत्त्वं मनोऽहमस्मि वाक्त्वँ सामाहमस्यमृक्त्वँ सा मामनुव्रता
भव पुँसे पुत्राय वेत्तवै श्रियै पुत्राय वेत्तवा एहि सूनृते ॥

२.५.१. सोमाय जनिविदे स्वाहा ।
गन्धर्वाय जनिविदे स्वाहा ।
अग्नये जनिविदे स्वाहा ।

कन्यला पितृभ्यो यती पतिलोकमव दीक्षादास्थ स्वाहा ।

प्रेतो मुञ्चाति नामुतस्सुबद्धाममुनुस्करत् ।
यथेयमिन्द्र मीढ्वस्सुपुत्रा सुभगासति ॥

इमां त्वमिन्द्र मीढ्वस्सुपुत्रां सुभगां कुरु ।
दशाभ्यां पुत्रानाधेहि पतिमेकादशं कृधि ॥

अग्निरैतु प्रथमो देवतानाम् सोऽस्यै प्रजां मुञ्चतु मृत्युपाशात् ।
तदयं राजा वरुणोऽनुमन्यतां यथेयम् स्त्री पौत्रमघं न रोदात् ।
इमामग्निस्त्रायतां गार्हपत्यः प्रजामस्यै नयतु दीर्घमायुः ।
अशून्योपस्था जीवतामस्तु माता पौत्रमानन्दमभिविबुध्यामियम् ।
मा ते गृहे निशि घोष उत्थादन्यत्र त्वद्रुदत्यस्संविशन्तु ।
मा त्वं विकेश्युर अवधिष्टा जीवपत्नी पतिलोके विराज पश्यन्ती प्रजां सुमनस्यमानां ॥

द्योस्ते पृष्टं रक्षतु वायुरूरू अश्विनौ च स्तनं धयन्तँ सविताभि रक्षतु ।
आ वाससः परिधानाद्बृहस्पतिर्विश्वे देवा अभिरक्षन्तु पश्चात् ॥

अप्रजस्तां पौत्रमृत्युं पाप्मानमुत वाघम् ।
शीर्णा स्रजमिवोन्मुच्य द्विषद्भ्यः प्रति मञ्चामि पाशम् ॥

इमं मे वरुण श्रुधी हवमद्या च मृडय । त्वामवस्युरा चके ॥

तत्वा यामि ब्रह्मणा वन्दमानस्तदा शास्ते यजमानो हविर्भिः ।
अहेडमानो वरुणेह बोध्युरुशँस मा न आयुः प्र मोषीः ॥

त्वं नो अग्ने वरुणस्य विद्वान्देवस्य हेडोऽवं यासिसीष्ठाः ।
यजिष्ठो वह्नितमश्शोश्रुचानो विश्वा द्वेषाँसि प्र मुमुग्ध्यस्मत् ॥

स त्वं नो अग्नेऽवमो भवोती नेदिष्ठो अस्या उषसो व्युष्टौ ।
अव यक्ष्व नो वरुणँ रराणो वीहि मृडीकँ सुहवो न एधी ॥

त्वमग्ने अयास्ययासन्मनसा हितः ।
अयासन्हव्यसूहिषेऽया नो धेहि भेषजम् ॥

२.५.२. आतिष्ठेममश्मानमश्मेव त्वं स्थिरा भव ।
अभितिष्ठ पृतन्यतस्सहस्व पृतनायतः ॥

२.५.५. इयं नार्युप ब्रूते कुल्यान्यावपन्तिका ।
दीर्घायुरस्तु मे पतिर्जीवातु शरदश्शतं ॥

२.५.७. तुभ्यमग्ने पर्यवहन् सूर्याम् वहतुना सह ।
पुनः पतिभ्यो जायां दा अग्ने प्रजया सह ॥

पुनः पत्नींमग्निरदादायुषा सह वर्चसा ।
दीर्घायुर्स्या यः पतिस्म एतु शरदशतम् ॥

विश्वा उत त्वया वयं धारा उदन्या इव ।
अति गाहेमहि द्विषः ॥ आतिष्ठेममश्मानम् ॥

२.५.८. अर्यमणं नु देवं कन्या अग्निमयक्षत ।
स इमां देवो अध्वरः प्रेतो मुञ्चाति नामुतस्सुबद्धाममुतस्करत् ॥

२.५.९. तुभ्यमग्ने पर्यवहन् ॥
पुनः पत्नीमग्निरदात् ॥
विश्वा उत त्वया वयम् ॥
आतिष्ठेममश्मानम् ॥

त्वमर्यमा भवसि यत्कनीनां नाम स्वधावत्स्वर्ये बिभार्षि ।
अञ्जन्ति वृक्षं सुधितं त गोभिर्यद्दंपती समनसा कृणोषि ॥

२.५.१०. तुभ्यमग्ने पर्यवहन् ॥
पुनः पत्नीमग्निरदात् ॥
विश्वा उत त्वया वयम् ॥

२.५.१३. प्र त्वा मुञ्चामि वरुणस्य पाशाद् येन त्वाबध्नात् सविता सुकेतः ।
धातुश्च योनौ सुकृतस्य लोके स्योनं ते सह पत्या कृणोमि ॥

इमं वि ष्यामि वरुणस्य पाशं यमबध्नीत सविता सुशेवः ।
धातुश्च योनौ सुकृतस्य लोकेऽरिष्टां त्वा सह पत्या कृणोमि ॥

२.५.२०. अयाश्चाग्नेऽस्यनभिशस्तीश्च सत्यमित्त्वमया असि ।
अयसा मनसा धृतोऽयसा हव्यमूहिषेऽया नो धेहि भेषजम् ॥

२.५.२१. सत्येनोत्तभिता भूमिस्सूर्येणोत्तभिता द्यौः ।
ऋतेनादित्यास्तिष्ठन्ति दिवि सोमो अधि शितः ॥

२.५.२२. युञ्जन्ति ब्रध्नमरुषं चरन्तं परि तस्थुषः । रोचन्ते रोचना दिवि ॥
योगेयोगे तवस्तरं वाजेवाजे हवामहे । सखाय इन्द्रमूतये ॥

२.५.२३. सुकिँशुकँ शल्मलिं विश्वरूपँ हिरण्यवर्णँ सुवृतँ सुचक्रम् ।
आरोह वध्वमृतस्य लोकं स्योनं पत्ये वहतुं कृणुष्व ॥

उदुत्तरमारोहन्ती व्यस्यन्ती पृतन्यतः ।
मूर्धानं पत्युरा रोह प्रजया च विराड्भव ॥

सम्राज्ञी श्वशुरे भव सम्राज्ञी श्वश्र्वां भव ।
ननान्दरि सम्राज्ञी भव सम्राज्ञी अधि देवृषु ॥

स्नुषाणाँ श्वश्रुराणां प्रजायाश्च धनस्य च ।
पतीनां च देवृणां च सजातानां विराड्भव ॥

२.५.२४. नीललोहितं भवतः कृत्यासक्तिर्व्यज्यते ।
एधन्ते अस्या ज्ञातयः पतिर्बन्धेषु बध्यते ॥

२.५.२५. ये वध्वश्चन्द्रं वहतुं यक्ष्मा यन्ति जनाँ अनु ।
पुनस्तान्यज्ञिया देवा नयन्तु यत आगताः ॥

मा विदन्परिपन्थिनो य असीदन्ति दम्पती ।
सुगेभिर्दुर्गमतीतामप द्रान्त्वरातयः ॥

सुगं पन्थानमारुक्षमरिष्टँ स्वस्तिवाहनम् ।
यस्मिन्वीरो न रिष्यत्यन्येषां विन्दते वसु ॥

२.५.२६. ता मन्दसाना मनुषो दुरोण आ धत्तँ रयिं दशवीरं वचस्यवे ।
कृतं तीर्थँ सुप्रमाणँ शुभस्पती स्थाणुं पथेष्ठामप दुर्मतिँ हतम् ॥

२.६.१. अयं नो मह्याः पारँ स्वस्ति नेषड्वनस्पतिः ।
सीरा नस्सुतरा भव दीर्घायुत्वाय वर्चसे ॥

२.६.३. अस्य पारे निर्‌ऋथस्य जीवा ज्योतिरशीमहि । मह्या इन्द्र स्वस्तये ॥

२.६.४. यदृते चिदभिश्रिषः पुरा जर्तुभ्य आतृदः ।
संधाता सन्धिं मघवा पुरोवसुर्निष्कर्ता विह्रुतं पुनः ॥

इडामग्ने पुरुदँसँ सनिं गोश्शश्वत्तमँ हवमानाय साध ।
स्यान्नस्सूनुस्तनयो विजावाग्ने सा ते सुमतिर्भूत्वस्मे ॥
इमं मे वरुण ॥ तत्वा यामि ॥ त्वं नो अग्ने ॥ स त्वं नो अग्ने ॥ त्वमग्ने अयासि ॥

२.६.५. ये गन्धर्वा अप्सरसश्च देवीरेषु वृक्षेषु वानस्पत्येष्वासते ।
शिवास्त अस्यै वध्वै भवन्तु मा हिँसिषुर्वहतुमूह्यमानाम् ॥

या ओषधयो या नद्यो यानि धन्वानि ये वनां ।
ते त्वा वधु प्रजावतीं प्र त्वे मुञ्चन्त्वँहसः ॥

२.६.६. सं काशयामि वहतुं ब्रह्मणा गृहैरघोरेण चक्षुषा मैत्रेण ।
पर्याणद्धं विश्वरूपं यदस्याँ स्योनं पतिभ्यस्सविता कृणोतु तत् ॥

२.६.७. आ वामगन्त्सुमतिर्वाजिनीवसू न्यश्विना हृत्सु कामाँ अयँसत ।
आभूतं गोपा मिथुना शुभस्पती प्रिया अर्यम्णो दुर्याँ अशीमहि ॥

अयं नोदेवस्सविता ब्रहस्पतिरिन्द्राग्नी मित्रावरुणा स्वस्तये ।
त्वष्टा विष्णुः प्रजया संरराणः काम आयातं त्वा विमुञ्चतु ॥

२.६.७. शर्म वर्मेदमा भरास्यै नार्या उपस्तिरे ।
सिनीवालि प्र जायतामियं भगस्य सुमतावसत् ॥

गृहान्भद्रान्त्सुमनसः प्र पद्येऽवीरघ्नी वीरवतस्सुवीरान् ।
इरां वहतो घृतमुक्षुमाणस्तेष्वहँ सुमनास्संविशामि ॥

२.६.१०. आगन्गोष्ठं महिषी गोभिरश्वैरायुष्मत्पत्नी प्रजया स्वर्वित् ।
वह्वीं प्रजां जनयन्ती सुरत्नेममग्निँ शतहिमास्सपर्यात् ॥

अयमग्निर्गृहपतिस्सुसँत्पुष्टिवर्धनः ।
यथा भगस्याभ्यां ददद्रयिं पुष्टिमथो प्रजाम् ॥

प्रजाया आभ्यां प्रजापत इन्द्राग्नी शर्म यच्छतम् ।
यथैनर्योन प्रमीयातां उभयोर्जीवतोः प्रजा ॥

तेन भूतेन हविषायमा प्यायतां पुनः ।
जायतां यामस्मा आवाक्षुस्ताँ रसेनाभि वर्धताम् ॥

अभि वर्धातां पयसाभि राष्ट्रेण वर्धताम् ।
रय्या सहस्रपोषसेमौ स्तामनपोक्षितौ ॥

इहैव स्तं मा वि योष्टं विश्वमायुर्व्यश्नुतम् । मह्या इन्द्र स्वस्तये ॥

ध्रुवैधि पोष्या मयि मह्यं त्वादाद्बृहस्पतिः ।
मया पत्या प्रजावती सं जीव शरदशतम् ॥

त्वष्टा जायामजनयत्त्वष्टास्यै त्वां पतिम् ।

त्वष्टा सहस्रमायूँषि दीर्घमायुः कृणोतु वाम् ॥ इमं मे वरुण ॥
तत्वा मयि ॥ त्वं नो अग्ने ॥ स त्वं नो अग्ने ॥ त्वमग्ने अयासि ॥

इह गावः प्र जायध्वमिहाश्वा इह पुरुषाः ।
इहो सहस्रदक्षिणो रायस्पोषो निषीदतु ॥

२.६.११. सोमेनादित्या बलिनस्सोमेन पृथिवी दृढा ।
अथो नक्षत्राणामेषामुपस्थे सोम आधितः ॥
प्रस्व स्थः प्रेयं प्रजया भुवने शोचेष्ट ॥

इह प्रियं प्रजया ते समृध्यतामस्मिन्गृहे गार्हपत्याय जागृहि ।
एना पत्या तन्वँ सँ सृजस्वाथा जीव्री विदथमा वदासि ॥

सुमङ्गलीरियं वधूरिमां समेत पश्यत ।
सौभाग्यामस्यै दत्वायाथास्तं विपरेतन ॥

२.६.१२. ध्रुवक्षितिर्ध्रुवयोनिर्ध्रुवमसि ध्रुवत स्थितम् ।
त्वं नक्षत्राणां मेथ्यसि स मा पाहि पृतन्यतः ॥

सप्तर्षयः प्रथमां कृत्तिकानामरुन्धतीं यद्ध्रुवताँ ह नित्युः ।
षट् कृत्तिकां मुख्ययोगं वहन्तीयमस्माकमेधत्वष्टमी ॥

३.८.२. सदसस्पतिमद्भुतम् प्रियमिन्द्रस्य काम्यम् ।
सनिं मेधामयासिषम् ॥

३.८.५. उद्दीप्यस्व जातवेदोऽपघ्नन्निर्ऋतिं मम ।
पशूँश्च मह्यमा वह जीवनं च दिशे दिश ॥

मा नो हिँसीज्जातवेदो गामश्वं पुरुषं जगत् ।
अबिभ्रदग्न आ गाहि श्रिया मा परि पातय ॥

३.८.१०. उदीर्ष्वातो विश्वावसो नमसेडामहे त्वा ।
अन्यामिच्छ प्रभर्व्यँ सं जायां पत्या सृज ॥

उदीर्ष्वात पतिवति ह्येषा विश्वावसुं नमसा गीर्भिरिट्टे ।
अन्यामिच्छ पितृषदं वित्ताँ स ते भागो जनुषा तस्य विद्धि ॥

अग्ने प्रायश्चित्ते त्वं देवानां प्रायश्चित्तिरसि ब्राह्मणस्त्वां नाथकामः प्र पद्ये यास्यां पतिघ्नी तनूः प्रजाघ्नी पशुघ्नी लक्ष्मिघ्नी जारघ्नीमस्यै तां कृणोमि स्वाहा ॥

वायो प्रायश्चित्ते . . . ॥

आदित्य प्रायश्चित्ते . . . ॥

प्रजापते प्रायश्चित्ते त्वं देवानां प्रायश्चित्तिरसि ब्राह्मणस्त्वां नाथकामः प्र पद्ये यास्यां पतिघ्नी तनूः प्रजाघ्नी पशुघ्नी लक्ष्मिघ्नी जारघ्नीमस्यै तां कृणोमि स्वाहा ॥

प्रसवश्चोपयामश्च काटश्चार्णवश्च धर्णसिश्च द्रविणं च भगश्चान्तरिक्षं च सिन्धुश्च समुद्रश्च सरस्वाँश्च विश्वव्यचाश्च ते यं द्विष्मो यश्च नो द्वेष्टि तमेषां जम्भे दध्म स्वाहा ॥

मधुश्च माधवश्च शुक्रश्च शुचिश्च नभश्च नभस्यश्चेषश्चोर्जश्च सहश्च सहस्यश्च

तपश्च तपस्यश्च ते यं द्विष्मो यश्च नो द्वेष्टि तमेषां जम्भे दध्म स्वाहा ॥

चित्तं च चित्तिश्चाकूतं चाकूतिश्चाधीतं चाधीतिश्च विज्ञातं च विज्ञानं च नाम च क्रतुश्च दर्शश्च । पूर्णमासश्च ते यं द्विष्मो यश्च नो द्वेष्टि तमेषां जम्भे दध्म स्वाहा ॥

भू स्वाहा ॥ भुव स्वाहा ॥ सुव स्वाहा ॥ ॐ स्वाहा ॥

अपश्यं त्वा मनसा चेकितानं तपसो जातं तपसो विभूतम् ।
इह प्रजामिह रयिं रराणः प्र जायस्व प्रजयां पुत्रकाम ॥

अपश्यं त्वा मनसा दीध्यानाँ स्वायां तनूँ ऋत्विये नाथमानाम् ।
उप मामृच्चा युवतिर्बभूयाः प्र जायस्व प्रजयां पुत्रकाम ॥

समञ्जन्तु विश्वे देवाः समापो हृदयानि नौ ।
सं मातरिश्वा सं धाता समु देष्ट्री दिदेष्टु नौ ॥

प्रजापते तन्वं मे जुषस्व त्वष्टर्देवेभिसहसाम इन्द्र ।
विश्वैर्देवै एतिभिसाँरराणः पुँसां बहूनां मातरं स्याम ॥

आ नः प्रजां जनयतु प्रजापतिराजरसाय समनक्त्वर्यमा ।
अदुर्मङ्गलीः पतिलोकमा विश शं न एधि द्विपदे शं चतुष्पदे ॥

तां पूषञ्छिवतमामेरयस्व यस्यां बीजं मनुष्या वपन्ति ।
या न ऊरू उशति विस्रयातै यस्यामुशन्त प्रहरेम शेपम् ॥

आ रोहोरुमुप बर्हस्व बाहुं परि ष्वजस्व जायाँ सुमनस्यमानः ।
तस्यां पुष्यतं मिथुनौ सयोनी बह्वीं प्रजां जनयन्तौ सरेतसा ॥

आर्द्रयारण्या यत्रामन्थत्पुरुषं पुरुषेण शक्रः ।
तदेतौ मिथुनौ सयोनी प्रजयामृतेनेह गच्छतम् ॥

अहं गर्भमदधामोषधीष्वहं विश्वेषु भुवनेष्वन्तः ।
अहं प्रजा अजनयं पितॄणामहं जनिभ्यो अपरीषु पुत्रान् ॥
पुत्रिणेमा कुमारिणा विश्वमायुर्व्यश्नुतम् । उभा हिरण्यपेशसा ॥

वीतिहोत्रा कृतद्वसू दशस्यन्त्वामृताय कम् ।
शमूधो रोमशँ हथो देवेषु कृणुतो दुवः ॥

३.८.१३. विष्णुर्योनिं कल्पयतु त्वष्टा रूपाणि पिंशतु ।
आसिञ्चतु प्रजापतिर्धाता गर्भं दधातु ते ॥

गर्भं धेहि सिनीवालि गर्भं धेहि सरस्वति ।
गर्भं ते अश्विनौ देवावाधत्तां पुष्करस्रजा ॥

हिरण्ययी अरुणी यं निर्मन्थतो अश्विना ।
तंते गर्भं दधाम्यहं दशमे मासि सूतवे ॥

मथेयं पृथिवी मही तिष्ठन्ती गर्भमादधे ।
एवं त्वं गर्भमा धत्स्व दशमे मासि सूतवे ॥

यथा पृथिव्यऽग्निगर्भा द्यौर्यथेन्द्रेण गर्भिणी ।
वायुर्यथा दिशां गर्भ एवं गर्भं दधातु ते ॥

विष्णो श्रेष्ठेन रूपेणास्यां नार्या गवीन्याम् ।

पुमाँसं गर्भमा धेहि दशमे मासि सूतवे ॥

नेजमेष परा पत सुपुत्रः पुतरा पत ।
अस्यै मे पुत्रकामायै गर्भमा धेहि यः पुमान् ॥

व्यस्य योनिं प्रति रेतो गृहाण पुमान्पुत्रो धीयतां गर्भो अन्तः ।
तं माता दश मासो बिभर्तु स जायतां वीरतम स्वानाम् ॥

आ ते गर्भो योनिमेतु पुमान्बाण इवेषुधिम् ।
आ वीरो जायतां पुत्रस्ते दशमास्यः ॥

करोमि ते प्राजापत्यमा गर्भो योनिमेतु ते ।
अनूनः पूर्णो जायतामश्लोणोऽपिशाचधीतः ॥

पुमाँस्ते पुत्रो नारि तं पुमाननु जायताम् ।
तानि भद्राणि बीजान्यृषभा जनयन्तु नौ ॥

यानि भद्राणि बीजान्यृषभा जनयन्तु नः ।
तैस्त्वं पुत्रान्विन्दस्व सा प्रसुर्धेनुका भव ॥

कामप्रभुध्यतां मह्यमपराजितमेव मे ।
यं कामं कामयेदेव तं मे वायो समर्धय ॥

जरां गच्छ परिधत्स्व वासो भवाकृष्टीनामभिशस्तिपावा ।
शतं च जीव शरदः सुवर्च्चा रयिं च पुत्राननुसंव्ययस्व ॥

हिरण्यकेशि गृह्यसूत्र विवाह मन्त्राः

१.१९.४. सुमङ्गलीरियं वधूरिमां समेत पश्यत ।
सौभाग्यमस्यै दत्त्वायाथास्तं विपरेतन ॥

१.१९.७. अग्निरैतु प्रथमो देवतानां सोस्यै प्रजां मुञ्चतु मृत्युपाशात् । तदयं राजा वरुणोनुमन्यतां यथेयं स्त्री पौत्रमघं न रोदात् । स्वाहा ॥ इमामग्निस्त्रायतां गार्हपत्यः प्रजामस्यै नयतु दीर्घमायुः । अशून्योपस्था जीवतामस्तु माता पौत्रमानन्दमभिप्रबुध्यतामियम् स्वाहा ॥ मा ते गृहे निशि घोष उत्थादन्यत्र त्वद्रुदत्यः संविशन्तु । मा त्वं विकेश्युर आवधिष्ठा जीवपत्नी पतिलोके विराज प्रजां पश्यन्ती सुमनस्यमानाम् । स्वाहा ॥ द्योस्ते पृष्ठं रक्षतु वायुरूरू अश्विनौ च स्तनं धयतस्ते पुत्रान्सविताभिरक्षतु । आ वाससः परिधानाद्बृहस्पतिर्विश्वे देवा अभिरक्षन्तु पश्चात् । स्वाहा ॥ अप्रजस्तां पौत्रमृत्युं पाप्मानमुत वाधम् । शीर्ष्णाः स्रजमिवोन्मुच्य द्विषद्भ्यः प्रतिमुञ्चामि पापम् । स्वाहा ॥ देवकृतं ब्राह्मणं कल्पमानं तेन हन्मि योनिषदः पिशाचान् । क्रव्यादो मृत्यूनधरान्पादयामि दीर्घमायुस्तव जीवन्तु पुत्राः । स्वाहा ॥

१.१९.८. आतिष्ठेममश्मानमश्मेव त्वं स्थिरा भव ।
प्रमृणीहि दुरस्यून्सहस्व पृतनायतः ॥

१.२०.१. गृह्णामि ते सुप्रजास्त्वाय हस्तं मया पत्या जरदष्टिर्यथासत् ।
भगो अर्यमा सविता पुरन्धिर्मह्यं त्वादुर्गार्हपत्याय देवाः ॥

१.२०.२. अघोरचक्षुरपतिघ्न्येधि शिवा पशुभ्यः सुवर्चाः । जीवसूर्वीरसूः स्योना शं न एधि द्विपदे शं चतुष्पदे ॥ तां नः पूषञ्छिवतमामेरयस्व यस्यां बीजं मनुष्या

वपन्ति । या न ऊरू उशती विस्रयातै यस्यामुशन्तः प्रहरेम शेपम् ॥ सोमः प्रथमो विविदे गन्धर्वो विविद उत्तरः । तृतीयो अग्निष्टे पतिस्तुरीयोहं मनुष्यजाः ॥ सोमोददाद्गन्धर्वाय गन्धर्वोग्नयेददात् । पशूंश्च मह्यं पुत्रांश्चाग्निर्ददात्यथो त्वाम् ॥ अमूहमस्मि सा त्वं द्यौरहं पृथिवी त्वं सामाहमृक्त्वं तावेहि संभवाव सह रेतो दधावहै पुंसे पुत्राय वेत्तवै रायस्पोषाय सुप्रजास्त्वाय सुवीर्याय ॥ इमां त्वमिन्द्र मीढ्वः सुपुत्रां सुभगां कुरु । दशास्यां पुत्रानादेहि पतिमेकादशं कुरु ॥

१.२०.३. इमाँल्लाजानावपामि समृद्धिकरणान्मम ।
तुभ्यं च संवननं तदाग्निरनुमन्यतामयम् ॥

१.२०.४. इयं नार्युपब्रूतेग्नौ लाजानावपन्ती ।
दीर्घायुरस्तु मे पतिरेधन्तां ज्ञातयो मम ॥

१.२०.५. विश्वा उत त्वया वयं धारा उदन्या इव । अतिगाहेमहि द्विषः ॥

१.२१.१. एकमिषे विष्णुस्त्वान्वेतु । द्वे ऊर्जे विष्णुस्त्वान्वेतु । त्रीणि व्रताय विष्णुस्तान्वेतु । चत्वारि मायोभवाय विष्णुस्तान्वेतु । पञ्च पशुभ्यो विष्णुस्तान्वेतु । षड्रायस्पोषाय विष्णुस्तान्वेतु । सप्त सप्तभ्यो होत्राभ्यो विष्णुस्तान्वेतु ॥

१.२१.२. सखायौ सप्तपदाबभूव सख्यं ते गमेयं सख्यात्रे मा योषं सख्यान्मे मा योष्ठाः ॥

१.२१.४. प्राणानां ग्रन्थिरसि स मा विस्रसः ॥

१.२१.५. आपो हि ष्ठा मयोभुवस्ता न ऊर्जे दधातन । महे रणाय चक्षसे ॥

यो वः शिवतमो रसस्तस्य भाजयतेह नः । उशतीरिव मातरः ॥

तस्मा अरं गमाम वो यस्य क्षयाय जिन्वथ । आपो जनयथा च नः ॥

हिरण्यवर्णाः शुचयः पावका यासु जातः कश्यपो यास्विग्निः ।
या अग्निं गर्भं दधिरे सुवर्णास्तास्त आपश्शँ स्योना भवन्तु ॥

पवमानः सुवर्जनः । पवित्रेण विचर्षणिः । यः पोता स पुनातु मा । पुनन्तु मा देवजनाः । पुनन्तु मनवो धिया । पुनन्तु विश्व आयवः । जातवेदः पवित्रवत् । पवित्रेण पुनाहि मा । शुक्रेण देव दीद्यत् । अग्ने क्रत्वा क्रतूँरनु ॥ (अनूवाक् – तै.ब्रा. १.४.८)

१.२२.११. देवीः षडुर्वीरुरु णः कृणोत विश्वे देवास इह वीरयध्वम् ।

१.२२.१२-१३. मा हस्महि प्रजया मा तनूभिर्मा रधाम द्विषते सोम राजन् ॥

१.२२.१४. सप्तर्षयः प्रथमां कृत्तिकानामरुन्धती ये ध्रुवतां ह निन्युः ।
षट्कृत्तिकामुख्ययोगं वहन्तीयमस्माकं भ्रजत्वष्टमी ॥

ध्रुवक्षितिर्ध्रुवयोनिर्ध्रुवमसि ध्रुवत स्थितम् ।
त्वं नक्षत्राणां मेथ्यसि स मा पाहि पृतन्यतः ॥

नमो ब्रह्मणे ध्रुवायाच्युतायास्तु नमो ब्रह्मणः पुत्राय प्रजापतये नमो ब्रह्मणः पुत्रेभ्यो देवेभ्यस्त्रयस्त्रिंशेभ्यो नमो ब्रह्मणः पुत्रपौत्रेभोङ्गिरोभ्यः ॥

यस्त्वा ध्रुवमच्युतं सपुत्रं सपौत्रं ब्रह्म वेद ध्रुवा अस्मिन्पुत्राः पौत्रा भवन्ति । प्रेष्यान्तेवासिनो वसनं कम्बलानि कंसं हिरण्यं स्त्रियो राजानोन्नमभयमायुः

कीर्तिर्वर्चो यशो बलं ब्रह्मवर्चसमन्नाद्यमित्येयातानि मयि सर्वाणि ध्रुवाण्यच्युतानि सन्तु ॥

१.२३.१. ध्रुवं त्वा ब्रह्म वेद ध्रुवोहमस्मिँल्लोकेस्मिंश्च जनपदे भूयासम् ॥ अच्युतं त्वा ब्रह्म वेद माहमस्माल्लोकादस्माच्च जनपदाच्च्योषि द्विषन्मे भ्रातृव्योस्माल्लोकादस्माच्च जनपदाच्च्यवताम् । अचेष्टं त्वा ब्रह्म वेद माहमस्माल्लोकादस्माच्च जनपदाच्चेष्टिषि द्विषन्मे भ्रातृव्योस्माल्लोकादस्माच्च जनपदाच्छेष्टिताम् । अव्यथमानं त्वा ब्रह्म वेद माहमस्माल्लोकादस्माच्च जनपदाद्व्यथिषि द्विषन्मे भ्रातृव्योस्माल्लोकादस्माच्च जनपदाद्व्यथताम् ॥ नभ्यं त्वा सर्वस्य नभ्यमहमस्य जनपदस्य भूयासम् । मध्यं त्वा सर्वस्य वेद मध्यमहमस्य जनपदस्य भूयासम् । तन्तिं त्वा सर्वस्य वेद तन्तिरहमस्य जनपदस्य भूयासम् । मेथीं त्वा सर्वस्य वेद मेथ्यहमस्य जनपदस्य भूयासम् । नाभिं त्वा सर्वस्य वेद नाभिरहमस्य जनपदस्य भूयासम् । यथा नाभिः प्राणानां विषूवानेवहमहं विषूवान् । एकशतं तं पाप्मानमृच्छतु योस्मान्द्वेष्टि यं च वयं द्विष्मो भूयांसि मामेकशतात्पुण्यान्यागच्छन्तु ॥

१.२४.१. अग्ने प्रायश्चित्ते त्वं प्रायश्चित्तिरसि ब्राह्मणस्त्वा नाथकाम उपधावामि यास्यै घोरा तनूस्तामितो नाशय स्वाहा ॥ वायो प्रायश्चित्ते त्वं प्रायश्चित्तिरसि ब्राह्मणस्त्वा नाथकाम उपधावामि यास्यै निन्दिता तनूस्तामितो नाशय स्वाहा ॥ आदित्य प्रायश्चित्ते त्वं प्रायश्चित्तिरसि ब्राह्मणस्त्वा नाथकाम उपधावामि यास्यै पतिघ्नी तनूस्तामितो नाशय स्वाहा ॥ आदित्य प्रायश्चित्ते वायो प्रायश्चित्तेग्ने प्रायश्चित्तेग्ने प्रायश्चित्ते वायो प्रायश्चित्त आदित्य प्रायश्चित्ते ॥

१.२४.२. भूर्भगं त्वयि जुहोमि स्वाहा ॥ भुवो यशस्त्वयि जुहोमि स्वाहा ॥ सुवः श्रियं त्वयि जुहोमि स्वाहा ॥ भूर्भुवः सुवस्त्विषिं त्वयि जुहोमि स्वाहा ॥

१.२४.३. अभि त्वा पञ्चशाखेन शिवेनाविद्विषावता ।
साहस्रेण यशस्विना हस्तेनाभिमृशामसि सुप्रजास्त्वाया ॥

१.२४.४. सं त्वा सं हृदयानि सं नाभिः सं त्वचः ।
सं त्वा कामस्य योक्त्रेण युञ्जान्यविमोचनाय ॥

१.२४.५. मामनुव्रता भव सहचर्या मया भव । या ते पतिघ्नी तनूर्जारघ्नीं त्वेतां करोमि । शिवा त्वं गह्यगेधि क्षुरगतिजरिभ्यः ॥

१.२४.६. मधु हे मध्विदं मधु जिह्वा मे मधुवादिनी ।
मुखे मे सारघं मधु दत्सु संवननं कृतम् ॥

चाक्रवाकं संवननं यन्नदीभ्य उदाहृतम् ।
यद्युक्तो देवगन्धर्वस्तेन संवनिनौ स्वके ॥

१.२५.१. विष्णुर्योनिं कल्पयतु त्वष्टा रूपाणि पिंशतु ॥ आसिञ्चतु प्रजापतिधाता गर्भं दधातु ते ॥ गर्भं देहि सिनीवालि गर्भं देहि सरस्वति । गर्भं ते अश्विनावुभावाधत्तां पुष्करस्रजौ । हिरण्ययी अरणीं यं निर्मन्थतो अश्विना । तं ते गर्भं हवामहे दशमास्याय सूतवे ॥ यथाग्निगर्भा पृथिवी द्यौर्यथेन्द्रेण गर्भणी । वायुर्यथा दिशां गर्भ एवं दधामि ते ॥ यस्य योनिं प्रति रेतो गृहाण पुमान्पुत्रो जायतां गर्भो अन्तः । तं माता दश मासो बिभर्तु स जायतां वीरतमः स्वानाम् ॥ आ ते गर्भो योनिमेतु पुमान्बाण इवेषुधिम् । आ वीरो अत्र जायतां पुत्रस्ते दशमास्यः ॥ करोमि ते प्रजापत्यमा गर्भो योनिमेतु ते।

अनूनः पूर्णो जायतामनन्धोऽश्लोणोपिशाचधीरः ॥ यानि प्रभूणि वीर्याण्यृषभा जनयन्तु नः । तैस्त्वं गर्भिणी भव स जायतां वीरतमः स्वानाम् ॥ यो वशायां गर्भो यश्च वेहतीन्द्रस्तं निदधे वनस्पतौ । तेन त्वं गर्भिणी भव सा प्रसूर्धेनुगा भव ॥

१.२५.२. भूः प्रजापतिनात्यृषभेण स्कन्दयामि वीरं धत्स्वासौ । भुवः प्रजापतिनात्यृषभेण स्कन्दयामि वीरं धत्स्वासौ । सुवः प्रजापतिनात्यृषभेण स्कन्दयामि वीरं धत्स्वासौ ॥

बौधायन गृह्यसूत्र विवाह मन्त्राः

१.१.१५. अनृक्षरा ऋजवस्सन्तु पन्था येभिस्सखायो यन्ति नो वरेयम् ।
समर्यमा सम्भगो नो निनीयात्सञ्जास्पत्यँ सुयममस्तु देवाः ॥

१.१.१७. प्रजापतिः स्त्रियां यशः । मुष्कयोरदधात्सपम् । कामस्य तृप्तिमानन्दम् । तस्याग्ने भाजयेह मा । मोदः प्रमोद आनन्दः । मुष्कयोर्निहितः सपः । सृत्वेव कामस्य तृप्याणि । दक्षिणानां पतिग्रहे । मनसश्चित्तमाकूतिम् । वाचः सत्यमशीमहि। पशूनाँ रूपमन्नस्य । यशः श्रीः श्रयतां मयि । यथाऽहमस्या अतृपँ स्त्रियै मयि । यथा स्त्री तृप्यति पुँसि प्रिये प्रिया । एवं भगस्य तृप्याणि । यज्ञस्य काम्यः प्रियः । ददामीत्यग्निर्वदति । तथेति वायुराह तत् । हन्तेति सत्यं चन्द्रमाः । आदित्यः सत्यमोमिति । आपस्तत्सत्यमाभरन् । यशो यज्ञस्य दक्षिणाम् । असौ मे कामः समृध्यताम् ॥

(तै.ब्रा.२.४.५,६,७)

१.१.२४. अभ्रातृघ्नीं वरुणापतिघ्नीं बृहस्पते ।
इन्द्रापुत्रघ्नीं लक्ष्म्यं तामस्यै सवितस्सुव ॥

१.१.२५. अघोरचक्षुरपतिघ्न्येधि शिवा पतिभ्यऽस्सुमनास्सुवर्चाः ।
जीवसूर्देवकामा शं नो भव द्विपदे शं चतुष्पदे ॥

१.१.२६. इदमहं या त्वयि पतिघ्न्यलक्ष्मिस्तां निर्दिशामि ॥

१.१.२८. एकमिषे विष्णुस्त्वाऽन्वेतु । द्वे ऊर्जे विष्णुस्त्वाऽन्वेतु । त्रीणि व्रताय विष्णुस्त्वाऽन्वेतु । चत्वारि मायोभवाय विष्णुस्त्वाऽन्वेतु । पञ्च पशुभ्यो विष्णुस्त्वाऽन्वेतु । षड्रायस्पोषाय विष्णुस्त्वाऽन्वेतु । सप्त सप्तभ्यो होत्राभ्यो विष्णुस्त्वाऽन्वेतु ॥

१.१.२९. सखायस्सप्तपदा अभुम सख्यं ते गमेयं सख्यात्ते मा योषं मा योष्ठाः ॥

१.२.२०. आपः पादावनेजनीर्द्विषन्तं नाशयन्तु मे ॥
अस्मिन् कुले ब्रह्मवर्चस्यानि ॥

१.२.२४. मयि महो मयि भगो मयि भर्गो मयि यशः ॥

१.२.२७. आम आगाद्वर्चसा यशसा संसृज पयसा तेजसा च ।
तं मा प्रियं प्रजानां कुर्वधिपतिं पशूनाम् ॥

१.२.२८. विराजोऽसि विराजो दोहमशीय । मम पद्याय विराज ॥

१.२.२९. समुद्रं वः प्रहिणोम्यक्षिताः स्वां योनिमपि गच्छत ।
अच्छिद्रः प्रजया भूयासं मा परासोचि मत्पयः ॥

१.२.३१. अमृतोपस्तरणमसि ॥

१.२.३४. त्रय्यै विद्यायै यशोऽसि यशसो यशोऽसि ब्रह्मणो दीप्तिरसि ।
तं मा प्रियं प्रजानां कुर्वधिपतिं पशूनाम् ॥

१.२.३५. देवस्य त्वा सवितुः प्रसवेऽश्विनोर्बाहुभ्यां पूष्णो हस्ताभ्यां प्रतिगृह्णामि ॥

१.२.३६. नेष्टावृद्धिं कृन्तामि या ते घोरा तनूः।
तया तमाविश योस्मान् द्वेष्टि यं च वयं द्विष्मः ॥

१.२.३७. यन्मधुनो मधव्यं परममनाद्यं वीर्यम् ।
तेनाहं मधुनो मधव्येन परमेणात्राद्येन वीर्येण परमोऽन्नादो मधुव्योऽसानि ॥

१.२.४४. गौरस्यपहतपाप्माऽप पाप्मानं नुद मम चामुष्य च ॥

१.२.४८. अग्निः प्रथमः प्राश्नातु स हि वेद यथा हविः ।
शिवा अस्मभ्यमोपधीः कृणोतु विश्वचर्षणिः ॥

१.२.४९. अग्निः प्रथमः प्राश्नातु स हि वेद यथा हविः।
अरिष्टमस्माकं कृणोत्वसौ ब्राह्मणो ब्राह्मणेषु ॥

१.२.५०. गौर्धेनुभव्या माता रुद्राणां दुहिता वसूनां स्वसाऽऽदित्यानाममृतस्य नाभिः ।
प्रणुवोचं चिकितृषे जनाय मा गामनागामदितिं वधिष्ट । पिबतूदकं तृणान्यत्तु।
ओमुत्सृजत ॥

१.२.५७. भूतं सुभूतं सा विराट् तन्मा क्षायि तन्मेऽशीय तन्म ऊर्जं धा ओं कल्पयत ॥

१.२.६०. विराडसि विराडन्नं विराड्विराजो मयि धेहि ॥

१.४.१. मम हृदये हृदयं ते अस्तु मम चित्ते चित्तमस्तु ते ।
मम वाचकमेकमनाः शृणु मामेवानुव्रता सहचर्या मया भव ॥

१.४.३. मां ते मनः प्रविशतु मां चक्षुर्मामु ते भगः मयि सर्वाणि भूतानि मयि प्रज्ञानमस्तु त ॥

१.४.४. मधुगो मध्वगाहे जिह्वा मे मधुवादिनी ।
मुखे मे सारघं मधु दत्सु संवननं कृतम् ॥

१.४.५. चाक्रवाकं संवननं यन्नदीभ्य उदाहृतम् ।
यद्वित्तौ देवगान्धर्वौ तेन संविननौ स्वः ॥

१.४.६. स्पृशामि तेऽहमङ्गानि वायुरापश्च मा परः ।
मां चैव पश्य सूर्यं च मा चान्येषु मनः कृथाः ॥

१.४.७. सोमः प्रथमो विविदे गन्धर्वो विविद उत्तरः ।
तृतीयो अग्निष्टे पतिस्तुरीयस्ते मनुष्यजाः ॥

१.४.८. सोमोऽददद्गन्धर्वाय गन्धर्वोऽददग्नये ।
रयिं च पुत्रांश्चा दादग्निर्मह्यमथो इमाम् ॥

१.४.९. सरस्वति प्रेदमव सुभगे वाजिनीविति ।
तां त्वा विश्वस्य भूतस्य प्रगायामस्यग्रतः ॥

१.४.१०. गृभ्णामि ते सुप्रजस्त्वाय हस्तं मया पत्या जरदिष्टिर्यथाऽसः ।
भगो अर्यमा सविता पुरन्धिर्मह्यं त्वाऽदुर्गार्हपत्याय देवाः ॥

१.४.११. परित्वाऽग्ने पुरं वयं विप्रं सहस्य धीमहि ।
धृषद्वर्णं दिवोदिवे भेत्तारं भङ्गुरावतः ॥

१.४.१३. अग्ने शर्ध महते सौभागाय तव द्युम्नान्युत्तमानि सन्तु ।
सञ्जास्पत्यं सुयममाकृणष्व शत्रूयताभितिष्ठा महांसि ॥

१.४.१४. सोमाय जनिविदे स्वाहा ॥

१.४.१५. गन्धर्वाय जनिविदे स्वाहा ॥

१.४.१६. अग्नये जनिविदे स्वाहा ॥

१.४.१७. कन्यला पितृभ्यो यती पतिलोकमव दक्षिणमदास्थ स्वाहा ॥

१.४.१८. प्रेतो मुञ्चाति नामुतस्सुबद्धाममुतस्करत् ।
यथेयमिन्द्रमीढ्वस्सुपुत्रा सुभगा सती ॥

१.४.१९. इमां त्वमिन्द्र मीढ्वस्सुपुत्रां सुभगां कुरु ।
दशाभ्यां पुत्रानाधेहि पतिमेकादशं कृधि ॥

१.४.२०. अग्निरैतु प्रथमो देवतानां सोऽस्यै प्रजां मुञ्चतु मृत्युपाशात् ।
तदयं राजा वरुणोऽनुमन्यतां यथेयं स्त्री पौत्रमघं न रोदात् ॥

१.४.२१. इमामग्निस्त्रायतां गार्हपत्यः प्रजामस्यै नयतु दीर्घमायुः ।
अशून्योपस्था जीवतामस्तु माता पौत्रमानन्दमयि प्रबुध्यतामियम् ॥

१.४.२२. मा ते गृहे निशि घोष उत्थादन्यत्र त्वद्रुदत्यस्संविशन्तु । मा त्वं विकेश्युर
अवधिष्टा जीवपत्नी पतिलोके विराज पश्यन्ती प्रजां सुमनस्यमानाम् ॥

१.४.२३. अप्रजस्तां पौत्रमृत्यं पाप्मानमुत वाऽघम् ।
शीर्ष्णस्स्रजमिवोन्मुच्य द्विषद्भ्यः प्रतिमुञ्चामि पाशम् ॥

१.४.२४. आतिष्ठेममश्मानमश्मेव त्वं स्थिरा भव ।
अभितिष्ठ पृतन्यतस्सहस्व पृतनायतः ॥

१.४.२६. इयं नार्युपब्रूतेऽग्नौ लाजानावपन्ती ।
दीर्घायुरस्तु मे पतिर्जीवातु शरदश्शतम् ॥

१.४.२७. तुभ्यमग्ने पर्यवहन् सूर्याम् वहतुना सह ।
पुनः पतिभ्यो जायां दा अग्ने प्रजया सह ॥

१.४.२९. पुनः पत्नीमग्निरदादायुषा सह वर्चसा ।
दीर्घायुरस्या यः पतिस्स एतु शरदश्शतम् ॥

१.४.३१. विश्वा उत त्वया वयं धारा उदन्या इव । अतिगाहेमहि द्विषः ॥

१.४.३३. प्रजापते न त्ववेतान्यन्यो विश्वा जातानि परि ता बभूव ।
यत्कामास्ते जुहुमस्तन्नो अस्तु वयं स्याम पतयो रयीणाम् ॥

१.४.३४. यदस्य कर्मणोऽत्यरीरिचं यद्वा न्यूनमिहाकरम् ।
अग्निस्तत्स्विष्टकृद्विद्वान् सर्वं स्विष्टं सुहुतं करोतु मे ।
अग्नये स्विष्टकृते सुहुतहुत आहुतीनां कामानां समर्धयित्रे ॥

१.५.२. ये वध्वश्चन्द्रं वहतुं यक्ष्मा यन्ति जनाँ अनु ।
पुनस्तान्यज्ञिया देवा नयन्तु यत आगताः ॥

१.५.४. पूषा त्वेतो नयतु हस्तगृह्याश्विनौ त्वा प्रवहतां रथेन ।
गृहान् गच्छ गृहपत्नी यथाऽसो वशिनी त्वं विदथमावदासि ॥

१.५.५. सु गं पन्थानमारुक्षमरिष्टं स्वस्तिवाहनम् ।
यस्मिन् वीरो न रिष्यत्यन्येषां विन्दते वसु ॥

१.५.६. या ओषधयो या वनस्पतयो या नद्यो यानि धन्वानि ये वना ।
ते त्वा वधु प्रजावतीं प्रत्वे मुञ्चन्त्वंहसः ॥

१.५.७. भद्रान् गृहान् सुमनमः प्रपद्येऽवीरघ्नी वीरवतस्सुवीरान् ।
इरां वहतो घृतमुक्षमाणास्तेष्वहं सुमनास्संविशानि ॥

१.५.८. इह गावः प्रजायध्वमिहाश्वा इह पुरुषाः ।
इहो सहस्रदक्षिणो रायप्सोषो निषीदत ॥

१.५.११. नीललोहिते भवतः कृत्या सक्तिर्व्यज्यते ।
एधन्तेऽस्या ज्ञातयः पतिर्बन्धेषु वध्यताम् ॥

१.५.१३. ध्रुवोऽसि ध्रुवक्षितिर्ध्रुवमसि ध्रुवतस्स्थितम् ।
त्वं नक्षत्राणां मेथ्यसि स मा पाहि पृतन्यतः ॥

१.५.१४. सप्त ऋषयः प्रथमां कृत्तिकानामरुन्धतीं यद्ध्रुवतां ह नित्युः ।
षट्कृत्तिका मुख्ययोगं वहन्तीयमस्माकमेधत्वष्टम्यरुन्धती ॥

१.५.१५. अग्ने व्रतपते उपयमनं व्रतं चरिष्यामि तच्छकेयम् तन्मे राध्यताम् ।
वायो व्रतपत आदित्य व्रतपते व्रतानां व्रतपते उपयमनं व्रतं चरिष्यामि तन्मे राध्यानाम् ॥

१.५.१८. ऊर्जः पृथिव्या अध्युत्थितोऽसि वनस्पते शतवल्शो विरोह ।
त्वया वयमिषमूर्जं वदन्तो रायस्पोषेण समिषा मदेम ॥

१.५.१९. प्रजया त्वा संसृजामि मासरेण सुरामिव ॥

१.५.२०. प्रजावती भूयासम ॥

१.५.२१. प्रजया त्वा पशुभिस्संसृजामि मासरेण सुरामिव ॥

१.५.२२. प्रजावान् पशुमान् भूयासम् ॥

१.५.३०. सुमङ्गलीरियं वधूरिमां समेत पश्यत ।
सौभाग्यामस्यै दत्वायाथास्तं विपरेतन ॥

१.५.३१. सं ना मनस्सं हृदयानि सं नाऽभि सं तनुत्यजः ।
सं त्वा कामस्य याक्त्रेणे युञ्जत्यविमोचनाय ॥

१.६.१०. यस्त्वा दा कीरिणा मन्यमानो मर्त्यं मर्त्यो जोहवीमि ।
जातवेदा यशो अरगारा धेहि प्रजाभिरग्ने अमृतत्वमश्याम् ॥

यस्मै त्वं सुकृते जातवेद उ लोकमग्ने कृणवः स्योनम् ।
अश्विनं स पुत्रिणं वीरवन्तं गोमन्तं रयिं नशते स्वस्ति ॥

१.६.१२. अग्ने प्रायश्चित्ते त्वं देवानां प्रायश्चित्तिरसि । ब्राह्मणस्त्वा नाथकाम उपधावामि ।
यास्याः पापी लक्ष्मिस्तामस्या अपजहि ॥

१.६.१३. वायो प्रायश्चित्ते त्वं देवानां प्रायश्चित्तिरसि । ब्राह्मणस्त्वा नाथकाम उपधावामि ।
यास्याः पतिघ्नी तनूस्तामस्या अपजहि ॥

१.६.१४. आदित्ये प्रायश्चित्ते त्वं देवानां प्रायश्चित्तिरसि । ब्राह्मणस्त्वा नाथकाम उपधावामि । यास्याः अपुत्र्या तनूस्तामस्या अपजहि ॥

१.६.१५. प्रजापते प्रायश्चित्ते त्वं देवानां प्रायश्चित्तिरसि । ब्राह्मणस्त्वा नाथकाम उपधावामि । यास्याः अपशव्या तनूस्तमस्या अपजहि ॥

१.६.२१. अर्यम्णो अग्निं परियन्तु क्षिप्रं प्रतिक्षन्तां श्वश्र्वो देवराश्च ॥

१.६.२३. उदीर्ष्वातो विश्वावसो नमसेडामहे त्वा । अन्यामिच्छ प्रफर्व्यं सं जायां पत्या सृज । उदीर्ष्वातः पतिवती ह्येषा विश्वावंसु नमसा गीर्भिरी । अन्यामिच्छ पितृपदं व्यक्तां स ते भागो जनुषा तस्य विद्धि ॥

१.६.२४. प्रजापतिः स्त्रियां यशः । मुष्कयोरदधात्सपम् । कामस्य तृप्तिमानन्दम् । तस्याग्ने भाजयेह मा । मोदः प्रमोद आनन्दः । मुष्कयोर्निहितः सपः । सृत्वेव कामस्य तृप्याणि । दक्षिणानां पतिग्रहे । मनसश्चित्तमाकूतिम् । वाचः सत्यमशीमहि । पशूनाँ रूपमन्नस्य । यशः श्रीः श्रयतां मयि । यथाऽहमस्या अत्रुपँ स्त्रियै मयि । यथा स्त्री तृप्यति पुँसि प्रिये प्रिया । एवं भगस्य तृप्याणि। यज्ञस्य काम्यः प्रियः । ददामीत्यग्निर्वदति । तथेति वायुराह तत् । हन्तेति सत्यं चन्द्रमाः । आदित्यः सत्यमोमिति । आपस्तत्सत्यमाभरन् । यशो यज्ञस्य दक्षिणाम् । असौ मे कामः समृध्यताम् ॥

१.६.२६. जीवां रुदन्ती विमयन्तो अध्वरे दीर्घामनुप्रसिति दीधियुर्नरः ।
वामं पितृभ्यो य इदं समेरिरे मयः पतिभ्यो जनयः परिष्वजे ॥

१.७.३७. विष्णुर्योनिं कल्पयतु त्वष्टा रूपाणि पिंशतु ।
आसिञ्चतु प्रजापतिर्धाता गर्भं दधातु ते ॥

१.७.३८. यथाऽग्निगर्भा पृथिवी द्यौर्यथेन्द्रेण गर्भिणी ।
वायुर्यथा दिशां गर्भ एवं गर्भं दधातु ते ॥

१.७.३९. गर्भं धेहि सिनीवालि गर्भं धेहि सरस्वति ।
गर्भं ते अश्विनौ देवावाधत्तां पुष्करस्रजा ॥

१.७.४०. हिरण्ययी अरुणी यं निर्मन्थतो अश्विना ।
तंते गर्भं दधाम्यहं दशमे मासि सूतवे ॥

१.७.४१. नेजमेष परापत सपुत्रः पुनरापत ।
अस्यै मे पुत्रकामायै गर्भमाधेहि यः पुमान् ॥

१.७.४२. अमूहमस्मि सा त्वं द्यौरहं पृथिवी त्वं रेतोऽहं रेतोभृत्त्वं मनोऽहमस्मि वाक्त्वं सामाहमस्मि ऋक्त्वं तावेहि सम्भवाव सह रेतो दधावहै पुंसे पुत्राय वेत्तवै रायस्पोषाय सुप्रजास्त्वाय सुवीर्याय ॥

१.७.४३. अहं गर्भमदधामोषधीष्वहं विश्वेषु भुवनेष्वन्तः ।
अहं प्रजा अजनयन्पितृणामहं जनिभ्यो अपरिषु पुत्रान् ॥

१.७.४४. तां पूषच्छिवतमोमरयस्व यस्यां बीजं मनुष्या वपन्ती ।
या न ऊरू उशती विस्रयातै यस्यामुशन्तः प्रहरेम शेफम् ॥

१.८.१. यथा त्वं वनस्पत ऊर्जा अभ्युत्थितो वनस्पते ।
शतवल्शो विरोहस्येवमहं पुत्रैश्च पशुभिश्च सहस्रवल्शा वि वयं रुहेम ॥

१.८.३. यथा त्वं वनस्पते फलवानस्येवमहं पुत्रैश्च पशुभिश्च फलवान् भवानि ॥

१.८.५. ऊर्जस्वान् पयस्वान् पयसा पिन्वमानोऽस्मान् वनस्पते पयसाऽभ्याववृत्स्व ॥

१.८.१०. प्रतियुतो वरुणस्य पाशः प्रत्यस्तो वरुणस्य पाशः ॥

वाराह गृह्यसूत्र विवाह मन्त्राः

१०.७. अनृक्षरा ऋजवः सन्तु पन्था येभिस्सखायो यन्ति नो वरेयम् ।
समर्यमा सं भगो नो निनीयात् सञ्जास्पत्यं सुयममस्तु देवाः ॥

३.५. विराजो दोहोऽसि विराजो दोहोऽसि विराजो दोहमशीय मयि दोहः पद्यायै विराज ॥

११.७. अहं वर्ष्म सदृशानामुद्यतामिव सूर्यः ।
इदमहं तमधरं करोमि यो मा कश्चाभिदासति ॥

११.१२. अमृतोपस्तरणमसि ॥

११.१६. आदित्यास्त्वा पृष्ठे सादयामि ॥ सुपर्णस्य त्वा गरुत्मतश्चक्षुषाऽवेक्ष ॥ नमो रुद्राय पात्रसदे ॥ ये अग्नेषु विविध्यन्ति पात्रेषु पिबतो जनान् ॥ नमो रुद्राय ग्रामसदे ॥ नमो रुद्रायैकवृक्षसदे ॥ नमो रुद्राय श्मशानसदे ॥ नमो रुद्राय चतुष्पथसदे ॥ नमो रुद्राय तीर्थसदे ॥

मधु वाता ऋतायते मधु क्षरन्ति सिन्धवः । माध्वीर्नः सन्त्वोषधीः ॥
मधुनक्तमुतोषसो मधुमत् पार्थिवं रजः । मधु द्यौरस्तु नः पिता ॥
मधुमान्नो वनस्पतिर्मधुमाँ अस्तु सूर्यः । माध्वोर्गावो भवन्तु नः ॥

११.१७. सत्यं यशः श्रीर्मयि श्रीरश्रयतामिति त्रिः प्राश्नाति भूयिष्ठम् ॥

११.२१. हतो मे पाप्मा पाप्मानं मे हत । यां त्वा देवा वसवोऽन्वजीविषुरादित्यानां स्वसारं रुद्रमातरम् । दैवीं गामादितिं जनानामारभन्तामर्हतामर्हणाय ॥

११.२३. माता रुद्राणां दुहिता वसूनां स्वसादित्यानामृतस्य नाभिः । प्र नु वोचं चिकितुषे जनाय मा गामनागामदितिं वधिष्ठ । ॐ उत्सृजत तृणान्यत्तूदकं पिबत ॥

१२.१. अलङ्करणमसि सर्वस्मा अलं भूयासम् ॥

१२.२. प्राणापानौ मे तर्पयामि समानव्यानौ मे तर्पयामि ।
उदानरूपे मे तर्पयामि चक्षुःश्रोत्रे मे तर्पयामि ।
सुवर्चा अहमक्षिभ्यां भूयासं सुवर्चा मुखेन सुश्रुत्कर्णाभ्यामिति ॥

१२.३. परिधास्ये यशो धास्ये दीर्घायुत्वाय जरदिष्टरस्मि ।
शतं च जीव शरदः पुरूचीर्वसूनि चाय्यो विभजाय जीयाम् ॥

१२.४. शुभं वद दुन्दुभे सुप्रजास्त्वाय गोमुख ।
प्रक्रीडन्तु कन्यास्सुमनस्यमानास्सहेन्द्राण्या सवयसः सनीडाः ।
प्रजापतिर्यो वसति प्रजासु प्रजास्वन्वते सुमनस्यमानाः ।
स इमाः प्रजां रमयतु प्रजात्यै स्वयं च नोरमतां शं दधानः ॥

१४.१. खे रथस्य खेऽनसः खे युगस्य शतक्रतोः ।
अपालामिन्द्रस्त्रिः पूर्त्यवकृणोत्सूर्यत्वचसः ॥

१४.२. सं त्वा नह्यामि पयसा पृथिव्याः सं त्वा नह्याम्याद्भिरोषधीभिः ।
सं त्वा नह्यामि प्रजया धनेन सह संनद्धा सुनुहि भागधेयम् ॥

१४.३. अघोरचक्षुरपतिध्न्येधि । एहि शिवा पशुभ्यः सुमना सुवर्चाः ।
दीर्घायुपत्नी प्रजया स्वर्विदिन्द्रप्रणयीरुप नो वस्तुमेहि ॥

१४.१०. अग्नये जनविदे स्वाहा । सोमाय जनविदे स्वाहा । गन्धर्वाय जनविदे स्वाहा।

सोमः प्रथमो विविदे गन्धर्वो विविद उत्तरः ।
तृतीयोऽग्निष्टे पतिस्तुर्योऽहं मनुष्यजाः॥

सोमाऽददद्गन्धर्वाय गन्धर्वोऽदददग्नये ।
रयिं च पुत्राँश्चादादग्निर्मह्यमथो इमाम् ॥

१४.११. हिरण्यगर्भः समवर्तताग्रे भूतस्य जातः पतिरेक आसीत् ।
स दाधार पृथिवीं द्यामुतेमां कस्मै देवाय हविषा विधेम ॥

प्रद्भ्यः सम्भृतः पृथिव्यै रसाच्च विश्वकर्मणः समवर्तताग्रे ।
तस्य त्वष्टा विदधद्रूपमेति तन्मर्त्यस्य देवत्वमाजानमग्रे ॥

१४.१२. आकूत्यै त्वा स्वाहा । भूत्यै त्वा स्वाहा । कामायै त्वा स्वाहा । रक्षायै त्वा स्वाहा । समृधे त्वा स्वाहा । समृद्ध्यै त्वा स्वाहा । ऋचा स्तोमम् । प्रजापतये । भूः स्वाहा । अयाश्चाग्नेऽसीत् ॥

१४.१४. देवस्य ते सवितुः प्रसवेऽश्विनोर्बाहुभ्यां पूष्णो हस्ताभ्याँ हस्तं गृह्णाम्यहम् ॥

गृह्णामि ते सौभगत्वाय हस्तं मया पत्या जरदष्टिर्यथासत् ।
भगो अर्यमा सविता पुरन्धिर्मह्यम् त्वादुर्गार्हपत्याय देवाः ॥

ऊर्ध्वा वाक्समभवत्पुरा देवासुरेभ्यः ।
यां त्वा विश्वस्य भूतस्य प्रागायाम्यस्या अग्रतः ॥

सरस्वति प्रेदमव सुभगे वाजीनावति ।
येन भूतँ समभवद्येन विश्वामिदं जगत् ।
तामद्य गाथां गास्यामो या स्त्रीणामुत्तमं मनः ॥

सा त्वमस्यमोऽहमोऽहमसि सा त्वम् ।
द्यौरहं पृथिवी त्वं बृहदहं रथन्तरं त्वम् । रेतोऽहमस्मि रेतोधृक्त्वम् ॥

सामाहमस्मि ऋक्त्वं मनोऽहमस्मि वाक्त्वम् ।
सा मामनुव्रता भव सा मामनुप्रजायस्व ॥

प्रजाँ सृजावहा उभौ पुँसे पुत्राय कर्तवे ।
श्रियै पुत्राय वेथवेह सूनृते ॥

१४.१५. आतिष्ठेममश्मानमश्मेव त्वँ स्थिरा भव ।
कृण्वन्तु विश्वे देवा आयुष्टे शरदः शतम् ॥

१४.१७. इयं नार्युपब्रूते लाजानावपन्तिका ।
दीर्घायुरस्तु मे पतिरेधान्तां ज्ञातयो मम ॥

अर्यमणं नु देवं कन्याग्निमयक्षत ।
सोऽस्मान्देवोऽर्यमा प्रेतो मुञ्चातु मामुत ॥

१४.२०. तुभ्यमग्रे पर्यण्यँ सूर्याँ वहुतना सह ।
पुनः पतिभ्यो जायां दा अग्ने प्रजया सह ॥

१४.२३. एकमिषे विष्णुस्त्वां नयतु । द्वे ऊर्जे । त्रीणि रायस्पोषाय । चत्वारि मायोभवाय ।
पञ्च प्रजाभ्यः । षड्तुभ्यः । सप्त सप्तभ्यो होत्राभ्यः ॥ सखी सप्तपदी भव
सख्यं ते गमेयँ सख्यात्ते मा रिषिम् ॥

१४.२४. प्र त्वा मुञ्चातु वरुणस्य पाशाद्येन त्वाबध्नात्सविता सुशेवः ।
धातुश्च योनौ सुकृतस्य लोके हृष्टा सँ सह पात्या भूयासम् ॥

१४.२५. सुमङ्गलीरियँ वधुरिमाँ समेत्य पश्यत ।
सौभाग्यमस्यै दत्वा यथार्थँ विपरेतन ॥

१५.१. अङ्कौ न्यङ्कावभितो रथँ ये ध्वान्ता वाता अग्रमभि ये संपतन्ति ।
दूरेहेतिः पतत्री वाजीविनाँस्ते नोऽग्नयः पप्रयः पारयन्तु ॥

१५.२. सुकिँशुकँ शल्मलिं विश्वरूपँ हिरण्यवर्णँ सुधुरँ सुचक्रम् ।
आरोह सूर्ये अमृतस्य पन्थाँस्तेन याहि गृहान्स्वस्ति ॥

१५.३. उप मायन्तु देवता उप ब्रह्म सुवीर्यम् ।
उप क्षत्रं च यद्बलमुप मामैतु यद्बलम् ॥

१५.४. अनु मायन्तु देवता अनु ब्रह्म सुवीर्यम् ।
अनु क्षत्रं च यद्यशमनु मामैतु यद्यशम् ॥

१५.५. नमो रुद्रायैकवृक्षसद । ये वृक्षेषु शष्पिञ्जरा ॥

१५.६. नमो रुद्राय चतुष्पथसद । ये पथां पथिरक्षय ॥

१५.७. नमो रुद्राय श्मशानसद । ये भूतानामधिपतय ॥

१५.८. नमो रुद्राय पात्रसद । ये अन्नेषु विविध्यनति ॥

१५.९. ये तीर्थानि ॥

१५.१०. समुद्राय वयुनाय सिन्धूनां पतये नमः ।
नदीनाँ सर्वासां पित्वे जुहुता विश्वकर्मणे । विश्वहादाभ्यँ हविः ॥

१५.११. अमृतमास्ये जुहोम्यायुः प्राणे परिदधामि ।
अमृतं ब्रह्मणा सह मृत्युं तरेम । प्रासहादितीष्टरस्यादितिरेव मृत्युन्धय ॥

१५.१७. गृहानहँ सुमनसः प्रपद्येऽवीरघ्नी वीरवतः सुशेवा ।
इराँ वहन्ती घृतमुक्षमाणाँस्तेष्वहँ सुमनाः सँविशामि ॥

१५.२१. अच्युता ध्रुवा ध्रुवपत्नी ध्रुवं पश्येम विश्वत ॥

दधिक्राव्णो अकारिषं जिष्णोरश्वस्य वाजिनः ।
सुरभि नो मुखा करत् प्र ण आयूंषी तारिषत् ॥

१५.२२. चक्रमिवानडुहः पदं मामेवान्वेतु ते मनः ।
मां च पश्यसि सूर्यं च मा चान्येषु मनस्कृथाः ॥
चाक्रावाकं सँवसनं तन्नौ सँवननं कृतम् ॥

मानव गृह्यसूत्र विवाह मन्त्राः

१.८.९. क इदं कस्मा अदात् कामः कामायादात् ।
कामो दाता कामः प्रतिग्रहीता कामः समुद्रमाविवेश ।
कामेन त्वा प्रतिगृह्णामि कामैतत्ते ॥

१.८.१०. समाना व आकूतानि समाना हृदयानि वः ।
समानमस्तु वो मनो यथा वः सुसहासति ॥

१.८.११. खे रथस्य खेऽनसः खे युगस्य शतक्रतो ।
अपालामिन्द्रस्त्रिः पूर्त्यवकृणोत्सूर्यत्वचम् ॥

१.९.७. विराजो दोहोसि । विराजो दोहमशीय । मयि दोहः पद्यायै विराजः ॥

१.९.८. अहं वर्ष्म सदृशानामुद्यतामिव सूर्यः ।
इदं तमभितिष्ठामि यो मा कश्चाभिदासत् ॥

१.९.१३. नमो रुद्राय पात्रसदे । नमो रुद्राय पात्रसद ॥

१.९.१४. मधु वाता ऋतायते मधु क्षरन्ति सिन्धवः । माध्वीर्नः सन्त्वोषधीः ॥
मधुनक्तमुतोषसो मधुमत् पार्थिवं रजः । मधु द्यौरस्तु नः पिता ॥
मधुमान्नो वनस्पतिर्मधुमाँ अस्तु सूर्यः । माध्वोर्गावो भवन्तु नः ॥

१.९.२०. हतो मे पाप्मा पाप्मानं मे हत । यां त्वा देवा वसवोऽन्वजीविषुरादित्यानां
स्वसारं रुद्रमातरम् । दैवीं गामादितिं जनानामारभन्तामर्हतामर्हणाय ॥

१.९.२३. माता रुद्राणां दुहिता वसूनां स्वसादित्यानामृतस्य नाभिः । प्र नु वोचं
चिकितुषे जनाय मा गामनागामदितिं वधिष्ठ । ॐ उत्सृजत तृणान्यत्तूदकं
पिबत ॥

१.९.२४. अलंकरणमसि सर्वस्मा अलं मे भूयासम् ॥

१.९.१५. प्राणापानौ मे तर्पय समान व्यानौ मे तर्पय उदानरूपे मे तर्पय ।
सुचक्षा अह मक्षिभ्यां भूयासं सुवर्चा मुखेन सुश्रुत्कर्णाभ्यां भूयासम् ॥

१.९.२७. परिधास्ये यशो धास्ये दीर्घायुत्वाय जरदष्टिरस्तु शतं जीवमेशरदः ।
पुरूची रायस्पोषमभिसँव्ययिष्ये यशसा माऽद्यावा पृथिवी ।
यशसेन्द्रा बृहस्पती यशो भगश्च मारिषद्यशो मा प्रति मुच्यताम् ॥

१.१०.६. अघोर चक्षुरपतिघ्न्येधि शिवा पशुभ्यः सुमनाः सुवर्चाः ।
वीरसूर्देवकामा स्योना शं नो भव द्विपदे शं चतुस्पदे ॥

१.१०.७. हिरण्यवर्णाः शुचयः पावका यासु जातः कश्यपो यास्विन्द्रः ।
अग्निं या गर्भं दधिरे विरूपास्ता न आपः शं स्योना भवन्तु ॥

१.१०.८. या अकृन्तन्या अतन्वन्या अवाहरन् याश्चाग्नादेव्योऽन्तानभितोऽततनन्त ।
तास्त्वादेव्यो जरसे सँव्ययन्त्वायुष्मतीदं परिधत्स्व वासः ॥

१.१०.१०. सोमोददद्गन्धर्वाय गन्धर्वो दददग्नये ।
रयिं च पुत्रांश्चादादग्निर्मह्यमथो इमाम् ॥

अग्निरस्याः प्रथमो जातवेदाः सोऽस्याः प्रजा मुञ्चतु मृत्युपाशात् ।
तदिदं राजा वरुणोऽनुमन्यताम् । यथेदँस्त्रीपौत्रमगन्म रुद्रियाय ॥

हिरण्यगर्भः समवर्तताग्रे भूतस्य जातः पतिरेक आसीत् ।
स दाधार पृथिवीं द्यामुतेमां कस्मै देवाय हविषा विधेम ॥

प्रद्भ्यः सम्भृतः पृथिव्यै रसाच्च विश्वकर्मणः समवर्तताग्रे ।
तस्य त्वष्टा विदधद्रूपमेति तन्मर्त्यस्य देवत्वमाजानमग्रे ॥

१.१०.१३. तस्याँ व्रते ते हृदयं दधातु मम चित्तमनुचितं तेऽस्तु ।
मम वाचमेकमना जुषस्व प्रजापतिष्ट्वा नियुनक्तुमह्याम् ॥

१.१०.१४. देवस्य त्वा सवितुः प्रसवेऽश्विनोर्बाहुभ्यां पूष्णो हस्ताभ्याँहस्तं गृह्णाम्यसाव ।

गृभ्णामि ते सौभगत्वाय हस्तं मया पत्या जरद्दष्टिर्यथासत् । भगो अर्यमा सविता पुरन्धि र्मह्यं त्वादुर्गार्हपत्याय देवाः । सरस्वति प्रेदमव सुभगे वाजिनीवति। यां त्वा विश्वस्य भुतस्य भव्यस्य प्रगायाम्यस्याग्रतः ॥

अमोह मस्मि सा त्वं सा त्वमस्यप्यमोहम् ।
द्योरहं पृथिवी त्वमृक् त्वमसि सामाऽहम् रेतोह मस्मि रेतो धत्तम् ॥

ता एव विवाहवहै पुँसे पुत्राय कर्त्तवै । श्रीये पुत्राय वेधवै ॥
रायस्पोषाय सुप्रस्त्वाय सुवीर्याय ॥

१.१०.१६. एतमश्मानमातिष्ठतमश्वेव युवां स्थिरौ भवतम् कृण्वन्तु विश्वे देवा आयुर्वा शरदः शतम् ॥

१.१०.१७. यथेन्द्रः सहेन्द्राण्या अवारुहद् गन्धमादनात् ।
एवं त्वमस्मादश्मनो अवरोह सह पत्न्या ॥

१.१०.१८. आरोहस्व समे पादौ प्र पूर्व्यायुष्मती कन्ये पुत्रवती भव ॥

१.११.६. सं त्वा नह्यामि पयसा पृथिव्याः संत्वा नह्याम्यद्भिरोषधीभिः ।
सं त्वा नह्यामि प्रजया धनेन सा सन्नद्धा सुनुहि भगधेयम् ॥

१.११.९. यानिरक्षाँस्यभितो व्रजन्त्यस्या वध्वा अग्निसकाश मागच्छन्त्याः ।
तेषामहं प्रतिविध्यामि चक्षुः स्वस्ति वध्वै भूतपतिर्दधातु ॥

१.११.१२. अर्यमणं नु देवं कन्या अग्निमयक्षत ।
सोस्मान्देवोऽर्यमा प्रेतो मुञ्चातु मामुतः ॥

तुभ्यमग्ने पर्यवहन्त्सूर्यॅंविहतुना सह ।
पुनः पतिभ्यो जायां दा अग्नेः प्रजया सह ॥

पुनः पत्नी मग्निरदादायुषा सह वर्चसा ।
दीर्घायुरस्या यः पतिर्जीवाति शरदः शतम् ॥

इयं नार्युपब्रूतेऽनौलाजावपन्तिका ।
दीर्घायुरस्तु मे पतिरेधन्तां ज्ञातयो मम ॥

१.११.१८. एकमिषे द्वे ऊर्जे त्रीणि प्रजाभ्यश्चत्वारि रायस्पोषाय पञ्च भवाय षड्तुभ्यः। सखा सप्तदीभव सुमृडीका सरस्वती । सा ते व्योम संदृशी । विष्णुस्त्वा मुन्नयत्विति सर्वत्रानुषजति ॥

१.११.२०. इमँ विष्यामि वरुणस्य पाशँ यज्जग्रन्थ सविता सत्यधर्मा ।
धातुश्च योनौ सुकृतस्य लोके रिष्टां मा सह पत्या दधातु ॥

१.१२.१. सुमङ्गलीरियँ वधूरिमां समेत पश्यतः ।
सौभाग्यमस्यै दत्वायाथास्त्वं विपरेतन ॥

१.१२.३. अभ्यज्य केशान् सुमनस्यमानाः प्रजावरीर्यशसे बहुपुत्रा अघोराः ।
शिवा भर्त्तुः श्वशुरस्यावदायायुष्मतीः श्वश्रूमतीश्चिरायुः ॥

१.१२.४. समस्य केशानवृजिनानघोरान् शिखा सखिभ्यो भव सर्वाभ्यः ।
शिवा भव सुकुलोह्यमाना शिवा जनेषु सहवाहनेषु ॥

१.१३.४. अङ्कून्यङ्कवभितो रथँ ये ध्वान्ता वाता अग्निमभिये संचरन्ति ।
दूरे हेतिः पतत्री वाविनी वाँस्ते नोऽग्नयः पप्रयः पालयन्तु ॥

१.१३.६. सुकिँशुकँ शल्मलिँ विश्वरूपँ हिरण्यवर्णँ सुवृतँ सुचक्रम् ।
आरोह सूर्ये अमृतस्य लोकँ स्योनं पत्ये वहतं कृणुष्व ॥

१.१३.७. अनुमायन्तु देवता अनुब्रह्म सुवीर्यम् ।
अनुक्षत्रं तु यद्बल मनुमामैतु मद्यशः ॥

१.१३.८. प्रतिमायन्तु देवताः प्रतिब्रह्म सुवीर्यम् ।
प्रतिक्षत्रं तु यद्बलं प्रति मामैतु यद्यशः ॥

१.१३.१०. नमो रुद्राय ग्रामसद ॥

१.१३.११. नमो रुद्रायैक वृक्षसद । ये वृक्षेषु शष्पिञ्जरा ॥

१.१३.१२. नमो रुद्राय श्मशानसद । ये भूताना मधिपतय ॥

१.१३.१३. नमो रुद्राय चतुष्पथसद । ये पथां पथि रक्षय ॥

१.१३.१४. नमो रुद्राय तीर्थसद । ये तीर्थानि प्रचरन्तीति ॥

१.१३.१५. समुद्राय वैणवे सिन्धूनां पतये नमः । नमो नदीनाँ सर्वासां पत्ये । विश्वाहा
जुषताँ विश्वकर्मणामिदँ हविः स्वः स्वाहेत्यप्सूदकाञ्जलीन्निनयति । अमृतं
वा आस्ये जुहोम्यायुः प्राणेऽप्यमृतं ब्रह्मणा सह मृत्युन्तरति । प्रासहादिति
रिष्टिरिति मुक्तिरिति मुक्षीयमाणः सर्वं भयं नुदस्व ॥

१.१३.१८. जवेन शिवेन वैश्वानर इडयास्याग्रतः ।
आचार्यो येन येन पथा प्रयाति तेन तेन सह ॥

१.१४.५. येष्वध्येति प्रवसन्येषु सौमनसं महत् ।
तेनोपव्हयामहे ते नो जानन्त्वागतम् ॥

१.१४.६. गृहानहँ सुमनसः प्रपद्ये वीरँहि वीरवतः सुशेवा ।
इराँवहन्ती घृतमुक्षमाणास्तेष्वहँ सुमनाः सँवसाम ॥

१.१४.८. सोमेनदित्या बलिनः सोमेन पृथिवी मही ।
असौ नक्षत्राणामेषामुपस्थे सोम आहितः ॥

१.१४.१०. अच्युता ध्रुवा ध्रुवपत्नी ध्रुवं पश्येम सर्वतः ।
ध्रुवासः पर्वता इमे ध्रुवा स्त्री पतिकुलेयम् ॥

१.१४.१२. चक्रीवानडुहौ वा मे वाङ्मैतु ते मनः ।
चाक्रवाकँ सँ वननं तन्नौ सं वननं कृतम् ॥

१.१४.१६. अपश्यं त्वा मनसा चेकितानां तपसो जातं तपसो विभूतम् ॥
इह प्रजामिह रयिँरराणः प्रजायस्व प्रजया पुत्रकाम ॥

अपश्यं त्वा मनसा दीध्यानां स्वायां तनूँ ऋत्विये बाधमानम् ।
उप मामूच्चा युवतिर्बभुयाः प्रजायस्व प्रजया पुत्रकामे ॥

प्रजापतिस्तन्वं मे जुषस्व त्वष्टा देवैः सहमान इन्द्रः ।
विश्वेदेवैर्ऋतुभिः सँ विदानः पुँसां बहूनां मातरौ स्याव ॥

अहं गर्भं मदधामोषधीष्वहँ विश्वेषु भुवनेष्वन्तः ।
अहं प्रजा अजनयं पृथिव्या अहं जनिभ्यो अपरिषु पुत्रान् ॥

आग्निवेश्य गृह्यसूत्र विवाह मन्त्राः

१. अनृक्षरा ऋजवः सन्तु पन्था येभिः सखायो यन्ति नो वरेण्यम् ।
समर्यमा संभगो नो निनीयात् सञ्जास्पत्यं सुयममस्तु देवाः ॥

२. मयि गृह्णाम्यग्रे अग्निं रायस्पोषाय सुप्रजस्त्वाय सुवीर्याय ।
मयि प्रजां मयि वर्चो दधाम्यरिष्टाः स्याम तनुवा सुवीराः ॥

३. यो नो अग्निः पितरो हृत्स्वन्तरमर्त्यो मर्त्यों आविवेश ।
तमात्मन् परिगृह्णीमहे वयं मा सो अस्मां अवहाय परागात् ॥

१. प्रजापतिः स्त्रियां यशो मुष्कयोरदधात् सपम् । कामस्य तृप्तिमानन्दं तस्याग्ने भाजयेह मा । मोदः प्रमोद आनन्दो मुष्कयोर्निहितः सपः । सृत्वेव कामस्य तृप्याणि दक्षिणानां प्रतिग्रहे । मनसश्चित्तमाकूतिं वाचः सत्यमशीमहि । पशूनां रूपमन्नस्य यशः श्रीः श्रयतां मयि । यथाहमस्या अतृपं स्त्रियै पुमान् यथा स्त्री तृप्यति पुंसि प्रिये प्रिया । एवं भगस्य तृप्याणि यज्ञस्य काम्यः प्रियाम् । आदित्यः सत्यभोमिति । आपस्तत् सत्यमाभरन् । यशो यज्ञस्य दक्षिणाम् । असौ मे कामः समृध्यताम् ॥

२. आपो हि ष्ठा मयोभुवस्ता न ऊर्जे दधातन । महे रणाय चक्षसे ॥

यो वः शिवतमो रसस्तस्य भाजयतेह नः । उशतीरिव मातरः ॥

तस्मा अरं गमाम वो यस्य क्षयाय जिन्वथ । आपो जनयथा च नः ॥

३. हिरण्यवर्णाः शुचयः पावका यासु जातः कश्यपो यास्विन्द्रः ।
अग्निं या गर्भं दधिरे विरूपास्ता न आपः शं स्योना भवन्तु ॥

४. पवमानः सुवर्जनः । पवित्रेण विचर्षणिः । यः पोता स पुनातु मा । पुनन्तु मा देवजनाः । पुनन्तु मनवो धिया । पुनन्तु विश्व आयवः । जातवेदः पवित्रवत् । पवित्रेण पुनाहि मा । शुक्रेण देव दीद्यत् । अग्ने क्रत्वा क्रतूँरनु ॥

५. या अकृन्तन्नवयन् या अतन्वत याश्च देवीरन्तानभितोऽददन्त ।
तास्त्वा देवीर्जरसा संव्ययन्त्वायुष्मतीदं परिधत्स्व वासः ।

६. परिधत्त धत्त वाससैनां शतायुषीं कृणुत दीर्घमायुः ।
बृहस्पतिः प्रायच्छद्वास एतत् सोमाय राज्ञे परिधातवा उ ।

७. जरां गच्छासि परिधत्स्व वासो भवा कृष्टीनामभिशस्तिपावती ।
शतं च जीव शरदः सुवर्चा रायश्च पोषमुपसंव्ययस्व ।

८. परीदं वासो अधिपाः स्वस्तयेऽभूरापीनागभिशस्तिपावति ।
शतं च जीव शरदः पुरूचीर्वसूनि चार्यो विभजासु जीवति ।

९. अनया सह मया कर्माणि कर्तव्यानि । प्रजाश्चोत्पदयितव्याः । तदर्थमेनां परिणेष्ये ॥

१०. इन्द्राय नमः । अग्नये नमः । यमाय नमः । निरृतये नमः । वरुणाय नमः । सोमाय नमः । ईशानाय नमः । ब्रह्मणे नमः । अद्भ्यो नमः । अग्नये नमः । आत्मने नमः ॥

११. अदितेऽनुमन्यस्व । अनुमतेऽनुमन्यस्व । सरस्वतेऽनुमन्यस्व ।

१२. देवसवितः प्रसुव यज्ञं प्रसुव यज्ञपतिं भगाय ।
दिवो गन्धर्वः केतपूः केतं नः पुनातु वाचस्पतिर्वाचं न स्वदतु ॥

१३. अयं त इध्म आत्मा जातवेदस्तेनेध्यस्व वर्धस चेद्ध वर्धय चास्मान् प्रजया पशुभिर्ब्रह्मवर्चसेनानाध्येन समेधय स्वाहा ॥

१४. प्रजापतये स्वाहा । इन्दाय स्वाहा । अग्नये स्वाहा । सोमाय स्वाहा । भूः स्वाहा । भुवः स्वाहा । स्वः स्वाहा । भूर्भुवःस्वः स्वाहा ॥

१५. या तिरश्ची निपद्यसेऽहं विधरणी इति ।
तां त्वा घृतस्य धारया जुहोति वैश्वकर्मणि ॥

१६. यानूची निपद्यसेऽहं विधरणी इति । तां त्वा घृतस्य धारया अग्नौ ।
संराधन्यै देव्यै स्वाहा । प्रसाधन्यौ देव्यै स्वाहा ॥

२०. युक्तो वह जातवेदः पुरस्तादग्ने विद्धि कर्म क्रियमाणं ययेदम् ।
त्वं भिषग् भेषजस्यासि कर्ता त्वया गा अश्वान् पुरुषान् सनेमि ॥

विरुपाक्षाय स्वाहा । दन्तान् जये स्वाहा ।

२१. विरूपाक्षमहं यजे निजङ्गं शबळोदरम् ।
यो मायं परिबाधते श्रियै पुष्ट्यै च तस्मै स्वाहा ॥

२२. परिबाध मा विबाधिष्ठा मा विबाध विबाधिथाः ।
निरॠत्यै त्वा पुत्रमाहुः स नः कर्माणि साध्य ॥

२३. सदस्पतिमद्भुतं प्रियमिन्द्रस्य काम्यम् । सनिं मेधामयासिषं ॥

२४. यावन्तो देवास्त्वयि जातवेदः स्त्रियं चोद्घ्नन्ति पुरुषस्य कर्म ।
तेभ्य एतद्धूयते भागधेयं ते मा तृप्तास्तर्पयन्तु कामैः ॥

२५. आकूत्यै त्वा कामाय त्वा समृधे त्वा । पुरो दधे अमृतत्वाय जीवसे ॥

२६. आकूतिमस्यावसे । काममस्य समृद्ध्यै । इन्द्रस्य युञ्जते धियः ॥

२७. आकूतिं देवीं मनसः पुरो दधे । यज्ञस्य माता सुहवा मे अस्तु । यदिच्छामि मनसा स कामः । विदेयमेनद्धृदये निविष्टं ॥

इष्टेभ्यः स्वाह । वषडनिष्टेभ्यः स्वाहा । भेषजं दुरिष्ट्यै स्वाहा । निष्कृत्यै स्वाहा । दौराध्यै स्वाहा । देवीभ्यस्तनूभ्यः स्वाहा । ॠद्ध्यै स्वाहा । समृद्ध्यै स्वाहा । चित्ताय स्वाहा । चित्तये स्वाहा । आकूताय स्वाहा । आकूत्यै स्वाहा। विज्ञाताय स्वाहा । विज्ञानाय स्वाहा । मनसे स्वाहा । शकरीभ्यः स्वाहा । दर्शाय स्वाहा । पूर्णमासाय स्वाहा । बृहते स्वाहा । रथन्तराय स्वाहा ॥

२८. प्रजापतिर्जयानिन्द्राय वृष्णे प्रायच्छदुग्रः पृतनाज्येषु ।
तस्मै विशः समनमन्त सर्वाः स उग्रः स हि हव्यो बभूव ॥

२९. अग्निर्भुतानामधिपतिः स मावतु स्वाहा । पितरः इन्द्रो ज्येष्टानामधिपतिः स मावतु स्वाहा । यमः पृथिव्या अधिपतिः स मावतु स्वाहा । वायुरन्तरिक्षस्याधिपतिः स मावतु स्वाहा । सूर्यो दिवोऽधिपतिः स मावतु स्वाहा । चन्द्रो नक्षत्राणामधिपतिः स मावतु स्वाहा । बृहस्पतिर्ब्रह्मणोऽधिपतिः स मावतु स्वाहा । मित्रः

सत्यानामाधिपतिः स मावतु स्वाहा । वरुणोऽपामधिपतिः स मावतु स्वाहा । समुद्रः स्त्रोत्यानामधिपतिः स मावतु स्वाहा । अन्नँ साम्राज्यानामधिपति तन्मावतु स्वाहा । सोम ओषधीनामधिपतिः स मावतु स्वाहा । सविता प्रसवानामधिपतिः स मावतु स्वाहा । रुद्रः पशूनामधिपतिः स मावतु स्वाहा । त्वष्टा रुपाणामधिपतिः स मावतु स्वाहा । विष्णुः पर्वतानामधिपतिः स मावतु स्वाहा । मरुतो गणनामधिपतयस्ते मावन्तु स्वाहा । पितरः पितामाहाः परेऽवरे ततास्ततामहा इह मावत । अस्मिन् ब्रह्मचारिन् क्षत्रेऽस्यामाशिष्यस्यां पुरोधायामस्मिन् कर्मस्यां देवहूत्यां स्वाहा ॥

३०. ऋताषाड़तधामाग्निगन्धर्वस्तस्यौषधयोऽप्सरस ऊर्जो नाम स इदं ब्रह्म क्षत्रं पातु ता इदं ब्रह्म क्षत्रं पान्तु तस्मै स्वाहा । ताभ्यः स्वाहा । सँहितो विश्वसामा सूर्यो गन्धर्वस्तस्य मरीचयोऽप्सरस आयुवो नाम स इदं ब्रह्म क्षत्रं पातु ता इदं ब्रह्म क्षत्रं पान्तु तस्मै स्वाहा । ताभ्यः स्वाहा । सुषुम्नः सूर्यरश्मिश्चन्द्रमा गन्धर्वस्तस्य नक्षत्राण्यप्सरसो बेकुरयो नाम स इदं ब्रह्म क्षत्रं पातु ता इदं ब्रह्म क्षत्रं पान्तु तस्मै स्वाहा । ताभ्यः स्वाहा । भुज्युः सुपर्णो यज्ञो गन्धर्वस्तस्य दक्षिणा अप्सरसः स्तवा नाम स इदं ब्रह्म क्षत्रं पातु ता इदं ब्रह्म क्षत्रं पान्तु तस्मै स्वाहा । ताभ्यः स्वाहा । प्रजापतिर्विश्वकर्मा मनो गन्धर्वस्तस्यर्कूसामान्यप्सरसो वह्वयो नाम स इदं ब्रह्म क्षेत्रं पातु ता इदं ब्रह्म क्षत्रं पान्तु तस्मै स्वाहा । ताभ्यः स्वाहा । इषिरो विश्वव्यचा वातो गन्धर्वस्तस्यापोऽप्सरसो मुदा नाम स इदं ब्रह्म क्षत्रं पातु ता इदं ब्रह्म क्षत्रं पान्तु तस्मै स्वाहा । ताभ्यः स्वाहा ।

३१. अग्निरेतु प्रथमो देवतानां सोऽस्यै प्रजां मुञ्चतु मृत्युपाशात् ।
तदयँ राजा वरुणोऽनुमन्यतां यथेयं स्त्री पौत्रमघं न रोदात् ॥

३२. इमामग्निस्त्रायतां गार्हपत्यः प्रजामस्यै नयतु दीर्घमायुः ।
अशून्योपस्था जीवतामस्तु माता पौत्रमानन्दमभिप्रबुद्ध्यतामियं ॥

३३. मा ते गृहे निशि घोष उत्थादन्यत्र त्वद्रुदत्यः संविशन्तु ।
मा त्वं विकेश्युर आवधिष्ठा जीवपत्नी पतिलोके विराज पश्यन्ती प्रजां सुमनस्यमानां ॥

३४. स्तनन्धयतस्ते पुत्रान् सविताभिरक्षतु ।
आ वाससः परिधानाद् बृहस्पतिर्विश्वदेवा अभिरक्षन्तु पश्चात् ॥

३५. अप्रजस्तां पौत्रमृत्युं पाप्मानमुत वाघम् ।
शीर्ष्णः स्रजमिवोन्मुच्य द्विषद्भ्यः प्रतिमुञ्चामि पाशं ॥

३६. ब्राह्मणं देवकृतं कल्पमानं तेन हन्ये निषदः पिशाचात् ।
क्रव्यादो मृत्युरधरान् पातयामि दीर्घमायुस्तव जीवन्तु पुत्रान् स्वाहा ॥

३७. शन्नो देविरभिष्टय आपो पीतये शंयोरभिस्रवन्तु नः॥

३८. देवस्य त्वा सवितुः प्रसवेऽश्विनोर्बाहुभ्यां पूष्णो हस्ताभ्याम् ।

३९. गृभ्णामि ते सौभग्त्वाय हस्तं मया पत्या जरदिष्टिर्यथासत् ।
भगो अर्यमा सविता पुरन्धिस्ते त्वा देवा अदुर्मह्यं पत्नीम् ॥

४०. अघोरचक्षुरपतिघ्न्येधि शिवा पशुभ्यः सुमनाः सुचर्चाः ।
वीरसूर्देवकामा स्योना शं नो भव द्विपदे शं चतुष्पदे ॥

४१. यां पूषन् शिवतमामेरयस्व यस्यां बीजं मनुष्या वपन्ति ।
या न ऊरू उशति विस्रयातै यस्यामुशन्तः प्रहरेम शेफम् ॥

४२. सोमोऽददात् गन्धर्वाय गन्धर्वोऽग्नयेऽददात् ॥

४३. पशूंश्च मह्यं पुत्रांश्च ददावग्निरथो त्वा असावहम् ॥

४४. सोमः पथमो विविदे गन्धर्वो विविद उत्तरः ।
तृतीयो अग्निष्टे पतिस्तुर्योऽहं मुनुष्यजाः ॥

४५. सरस्वति प्रेदमव सुभगे वाजीनीवति ।

४६. तां त्वा विश्वस्य भूतस्य प्रगायामस्यग्रतः ॥

४७. आतिष्ठेममश्मानमश्मेव त्वं स्थिरा भव ।
प्रमृणीहि दुरस्यून् सहस्व पृतनायतः ॥

४८. विश्वा उत त्वया वयं धारा उदन्या इव । अतिगाहेमहि द्विषः ॥

४९. इमान् लाजानावपामि समृद्धिकरणान्मम ।
मम तुभ्यं च संवननं तदग्निरनुमन्यताम् ॥

५०. भगेन त्वा संसृजामि मासरेण सुरामिव ॥

५१. इयं नार्यपब्रूते अग्नौ लाजानावपन्ती ।
दीर्घायुरस्तु मे पतिरेधन्तां ज्ञातयो मम ॥

५२. इमं मे वरुण श्रुधी हवमद्या च मृडय । त्वामवस्युराचके ॥

५३. तत्वा यामि ब्रह्मणा वन्दमानस्तदाशास्ते यजमानो हविर्भिः ।
अहेडमानो वरुणेह बोध्युरुशंस मा न आयुः प्रमोषीः ॥

५४. त्वन्नो अग्ने वरुणस्य विद्वान् देवस्य हेडोऽवयासिसीष्ठाः ।
यजिष्ठो वह्नितम शोशुचानो विश्वा द्वेषाँसि प्रमुमुग्ध्यस्मत् ॥

५५. स त्वं नो अग्नेऽवमो भवेती नेदिष्ठो अस्या उषसो व्युष्टौ ।
अवयक्ष्व नो वरुणं रराणो वीहि मृडिकं सुहवो न एधि ॥

५६. त्वमग्ने अयास्ययासन्मनसा हितः ।
अयासन् हव्यमूहिषेऽयानो धेहि भेषजं ॥

५७. प्रजापते न त्वदेतान्यन्यो विश्वा जातानि परिता बभूव ॥

५८. यत्कामास्ते जुहुमस्तन्नो अस्तु वयँ स्याम पतयो रयीणां ।
यन्म आत्मनो मिन्दाभूदग्निस्तत्पुनराहार्जातवेदा विचर्षणिः ॥

५९. पुनरग्निश्चक्षुरदात् पुनरिन्द्रो बृहस्पतिः ।
पुनर्मे अश्विना युवं चक्षुराधत्तमक्ष्योः ॥

६०. अनाज्ञातं यदाज्ञातं यज्ञस्य क्रियते मधु ।
अग्ने तदस्य कल्पय त्वं हि वेत्थ यथातथं ॥

६१. पुरुषसम्मितो यज्ञो यज्ञः पुरुषसम्मितः ।
अग्ने तदस्य कल्पय त्वं हि वेत्थ यथातथं ॥

६२. यत्पाकत्रा मनसा दीनदक्षान यज्ञस्य मन्वते मर्त्तासः ।
अग्निष्टद्धीता क्रतुविद्विजानन् यजिष्ठो देवां ऋतुशो यजाति ॥

६३. पाहि नो अग्न एनसे स्वाहा । पाहि नो विश्वेदसे स्वाहा । यज्ञं पाहि विभावसो स्वाहा । सर्वं पाहि शतक्रतो स्वाहा । भुरग्नये च पृथिव्यै च महते च स्वाहा । भुवो वायवे चान्तरिक्षाय च महते च स्वाहा । सुवरादित्याय च दिवे च महते च स्वाहा । भूर्भुवः स्वश्चन्द्रमसे च नक्षत्रेभ्यश्च दिग्भ्यश्च महते च स्वाहा । नमो देवेभ्यः स्वधा पितृभ्यो भूर्भुवस्वर्महरों स्वाहा । ओं स्वाहा । भूः स्वाहा। भुवः स्वाहा । स्वः स्वाहा । भुर्भुवःस्वः स्वाहा ॥

६४. यदस्य कर्मणोऽत्यरीरिचं यद्वा न्यूनमिहाकरम् ।
अग्निष्टत् स्विष्टकृद्विद्वान् सर्वं स्विष्टं सुहुतं करोतु मे ॥

६५. अग्नये स्विष्टकृते सुहुतहुते सर्वहुते ।
सर्वप्रायश्चित्ताहुतीनां कामानां समर्धयित्रे ॥

६५. अदितेऽन्वमंस्थाः । अनुमतेऽन्वमंस्थाः । सरस्वतेऽन्वमंस्था ॥

६६. देवसवितः प्रसुव यज्ञं प्रसुव यज्ञपतिं भगाय ।
दिवो गन्धर्वः केतपूः केतं नः पुनातु वाचस्पतिर्वाचं न स्वदतु ॥

६७. अग्ने व्रतपते व्रतं चरिष्यामि तच्छकेयं तन्मे राध्यताम् । वायो व्रतपते व्रतं चरिष्यामि तच्छकेयं तन्मे राध्यताम् । आदित्य व्रतपते व्रतं चरिष्यामि तच्छकेयं तन्मे राध्यताम् । व्रतानाम् व्रतपते व्रतं चरिष्यामि तच्छकेयं तन्मे राध्यताम् ॥

६८. अमूहमस्मि सा त्वं सा त्वमस्यमूहं ऋगहमस्मि साम त्वं द्योरहं पृथिवी त्वम् ॥

६९. मम हृदये हृदयं ते अस्तु । मम चित्ते चित्तमस्तु ते । मम वाचमेकमनाः श्रुणु । मामेवानुव्रता सहचर्या मया भव । चाक्रवाकं संवननं यन्नदीभ्य उदाहृतम्। यद्देवगन्धर्वो वित्तः संवनन् तेन संवनिनौ स्वः ॥

७०. एकमिषे विष्णुस्त्वान्वेतु द्वे ऊर्जे विष्णुस्त्वान्वेतु त्रीणि व्रताय विष्णुस्त्वान्वेतु चत्वारि मायोभवाय विष्णुस्त्वान्वेतु पञ्च पशुभ्यो विष्णुस्त्वान्वेतु षड् रायस्पोषाय विष्णुस्त्वान्वेतु सप्त सप्तभ्यो होत्राभ्यो विष्णुस्त्वान्वेतु । सखायौ सप्तपदाबभूव सख्यं ते गमेयं सख्यात्ते मा योषं सख्यान्मे मा योष्ठाः ॥

७१. सप्तऋषयः प्रथमां कृत्तिकानामरुन्धतीम् । ध्रुवतां ये ह निन्युः । षट् कृत्तिका मुख्ययोगं वहन्तीयमस्माकं भ्राजत्वष्टमी ॥

६९. ध्रुवं नमस्यामि मनसा ध्रुवेण ध्रुवं नो सख्यं दीर्घमायुश्च भुयात् । अद्रुग्धावस्मिंश्च परे च लोके ध्रुवं प्रविष्टौ स्याम शरणं सुखार्तौ । शन्न एधि द्विपदे शं चतुष्पदे ॥

७४. इह गावो निषीदन्त्विहाश्वा इह पुरुषाः । इहो सहस्रदक्षिणो अधिपूषा निषीदतु ॥

७५. अग्ने प्रायश्चित्ते त्वं देवानां प्रायश्चित्तिरसि ब्राह्मणस्त्वा नाथकाम उपधावामि यास्यै पतिघ्नी तनूस्तामितो नाशयामसि स्वाहा । वायो प्रायश्चित्ते त्वं देवानां प्रायश्चित्तिरसि (ब्राह्मणस्त्वा नाथकाम उपधावामि) यास्यै पुत्रघ्नी तनूस्तामिते नाशयामसि स्वाहा । आदित्य प्रायश्चित्ते त्वं देवानां प्रायश्चित्तिरसि ब्राह्मणस्त्वा नाथकाम उपधावामि यास्यै पशुघ्नी तनूस्तामितो नाशयामसि स्वाहा । सर्व प्रायश्चित्ते त्वं प्रायश्चित्तिरसि ब्राह्मनस्त्वा नाथकाम उपधावामि योस्यै पतिघ्नी पुत्रघ्नी पशुघ्नी निन्दिता तनूस्तामितो नाशयामसि स्वाहा ।

७६. अग्ने व्रतपते उपयमनं व्रतं चरिष्यामि तच्छकेयम् तन्मे राध्यताम् । वायो व्रतपत आदित्य व्रतपते व्रतानां व्रतपते उपयमनं व्रतं चरिष्यामि तन्मे राध्यानाम् ॥

७७. आवाभ्यां दम्पतिभ्यां स्वस्ति भवन्तो ब्रुवन्तु ।
युवाभ्यां दम्पतिभ्यां स्वस्ति ॥

७८. तशिने शिवेन त्वाभिमृशति हस्तेनाविद्विषाणिना । यथा न विद्विषेमहि ॥

७९. ऋषभेण स्कन्दामि व्यस्य योनिं पतिरेतो गृहाण ।
पुमांस्त्री जायतां गर्भो अन्तः ॥

८०. आ ते योनिं गर्भ एतु पुमांसं गर्भमाधत्स्व । यन्तुभ्यं शिमिवाससि पुमांस्ते पुत्रो नारितं पुमाननुजायताम् । स संवर्धतां गर्भो दशमे मासि सूतवे ॥

भारद्वाज गृह्यसूत्र विवाह मन्त्राः

१.११.१७. यस्यां मनोऽनुरमते चक्षुश्च प्रतिबद्यते ।
तां विद्यात्पुण्यलक्ष्मीकां किं ज्ञानेन करिष्यति ॥

१.१३.२. या अकृन्तन्नवयन्या अतन्वत याश्च देविरन्तानभितोऽददन्त ।
तास्त्वा देवीर्जरसे संव्ययन्त्वायुष्मतीदं परिधत्स्व वासः ॥

१.१३.३. परिधत्त धत्त वाससैनां शतायुर्षीं कृणुत दीर्घमायुः ।
बृहस्पतिः प्रयच्छद्वास एतत्सोमाय राज्ञे परिधातवा उ ॥

जरां गच्छासि परिधत्स्व वासो भवा कृष्टीनामभिशस्तिपावती ।
शतं च जीव शरदः सुवर्चा रायश्च पोषमुपसंव्ययस्व ॥

१.१३.४. परीदं वासो अधिधाः स्वस्तयेऽभूरापीनामभिशस्तिपावती ।
शतं च जीव शरदः परूचीर्वसूनि चार्या विभजासि जीवती ॥

१.१३.५. अग्नये जनिविदे स्वाहा । सोमाय जनिविदे स्वाहा ॥

१.१३.६. या तिरश्ची यानूची संराधन्ये प्रसाधन्ये सदसस्पतीं युक्तौ वह जातवेद इति ॥

१.१४.१. अग्निरैतु प्रथमो देवतानां सोऽस्यै प्रजां मुञ्चतु मृत्युपाशात् ।
तदयं राजा वरुणोऽनुमन्यतां यथेयं स्त्री पौत्रमघं न रोदात् ॥

इमामग्निस्त्रायतां गार्हपत्यः प्रजामस्यै नयतु दीर्घमायुः ।
अशून्योपस्था जीवतामस्तु माता पौत्रमानन्दमभिप्रबुध्यतामियम् ॥

मा ते गृहे निशि घोष उत्थादन्यत्र त्वद्रुदत्यः संविशन्तु ।
मा त्वं विकेश्युर आवधिष्ठा जीवपत्नी पतिलोके विराज पश्यन्ती प्रजां सुमनस्यमानां ॥

द्योस्ते पुष्ठं रक्षतु वायुरूरू अश्विनौ च स्तनं धयन्तं सविताभिरक्षतु ।
आ वाससः परिधानाद्बृहस्पतिर्विश्वे देवा अभिरक्षन्तु पश्चात् ॥

अप्रजस्तां पौत्रमृत्युं पाप्मानमुत वाघम् ।
शीर्ष्णः स्रजमिवोन्मुच्य द्विषद्भ्यः प्रतिमुञ्चामि पाशम् ॥

पूर्णा पश्चादिमं मे वरुणा तत्त्वा यामि । त्वं नो अग्ने स त्वं नो अग्ने ।
त्वमग्ने अयास्ययाश्चाग्नेऽस्यनभिशस्तीश्च यदस्य कर्मणोऽत्यरीरिचं ॥

१.१५.४. शं नो देवीरभिष्ट्य आपो भवन्तु पीतये । शं योरभिस्रवन्तु न ॥

१.१५.५. देवस्य त्वा सवितुः प्रसवेऽश्विनोर्बाहुभ्यां पूष्णो हस्ताभ्यां ॥

हस्तेन ते हस्तं गृह्णामि सौभगत्वाय मया पत्या जरदिष्टिर्यथासः ।
भगो अर्यमा सविता पुरन्धिस्ते त्वा देवा अदुर्मह्यं पत्नीम् ॥

अघोरचक्षुरपतिघ्न्येधि शिवा पशुभ्यः शन्तमा प्रजायै ।
क्षुरपविर्जारिभ्यो जीवसूर्वीरसूः स्योना मह्यं त्वादुर्गार्हपयाय देवाः ॥

तां नः पूषञ्छिवतममेरयस्व यस्यां बीजं मनुष्या वपन्ति ।
या न ऊरू उशती विस्रयातै यस्यामुशन्तः प्रहरेम शेफम् ॥

सोमः प्रथमो विविदे गन्धर्वस्ततोऽपरः ।
तृतीयो अग्निष्टे पतिस्तुरीयस्ते मनुष्यजाः ॥

सोमो ददद्गन्धर्वाय गन्धर्वोऽग्नये ददत् ।
रीयं च पुत्रांश्चादादग्निर्मह्यमथो इमाम् ।

सरस्वति प्रेदमव सुभगो वाजिनीवति ।
तां त्वा विश्वस्य भूतस्य प्रगायामस्यग्रत इति ॥

१.१५.६. सं वां सृजामि हृदये । संसृष्टं मनो अस्तु वां संसृष्टः प्राणो अस्तु वां ॥

१.१५.७. आतिष्ठेममश्मानमश्मेव त्वं स्थिरा भव ।
प्रमृणीहि दुरस्यून्सहस्व पृतनायत इति ॥

१.१५.८. विश्वा उत त्वया वयं धारा उदन्या इव । अतिगाहेमहि द्विषः ॥

१.१५.९. इयं नार्युप्रब्रूतेऽग्नौ लाजानावपन्ती ।
दीर्घायुरस्तु मे पतिरेधन्तां ज्ञातयो मम ॥
भगेन त्वा संसृजामि मासरेण सुरामिव ॥

१.१५.१०. इमान्लाजानावपामि समृद्धिकरणान्मम ।
तुभ्यं च संवननांस्तदग्निरनुमन्यतामियम् ॥

१.१६.१. एकमिषे विष्णुस्त्वान्वेतु द्वे ऊर्जे विष्णुस्त्वान्वेतु त्रीणि व्रताय विष्णुस्त्वान्वेतु
चत्वारि मायोभवाय विष्णुस्त्वान्वेतु पञ्च पशुभ्यो विष्णुस्त्वान्वेतु षड्रायस्पोषाय
विष्णुस्त्वान्वेतु सप्त सप्तभ्यो होत्राभ्यो विष्णुस्त्वान्वेतु ॥

१.१६.२. सखा सप्तपदा भव सखायौ सप्तपदाबभूव ।
सख्यं ते गमेयं सख्यात्ते मा योषं सख्यान्मे मायोष्ठा ॥

१.१६.३. मम हृदये हृदयं ते अस्तु मम चित्ते चित्तमस्तु ते ।
मम वाचमेकमना शृणु मामेवानुव्रता भव सहचर्या मया भव ॥

१.१६.४. मां ते चित्तं प्रतिशतु मां चक्षुर्मामु ते मनः ।
मयि सर्वाणि भूतानि मयि प्रज्ञानमस्तु ते ॥

मधु हे मध्वागाहे जिह्वा मे मधुवादिनी ।
मुखे मे सारघं मधु दत्सु संवननं कृतम् ॥

चाक्रवाकं संवननं यन्नदीभ्य उदाहृतम् ।
यद्देवगन्धर्वो वितस्तेन संवनिनौ स्वः ॥

मां चैव पश्य सूर्यं च मान्येषु मनः कृथा ॥

१.१७.१. आपो हि ष्ठा मयोभुवस्ता न ऊर्जे दधातन । महे रणाय चक्षसे ॥

यो वः शिवतमो रसस्तस्य भाजयतेह नः । उशतीरिव मातरः ॥

तस्मा अरं गमाम वो यस्य क्षयाय जिन्वथ । आपो जनयथा च नः ॥

हिरण्यवर्णाः शुचयः पावका यासु जातः कश्यपो यास्विन्द्रः ।
अग्निं या गर्भं दधिरे विरूपास्ता न आपः शं स्योना भवन्तु ॥

पवमानः सुवर्जनः । पवित्रेण विचर्षणिः । यः पोता स पुनातु मा । पुनन्तु मा देवजनाः । पुनन्तु मनवो धिया । पुनन्तु विश्व आयवः । जातवेदः पवित्रवत् । पवित्रेण पुनाहि मा । शुक्रेण देव दीद्यत् । अग्ने क्रत्वा क्रतूँरनु ॥

१.१७.३. ये वध्वश्चन्द्रं वहतुं यक्ष्मा यन्ति जनामनु ।
पुनस्तान्यज्ञिया देवा नयन्तु यत आगता ॥

१.१७.४. इह गावो निषीदन्त्विहाश्वा इह पुरुषाः ।
इहो सहस्रदक्षिणोऽभि पूषा निषीदत्व ॥

१.१८.५ ध्रुवक्षितिर्ध्रुवयोनिर्ध्रुवमसि ध्रुवत स्थितम् ।
त्वं नक्षत्राणां मेथ्यसि स मा पाहि पुतन्यत ॥

सप्तर्षयः प्रथमां कृत्तिकानामरुन्धतीं ध्रुवतां ये ह नित्युः ।
षट्कृत्तिका मुख्ययोगं वहन्तीयमस्माकं भ्राजत्वष्टमीत्यरुन्धतीम् ॥

१.१८.७. अग्ने प्रायश्चित्ते त्वं देवानां प्रायश्चित्तिरसि ब्राह्मणस्त्वा नाथकामः प्रपद्ये । यास्यां पतिघ्नो तनूः प्रजाघ्नी पशुघ्नी लक्ष्मिघ्नो जारघ्नीमस्यै तां कृणोति स्वाहा ॥ वायो प्रायश्चित्त आदित्य प्रायश्चित्ते प्रजापते प्रायश्चित्ते त्वं देवानां प्रायश्चित्तिरसि ब्राह्मनस्त्वा नाथकामः प्रपद्ये । यास्यै निन्दिता तनूस्तामितो नाशयामसि स्वाहा ॥

१.१९.१. अमूहमस्मि सा त्वं द्योरहं पृथिवी त्वं सामाहमृक्त्वं तावेहि संभवाव सह रेतो दधावहै पुंसे पुत्राय वेत्तवै रायस्पोषाय सुप्रजस्त्वाय सुवीर्याय ॥

१.१९.६. सं ना मनस्सं हृदयानि सं नाऽभि सं तनुत्यजः ।
सं त्वा कामस्य याक्त्रेणे युञ्जत्यविमोचनाय ॥

काठक गृह्यसूत्र विवाह मन्त्राः

२.१४.५. ऋतमेव परमेष्ठ्यृतं नात्येति किञ्चन ।
ऋत इयं पृथिवी श्रिता सर्वामिदमियमसौ भूयात् ॥

२.१५.५. समाना व आकूतानि समाना हृदयानि वः ।
समानमस्तु वो मनो यथा वः सुसहासति ॥

सं वो मनांसि सं व्रता समु चित्तान्यकरम् ।
अमी ये विव्रताः स्थन तान्नः सन्नमयामसि ॥

२.१६.४. हिरण्यवर्णाः शुचयः पावका यासु जातः कश्यपो यास्विन्द्रः ।
अग्निं या गर्भं दधिरे विरूपास्ता न आपः शं स्योना भवन्तु ॥

२.१७.२. स्वनं वद दुन्दुभे सुप्रजस्त्वाय गोमुख ।
प्रक्रीडन्तु कन्याः सुमनस्यमानाः सहेन्द्राण्या कृतमंगलाः ॥

२.१८.१. या तेऽलक्ष्मीर्मातृमयी पितृमयी संक्रामणी सहजा वापि काचित्तां ॥
तिष्येण सह देवतया निर्भजामि निर्दुणामि ।
सा द्विषन्तं गच्छतु तिष्यबृहस्पतिभ्यां नमो नमः ॥

२.२१.१. क्रीडं वः शर्धो मारुतमनर्वाणं रथेशुभम् । कण्वा अभिप्रगायत ॥

२.२१.२. अग्निना रयिमश्नवत्पोषमेव दिवेदिवे । यशसं वीरवत्तमम् ॥

२.२४.६. मयि दोहोऽसि विराजो दोहः पाद्यायै विराजो दोहमशीय ॥

२.२४.७. विष्टरोऽसि मातरि सीद ॥

२.२४.१०. शन्नो देवीरभिष्ट्य आपो भवन्तु पीतये । शंयोरभिस्रवन्तु नः ॥
इदमहमस्मिन् कुले ब्रह्मवर्चसं ददामि ।
इदमहं मां मयि तेजो वीर्यमन्नाद्यं प्रजां पशून् ब्रह्मवर्चसं ददामि ॥

१.२४.११. आपो हि ष्ठा मयोभुवस्ता न ऊर्जे दधातन । महे रणाय चक्षसे ॥
यो वः शिवतमो रसस्तस्य भाजयतेह नः । उशतीरिव मातरः ॥
तस्मा अरं गमाम वो यस्य क्षयाय जिन्वथ । आपो जनयथा च नः ॥
मधु वाता ऋतायते मधु क्षरन्ति सिन्धवः । माध्वीर्नः सन्त्वोषधीः ॥
मधु नक्तमुतोषसो मधुमत् पार्थिवं रजः । मधु द्यौरस्तु नः पिता ॥
मधुमान्नो वनस्पतिर्मधुमाँ अस्तु सूर्यः । माध्वीर्गावो भवन्तु नः ॥

२.२४.१२. वसवस्त्वाग्निराजानो भक्षयन्तु पितरस्त्वा यमराजनो भक्षयन्तु रुद्रस्त्वा सोमराजानो भक्षयन्त्वादित्यास्त्वा वरुनराजानो भक्षयन्तु विश्वे त्वा देवा बृहस्पतिराजानो भक्षयन्तु ॥

२.२४.१३. यन्मधुनो मधव्यस्य परमस्यान्नाद्यस्य परममन्नाद्यं रूपं ॥
तेनाहं मधुनो मधव्यस्य परमस्यान्नाद्यस्य परमोऽन्नादो मधव्यो भूयासम् ॥
त्रय्यै विद्यायै यशोऽसि श्रियै यशोऽसि यशसे ब्रह्मणे दीप्तिरसि ॥
सत्यश्रीर्यशःश्रीर्मयि श्रीः श्रीः श्रयताम् ॥

१.२४.१४. अमृतोपस्तरणमसि ॥

१.२४.१७. हतो मे पाप्मा पाप्मानं मे हत ।
यां त्वा देवा वसवोऽन्वजीविषुरादित्यानां स्वसारं रुद्रमातरम् ।
दैवीं गामादितिं जनानामारभन्तामर्हतामर्हणाय ॥

१.२५.१८. गृभ्णामि ते सुप्रजस्त्वाय हस्तौ मया पत्या जरदष्टिर्यथासः ।
भगो अर्यमा सविता पुरन्धिर्मह्यं त्वादुर्गार्हपत्याय देवाः ॥

१.२४.२०. माता रुद्राणां दुहिता वसूनां स्वसादित्यानामृतस्य नाभिः ।
प्र नु वोचं चिकितुषे जनाय मा गामनागामदितिं वधिष्ठ ॥

१.२५.१. अनृक्षरा ऋजवः सन्तु पन्था येभिः सखायो यन्ति नो वरेयम् ।
समर्यमा सं भगो नो निनीयात् सं जास्पत्यं सुयमस्तु देवाः ॥

१.२५.४. शन्न आपो धन्वन्या शन्नं सन्त्वनूप्याः ।
शन्नः समुद्रिया आपः शमु नः सन्तु कूप्या ॥
या अकृन्तन्या अवयन्या अतन्वत याश्च देवीरन्तां अभितोऽततन्थ ।
तास्त्वा देवीर्जरसा संव्ययन्त्वायुष्मतीदं परिधत्स्व वासः ॥

१.२५.५. प्रेतो मुञ्चातु मामुतः सुबद्धाममृतस्करम् ।
यथेयमिंद्र मीढ्वः सुपुत्रा सुभगासति ॥

पूषा त्वेतो नयतु हस्तगृह्याश्विनौ त्वा प्रवहतां रथेन ।
गृहान्गच्छ गृहपत्नी यथासो वशिनी त्वं विदथे मा वदासि ॥

मा विदन्परिपंथिनो य आसीदन्ति दम्पती ।
सुगोभिर्दुर्गमतीतामपद्रान्त्वरातयः ॥

१.२५.८. योगे योगे तवस्तरं वाजे वाजे हवामहे । सखाय इन्द्रमूतये ॥

१.२५.९. खे रथस्य खेऽनसः खे युगस्य शतक्रतो ।
अपालामिन्द्रस्त्रिष्पूत्वा करोतु सूर्यवर्चसम् ॥

शं ते हिरण्यं शमु सन्त्वापः शं ते मेथी भवतु शं युगस्य तर्म ।
शं त आपः शतपवित्रा भवन्त्वेना पत्या तन्वा संसृजस्व ॥

१.२५.१०. अग्नये जनिविदे स्वाहा सोमाय जनिविदे स्वाहा गन्धर्वाय जनिविदे स्वाहा ॥

१.२५.१५. आकूत्यै त्वा कामाय त्वा समुद्ध्यै त्वा ॥
हिरण्यगर्भः समवर्तताग्रे भूतस्य जातः पतिरेक आसीत् ।
स दाधार पृथिवीं द्यामुतेमां कस्मै देवाय हविषा विधेम ॥

अग्न आयूंषि पवस आसुवोर्जमिषञ्च नः ।
आरे बाधस्व दुच्छुनान् ॥
अग्निर्ऋषिः पवमानः पाञ्चजन्यः पुरोहितः । तमीमहे महागयम् ॥

१.२५.१६. या ते पतिघ्नी तनूरपतिघ्नीं ते तां करोमि ।
या तेऽपुत्रिया तनूः पुत्रियां ते तां करोमि ।
या तेऽपशव्या तनूः पशव्यां ते तां करोमि ॥

१.२५.१९. देवस्य सवितुः प्रसवेऽश्विनोर्बाहुभ्यां पूष्णो हस्ताभ्याम् ॥

१.२५.२० इयं नार्युपब्रूतेऽग्नौ लाजानावपन्ती ।
दीर्घायुरस्तु मे पतिरेधन्तां ज्ञातयो मम ॥

तां पूषञ्शिवतमामेरयस्व यस्यां बीजं मनुष्या वपन्ति ।
या न ऊरू उशति विश्रयाते यस्यामुशन्तः प्रहराम शेपम् ॥

सोमो ददद्गन्धर्वाय गन्धर्वो दददग्नये ।
रयिं च पुत्रांश्चादादग्निर्मह्यमथो इमाम् ॥

सोमः प्रथमो विविदे गन्धर्वो विविद उत्तरः ।
तृतीयो अग्निष्टे पतिस्तुरियोऽहं मनुष्यज ॥

१.२५.१९. सरस्वति प्रेदमव सुभगो वाजिनीवती ।
श्या त्वा विश्वस्य भूतस्य प्रजायामस्याग्रतः ।

यस्यां भूतं समभवद्यस्यां विश्वमिदं जगत् ।
तामध्य गाथां गास्यामि या स्त्रीणामुत्तमं यशः ॥

१.२५.२३. सा त्वमस्यमोऽहममोऽहमस्मि सा त्वं ।
ता एहि विववाहवै पुंसे पुत्राय कर्तवे ।
रायस्पोषाय सुप्रजास्त्वाय सुवीर्याय ॥

१.२५.२४. अश्मानमातिष्ठाश्मेव त्वं स्थिरो भव ।
कृण्वन्तु विश्वेदेवा आयुष्टे शरदः शतम् ।
आतिष्ठेममश्मानमश्मेव त्वं स्थिरा भव ।
प्रमृणीहि दुवस्यवः सहस्व पृतन्यत इति ॥

१.२५.२६. अर्यमणं नु देवं कन्या अग्निमयक्षत ।
सोऽस्मान्देवो अर्यमा प्रेतो मुञ्चातु मामुष्य गृहेभ्यः ॥

१.२५.२८. इयं नार्यपब्रूते तोक्मान्यावपन्तिका । दीर्घायुरस्तु ज्ञातयो ममेति ॥

१.२५.३१. गन्धर्वं पतिदेवनं कन्या अग्निमयक्षत ।
सोऽस्मान्देवो गन्धर्वः प्रेतो मुञ्चातु मामुष्य गृहेभ्यः ॥

१.२५.३३. त्र्यम्बकं यजामहे सुगन्धिं पतिपोषणम् ।
उर्वारुकमिव बन्धनान्मृत्योर्मुक्षीय मामुष्य गृहेभ्यः ॥

१.२५.३४. पूषा मा पशुमाननया पशुमन्तं करोतु । जीवपत्नीर्भूयासम् ॥

१.२५.३८. एकमिषे द्वे ऊर्जे त्रीणि रायस्पोषाय चत्वारि मयोभवाय पञ्च प्रजाभ्यः
षड्तुभ्यो दीर्घायुत्वाय सप्तमं सखा सप्तपदा भव । सुमृडीका सरस्वति मा
ते व्योम सन्दृशि ॥ विष्णुस्त्वान्वेत्यनुषङ्गः ॥

१.२५.४२. सुमङ्गलीरियं वधूरिमां समेत पश्यत ।
सौभाग्यमस्यै दत्त्वायाथास्तं विपरेतन ॥

१.२५.४३. इमां त्वमिन्द्र मीढ्वः सुपुत्रां सुभगां कृणु ।
दशास्यां पुत्रानां धेहि पतिमेकादशं कृधि ॥
सम्राज्ञी श्वशुरे भव सम्राज्ञी श्वश्र्वां भव ।
ननान्दरि सम्राज्ञी भव सम्राज्ञी अधि देवृषु ॥
स्नुषाणां श्वशुराणां च प्रजायाश्च धनस्य च ।
पतिनां देवराणां च सजातानां विराड्भव ॥

१.२६.१. योगेयोगे तवस्तरं वाजेवाजे हवामहे । सखाय इन्द्रमूतये ॥

१.२६.२. अङ्क्न्यङ्का अभितो रथं ये ध्वान्ता वाताग्रमभि ये संपतन्ति ।
दूरहेतिः पतत्रिणीवाजिनीवांस्ते नोऽग्नयः प्रपयः पारयन्त्व ॥

१.२६.३. खे रथस्य खेऽनसः खे युगस्य च तर्मसु ।
खे अक्षस्य स्वे अवधामि ॥

१.२६.४. सुकीशुकं शल्मलिं विश्वरूपं हिरण्यवर्णं सुवृतं सुचक्रम् ।
आरोह सूर्ये अमृतस्य योनिं स्योनं पत्ये वहतुं कृणुष्व ॥

१.२६.४. मा विदन् परिपन्थिनो य आसीदन्ति दम्पती ।
सुगेभिर्दुर्गमतीताय द्रान्त्वरातयः ॥

१.२६.६. संकाशया विवहतं ब्रह्मणा गृहैरघोरेण चक्षुषा मैत्रेण ।
पर्याणद्धं विश्वरूपं यदस्याः स्योनं पतिभ्यः सविता कृणोतु ॥

१.२७.३. ऊर्जं बिभ्रति वसुवनिः सुमेधा गृहनागां मोदमाना सुवर्चाः ।
अघोरेण चक्ष्युषाहं मैत्रेण गृहाणां पश्यन्ती वय उत्तिरामि ॥

गृहाणामायुः प्र वयं तिराम गृहा अस्माकं प्रतिरन्त्वायुः ॥

गृहानहं सुमनसः प्रपद्ये वीरघ्नी वीरपतिः सुशेवा ।
इरां वहतो घृतमुक्षमाणांस्तेष्वहं सुमनाः संविशामि ॥

येषां मध्ये ऽधिप्रवसन्नेति सौमनसं बहु ।
गृहानुपह्वयामहे ते नो जानन्तु जानतः ॥

सूनृतावन्तः स्वधावन्त इरावन्तो ह सामदाः ।
अक्षुध्या अतृष्या गृहा मास्मद्बिभेतन ॥

उपहूता इह गाव उपहूता अजावयः ।
अथो अन्नस्य कीलाल उपहूतो गृहेषु मे ॥

उपहूता भूरिधनाः सखायः साधुसंमदाः ।
अरिष्टाः सर्वपुरुषा गृहा नः सन्तु सर्वद ॥

१.२८.४. अग्निरैतु प्रथमो देवतानां सो ऽस्याः प्रजां मुञ्चतु मृत्युपाशात् ।
अरिक्तोपस्था जीवितामस्तु माता पौत्रमानन्दमभिविबुध्यतामियम् ॥

मा ते गृहे निशि घोर उत्थादन्यत्र त्वद्रुत्यः संविशन्तु ।
जीवपुत्रा पतिलोके विराज पश्यन्ती प्रजां सुमनस्यमानाम् ॥

मा ते कुमारः स्तनधः प्रमायि मा त्वं विकेश्युर आवधिष्टाः ।
स्तनं धयन्तं सविताभिरक्षत्वा वाससः परिधानाद्बृहस्पतिर्विश्वे देवा अभिरक्षन्तु नित्यम् ॥

अग्ने प्रायश्चित्ते त्वं देवानां प्रायश्चित्तिरसि यास्यां भृशा तनूस्तामस्या नाशया॥ वायो प्रायश्चित्ते ॥ सूर्य प्रायश्चित्ते ॥ चन्द्र प्रायश्चित्ते ॥ विष्णो प्रायश्चित्ते ॥ विष्णो प्रायश्चित्ते ॥ चन्द्र प्रायश्चित्ते ॥ सूर्य प्रायश्चित्ते ॥ वायो प्रायश्चित्ते ॥ अग्ने प्रायश्चित्ते त्वं देवानां प्रायश्चित्तिरसि यास्यां भृशा तनूस्तामस्या नाशया स्वाहा॥ त्र्यायुषं जमदग्नेः कश्यपस्य त्र्यायुषं यद्देवानां त्र्यायुषं तन्मे अस्तु त्र्यायुषमिति ॥

१.२९.१. अन्नमेव विवननमन्नं संवननं स्मृतम् ॥
अन्नं पशूनां प्राणोऽन्नं ज्येष्ठं भिषक् स्मृतम् ॥

अन्नमयेन मणिना प्राणसूत्रेण पृश्निना ।
सिनोमि सत्यग्रन्थिना हृदयं च मनश्च ते ।
सह वाचा मनो अस्तु सह चित्तं सह व्रतम् ॥

चक्रमिवानडुहः सूर्यं च मा चान्येषु मनः कृथाः ।
चाक्रवाकं संवननं मम चामुष्याश्च भूयादिति ॥

वैखानस गृह्यसूत्र विवाह मन्त्राः

३.२.२. प्र सु ग्मन्ता धियसानस्य सक्षणि वरेभिर्वराँ अभि षु प्रसीदतः ।
अस्माकमिन्द्र उभयं जुजोषिति यत्सोम्यस्यान्धसो बुबोधति ॥

अभ्रातृघ्नीं वरुणापतिघ्नीं बृहस्पते ।
इन्द्रापुत्रघ्नीं लक्ष्म्यं तामस्यै सवितस्सुव ॥

धर्मप्रजासंपत्त्यर्थं यज्ञापत्त्यर्थं ब्रह्मदेवर्षिपितृतृप्त्यर्थं प्रजासहत्वकर्मभ्यो ददामि ॥

प्रजापतिः स्त्रियां यशो मुष्कयोरदधात् सपम् ।
कामस्य तृप्तिमानन्दं तस्याग्ने भाजयेह मा ॥

मोदः प्रमोद आनन्दो मुष्कयोर्निहितः सपः । सृत्वेव कामस्य तृप्याणि दक्षिणानां प्रतिग्रहे । मनसश्चित्तमाकूतिं वाचः सत्यमशीमहि । पशूनां रूपमन्नस्य यशः श्रीः श्रयतां मयि । यथाहमस्या अतृपं स्त्रियै पुमान् यथा स्त्री तृप्यति पुंसि प्रिये प्रिया । एवं भगस्य तृप्याणि यज्ञस्य काम्यः प्रियाम् । आदित्यः सत्यभोमिति । आपस्तत् सत्यमाभरन् । यशो यज्ञस्य दक्षिणाम् । असौ मे कामः समृध्यताम् ॥

तेज आयुः श्रियं धन्यं सुमङ्गलं यशस्विनम् । दशपुत्रमविध्वनं कामयते ।
इन्द्रापुत्रघ्नीं लक्ष्म्यं तामस्यै सवितः सुव ॥

३.२.३. सुमङ्गलीरियं वधूरिमां समेत पश्यत ।
सौभाग्यमस्यै दत्त्वायाथास्तं विपरेतन ॥

मा ते गृहे निशि घोष उत्थादन्यत्र त्वद्रुदत्यः संविशन्तु ।
मा त्वं विकेश्युर आवधिष्ठा जीवपत्नी पतिलोके विराज पश्यन्ती प्रजां सुमनस्यमानां ॥

द्योस्ते पृष्ठं रक्षतु वायुरूरू अश्विनौ च स्तनं धयन्तं सविताभिरक्षतु ।
आ वाससः परिधानाद्बृहस्पतिर्विश्वे देवा अभिरक्षन्तु पश्चात् ॥

सरस्वति प्रेदमव सुभगो वाजिनीवती ।
श्या त्वा विश्वस्य भूतस्य प्रजायामस्याग्रतः ।
यस्यां भूतं समभवद्यस्यां विश्वमिदं जगत् ।
तामध्य गाथां गास्यामि या स्त्रीणामुत्तमं यशः ॥

गृभ्णामि ते सौभगत्वाय हस्तं मया पत्या जरदिष्टिर्यथासत् ।
भगो अर्यमा सविता पुरन्धिस्ते त्वा देवा अदुर्मह्यं पत्नीम् ॥

अघोरचक्षुरपतिघ्न्येधि शिवा पशुभ्यः सुमनाः सुचर्चाः ।
वीरसूर्देवकामा स्योना शं नो भव द्विपदे शं चतुष्पदे ॥

इयं नार्युपब्रूतेऽग्नौ लाजानावपन्ती ।
दीर्घायुरस्तु मे पतिरेधन्तां ज्ञातयो मम ॥

३.२.४. विश्वा उत त्वया वयं धारा उदन्या इव अतिगाहेमहि द्विषः ॥
एकमिषे विष्णुरिति द्वे ऊर्जे इति त्रीणि व्रतायेति चत्वारिति पञ्च पशुभ्य इति षड्रायस्पोषायेति सप्त सप्तभ्य इति तान्पर्यायेणाक्रम्य गत्वा सखेति निवर्तेत ॥

मम दये दयं ते अस्तु मम चित्तं चित्तेनान्वेहि ।
मम वाचेकमना जुषस्व प्रजापतिष्ट्वा नियुनक्तु मह्यम् ॥

इह गावो निषीदन्त्विहाश्वा इह पुरुषाः ।
इहो सहस्रदक्षिणो अपि पूषा निषीदतु ॥

देवीः षडुर्वीरुरु णः कृणोत विश्वे देवास इह वीरयध्वन् ।
मा हास्महि प्रजया मा तनूर्भिर्मा रधाम द्विषते सोम राजन् ॥

सप्तर्षयः प्रथमां कृत्तिकानामरुन्धतीं ध्रुवतां ये ह नित्युः ।
षट्कृत्तिका मुख्ययोगं वहन्तीयमस्माकं भ्राजत्वष्टमीत्यरुन्धतीम् ॥

ध्रुवक्षितिर्ध्रुवयोनिर्ध्रुवमसि ध्रुवत स्थितम् ।
त्वं नक्षत्राणां मेथ्यसि स मा पाहि पुतन्यत ॥

गोभिल गृह्यसूत्र विवाह मन्त्राः

२.१.७. ऋतमेव प्रथममृतं नात्येति कश्चनर्त्त इयं पृथिवी श्रिता सर्वमिदमसौ भूयात्॥

२.१.१०. काम वेद ते नाम मदो नामसि समानयामुं सुरया ते अभवत् ।
परमत्र जन्माग्ने तपसो निर्म्मितोऽसि ॥

इमं त उपस्थं मधुना सँसृजामि प्रजापतेर् मुखमेतदद्वितीयम् ।
तेन पुंसोऽभिववासि सर्वान् अवशान् वशिनि असि राज्ञी ॥

२.१.१८. या आकृन्तन्नवयन् या अतन्वत याश्च देव्योऽन्तानभितो ततन्थ ।
तास्त्वा देव्यो जरसे संव्ययन्त्वायुष्मतीदं परिधत्व वासः ॥

परिधत्त धत्त वाससैनां शतायुषीं कृणुत दीर्घमायुः ।
शतं च जीव शरदः सुवर्चा वसूनिचार्ये विभृजासि जीवन् ॥

२.१.१९. सोमोऽददत् गन्धर्वाय गन्धर्वोऽददत् अग्नये ।
रयिं च पुत्राँश्चादादग्निर्मह्यमथो इमाम् ॥

२.१.२०. प्र मे पतियानः पन्थाः कल्पताँ शिवा अरिष्टा पतिलोकं गमेयम् ॥

२.१.२१. प्रास्याः पतियानः पन्थाः कल्पताँ शिवा अरिष्टा पतिलोकं गम्याः ॥

२.१.२४. अग्निरेतु प्रथमो देवताभ्यः सोऽसै प्रजां मुञ्चातु मृत्युपाशात् ।
तदयँ राजा वरुणोऽनुमन्यतां यथेयं स्त्री पौत्रमघं न रोदात् स्वाहा ॥

इमामग्निस्त्रायतां गार्हपत्यः प्रजामस्यै जरदष्टिं कृणोतु ।
अशून्योपस्थ जीवतामस्तु माता पौत्रमानन्दमभिविबुध्यतामियं स्वाहा ॥

द्यौस्ते पृष्ठं रक्षतु वायुरूरु अश्विनौ च । स्तनन्धयस्ते पुत्रान् सविताभिरक्षतु ।
आ वाससः परिधानत् बृहस्पतिर्विश्वे देवा अभिरक्षन्तु पश्चात् स्वाहा ॥

मा ते गृहेषु निशि घोष उत्थादन्यत्र त्वद्रुदत्यः संविशन्तु ।
मा त्वँ रुदत्युर आ बधिष्ठा जीवपत्नी पतिलोके विराज पश्यन्ती प्रजां
सुमनस्यमानां ॥

अप्रजस्यम् पौत्रमर्त्यं पाप्मानमुत वा अघम् ।
शीर्ष्णः स्रजमिवोन्मुच्य द्विषद्भ्यः प्रतिमुञ्चामि पाशँ स्वाहा ॥

परैतु मृत्युरमृतं म आगाद् वैवस्वतो नो अभयं कृणोतु ।
परं मृत्यो अनुपमेहि पन्थां यत्र नो अन्य इतरो देवयानात् ॥
चक्षुस्मते शृण्वते ते ब्रवीमि मानः प्रजां रीरिषो मोत वीरान् स्वाहा ॥

२.२.४. इममश्मानारोहाश्मेव त्वं स्थिरा भव ।
द्विषन्तमप बाधदस्व मा च त्वं द्विषतामधः ॥

२.२.६. इयं नार्यूपब्रूतेऽग्नौ लाजानापवन्ती ।
दीर्घायुरस्तु मे पतिः शतं वर्षाणि जीवतु ।
एधन्ताम् ज्ञातयो मम स्वाहा ॥

२.२.७. अर्यमणं नु देवं कन्या अग्निमयक्षत ।
स इमां देवो अर्यमा प्रेतो मुञ्चातु मामुतः स्वाहा ॥

पूषाणं नु देवं कन्या अग्निमयक्षत ।
स इमां देवो पूषा प्रेतो मुञ्चातु मामुतः स्वाहा ॥

२.२.८. कन्यला पितृभ्यः पतिलोकमयतीयमप दीक्षामयष्ट ।
कन्या उत त्वया वयं धारा उदन्या इवातिगहेमहि द्विषः ॥

२.२.११. एकं इषे विष्णुस्त्वा नयतु । द्वे ऊर्जे विष्णुस्त्वा नयतु । त्रीणि व्रताय विष्णुस्त्वा नयतु । चत्वारि मायोभवाय विष्णुस्त्वा नयतु । पञ्च पशुभ्यो विष्णुस्त्वा नयतु । षड्रायस्पोषाय विष्णुस्त्वा नयतु । सप्त सप्तभ्यो होत्राभ्यो विष्णुस्त्वा नयतु । सखा सप्तपदी भव सख्यं ते गमेयँ सख्यं ते मा योषाः सख्यं ते मा योष्ठाः ॥

२.२.१४. सुमङ्गलीरियं वधूरिमाँ समेत पश्यत ।
सौभाग्यमस्यै दत्तवायाथास्थं विपरेतन ॥

२.२.१५. समञ्जन्तु विश्वे देवाः समापो हृदयानि नौ ।
सं मातरिश्वा सं धाता समुदेष्ट्री दधातु नौ ॥

२.२.१६. गृभ्णामि ते सौभगत्वाय हस्तं मया पत्या जरदिष्टिर्यथासः ।
भगो अर्यमा सविता पुरंधिर्मह्यं त्वादुर्गार्हपत्याय देवाः ॥

अघोरचक्षुरपतिघ्नि एधि शिवा पशुभ्यः सुमनः सुवर्चः ।
वीरसर्जीवसूर्देवकामा स्योना शं नो भव द्विपदे शं चतुष्पदे ॥

आ नः प्रजां जनयतु प्रजापतिराजरसाय समनक्त्वार्यमा ।
अदुर्मङ्गलीः पतिलोकमाविश शं नो भव द्विपदे शं चतुष्पदे ॥

इमां त्वमिन्द्र मीढ्वः सुपुत्राँ सुभगां कृधि ।
दशास्यां पुत्राना धेहि पतिमेकदशां कुरु ॥

सम्राज्ञी श्वशुरे भव सम्राज्ञी श्वश्रवां भव ।
ननान्दरि सम्राज्ञी भव सम्राज्ञी अधि देवृषु ॥

मम व्रते ते हृदयं दधातु मम चित्तमनु चित्तं ते अस्तु ।
मम वाचमेकमना जुषस्व बृहस्पतिस्त्वा नियुनक्तु मह्यम् ॥

२.३.६. रेखासन्धिषु पक्ष्मस्वावर्तेषु च यानि ते ।
तानि ते पूर्णाहुत्या सर्वाणि शमयाम्यहम् ॥

केशेषु यच्च पापकमीक्षिते रुदिते च यत् ।
तानि ते पूर्णाहुत्या सर्वाणि शमयाम्यहम् ॥

शिले च यच्च पापकं भाषिते हसिते च यत् ।
तानि ते पूर्णाहुत्या सर्वाणि शमयाम्यहम् ॥

आरोकेषु च दन्तेषु हस्तयोः पादयोश्च यत् ।
तानि ते पूर्णाहुत्या सर्वाणि शमयाम्यहम् ॥

ऊर्वोरुपस्थे जङ्घयोः संधानेषु च यानि ते ।
तानि ते पूर्णाहुत्या सर्वाणि शमयाम्यहम् ॥

यानि कानि च घोराणि सर्वाङ्गेषु तवाभवन् ।
पूर्णाहुतिभिराज्यस्य सर्वाणि तान्यशीशमम् ॥

२.३.९. ध्रुवा द्यौर्ध्रुवा पृथिवी ध्रुवं विश्वमिदं जगत् ।
ध्रुवासः पर्वता इमे ध्रुवा स्त्री पतिकुले इयम् ॥

२.३.२१. अन्नपाशेन मणिना प्राणसूत्रेन पश्निना ।
बध्नामि सत्यग्रन्थिना मनश्च हृदयं च ते ॥

यदेतधृदयं तव तदस्तु हृदयं मम ।
यदिदं हृदयं मम तदस्तु हृदयं तव ॥
अन्नं प्राणस्य पड्विँशस्तेन बध्नामि त्वासौ ॥

२.४.१. सुकिँशुकं शल्मलिं विश्वरूपं सुवर्णवर्णँ सुकृतँ सुचक्रम् ।
आरोह सूर्ये अमृतस्य नाभिँ स्योनं पत्ये वहतुं कृणुष्व ॥

२.४.२. मा विदन् परिपन्थिनो य आसीदन्ति दम्पती ।
सुगेभिर्दुर्गमतीतामपद्रान्त्वरातयः ॥

२.४.६. इह गावः प्रजायध्वमिहाश्वा इह पूरूषाः ।
इहो सहस्रदक्षिणोऽपि पूषा निषीदतु ॥

इह धृतिरिह स्वधृतिरिह रन्तिरिह रमस्व ।
मयि धृतिर्मयि स्वधृतिर्मयि रमो मयि रमस्व ॥

२.५.२. अग्ने प्रायश्चित्ते त्वं देवानां प्रायश्चित्तिरसि । ब्राह्मणस्त्वा नाथकाम उपधावामि ।
यास्याः पापी लक्ष्मिस्तामस्या अपजहि ॥

वायो प्रायश्चित्ते त्वं देवानां प्रायश्चित्तिरसि । ब्राह्मणस्त्वा नाथकाम उपधावामि ।
यास्याः पतिघ्नी तनूस्तामस्या अपजहि ॥

चन्द्र प्रायश्चित्ते त्वं देवानां प्रायश्चित्तिरसि । ब्राह्मणस्त्वा नाथकाम उपधावामि ।
यास्याः अपुत्र्या तनूस्तामस्या अपजहि ॥

सूर्य प्रायश्चित्ते त्वं देवानां प्रायश्चित्तिरसि । ब्राह्मणस्त्वा नाथकाम उपधावामि ।
यास्याः अपशव्या तनूस्तमस्या अपजहि ॥

अग्निवायुचन्द्रसूर्याः प्रायश्चित्तयो यूयं देवानां प्रायश्चित्तयाः स्थ । ब्राह्मणो वो नाथकाम उपधावामि । यास्याः पापिलक्षीर्या पतिध्निया पुत्र्या या पशव्या तामस्या अपहत ॥

२.५.९. विष्णुर्योनिं कल्पयतु त्वष्टा रूपाणि पिँशतु ।
आसिञ्चतु प्रजापतिर्धाता गर्भं दधातु ते ॥

गर्भं धेहि सिनीवालि गर्भं धेहि सरस्वति ।
गर्भं ते अश्विनौ देवावाधत्तां पुष्करस्रजौ ॥

खादिर गृह्यसूत्र विवाह मन्त्राः

१.३.६. या आकृन्तन्नवयन् या अतन्वत याश्च देव्योऽन्तानभितो ततन्थ ।
तास्त्वा देव्यो जरसे संव्ययन्त्वायुष्मतीदं परिधत्व वासः ॥

परिधत्त धत्त वाससैनां शतायुषीं कृणुत दीर्घमायुः ।
शतं च जीव शरदः सुवर्चा वसूनिचार्ये विभृजासि जीवन् ॥

सोमोऽददत् गन्धर्वाय गन्धर्वोऽददत् अग्नये ।
रयिं च पुत्राँश्चादादग्निर्मह्यमथो इमाम् ॥

प्र मे पतियानः पन्थाः कल्पताँ शिवा अरिष्टा पतिलोकं गमेयम् ॥
प्रास्याः पतियानः पन्थाः कल्पताँ शिवा अरिष्टा पतिलोकं गम्याः ॥

१.३.११. अग्निरेतु प्रथमो देवताभ्यः सोऽसै प्रजां मुञ्चातु मृत्युपाशात् ।
तदयँ राजा वरुणोऽनुमन्यतां यथेयं स्त्री पौत्रमघं न रोदात् स्वाहा ॥

इमामग्निस्त्रायतां गार्हपत्यः प्रजामस्यै जरदष्टिं कृणोतु ।
अशून्योपस्थ जीवतामस्तु माता पौत्रमानन्दमभिविबुध्यतामियं स्वाहा ॥

द्यौस्ते पृष्ठं रक्षतु वायुरूरू अश्विनौ च । स्तनन्धयस्ते पुत्रान् सविताभिरक्षतु ।
आ वाससः परिधानत् बृहस्पतिर्विश्वे देवा अभिरक्षन्तु पश्चात् स्वाहा ॥

मा ते गृहेषु निशि घोष उत्थादन्यत्र त्वद्रुदत्यः संविशन्तु ।
मा त्वँ रुदत्युर आ बधिष्ठा जीवपत्नी पतिलोके विराज पश्यन्ती प्रजां
सुमनस्यमानां स्वाहा ॥

अप्रजस्यम् पौत्रमर्त्यं पाप्मानमुत वा अघम् ।
शीर्ष्णः स्रजमिवोन्मुच्य द्विषद्भ्यः प्रतिमुञ्चामि पाशँ स्वाहा ॥

परैतु मृत्युरमृतं म आगाद् वैवस्वतो नो अभयं कृणोतु ।
परं मृत्यो अनुपमेहि पन्थां यत्र नो अन्य इतरो देवयानात् ॥
चक्षुस्मते शृण्वते ते ब्रवीमि मानः प्रजां रीरिषो मोत वीरान् स्वाहा ॥

१.३.१९. इममश्मानारोहाश्मेव त्वं स्थिरा भव ।
द्विषन्तमप बाधदस्व मा च त्वं द्विषतामधः ॥

१.३.२२. इयं नार्यूपब्रूतेऽग्नौ लाजानापवन्ती ।
दीर्घायुरस्तु मे पतिः शतं वर्षाणि जीवतु ।
एधन्ताम् ज्ञातयो मम स्वाहा ॥

१.३.२३. अर्यमणं नु देवं कन्या अग्निमयक्षत ।
स इमां देवो अर्यमा प्रेतो मुञ्चातु मामुतः स्वाहा ॥

पूषाणं नु देवं कन्या अग्निमयक्षत ।
स इमां देवो पूषा प्रेतो मुञ्चातु मामुतः स्वाहा ॥

१.३.२४. कन्यला पितृभ्यः पतिलोक मयतीयमप दीक्षामयष्ट ।
कन्या उत त्वया वयं धारा उदन्या इवातिगहेमहि द्विषः ॥

१.३.२६. एकं इषे विष्णुस्त्वा नयतु । द्वे ऊर्जे विष्णुस्त्वा नयतु । त्रीणि व्रताय
विष्णुस्त्वा नयतु । चत्वारि मायोभवाय विष्णुस्त्वा नयतु । पञ्च पशुभ्यो
विष्णुरत्वा नयतु । षड्रायस्पोषाय विष्णुस्त्वा नयतु । सप्त सप्तभ्यो होत्राभ्यो
विष्णुस्त्वा नयतु । सखा सप्तपदी भव सख्यं ते गमेयँ सख्यं ते मा योषाः
सख्यं ते मा योष्ठाः ॥

१.३.२७. सुमङ्गलीरियं वधूरिमाँ समेत पश्यत ।
सौभाग्यमस्यै दत्तवायाथास्थं विपरेतन ॥

सुकिँशुकं शल्मलिं विश्वरूपं सुवर्णवर्णँ सुकृतँ सुचक्रम् ।
आरोह सूर्ये अमृतस्य नाभिँ स्योनं पत्ये वहतुं कृणुष्व ॥

मा विदन् परिपन्थिनो य आसीदन्ति दम्पती ।
सुगेभिर्दुर्गमतीतामपद्रान्त्वरातयः ॥

१.३.३०. समञ्जन्तु विश्वे देवाः समापो हृदयानि नौ ।
सं मातरिश्वा सं धाता समुदेष्ट्री दधातु नौ ॥

१.३.३१. गृभ्णामि ते सौभगत्वाय हस्तं मया पत्या जरदिष्टिर्यथासः ।
भगो अर्यमा सविता पुरंधिर्मह्यं त्वादुर्गार्हपत्याय देवाः ॥

अघोरचक्षुरपतिघ्नि एधि शिवा पशुभ्यः सुमनः सुवर्चः ।
वीरसर्जीवसूर्देवकामा स्योना शं नो भव द्विपदे शं चतुष्पदे ॥

आ नः प्रजां जनयतु प्रजापतिराजरसाय समनक्त्वार्यमा ।
अदुर्मङ्गलीः पतिलोक माविश शं नो भव द्विपदे शं चतुष्पदे ॥

इमां त्वमिन्द्र मीढ्वः सुपुत्राँ सुभगां कृधि ।
दशास्यां पुत्राना धेहि पतिमेकदशां कुरु ॥

सम्राज्ञी श्वशुरे भव सम्राज्ञी श्वश्र्वां भव ।
ननान्दरि सम्राज्ञी भव सम्राज्ञी अधि देवृषु ॥

मम व्रते ते हृदयं दधातु मम चित्तमनु चित्तं ते अस्तु ।
मम वाचमेकमना जुषस्व बृहस्पतिस्त्वा नियुनक्तु मह्यम् ॥

१.४.३. रेखासन्धिषु पक्षमस्वावर्तेषु च यानि ते ।
तानि ते पूर्णाहुत्या सर्वाणि शमयाम्यहम् ॥

केशेषु यच्च पापकमीक्षिते रुदिते च यत् ।
तानि ते पूर्णाहुत्या सर्वाणि शमयाम्यहम् ॥

शिले च यच्च पापकं भाषिते हसिते च यत् ।
तानि ते पूर्णाहुत्या सर्वाणि शमयाम्यहम् ॥

आरोकेषु च दन्तेषु हस्तयोः पादयोश्च यत् ।
तानि ते पूर्णाहुत्या सर्वाणि शमयाम्यहम् ॥

ऊर्वोरुपस्थे जङ्घयोः संधानेषु च यानि ते ।
तानि ते पूर्णाहुत्या सर्वाणि शमयाम्यहम् ॥

यानि कानि च घोराणि सर्वाङ्गेषु तवाभवन् ।
पूर्णाहुतिभिराज्यस्य सर्वाणि तान्यशीशमम् ॥

१.४.६. ध्रुवा द्यौर्ध्रुवा पृथिवी ध्रुवं विश्वमिदं जगत् ।
ध्रुवासः पर्वता इमे ध्रुवा स्त्री पतिकुले इयम् ॥

१.४.१०. अन्नपाशेन मणिना प्राणसूत्रेन पश्निना ।
बध्नामि सत्यग्रन्थिना मनश्च हृदयं च ते ॥

यदेतधृदयं तव तदस्तु दयं मम ।
यदिदं दयं मम तदस्तु दयं तव ॥
अन्नं प्राणस्य पड्विँशस्तेन बध्नामि त्वासौ ।

१.४.११. सुकिँशुकं शल्मलिं विश्वरूपं सुवर्णवर्णँ सुकृतँ सुचक्रम् ।
आरोह सूर्ये अमृतस्य नाभिँ स्योनं पत्ये वहतुं कृणुष्व ॥

मा विदन् परिपन्थिनो य आसीदन्ति दम्पती ।
सुगेभिर्दुर्गमतीतामपद्रान्त्वरातयः ॥

इह गावः प्रजायध्वमिहाश्वा इह पूरूषाः ।
इहो सहस्रदक्षिणोऽपि पूषा निषीदतु ॥

इह धृतिरिह स्वधृतिरिह रन्तिरिह रमस्व ।
मयि धृतिर्मयि स्वधृतिर्मयि रमो मयि रमस्व ॥

१.४.१२. अग्ने प्रायश्चित्ते त्वं देवानां प्रायश्चित्तिरसि । ब्राह्मणस्त्वा नाथकाम उपधावामि ।
यास्याः पापी लक्ष्मिस्तामस्या अपजहि ॥

वायो प्रायश्चित्ते त्वं देवानां प्रायश्चित्तिरसि । ब्राह्मणस्त्वा नाथकाम उपधावामि ।
यास्याः पतिघ्नी तनूस्तामस्या अपजहि ॥

चन्द्र प्रायश्चित्ते त्वं देवानां प्रायश्चित्तिरसि । ब्राह्मणस्त्वा नाथकाम उपधावामि ।
यास्याः अपुत्र्या तनूस्तामस्या अपजहि ॥

सूर्य प्रायश्चित्ते त्वं देवानां प्रायश्चित्तिरसि । ब्राह्मणस्त्वा नाथकाम उपधावामि ।
यास्याः अपशव्या तनूस्तमस्या अपजहि ॥

अग्निवायुचन्द्रसूर्याः प्रायश्चित्तयो यूयं देवानां प्रायश्चित्तयाः स्थ । ब्राह्मणो वो नाथकाम उपधावामि । यास्याः पापिलक्षीर्या पतिघ्निया पुत्र्या या पशव्या तामस्या अपहत ॥

१.४.१५. विष्णुर्योनिं कल्पयतु त्वष्टा रूपाणि पिँशतु ।
आसिञ्चतु प्रजापतिर्धाता गर्भं दधातु ते ॥

गर्भं धेहि सिनीवालि गर्भं धेहि सरस्वति ।
गर्भं ते अश्विनौ देवावाधत्तां पुष्करस्रजौ ॥

जैमिनि गृह्यसूत्र विवाह मन्त्राः

१.२०. अनृक्षरा ऋजवः सन्तु पन्था एभिः सखायो यन्ति नो वरेयम् ।
समर्यमा सं भगो नोऽनुनीयात्सं जास्पत्यं सुयममस्तु देवाः ॥

अग्निरेतु प्रथमो देवताभ्यः सोऽसै प्रजां मुञ्चातु मृत्युपाशात् ।
तदयँ राजा वरुणोऽनुमन्यतां यथेयं स्त्री पौत्रमघं न रोदात् स्वाहा ॥

इमामग्निस्त्रायतां गार्हपत्यः प्रजामस्यै जरदष्टिं कृणोतु ।
अशून्योपस्थ जीवतामस्तु माता पौत्रमानन्दमभिविबुध्यतामियं स्वाहा ॥

द्यौस्ते पृष्ठं रक्षतु वायुरूरु अश्विनौ च । स्तनन्धयस्ते पुत्रान् सविताभिरक्षतु ।
आ वाससः परिधानत् बृहस्पतिर्विश्वे देवा अभिरक्षन्तु पश्चात् स्वाहा ॥

मा ते गृहेषु निशि घोष उत्थादन्यत्र त्वद्रुदत्यः संविशन्तु ।
मा त्वँ रुदत्युर आ बधिष्ठा जीवपत्नी पतिलोके विराज पश्यन्ती प्रजां सुमनस्यमानां स्वाहा ॥

अप्रजस्यम् पौत्रमर्त्यं पाप्मानमुत वा अघम् ।
शीर्ष्णः स्रजमिवोन्मुच्य द्विषद्भ्यः प्रतिमुञ्चामि पाशँ स्वाहा ॥

परैतु मृत्युरमृतं म आगाद् वैवस्वतो नो अभयं कृणोतु ।
परं मृत्यो अनुपमेहि पन्थां यत्र नो अन्य इतरो देवयानात् ॥

चक्षुस्मते शृण्वते ते ब्रवीमि मानः प्रजां रीरिषो मोत वीरान् स्वाहा ॥

या आकृन्तन्नवयन् या अतन्वत याश्च देव्योऽन्तानभितो ततन्थ ।
तास्त्वा देव्यो जरसे संव्ययन्त्वायुष्मतीदं परिधत्व वासः ॥

परिधत्त धत्त वाससैनां शतायुषीं कृणुत दीर्घमायुः ।
शतं च जीव शरदः सुवर्चा वसूनिचार्ये विभृजासि जीवन् ॥

सोमोऽददत् गन्धर्वाय गन्धर्वोऽददत् अग्नये ।
रयिं च पुत्राँश्चादादग्निर्मह्यमथो इमाम् ॥

प्र मे पतियानः पन्थाः कल्पताँ शिवा अरिष्टा पतिलोकं गमेयम् ॥
प्रास्याः पतियानः पन्थाः कल्पताँ शिवा अरिष्टा पतिलोकं गम्याः ॥

या तिरश्ची निपद्यते अहं विधरणी इति ।
तां त्वा घृतस्य धारया संराधा राधायामसि संराधायै ॥

मा ते गृहेषु निशि घोष उत्थादन्यत्र त्वद्रुदत्यः संविशन्तु ।
मा त्वँ रुदत्युर आ बधिष्ठा जीवपत्नी पतिलोके विराज पश्यन्ती प्रजां सुमनस्यमानां॥

अन्वद्य नोऽनुमतिर्यज्ञं देवेषु मन्यताम् ।
अग्निश्च हव्यवाहनस्तत्करोतु समृध्यताम् ॥

द्यौस्ते पृष्ठं रक्षतु वायुरूरु अश्विनौ च । स्तनन्धयस्ते पुत्रान् सविताभिरक्षतु ।
आ वाससः परिधानत् बृहस्पतिर्विश्वे देवा अभिरक्षन्तु पश्चात् ॥

अप्रजस्यम् पौत्रमर्त्यं पाप्मानमुत वा अघम् ।
शीर्ष्णः स्रजमिवोन्मुच्य द्विषद्भ्यः प्रतिमुञ्चामि पाशँ स्वाहा ॥

यानि कानि च घोराणि सर्वाङ्गेषु तवाभवन् ।
पूर्णाहुतिभिराज्यस्य सर्वाणि तान्यशीशमम् ॥

१.२१. गृभ्णामि ते सौभगत्वाय हस्तं मया पत्या जरदिष्टिर्यथासः ।
भगो अर्यमा सविता पुरंधिर्मह्यं त्वादुर्गार्हपत्याय देवाः ॥

सोमोऽददद्गन्धर्वाय गन्धर्वोऽददग्नये ।
सोमः प्रथमो विविदे गन्धर्वो विविद उत्तरः ।
तृतीयोऽग्निष्टे पतिस्तुरीयोऽहं मनुष्यजा ॥

अघोरचक्षुरपतिघ्नि एधि शिवा पशुभ्यः सुमनः सुवर्चः ।
वीरसर्जीवसूर्देवकामा स्योना शं नो भव द्विपदे शं चतुष्पदे ॥

आ नः प्रजां जनयतु प्रजापतिराजरसाय समनक्त्वार्यमा ।
अदुर्मङ्गलीः पतिलोक माविश शं नो भव द्विपदे शं चतुष्पदे ॥

तां पूषच्छिवतमामेरयस्व यस्यां बीजं मनुष्या वपन्ति ।
या न ऊरु उशति विस्रयातै यस्यामुशन्तः प्रहरेम शेफम् ॥

अमोऽहमस्मि सा त्वं सामाहमस्म्यृक्त्वं मनोऽहमस्मि वाक्त्वं द्योरहं पृथिवी त्वं तावेहि संभवाव सह रेतो दधावहै पुंसे पुत्राय वैत्तवै मामनुव्रता भव सहशय्या मया भवासाव ॥

कन्यला पितृभ्यः पतिलोक मयतीयमप दीक्षामयष्ट ।
कन्या उत त्वया वयं धारा उदन्या इवातिगहेमहि द्विषः ॥

इयं नार्युपब्रूतेऽग्नौ लाजान्वपन्ती ।
दीर्घायुरस्तु मे पतिरेधन्तां ज्ञातयो मम ॥

अर्यम्णं नु देवं कन्याग्निमयक्षत ।
स इमां देवो अर्यमा प्रेतो मुञ्चातु मामुतः॥

विश्वा उत त्वया वयं धारा उदन्या इव । अतिगाहेमहि द्विषः ॥

एकमिषे विष्णुस्त्वान्वेतु । द्वे ऊर्जे विष्णुस्त्वान्वेतु । त्रीणि रायस्पोषाय विष्णुस्त्वान्वेतु । चत्वारि मयोभवाय विष्णुस्त्वान्वेतु । पञ्च प्रजाभ्यो विष्णुस्त्वान्वेतु । षड्तुभ्यो विष्णुस्त्वान्वेतु । सखा सप्तपदी भव ॥

सुमङ्गलीरियं वधूरिमां समेत पश्यत । सौभाग्यमस्यै दत्त्वायाथास्तं विपरेतन ॥

ध्रुवोऽसीति ध्रुवमुपतिष्ठते ध्रुवोऽसि ध्रुवाहं पतिकुले भूयासम् ॥

असावित्यात्मनोऽरुन्धतीमरुन्धत्यरुद्धाहं पत्या भूयासम् ॥

१.२२. पूषा त्वेतो नयतु हतगृह्याश्विना त्वा प्रवहतं रथेन ।
गृहान् गच्छ गृहपत्नी यथासो वशिनी त्वं विदथमा वदासि ॥

स्वं कुलं प्राप्तां कल्याणशीलाः कल्याणप्रजाः समवजीर्णाः प्रत्यवरोपयन्ति
इह प्रियं प्रजया ते समृध्यतामस्मिन्गृहे गार्हपत्याय जागृहि ।
एना पत्या तन्वं संसृजस्वाथाजीव्री विदथमावदासि ॥

इह गावः प्रजायध्वमिहाश्वा इह पूरुषाः ।
इहो सहस्रदक्षिणोऽपि पूषा निषीदतु ॥

इह धृतिरिह स्वधृतिरिह रन्तिरिह रमस्व ।
मयि धृतिर्मयि स्वधृतिर्मयि रमो मयि रमस्व ॥

इमां त्वमिन्द्र मीढ्वः सुपुत्राँ सुभगां कृधि ।
दशास्यां पुत्राना धेहि पतिमेकदशां कुरु ॥

सम्राज्ञी श्वशुरे भव सम्राज्ञी श्वश्वां भव ।
ननान्दरि सम्राज्ञी भव सम्राज्ञी अधि देवृषु ॥

मम व्रते ते हृदयं दधातु मम चित्तमनु चित्तं ते अस्तु ।
मम वाचमेकमना जुषस्व बृहस्पतिस्त्वा नियुनक्तु मह्यम् ॥

अग्ने प्रायश्चित्ते त्वं देवानां प्रायश्चित्तिरसि । ब्राह्मणस्त्वा नाथकाम उपधावामि ।
यास्याः पापी लक्ष्मिस्तामस्या अपजहि ॥

वायो प्रायश्चित्ते त्वं देवानां प्रायश्चित्तिररि । ब्राह्मणस्त्वा नाथकाम उगधावामि ।
यास्याः पतिघ्नी तनूस्तामस्या अपजहि ॥

चन्द्र प्रायश्चित्ते त्वं देवानां प्रायश्चित्तिरसि । ब्राह्मणस्त्वा नाथकाम उपधावामि ।
यास्याः अपुत्र्या तनूस्तामस्या अपजहि ॥

सूर्य प्रायश्चित्ते त्वं देवानां प्रायश्चित्तिरसि । ब्राह्मणस्त्वा नाथकाम उपधावामि ।
यास्याः अपशव्या तनूस्तमस्या अपजहि ॥

अग्निवायुचन्द्रसूर्याः प्रायश्चित्तयो यूयं देवानां प्रायश्चित्तयाः स्थ । ब्राह्मणो वो

नाथकाम उपधावामि । यास्याः पापिलक्षीर्या पतिघ्निया पुत्र्या या पशव्या तामस्या अपहत ॥

विष्णुर्योनिं कल्पयतु त्वष्टा रूपाणि पिंशतु ।
आसिञ्चतु प्रजापतिर्धाता गर्भं दधातु ते ॥

गर्भं धेहि सिनीवालि सरस्वति । गर्भं ते अश्विनौ देवावाधत्तां पुष्करस्रजौ ॥ हिरण्ययी अरणी यं निर्मन्थतामश्विनौ । तं ते गर्भं दधाम्यहं दशमे मासि सूतवे ॥

कौशिक गृह्यसूत्र विवाह मन्त्राः

१०.१.६. सत्येनोत्तभिता भूमिः सूर्येणोत्तभिता द्यौः ।
ऋतेनादित्यास्तिष्ठन्ति दिवि सोमो अधि श्रितः ॥

सोमेनादित्या बलिनः सोमेन पृथिवी मही ।
अथो नक्षत्राणामेषामुपस्थे सोम आहितः ॥

सोमं मन्यते पपिवान् यत् संपिषत्योषधिम् ।
सोमं यं ब्रह्मणो विदुर्न तस्याश्नाति पार्थिवः ॥

यत् त्वा सोम प्रपिबन्ति तत आ प्यायसे पुनः ।
वायुः सोमस्य रक्षिता समानां मास आकृतिः ॥

आच्छद्विधानैर्गुपितो बार्हतैः सोम रक्षितः ।
ग्राव्णामिच्छृण्वन् तिष्ठसि न ते अश्नाति पार्थिवः ॥

चित्तिरा उपबर्हणं चक्षुरा अभ्यञ्जनम् ।
द्यौर्भुमिः कोश आसीद् यदयात् सूर्या पतिम् ॥

रैभ्यासीदनुदेयी नाराशंसी न्योचनी ।
सूर्याया भद्रमिद् वासो गाथयैति परिष्कृता ॥

स्तोमा आसन् प्रतिधयः कुरीरं छन्द ओपशः ।
सूर्याया अश्विना वराग्निरासित् पुरोगवः ॥

सोमो वधुयुरभवदश्विनास्तामुभा वरा ।
सूर्यां यत् पत्ये शंसन्तीं मनसा सवितादादात् ॥

मनो अस्या अन आसीद् द्योरासीदुत च्छदिः ।
शुक्रावनड्वाहावास्तां यदायात् सूर्या पतिम् ॥

ऋक्सामाभ्यामभिहितौ गावौ ते सामनावैताम् ।
श्रोत्रे ते चक्रे आस्तां दिवि पन्थाश्चराचरः ॥

शुची ते चक्रे यात्या व्यानो अक्ष आहतः ।
अनो मनस्मयं सूर्यारोहत् प्रयती पतिम् ॥

सूर्याया वहतुः प्रागात् सविता यमवासृजत् ।
मघासु हन्यन्ते गावः फल्गुणिषु व्यु ह्यते ॥

यदश्विना पृच्छमानावयातं त्रिचक्रेण वहतुं सूर्यायाः ।
क्वैकं चक्रं वामासीत् क्व देष्ट्राय तस्थथुः ॥

यदयातं शुभस्पती वरेयं सूर्यामुप ।
विश्वे देवा अनु तद् वामजानन् पुत्रः पितरवृणाति पुषा ॥

द्वे ते चक्रे सूर्ये ब्रह्माण ऋतुथा विदुः ।
अथैकं चक्रं यद् गृहा तदद्धातय इद् विदुः ॥

पूर्वापरं चरतो माययैतौ शिशू क्रीडन्तौ परि यातोऽर्णवम् ।
विश्वान्यो भुवना विचष्ट ऋतूँरन्यो विदधज्जायसे नवः ॥
भागं देवेभ्यो वि दधास्यायन् प्र चन्द्रमस्तिरसे दीर्घमायुः ॥

१०.१.७. आ नो अग्ने सुमतिं सम्भलो गमेदिमां कुमारि सह नो भगेन ।
जुष्टा वरेषु समनेषु वल्गुरोषं पत्या सौभगमस्त्वस्यै ॥

१०.१.८. युवं भगं सं भरतं समृद्धमृतं वदन्तावृतोद्येषु ।

१०.१.९. ब्रह्मणस्पते पतिमस्यै रोचय चारु संभलो वदतु वाचमेतम् ॥

१०.१.१२. अनृक्षरा ऋजवः सन्तु पन्थानो येभिः सखायो यन्ति नो वरेयम् ।
सं भगेना समर्यम्णा सं धाता सृजतु वर्चसा ॥

१०.१.१४. यो अनिध्मो दीदयदप्स्वऽन्तर्यं विप्रास ईडते अध्वरेषु ।
अपां नपान्मधुमतीरिपो दा याभिरिन्द्रो वावृधे वीर्या वान् ॥

१०.१.१५. इदमहं रुशन्तं ग्राभं तनूदूषिमपोहामि ।

१०.१.१६. यो भद्रो रोचनस्तमुदचामि ॥

१०.१.१७. आस्यै ब्राह्मणाः स्नपनीर्हन्त्ववीरघ्नीरुदजन्त्वापः ।
अर्यम्णो अग्निं पर्येतु पूषन् प्रतिक्षन्ते श्वशुरो देवरश्च ॥

१०.१.२३. प्र त्वा मुञ्चामि वरुणस्य पाशाद् येन त्वाबध्नात् सविता सुशेवाः ।
ऋतस्य योनौ सुकृतस्य लोके स्योनं ते अस्तु सहसंभलायै ॥

१०.१.२४. उशती कन्यला इमाः पितृलोकात् पति यतीः ।
अव दीक्षामसृजत स्वाहा ॥

बृहस्पतिनावसृष्टां विश्वे देवा अधारयन् ।
वर्चो गोषु प्रविष्टं यत् तेनेमां सं सृजामसि ॥

बृहस्पतिनावसृष्टां विश्वे देवा अधारयन् ।
तेजो गोषु प्रविष्टं यत् तेनेमां सं सृजामसि ॥

बृहस्पतिनावसृष्टां विश्वे देवा अधारयन् ।
भगो गोषु प्रविष्टं यत् तेनेमां सं सृजामसि ॥

बृहस्पतिनावसृष्टां विश्वे देवा अधारयन् ।
यशो गोषु प्रविष्टं यत् तेनेमां सं सृजामसि ॥

बृहस्पतिनावसृष्टां विश्वे देवा अधारयन् ।
पयो गोषु प्रविष्टं यत् तेनेमां सं सृजामसि ॥

बृहस्पतिनावसृष्टां विश्वे देवा अधारयन् ।
रसो गोषु प्रविष्टं यत् तेनेमां सं सृजामसि ॥

१०.१.२६. यदासन्ध्यामुपधाने यद् वोपासने कृतम् ।
विवाहे कृत्यां यां चक्रुरास्ताने तां नि दध्मसि ॥

१०.१.२७. यच्च वर्चो अक्षेषु सुरायां च यदाहितम् ।
यद् गाष्वश्विना वर्चस्तेनेमां वर्चसावतम् ॥

यथा सिन्धुर्नदीनां साम्राज्यं सुषुवे वृषा ।
एवा त्वं सम्राज्येधि पत्युरस्तं परेत्य ॥

१०.२.१. यद् दुष्कृतं यच्छमलं विवाहे वहतौ च यत् ।
तत् सम्भलस्य कम्बले मृज्महे दुरितं वयम् ॥

सम्भले मलं सादयित्वा कम्बले दुरितं वयम् ।
अभूम यज्ञियाः शुद्धाः प्र ण आयूंषि तारिषत् ॥

१०.२.४. या अकृन्तन्नवयन् याश्च तत्निरे या देवीरन्तां अभितोऽददन्त ।
तास्त्वा जरसे सव्ययन्त्वायुष्मतीदं परिधत्स्व वासः ॥

त्वष्टा वासो व्यदधाच्छुभे कं बृहस्पतेः प्रशिषा कविनाम् ।
तेनेमां नारीं सविता भगश्च सूर्यामिव परि धत्तां प्रजया ॥

१०.२.५. कृत्रिमः कण्टकः शतदन् य एषः ।
अपास्याः केश्यं मलमप शीर्षण्यं लिखात् ॥

१०.२.७. आशासाना सौमनसं प्रजां सौभाग्यं रयिम् ।
पत्युरनुंव्रता भूत्वा सं नह्यस्वामृताय कम् ॥

सं त्वा नह्यामि पयसा पृथिव्याः सं त्वा नह्यामि पयसौषधीनाम् ।
सं त्वा नह्यामि प्रजया धनेन सह संनद्धा सुनुहि वाजमेमम् ॥

१०.२.८. इयं वीरुन्मधुजाता मधुना त्वा खनामसि ।
मधोरधि प्रजातासि सा नो मधुमतस्कृधि ॥

१०.२.१०. भगस्त्वेतो नयतु हतगृह्याश्विना त्वा प्र वहतां रथेन ।
गृहान् गच्छ गृहपत्नी यथासो वशिनी त्वं विदथमा वदासि ॥

१०.२.१२. शं ते हिरण्यं शमु सन्त्वापः शं मेथिर्भवतु शं युगस्य तर्द्म ।
शं त आपः शतपवित्रा भवन्तु शमु पत्या तहन्वं सं स्पृशस्व ॥

खे रथस्य खेऽनसः खे युगस्य शतक्रतो ।
अपालमिन्द्र त्रिष्पूत्व्यकृणोः सूर्यत्वचम् ॥

१०.२.१४. अङ्गादङ्गाद् वयमस्या अप यक्ष्मं नि दध्मसि ।
तन्मा प्रापत् पृथिवीं मोत देवान् दिवं मा प्रापदुर्वऽन्तरिक्षम् ।
अपो मा प्रापन्मलमेतदग्ने यमं मा प्रापत् पितृंश्च सर्वान् ॥

१०.२.१५. स्योनं ध्रुवं प्रजायै धारयामि तेऽश्मानं देव्याः पृथिव्या उपस्थे ।
तमातिष्ठानुमाद्या सुवर्चा दीर्घं त आयुः सविता कृणोतु ॥

१०.२.१७. इयं नार्युपब्रूते पूल्यान्यावपन्तिका ।
दीर्घायुरस्तु मे पतिर्जीवाति शरदः शतम् ॥

१०.२.१९. येनाग्निरस्या भूम्या हस्तं जग्राह दक्षिणम् ।
तेन गृह्णामि ते हस्तं मा व्यथिष्ठा मया सह प्रजया च धनेन च ॥

देवस्ते सविता हस्तं गृह्णातु सोमो राजा सुप्रजसं कृणोतु ।
अग्निः सुभगां जातवेदाः पत्ये पत्नी जरदिष्टं कृणोतु ॥

गृभ्णामि ते सौभगत्वाय हस्तं मया पत्या जरदष्टिर्यथासः ।
भगो अर्यमा सविता पुरंधिर्मह्यं त्वादुर्गार्हपत्याय देवाः ॥

भगस्ते हस्तमग्रहीत् सविता हस्तमग्रहीत् ।
पत्नी त्वमसि धर्मणाहं गृहपतिस्तव ॥

ममेयमस्तु पोष्या मह्यं त्वादाद् बृहस्पतिः ।
मया पत्या प्रजावति सं जीव शरदः शतम् ॥

१०.२.२०. अर्यम्णो अग्निं पर्येतु पूषन् प्रतिक्षन्ते श्वशुरो देवरश्च ॥

१०.२.२१. सप्तमर्यादाः कवयस्ततक्षुस्तासामिदेकामभ्यं हुरो गात् ।
आयोर्ह स्कम्भ उपमस्य नीडे पथां विसर्गे धरुणेषु तस्थौ ॥

१६.२.२३. इषे त्वा सुमङ्गलि प्रजावति सुसीम ।

१०.२.२४. ऊर्जे त्वा रायस्पोषाय त्वा सौभाग्याय त्वा साम्राज्याय त्वा संपदे त्वा जीवातवे
त्वा सुमङ्गलि प्रजावति सुसीम इति सप्तमं सखा सप्तपदी भव ॥

१०.२.२५. आ रोहरुमुप धस्त्व हस्तं परि षजस्व जायां सुमनस्यमानः ।
प्रजां कृण्वाथामिह मोदमानौ दीर्घं वामायुः सविता कृणोतु ॥

भगस्ततक्ष चतुरः पादान् भगस्ततक्ष चत्वार्युष्पलानि ।
त्वष्टा पिपेष मध्यतोऽनु वर्ध्रान्त्सा नो अस्तु सुमङ्गली ॥

१०.२.२८. अहं वि ष्यामि मयि रूपमस्या वेददित् पश्यन् मनसः कुलायम् ।
न स्तेयमद्मि मनसोदमुच्ये स्वयं श्रथ्नानो वरुणस्य पाशान् ॥

प्र त्वा मुञ्चामि वरुणस्य पाशाद् येन त्वाबध्नात् सविता सुशेवाः ।
उरुं लोकं सुगमत्र पन्थां कृणोमि तुभ्यं सहपत्न्यै वधु ॥

१०.२.३१. बृहस्पतिनावसृष्टां विश्वे देवा अधारयन् ।
वर्चो गोषु प्रविष्टं यत् तेनेमां सं सृजामसि ॥

बृहस्पतिनावसृष्टां विश्वे देवा अधारयन् ।
तेजो गोषु प्रविष्टं यत् तेनेमां सं सृजामसि ॥

बृहस्पतिनावसृष्टां विश्वे देवा अधारयन् ।
भगो गोषु प्रविष्टं यत् तेनेमां सं सृजामसि ॥

बृहस्पतिनावसृष्टां विश्वे देवा अधारयन् ।
यशो गोषु प्रविष्टं यत् तेनेमां सं सृजामसि ॥

बृहस्पतिनावसृष्टां विश्वे देवा अधारयन् ।
पयो गोषु प्रविष्टं यत् तेनेमां सं सृजामसि ॥

बृहस्पतिनावसृष्टां विश्वे देवा अधारयन् ।
रसो गोषु प्रविष्टं यत् तेनेमां सं सृजामसि ॥

१०.२.३२. उद्यच्छध्वमप रक्षो हनाथेमां नारी सुकृते दधात ।
धाता विपश्चित् पतिमस्यै विवेद भगो राजा पुर एतु प्रजानन् ॥

भगस्ततक्ष चतुरः पादान् भगस्ततक्ष चत्वार्युष्पलानि ।
त्वष्टा पिपेष मध्यतोऽनु वर्ध्रान्त्सा नो अस्तु सुमङ्गली ॥

अभ्रातृघ्नीं वरुणापशुघ्नीं बृहस्पतये ।
इन्द्रापतिघ्नीं पुत्रिणीमास्मभ्यं सवितर्वह ॥

१०.२.३३. प्रति तिष्ट विराडसि विष्णुरिवेह सरस्वति ।
सिनीवालि प्र जायतां भगस्य सुमतावसत् ॥

१०.३.१. सुकिंशुकं वहतुं विश्वरूपं हिरण्यवर्णं सुवृतं सुचक्रम् ।
आरोह सूर्ये अमृतस्य लोकं स्योनं पतिभ्यो वहतुं कृणु त्वम् ॥

रुक्मप्रस्तरणं वह्यं विश्वा रूपाणि बिभ्रतम् ।
आरोहत् सूर्या सावित्री बृहते सौभगाय कम् ॥

१०.३.२. एमं पन्थामरुक्षाम सुगं स्वस्तिवाहनम् ।
यस्मिन् वीरो न रिष्यत्यन्येषां विन्दते वसु ॥

ब्रह्मापरं युज्यतां ब्रह्म पूर्वं ब्रह्मान्ततो मध्यतो ब्रह्म सर्वतः ।
अनाव्याधां देवपुरां प्रपद्य शिवा स्योना पतिलोके विराज ॥

१०.३.३. मा विदन् परिपन्थिनो य आसीदन्ति दम्पती ।
सुगन दुर्गमतीताहमप द्रान्त्वरातयः ॥

अनृक्षरा ऋजवः सन्तु पन्था येभिः सखायो यन्ति नो वरेयम् ।
सं भगेन समर्यम्णा सं धाता सृजसु वर्चसा ॥

१०.३.४. येदं पूर्वागन् रशनायमाना प्रजामस्यै द्रविणं चेह दत्त्वा ।
तां वहत्वगतस्यानु पन्थां विराडियं सुप्रजा अत्यजैषीत् ॥

१०.३.५. सूर्यायै देवेभ्यो मित्राय वरुणाय च ।
ये भूतस्य प्रचेतसस्तेभ्य इदमकरं नमः ॥

१०.३.७. य ऋते चिदभिश्रिषः पुरा जत्रुभ्य आतृदः ।
संधाता संधिं मघवा पुरूवसुर्निष्कर्ता विह्रुतं पुनः ॥

१०.३.८. सा मन्दसाना मनसा शिवेन रयिं धेहि सर्ववीरं वचस्यम् ।
सुगं तीर्थं सुप्रपाणं शुभस्पती स्थाणुं पथिष्ठमप दुर्मतिं हतम् ॥

१०.३.९. इदं सु मे नरः शृणुत ययाशिषा दम्पती वाममश्नुतः ।
ये गन्धर्वा अप्सरसश्च देवीरेषु वानस्पत्येषु येऽधेहि तस्थुः ।
स्योनास्ते अस्यै वध्वै भवन्तु मा हिम्सिषुर्वहतुमुह्यमानम् ॥

१०.३.१०. सुमङ्गली प्रतरणी गृहाणां सुशेवा पत्ये श्वशुराय शंभूः ।
स्योना श्वश्र्वै प्र गृहान् वेशेमान् ॥

१०.३.११. या ओषधयो या नद्यो यानि क्षेत्राणि या वना ।
तास्त्वा वधु प्रजावतीं पत्ये रक्षन्तु रक्षसः ॥

१०.३.१२. ये पितरो वधूदर्शा इमं वहतुमागमन् ।
ते अस्यै वध्वै संपत्न्यै प्रजावच्छर्म यच्छन्तु ॥

१०.३.१३. प्र बुध्यस्व सुबुधा बुध्यमाना दीर्घायुत्वाय शतशारदाय ।
गृहान् गच्छ गृहपत्नी यथासो दीर्घं त आयुः सविता कृणोतु ॥

१०.३.१४. सं काशयामि वहतुं ब्रह्मणा गृहैरघोरेण चक्षुषा मित्रियेण ।
पर्याणद्धं विश्वरूपं यदास्ति स्योनं पतिभ्यः सविता तत् कृणोतु ॥

१०.३.१६. उद्व ऊर्मिः शम्या हन्त्वापो योक्त्राणि मुञ्चत ।
मादुष्कृतौ व्ये नसावघ्न्यावशुनमारताम् ॥

१०.३.१७. स्योनं ध्रुवं प्रजायै धारयामि तेऽश्मानं देव्याः पृथिव्या उपस्थे ।
तमातिष्ठानुमाद्या सुवर्चा दीर्घं त आयुः सविता कृणोतु ॥

१०.३.१९. तमातिष्ठानुमाद्या सुवर्चा दीर्घं त आयुः सविता कृणोतु ॥

१०.३.२०. सुमङ्गली प्रतरणी गृहाणां सुशेवा पत्ये श्वशुराय शंभूः ।
स्योना श्वश्र्वै प्र गृहान् वेशेमान् ॥

इह प्रियं प्रजायै ते समृध्यतामस्मिन् गृहे गार्हपत्याय जागृहि ।
एना पत्या तन्वं सं स्पृशस्वाथ जिर्विर्विदथमा वदासि ॥

मा हिंसिष्टं कुमार्यं स्थूणे देवकृते पथि ।
शालाया देव्या द्वारं स्योनं कृण्मो वधूपथम् ॥

ब्रह्मापरं युज्यतां ब्रह्म पूर्वं ब्रह्मान्ततो मध्यतो ब्रह्म सर्वतः ।
अनाव्याधां देवपुरां प्रपद्य शिवा स्योना पतिलोके विराज ॥

१०.३.२२. अघोरचक्षुरपतिघ्नी स्योना शग्मा सुशेवा सुयमा गृहेभ्यः ।
वीरसूदेवृकामा सं त्वयैधिषीमहि सुमनस्यमाना ॥

अदेवृघ्न्यपतिघ्नीहैधि शिवा पशुभ्यः सुयमा सुवर्चाः ।
प्रजावती वीरसूर्देवृकामा स्योनेममग्निं गार्हपत्यं सपर्य ॥

१०.३.२३. यदा गार्हपत्यमसपर्यैत् पूर्वमग्निं वधूरियम् ।
अधा सरस्वत्यै नारि पितृभ्यश्च नमस्कुरु ॥

सूर्यायै देवेभ्यो मित्राय वरुणाय च ।
ये भूतस्य प्रचेतसस्तेभ्य इदमकरं नमः ॥

१०.४.१. शर्म वर्मैतदा हरास्यै नार्या उपस्तरे ।
सिनीवालि प्र जायतां भगस्य सुमतावसत् ॥

१०.४.२. चर्म चोपस्तृणीथन ॥

१०.४.३. यं बल्बजं न्यस्यथ चर्म चोपस्तृणीथन ।
तदा रोहतु सुप्रजा या कन्या विन्दते पतिम् ॥

१०.४.४. उप स्तृणीहि बल्बजमधि चर्मणि रोहिते ।
तत्रोपविश्य सुप्रजा इममग्निं सपर्यतु ॥

१०.४.५. तदा रोहतु सुप्रजा या कन्या विन्दते पतिम् ॥

१०.४.६. तत्रोपविश्य सुप्रजा इममग्निं सपर्यतु ॥

१०.४.८. सुज्यैष्ठ्यो भवत् पुत्रस्त एषः ॥

१०.४.९. वि तिष्ठन्तां मातुरस्य उपस्थान्नानारूपाः पशवो जायमानाः ।
सुमङ्गल्युप सीदेममग्निं संपत्नी प्रति भूषेह देवान् ॥

१०.४.१०. तेन भूतेन हविषायमा प्यायतां पुनः ।
जायां यामस्मा आवाक्षुस्तां रसेनाभि वर्धताम् ॥

तुभ्यमग्ने पर्यवहन् सूर्यां वहतुना सह ।
स नः पतिभ्यो जायां दा अग्ने प्रजया सह ॥

पुनः पत्नीमग्निरदादायुषा सह वर्चसा ।
दीर्घायुरस्या यः पतिर्जीवाति शरदः शतम् ॥

सोमस्य जाया प्रथमं गन्धर्वस्तेऽपरः पतिः ।
तृतीयो अग्निष्टे पतिस्तुरीयस्ते मनुष्यजाः ॥

सोमो ददद् गन्धर्वाय गन्धर्वो दददग्नये ।
रयिं च पुत्रांश्चादादग्निर्मह्यमथो इमाम् ॥

आ वामगन्त्सुमतिर्वाजिनीवसू न्य श्विना हृत्सु कामा अरंसत ।
अभूतं गोपा मिथुना शुभस्पती प्रिया अर्यम्णो दुर्यां अशीमहि ॥

शुम्भनी द्यावापृथिवी अन्तिसुम्ने महिव्रते ।
आपः सप्त सुस्रुवुर्देवीस्ता नो मुञ्चन्त्वंहसः ॥

अग्नये जनविदे स्वाहा सोमाय वसुविदे स्वाहा पूष्णे जातिविदे स्वाहा
इन्द्राय सहीयसे स्वाहा ॥

आगच्छत आगतस्य नाम गृह्णाम्यायतः ।
इन्द्रस्य वृत्रघ्नो वन्वे वासवस्य शतक्रतोः ॥

सविता प्रसवानामधिपतिः स मावतु ।
अस्मिन् ब्रह्मण्यस्मिन् कर्मण्यस्यां पुरोधामस्यां प्रतिष्ठायामस्यां
चित्त्यामस्यामाकूत्यामस्यामाशिष्यस्यां देवहूत्यां स्वाहा ॥

१०.४.१३. शुम्भनी द्यावापृथिवी अन्तिसुम्ने महिव्रते ।
आपः सप्त सुस्रुवुर्देवीस्ता नो मुञ्चन्त्वंहसः ॥

१०.४.१४. तेन भूतेन हविषायमा प्यायतां पुनः ।
जायां यामस्मा आवाक्षुस्तां रसेनाभि वर्धताम् ॥

१०.४.१६. तेन भूतेन हविषायमा प्यायतां पुनः ।
जायां यामस्मा आवाक्षुस्तां रसेनाभि वर्धताम् ॥

१०.५.१. सप्तमर्यादाः कवयस्ततक्षुस्तासामिदेकामभ्यं हुरो गात् ।
आयोर्ह स्कम्भ उपमस्य नीडे पथां विसर्गे धरुणेषु तस्थौ ॥

१०.५.२. अक्ष्यौ नौ मधुसंकाशे अनीकं नौ समञ्जनम् ।
अन्तः कृणुष्व मां हृदि मन इन्नौ सहासति ॥

१०.५.३. महीमू षु मातरं सुवृतानामृतस्य पत्नीमवसे हवामहे ।
तुविक्षत्रामजरन्तीमुरुचीं सुशर्माणमदितिं सुप्रणीतिम् ॥

१०.५.४. आ रोह तल्पं सुमनस्यमानिह प्रजां जनय पत्ये अस्मै ।
इन्द्राणीव सुबुधा बुध्यमाना ज्योतिरग्रा उषसः प्रति जागरसि ॥

१०.५.५. तत्रोपविश्य सुप्रजा इममग्निं सपर्यतु ॥

१०.५.६. देवा अग्रे न्य पद्यन्त पत्नीः समस्पृशन्त तन्व स्तनूभिः ।
सूर्येव नारि विश्वरूपा महित्वा प्रजावती पत्या सं भवेह ॥

१०.५.७. अभित्वा मनुजातेन दधामि मम वाससा ।
यथासो मम केवलो नान्यासां कीर्तियाश्चन ॥

१०.५.८. सं पितरावृत्विये सृजेथां माता पिता च रेतसो भवाथः ।
मर्य इव योषामधिरोहयैनां प्रजां कृण्वाथामिह पुष्यतं रयिम् ॥

तां पूषञ्छिवतमामेरयस्व यस्यां बीजं मनुष्या वपन्ति ।
या न ऊरू उशती विश्रयाति यस्यामुशन्तः प्रहरेम शेपः ॥

आ रोहोरुमप धत्स्व हस्तं परि ष्वजस्व जायां सुमनस्यमानः ।
प्रजां कृण्वाथामिह मोदमानौ दीर्घं वामायुः सविता कृणोतु ॥

आ वां प्रजां जनयतु प्रजापतिरहोरात्राभ्यां समनक्त्वर्यमा ।
अदुर्मङ्गली पतिलोकमा विशेमं शं नो भव द्विपदे शं चतुष्पदे ॥

१०.५.९. इहेमाविन्द्र सं नुद चक्रवाकेव दम्पती ।
प्रजयैनौ स्वस्तकौ विश्वमायुर्व्य श्नुताम् ॥

१०.५.१०. इयं वीरुन्मधुजाता मधुना त्वा खनामसि ।
मधोरधि प्रजातासि सा नो मधुमतस्कृधि ॥

अमोऽहमस्मि सा त्वं सामाहमस्म्यृक् त्वं द्यौरहं पृथिवी त्वं ।
ताविह सं भवाय प्रजामा जनयावहै ॥

जनियन्ति नावग्रवः पुत्रियन्ति सुदानवः ।
अरिष्टास् सचेवहि बृहते वाजसातये ॥

१०.५.११. ब्रह्म जज्ञानं प्रथमं पुरस्ताद् वि सीमतः सुरुचो वेन आवः ।
स बुध्न्या उपमा अस्य विष्ठाः सतश्च योनिमसतश्च वि वः ॥

रात्री माता नभः पितार्यमा ते पितामहः ।
सिलाची नाम वा असि सा देवानामसि स्वसा ॥

१०.५.१२. स्योनाद्योनेरधि बुध्यमानौ हसामुदौ महसा मोदमानौ ।
सुगू सुपुत्रौ सुगृहौ तराथो जीवावुषसो विभाति ॥

१०.५.१३. या अकृन्तन्नवयन् याश्च तत्निरे या देवीरन्तां अभितोऽददन्त ।
तास्त्या जरसे सव्ययन्त्वायुष्मतीदं परिधत्स्व वासः ॥

त्वष्टा वासो व्यदधाच्छुभे कम् बृहस्पतेः प्रशिषा कवीनाम् ।
तेनेमां नारीं सविता भगश्च सूर्यामिव परि धत्तां प्रजया ॥

१०.५.१४. बृहस्पतिः प्रथमः सूर्यायाः शीर्षे केशाँ अकल्पयत् ।
तेनेमामश्विना नारीं पत्ये सं शोभयामसि ॥

इदं तद्रूपं यदवस्त योषा जायां जिज्ञासे मनसा चरन्तीम् ।
तामन्वर्तिष्ये सखिभिर्नवग्वैः क इमान् विद्वान् वि चर्चत पाशान् ॥

१०.५.१६. सत्येनोत्तभिता भूमिः सूर्येणोत्तभिता द्यौः ।
ऋतेनादित्यास्तिष्ठन्ति दिवि सोमो अधि श्रितः ॥

सोमेनादित्या बलिनः सोमेन पृथिवी मही ।
अथो नक्षत्राणामेषामुपस्थे सोम आहितः ॥

१०.५.१७. इहेदसाथ न पुरो गमाथेमं गावः प्रजया वर्धयाथ ।
शुभं यतीरुस्रियाः सोमवर्चसो विश्वे देवाः क्रन्निह वो मनांसि ॥

१०.५.१९. इहेदसाथ न पुरो गमाथेमं गावः प्रजया वर्धयाथ ।
शुभं यतीरुस्रियाः सोमवर्चसो विश्वे देवाः क्रन्निह वो मनांसि ॥

इमं गावः प्रजया सं विशाथायं देवानां न मिनाति भागम् ।
अस्मै वः पूषा मरुतश्च सर्वे अस्मै वो धाता सविता सुवाति ॥

१०.५.२०. परा देहि शामुल्यं ब्रह्माभ्यो वे भजा वसु ।
कृत्यैषा पद्वती भूत्वा जाया विशते पतिम् ॥

नीललोहितं भवति कृत्यासक्तिर्व्य ज्यते ।
एधन्ते अस्या ज्ञातयः पतिर्बन्धेषु बध्यते ॥

अश्लीला तनूर्भवति रुशती पापयामुया ।
पतिर्यद् वध्वो वाससः स्वमङ्गमभ्यूर्णुते ॥

आशासनं विशासनमथो अधिविकर्तनम् ।
सूर्यायाः पश्य रूपाणि तानि ब्रह्मोत शुम्भति ॥

तृष्टमेतत् कटुकमपाष्ठवद् विषवन्नैतदत्तवे ।
सूर्यां यो ब्रह्मा वेद स इद् वाधूयमर्हति ॥

स इत् तत् स्योनं हरति ब्रह्मा वासः सुमङ्गलम् ।
प्रायश्चित्तिं यो अध्येति येन जाया न रिष्यति ॥

१०.५.२१. देवैर्दत्तं मनुना साकमेतद् वाधूयं वासो वध्वश्च वस्त्रम् ।
यो ब्रह्मणे चिकितुषे ददाति स इद् रक्षांसि तल्पानि हन्ति ॥

यं मे दत्तो ब्रह्मभागं वधूयोर्वाधूयं वासो वध्वश्च वस्त्रम् ।
युवं ब्रह्मणेऽनुमन्यमानौ ब्रहस्पते साकमिन्द्रश्च दत्तम् ॥

१०.५.२२. अपास्मत् तम उच्छतु नीलं पिशङ्गमुत लोहितं यत् ।
निर्दहनी या पृषातक्यऽस्मिन् तां स्थाणावध्या सजामि ॥

१०.५.२३. यावतीः कृत्या उपवासने यावन्तो राज्ञो वरुणस्य पाशाः ।
व्यृद्धयो या असमृद्धयो या अस्मिन् ता स्थाणावधि सादयामि ॥

१०.५.२४. या मे प्रियतमा तनूः सा मे विभाय वाससः ।
तस्याग्रे त्वं वनस्पते नीविं कृणुष्व मा वयं रिषाम ॥

१०.५.२५. शुम्भनी द्यावापृथिवी अन्तिसुम्ने महिव्रते ।
आपः सप्त सुस्रुवुर्देवीस्ता नो मुञ्चन्त्वंहसः ॥

१०.५.२६. ये अन्ता यावतीः सिचो य ओतवो ये च तन्तवः ।
वासो यत् पत्नीभिरुतं तन्नः स्योनमुप स्पृशात् ॥

१०.५.२७. नवं वसानः सुरभिः सुवासा उदागां जीव उषसो विभातीः ।
आण्डात् पतत्रीवामुक्षि विश्वस्मादेनस्परि ॥

१०.५.३०. जीवं रुदन्ती वि नयन्त्यध्वरं दीर्घामनु प्रसितिं दीध्युर्नरः ।
वामं पितृभ्यो य इदं समेरिरे मयः पतिभ्यो जनयः परिष्वजे ॥

यदीमे केशिनो जना गृहे ते समनर्तिषू रोदेन कृण्वन्तोऽधम् ।
अग्निष्टवा तस्मादेनसः सविता च प्र मुञ्चताम् ॥

यदीयं दुहिता तव विकेश्यरुदद गृहे रोदेन कृण्वन्तोऽधम् ।
अग्निष्टवा तस्मादेनसः सविता च प्र मुञ्चताम् ॥

यज्जामयो यद्युवतयो गृहे ते समनर्तिषु रोदेन कृण्वन्तोऽधम् ।
अग्निष्टवा तस्मादेनसः सविता च प्र मुञ्चताम् ॥

यत् ते प्रजायां पशुषु यद्वा गृहेषु निष्ठितमघकृद्भिरघं कृतम् ।
अग्निष्टवा तस्मादेनसः सविता च प्र मुञ्चताम् ॥

१०.५.३२. ब्रह्मापरं युज्यतां ब्रह्म पूर्वं ब्रह्मान्ततो मध्यतो ब्रह्म सर्वतः ।
अनाव्याधां देवपुरां प्रपद्य शिवा स्योना पतिलोके विराज ॥

Appendix B

Vivāha Mantras from Mantra-Pāṭha of Āpastambins (Winternitz)

(आपस्तम्बीय मन्त्रपाठः)

१.१.१. प्र सु ग्मन्ता धियसानस्य सक्षणि वरेभिर्वराँ अभि षु प्रसीदतः ।
अस्माकमिन्द्र उभयं जुजोषिति यत्सोम्यस्यान्धसो बुबोधिति ॥

१.१.२. अनृक्षरा ऋजवः सन्तु पन्था येभिः सखायो यन्ति नो वरेयम् ।
समर्यमा सम्भगो नो निनीयात् सं जास्पत्यं सुयममस्तु देवाः ॥

१.१.३. अभ्रातृघ्नीं वरुणापतिघ्नीं बृहस्पते ।
इन्द्रापुत्रघ्नीं लक्ष्म्यं तामस्यै सवितस्सुव ॥

१.१.४. अघोरचक्षुअरपतिध्न्ये धि शिवा पशुभ्यः सुमना सुवर्चाः ।
वीरसूर्देवकामा स्योना शं नो भव द्विपदे शं चतुष्पदे ॥

१.१.५. इदमहं या त्वयिं पतिघ्न्यलक्ष्मिस्तां निर्दिशामि ॥

१.१.६. जीवां रुदन्ती विमयन्तो अध्वरे दीर्घामनुप्रसितिं दीधियुर्नरः ।
वामं पितृभ्यो य इदं समेरिरे मयः पतिभ्यो जनयः परिष्वज ॥

१.१.७. व्युक्षत्क्रूरमुदचन्त्वाप आस्यै ब्राह्मणा स्नपनँ हरन्तु ।
अवीरघ्नीरुदचन्त्वापः ॥

१.१.८. अर्यम्णो अग्निं परिं यन्तु क्षिप्रं प्रतीक्षान्ताँ श्वश्रुवो देवरार्श्च ॥

१.१.९. खेऽनसः खे रथः खे युगस्य शचीपते ।
अपालमिन्द्र त्रिः पूत्व्यकरत्सूर्यवर्चसम् ॥

१.१.१०. शं ते हिरण्यँ समु शन्त्वापश्शं ते मेथी भवतु शं युगस्य तृत्म ।
शं त आपश्शतपवित्रा भवन्त्वथा पत्या तन्वँ सँ सृजस्व ॥

१.२.१. हिरण्यवर्णाः शुचयः पावकाः प्र चक्रमुर्हित्वावद्यमापः ।
शतं पवित्रा वितता ह्यासु ताभिष्ट्वा देवस्सविता पुनातु ॥

१.२.२. हिरण्यवर्णाः शुचयः पावका यासु जातः कश्यपो यास्विग्निः ।
या अग्निं गर्भे दधिरे सुवर्णास्तास्त आपश्शँ स्योना भवन्तु ॥

१.२.३. यासाँ राजा वरुणो याति मध्ये सत्यानृते अवपश्यञ्जनानाम् ।
या अग्निं गर्भे दधिरे सुवर्णास्तास्त आपश्शँ स्योना भवन्तु ॥

१.२.४. यासाँ देवा दिवि कृण्वन्ति भक्ष्यं या अन्तरिक्षे बहुधा निविष्टाः ।
या अग्निं गर्भे दधिरे सुवर्णास्तास्त आपश्शँ स्योना भवन्तु ॥

१.२.५. शिवेन त्वा चक्षुषा पश्यन्त्वापश्शिवयां तन्वोपं स्पृशन्तु त्वचं ते ।
घृतश्च्युतश्शुचयो याः पावकास्तास्त अपश्शँ स्योना भवन्तु ॥

१.२.६. परि त्वा गिर्वणो गिर इमा भवन्तु विश्वतः ।
वृद्धायुमनु वृद्धयो जुष्टा भवन्तु जुष्टयः ॥

१.२.७. आशासाना सौमनसं प्रजाँ प्रजाँ सौभाग्यं तनूम् ।
अग्नेरनुव्रता भूत्वा सं नह्ये सुकृताय कम् ॥

१.२.८. पूषा त्वेतो नयतु हस्तगृह्याश्विनौ त्वा प्र वहतां रथेन ।
गृहान्गच्छ गृहपत्नी यथासो वशिनी त्वं विदथमा वदासि ॥

१.३.१. सोमः प्रथमो विविदे गन्धर्वो विविद उत्तरः ।
तृतीयो अग्निष्टे पतिस्तुरीयस्ते मनुष्यजाः ॥

१.३.२. सोमो ददद्गन्धर्वाय गन्धर्वो दददग्नये ।
रयिं च पुत्राँश्चादादग्निर्मह्यमथो इमाम् ॥

१.३.३. गृभ्णामि ते सुप्रजस्त्वाय हस्तं मया पत्या जरदष्टिर्यथासः ।
भगो अर्यमा सविता पुरन्धिर्मह्यं त्वादुर्गार्हपत्याय देवाः ॥

१.३.४. ते ह पूर्वे जनासो यत्र पूर्ववतो हिताः ।
मूर्धन्वान्यत्र सौभ्रवः पूर्वो देवेभ्य आतपत् ॥

१.३.५. सरस्वति प्रेदमव सुभगे वाजीनीवति ।
तां त्वा विश्वस्य भूतस्य प्र गायामस्यग्रतः ॥

१.३.६. य एतिं प्रदिशस्सर्वा दिशोऽनु पवमानः ।
हिरण्यहस्त एरम्मस्स त्वा मन्मनसं कृणोतु ॥

१.३.७. एकमिषे विष्णुस्त्वान्वेतु ।

१.३.८. द्वे ऊर्जे विष्णुस्त्वान्वेतु ।

१.३.९. त्रीणि व्रताय विष्णुस्तान्वेतु ।

१.३.१०. चत्वारि मायोभवाय विष्णुस्तान्वेतु ।

१.३.११. पञ्च पशुभ्यो विष्णुस्तान्वेतु ।

१.३.१२. षड्तुभ्यो विष्णुस्तान्वेतु ।

१.३.१३. सप्त सप्तभ्यो होत्राभ्यो विष्णुस्तान्वेतु ।

१.३.१४. सखा सप्तपदा भव सखायौ सप्तपदा बभूव । सख्यं ते गमेयँ सख्यात्ते मा योषं सख्यान्मे मा योष्ठाः । समयाव सं कल्पावहै संप्रियौ रोचिष्णू सुमनस्यमानौ। इषमूर्जमभि संवसानौ । सं नो मनाँसि सं व्रता समु चित्तान्या करम् । सा त्वमस्यमूहममूहमस्मि सा त्वं द्यौरहं पृथिवी त्वं रेतोऽहं रेतोभृत्त्वं मनोऽहमस्मि वाक्त्वँ सामाहमस्म्यृक्त्वँ सा मामनुव्रता भव पुँसे पुत्राय वेत्तवै श्रियै पुत्राय वेत्तवा एहि सूनृते ॥

१.४.१. सोमाय जनिविदे स्वाहा ।

१.४.२. गन्धर्वाय जनिविदे स्वाहा ।

१.४.३. अग्नये जनिविदे स्वाहा ।

१.४.४. कन्यला पितृभ्यो यती पतिलोकमव दीक्षादास्थ स्वाहा ।

१.४.५. प्रेतो मुञ्चाति नामुतस्सुबद्धाममुनुस्करत् ।
यथेयमिन्द्र मीढ्वस्सुपुत्रा सुभगासति ॥

१.४.६. इमां त्वमिन्द्र मीढ्वस्सुपुत्रां सुभगां कुरु ।
दशाभ्यां पुत्रानाधेहि पतिमेकादशं कृधि ॥

१.४.७. अग्निरैतु प्रथमो देवतानाम् सोऽस्यै प्रजां मुञ्चतु मृत्युपाशात् ।
तदयं राजा वरुणोऽनुमन्यतां यथेयम् स्त्री पौत्रमघं न रोदात् ।

१.४.८. इमामग्निस्त्रायतां गार्हपत्यः प्रजामस्यै नयतु दीर्घमायुः ।
अशून्योपस्था जीवतामस्तु माता पौत्रमानन्दमभिविबुध्यामियम् ।

१.४.९. मा ते गृहे निशि घोष उत्थादन्यत्र त्वद्रुदत्यस्संविशन्तु ।
मा त्वं विकेश्युर अवधिष्टा जीवपत्नी पतिलोके विराज पश्यन्ती प्रजां सुमनस्यमानां ॥

१.४.१०. द्यौस्ते पृष्ठं रक्षतु वायुरूरू अश्विनौ च स्तनं धयन्तँ सविताभि रक्षतु ।
आ वाससः परिधानाद्बृहस्पतिर्विश्वे देवा अभिरक्षन्तु पश्चात् ॥

१.४.११. अप्रजस्तां पौत्रमृत्युं पाप्मानमुत वाघम् ।
शीर्णा स्रजमिवोन्मुच्य द्विषद्भ्यः प्रति मञ्चामि पाशम् ॥

१.४.१२. इमं मे वरुण श्रुधी हवमद्या च मृडय ।
त्वामवस्युरा चके ॥

१.४.१३. तत्वा यामि ब्रह्मणा वन्दमानस्तदा शास्ते यजमानो हविर्भिः ।
अहेडमानो वरुणेह बोध्युरुशँस मा न आयुः प्र मोषीः ॥

१.४.१४. त्वं नो अग्ने वरुणस्य विद्वान्देवस्य हेडोऽवं यासिसीष्ठाः ।
यजिष्ठो वह्नितमश्शोश्रुचानो विश्वा द्वेषाँसि प्र मुमुग्ध्यस्मत् ॥

१.४.१५. स त्वं नो अग्नेऽवमो भवोती नेदिष्ठो अस्या उषसो व्युष्टौ ।
अव यक्ष्व नो वरुणँ रराणो वीहि मृडीकँ सुहवो न एधी ॥

१.४.१६. त्वमग्ने अयास्ययासन्मनसा हितः ।
अयासन्हव्यसूहिषेऽया नो धेहि भेषजम् ॥

१.५.१. आतिष्ठेममश्मानमश्मेव त्वं स्थिरा भव ।
अभितिष्ठ पृतन्यतस्सहस्व पृतनायतः ॥

१.५.२. इयं नार्युप ब्रूते कुल्यान्यावपन्तिका ।
दीर्घायुरस्तु मे पतिर्जीवातु शरदश्शतं ॥

१.५.३. तुभ्यमग्ने पर्यवहन् सूर्याम् वहतुना सह ।
पुनः पतिभ्यो जायां दा अग्ने प्रजया सह ॥

१.५.४. पुनः पत्नीमग्निरदादायुषा सह वर्चसा ।
दीर्घायुर्स्या यः पतिस्म एतु शरदशतम् ॥

१.५.५. विश्वा उत त्वया वयं धारा उदन्या इव ।
अति गाहेमहि द्विषः ॥

१.५.६. आतिष्ठेममश्मानम् ॥

१.५.७. अर्यमणं नु देवं कन्या अग्निमयक्षत ।
स इमां देवो अध्वरः प्रेतो मुञ्चाति नामुतस्सुबद्धाममुतस्करत् ॥

१.५.८. तुभ्यमग्ने पर्यवहन् ॥

१.५.९. पुनः पत्नीमग्निरदात् ॥

१.५.१०. विश्वा उत त्वया वयम् ॥

१.५.११. आतिष्ठेममश्मानम् ॥

१.५.१२. त्वमर्यमा भवसि यत्कनीनां नाम स्वधावत्स्वर्ये बिभार्षि ।
अञ्जन्ति वृक्षं सुधितं त गोभिर्यद्दंपती समनसा कृणोषि ॥

१.५.१३. तुभ्यमग्ने पर्यवहन् ॥

१.५.१४. पुनः पत्नीमग्निरदात् ॥

१.५.१५. विश्वा उत त्वया वयम् ॥

१.५.१६. प्र त्वा मुञ्चामि वरुणस्य पाशाद् येन त्वाबध्नात् सविता सुकेतः ।
धातुश्च योनौ सुकृतस्य लोके स्योनं ते सह पत्या कृणोमि ॥

१.५.१७. इमं वि ष्यामि वरुणस्य पाशं यमबध्नीत सविता सुशेवः ।
धातुश्च योनौ सुकृतस्य लोकेऽरिष्टां त्वा सह पत्या कृणोमि ॥

१.५.१८. अयाश्चाग्नेऽस्यनभिशस्तीश्च सत्यमित्त्वमया असि ।
अयसा मनसा धृतोऽयसा हव्यमूहिषेऽया नो धेहि भेषजम् ॥

१.६.१. सत्येनोत्तभिता भूमिस्सूर्येणोत्तभिता द्यौः ।
ऋतेनादित्यास्तिष्ठन्ति दिवि सोमो अधि शितः ॥

१.६.२. युञ्जन्ति ब्रध्नमरुषं चरन्तं परि तस्थुषः ।
रोचन्ते रोचना दिवि ॥

१.६.३. योगेयोगे तवस्तरं वाजेवाजे हवामहे ।
सखाय इन्द्रमूतये ॥

१.६.४. सुकिँशुकँ शल्मलिं विश्वरूपँ हिरण्यवर्णँ सुवृतँ सुचक्रम् ।
आरोह वध्वमृतस्य लोकं स्योनं पत्ये वहतुं कृणुष्व ॥

१.६.५. उदुत्तरमारोहन्ती व्यस्यन्ती पृतन्यतः ।
मूर्धानं पत्युरा रोह प्रजया च विराड्भव ॥

१.६.६. सम्राज्ञी स्वशुरे भव सम्राज्ञी स्वश्र्वां भव ।
ननान्दरि सम्राज्ञी भव सम्राज्ञी अधि देवृषु ॥

१.६.७. स्नुषाणाँ श्वशुराणां प्रजायाश्च धनस्य च ।
पतीनां च देवृणां च सजातानां विराड्भव ॥

१.६.८. नीललोहितं भवतः कृत्यासक्तिर्व्यज्यते ।
एधन्ते अस्या ज्ञातयः पतिर्बन्धेषु बध्यते ॥

१.६.९. ये वध्वश्चन्द्रं वहतुं यक्ष्मा यन्ति जनाँ अनु ।
पुनस्तान्यज्ञिया देवा नयन्तु यत आगताः ॥

१.६.१०. मा विदन्परिपन्थिनो य असीदन्ति दम्पती ।

सुगेभिर्दुर्गमतीतामप द्रान्त्वरातयः ॥

१.६.११. सुगं पन्थानमारुक्षमरिष्टँ स्वस्तिवाहनम् ।
यस्मिन्वीरो न रिष्यत्यन्येषां विन्दते वसु ॥

१.६.१२. ता मन्दसाना मनुषो दुरोण आ धत्तँ रयिं दशवीरं वचस्यवे ।
कृतं तीर्थँ सुप्रमाणँ शुभस्पती स्थाणुं पथेष्ठामप दुर्मतिँ हतम् ॥

१.६.१३. अयं नो मह्याः पारँ स्वस्ति नेषद्वनस्पतिः ।
सीरा नस्सुतरा भव दीर्घायुत्वाय वर्चसे ॥

१.६.१४. अस्य पारे निरृथस्य जीवा ज्योतिरशीमहि ।
मह्या इन्द्र स्वस्तये ॥

१.७.१. यदृते चिदभिश्रिषः पुरा जर्तृभ्य आतृदः ।
संधाता सन्धिं मघवा पुरोवसुर्निष्कर्ता विहृतं पुनः ॥

१.७.२. इडामग्ने पुरुदँसँ सनिं गोश्शश्वत्तमँ हवमानाय साध ।
स्यान्नस्सूनुस्तनयो विजावाग्ने सा ते सुमतिर्भूत्वस्मे ॥

१.७.३. इमं मे वरुण ॥

१.७.४. तत्वा यामि ॥

१.७.५. त्वं नो अग्ने ॥

१.७.६. स त्वं नो अग्ने ॥

१.७.७. त्वमग्ने अयासि ॥

१.७.८. ये गन्धर्वा अप्सरसश्च देवीरेषु वृक्षेषु वानस्पत्येष्वासते ।
शिवास्त अस्यै वध्वै भवन्तु मा हिँसिषुर्वहतुमूह्यमानाम् ॥

१.७.९. या ओषधयो या नद्यो यानि धन्वानि ये वनां ।
ते त्वा वधु प्रजावतीं प्र त्वे मुञ्चन्त्वँहसः ॥

१.७.१०. सं काशयामि वहतुं ब्रह्मणा गृहैरघोरेण चक्षुषा मैत्रेण ।
पर्याणद्धं विश्वरूपं यदस्याँ स्योनं पतिभ्यस्सविता कृणोतु तत् ॥

१.७.११. आ वामगन्त्सुमतिर्वाजिनीवसू न्यश्विना हृत्सु कामाँ अयँसत ।
आभूतं गोपा मिथुना शुभस्पती प्रिया अर्यम्णो दुर्याँ अशीमहि ॥

१.७.१२. अयं नोदेवस्सविता ब्रहस्पतिरिन्द्राग्नी मित्रावरुणा स्वस्तये ।
त्वष्टा विष्णुः प्रजया संरराणः काम आयातं त्वा विमुञ्चतु ॥

१.८.१. शर्म वर्मेदमा भरास्यै नार्या उपस्तिरे ।
सिनीवालि प्र जायतामियं भगस्य सुमतावसत् ॥

१.८.२. गृहान्भद्रान्त्सुमनसः प्र पद्येऽवीरघ्नी वीरवतस्सुवीरान् ।
इरां वहतो घृतमुक्षमाणस्तेष्वहँ सुमनास्संविशामि ॥

१.८.३. आगन्गोष्ठं महिषी गोभिरश्वैरायुष्मत्पत्नी प्रजया स्वर्वित् ।
वह्वीं प्रजां जनयन्ती सुरत्नेममग्निँ शतहिमास्सपर्यात् ॥

१.८.४. अयमग्निर्गृहपतिस्सुसँत्पुष्टिवर्धनः ।
यथा भगस्याभ्यां ददद्रयिं पुष्टिमथो प्रजाम् ॥

१.८.५. प्रजाया आभ्यां प्रजापत इन्द्राग्नी शर्म यच्छतम् ।
यथैनर्योन प्रमीयातां उभयोर्जीवतोः प्रजा ॥

१.८.६. तेन भूतेन हविषायमा प्यायतां पुनः ।
जायतां यामस्मा आवाक्षुस्ताँ रसेनाभि वर्धताम् ॥

१.८.७. अभि वर्धातां पयसाभि राष्ट्रेण वर्धताम् ।
रय्या सहस्रपोषसेमौ स्तामनपोक्षितौ ॥

१.८.८. इहैव स्तं मा वि योष्टं विश्वमायुर्व्यश्नुतम् ।
मह्या इन्द्र स्वस्तये ॥

१.८.९. ध्रुवैधि पोष्या मयि मह्यं त्वादाद्बृहस्पतिः ।
मया पत्या प्रजावती सं जीव शरदशतम् ॥

१.८.१०. त्वष्टा जायामजनयत्त्वष्टास्यै त्वां पतिम् ।
त्वष्टा सहस्रमायूँषि दीर्घमायुः कृणोतु वाम् ॥

१.८.११. इमं मे वरुण ॥

१.८.१२. तत्त्वा मयि ॥

१.८.१३. त्वं नो अग्ने ॥

१.८.१४. स त्वं नो अग्ने ॥

१.८.१५. त्वमग्ने अयासि ॥

१.९.१. इह गावः प्र जायध्वमिहाश्वा इह पुरुषाः ।
इहो सहस्रदक्षिणो रायस्पोषो निषीदतु ॥

१.९.२. सोमेनादित्या बलिनस्सोमेन पृथिवी दृढा ।
अथो नक्षत्राणामेषामुपस्थे सोम आधितः ॥

१.९.३. प्रस्व स्थः प्रेयं प्रजया भुवने शोचेष्ट ॥

१.९.४. इह प्रियं प्रजया ते समृध्यतामस्मिन्गृहे गार्हपत्याय जागृहि ।
एना पत्या तन्वँ सँ सृजस्वाथा जीव्री विदथमा वदासि ॥

१.९.५. सुमङ्गलीरियं वधूरिमां समेत पश्यत ।
सौभाग्यमस्यै दत्वायाथास्तं विपरेतन ॥

१.९.६. ध्रुवक्षितिर्ध्रुवयोनिर्ध्रुवमसि ध्रुवत स्थितम् ।
त्वं नक्षत्राणां मेथ्यसि स मा पाहि पृतन्यतः ॥

१.९.७. सप्तर्षयः प्रथमां कृत्तिकानामरुन्धतीं यद्ध्रुवताँ ह नित्युः ।
षट् कृत्तिकां मुख्ययोगं वहन्तीयमस्माकमेधत्वष्टमी ॥

१.९.८. सदसस्पतिमद्भुतम् प्रियमिन्द्रस्य काम्यम् ।
सनिं मेधामयासिषम् ॥

१.९.९. उद्दीप्यस्व जातवेदोऽपघ्नन्निर्ऋतिं मम ।
पशूँश्च मह्यमा वह जीवनं च दिशो दिश ॥

१.९.१०. मा नो हिँसीज्जातवेदो गामश्वं पुरुषं जगत् ।
अबिभ्रदग्न आ गाहि श्रिया मा परि पातय ॥

१.१०.१. उदीर्ष्वातो विश्वावसो नमसेडामहे त्वा ।
अन्यामिच्छ प्रभर्व्यँ सं जायां पत्या सृज ॥

१.१०.२. उदीर्ष्वात पतिवति ह्येषा विश्वावसुं नमसा गीर्भिरिट्टे ।
अन्यामिच्छ पितृषदं वित्ताँ स ते भागो जनुषा तस्य विद्धि ॥

१.१०.३. अग्ने प्रायश्चित्ते त्वं देवानां प्रायश्चित्तिरसि ब्राह्मणस्त्वां नाथकामः प्र पद्ये यास्यां पतिघ्नी तनूः प्रजाघ्नी पशुघ्नी लक्ष्मिघ्नी जारघ्नीमस्यै तां कृणोमि स्वाहा ॥

१.१०.४. वायो प्रायश्चित्ते . . . ॥

१.१०.५. आदित्य प्रायश्चित्ते ॥

१.१०.६. प्रजापते प्रायश्चित्ते त्वं देवानां प्रायश्चित्तिरसि ब्राह्मणस्त्वां नाथकामः प्र पद्ये यास्यां पतिघ्नी तनूः प्रजाघ्नी पशुघ्नी लक्ष्मिघ्नी जारघ्नीमस्यै तां कृणोमि स्वाहा ॥

१.१०.७. प्रसवश्चोपयामश्च काटश्चार्णवश्च धर्णसिश्च द्रविणं च भगश्चान्तरिक्षं च सिन्धुश्च समुद्रश्च सरस्वाँश्च विश्वव्यचाश्च ते यं द्विष्मो यश्च नो द्वेष्टि तमेषां जम्भे दध्म स्वाहा ॥

१.१०.८. मधुश्च माधवश्च शुक्रश्च शुचिश्च नभश्च नभस्यश्चेषश्चोर्जश्च सहश्च सहस्यश्च तपश्च तपस्यश्च ते यं द्विष्मो यश्च नो द्वेष्टि तमेषां जम्भे दध्म स्वाहा ॥

१.१०.९. चित्तं च चित्तिश्चाकूतं चाकूतिश्चाधीतं चाधीतिश्च विज्ञातं च विज्ञानं च नाम च क्रतुश्च दर्शश्च पूर्णमासश्च ते यं द्विष्मो यश्च नो द्वेष्टि तमेषां जम्भे दध्म स्वाहा ॥

१.१०.१०. भू स्वाहा ॥

१.१०.११. भुव स्वाहा ॥

१.१०.१२. सुव स्वाहा ॥

१.१०.१३. ॐ स्वाहा ॥

१.११.१. अपश्यं त्वा मनसा चेकितानं तपसो जातं तपसो विभूतम् ।
इह प्रजामिह रयिं रराणः प्र जायस्व प्रजयां पुत्रकाम ॥

१.११.२. अपश्यं त्वा मनसा दीध्यानाँ स्वायां तनूँ ऋत्विये नाथमानाम् ।
उप मामृच्चा युवतिर्बभूयाः प्र जायस्व प्रजयां पुत्रकाम ॥

१.११.३. समञ्जन्तु विश्वे देवाः समापो हृदयानि नौ ।
सं मातरिश्वा सं धाता समु देष्ट्री दिदेष्टु नौ ॥

१.११.४. प्रजापते तन्वं मे जुषस्व त्वष्टर्देवेभिसहसाम इन्द्र ।
विश्वैर्देवै एतिभिसाँरराणः पुँसां बहूनां मातरं स्याम ॥

१.११.५. आ नः प्रजां जनयतु प्रजापतिराजरसाय समनत्वर्यमा ।
अदुर्मङ्गलीः पतिलोकमा विश शं न एधि द्विपदे शं चतुष्पदे ॥

१.११.६. तां पूषञ्छिवतमामेरयस्व यस्यां बीजं मनुष्या वपन्ति ।
या न ऊरू उशति विस्रयातै यस्यामुशन्त प्रहरेम शेपम् ॥

१.११.७. आ रोहोरुमुप बर्हस्व बाहुं परि ष्वजस्व जायाँ सुमनस्यमानः ।
तस्यां पुष्यतं मिथुनौ सयोनी बह्वीं प्रजां जनयन्तौ सरेतसा ॥

१.११.८. आर्द्रयारण्या यत्रामन्थत्पुरुषं पुरुषेण शक्रः ।
तदेतौ मिथुनौ सयोनी प्रजयामृतेनेह गच्छतम् ॥

१.११.९. अहं गर्भमदधामोषधीष्वहं विश्वेषु भुवनेष्वन्तः ।
अहं प्रजा अजनयं पितृणामहं जनिभ्यो अपरीषु पुत्रान् ॥

१.११.१०. पुत्रिणेमा कुमारिणा विश्वमायुर्व्यश्नुतम् ।
उभा हिरण्यपेशसा ॥

१.११.११. वीतिहोत्रा कृतद्वसू दशस्यन्त्वामृताय कम् ।
शमूधो रोमशँ हथो देवेषु कृणुतो दुवः ॥

१.१२.१. विष्णुर्योनिं कल्पयतु त्वष्टा रूपाणि पिंशतु ।
आसिञ्चतु प्रजापतिर्धाता गर्भं दधातु ते ॥

१.१२.२. गर्भं धेहि सिनीवालि गर्भं धेहि सरस्वति ।
गर्भं ते अश्विनौ देवावाधत्तां पुष्करस्रजा ॥

१.१२.३. हिरण्ययी अरुणी यं निर्मन्थतो अश्विना ।
तंते गर्भं दधाम्यहं दशमे मासि सूतवे ॥

१.१२.४. मथेयं पृथिवी मही तिष्ठन्ती गर्भमादधे ।
एवं त्वं गर्भमा धत्स्व दशमे मासि सूतवे ॥

१.१२.५. यथा पृथिव्यऽग्निगर्भा द्यौर्यथेन्द्रेण गर्भिणी ।
वायुर्यथा दिशां गर्भ एवं गर्भं दधातु ते ॥

१.१२.६. विष्णो श्रेष्ठेन रूपेणास्यां नार्या गवीन्याम् ।
पुमाँसं गर्भमा धेहि दशमे मासि सूतवे ॥

१.१२.७. नेजमेष परा पत सुपुत्रः पुतरा पत ।
अस्यै मे पुत्रकामायै गर्भमा धेहि यः पुमान् ॥

१.१२.८. व्यस्य योनिं प्रति रेतो गृहाण पुमान्पुत्रो धीयतां गर्भो अन्तः ।
तं माता दश मासो बिभर्तु स जायतां वीरतम स्वानाम् ॥

१.१२.९. आ ते गर्भो योनिमेतु पुमान्बाण इवेषुधिम् ।
आ वीरो जायतां पुत्रस्ते दशमास्यः ॥

१.१३.१. करोमि ते प्राजापत्यमा गर्भो योनिमेतु ते ।
अनूनः पूर्णो जायतामश्लोणोऽपिशाचधीतः ॥

१.१३.२. पुमाँस्ते पुत्रो नारि तं पुमाननु जायताम् ।
तानि भद्राणि बीजान्यृषभा जनयन्तु नौ ॥

१.१३.३ यानि भद्राणि बीजान्यृषभा जनयन्तु नः ।
तैस्त्वं पुत्रान्विन्दस्व सा प्रसुर्धेनुका भव ॥

१.१३.४. कामप्रभुध्यतां मह्यमपराजितमेव मे ।
यं कामं कामयेदेव तं मे वायो समर्धय ॥

Appendix C

Vivāha Mantras from Sāmaveda Mantra Brāhmaṇa

(सामवेदीय मन्त्र ब्राह्मण)

१.१.१. देव सवितः प्रसुव यज्ञं प्रसुव यज्ञपतिं भगाय ।
दिव्यो गन्धर्वः केतपूः केतं नः पुनतु वाचस्पतिर्वाचं नः स्वदतु ॥

१.१.२. काम वेद ते नाम मदो नामासि सामानयामुँ सुरा ते अभवत् ।
परमत्र जन्माग्ने तपसो निर्मितोऽसि स्वाहा ॥

१.१.३. इमं त उपस्थं मधुना सँसृजामि प्रजापतेर् मुखमेतदद्वितीयम् ।
तेन पुंसोऽभिववासि सर्वान् अवशान् वशिनि असि राज्ञी स्वाहा ॥

१.१.४. अग्निं क्रव्यादमकृण्वन् गुहानाः स्त्रीणामुपस्थं ऋषयः पुराणाः ।
तेनाज्यमकृण्वस्त्रैशृङ्गं त्वाष्ट्रं त्वयि तद्दधातु स्वाहा ॥

१.१.५. या आकृन्तन्नवयन् या अतन्वत याश्च देव्योऽन्तानभितो ततन्थ ।
तास्त्वा देव्यो जरसे संव्ययन्त्वायुष्मतीदं परिधत्व वासः ॥

१.१.६. परिधत्त धत्त वाससैनां शतायुषीं कृणुत दीर्घमायुः ।
शतं च जीव शरदः सुवर्चा वसूनिचार्ये विभृजासि जीवन् ॥

१.१.७. सोमोऽददत् गन्धर्वाय गन्धर्वोऽददत् अग्नये ।
रयिं च पुत्राँश्चादादग्निर्मह्यमथो इमाम् ॥

१.१.८. प्र मे पतियानः पन्थाः कल्पताँ शिवा अरिष्टा पतिलोकं गमेयम् ॥

१.१.९. प्रास्याः पतियानः पन्थाः कल्पताँ शिवा अरिष्टा पतिलोकं गम्याः ॥

१.१.१०. अग्निरेतु प्रथमो देवताभ्यः सोऽसै प्रजां मुञ्चातु मृत्युपाशात् ।
तदयँ राजा वरुणोऽनुमन्यतां यथेयं स्त्री पौत्रमघं न रोदात् स्वाहा ॥

१.१.११. इमामग्निस्त्रायतां गार्हपत्यः प्रजामस्यै जरदष्टिं कृणोतु ।
अशून्योपस्थ जीवतामस्तु माता पौत्रमानन्दमभिविबुध्यतामियं स्वाहा ॥

१.१.१२. द्यौस्ते पृष्ठं रक्षतु वायुरूरू अश्विनौ च । स्तनन्धयस्ते पुत्रान् सविताभिरक्षतु ।
आ वाससः परिधानत् बृहस्पतिर्विश्वे देवा अभिरक्षन्तु पश्चात् स्वाहा ॥

१.१.१३. मा ते गृहेषु निशि घोष उत्थादन्यत्र त्वद्रुदत्यः संविशन्तु ।
मा त्वँ रुदत्युर आ बधिष्ठा जीवपत्नी पतिलोके
विराज पश्यन्ती प्रजां सुमनस्यमानां स्वाहा ॥

१.१.१४. अप्रजस्यम् पौत्रमर्त्यं पाप्मानमुत वा अघम् ।
शीर्ष्णः स्रजमिवोन्मुच्य द्विषद्भ्यः प्रतिमुञ्चामि पाशँ स्वाहा ॥

१.१.१५. परैतु मृत्युरमृतं म आगाद् वैवस्वतो नो अभयं कृणोतु ।

परं मृत्यो अनुपमेहि पन्थां यत्र नो अन्य इतरो देवयानात् ॥
चक्षुस्मते शृण्वते ते ब्रवीमि मानः प्रजां रीरिषो मोत वीरान् स्वाहा ॥

१.२.१. इममश्मानारोहाश्मेव त्वं स्थिरा भव ।
द्विषन्तमप बाधदस्व मा च त्वं द्विषतामधः ॥

१.२.२. इयं नार्यूपब्रूतेऽग्नौ लाजानापवन्ती ।
दीर्घायुरस्तु मे पतिः शतं वर्षाणि जीवतु ।
एधन्ताम् ज्ञातयो मम स्वाहा ॥

१.२.३. अर्यमणं नु देवं कन्या अग्निमयक्षत ।
स इमां देवो अर्यमा प्रेतो मुञ्चातु मामुतः स्वाहा ॥

१.२.४. पूषाणं नु देवं कन्या अग्निमयक्षत ।
स इमां देवो पूषा प्रेतो मुञ्चातु मामुतः स्वाहा ॥

१.२.५. कन्यला पितृभ्यः पतिलोक मयतीयमप दीक्षामयष्ट ।
कन्या उत त्वया वयं धारा उदन्या इवातिगहेमहि द्विषः ॥

१.२.६. एकं इषे विष्णुस्त्वा नयतु ।

१.२.७. द्वे ऊर्जे विष्णुस्त्वा नयतु ।

१.२.८. त्रीणि व्रताय विष्णुस्त्वा नयतु ।

१.२.९. चत्वारि मायोभवाय विष्णुस्त्वा नयतु ।

१.२.१०. पञ्च पशुभ्यो विष्णुस्त्वा नयतु ।

१.२.११. षड्रायस्पोषाय विष्णुस्त्वा नयतु ।

१.२.१२. सप्त सप्तभ्यो होत्राभ्यो विष्णुस्त्वा नयतु ।

१.२.१३. सखा सप्तपदी भव सख्यं ते गमेयँ सख्यं ते मा योषाः सख्यं ते मा योष्ठाः ॥

१.२.१४. सुमङ्गलीरियं वधूरिमाँ समेत पश्यत ।
सौभाग्यमस्यै दत्तवायाथास्थं विपरेतन ॥

१.२.१५. समञ्जन्तु विश्वे देवाः समापो हृदयानि नौ ।
सं मातरिश्वा सं धाता समुदेष्ट्री दधातु नौ ॥

१.२.१६. गृभ्णामि ते सौभगत्वाय हस्तं मया पत्या जरदिष्टिर्यथासः ।
भगो अर्यमा सविता पुरंधिर्मह्यं त्वादुर्गार्हपत्याय देवाः ॥

१.२.१७. अघोरचक्षुरपतिघ्नि एधि शिवा पशुभ्यः सुमनः सुवर्चः ।
वीरसर्जीवसूर्देवकामा स्योना शं नो भव द्विपदे शं चतुष्पदे ॥

१.२.१८. आ नः प्रजां जनयतु प्रजापति राजरसाय समनक्त्वार्यमा ।
अदुर्मङ्गलीः पतिलोक माविश शं नो भव द्विपदे शं चतुष्पदे ॥

१.२.१९. इमां त्वमिन्द्र मीढ्वः सुपुत्राँ सुभगां कृधि ।
दशास्यां पुत्राना धेहि पतिमेकदशां कुरु ॥

१.२.२०. सम्राज्ञी श्वशुरे भव सम्राज्ञी श्वश्वां भव ।
ननान्दरि सम्राज्ञी भव सम्राज्ञी अधि देवृषु ॥

१.२.२१. मम व्रते ते हृदयं दधातु मम चित्तमनु चित्तं ते अस्तु ।
मम वाचमेकमना जुषस्व बृहस्पतिस्त्वा नियुनक्तु मह्यम् ॥

१.३.१. लेखासन्धिषु पक्षमस्वावर्तेषु च यानि ते ।
तानि ते पूर्णाहुत्या सर्वाणि शमयाम्यहम् ॥

१.३.२. केशेषु यच्च पापकमीक्षिते रुदिते च यत् ।
तानि ते पूर्णाहुत्या सर्वाणि शमयाम्यहम् ॥

१.३.३. शिले च यच्च पापकं भाषिते हसिते च यत् ।
तानि ते पूर्णाहुत्या सर्वाणि शमयाम्यहम् ॥

१.३.४. आरोकेषु च दन्तेषु हस्तयोः पादयोश्च यत् ।
तानि ते पूर्णाहुत्या सर्वाणि शमयाम्यहम् ॥

१.३.५. ऊर्वोरुपस्थे जङ्घयोः संधानेषु च यानि ते ।
तानि ते पूर्णाहुत्या सर्वाणि शमयाम्यहम् ॥

१.३.६. यानि कानि च घोराणि सर्वाङ्गेषु तवाभवन् ।
पूर्णाहुतिभिराज्यस्य सर्वाणि तान्यशीशमम् ॥

१.३.७. ध्रुवा द्यौर्ध्रुवा पृथिवी ध्रुवं विश्वमिदं जगत् ।
ध्रुवासः पर्वता इमे ध्रुवा स्त्री पतिकुले इयम् ॥

१.३.८. अन्नपाशेन मणिना प्राणसूत्रेन पश्निना ।
बध्नामि सत्यग्रन्थिना मनश्च हृदयं च ते ॥

१.३.९. यदेतधृदयं तव तदस्तु हृदयं मम ।
यदिदं हृदयं मम तदस्तु हृदयं तव ॥

१.३.१०. अन्नं प्राणस्य पड्विँशस्तेन बध्नामि त्वासौ ।

१.३.११. सुकिँशुकं शल्मलिं विश्वरूपं सुवर्णवर्णँ सुकृतँ सुचक्रम् ।
आरोह सूर्ये अमृतस्य नाभिँ स्योनं पत्ये वहतुं कृणुष्व ॥

१.३.१२. मा विदन् परिपन्थिनो य आसीदन्ति दम्पती ।
सुगेभिर्दुर्गमतीतामपद्रान्त्वरातयः ॥

१.३.१३. इह गावः प्रजायध्वमिहाश्वा इह पूरूषाः ।
इहो सहस्रदक्षिणोऽपि पूषा निषीदतु ॥

१.३.१४. इह धृतिरिह स्वधृतिरिह रन्तिरिह रमस्व ।
मयि धृतिर्मयि स्वधृतिर्मयि रमो मयि रमस्व ॥

१.४.१. अग्ने प्रायश्चित्ते त्वं देवानां प्रायश्चित्तिरसि । ब्राह्मणस्त्वा नाथकाम उपधावामि ।
यास्याः पापी लक्ष्मिस्तामस्या अपजहि ॥

१.४.२. वायो प्रायश्चित्ते त्वं देवानां प्रायश्चित्तिरसि । ब्राह्मणस्त्वा नाथकाम उपधावामि ।
यास्याः पतिघ्नी तनूस्तामस्या अपजहि ॥

१.४.३. चन्द्र प्रायश्चित्ते त्वं देवानां प्रायश्चित्तिरसि । ब्राह्मणस्त्वा नाथकाम उपधावामि ।
यास्याः अपुत्र्या तनूस्तामस्या अपजहि ॥

१.४.४. सूर्य प्रायश्चित्ते त्वं देवानां प्रायश्चित्तिरसि । ब्राह्मणस्त्वा नाथकाम उपधावामि ।
यास्याः अपशव्या तनूस्तमस्या अपजहि ॥

१.४.५. अग्निवायुचन्द्रसूर्याः प्रायश्चित्तयो यूयं देवानां प्रायश्चित्तयाः स्थ । ब्राह्मणो वो नाथकाम उपधावामि । यास्याः पापिलक्ष्मीर्या पतिघ्निया पुत्र्या या पशव्या तामस्या अपहत ॥

१.४.६. विष्णुर्योनिं कल्पयतु त्वष्टा रूपाणि पिँशतु ।
आसिञ्चतु प्रजापतिर्धाता गर्भं दधातु ते ॥

१.४.७. गर्भं धेहि सिनीवालि गर्भं धेहि सरस्वति ।
गर्भं ते अश्विनौ देवावाधत्तां पुष्करस्रजौ ॥

१.४.८. पुमाँसौ मित्रावरुणौ पुमाँसावश्विनावुभौ ।
पुमानग्निश्च वायुश्च पुमान्गर्भस्तवोदरे ॥

१.४.९. पुमानग्निः पुमानिन्द्रः पुमान्देवो ब्रहस्पतिः ।
पुमाँसं पुत्रं विन्दस्व तं पुमाननुजायताम् ।

१.५.१. अयमूर्जावतो वृक्ष ऊर्जिव फलिनी भव ।
पर्णं वनस्पतेऽनु त्वानु त्वा सूयताँ रयिः ॥

१.५.२. येनादितेः सीमानं नयति प्रजापतिर्महते सौभगाय ।
तेनाहमस्यै सीमानं नयामि प्रजामस्यै जरदष्टिं कृणोमि ॥

१.५.३. राकामहँ सुहवाँ सुष्टुति हुवे शृणोतु नः सुभगा बोधतुऽऽत्मना ।
सीव्यत्वपः सूच्याच्छिद्यमानाय ददातु वीरं शतदायुमुख्यम् ॥

१.५.४. यास्ते राके सुमतयः सुपेशसो याभिर्ददासि दाशूषे वसूनि ।
ताभिर्नो अद्य सुमना उपागहि सहस्रपोषँ सुभग रराणा ॥

१.५.५. किं पश्यसि । प्रजां पशून् सौभाग्यं मह्यं दीर्घायुष्ट्वं पत्युः ॥

१.५.६. या तिरश्ची निपद्यते अहं विधरणी इति ।
तां त्वा घृतस्य धारया यजे सँराधनीमहम् सँराधन्यै देव्यै देष्ट्र्यै ॥

१.५.७. विपश्चित् पुच्छमभरत् तद्धाता पुनराहरत् ।
परेहि त्वं विपश्चित् पुमानयं जनिष्यतेऽसौ नाम ॥

१.५.८. इयमाज्ञेदमिन्नमिदमायुरिदममृतम् ।

१.५.९. मेधां ते मित्रावरुणौ मेधामग्निर्दधातु ते ।
मेधां ते अश्विनौ देवावाधत्तां पुष्करस्रजौ ॥

१.५.१०. यत्ते सुसीमे हृदयँ हितमन्तः प्रजापतौ ।
वेदाहं मन्ये तद्ब्रह्माहं पौत्रमधं निगाम् ॥

१.५.११. यत्पृथिव्या अनामृतं दिवि चन्द्रमसि श्रितम् ।
वेदामृतस्याहं नाम माहं पौत्रमघँ रिषम् ॥

१.५.१२. इन्द्राग्नि शर्म यच्चतं प्रजायै मे प्रजापति ।
यथायं न प्रमीयेत पुत्रो जनित्र्या अधि ॥

१.५.१३. यददश्चन्द्रमसि कृष्णं पृथिव्या हृदयं श्रितम् ।
तदहं विद्वाँस्तत् पश्यन् माहं पौत्रं अघँ रुदम् ॥

१.५.१४. कोऽसि कतमोऽस्येषोऽस्यमृतोऽसि ।

आहस्पत्यं मासं प्रविशासौ ॥

१.५.१५. स वाह्ने परिददात्वहस्त्वा रात्रै परिददातु रात्रिस्त्वाहोरात्राभ्यां परिददात्वहोरात्रौ त्वार्धमासेभ्यः परिदत्तामर्धमासास्त्वा मासेभ्यः परिददतु मासास्त्व र्तुभ्यः परिददत्वृतवस्त्वा संवत्सराय परिददतु सँवत्सरस्त्वायुषे जरायै परिददात्वसौ ॥

१.५.१६. अङ्गादङ्गात्सँश्रवसि हृदयादधि जायसे ।
प्राणं ते प्राणेन सन्दधामि जीव मे यावदायुषम् ॥

१.५.१७. अङ्गादङ्गात्सँभवसि हृदयादधि जायसे ।
वेदो वै पुत्रनामासि स जीव शरदः शतम् ॥

१.५.१८. अश्मा भव परशुर्भव हिरण्यमस्तृतं भव ।
आत्मासि पुत्र मा मृथा स जीव शरदः शतम् ॥

१.५.१९. पशूनां त्वा हिङ्कारेणाभिजिघ्राम्यसौ ॥

Bibliography

Primary Texts

Atharvaveda Saṁhitā.

Ekāgni Kāṇḍa.

Ṛgveda Saṁhitā.

Sāmaveda Saṁhitā.

Taittirīya Brāhmaṇa.

Taittirīya Saṁhitā.

Secondary Texts

A Vedic Concordance, Maurice Bloomfield, Delhi: Motilal Banarsidass, 1996.

Agniveśya Gṛhya-Sūtra, ed. Pandit L.A. Ravi Varma, Trivandrum: Trivandrum Sanskrit Series, 1940.

Āpastamba Gṛhya-Sūtra, Commentary by Sudarśanācārya, ed. A. Mahadeva Shastri, Mysore: ORI, 1987.

Āpastamba Gṛhya-Sūtram, Commentary by Haradatta and Sudarśanācārya, tr. in Hindi by Umeshcandra Pandey, Varanasi: Chaukhambha Sanskrit Sansthan, 2005.

Ārṣeya Brāhmaṇa with Vedārthaprakāśa of Sāyaṇa, Critical ed. Bellikoth Ramacandra Sharma, Tirupati: Kendriya Sanskrit Vidyapitha, 1984.

Āśvalāyana Gṛhya Sūtram, Commentary by Nārāyaṇa, tr. Narendra Nath Sharma, Delhi: Eastern Book Linkers, 1997.

Atharvaveda Saṁhitā, tr. W.D. Whitney and *Bhāṣya* by Sāyaṇācārya, ed. and rev. K.L. Joshi, vols. 1-3, Delhi: Parimal Publications, 2009.

Atharvavedīya Kauśika Gṛhya-Sūtram, Commentary by Dārila and Keśava, tr. in Hindi by Udaya Narain Singh, Varanasi: Chaukhambha Sanskrit Series, 2009.

Baudhāyana Gṛhya-Sūtra, ed. R. Sama Shastri, Mysore: ORI, 1920.

Baudhāyana Gṛhya Sūtrānusārī Mantra Kośa, ed. Ramachandra Shastri Suri, Kavalakki (Kar): Sri Subramanya Prachya Vidya Pitham, 1988.

Bhāradvājīya Gṛhya-Sūtra Bhāṣyam, Kumbhakodam: Veda Dharma Shastra Paripalana Sabha, 1966.

Bhāradwāja Gṛhya Sūtram, Henriette J.W. Solomons, New Delhi: Meharchand Lachhmandas, 1981.

Chāndogya Brāhmaṇa, With commentaries of Guṇaviṣṇu and Sāyaṇa, ed. Durgamohan Bhattacarya, Calcutta: Sanskrit College, 1958.

Dās Brāhmana (German), Heinrich Stonner, Halle A.S., 1901.

Evolution of Hindu Marriage, Nilakshi Sen Gupta, Bombay: Popular Prakshan, 1965.

Gautama Dharma-Sūtra, Commentary by Haradatta, Vṛtti by Mitākṣarā, Hindi tr. Umeshchandra Pandeya, Varanasi: Chaukhambha Sanskrit Sansthan, 2005.

Gobhila Gṛhya-Sūtram, Pandit Satyavrata Samashrami, tr. Thakur Udaya Narain Singh, Delhi: Chaukhambha Sanskrit Pratisthan, 1992.

Gobhila Gṛhya-Sūtram, tr. Sudhakara Malaviya, Varanasi: Chaukhambha Sanskrit Sansthan, 1997.

Gṛhya Mantra aur Unkā Viniyoga (Hindi), Krishna Lal, Delhi: National Publishing House, 1970.

Gṛhya-Sūtras, tr. Hermann Olderberg, Sacred Books of the East, part 1 & 2, vol. 29 & 30, Delhi: Motilal Banarsidass, 2007.

Hindu Domestic Rituals at a Glance, Sindhu S. Dange, Delhi: Ajanta Publications, 1985.

Hindu Marriage Saṁskāra, Prem Sahni, Allahabad: A.H. Wheeler & Co., 1993.

Hindu Saṁskāras, Rajbali Pandey, Delhi: Motilal Banarsidass, 1969.

Hindu Saṁskāras in a Nutshell, G.H. Ananthanarayanan, Wadakanchery (Ker): Kerala Brahmana Samaja, 2004.

Hiraṇyakeśin Gṛhya-Sūtra, Commentary by Matridatta, ed. J. Kirste.

History of DharmaŚāstra, P.V. Kane, vol. I, part I and vol. II, part I, Pune: Bhandarkar Oriental Research Institute, 1990.

History of Indian Literature, M. Winternitz, tr. Subhadra Jha, vol. III, part 2, Delhi: Motilal Banarsidass, 1967.

India of Vedic Kalpa-Sūtras, Ram Gopal, Delhi: Motilal Banarsidass, 1959.

Jaimini Gṛhya-Sūtra, ed. and tr. W. Caland, Delhi: Motilal Banarsidass, 1984.

Kauśika Paddhati, Kesava, Critical ed. V.P. Limaye, R.N. Dandekar, C.G. Kasikar, V.V. Bhide, and S.S. Bahulkar, Pune: Tilak Mahaarastra Vidya Pitha, 1982.

Kauṣītaka Gṛhya Sūtrāṇi, commentary by Bhavatrāta, ed. T.R. Chintamani, Madras: University of Madras, 1944.

Kauthuma Gṛhya-Sūtra, Suryakant, Calcutta: Asiatic Society, 1954.

Khādira (Drāhyāyaṇa) Gṛhya-Sūtram, Commentary of Rudraskanda, Hindi tr. Udaya Narain Singh, Delhi: Chaukhambha Sanskrit Pratisthan, 1995.

Khādira Gṛhya-Sūtra, Commentary by Rudraskanda, ed. A. Mahadeva Shastri and L. Srinivasacarya, Mysore: ORI, 1913.

Khādira Gṛhya-Sūtra, Pattabhiramayya, Madras: P. Ramadoss, 1955.

Laugākṣi Gṛhya-Sūtras, Commentary by Devapāla, ed. Pandit Madhusudan Kaul Shastri, vol. I & II, Srinagar: Research Dept. of Jammu & Kashmir State, 1934.

Mānava Gṛhya-Sūtra: A Vedic Manual of Domestic Rites Translation, Commentary & Preface, Mark Jan Dresden, Bij J.B. Woolters', Groningen, Batavia: Uitgevers Maatschappi N.V., 1941.

Mānava Gṛhya-Sūtra, Commentary by Aṣṭāvakra, R.K.H. Shastri, New Delhi: Panini, 1982.

Mānava Gṛhya-Sūtra, Commentary of Aṣṭāvakra, ed. Ramakrishna Harsaji Shastri, New Delhi: Padini, 1982.

Pāṇigrahaṇa (Kannada), Mathur Krishnamurti, Bangalore: B.R. Narayana Shetty & Family, 2006.

Pāraskara Gṛhya-Sūtram, Bhāṣya by Harihara, Gadādhara and Jayarāma, tr. in Hindi, Sudhakar Malaviya, Varanasi: Chaukhambha Sanskrit Series, 2007.

Pūjā and Saṁskāra, Musashi Tachikawa, Shoun Hino, Lalitha Deodhar, Delhi: Motilal Banarsidass, 2007.

Religious Rites and Festivals of India, G.V. Sholapurkar, New Delhi: Bharatiya Vidya Prakashan.

Ṛgveda Prayoga Dīpikā (Kannada), Dhali Lakshminarasimha Bhatta, Bangalore: Praja Printers P. Ltd., 2003.

Ṛgveda Saṁhita, tr. H.H. Wilson and *Bhāṣya* by Sāyaṇācārya, ed. and rev. Ravi Prakash Arya and K.L. Joshi, Delhi: Parimal Publications, 2001

Saṁskāra Ratnamālā, Kashinath Shastri Agashee, vols. I and II, Varanasi: Chaukhambha Sanskrit Series, 2009.

Saṁskāra Sanjīvini (Kannada), Vasudeva Paranjape, Sonda (Kar): Bharati Prabodha Shodha Sanstha, 2006.

Saṁskāragalu Hāgū Mānavīya Maulyagalu (Kannada), R.K. Shrikanthakumaraswami, Bangalore: Apastamba Prakashan, 2009.

Saṁskāras in Indian Tradition & Culture, Ramashray Roy, Delhi: Shilpa Publications, 2003.

Sāṅgo-Pāṅga Vivāha Paddhati (Hindi), Pandit Shri Deviprasad Mishra, Varanasi: Kadas Academy, 1999.

Śāṅkhāyana Gṛhya Saṁgraha and Kauṣītaki Gṛhya-Sūtras, Pandit Vasudeva, ed. Somanathopadhyay and Ratna Gopala Bhatta, Benares: Vidya Vilas Press, 1908.

Śāṅkhāyana Gṛhya-Sūtra, Bhāṣya by Narayana, Śāṅkhāyana Gṛhya Saṁgraha by Vasudeva, tr. Ganga Sagar Rai, Varanasi: Ratna Publications, 1995.

Śāṅkhāyana Gṛhya-Sūtra, S.R. Sehgal, Crit. edn. Delhi: Sri Satguru Publications, 1987.

Sārtha Ṣoḍaśa Saṁskāra Ratnamāla, Padmakara Shastri Balashastri Ksheersagara, tr. in Kannada by Guru Krishan Bhatta, Mudubidre (Kar): Shri Nagalingaswamy Sanskrti Veda Pathsala, 1979.

Studies in the Rites & Rituals of Hindu Marriage in Ancient India, Chanchal Kumar Chatterjee, Calcutta: Sanskrit Pustak Bhandar, 1978.

Symbolism of Marriage, R.V. Jahagirdhar, Bangalore: Sri Aurubindo Kapali Shastri Inst. of Vedic Culture, 2005.

The Āryan Marriage, R. Raghunatha Rao, Delhi: Cosmo Publications, 1975.

The Essence of Vivāha Mantras, Swami Paramatmananda, Chennai: Shastraprakashika Trust, 2006.

The Kāṭhaka Gṛhya-Sūtra, W. Caland, Lahore: The Research Dept., D.A.V. College, 1925.

The Kauśika Sūtra of Atharvaveda, With extracts from Darila and Keshav, Delhi: Motilal Banarsidass, 1972.

The Mantra Pāṭha of Āpastambins, Commentary by Haradatta, M. Winternitz, Oxford: Clarendon Press, 1897.

The Mantras of Kauśika Sūtra 10.52, J. Gonda, Studio Orientalia 47, 1977.

The Marriage Section of Agniveśya Gṛhya-Sūtra, Memoirs of the Research Department of the Toyo Bunko, No. 19, Tokyo: The Toyo Bunkoo, 1960.

The Sacrament of Marriage in Hindu Society, Usha M. Apte, Delhi: Ajanta Publications, 1978.

The Upaniṣads, tr. and ed. Valerie Roebuck, London: Penguin, 2003.

The Vivāha, Pandit Bhaiyaram Sharma, tr. R.C. Prasad, Delhi: Motilal Banarsidass, 1999.

Vaikhānasa Smārta Sūtram, tr. W. Caland, Delhi: Ramanand Vidya Bhavan, 1982.

Vārāha Gṛhya-Sūtra, Extracts from *paddhatis* of Gangādhara & Vasiṣṭha, Critical ed. Raghu Vira, Lahore: University of Punjab, 1932.

Vārāha Gṛhya-Sūtram, tr. in Hindi by Udaya Narain Singh, Muzaffarpur: Shastra Publishing House, 1934.

Vārāha Gṛhya-Sūtram, tr. in Hindi Thakur Narain Singh, Varanasi: Chowkhamba Sanskrit Series Office, 2007.

Vivāha Mantrārthaṅgal (Tamil), K. Balasubramanya Iyer, Madras: Subam Process, 1978.

Vivāha Paddhati, With Hindi tr. Pandit Daulatram Gaur Devacarya, Varanasi: Thakur Prasad Kailashnath Bookseller.

Vivāha Saṁskāra (Marathi), Siddheshwara Shastri Citrava, Pune: Bharatiya Caritra Kosh Mandal, 2005.

Vivāhārtha Pradīpikā (Kannada), Banavati Ramakrishna Shastri, Bangalore: Banavati Prakasana, 1998.

Journals

"Baijavāpa Gṛhya-Sūtra Sankalanam", C.G. Kashikar Bhagavadatta, *All India Oriental Conference* **IV**, Allahabad, 1926.

"Gṛhya-Sūtras *vis-à-vis* Atharvaṇic Tradition", S.S. Bahulkar Sp. *All India Oriental Confrence* **27**, Kurukshetra, 1974.

"On the Bhāradvāja Gṛhya-Sūtra and its Commentary", *Bulletin of Deccan College Research Institute* **35** (1-2), 1975.

"The Aśvalāyana Mantra Saṁhitā", V.M. Apte, *Annals of the Bhandarkar Oriental Research Institute.*

"The Ṛgveda Mantras in their Ritual setting in the Gṛhya-Sūtras", V.M. Apte, *Bulletin of Deccan College Research Institute* **1**, Dec 1939-Mar 1940.

Internet Sites

- http:// is1.mum.edu/vedicreserve
- http:// www.hinduwebsite.com
- http:// www.sanskritdocuments.org
- http:// www.sanskritweb.net